PRINCIPLES OF
AUTOMATED
THEOREM
PROVING

PRINCIPLES OF
AUTOMATED
THEOREM
PROVING

David A. Duffy
University of Strathclyde
Glasgow, Scotland

JOHN WILEY & SONS
Chichester · New York · Brisbane · Toronto · Singapore

Other Wiley Editorial Offices

John Wiley & Sons, Inc., 605 Third Avenue,
New York, NY 10158-0012, USA

Jacaranda Wiley Ltd, G.P.O. Box 859, Brisbane,
Queensland 4001, Australia

John Wiley & Sons (Canada) Ltd, 22 Worcester Road,
Rexdale, Ontario M9W 1L1, Canada

John Wiley & Sons (SEA) Pte Ltd, 37 Jalan Pemimpin 05-04,
Block B, Union Industrial Building, Singapore 2057

Library of Congress Cataloging-in-Publication Data:

Duffy, David A.
    Principles of automated theorem proving / David A. Duffy.
        p. cm.
    Includes bibliographical references and index.
    ISBN 0 471 92784 8
    1. Automatic theorem proving. I. Title.
QA76.9.A96D84 1991
511.3—dc20   91-9103
                                                        CIP

A catalogue record for this book is available
from the British Library

Printed in Great Britain by Biddles of Guildford

*To my mother
and to the memory of
my late father*

CONTENTS

PART 3: SPECIAL PURPOSE THEOREM PROVERS

PART 4: CONCLUSIONS

PREFACE

Automated theorem proving is an important area of research having many applications within computer science. Perhaps the most prominent of these applications are verification, program synthesis and programming; also new insights have been provided in related areas such as database theory, artificial intelligence and expert systems. In addition, implemented theorem-proving systems have been employed to prove previously unsolved conjectures in mathematics. This book is a study of automatic theorem-proving techniques (for first-order logic) which are currently attracting widespread interest.

SCOPE AND INTENDED AUDIENCE

The aim of this book is to serve as both an introduction to automated theorem proving (ATP) in first-order logic, and as a guide to current work on particular aspects of ATP. The intention is to give full details of the principles involved, whilst keeping the non-specialist in mind. The book is aimed at, in particular, computer scientists and mathematicians who would like a detailed discussion of the general themes and aims in this area of research, but who are not concerned with the technical proofs associated with the correctness of the different approaches. It would serve as an introduction to the major principles involved for postgraduates intending to move into this area of research, and also as a text for advanced undergraduate computer science students.

There are two main themes in the book. The first concerns general techniques for performing proofs automatically, while the second concerns particular implemented systems that apply these techniques for specific purposes. With regard to the first theme, the major approaches—natural deduction, sequentzen, resolution, and the connection calculi—are discussed in detail, together with some strategies for their application. Throughout this discussion an attempt is made to bring out the underlying relationships between these diverse approaches to proof, pointing out both their analogies and their distinctions.

With regard to the second theme, three major systems are described: Prolog, the Knuth-Bendix completion procedure, and the Boyer-Moore theorem prover. Part of the discussion of these three systems will concern their relationships to the techniques previously discussed, and to each other. In particular, Prolog is related both to resolution and to (cut-free) sequent calculi, while the distinct approaches to proof by induction applied by the Knuth-Bendix procedure and the Boyer-Moore system are shown to have fundamental connections.

This is the first time almost all the major approaches to theorem proving have been discussed in a single text aimed at the non-specialist. It is, of course, impossible to look at every possible proof method available, but, hopefully, the diversity of those discussed will mean that the general area and general aims of ATP will be covered. Little mathematical background is required for an understanding of the text since the relevant notions of first-order logic are summarised in an introductory chapter. However, a useful prerequisite is an acquaintance with formal systems.

One of the original motivations that led to the writing of this book was the need to find the most suitable theorem-proving systems and techniques to tackle the verification problems that arose in the PROSPECTRA project, a software-technology project funded by the European Commission under the ESPRIT programme [Kr90]. This project provided a wealth of interesting applications for theorem proving, and inspired much of the study involved in the development of this text. In particular, the studies of the Boyer-Moore theorem prover, the Knuth-Bendix completion procedure and its application to proof by induction, and the application of automated theorem-proving principles to logic programming in Prolog were motivated by the verification tasks involved in the methodology. It also inspired some of the secondary discussion and examples in the book. This explains why the book covers in detail certain topics that might normally be considered to be outside the scope of an introductory text on automated theorem proving. It is hoped that, rather than detracting from the introductory nature of the text, the treatment of these subjects will provide additional interest and motivation for the general reader. On the other hand, the reader will perhaps be relieved to know that no knowledge whatsoever of the methodology of the PROSPECTRA project is required in order to understand the text, as the project will rarely even be mentioned from here on.

OUTLINE OF CONTENTS

Part 1 of this book is concerned with some preliminary issues. The first chapter is intended to provide motivation and background for the general reader, and to outline some of the basic ideas to be introduced in the chapters to follow. In the second chapter the basic definitions and concepts necessary to the rest of the book will be introduced. It discusses the main ideas from first-order logic and will serve to clarify what is meant by "theoremhood" and what is meant by "proof".

In Part 2 the basic theorem-proving techniques are discussed; not all known methods are described, but what seem to be the major approaches are presented. The main aim in these chapters is to explain the underlying principles involved in these techniques, and to discuss their associated correctness issues and limitations. The implementation details of these systems are not discussed, but the descriptions are, for the most part, "algorithmic", and thus there will generally be no conceptual difficulties in relating the ideas explained to the problems of actual implementation. Generally, in those cases where problems may arise, such as in the case of the natural deduction systems, further clarification is given. A secondary issue will be to bring out the relationships between the different approaches, and there will be regular asides that attempt to point out the connections.

Chapter 3 describes what are referred to as "fundamental systems". It may be disputed that these are fundamental to all theorem provers currently being developed, but the major ideas presented in this chapter are, at the very least, necessary for the chapters to follow. The three systems discussed in this chapter—natural deduction, sequent calculi, and resolution—are perhaps the most well-known amongst computer scientists, and thus it is worthwhile discussing them first, explaining the fundamental principles in terms of these systems. A particularly important aspect of Chapter 3 is the discussion of sequent calculi in Section 3.2. The main system discussed here will be referred to regularly throughout the rest of the book for the purpose of relating the diverse approaches. Other important features of this chapter are the introduction of the ideas of "deriving inference rules", "backward proof" and "unification" (a mechanism that is used in some form or other by every system to follow, except the Boyer-Moore theorem prover).

Throughout the short history of ATP (since the construction of the first mechanical provers in the late 1950s) two distinct approaches to the problem have been advocated. On the one hand are the complete and machine-oriented strategies, and on the other are the "heuristic" or "natural" strategies. The resolution community has commonly advocated and designed complete systems, while heuristic methods have more often been associated with natural deduction. However, this is not absolutely the case since some proposed resolution strategies have been of a heuristic nature and conversely many "natural strategies" may be incorporated into theorem provers in a completeness-preserving manner. For this reason, Chapter 4, which discusses these strategies, is separated into sections on "resolution" and "natural" strategies, respectively, rather than "complete" and "heuristic".

Chapter 5 describes two approaches to theorem proving that are referred to as "connection methods". Section 5.1 on the connection-graph proof procedure discusses the idea of structuring formulae by treating them as nodes of a graph, and describes the proof procedure of Kowalski [Ko75] which uses this structure in a powerful way. Section 5.2 on the connection-matrix method describes a method of proof that is very different from those described previously. Here no formulae are deduced, but instead lines through a "graph" or "matrix" are checked for contradiction. It will be shown that these two approaches are very different from each other, for the connection-graph method is essentially a strategy for applying the resolution rule, while the connection-matrix method is an alternative to resolution. What they have in common is that they both give a more global structure to the problem of proving a theorem. They do this in different ways, but the fundamental point is that each step of the proof in both approaches has an explicit effect on the problem as a whole. This global effect of a single proof step is not so apparent in other approaches.

Currently, there are many important new directions being taken in ATP work. Most of these (for example, systems that support higher-order logics or systems that present frameworks in which a variety of logics may be defined) are felt to be outside the scope of this text. However, two very important topics, namely "logic programming" and "proof by induction", are just within the scope of a book on ATP in first-order logic and will be discussed in Part 3 of this book.

Chapter 6 is concerned with logic programming, and, in particular, with the programming language Prolog. Here the theoretical underpinnings of this language will be described and its relationship to resolution theorem proving and to sequent calculi made clear. The failure of standard implementations of Prolog to conform to the requirements of a theorem prover will be explicitly covered, and some of the "impure" features, added to the underlying logic-based language to increase Prolog's capabilities as a programming language, will be highlighted. Although this chapter is concerned with how a theorem prover may be treated as a programming system, many of the ideas presented are very relevant to other theorem-proving environments. The most important example of this is the concept of the search tree and the associated notions of depth-first and breadth-first creation of this tree.

The completion procedure due to Knuth and Bendix is a fairly recent development which, though originally designed for a very specific purpose, has been found to have many and varied applications in computer science, such as in programming and proof by induction [De85]. Chapter 7 of this book will explain the principles behind this procedure and discuss in detail its application to proof by induction, as well as highlighting its other applications to theorem proving. The concentration on the aspect of inductive theorem proving will be adequate to show how, on the one hand, Knuth-Bendix completion may be applied to a task not obviously within its domain, and, on the other hand, how it can often be inadequate as it stands for many applications, thus giving rise to restrictions.

The final chapter on theorem proving discusses the Boyer-Moore theorem prover, another implemented system for performing inductive proofs. This is generally considered to be one of the most successful non-interactive systems currently available, and is an important example of the heuristic approach to theorem proving. A detailed overview of the system is presented together with some discussion of the limited interaction afforded by it, and hence the problems a novice may have in trying to prove theorems using it. This chapter follows naturally the discussion of induction in Chapter 7, and illustrates concepts not fully covered there.

Finally, in Part 4, the main issues are reviewed and some conclusions are drawn.

READING ORDER

Rather than introduce all the main theoretical concepts in the first two or three chapters, and then merely apply these in the subsequent chapters, this book tries, as far as possible, to introduce new ideas as they are required in a particular context. This means that, on reading through the book, the reader should be able to build up progressively an overall picture of automated theorem proving. Unfortunately, it also means that there is a certain degree of sequentiality required in reading the text, for to understand concepts fully in one chapter may require an understanding of concepts in some of the preceding chapters. To alleviate this problem as far as possible, an attempt has been made to ensure a certain degree of independence between chapters. This has been done by describing new methods using ideas introduced previously as little as possible. Thus, while it may be possible to explain a particular method directly in terms of an approach discussed earlier, in the main discussion of the new method it will generally be described on its own terms, hopefully in the simplest way possible.

The relationships between the different methods, which is, of course, an important issue in its own right, will usually be left to asides from the main text. These asides will generally have in their title the phrase "Connections to" or "Relationship to", and may be safely ignored by the reader who is not concerned about the interconnections of the different approaches. As an additional aid, in Chapter 1 an overview of some of the main ideas is presented; this should allow at least Chapter

2 to be skipped if only an intuitive overview is desired or only special topics are of interest to the reader. In this respect, the final chapter should also be of help, as it provides a review of the main principles introduced earlier in the book.

A NOTE ON THE EXERCISES

Throughout this text there are exercises. Generally, these add new information to the text and thus are not merely bookwork problems. However, they are not designed to require deep insight, but merely to test the reader's understanding of the preceding technical discussion. On the other hand, because they do extend the text, they are generally expressed in an imperative form such as "Show that it holds that...", rather than in an interrogative form such as "Does it hold that...?". For this reason the reader is free simply to assume the result proposed in the exercise and thus to treat it as part of the technical discussion. Answers to many of the exercises are supplied at the back of the book.

ACKNOWLEDGEMENTS

It is unlikely that this book would have reached publication without the efforts of Craig Renfrew. It was he who initially contacted the publishers (without informing me beforehand), and who performed most of the early correspondence (thus bringing new meaning to the phrase "free agent"). I am also grateful for his encouragement, and for his helpful suggestions and technical assistance concerning various aspects of the presentation of this book.

I am indebted to Dr. Brian Duffy for the hard work he put into reading and providing detailed suggestions on the final draft of this text (and then carefully explaining his corrections to me). His comments, particularly on my free-form grammatical constructions, substantially improved the original text, indicating many places where confusion might arise and also highlighting several technical deficiencies. His moral support and assistance during the latter stages of the writing of this book, particularly through the ordeal of trying to meet a deadline that had run out several months previously, are also appreciated.

This book started life as an MPhil thesis. I would like to express my gratitude to Professor Andrew McGettrick and Dr. Owen Traynor for their help and for the many technical discussions on various aspects of theorem proving that we had during the writing of the original thesis.

The constructive comments made by my MPhil examiners Dr. M. Livesey and Dr. J. McInnes, and by the anonymous referees for the original version of this book were also helpful, providing corrections, new references to important work, and also motivation to extend the original thesis to include more informal discussion, technical asides, examples and exercises.

I would also like to thank the many other people working in the Department of Computer Science at the University of Strathclyde who lent support and assistance in various ways during the writing of the original thesis and the completion of the book. In particular, Veronica Koh provided the philosophical discussions concerning the nature and meaning of existence (and related matters) in between the writing of the pages of this text—how these discussions contributed to the content of the text is uncertain. On the more technical side, the Strathclyde "IKBS" group allowed me access to their facilities and provided incidental assistance in various ways (such as helping to save some of my files from oblivion). In addition, Dr. Murray Wood, in particular, moved my files between systems as the mood took me; Dr. Faron Moller provided a version of one of my chapters formatted with a different system, which I used as an initial guide in formatting this text, and also supplied some important references; Joseph McClean made some helpful suggestions on the early chapters of the original thesis; and Agnes Wisley provided secretarial assistance in a variety of ways (such as typing most of my letters).

I am also grateful to the Department of Computer Science at the University of Strathclyde through whom my original MPhil thesis was funded.

Finally, I would like to thank the publishing staff of John Wiley & Sons for their patience during the extra few months it took to complete this book.

BASIC NOTATION

In the rest of this text some standard mathematical notation will be employed to express the main ideas in a more precise and concise form. An intuitive understanding of these symbols is assumed, but here the main abbreviations will be indicated with informal explanations of their meanings.

The set-theoretic notation to be used is as follows.

$\emptyset$: the *empty set*.

$\{x : ...x... \}$: the set of elements "x" that have the property that ...x....

$x \in S$: x is a *member of* S.

$S \subseteq S'$: S is a *subset of* (*and possibly equal to*) S'.

$S \cup S'$: the *union of* S and S'.

$S - S'$: (for $S \subseteq S'$) the set S excluding the members of S'.

The following abbreviations will also have fixed meanings throughout the rest of the book.

iff : "if and only if" or "is equivalent to".

$\mathbb{N}$: $\{0, 1, 2, ... \}$ or the "natural numbers".

$=$: "is identical to".

PART 1

INTRODUCTION

CHAPTER 1

BACKGROUND AND MOTIVATION

Automated theorem proving (ATP) is concerned with the task of mechanising mathematical (or "logical") reasoning. Proofs of mathematical theorems are performed by a computer, analogously to the way arithmetical problems are solved by a calculator. A theorem-proving system may be employed merely to perform routine proofs of trivial theorems, thus relieving theoreticians from the burden of performing these proofs themselves, but it may also (perhaps with some human guidance) uncover proofs of previously unsolved conjectures. More generally, tasks normally solved by humans via logical reasoning may be performed mechanically; for this reason, the processes involved are sometimes also referred to as "automated reasoning". This book is a study of the principles involved in such proof systems, paying special regards to efficiency and "naturalness", to the treatment of the special relation of equality, and to the construction of inductive proofs. It will be shown how the process of proof may be automated, and how this may be done in many different ways, each with its own advantages and limitations. Some applications in programming and formal methods will also be highlighted.

The intention in this first chapter is to provide additional motivation and background for the general reader. It will be concerned with three issues. First it will give an informal characterisation of what constitutes a theorem-proving system, and will indicate the inherent practical and theoretical limitations of such systems. Secondly, it will outline some of the potential applications of ATP, particularly in formal methods; some of these applications will be the subject of more detailed study in later chapters. Thirdly, it will provide an overview of the major ideas to be presented in the rest of the text. The purpose of this overview is not only to provide an informal introduction to the main ideas, but also to allow those readers who are concerned only with acquiring an intuitive understanding of the principles involved or who are interested only in certain topics to skip chapters. In particular, the overview should enable some readers to skip the next chapter, which merely provides technical background to the main discussion.

1.1 SCOPE AND LIMITATIONS

Concerning the scope of automated theorem proving various issues arise. Questions naturally spring to mind as to the diversity of the tasks solvable, the "depth" and "elegance" of the proofs that may be found, the necessity for human guidance in solving anything other than trivial problems, and the practical and theoretical limitations. It might be supposed, for instance, that while computers may be of assistance in proving certain "deep" theorems their use in any particular problem is necessarily ad hoc (each new problem requiring a new computer program), and that their rôle is limited purely to performing tedious "calculations".

A well-known example of this limited application of computers to aiding in the construction of mathematical proofs is the work of Appel and Haken on the four-colour problem [AH76]. The task in their case was to show that four colours are sufficient to colour any "simple" map in such a way that any two countries having a common boundary (other than a single point) are not given the same colour. This task was first reduced to the problem of showing that a finite number of maps of a special form could be coloured in this manner. At this stage, because of the large number of these maps and the complexity of the task of checking each of them, the completion of the proof depended upon the use of a computer. On the other hand, while the task was humanly impossible and certainly required the speed and accuracy of a computer to complete the process in a reasonable time, all the "theoretical" work had been done by Appel and Haken, and the computer was employed merely to perform a mundane and purely "computational" task. The algorithm devised may be viewed as a specialised theorem-proving system, but it does not constitute an application (or even a demonstration) of the main results in the field of automated theorem proving. While ad hoc procedures for solving problems in special domains (such as, for instance, geometry) are of interest in ATP, and there is much work on developing such procedures and incorporating them into more powerful systems, the reasons for developing them are pragmatic rather than due to any limitations of the general theory. Specialised procedures may be more efficient or may find more "elegant" proofs, but the main positive results in ATP show that there are general procedures that can solve these problems without the need for special mechanisms to deal with each task.

These positive results stem from the formalist approach to mathematics initiated by Hilbert et al, and more particularly from the consequential development of the "formal axiomatic method" (see [De70]). This approach to mathematics provides a "mechanistic" formulation of proof in which no reference to "intuition" is allowed. It was originally developed as part of a strategy to eliminate the paradoxes that had appeared in classical mathematical theories and to overcome the inadequacies of earlier formal developments of mathematics such as Euclid's "Elements"; see [De70]. The aim was to reduce mathematical reasoning to a mechanical process expressible in terms of "transformation rules" that allow consequences to be derived automatically from given assumptions. This work provided the underlying framework for computerised reasoning and led to the main positive result characterising the scope of ATP. This result, the "completeness theorem", essentially states that there is a general computational procedure such that for any set of assumptions that may be expressed in first-order logic (see Section 1.3), the set of consequences of these assumptions may be derived by the procedure. In practice (for the purposes of mechanisation) the assumptions must be further restricted to those for which there is an algorithm that is able to determine whether a formula does or does not constitute one of the assumptions. This requirement may seem limiting but, in fact, it covers a very wide range of mathematical theories (concepts); and it is uncertain whether human "intuition" goes beyond this limit (cf. [De70]).

On the other hand, the principles behind the axiomatic method were not developed with either efficiency or even naturalness in mind. It was simply required to show that proofs could be performed this way; in fact, even Hilbert did not intend that mathematics should be done this way. Later, people such as Gerhard Gentzen pointed out the contrived nature of the transformation rules described by logicians such as Hilbert and proposed more natural rules. With the advent of real computers (as opposed to the abstract computers of Turing et al), the drive for efficiency in proof construction became of much more concern. For a time this led researchers completely away from the requirement for "natural proofs", but it was soon realised that there are massive hurdles to full automation (even apart from the negative theoretical results concerning "undecidability"). Nowadays, researchers generally try to develop systems in which both efficiency and naturalness may be accounted for.

Even with these developments, however, the intention behind the development of the formal axiomatic approach to banish "intuition" was not fully realised, and is unlikely ever to be realised. There are both theoretical and practical difficulties that arise. The major results are the "undecidability" and "incompleteness" theorems. The former states that there is no algorithm that is able to decide whether an arbitrary conjecture is or is not a theorem—this does not contradict the previous claim that if a conjecture is a theorem then a procedure will be able to determine that it is. The incompleteness theorem states (in the context of arithmetic) that for any set of assumptions that is "consistent" (i.e. does not "contradict" itself), decidable by an algorithm, and sufficiently general (e.g. it contains adequate definitions of addition and multiplication—cf. Section 1.3.1 below), there is a (first-order) conjecture that is *true* for every natural number (and may be proved for each number individually) but which does not follow from the assumptions. The effects of these two results becomes most apparent when well-known unsolved problems in mathematics are considered for treatment by an automated system.

Suppose, for instance, that an implemented theorem-proving system is presented with "Fermat's last theorem" (which is in fact an unproved conjecture) which states that for any integer n greater than 2, there are no integers x, y and z greater than 0 such that $x^n + y^n = z^n$. What are the chances that the theorem-proving system will return an answer to this problem, and, moreover, will return an answer within a "reasonable" time? Given the completeness theorem indicated above, it follows that if Fermat's last theorem is a consequence of the axioms specified by the user, then an answer will eventually be returned. However, the undecidability theorem states that if Fermat's theorem does not follow from the axioms then it may be that no automated system will be able to determine this fact. Furthermore, the incompleteness theorem states that Fermat's theorem may hold for every natural number $n > 2$, and yet still not follow from the given axioms; of course, in this case Fermat's theorem could just be added as an extra axiom without fear of introducing inconsistency—though, of course, it may be preferable to find a "simpler" axiom that implies Fermat's theorem.

Even if it turns out that Fermat's theorem does follow from the given axioms, the proof system may still take an "unreasonable" length of time to perform the proof. In fact, by the undecidability result there can be no general algorithmically specifiable relationship between, say, the length of any given conjecture and the length of its proof that would determine a bound on the size of the proof; for otherwise its theoremhood would be decidable: simply construct all proof sequences of length smaller than the proposed bound. Such problems as these are considered in more detail in [De70]. Here it will merely be pointed out that the practical intractability of certain tasks is perhaps more of a hurdle for automated proof systems than theoretical undecidability or incompleteness results; and intractability seems to hold even for decidable subsystems of first-order logic such as propositional logic.

Apart from the theoretical and practical limitations of automated theorem-proving systems, what of the more pragmatic issues such as: will the proofs derived by a machine provide "insight" to a human user, or are they essentially "plodding" and "tedious", essentially "trying all possible combinations" and providing nothing more than an answer of "true"? These are, of course, subjective issues, but even so they are of importance to designers building systems for practical applications. With regard to elegance, it may be said that there have been proofs performed by computers of well-known theorems that have both generalised the known results and been more "elegant" than the human proofs (though it is usually the case that these are proofs by specialised systems—if only by the addition of heuristics). In general, however, the practicability of a system is perhaps more dependent upon the "naturalness" of its modes of inference and its interactiveness rather than the subtlety of its reasoning. The naturalness of proof systems will be of more concern than elegance in this book.

The reader more dubious of a theorem prover's capabilities may also enquire: what of the problem of providing all the necessary information? Of course, the incompleteness theorem mentioned above has a bearing on this issue from a more theoretical point of view, but even what may seem an everyday task to a human may require a mass of explicit instructions for a computer. With regard to this "axiomatisation" task it has to be admitted that, while there is research being done on the design of systems that will invent new concepts, the requirement to supply all the relevant information is unavoidable for the type of proof systems of concern in this book. This task may not only be tedious, but may also be very difficult in many cases (and is sometimes the main problem), but it is a subject outside the scope of the current book. What should be noted, however, is that providing the necessary information does not necessarily involve also providing all the hints and tricks that would be used by a human working on the same problem. For instance, to prove that an isosceles triangle (defined as a triangle with two equal sides) has two equal angles, a mathematician may use the trick of dividing the triangle into two using a line perpendicular to the base. It may be thought that an automated theorem prover attempting to prove the same theorem would have to be supplied also with this hint together with the "description" of an isosceles triangle, but this is not the case. Any sufficiently powerful system will not only manage to prove the theorem without any hints, but it may also derive the perpendicular line as part of its solution. This is not because the system will "purposely" intend to derive the line (unless some heuristic techniques are built into it), but will simply depend upon its general method of proof and the initial specification of the problem.

Perhaps also it may be asked: to what degree can a mechanical proof be trusted? This was a problem that arose in the case of Appel and Haken's proof, since it was inconceivable, in their case, that a human could validate the computer's computation except by recourse to a second computer. Here there are issues with regard to the correctness of the algorithms, the correctness of the input to the computer, and the possibility of undetected hardware errors. Naturally, these problems also apply to general theorem-proving systems. This is not a real concern in the current context, since the aim is to describe different methods of proof, not to claim the reliability of any particular implementations; however, from a practical viewpoint there are perhaps two outstanding issues: the correctness of the proof system and the possibility of hardware failures. Concerning the first issue it is pointed out in [BM79] that while their own system (see Chapter 8) may not be of sufficient power to warrant a concerted effort by the mathematical community to prove its correctness, perhaps future systems will merit such interest. As concerns the possibility of undetected hardware errors, several runs should overcome any doubts in this case. For the interested reader the reliability issues regarding computer-assisted proofs are discussed further in [La90]. The overall answer is perhaps that there is no real reason to doubt a proof performed by a computer any more than one performed by human beings (who tend to be less reliable even for trivial tasks such as performing arithmetic operations).

1.2 APPLICATIONS

As has been indicated, difficult and important results in mathematics have already been proven by (or with the assistance of) implemented theorem-proving systems. In terms of the less significant results, they have been used to solve combinatorial problems such as the "cannibals and missionaries" puzzle (see [WO84]), and to prove well-known results in, for example, geometry. These in themselves are quite impressive, but theorem provers have also been employed (at least as assistants) to prove much deeper results, such as previously unsolved conjectures and "meta-theorems" corresponding to proofs concerning their own capabilities. Examples of proofs of new results may be found in, for example, [WO84]: deep problems from both algebra and logic solved with the assistance of an implemented system, AURA, are discussed. As examples of the proofs of meta-theorems, the Boyer-Moore theorem prover, to be discussed in Chapter 8 of this text, has been guided to prove the well-known undecidability and incompleteness results related to the mechanisation of proof. It has thus proven results expressing its own limitations.

Naturally, as might be expected, in both of these applications there was a certain degree of human endeavour involved. In the case of the AURA proofs it is indicated in [WO84] that various "heuristics" and special techniques were implemented in the AURA theorem prover to allow it to complete the proofs of the previously unsolved conjectures. Similarly, in the case of the Boyer-Moore system, as will become apparent in Chapter 8, though it is not designed for "interactive" proof construction, a massive degree of user guidance is required to indicate the lemmas that are required and the most suitable techniques that should be employed even for relatively simple theorems. Furthermore, in the case of the proofs of the undecidability and incompleteness theorem the task of setting up the necessary axioms was half the problem. On the other hand, as is pointed out in [WO84], apart from the fact that the theorems performed with assistance from AURA had previously defied solution by competent mathematicians, the people involved in guiding this system to its proofs were not experts in the fields (of algebra and logic) from which the theorems were taken. Overall, these results may be seen as an indication of the potential for automated theorem provers when employed as assistants by experts in a field of research.

With regard to computer science, one of the most significant applications of automated theorem-proving techniques is in the new field of "logic programming". As noted in the Preface, in Chapter 6 of this book a language called Prolog is described which has its roots in the early work on the development of theorem-proving systems. In particular, its underlying mechanism of computation is based upon the proof principle of "resolution" to be discussed in Chapter 3. This work has also carried over in to the study of database systems. In fact, Prolog itself is used in such systems. A database may, in its most general form, be viewed as a collection of facts and rules, and the programs of the Prolog language are expressed in exactly this form.

The rest of this section will consider some other potential applications in computer science, and more particularly, in the field of "formal methods". These particular applications were each aspects of the PROSPECTRA project mentioned in the Preface, and they form the motivation for the study of many of the ideas to be discussed in the book, particularly in Part 3. Furthermore, some of them will be used as the basis for illustrations of the theorem-proving techniques.

1.2.1 Algebraic Specifications

A fundamental aspect of the new formal methodologies for program construction are formal specifications. For this purpose, the techniques of algebraic specification of abstract data-types [EM85] are one well accepted paradigm (though there are others). In this approach, requirements are specified at a completely formal and abstract level without reference to implementation details. An abstract data-type specification consists of a "signature" and a set of axioms. The signature specifies the syntax and types of the functions and relations, while the axioms define the meaning of these functions and relations. For example, a signature for the binary infix addition function symbol '+' may be given as '$\_+\_$: *nat nat $\rightarrow$ nat*', which denotes the fact that + acts on two natural numbers and returns a natural number; the definition of addition may then be given as $\{x + 0 = x, x + s(y) = s(x + y)\}$, which characterises the function + in terms of the primitives 0 and s (denoting successor) with signatures '$\rightarrow$ *nat*' and '*nat $\rightarrow$ nat*', respectively. (See Section 1.3.1 below for further discussion of the axiomatisation of such concepts as addition.)

An initial formal specification (which will be a set of axioms) may be tested in various ways in order to check that it exhibits the kinds of properties that are required for the intended theory (that is, the specification satisfies the informal requirements). If the specification corresponds (or can be made to correspond) to a program in the sense of Prolog (see Chapter 6), or a rewrite system in the sense of REVE (Chapter 7), then the evaluation of particular queries is an immediate possibility; in this way, the specification is treated as a prototype system. Also, general theorems may be shown to follow from the axioms, assuring that the specification is "correct" for whole classes of problems; these proofs will generally involve a component of induction, a subject that is studied in detail in Part 3 of this text. Apart from tests for the required functionality, there are also deeper questions concerning completeness and consistency. It is impossible to answer such questions in general, but here a system like REVE might suggest additional axioms that may be considered.

1.2.2 Program Synthesis

Once the initial specification has been constructed and shown to be "correct", the next step is to produce an implementation. This task is usually difficult. The problem is that, as indicated above, requirements specifications are intended to be an abstract description of what is required. They should not be concerned with issues of implementation, because these simply cloud the details of the specification, and, worse, restrict the class of programs that would satisfy the intended requirements. This means that, although such specifications present a precise description of what is required, they generally give no indication of how to produce a program (in the normal sense) that will satisfy those requirements.

One of the major tasks involved in the implementation step is to produce a "design" specification of the desired functions that is constructive and readily amenable to implementation [Kr87]. Producing from this an implementation in Ada, say, will then present little problem and could be performed by a compiler-like system. But how will the transition from one style of specification to another be made? Consider, for example, the following abbreviated version of an example in [Kr85] (also to be found in [Kr87]):

Suppose we require functions "mod" and "/" on the natural numbers that satisfy the following formal requirements specification: for $N > 0$,

$$M \bmod N < N, \text{ and} \qquad\qquad\qquad\qquad \text{(I)}$$
$$M = N * (M / N) + (M \bmod N).$$

From this a design specification needs to be constructed, such as

$$M / N = \begin{cases} 0 & \text{if } M < N \\ ((M - N) / N) + 1 & \text{if } M \geq N, \text{ and} \end{cases}$$

$$\qquad\qquad\qquad\qquad\qquad\qquad\qquad\qquad\qquad \text{(II)}$$

$$M \bmod N = \begin{cases} M & \text{if } M < N \\ (M - N) \bmod N & \text{if } M \geq N. \end{cases}$$

How may the transition from (I) to (II) be made and how may it be verified? A possible approach is to attempt to derive the design specification from the formal requirements specification using theorem-proving techniques (commonly referred to as "program synthesis"). In Chapter 7 it will be shown how, for a slightly simpler example, the "design" may be synthesized from the "requirements".

1.2.3 Program Transformations

In the "transformational" approach to programming, programs are constructed from their specifications in stages according to formal rules. The process is analogous to the bottom-up construction of proofs in mathematics, where theorems are derived from a set of axioms via the application of formal inference rules. The validity of the program/theorem with respect to the specification/axioms is ensured by the correctness of the rules. Given an initial formal specification, the computer applies a sequence of correctness-preserving transformation rules, individually or as a group, to derive the desired program, with interactive guidance from the programmer. The programmer makes design decisions in selecting the preconceived transformation rules to achieve a particular purpose, e.g. to optimise according to certain criteria [Kr87]. In this way, program construction and verification are integrated so that the resulting program is automatically correct in the sense that it conforms to the initial formal specification. Also, since the transitions can be described by schematic rules they can be reused for whole classes of problems [BM86]. Equally important, since the whole process is formalised it can be supported by a computer [BM86].

Considered individually, these transformation rules take the form of schema for development steps which have been proven to be correctness-preserving. For example, the following (taken from [Kr85], and also to be found in [Kr87]) is a schema for removing one type of recursion:

```
function F(X: S) return R is        function F(X: S) return R is
                                     Y: S := X;
  begin                               begin
    if B(X) then                        while not B(Y) loop
      return T(X);                        Y := H(Y);
    else                                end loop;
      return F(H(X));                   return T(Y);
    end if;                          end F;
  end F;
```

Here F is a function acting on an arbitrary number of parameters X of type S (numbers or lists or records, etc.) and returning a value of type R; B is a relation on X (e.g. "<"); and T and H are functions that act on the relevant types and return values of the types R and S respectively. For a given function fitting the recursive schema on the left (e.g. $M \bmod N = $ if $M < N$ then M else $(M - N) \bmod N$), by transliteration to a form that fits the schema on the right a loop construct can be automatically produced that computes the same function.

The correctness of the transformations themselves ultimately relates back to the definition of the programming language. In general, a verifier needs to be able to manipulate this formal definition of the language to enable proofs to be carried out. The proof of the equivalence of two program schemas (corresponding to the proof of correctness of a program transformation) will be described in Chapter 8 of this book. However, in this study only a very simple functional language will be treated which will avoid the many problems involved in proving transformations correct for languages such as Ada.

Apart from the correctness of the program transformations themselves, there are also verification issues concerning the *applicability conditions* associated with each transformation. These conditions ensure that the application of the transformation preserves some relation (equivalence, say), that is, that the program fragment to which the transformation is applied and the produced fragment satisfy the required relation. They are essentially of two types: syntactic and semantic. An example of a syntactic condition is the requirement that some variable must not appear in the initial program (since it is to be introduced as a new variable in the produced program). An example of a semantic condition is that some function symbol must be associative. There will usually be algorithms that can determine whether syntactic conditions are satisfied, and thus these conditions are not dealt with by a verifier. That semantic conditions are satisfied, on the other hand, will generally require proof. These proofs must be carried out by some sort of theorem prover, and will generally require induction.

1.3 REPRESENTATION AND REASONING

This section will provide an overview of the major ideas to be discussed in this book. It will be concerned with the three main aspects of the mechanical solution to any proposed problem:

- how the problem may be represented for the purposes of mechanical manipulation by a computer,
- in what sense the problem may constitute a "theorem", and
- how the theorem may be proved mechanically.

In particular, the discussion of the first two aspects will naturally lead to an informal account of the "system of logic" taken as the basis for the current study, generally referred to as "classical first-order predicate logic (with equality)". It will be shown how mathematical problems may be represented in this logic, and indicated, by example, how its expressive power is limited. It will also be compared with some other logics, thus explaining its name, and indicated why this logic was chosen rather than another. With regard to the third aspect of the proposed problems, the theorem-proving task, a simple but non-trivial classical theorem and its proof will be presented and the first steps to its automated proof outlined.

1.3.1 Representing Theories

A system of logic is given by a *language* and a *semantics* for this language. The language specifies the set of *well-formed* (or, grammatically correct) sentences constructed from a given set of symbols (an alphabet), while the semantics specifies the meaning of these well-formed expressions. The expressiveness of the logic is determined by these two components. It is usual, however, simply to speak of the expressiveness of the language, as in talking of the expressiveness of "natural" languages such as English.

The language of first-order logic is very expressive. In fact, some logicians maintain that once theoreticians attempt to formalise their intuitions about the structures they are intending to capture, the axioms they construct will always be expressible in first-order logic (cf. [Ba77]). There are good technical reasons for taking this view. Many other logics, such as many-sorted logic, which are more expressive in practice, may be represented within (unsorted) first-order logic (see [En72]), while there are certain properties of first-order logic that are not exhibited by truly more expressive logics such as second-order logic. In particular, there is no mechanisable system of proof (according to current understanding of mechanisation, i.e. Turing machines, etc.) for full second-order logic, a property that is, of course, of fundamental importance in the current context. Essentially, the view may be taken that logics more expressive than first-order logic simply provide a more concise and elegant mechanism for representing certain concepts (or theories). This section will outline the essential aspects of first-order logic (explaining the reason for its name), and will illustrate its power by discussing some typical theories; examples of the limitations of its expressiveness may be found in [Ba77] and in most textbooks on logic, such as [En72].

The basic symbols of first-order logic are divided into two groups: the *logical* symbols which have predefined meanings, and the *non-logical* symbols whose meanings are determined by the context (that is, the problem of concern). In this book, the following logical symbols will be used:

the propositional connectives: ¬ (not), ∨ (or), ∧ (and), → (if..then),
the first-order quantifiers: ∀ (for all), ∃ (there exists),
the equality relation: = (equals),
variables: $x, y, z, x_1, y_1, z_1, ...,$ and
some punctuation symbols: (,) and ,.

The name in brackets next to each symbol indicates its intended meaning; a more formal explanation of each symbol may be found in Chapter 2.

The non-logical symbols are "function" and "predicate" symbols (other than =). Examples of non-logical symbols are the constant 0, the function symbol + (usually used to represent addition) and the predicate (or relation) symbol < (usually used to represent the relation "less than"). In general, if well-known symbols such as 0, +, and < are not used, then the function symbols will be represented by small letters (other than the letters for variables) such as f, g and h, while the predicate symbols will be represented by capital letters such as P, Q and R. Usually function symbols specifically intended to denote constants (i.e. "nullary" function symbols) will be taken from the set $\{a, b, c, d, e\}$.

Since the meanings of the non-logical symbols are not predefined (and are not "built-in" to the choice of symbols, such as '+'), axioms (or assumptions) have to be introduced which express (as far as is possible) their intended meaning. These axioms are stated with well-formed expressions (or "sentences") of the language. The technical details of the construction of the well-formed expressions are not particularly interesting from a pedagogical point of view, and are, in fact, no different from what would be expected from normal mathematical usage, apart from their precision. To illustrate the form these expressions take and the manner in which meaning is assigned to them, some example "theories" will be discussed.

Groups

A group is given by a set S together with a function on S, denoted by the symbol *, which satisfies the following two axioms

$$\{\exists y \forall x (x * y = x \land \exists z \, x * z = y), \forall x \forall y \forall z \, x * (y * z) = (x * y) * z\}.$$

The first axiom, for instance, may be read as follows:

there exists *a* **y** *such that* **for all x** *it holds that*
    (x * y equals x, and there exists *a* **z** *such that* **x * z equals y).**

The emboldened parts of this sentence correspond to a symbol-by-symbol translation of the original expression; the italic parts have been included merely to make the sentence more readable from a grammatical point of view.

It is more usual for two further functions, denoted by the constant e and the unary function symbol $-$, to be included in the definition of a group and for the first axiom in the above set then to be re-expressed as the pair of axioms (in this case, *equations*) $\forall x\, x * e = x$ and $\forall x\, x * -x = e$. This is an example of the process of Skolemisation: the existentially quantified variables in the axioms are replaced by functions. Note that a constant was introduced to replace y, while a function of one parameter, x, was introduced for z; this corresponds to the fact that the value of z depends upon the value of x (since z is the "inverse" of x), while the value of y is the same no matter what the value of x is. Once the existential quantifiers have been removed in this way, the universal quantifiers may then be omitted for the sake of brevity, and the conjunction symbol $\wedge$ may also be removed and the single axiom thus replaced by two.

When the axioms are expressed in this alternative form, a group requires two other components: a selection of some particular value (from the set S) to be assigned to the constant e, and a unary function on S to be assigned to $-$. A set S together with an assignment of a function to each of the symbols in $\{e, -, *\}$ is said to be an *interpretation* of the symbols; the set S is said to be the *domain* of the interpretation. If the axioms are *true* for a particular interpretation then the interpretation is said to be a *model* of the axioms; also the axioms are said to be *satisfied* by the interpretation. For example, the interpretation given by taking the non-zero rational numbers as the domain, and by assigning to the symbols $*$, $-$ and e, respectively, the *multiplication* function, the *inverse* function, and the value 1, is clearly a model of the axioms. The axioms are also satisfied if S is taken to be the set of integers, and $*$, $-$ and e are assigned, respectively, the *addition* function, the unary *minus* function and the value 0. However, the axioms are not satisfied if, for example, S is taken to be the set of integers and $*$ is assigned the *multiplication* function, no matter what assignments are provided for $-$ and e: to satisfy the axiom $x * e = x$ the constant e must be assigned the value 1, but then there is no integer n such that 2, say, multiplied by n is 1, and thus the equation $x * -x = e$ cannot be satisfied.

Group theory is concerned with reasoning about subsets of the models of these axioms. For instance, commutative groups are one important subset of the models of these axioms; they may be characterised by adding the axiom $x * y = y * x$ to the above set. Examples of submodels of the set of groups that cannot be characterised by any set of first-order axioms may be found in [Ba77].

Number Theory

For the purposes of symbolic manipulation, the notations 1, 2, 3,... usually used for the natural numbers are not very appropriate. The problem lies in the fact that there is no explicit connection between each of these symbols. A preferable notation may be based upon the use of the constant "0" and a unary function symbol s. Any number may be expressed in the form $s(...s(0)...)$ (represented by $s^n(0)$ for brevity) where the number n of s's is determined by the size of the number. This notation is more cumbersome, but is easier to manipulate. For example, with this notation the addition function, denoted $+$, may be defined as follows:

$$\{x + 0 = x, \; x + s(y) = s(x + y)\}$$

(where the variables are universally quantified, but these quantifiers have been omitted since there are no existential quantifiers involved). These equations may be used to evaluate the sum of any pair of numbers. For example, $3 + 2$ may be represented as $s(s(s(0))) + s(s(0))$, and this in turn may be evaluated as follows:

$$s(s(s(0))) + s(s(0)) \quad = s(s(s(s(0))) + s(0)) \qquad \text{by the second axiom}$$
$$= s(s(s(s(s(0))) + 0)) \qquad \text{by the second axiom again}$$
$$= s(s(s(s(s(0))))) \qquad \text{by the first axiom.}$$

On the other hand, it should not be thought that the only possible model of these axioms is the one given by taking the natural numbers together with the functions "zero", "successor" and "addition". Even if the set of natural numbers is assumed as the "domain" of the interpretation, there are still other functions that satisfy the equations above. For example, s could be assigned the function "$+ 2$", rather than "$+ 1$", and the axioms clearly would still be satisfied. Alternatively, s could be assigned the "identity" function defined by $I(x) = x$, and $+$ could be assigned the "subtraction" function, $--$, for natural numbers, defined by

$$x -- y = \begin{cases} 0 & \text{if } y > x \\ x - y & \text{otherwise,} \end{cases}$$

where '$-$' denotes the usual subtraction for real numbers. It is not difficult to see that this interpretation is also a model for the axioms. Also, while this model is very different from the first, the equation $s(s(s(0))) + s(s(0)) = s(s(s(s(s(0)))))$ still holds, for in this case $s^n(0) = I^n(0) = 0$ for any n and hence the equation reduces to $0 -- 0 = 0$, which is true. In fact, the reasoning used above to verify the equation $s(s(s(0))) + s(s(0)) = s(s(s(s(s(0)))))$ corresponds to a simple proof that it is a "logical consequence" of the axioms (see the discussion in the next section), and hence that it holds for any model of the axioms.

Note, on the other hand, that the equation $s(0) = 0$ is not a logical consequence of the given axioms, and thus, while it is true for the third model described, it is not true of all models; this is not surprising, since it is obviously not true for the "intended model". Naturally, the equation $s(0) = 0$ could be added as an extra axiom, thus excluding the first and second proposed interpretations as models. On the other hand, to eliminate the third interpretation as a model the axiom $\neg 0 = s(0)$ may be added. To exclude also the second model, the axiom $\forall x(\neg x = 0 \to \exists y x = s(y))$ could be added; for in the second model the odd numbers fail to satisfy this axiom. Unfortunately, it is not possible to exclude all models other than the first (the originally intended) model with the addition of first-order axioms. On the other hand, it is possible to exclude all "non-isomorphic" models that take any subset of the natural numbers as their domain; *isomorphic* essentially means identical apart from the names for the symbols. (An example of a model of the original axioms that is isomorphic to the first model above is given by taking the domain to be the even natural numbers, s to be "$+ 2$", and $+$ to be addition; for instance, there is no axiom (involving only the functions given) that distinguishes this model from the first model—as the reader may like to verify.) See [En72] for more discussion of the models of an extended set of axioms for 0, s and $+$.

Databases; The Family Relationships Example

As a non-numeric example (under the "natural" interpretation), consider the following characterisation of the relation of being a "grandparent" in terms of the "simpler" relation of being a "parent":

$$\forall x \forall y (Gparent(x, y) \leftrightarrow \exists z(Parent(x, z) \wedge Parent(z, y))).$$

Given the additional "facts" that $Parent(jack, jane)$ and $Parent(jane, tom)$ hold (are axioms) then it follows that $Gparent(jack, tom)$ holds. It is not difficult to see how this definition of $Gparent$ together with the definitions of other relationships and individual "facts" may be used as the basis for a database containing hereditary information. It should be noted, however, that there are (infinitely) many other models of these axioms apart from the one indicated by the choice of symbols. The construction of examples of such models is left to the reader.

Note that in each of the above examples, the domain in each case was taken to be a set of values (or "individuals"). This is expressed by saying that the first-order quantifiers "range over" the elements of a set. This is what distinguishes first-order logic from, say, second-order logic in which the quantifiers may range over sets (or, in other words, properties) themselves. For example, the expression $\forall P \exists y P(y)$ is a statement of second-order logic which claims that for every property P there is some value that satisfies P. In first-order logic this second-order formula would have to be replaced by a (probably infinite) set of formulae $\{\exists y \alpha_1(y), \exists y \alpha_2(y), ...\}$ for each formula α_i in the language of the current sets of axioms. Unfortunately, this set of first-order formulae does not completely capture the meaning of the second-order formula even for the given set of axioms, for it applies only to those properties definable in first-order logic, and not to all possible properties (see, for example, [En72]). This issue (which is related to the incompleteness theorem mentioned above) will crop up several times in this text, but it is not an integral part of the current study from a pragmatic point of view, and may be safely ignored by the reader.

1.3.2 A Simple Theorem and Its Proof

The following example theorem and its proof will serve to illustrate several aspects of the current study of theorem proving. In particular, it will explain the use of the term "classical" for the system of logic taken as the basis for the current study.

The example chosen is a classical theorem concerning the "irrational" numbers. A number is said to be *rational* if it may be represented in the form m/n where m and n $(n \neq 0)$ are integers, and is said to be *irrational* otherwise. It is well known that, for example, the square root of 2, denoted $\sqrt{2}$, is irrational. The theorem is the following.

Theorem: There are two irrational numbers, q and r, such that q^r is rational.

Classical proof: Consider the number $\sqrt{2}^{\sqrt{2}}$. It is either rational or irrational. If it is rational, then let $q = \sqrt{2}$ and $r = \sqrt{2}$, and the problem is solved. If it is irrational, then let

$$q = \sqrt{2}^{\sqrt{2}} \text{ and } r = \sqrt{2};$$

then

$$q^r = \left(\sqrt{2}^{\sqrt{2}}\right)^{\sqrt{2}} = \sqrt{2}^{\left(\sqrt{2} \, * \, \sqrt{2}\right)} = \left(\sqrt{2}\right)^2 = 2$$

and thus q^r is again rational.

This is a "non-constructive" proof; that is, it does not determine the values of q and r required in the result. The solution may be either the pair $\left(\sqrt{2}, \sqrt{2}\right)$ or the pair $\left(\sqrt{2}^{\sqrt{2}}, \sqrt{2}\right)$; the proof does not indicate which. The proof depended upon the assumption that a number is either rational or irrational (i.e. not rational); this is a special case of the more general assumption that every proposition is either *true* or not *true*. This may seem to be a reasonable assumption to make, but there is a system of logic called *intuitionistic logic* [Du77] which does not accept this claim as a basis for mathematical reasoning. This logic requires that every proof must provide an algorithm for constructing the objects stipulated to exist in the theorem. In the system of logic used in this book, however, the assumption that a proposition is either *true* or not *true* is accepted; this explains the use of the term "classical" to refer to this logic.

The first step toward a mechanical proof of this theorem is to represent it in a "symbolic" form that may be manipulated by a computer. Naturally, different theorem-proving systems may not only use different symbols, but may even require different formulations of a conjecture (as will become apparent in later chapters). For the moment, however, full first-order logic with the standard symbols will be used to represent problems.

1.3.2.1 Representing the Theorem

The claim that some number n is rational may be denoted by the expression $R(n)$, while the "exponentiation" function x^y may be denoted by $exp(x, y)$. The theorem to be proved may then be represented by the formula

$$\exists x \exists y (\neg R(x) \land \neg R(y) \land R(exp(x, y))).$$

In this particular example the variables are intended to range over the real numbers. The formula may be read (in a "quasi-English") as

there exists *an* x *and* **there exists** *a* y *such that*
not Rational x **and not R**ational y **and R**ational **exp**onentiation of x to y.

From this informal translation, it may be seen that the formula expresses the content of the original theorem.

1.3.2.2 The Truth of the Theorem

The first task is to determine in what sense the conjecture is *true*. This will depend upon the way in which the non-logical symbols are "interpreted" and also on the semantics of the underlying logic. In this case it is known, given the classical proof above, that the conjecture is *true* according to the semantics of classical logic if the symbol R is interpreted to mean "rational" and *exp* is interpreted to mean "exponentiation". This interpretation is clearly not "built into" the symbols, and (infinitely) many other interpretations could be given to them. If, for instance, R was intended to mean "prime" and the symbol *exp* was assigned the multiplication function, then the conjecture would correspond to the claim that there exist non-primes x and y such that x^y is prime, which is obviously *false*.

Since the intended meaning of a particular symbol does not follow automatically from the choice of notation, axioms have to be introduced that restrict the class of interpretations allowed. In the current example, it is required to restrict R and *exp* sufficiently to capture the features of the property "rational" and the "exponentiation" function, respectively, to ensure that the proposed conjecture holds. It turns out, in fact, that very few assumptions about the property "rational" and the "exponentiation" function are required for the theorem to hold.

Suppose that the "axioms" $\neg R(a)$ and $R(exp(exp(a, a), a))$ are given, where a is just a constant representing, in the intended interpretation, the square root of 2. These assumptions may in fact follow from more basic axioms describing the rational numbers, and thus correspond to *lemmas* (i.e. theorems required for the proof of the main theorem), but for the current purposes they will be given axiom status. It follows from these two assumptions that the theorem holds. In other words, the formula proposed as the conjecture is a "logical consequence" of these two axioms in the following sense: whenever $\neg R(a)$ and $R(exp(exp(a, a), a))$ are *true* for a given interpretation of the symbols R, a and *exp*, the conjecture is also *true* for this interpretation. This fact is represented by the following "consequence" statement:

$$\neg R(a), R(exp(exp(a, a), a)) \models \exists x \exists y (\neg R(x) \wedge \neg R(y) \wedge R(exp(x, y))).$$

For example, it is clear that the axioms hold if R means rational, a denotes the square root of 2 and *exp* means exponentiation, for these axioms were exactly the assumptions used in the original proof. On the other hand, the axioms do not hold if R is interpreted to mean "prime" and *exp* is interpreted to mean "multiplication", no matter what number a is intended to represent; thus the fact that the conjecture does not hold in this interpretation does not contradict the "consequence" claim. However, the axioms do hold also if R represents the property "perfect_square", *exp* represents "addition" and a denotes the number "3"; and it is easy to see that the conjecture also holds for this interpretation of the symbols. It is also not difficult to see that many other (including "non-numeric") interpretations satisfy the axioms, and hence the conjecture. Thus the result is now more general than was apparent from its original statement and proof. This generalisation has followed naturally from the symbolic representation: it has been determined that the conjecture holds whenever the proposed axioms hold, and that this is *true* irrespective of the meanings assigned to the symbols.

In general, following the translation of a theorem to symbolic form, axioms must be introduced that express the required properties of the symbols. These axioms must at least be sufficient for the conjecture to be a logical consequence of them, irrespective of the meanings assigned to the symbols. While the mathematician is free (in most cases) simply to assume the intended meaning of the symbols, they must be explicitly axiomatised (or, perhaps, implicitly "built-in" via a special procedure or algorithm) if the proof is to be performed by a computer. As already noted, this means that the user of the system is required to tell the computer "everything" about the domain of discourse in the initial phase; but once this specification is provided usually many results may be proved to follow, not just a single proposition.

1.3.2.3 Proving the Theorem

The next task is to indicate how $\exists x \exists y(\neg R(x) \wedge \neg R(y) \wedge R(exp(x, y)))$ may be mechanically proved to follow from the axioms $\neg R(a)$ and $R(exp(exp(a, a), a))$. It will become apparent in Part 2 of this book that each of the main systems to be described is powerful enough to prove this particular theorem. The current aim, however, is not to provide all the details of how some particular system might prove it, but to give an overview of the general form a proof might take.

There are essentially four aspects to any proof system:

- a (possibly empty) set of "logical" or "formal" axioms,
- a set of "inference rules",
- a proof development method, and
- a proof strategy.

The logical axioms are "universal truths" (i.e. formulae *true* in all interpretations). For example, $P \to P$, $\forall x P(x) \to \exists x P(x)$ and (in classical logic) $\neg P \vee P$ may be taken as logical axioms. These axioms may be included with the "non-logical" axioms assumed for the particular problem (such as those discussed in the preceding subsections). The inference rules are "transformation" rules that, essentially, are intended to map valid formulae to a valid formula. For example, the inference rule *modus ponens* 'from P and $P \to Q$ infer Q' allows the statement Q to be accepted as *true* if P and $P \to Q$ have already been shown to hold.

The proof development method concerns the "methodology" or the "style" of proof employed. There are several aspects to this. For instance, the proof may be performed "bottom-up" or "top-down". The classical "bottom-up" (or *synthetic*) approach to proof development starts with the axioms and applies the rules until the goal conjecture is deduced. The more practical "top-down" (or *analytic*) approach starts with the conjecture and applies the rules "backwards" (reducing the conjecture to subgoals) until axioms are derived. Sometimes a combination of the synthetic and analytic approaches is more appropriate. Apart from this there is also the question of what is in fact proved. To take the conjecture proposed above as an example, the system may be designed to prove any of the following:

- $\exists x \exists y(\neg R(x) \wedge \neg R(y) \wedge R(exp(x, y)))$ may be "deduced" from the axioms $\neg R(a)$ and $R(exp(exp(a, a), a))$,
- the single formula

$$(\neg R(a) \wedge R(exp(exp(a, a), a))) \to \exists x \exists y(\neg R(x) \wedge \neg R(y) \wedge R(exp(x, y)))$$

  is valid (i.e. a "logical truth", as for the logical axioms), or
- the set of formulae

$$\{\neg R(a), R(exp(exp(a, a), a)), \neg \exists x \exists y(\neg R(x) \wedge \neg R(y) \wedge R(exp(x, y)))\}$$

  has no models (i.e. is unsatisfiable).

These are slightly different approaches, each of which requires a slightly different mechanism for proof. The first approach requires a "deductive" system of proof, such as the usual style of "natural deduction" systems (see Section 3.1), and is perhaps the most natural approach. The correctness of the second style of proof depends upon the fact that a formula α is a logical consequence of a finite set of formulae $\beta_1, \beta_2,..., \beta_n$ if and only if the formula $(\beta_1 \wedge \beta_2 \wedge...\wedge \beta_n) \to \alpha$ is valid;

this style of proof is performed by "affirmation" systems such as cut-free sequent calculi (see Section 3.2). The third style of proof corresponds to a "proof by contradiction" method; it assumes the conjecture is false (in other words, it assumes the "negation" of the conjecture as an additional assumption—as in the example above) and then shows that this leads to a contradiction. Its correctness depends upon the classical assumption that if the axioms together with the formula $\neg\alpha$ is inconsistent then α must be a logical consequence of the axioms. Many methods of proof such as the "resolution" method to be described in Section 3.3 use this style of proof. While there are differences between these three approaches to proof, it will be seen that for the systems discussed in this book there are also remarkable similarities.

On top of the development method, a strategy for performing proofs is imposed. This may include using "derived" rules of inference, providing directions as to how to apply the given rules, or using special procedures for dealing with subtasks. The derived rules are simply new rules that combine several inferences in the original system into one step; they do not increase the power of the system in a technical sense, but save time in practice. The "direction" component of a theorem prover, on the other hand, determines which rules should be applied and to which formulae. The choice of "direction component" can have a dramatic effect both on the speed with which a proof is produced and on the "naturalness" of the derived proof. Many examples of such strategies will be discussed in Chapter 4, where both "complete" strategies (which are assured always to prove any theorem) and "heuristics" strategies (which are not assured to prove any theorem, but may be more efficient and natural in the cases they do succeed) are described.

With regard to the treatment of special subtasks, the mechanisms employed may include decision procedures mentioned in Section 1.1, but may also include procedures for reasoning about special relations (such as equality) in a more efficient or natural manner, or for dealing with difficult tasks such as proving theorems by induction. In particular cases, such as in proving inductive theorems, a combination of individual procedures for dealing with different aspects of a proof may lead to a "proof plan" according to which all proofs have an almost identical structure; this is an issue outside the scope of this book, but the idea is implicit in the system to be discussed in Chapter 8, which has proved many theorems using the same basic set of "heuristic" mechanisms.

It is hoped that this discussion has given some idea of the issues involved in the mechanisation of proof. For further details on how the proposed theorem may be proved mechanically, the reader will have to proceed to the main text.

CHAPTER 2

THE UNDERLYING LOGIC

This preliminary chapter is concerned with the basic notation and underlying concepts to be used in the rest of the book. Apart from clarifying the mathematical notions of relation and function, the main purpose is to introduce the required details of first-order logic.

2.1 FUNDAMENTAL CONCEPTS

In this section some standard notation and definitions concerning sets, relations and functions are reviewed for reference.

2.1.1 Enumerable and Recursive Sets

Some important concepts regarding "enumerability" will be referred to in the text, and are defined (informally) here.

Enumerable Sets: A set is said to be enumerable or *countable* if it may be put into a one-to-one correspondence with a subset of the natural numbers.

(The term "one-to-one correspondence" is defined formally below.) Examples of enumerable sets are: any (possibly finite) subset of the natural numbers, the rationals, and the set of all finite strings of letters from an enumerable alphabet. Examples of non-enumerable sets are: the real numbers, the set of all subsets of the natural numbers, and the set of all infinite strings of letters from an alphabet of two or more letters. This book will be concerned principally with enumerable sets: unless otherwise stated, any given infinite set will be assumed to be enumerable.

Recursive Sets: A set is said to be recursive or *decidable* if there is an algorithm (a program/procedure that terminates for all input) that can determine whether an element is in the set or not. Otherwise it is *undecidable*.

Recursively Enumerable Sets: A set is said to be recursively enumerable or *semi-decidable* if there is a procedure (program) that can determine if an element is in the set, but which possibly will not terminate for an element not in the set.

Clearly, recursive sets are recursively enumerable, and these, in turn, are enumerable, though the converse containments do not hold. The set of all programs in a standard programming language is, of course, recursive, since it is possible to determine whether an arbitrary (finite) string of symbols constitutes a program in a particular language. The set of all programs that terminate for a given input is an example of a set that is recursively enumerable but not recursive, since it is *not* possible to decide whether an arbitrary program will terminate for a given input, but if it does happen to terminate then it is possible to show that it does (simply by running the program). On the other hand, the set of all programs that do not terminate for a given input is not even recursively enumerable (though it is clearly enumerable); if it was, then termination would be decidable, as follows from the following exercise.

Exercise 2.1: Let S be a recursive set, and let S' be some subset of S. Show that if both S' and $S - S'$ are recursively enumerable, then they are also recursive.

The reader is referred to Enderton's book [En72], or any other good (modern) book on logic, for more details on these issues.

2.1.2 Relations

For technical simplicity, relations will be defined as sets of sequences. An n-place relation is thus a set of sequences, or, more accurately, n-tuples, each of n objects. An n-tuple satisfies the n-place (or n-ary) relation R if it is in the set corresponding to R, and does not satisfy R otherwise.

Ordered N-tuple: For $n \geq 2$, if $a_1, a_2,..., a_n$ are objects, then $(a_1, a_2,..., a_n)$ is their ordered n-tuple. By definition,

$$(a_1, a_2,..., a_n) = (b_1, b_2,..., b_n) \quad \text{iff} \quad a_1 = b_1, a_2 = b_2,..., a_n = b_n.$$

An ordered 2-tuple will also be referred to as an *ordered pair*.

Cartesian Product: If $S_1, S_2,..., S_n$ ($n \geq 2$) are sets then their Cartesian product is defined by

$$S_1 \times S_2 \times \cdots \times S_n = \{(s_1, s_2,..., s_n) : s_1 \in S_1,..., s_n \in S_n\}.$$

The Cartesian product $S \times S \times \cdots \times S$ will be denoted S^n, where n is the number of S's.

N-ary Relation: For $n \geq 2$, R^n is an n-ary relation on the sets $S_1, S_2,..., S_n$ if

$$R^n \subseteq S_1 \times S_2 \times \cdots \times S_n.$$

Example: The relation "<" on the set $\mathbf{N}$ of natural numbers is given by the following enumerably infinite set:

$$\{(0, 1), (0, 2), (1, 2), (0, 3), (1, 3), (2, 3),...\}.$$

This is a subset of the Cartesian product of the set $\mathbf{N}$ with itself.

Rather than writing $(s_1, s_2,..., s_n) \in R^n$, membership of a relation will usually be denoted by $R^n(s_1, s_2,..., s_n)$. Also, the superscript numeral, since superfluous, will usually be omitted. For some particular binary relations such as "<" and "=" the infix notation "aRb" (e.g. $a < b$) may be used rather than $R(a, b)$. Note that, in fact, the general characterisation of a relation above in terms of n-tuples of objects taken from n possibly different sets will not be required in this book, since an "untyped" logic is assumed. Thus, throughout this text the S_i in the definition of relation will always be assumed to be the same set.

Predicate: The term predicate will be used to denote *proposition letters* (i.e. "nullary relations"), *properties* (i.e. "unary relations"), and n-ary relations ($n \geq 2$).

Note that the nullary relations must be either "*true*" or "*false*" for the empty sequence of objects, and thus correspond to the symbols of propositional logic (hence their name). For this reason, a proposition letter with the name P, say, will always be written P as opposed to $P()$. The unary relations, on the other hand, are distinguished from the general class of relations because they do not "relate" objects, but only determine a set of objects (those that satisfy them). For example, the property "is_a_dog" determines the set of dogs.

2.1.3 Functions

Functions will be defined as special kinds of relations.

Function: An n-ary function f from A to B, where $A = A_1 \times A_2 \times \cdots \times A_n$, is a relation between A and B, such that for each $a \in A$ there is exactly one $b \in B$ such that $(a, b) \in f$.

The standard notation $f(a_1,..., a_n)$ for $a_1 \in A_1,..., a_n \in A_n$ will be used to denote the unique element b of B such that $(a_1,..., a_n, b) \in f$. Intuitively, $f(a_1,..., a_n)$ denotes the "application" of f to $a_1,..., a_n$ to "produce" a unique b in B. The elements $a_1,..., a_n$ are said to be the *arguments* of the function application. To denote the fact that f is from A to B, the notation $f : A \rightarrow B$ will be used, rather than $A \times B \subseteq f$. Functions will generally be defined by equations in the usual manner, as illustrated in the next example below.

Domain, Codomain and Range: A (i.e. $A_1 \times A_2 \times \cdots \times A_n$) is said to be the domain of the function f, while B is said to be the codomain. The subset of B such that at least one element of A is mapped to an element of this subset is said to be the range of the function.

Example: For the unary function "sq" on $\mathbf{N}$, given by $sq(n) = n * n$ for n (where '$*$' here denotes the binary function of multiplication on the natural numbers), the set $\mathbf{N}$ is both the domain and codomain, while the set $\{0, 1, 4, 9,...\}$ is the range.

One-to-one, Onto Functions: A function $f : A \rightarrow B$ is said to be one-to-one if for every $b \in B$ there is at most one $a \in A$ such that $f(a) = b$. It is said to be onto if for every $b \in B$ there is at least one $a \in A$ such that $f(a) = b$ (in other words, B is the range of f).

One-to-one Correspondence: A function $f : A \rightarrow B$ is said to be a one-to-one correspondence, or just a *correspondence*, if it is both one-to-one and onto.

Examples: The function "sq" of the previous example is one-to-one, but is not a one-to-one correspondence on the natural numbers. The addition function from the set of pairs of natural numbers to the set of natural numbers is onto, but it too is not a correspondence.

If there is a one-to-one correspondence between two sets, then it means that, in particular, the sets have the same "number of elements" (or *cardinality*).

2.2 FIRST-ORDER PREDICATE LOGIC

In this section the syntax and semantics of formulae of first-order logic will be described semi-formally. For more detail see, for instance, [En72] or [Ro69].

2.2.1 Syntax

The syntax (or *lexical analysis*) of formulae is concerned purely with their grammatical structure. It specifies the set of correctly formed formulae, without distinguishing the "*true*" from the "*false*" formulae.

Basic Symbols

The symbols from which formulae are constructed are divided into two (disjoint) sets, *logical* and *non-logical*. Essentially, a symbol is logical if it has a predefined meaning and is non-logical otherwise. The logical symbols are:

- the connectives: $\neg, \wedge, \vee, \rightarrow, \leftrightarrow$
- the quantifiers: $\forall, \exists$
- the predicate: $=$
- an infinite set of variables: $x_1, x_2, x_3,...$, and
- the punctuation symbols: '(', ')' and ','.

The variables will be represented by names beginning with the letters u, v, w, x, y, z. Informally, the logical symbols other than the variables and punctuation symbols have, respectively, the meanings **not, and, or, if..then, if and only if, for all, there exists** and **equals**.

The non-logical symbols are function symbols and predicate symbols, apart from =, each of which has an associated number of arguments referred to as its *arity*. Unless otherwise stated, function symbols will begin with either lower-case letters, other than the letters for variables, or with symbols such as '+', while predicate symbols will begin with either capital letters or symbols such as '<'. Function symbols of arity 0 will be called *constants*. Function symbols specifically assumed to be constants will begin with one of the letters a, b, c, d, e. A constant with the name "c", say, will generally be denoted simply by c as opposed to $c()$.

Well-Formed Expressions
An expression is simply any string of symbols. The well-formed expressions (with respect to a given collection of non-logical symbols) are as follows.

Terms:
- Constants and variables are terms.
- If f is a function symbol of arity n and $t_1,..., t_n$ are terms, then $f(t_1,..., t_n)$ is a term.

Atomic Formulae (Atoms):
- $t_1 = t_2$ is an atomic formula if t_1 and t_2 are terms.
- P is an atomic formula if P is a proposition letter.
- $P(t_1,..., t_n)$ is an atomic formula if P is a predicate symbol of arity $n > 0$, and $t_1,..., t_n$ are terms.

Infix notation may also be used for binary function and predicate symbols.

Examples: The expression $f(g(x), b)$ is a term if g and f are, respectively, unary and binary function symbols. The expression $P(f(g(x), b), a, z)$ is then an atomic formula if the symbol P is a ternary predicate symbol. Also, the two expressions $f(x + a, g(b) * z)$ and $g(x) + y < z$ are allowed as abbreviations of, respectively, the term $f(+(x, a), *(g(b), z))$, and the atomic formula $<(+(g(x), y), z)$.

To disambiguate expressions such as $x + y * z$, terms involving infix function symbols will be appropriately bracketed (for example, $x + (y * z)$). This idea may be formalised, if desired, as is done for formulae in the next definition.

(Well-Formed) Formulae:
- An atomic formula is a formula.
- If α and β are formulae, then so are

$$\neg\alpha, \ (\alpha \vee \beta), \ (\alpha \wedge \beta), \ (\alpha \rightarrow \beta), \ (\alpha \leftrightarrow \beta), \ \forall x\, \alpha, \ \text{and} \ \exists x\, \alpha.$$

Brackets have been included in the definition of formulae in order to avoid ambiguities. For instance, the expression $\alpha \vee \beta \wedge \gamma$ is ambiguous unless the appropriate brackets are introduced (or some other convention regarding the reading of formulae is applied). Often in this book, brackets (particularly outermost brackets) will be omitted if no confusion may arise. For instance, the formula $(\neg P \vee Q)$ would be abbreviated to $\neg P \vee Q$. Note that brackets are not required for α in the expressions $\neg\alpha$, $\forall x\, \alpha$ and $\exists x\, \alpha$ to avoid ambiguity.

Exercise 2.2: The (completely bracketed) formula $\neg\neg\forall x\neg\forall y(\exists z P(x, z) \rightarrow Q(y))$ is not ambiguous without additional brackets. Why?

The next few definitions concerning syntactical issues will also be of use in the rest of the text.

Language: A language is an enumerable set of non-logical symbols. The terms and formulae of a language L are those constructed from the logical symbols and the non-logical symbols of L.

Operator: All symbols, other than the variables and punctuation symbols, will be referred to as operators.

Subformula, Subterm: A subformula (subterm) of a formula (term) E is any formula (term) contained in E. In particular, E is a subformula (subterm) of itself.

Ground Expression: This is an expression that contains no variables.

Scope: In the definition of well-formed formulae above, α is the scope of $\neg$, $\forall x$ and $\exists x$, while α and β are the scope of $\vee$, $\wedge$, $\rightarrow$ and $\leftrightarrow$.

Free and Bound Variables: An occurrence of a variable in a formula is said to be bound if it is in the scope of a quantifier with the same variable name, or *is* the variable name of a quantifier. Otherwise it is free.

To indicate that the variables $x_1,..., x_n$ occur free in a formula α, the formula may be written $\alpha(x_1,..., x_n)$. A variable may have both bound and free occurrences within a formula.

Example: In the formula, $\forall y(P(x, y) \vee \exists x Q(x)) \wedge \exists x P(x, z)$, the first occurrence of x is free while the rest are bound; also the two occurrences of y and the single occurrence of z are, respectively, bound and free.

A formula containing a free variable is an incomplete statement. For example, the atomic formula $happy(x)$ says that "x is happy" without indicating "who" x is.

Sentence (or Closed Formula): This is a formula containing no free variables.

Closure: If α is a formula containing exactly the n free variables $x_1,..., x_n$, then
- $\forall x_1 \forall x_2 ... \forall x_n \alpha$ is called the *universal* closure of α.
- $\exists x_1 \exists x_2 ... \exists x_n \alpha$ is called the *existential* closure of α.

For brevity, these are written $\forall x\, \alpha$ and $\exists x\, \alpha$, respectively.

2.2.2 Semantics

While Section 2.2.1 was concerned purely with the syntax of formulae, this section is concerned with their semantics (or meaning).

2.2.2.1 Interpretations

The intention is to define what it means for a formula to be *true* or *false*. This is done using the notion of an *interpretation* (or *structure*), which assigns meanings to the symbols occurring in a formula. For a language L an interpretation $\mathbf{I}$ of L thus consists of the following.

1. A non-empty set, D, called the *domain* of interpretation. The elements of D will be called *values*.

2. An assignment of a function $f_{\mathbf{I}}: D^n \to D$ ($n \geq 0$) to each n-ary function symbol $f \in L$. In particular, each constant is assigned some value from D.

3. An assignment of one of the truth values **T** or **F** to each proposition letter in L.

4. An assignment of a predicate $P_{\mathbf{I}} \subseteq D^n$ ($n > 0$) to each n-ary predicate symbol $P \in L$.

Example: Consider the language $L_{\mathbf{N}} = \{0, s, +, <\}$, where 0, s and $+$ are nullary, unary and binary function symbols, respectively, and $<$ is a binary predicate symbol. One particular interpretation of $L_{\mathbf{N}}$ is given by

- $D = \mathbf{N}$
- 0 is assigned the value 0
- s is assigned the "successor" function $s_{\mathbf{N}}: \mathbf{N} \to \mathbf{N}$
- $+$ is assigned the "addition" function $+_{\mathbf{N}}: \mathbf{N}^2 \to \mathbf{N}$
- $<$ is assigned the "less than" predicate $<_{\mathbf{N}} \subseteq \mathbf{N}^2$.

In this example, the "standard interpretation" has been assigned to the symbols, but it should be noted that there are many other possible interpretations of this language. Even if $\mathbf{N}$ is taken as the domain of interpretation, there are non-enumerably many functions from $\mathbf{N}$ to $\mathbf{N}$ that could be assigned to the function symbol s. This is proven in the following exercise.

Exercise 2.3: Suppose that the set of unary functions from $\mathbf{N}$ to $\mathbf{N}$ may be enumerated as $f_1, f_2,...$, and then define the new unary function f by $f(i) = f_i(i) + 1$ for each $i \in \mathbf{N}$. Show that f cannot be in the enumeration, and hence that the set is not enumerable.

2.2.2.2 Semantics of Well-Formed Expressions

For a given well-formed expression E of a language L the task is to define the meaning of E in an interpretation $\mathbf{I}$ of L. To do this it is necessary to consider the problem of assigning values of the domain of interpretation to any free variables appearing in E. This means that, in general, the meaning of an expression will be different for different assignments of values of $\mathbf{I}$ to its free variables. Before proceeding, note that for a term t all of the variables appearing in t may be considered to be free variables.

Let E be a well-formed expression of the language L containing the m (≥ 0) free variables $x_1,..., x_m$ (the case $m = 0$ corresponding to the empty sequence), and let $d_1,..., d_n$ ($n \geq m$) be n values of D, the domain of an interpretation $\mathbf{I}$ of L. Then the meaning of E in $\mathbf{I}$ under the assignment of d_i ($1 \leq i \leq n$) to x_i ($1 \leq i \leq m$), that is, d_1 to x_1, d_2 to x_2,..., d_m to x_m, is denoted $\mathbf{I}(\alpha)[d_1,..., d_n]$ or, for brevity, $\mathbf{I}(\alpha)[d]$, where d denotes the sequence of n values of D, i.e. $d \in D^n$.

The meanings of terms and formulae of a language L in an interpretation $\mathbf{I}$ of L are now defined in an inductive manner.

Semantics of Terms

The meaning of a term t is distinguished into cases according to its form. In the following definition, let t be a term containing exactly the n variables $x_1,..., x_n$, let d be $d_1,..., d_n$ (n values of D, the domain of $\mathbf{I}$), and let t' be a subterm of t.

- If t' is a constant c then $\mathbf{I}(t')[d] = c_{\mathbf{I}}$
- if t' is a variable x_i then $\mathbf{I}(t')[d] = d_i$
- if t' has the form $f(t_1,..., t_k)$ then $\mathbf{I}(t')[d] = f_{\mathbf{I}}(\mathbf{I}(t_1)[d],..., \mathbf{I}(t_k)[d])$,

where $c_{\mathbf{I}}$ denotes the value from D assigned to c (and similarly for $f_{\mathbf{I}}$).

Example: Let the interpretation for the symbols '0', 's' and '+' be as in the previous example, and let $[d] = [2, 1]$. The meaning of the term $x_1 + s(0 + x_2)$ in this interpretation, under the given assignment to the variables, may be determined as follows:

$$
\begin{aligned}
\mathbf{I}(x_1 + s(0 + x_2))[2, 1] &= \mathbf{I}(x_1)[2, 1] +_{\mathsf{N}} \mathbf{I}(s(0 + x_2))[2, 1] \\
&= 2 +_{\mathsf{N}} \mathbf{I}(s(0 + x_2))[2, 1] \\
&= 2 +_{\mathsf{N}} s_{\mathsf{N}}(\mathbf{I}(0 + x_2)[2, 1]) \\
&= 2 +_{\mathsf{N}} s_{\mathsf{N}}(\mathbf{I}(0)[2, 1] +_{\mathsf{N}} \mathbf{I}(x_2)[2, 1]) \\
&= 2 +_{\mathsf{N}} s_{\mathsf{N}}(0 +_{\mathsf{N}} 1) \\
&= 4
\end{aligned}
$$

Semantics of Formulae

Intuitively, the truth value $\mathbf{T}$ is assigned to each "*true*" formula and $\mathbf{F}$ to each "*false*" formula. For the following definition, let α be a formula containing exactly the n free variables $x_1,..., x_n$, and let $d_1,..., d_n$ be n values of D. As for terms, the meaning of a formula is distinguished into cases according to its form.

If α is atomic it must have one of the forms P or $P(t_1,..., t_n)$ (for some non-logical n-ary predicate P) or $t_1 = t_2$.

- $\mathbf{I}(P)[d] = \mathbf{T}$ iff $P_{\mathbf{I}} = \mathbf{T}$
- $\mathbf{I}(P(t_1,..., t_n))[d] = \mathbf{T}$ iff $P_{\mathbf{I}}(\mathbf{I}(t_1)[d],..., \mathbf{I}(t_n)[d])$
- $\mathbf{I}(t_1 = t_2)[d] = \mathbf{T}$ iff $\mathbf{I}(t_1)[d] = \mathbf{I}(t_2)[d]$

(the latter meaning that t_1 and t_2 denote the same value from D under the given assignment).

If α is not atomic then it must have one of the forms $\neg\beta$, $(\beta \vee \gamma)$, $(\beta \wedge \gamma)$, $(\beta \rightarrow \gamma)$, $(\beta \leftrightarrow \gamma)$, $\forall x\beta$ or $\exists x\beta$, where β and γ are (well-formed) formulae.

- $\mathbf{I}(\neg\beta)[d] = \mathbf{T}$ iff $\mathbf{I}(\beta)[d] = \mathbf{F}$
- $\mathbf{I}(\beta \vee \gamma)[d] = \mathbf{F}$ iff $\mathbf{I}(\beta)[d] = \mathbf{F}$ and $\mathbf{I}(\gamma)[d] = \mathbf{F}$
- $\mathbf{I}(\beta \wedge \gamma)[d] = \mathbf{T}$ iff $\mathbf{I}(\beta)[d] = \mathbf{T}$ and $\mathbf{I}(\gamma)[d] = \mathbf{T}$
- $\mathbf{I}(\beta \rightarrow \gamma)[d] = \mathbf{F}$ iff $\mathbf{I}(\beta)[d] = \mathbf{T}$ and $\mathbf{I}(\gamma)[d] = \mathbf{F}$
- $\mathbf{I}(\beta \leftrightarrow \gamma)[d] = \mathbf{T}$ iff $\mathbf{I}(\beta)[d] = \mathbf{I}(\gamma)[d]$

Note that the above definitions merely restate for general first-order formulae the well-known laws of propositional logic. The next two define the meanings of the quantifiers.

- $\mathbf{I}(\forall x\beta)[d] = \mathbf{T}$ iff $\mathbf{I}(\beta)[d, d] = \mathbf{T}$ for every $d \in D$
- $\mathbf{I}(\exists x\beta)[d] = \mathbf{T}$ iff $\mathbf{I}(\beta)[d, d] = \mathbf{T}$ for at least one $d \in D$

where $[d, d]$ denotes the sequence $[d_1,..., d_n, d]$ and x is referenced as the $(n + 1)$th free variable of β.

Examples:
1. Consider $\forall x\ x + 0 = x$. Here are three interpretations of this sentence, with $D = \mathbf{N}$ in each case and with '$\rightarrow$' taken to mean "is assigned":

    (a) $0 \rightarrow 0$, $+ \rightarrow$ addition. Sentence is *true*.
    (b) $0 \rightarrow 0$, $+ \rightarrow$ multiplication. Sentence is *false*.
    (c) $0 \rightarrow 1$, $+ \rightarrow$ multiplication. Sentence is *true*.

If the formula had been $x + 0 = x$ then in case (b) above it would have been *true* if x was assigned the value 0 but *false* otherwise, whereas the sentence had only one possible meaning in the interpretation.

2. Consider the sentence $\forall x\forall y(\exists z(P(x, z) \wedge P(z, y)) \rightarrow Gp(x, z))$. One interpretation in which this is *true* is given as follows: $D =$ the set of human beings, P is assigned the predicate "parent_of", and Gp is assigned the predicate "grandparent_of". Another interpretation in which it is *true* is: $D = \mathbf{N}$, $P \rightarrow$ "greater_than", $Gp \rightarrow$ "greater_than".

Exercise 2.4: Find an interpretation in which the sentence $\forall x\exists yP(x, y) \rightarrow \exists y\forall xP(x, y)$ is *true*, and an interpretation in which it is *false*.

A binary operator "*op*" is said to be *commutative* if for all appropriate arguments p and q, the expressions $op(p, q)$ and $op(q, p)$ have the same (truth, or domain) value in any interpretation (under the same assignments of domain values for any free-variable occurrences), and is said to be *associative* if for all appropriate arguments p, q and r, the expressions $op(op(p, q), r)$ and $op(p, op(q, r))$ have the same value in any interpretation (use of infix notation being superfluous to these definitions). According to their semantics, the connectives '$\vee$' and '$\wedge$' are both commutative and associative. This means that, for example, the formula $\alpha \vee (\beta \vee \gamma)$ may be written without any bracketing and with α, β and γ in any order. For a set of formulae

$\{\alpha_1, \alpha_2,..., \alpha_n\}$, the formula $\alpha_1 \wedge \alpha_2 \wedge ... \wedge \alpha_n$ is referred to as their *conjunction*, while the formula $\alpha_1 \vee \alpha_2 \vee ... \vee \alpha_n$ is referred to as their *disjunction*.

2.2.2.3 Satisfiability, Validity and Implication

Now that the meanings of formulae have been characterised according to interpretations, this subsection is concerned with those interpretations in which a particular formula is "*true*".

Valid in an Interpretation: Let L be a language, $\mathbf{I}$ be an interpretation of L, D be the domain of $\mathbf{I}$, and α be a formula of L. If α has the value $\mathbf{T}$ in $\mathbf{I}$ for every assignment of the values of D to the free variables of α, then α is said to be valid in $\mathbf{I}$. Equivalently, $\mathbf{I}$ is said to *satisfy* α.

Model: If a formula α is valid in an interpretation $\mathbf{I}$ then $\mathbf{I}$ is said to be a model of α.

Satisfiable formula: If a formula has at least one model then it is said to be satisfiable, otherwise it is *unsatisfiable*.

Valid formula: If a formula is valid in all interpretations then it is simply said to be valid (or *logically valid*).

Example: The sentence $\exists y \forall x P(x, y) \rightarrow \forall x \exists y P(x, y)$ is valid, as the following reasoning shows:
- $\mathbf{I}(\exists y \forall x P(x, y) \rightarrow \forall x \exists y P(x, y)) = \mathbf{F}$ iff $\mathbf{I}(\exists y \forall x P(x, y)) = \mathbf{T}$ and $\mathbf{I}(\forall x \exists y P(x, y)) = \mathbf{F}$.

Expanding gives:
- $\mathbf{I}(\exists y \forall x P(x, y)) = \mathbf{T}$ iff there is some d' in the domain D of $\mathbf{I}$, such that for every $d \in D, P_{\mathbf{I}}(d, d')$ holds, while
- $\mathbf{I}(\forall x \exists y P(x, y)) = \mathbf{F}$ iff it is not the case that for all $e \in D$, there is some $e' \in D$ such that $P_{\mathbf{I}}(e, e')$ holds.

With the choice $d' = e'$ it can be seen that these statements are contradictory, and hence the original sentence must be valid.

Exercise 2.5: Show, by similar reasoning, that the sentence $\exists y \forall x P(x, y) \wedge \neg \forall x \exists y P(x, y)$ is unsatisfiable.

Exercise 2.6: Show that the following are consequences of the definitions above:
- α is valid in $\mathbf{I}$ iff $\forall x \alpha$ is valid in $\mathbf{I}$,
- (hence) α is valid iff $\forall x \alpha$ is valid,
- α is valid iff $\neg \alpha$ is unsatisfiable,
- α is (un)satisfiable iff $\exists x \alpha$ is (un)satisfiable.

These definitions are extended to (possibly infinite) sets of formulae in a natural way. For example:

Model: A set of formulae has a model if there is an interpretation in which all of the formulae are valid.

The next definition concerns an important relationship between formulae.

Implication: Let Γ be a set of formulae and let α be a formula of the same language. Γ *(logically) implies* α if there is no interpretation of the language of Γ and α in which every member of Γ is valid but in which α is not valid. In other words there is no model of Γ that is not also a model of α. This is written $\Gamma \models \alpha$ or $\Gamma \Rightarrow \alpha$, which may also be read as

"α follows from Γ" or "α is a (logical) consequence of Γ".

If α is valid then this is written $\models \alpha$, which is the same as $\{\} \models \alpha$, since every interpretation satisfies the empty set of formulae.

Example: It may be seen that the sentence $\forall x \exists y P(x, y)$ is a logical consequence of the set of sentences $\{\exists y \forall x P(x, y)\}$ since, as was shown in the previous example, there is no model of $\exists y \forall x P(x, y)$ that is not also a model of $\forall x \exists y P(x, y)$.

The symbol '$\rightarrow$' defined earlier is commonly referred to as "implies", partly due to misunderstanding and partly due to the following theorem:

$$\Gamma \cup \{\alpha\} \models \beta \quad \text{iff} \quad \Gamma \models \alpha \rightarrow \beta.$$

In particular, β follows from $\{\alpha\}$ iff the formula $\alpha \rightarrow \beta$ is logically valid. This theorem holds by the following reasoning:

"$\Rightarrow$": If $\Gamma \cup \{\alpha\} \models \beta$, then whenever Γ and α are *true* in a particular interpretation so is β. Hence $\alpha \rightarrow \beta$ is *true* whenever Γ is *true*, for if α is *true* then so is β by the previous claim, and if α is *false* then $\alpha \rightarrow \beta$ is automatically *true*. Thus the conclusion $\Gamma \models \alpha \rightarrow \beta$ follows.

"$\Leftarrow$": If $\Gamma \models \alpha \rightarrow \beta$ then $\alpha \rightarrow \beta$ is *true* in an interpretation whenever Γ is. Hence if Γ and α are *true* then β must also be true, for otherwise $\alpha \rightarrow \beta$ would necessarily be *false*. Thus $\Gamma \cup \{\alpha\} \models \beta$.

However, this theorem does not represent identity between the two forms of "implication". To see the distinction between the two, simply compare the propositional sentence $P \rightarrow Q$ with the statement $\{P\} \models Q$. While the sentence has the truth value **F** in an interpretation in which P is assigned **T** and Q is assigned **F**, and **T** in any other interpretation, the statement $\{P\} \models Q$ is *false* because Q does not follow from $\{P\}$. However, due to common practice, the term "implies" will occasionally be used to refer to the if..then connective in this book, while "logically implies" will normally be used for the notion of logical consequence. Correspondingly, for a formula of the form $\alpha \rightarrow \beta$ it is useful to refer to the sub-formula α as the *hypothesis* of the formula, and to refer to β as the *conclusion*.

Another very important fact regarding logical consequence that will be used frequently in this book is given by the following exercise:

Exercise 2.7: Show that $\Gamma \models \alpha$ iff $\Gamma \cup \{\neg\alpha\}$ is unsatisfiable.

2.2.3 The Mechanisation of Proof

Now that the concept of logical consequence has been defined, it is natural to look for a general method of showing that a formula follows from a given set of formulae. Such a method should apply universally (that is, it should not have to be modified for each new conjecture presented to it), and it should be possible to apply it in a mechanical fashion, without "intuitive reasoning". Fortunately, it turns out that for first-order logic it is possible to construct such mechanical methods of "proof".

This section will provide a basic characterisation of the concepts of "proof" and "proof procedures". In later chapters some minor modifications and extensions of these concepts will be made, but the present section should form an adequate background for the future developments.

2.2.3.1 Calculi and Proof

To construct proofs in a mechanical way, syntactic rules are required to derive new formulae from given (or assumed) formulae. A collection of such rules is referred to as a calculus. For a particular calculus to be of use, it must satisfy certain properties: it must correspond, in some way, to the semantics of the underlying logic. The concern of this subsection is to give a technically straightforward expression of calculi and proof, and to discuss the associated "correctness" issues with respect to the underlying semantics of first-order logic.

Inference Rules: An inference rule may be viewed simply as a mapping (or, more accurately, a relation) between expressions, such that a non-empty set of formulae (the *premisses*) are "mapped" to a single formula (the *conclusion*). The basic form for an inference rule is: from $\alpha_1,..., \alpha_n$ infer β.

Soundness: An inference rule will be called sound if the conclusion is a logical consequence of the premisses.

Examples: *Modus ponens*, 'from $\alpha, \alpha \rightarrow \beta$ infer β', is a sound inference rule, while 'from $\alpha \vee \beta$ infer β' is an inference rule that is clearly unsound. The sound inference rule 'from α infer $\alpha \vee \beta$' shows that, in general, an inference rule may be merely a relation between formulae, rather than a mapping (i.e. a function).

It is not in fact necessary for an inference rule to satisfy the above strong notion of soundness for it to be "useful". It is sufficient that it has the weaker properties given in the following definition.

Preservation of Satisfiability/Validity: An inference rule is said to preserve satisfiability/validity if whenever the premisses are satisfiable/valid then so is the conclusion.

Example: The rule 'from $\alpha(x)$ infer $\forall x\,\alpha(x)$' preserves validity, since if $\alpha(x)$ is valid then so is $\forall x\,\alpha(x)$, but it is not sound since $\alpha(x)$ does not imply $\forall x\,\alpha(x)$.

Another example is given in the following exercise.

Exercise 2.8: Find an unsound inference rule that preserves satisfiability. (Hint: use Exercise 2.6.)

Invertibility: An inference rule is said to be invertible if each of the premisses is a logical consequence of the conclusion.

Predicate Calculi: A calculus (or proof system) consists of
- a recursive set of valid formulae (called the *logical axioms*), and
- a finite set of inference rules.

Deduction: A formula β may be deduced (or *proved*) from a set of formulae Γ in a given calculus C if there is a finite sequence of formulae $\alpha_1,..., \alpha_n$ such that α_n is β and each α_i is either an axiom of C, a formula of Γ, or has been inferred from some of the previous formulae in the sequence by application of one of the rules of inference of C.

If β is provable from a set of formulae Γ in a calculus C, then this is written $\Gamma \vdash_C \beta$, or simply $\Gamma \vdash \beta$ if C is understood from the context. This may be read as "β *may be proved from* Γ", or "β *is a theorem of* Γ". The axioms of Γ, a set of non-valid formulae, will be referred to as *non-logical axioms*. These axioms are intended to be valid in the interpretations of interest (such as "groups" or "Peano arithmetic"). A set of non-logical axioms will generally be referred to either as an *axiomatisation* or as a *specification*. Associated with any set of non-logical axioms is a theory determined by the given calculus. In particular, an equational theory is any theory generated from a set of axioms that are universally closed equality atoms (*equations*).

Theory: If Γ is a set of non-logical axioms then the theory generated by Γ is the set of all possible theorems of Γ (according to the given calculus).

Soundness: A calculus is said to be sound if only logical consequences of any set of formulae are provable.

Completeness: A calculus is said to be complete if every logical consequence of any set of formulae is provable.

Adequacy: A calculus is adequate if it is both sound and complete.

The important theorem for first-order predicate calculi is the **completeness theorem**: it is possible to construct a calculus C such that

$$\Gamma \vdash_C \alpha \quad \text{iff} \quad \Gamma \models \alpha$$

for any set of formulae Γ and formula α. In fact, there are many such calculi, as will be shown in this book. Proofs of this theorem for classical "Hilbert calculi" may be found in [En72] and [Ro69]. The left to right direction of the theorem ensures the soundness of the calculus because it says that if α is proved from Γ using calculus C then α is a logical consequence of Γ. The right to left direction ensures the completeness of the calculus because it says that if α is a logical consequence of Γ then it can be proved to be so using the calculus **C**. It is clearly more important to prove the soundness of a calculus than to prove its completeness.

There are two important consequences of the completeness theorem that will be used throughout this book. The first of these is the **compactness theorem**; this may be expressed in several ways, but, in the current context, is perhaps most naturally stated as

$$\Gamma \models \alpha \quad \text{iff} \quad \text{there is some finite subset } \Gamma' \text{ of } \Gamma \text{ such that } \Gamma' \models \alpha.$$

This follows automatically from the completeness theorem given the fact that proofs must be finite. The second theorem concerns the calculus itself and relates to the concept of *consistency*.

Consistency: A specification Γ is said to be consistent if there is no formula α such that $\Gamma \vdash \alpha$ and $\Gamma \vdash \neg\alpha$; otherwise it is *inconsistent*. Correspondingly, a theory **T** is said to be consistent if there is no α such that $\alpha \in$ **T** and $\neg\alpha \in$ **T**, and is said to be inconsistent otherwise.

The second important consequence of the completeness theorem will be referred to as the **consistency theorem**:

$$\Gamma \text{ is consistent} \quad \text{iff} \quad \Gamma \text{ is satisfiable.}$$

The proof of this may be found in [En72]. Usually, in standard texts on logic, the consistency theorem is proven and the completeness theorem shown to follow. However, the completeness theorem follows from the consistency theorem only under certain conditions, while the reverse implication always holds. These facts are expressed in the following exercise.

Exercise 2.9: Show that if a given calculus satisfies the completeness theorem then it satisfies the consistency theorem. Using the result of Exercise 2.7, show that the converse also holds if the calculus has the following property:

$$\Gamma \vdash \alpha \quad \text{iff} \quad \Gamma \cup \{\neg\alpha\} \text{ is inconsistent.}$$

The converse implication of this exercise need not hold if the extra condition is not satisfied. For instance, the *resolution* calculus, to be described in Chapter 3, satisfies the consistency theorem but not the completeness theorem. If a calculus does satisfy the consistency theorem then it is clear that a given set of formulae is inconsistent if it is unsatisfiable. This motivates the next definition.

Refutation Completeness: A calculus is said to be refutation complete if it satisfies the left to right direction (the 'only if' part) of the consistency theorem.

There are two other types of calculi that do not satisfy the completeness theorem but which are still adequate mechanisms for proving theorems. There are the "duals" of refutation-complete calculi, called *affirmation-complete* calculi, and there are calculi designed purely for deducing valid formulae, which will be referred to as *assertion-complete* calculi.

Affirmation Completeness: A calculus is said to be affirmation complete if for any valid formula α there is a deduction of a logical axiom from α.

Assertion Completeness: A calculus is said to be assertion complete if it satisfies the implication 'if $\models \alpha$ then $\vdash \alpha$' for any formula α.

The affirmation-complete calculus is the dual of the refutation-complete calculus in the sense that the former deduces a valid formula while the latter deduces an unsatisfiable pair of formulae. Both are special cases of what may be referred to as *recognition calculi* (analogously to [Bi87]), since they apply to calculi designed for showing that a given set of formulae satisfy a required property, rather than for deducing a formula satisfying the property. An example of an affirmation-complete calculus is the "affirmation-resolution rule" which will be discussed following the main discussion of the resolution rule. An assertion complete calculus, on the other hand, is designed for deducing valid formulae rather than simply recognising validity. (Such a deduction will be referred to as an *assertion proof*.) An example of a calculus that is assertion complete but does not satisfy the completeness theorem is the "cut-free sequent calculus", also to be described in Chapter 3.

Of course, calculi that do satisfy the completeness theorem also satisfy the three other types of "completeness" just described. To distinguish these sort of calculi from the other "less powerful" types they will generally be referred to as *deductively complete*. Examples of such calculi are "natural deduction systems" and sequent calculi with the "cut rule", both of which are discussed in Chapter 3. Apart from describing examples of each type of calculus, Chapter 3 will also bring out the relationships between the different types.

2.2.3.2 Undecidability

The completeness theorem above states that if a given formula is a consequence of a set of first-order non-logical axioms then it may be shown to be so by applying the inference rules of a predetermined well-constructed calculus. However, in practice, for the purposes of proving theorems on a computer, the theories acceptable are further limited to those that are generated by a recursively enumerable set of non-logical axioms, since otherwise there is no way of representing them on the computer. The completeness theorem should thus be read in the current context as stating: if the set of non-logical axioms are recursively enumerable then so is the set of consequences (that is, so is the theory generated by the axioms). Of course, by the compactness theorem, in practice only finite subsets of the set of non-logical axioms need be of concern for the purposes of proving any particular theorem, and in this book usually only finite sets of formulae will ever be considered.

On the other hand, the completeness theorem does not ensure that first-order theories are necessarily decidable. It turns out that even when the set of non-logical axioms are limited to finite (and hence recursive) sets it is not guaranteed that the theory generated is decidable. This means that it is possible that any procedure designed to prove theorems of some theory will not terminate when attempting to prove that a particular formula is or is not in the theory. In particular, there can be no algorithm that is able to determine whether an arbitrary formula (or sentence) of first-order logic is valid. The corresponding results for unsatisfiable and satisfiable formulae are given in the following straightforward exercise.

Exercise 2.10: Assuming the undecidability of validity, show that unsatisfiability is also undecidable, and hence (by Exercise 2.1) that satisfiability is not even semi-decidable.

The obvious consequence of these facts is that if a particular calculus is programmed on a computer then for some formulae given to the theorem prover an infinite computation may occur. In general, by the theorem of undecidability, there is no way of telling, after a finite amount of time, whether the machine will or will not stop. Proofs of this fact may be found in most (modern) books on logic.

On the other hand, it is not the case that all first-order theories are undecidable. In fact, there are subsets of first-order logic for which all theories are decidable. Theories known to be decidable are of importance to mechanical theorem proving because special efficient algorithms may be built into a theorem prover to deal with them, thus avoiding the redundancy involved in treating them in the normal manner. Examples of decidable theories will be considered later in this book.

2.2.3.3 Proof Procedures

Proof procedures are concerned with the way in which calculi are applied. In the following let **C** be a given calculus.

Search Space: The search space for a set of formulae (corresponding to some conjecture perhaps) is the set of all possible ways of applying the rules of the calculus **C** to the formulae themselves and to the formulae deduced from them.

Search Strategy: This is a strategy for determining at each stage of a proof which rule of **C** should be applied and to which formulae, or subformulae of formulae, it should be applied.

Proof Procedure: A calculus together with a search strategy for the calculus is called a proof procedure [Ko79].

It is possible to talk about a search strategy being complete or incomplete, since the way in which the given rules are applied may determine whether a proof is found even if the chosen calculus has the completeness property. Of course, the most basic and complete strategy is to apply the rules of the (sound and complete) calculus in all possible ways to the given formulae (in some parallel manner, say). The main discussion of strategies, both complete and incomplete (or "heuristic"), will follow the chapter on "resolution" and "natural deduction", for which most strategies have been devised (see Chapter 4).

2.2.3.4 Herbrand's Theorem

Fundamental to most of the theorem-proving systems to be reviewed in this book is a theorem generally attributed to J. Herbrand. This theorem determines a particular domain of interpretation (the "Herbrand universe") for a sentence σ, such that σ is satisfiable iff σ is *true* in some interpretation with this domain. This gives rise to a method of effectively reducing conjectures of first-order logic to formulae of propositional logic, which may be tested for unsatisfiability using standard procedures, such as truth-tables. More importantly, with this theorem as basis, methods of proof for first-order logic may be formulated that do not require formulae to be reduced to propositional logic. The essential details of the commonly cited version of Herbrand's theorem will be described here.

Prenex Normal Form: A sentence is in prenex normal form (pnf) if it has the form

$$Æ_1x_1 \, Æ_2x_2 \, ... \, Æ_nx_n\alpha,$$

where
- each $Æ_i$ is either a universal quantifier or an existential quantifier,
- the x_i are distinct variables,
- each of the x_i occurs at least once in α, and
- α is quantifier-free (i.e. contains no quantifiers).

The subformula α is called the *matrix* of the sentence. Any sentence may be converted into an equivalent sentence in prenex normal form (see [BJ89]).

Example: The sentence $\forall v \exists w \forall x \forall y \exists z (P(x, w) \vee \neg Q(z, y, w, v))$ is in pnf.

Skolemisation: Let σ be a sentence in pnf. Skolemisation of σ involves deleting each existential quantifier and its attached variable from the prefix of σ and then replacing the ensuing free variables occurring in the matrix of σ by terms referred to as *Skolem functions*. If $\exists x_i$ was in the scope of the sequence of universal quantifiers $\forall x_1,..., \forall x_j$, then the Skolem function that replaces the free occurrences of x_i will be a term of the form $f(x_1,..., x_j)$, where f is a function symbol that does not already occur in σ (or in any other of the formulae of the conjecture of concern). In particular, if $\exists x_i$ is not in the scope of any universal quantifier then the free occurrences of x_i are replaced by constants.

For a sentence in pnf, Skolemisation may be expressed more succinctly in the form of a straightforward transformation rule:

$$\forall x \exists y \, Æz \, \alpha(x, y, z) \quad \longrightarrow \quad \forall x \, Æz \, \alpha(x, f(x), z)$$
- condition: the symbol f does not occur in α

where $\alpha(x, f(x), z)$ denotes the replacement of the Skolem function $f(x)$ for all free occurrences of y in the formula $\alpha(x, y, z)$.

Example: If σ is $\forall v \exists w \forall x \forall y \exists z (P(x, w) \vee \neg Q(z, y, w, v))$, then a Skolemised form of σ might be $\forall v \forall x \forall y (P(x, f(v)) \vee \neg Q(g(v, x, y), y, f(v), v))$. Intuitively, w and z have been replaced by functions that select one of the objects said to exist.

The parameters of the Skolem functions introduced are indicative of the dependence of the objects referred to by the existential quantifiers on the objects referred to by universal quantifiers. For example, in the sentence $\forall x \exists y \, Parent(y, x)$, the "parent" y is dependent upon the "child" x. Though the Skolemised form of a sentence σ in prenex normal form is not equivalent to σ (unless σ contains no existential quantifiers) it can be proven that

$$\sigma \text{ is satisfiable} \quad \text{iff} \quad \text{the Skolemisation of } \sigma \text{ is satisfiable.}$$

A proof of this may be found in [Lo78]. It is not in fact necessary to convert σ to pnf before Skolemising, but it simplifies the presentation. In Chapter 5 a transformation sequence is described in which Skolemisation is performed before converting to pnf but after certain other changes have been made to the sentence. In general, Skolemising before converting to pnf will reduce the arity of the Skolem functions introduced, because each of the existential quantifiers will often be in the scope of fewer universal quantifiers before conversion to pnf.

Herbrand Universe: The Herbrand universe of a Skolemised sentence σ is the set of all terms that may be constructed from the function symbols in σ, with the proviso that if σ does not contain any constants then a constant, c say, is included as the basic "building block". Formally then, the Herbrand universe of σ, denoted $H\sigma$, is defined by

- any constant in σ (or, if there are none, c) is in $H\sigma$,
- if f is an n-ary function symbol in σ and $t_1,..., t_n$ are in $H\sigma$, then $f(t_1,..., t_n)$ is in $H\sigma$.

Example: In the Skolemised formula of the previous example, the function symbols are the unary symbol f and the ternary symbol g. The Herbrand universe of this sentence may be enumerated as:

$$\{c, f(c), g(c, c, c), f(f(c)), f(g(c, c, c)), g(f(c), c, c), g(c, f(c), c),...\}.$$

Ground Instance: Let σ be a sentence of the form $\forall x_1...\forall x_n\alpha$, where α is quantifier-free, and where each of $x_1,..., x_n$ occurs at least once in α. If $t_1,..., t_n$ are (not necessarily distinct) terms of the Herbrand universe of σ then $\alpha(t_1,..., t_n)$ denotes the replacement of each occurrence of $x_1,..., x_n$ by $t_1,..., t_n$ respectively. The ground formula $\alpha(t_1,..., t_n)$ is then said to be a ground instance of σ.

Based on the construction of the Herbrand universe, and the associated concept of ground instances, it is possible to construct a particular model for any satisfiable set of Skolemised sentences. If the set of sentences is satisfiable then it must have some model M (say). Furthermore, M must assign some value to every ground term. Now if those values from the domain of M that are not assigned to some ground term are deleted, a new "ground" model G (say) is automatically derived: simply let the ground terms be assigned the values they were assigned in M, and define the relations of G to hold for any sequence of values in the domain of G iff the same relations held for the same values in M. The model appropriated in this way is also referred to as the *standard* (or *normal*) model of the sentences. The idea of the standard model combined with a variation of the *compactness theorem*, 'a set of formulae has a model iff every finite subset has a model', leads to **Herbrand's theorem:**

$$\sigma \text{ is satisfiable} \quad \text{iff}$$
$$\text{every finite subset of } \{\alpha(t_1,..., t_n) : t_1,..., t_n \in H\sigma\} \text{ is satisfiable.}$$

This may be restated more usefully as: σ is unsatisfiable iff the conjunction

$$\alpha(t_{11},..., t_{1n}) \wedge \alpha(t_{21},..., t_{2n}) \wedge ... \wedge \alpha(t_{m1},..., t_{mn})$$

is unsatisfiable, for some finite sequence of elements $t_{11},..., t_{mn}$ of $H\sigma$.

A proof of this theorem may be found in, for example, [CL73] and [Lo78]. From it a proof procedure is immediate for first-order logic without equality: enumerate the sequence of ground instances of σ until (if σ is unsatisfiable) a set of instances is produced which may be shown to be unsatisfiable by assigning the truth values **T** and **F** to the ground atomic subformulae of each $\alpha(t_{i1},..., t_{in})$ and then using the rules of propositional logic to determine the truth value of the conjunction of ground formulae. This idea may be extended to include equality, as will become apparent in the next section.

Example: Consider the unsatisfiable sentence $\forall x \forall y((P(a) \vee P(f(x))) \wedge \neg P(y))$. The Herbrand universe for this sentence is simply the set $\{a, f(a), f(f(a)),...\}$. Based on this particular enumeration of the Herbrand universe, the ground instances of the sentence may be enumerated:

$$\{(P(a) \vee P(f(a))) \wedge \neg P(a), \quad (P(a) \vee P(f(f(a)))) \wedge \neg P(a),$$
$$(P(a) \vee P(f(a))) \wedge \neg P(f(a)), \quad (P(a) \vee P(f(f(a)))) \wedge \neg P(f(a)),...\}.$$

Now consider the following conjunction of two elements of this enumeration:

$$((P(a) \vee P(f(a))) \wedge \neg P(a)) \wedge ((P(a) \vee P(f(a))) \wedge \neg P(f(a))).$$

It is not difficult to show that this conjunction is unsatisfiable. This may be done by building up a "truth-table" for the formula (see [En72], p.35), but more succinctly it may be reasoned as follows. For the conjunction of formulae to be *true* (that is, to have the truth value **T**) in some interpretation, it must be the case that the two formulae themselves are *true* in this interpretation. Analogously, since the formulae themselves are conjunctions it must be the case that each element of the set $\{P(a) \vee P(f(a)), \neg P(a), \neg P(f(a))\}$ is *true*. But if $P(a) \vee P(f(a))$ is *true* then either $P(a)$ or $P(f(a))$ (or both) must be *true*. But in that case either $\neg P(a)$ or $\neg P(f(a))$ (or both) must be *false*, contradicting the assumption that they were *true*. Hence the original conjunction cannot be *true* in any interpretation and is therefore unsatisfiable. Since a subset of the enumeration of ground instances is unsatisfiable it automatically follows that the whole set is unsatisfiable. Hence the original sentence must be unsatisfiable.

Exercise 2.11: The sentence $\exists y \forall x P(x, y) \wedge \neg \forall x \exists y P(x, y)$ has as a prenex normal form the sentence $\exists y \forall x \exists u \forall v (P(x, y) \wedge \neg P(u, v))$. Show that the pnf sentence is unsatisfiable by Skolemising it and then performing the process illustrated in the example above (using truth-tables, or some other device, for the final part, if preferred).

The reasoning used to show that the conjunction of the pair of ground formulae is unsatisfiable in the above example may be compared to the backward application of the inference rules of a sequent calculus as will be discussed in detail in Chapter 3. Also, it should be noted that the whole discussion presented above may have been expressed in a "dual" form for validity as opposed to unsatisfiability. In this case, it would have been necessary merely to Skolemise the universally quantified rather than the existentially quantified variables, and then to express the above version of Herbrand's theorem in the alternative form:

$$\sigma \text{ is valid} \quad \text{iff} \quad \alpha(t_{11},..., t_{1n}) \vee \alpha(t_{21},..., t_{2n}) \vee ... \vee \alpha(t_{m1},..., t_{mn}) \text{ is valid,}$$

for some sequence of elements $t_{11},..., t_{mn}$ of Hσ. This point will be clarified in the discussion of sequent calculi in Chapter 3 and their extension to include the mechanism of "unification" in Chapter 4.

Finally, simply for historical accuracy, two points may be made about the reference to the above theorem as "Herbrand's theorem". The first is that it would seem that T. Skolem completed many of the details of the above theorem some years before Herbrand submitted his thesis, and, in particular, the Herbrand universe might more accurately be referred to as the Skolem (or Skolem-Herbrand) universe of a sentence (see [Pr69]). The second point is that Herbrand's actual version of this theorem differed markedly from the commonly cited version. In particular, he gave a constructive "syntactic" proof of his corresponding theorem (cf. [An86]), closely related to G. Gentzen's "cut-elimination" theorem of a few years later, which will be discussed in Section 3.2 on sequent calculi.

2.2.3.5 Building-in the Equality Relation

There are three reasons for giving equality a special status, setting it apart from the other predicates, in a book such as this. The first is the fundamental importance of equality in expressing theories. For example, equality is commonly used in expressing mathematical theories (such as group theory), in specifying data-types (as in algebraic specifications), and in defining functions (as in functional programs and algebraic specifications).

The second reason for taking equality as a given predicate (that is, with predefined meaning) is that it is not possible to define equality (as the identity relation) in first-order logic. To illustrate the difficulty that arises, consider the sentence $\forall x \forall y \, x = y$. This sentence is *true* in only those interpretations that have a domain of exactly one element, since it states that every pair of (and hence all) values are identical. However, it may be shown that a model of any set of first-order formulae (without equality) may have a domain of arbitrary cardinality (see [BJ89] pp. 151).

Fortunately, it is possible to define a binary relation $\approx$ so that it has the necessary properties of equality for the purposes of theorem proving via the following enumerable set of *equality axioms*:

$$x \approx x,$$

for each n-ary function symbol of the language

$$x_1 \approx y_1 \rightarrow f(x_1, x_2,..., x_n) \approx f(y_1, x_2,..., x_n)$$
$$\vdots$$
$$x_n \approx y_n \rightarrow f(x_1, x_2,..., x_n) \approx f(x_1, x_2,..., y_n),$$

for each n-ary predicate symbol of the language, and also $\approx$ itself

$$x_1 \approx y_1 \rightarrow (P(x_1, x_2,..., x_n) \rightarrow P(y_1, x_2,..., x_n))$$
$$\vdots$$
$$x_n \approx y_n \rightarrow (P(x_1, x_2,..., x_n) \rightarrow P(x_1, x_2,..., y_n)).$$

These axioms are clearly valid in any interpretation in which ≈ is assigned the identity relation. Also, it is not difficult to show that in any interpretation in which these axioms are valid (or, in other words, the universal closure of each of them has the truth value **T**) the relation ≈ must be an *equivalence relation*.

Exercise 2.12: Substituting ≈ for P in the predicate symbol axioms, show that any relation that satisfies the universal closure of each of the axioms is an equivalence relation. That is, it must be

- reflexive: $\forall x\; x \approx x$ (which is just the universal closure of the first axiom),
- symmetric: $\forall x \forall y (x \approx y \rightarrow y \approx x)$, and
- transitive: $\forall x \forall y \forall z ((x \approx y \wedge y \approx z) \rightarrow x \approx z)$.

The substitution property for function symbols gives ≈ the stronger property of being a *congruence* relation. However, the important result associated with the above axioms is the following ([Lo78], [CL73]): if α is a formula involving =, β is the same as α except that each occurrence of = has been replaced by ≈, and EQ is the conjunction of the universal closures of each of the equality axioms for the language of α, then

$$\alpha \text{ is valid} \quad \text{iff} \quad EQ \rightarrow \beta \text{ is valid.}$$

As a consequence, the axioms EQ may be added to the axioms defining the underlying theory, and then the inference rules of the given calculus applied without modification. However, this approach leads naturally to the third reason for giving special status to equality. While the axiomatisation approach is adequate for theoretical purposes it is inadequate for automated theorem proving. There are various reasons for this, the first and most important of which is the inefficiency involved in using the axioms themselves, with regard to the time taken to perform proofs, the length of proofs, and other factors (see [RW69] and [Lo78]). Another important reason is the unnaturalness of using the axioms for a human who would normally rely upon a more intuitive understanding of the equality of terms.

To overcome the limitations of the axiomatisation approach, once a system has been designed for proving theorems, the usual practice is then to devise specialised mechanisms for dealing with equality. For this reason, this book will consider, for each system described, possible extensions for dealing with equality. Naturally, specialised procedures have also been designed for other important relations and theories (such as partial orderings and set theory), and some of these will be indicated in this book. However, extension for equality is certainly the most important development of any theorem-proving system, and this book will concentrate on this issue.

PART 2

APPROACHES TO PROOF

CHAPTER 3

FUNDAMENTAL SYSTEMS

This chapter will describe three theorem-proving systems, the main aspects of which will form the basis for the ideas to be presented in the rest of the book. The first is specifically human oriented whilst the third is machine oriented; the second may be seen as a mediation between these two extremes.

As mentioned in Chapter 1, there are technical problems associated with the implementation of the first proof system to be described in this chapter and there will be some discussion on this issue. In contrast, basic implementations of the other two proof methods to be discussed should be naturally derivable from their descriptions; however, any issues that seem outstanding in this regard will be clarified.

3.1 NATURAL DEDUCTION

In standard texts on logic, Hilbert-style calculi, consisting of a set of logical axioms together with a few rules of inference, are generally taken as the basic characterisation of a proof system. The purpose of such systems is merely to provide a purely theoretical basis for proving the completeness theorem for first-order logic. The problem with these systems is that in practice proofs tend to be long, tedious and difficult both to perform and to understand.

Referring to these calculi as "logistic", Gerhard Gentzen [Ge69] pointed out that they fail completely to capture the reasoning performed in practice by mathematicians. Based on a study of mathematical proofs he proceeded, during 1934-35, to develop a system of "natural deduction", intended to allow proofs to be performed in a manner that was felt to correspond to human reasoning. The major principle that characterises these "natural deduction" calculi is that for each logical symbol (of the chosen logic) there should be separate rules that allow its introduction and its removal. Thus in Gentzen systems there are many rules of inference (at least two for each logical symbol), and few (if any) axioms. The naturalness of these systems stems from the way in which proofs proceed from the assumed (that is, non-logical) axioms to the goal (the desired theorem) via application of intuitively understandable rules of inference.

An additional feature of the principal system to be described in this section is that the rules are specified in terms of constructs called *judgements*, as opposed to formulae. This style of system allows the current set of assumptions at each stage of the proof to be made explicit. In particular, at the end of the proof, the deduced judgement consists of the assumptions adopted for the particular application (the non-logical axioms—see Chapter 2), and the theorem proven from these axioms. These points will be clarified by looking at the basic construct for the system, the judgement, and the derivation of the rules of inference.

3.1.1 Judgements and Their Semantics

A **judgement** is an expression of the form $\Gamma \vdash \alpha$, where Γ is a finite set of formulae and α is a single formula. In such a judgement the elements of Γ are called the **antecedents**, while α is called the **consequent**. The antecedents are a set of assumptions under which the consequent must hold. There are several possible interpretations for judgements. With the symbol $\vdash$ taken to denote deduction (as in Chapter 2), a judgement $\Gamma \vdash \alpha$ may be read as: there is a proof of α from Γ. Under this interpretation, assumed by Kleene [Kl62] and Andrews [An86], the rules of the natural deduction system are statements about an underlying Hilbert (say) calculus, applied as derived rules of inference. An alternative interpretation of the judgement, assumed by Manna in [Ma74], is that it is simply a special representation (an abbreviation) of the formula-schema $\gamma_1 \wedge \dots \wedge \gamma_n \rightarrow \alpha$ (where the γ_i are the finite set of formulae in Γ). This allows the natural deduction system to be treated as a system in its own right independent of Hilbert systems, but it also means that judgements are no longer either *true* or *false*, but only *true* or *false* in a particular interpretation (see Chapter 2). Furthermore, the fact that a judgement $\Gamma \vdash \alpha$ may be viewed as an abbreviation for the corresponding formula in this interpretation does not mean that formulae may be built up from them, as in, for example, the expression $\forall x(\Gamma \vdash \alpha \wedge \Sigma \vdash \beta)$.

To overcome the limitations of both of the above representations, a judgement may be read informally as Γ entails α, and may be deemed to hold whenever it is the case that if the formulae of Γ are *true* then so is α. In this way, it is equated informally with the semantic consequence symbol $\models$. This means that both of the previous interpretations for $\vdash$ are captured: Manna's interpretation is satisfied because of the fact that $\{\gamma_1, \dots, \gamma_n\} \models \alpha$ iff $\models (\gamma_1 \wedge \dots \wedge \gamma_n) \rightarrow \alpha$, while the completeness result for Hilbert calculi (that is, $\Gamma \vdash_H \alpha$ iff $\Gamma \models \alpha$) means that the original interpretation of $\vdash$ as the deduction symbol is also captured.

Each of these three interpretations may be illustrated by the natural deduction rule for introducing the symbol $\rightarrow$:

$$\text{if } \Gamma \cup \{\alpha\} \vdash \beta \quad \text{then} \quad \Gamma \vdash \alpha \rightarrow \beta.$$

In the first interpretation this corresponds to the **deduction theorem** for Hilbert calculi, and may be read: if there is a proof of β from Γ and α in the Hilbert system, then there is a proof of $\alpha \rightarrow \beta$ from Γ in the Hilbert system. In the second interpretation, it may be re-expressed as

$$\text{if } (\Gamma^c \wedge \alpha) \rightarrow \beta \quad \text{then} \quad \Gamma^c \rightarrow (\alpha \rightarrow \beta),$$

where Γ^c denotes the conjunction of the members of Γ. In the third interpretation it reads: if Γ and α together entail β, then it may be inferred that Γ entails $\alpha \rightarrow \beta$. The third interpretation will generally be taken here, though sometimes the second may be preferred.

To express judgements—and inference rules involving them—in a more concise and natural form some notational abbreviations will be introduced. As above, Γ will be used to denote a finite set of formulae rather than a possibly infinite set (in contrast to Chapter 2). Also, rather than 'from X infer Y', where X and Y are, respectively, a finite set of judgements (i.e. $\Gamma_1 \vdash \alpha_1,..., \Gamma_n \vdash \alpha_n$) and a single judgement (i.e. $\Gamma \vdash \alpha$), the standard notation

$$\frac{\Gamma_1 \vdash \alpha_1 \text{ and } ... \text{ and } \Gamma_n \vdash \alpha_n}{\Gamma \vdash \alpha}$$

will be used. Similarly, the notation $\Gamma, \alpha \vdash \beta$ will be used as an abbreviation for $\Gamma \cup \{\alpha\} \vdash \beta$. To denote the replacement of all free occurrences of a variable x in a formula $\alpha(x)$ by a term t, the notation $\alpha(t)$ will be used. In this regard, the following definition will also be required: a term t is said to be **free for** x in a formula α if on replacing all free occurrences of the variable x in α by t no variable in t becomes bound in α. For example, the term $f(y)$ is free for x in the formula $\forall z P(x, z)$, but not in the formula $\forall y P(x, y)$.

3.1.2 A Complete Natural Deduction System

The following system is virtually that of [Ma74]. In [Kl62] a very similar system is presented. One of the main differences is that many of the rules of [Ma74] are represented as axioms in [Kl62]. For example, the $\wedge$-introduction rule becomes the axiom $\alpha, \beta \vdash \alpha \wedge \beta$. The preference for rules here is that they seem simpler to work with. The discussion in this section will be principally concerned with the technical aspects of the system; the problems that arise in the construction of proofs in a natural deduction calculus will be considered in more detail in Section 3.1.3 below.

3.1.2.1 The Inference Rules

The basic rules of the system are the "judgement" (or "assumption") axiom, and a rule for introducing arbitrary assumptions into judgements. The main rules are those for introducing and eliminating each logical operator. This particular system also contains separate rules for introducing and eliminating double negations $\neg\neg$.

Basic Axiom and Rule

Assumption axiom (ass): $\dfrac{}{\Gamma, \alpha \vdash \alpha}$

Assumption introduction rule (air): $\dfrac{\Gamma \vdash \beta}{\Gamma, \alpha \vdash \beta}$

Introduction and Elimination Rules

	Introduction	**Elimination**
$\neg$	$\dfrac{\Gamma, \alpha \vdash \beta \text{ and } \Gamma, \alpha \vdash \neg\beta}{\Gamma \vdash \neg\alpha}$	$\dfrac{\Gamma \vdash \alpha \text{ and } \Gamma \vdash \neg\alpha}{\Gamma \vdash \beta}$
$\neg\neg$	$\dfrac{\Gamma \vdash \alpha}{\Gamma \vdash \neg\neg\alpha}$	$\dfrac{\Gamma \vdash \neg\neg\alpha}{\Gamma \vdash \alpha}$
$\vee$	$\dfrac{\Gamma \vdash \gamma}{\Gamma \vdash \alpha \vee \beta}$ where γ is either α or β	$\dfrac{\Gamma, \alpha \vdash \gamma \text{ and } \Gamma, \beta \vdash \gamma \text{ and } \Gamma \vdash \alpha \vee \beta}{\Gamma \vdash \gamma}$
$\wedge$	$\dfrac{\Gamma \vdash \alpha \text{ and } \Gamma \vdash \beta}{\Gamma \vdash \alpha \wedge \beta}$	$\dfrac{\Gamma \vdash \alpha \wedge \beta}{\Gamma \vdash \gamma}$ where γ is either α or β
$\rightarrow$	$\dfrac{\Gamma, \alpha \vdash \beta}{\Gamma \vdash \alpha \rightarrow \beta}$	$\dfrac{\Gamma \vdash \alpha \text{ and } \Gamma \vdash \alpha \rightarrow \beta}{\Gamma \vdash \beta}$
$\forall$	$\dfrac{\Gamma \vdash \alpha(c)}{\Gamma \vdash \forall x\, \alpha(x)}$ where c does not occur in any member of Γ	$\dfrac{\Gamma \vdash \forall x\, \alpha(x)}{\Gamma \vdash \alpha(t)}$ where t is free for x in $\alpha(x)$
$\exists$	$\dfrac{\Gamma \vdash \alpha(t)}{\Gamma \vdash \exists x\, \alpha(x)}$ where t is free for x in $\alpha(x)$	$\dfrac{\Gamma \vdash \exists x\, \alpha(x) \text{ and } \Gamma, \alpha(c) \vdash \beta}{\Gamma \vdash \beta}$ where c does not appear in Γ, $\exists x\, \alpha(x)$ or β
$=$	$\dfrac{}{\Gamma \vdash t = t}$	$\dfrac{\Gamma \vdash t_1 = t_2}{\Gamma \vdash \alpha(t_1) \rightarrow \alpha(t_2)}$ where t_1 and t_2 are free for x in $\alpha(x)$

What has been called above the assumption axiom is, in fact, an *axiom schema*. This means that it denotes all the (possibly infinitely many) axioms (of the language of interest) which have the form '$\Gamma, \alpha \vdash \alpha$'. The inference rules are also schemas.

The rules for the connectives are quite straightforward, and it is not difficult to prove their soundness, particularly if the second interpretation of a judgement (as an abbreviation for the corresponding formula) is assumed. The = introduction rule, which is in fact an axiom, is also unsurprising, since it is merely a restatement of the reflexivity axiom for equality. The rules of =-elim, $\forall$-elim and $\exists$-intro are also quite reasonable, apart, perhaps, from the associated "free for x" condition. The need for this condition will become apparent in the section on proofs below. If this condition is assumed, then it may be shown that these rules are also sound, regardless of the interpretation assumed for judgements. The $\forall$-intro and $\exists$-elim rules, on the other hand, require further consideration in this respect.

The condition on the $\forall$-intro and $\exists$-elim rules is referred to as the *eigenvariable condition* (on the variable x of the inference). The necessity for this condition will be illustrated in the discussion of proofs in the next subsection. The idea behind it is that, since the constant c does not already occur in the formulae involved in the deduction, it assumes the rôle of an "arbitrary constant", and hence is not restricted to denoting any particular value. In the case of $\forall$-intro, this means that once α has been shown to hold for c, it may be deduced that it holds for all x. Similarly, in the case of $\exists$-elim, since it has been shown that there exists an x that satisfies α, this value of x may be named c without restricting the range of possible values that may suffice.

Even so, it is not difficult to show that the $\forall$-intro and $\exists$-elim rules are, in fact, not sound in the sense of Chapter 2 if the second interpretation of a judgement is assumed. In other words, if judgements are assumed to be abbreviations for the corresponding formulae, then the conclusion of each of these rules does not follow from the premisses, even with the proviso on their application. On the other hand, it may be shown that they preserve validity; this is the technical justification to substantiate the preceding informal reasoning regarding the eigenvariable condition. Hence, for any conjecture, a proof assures the conjecture is a theorem. Thus the proof system as a whole is sound in the sense of Chapter 2. It follows from this that the $\forall$-intro and $\exists$-elim rules *are* sound if the third interpretation of a judgement (as an entailment) is assumed. Similarly, they may be shown to be sound under the first interpretation (as a deduction). It may be noted in passing that the eigenvariable condition has a close relationship to the Skolemisation mechanism, and this analogy will be developed further in reference to sequent calculi in Section 3.2.6 below, and also in Chapter 4.

The above system is assertion complete in the sense that a judgement $\Gamma \vdash \alpha$ may be deduced in the system iff $\Gamma \models \alpha$. In other words, with the deduction of a judgement J in the above system denoted by $\vdash_N J$, the system satisfies the equivalence: $\Gamma \models \alpha$ iff $\vdash_N \Gamma \vdash \alpha$. The system also happens to be deductively complete, in the sense that if a set of judgements are taken as non-logical axioms, then it is possible to derive any logical consequence of them in the system. The distinction between these two forms of completeness will be further clarified as the discussion proceeds.

3.1.2.2 Natural Deduction Proofs

A straightforward characterisation of natural deduction proofs is as follows. Proofs are performed in a bottom-up manner. Each line of a proof takes the form:

$$n. \quad \Gamma \vdash \alpha \qquad \text{justification},$$

where

- n is the number of the line
- $\Gamma \vdash \alpha$ is an instance of one of the axiom schemas (of which there is only one in this case), or has been inferred from previous lines in the proof by application of one of the inference rules
- 'justification' states which axioms, inference rules and previous lines in the proof have been used for the deduction of line n.

According to this characterisation, a natural deduction proof is an "assertion proof" (see Section 2.2.3.1). Furthermore, the representation as a sequence corresponds to a Hilbert-style approach. Alternative representations will be discussed in the next subsection.

Some examples will now be presented. Note that most of the theorems proved in the examples are in schematic form as opposed to involving particular formulae. Thus any instance of these schemas must also be a theorem. This is reasonable, as the inference rules themselves are in schematic form; also this approach serves to accentuate the generality of the result. Thus the use of schemas corresponds to a form of abstraction, where irrelevant details of the formulae involved are eroded for the purposes of the proof; the idea of abstraction is discussed further in Section 4.2, on natural strategies.

Examples:

1. A proof of $\neg\alpha \vee \beta \vdash \alpha \rightarrow \beta$

1.	$\neg\alpha \vee \beta, \alpha, \neg\alpha \vdash \alpha$	ass
2.	$\neg\alpha \vee \beta, \alpha, \neg\alpha \vdash \neg\alpha$	ass
3.	$\neg\alpha \vee \beta, \alpha, \neg\alpha \vdash \beta$	$\neg$-elim 1, 2
4.	$\neg\alpha \vee \beta, \alpha, \beta \vdash \beta$	ass
5.	$\neg\alpha \vee \beta, \alpha \vdash \neg\alpha \vee \beta$	ass
6.	$\neg\alpha \vee \beta, \alpha \vdash \beta$	$\vee$-elim 3, 4, 5
7.	$\neg\alpha \vee \beta \vdash \alpha \rightarrow \beta$	$\rightarrow$-intro 6

It may also be proved that $(\alpha \rightarrow \beta) \vdash (\neg\alpha \vee \beta)$, but this entailment is easier to prove once some further rules have been derived; see below.

2. A proof of $\vdash \alpha \vee \neg\alpha$

1.	$\neg(\alpha \vee \neg\alpha), \alpha \vdash \alpha$	ass
2.	$\neg(\alpha \vee \neg\alpha), \alpha \vdash \alpha \vee \neg\alpha$	$\vee$-intro 1
3.	$\neg(\alpha \vee \neg\alpha), \alpha \vdash \neg(\alpha \vee \neg\alpha)$	ass
4.	$\neg(\alpha \vee \neg\alpha) \vdash \neg\alpha$	$\neg$-elim 2, 3
5.	$\neg(\alpha \vee \neg\alpha), \neg\alpha \vdash \neg\alpha$	ass
6.	$\neg(\alpha \vee \neg\alpha), \neg\alpha \vdash \alpha \vee \neg\alpha$	$\vee$-intro 5
7.	$\neg(\alpha \vee \neg\alpha), \neg\alpha \vdash \neg(\alpha \vee \neg\alpha)$	ass
8.	$\neg(\alpha \vee \neg\alpha) \vdash \neg\neg\alpha$	$\neg$-elim 6, 7
9.	$\vdash \neg\neg(\alpha \vee \neg\alpha)$	$\neg$-intro 4, 8
10.	$\vdash \alpha \vee \neg\alpha$	$\neg\neg$-elim 9

It may reasonably be claimed that this proof is unacceptably complex for such an apparently simple theorem. Later the derivation of new rules of inference that serve to simplify the construction of proofs will be discussed. In this regard, it is worth mentioning that the corresponding proof of this theorem in the sequent calculus of the next section takes only three steps.

3. A proof of $\exists y \forall x\, \alpha(x, y) \vdash \forall x \exists y\, \alpha(x, y)$

   1. $\exists y \forall x\, \alpha(x, y) \vdash \exists y \forall x\, \alpha(x, y)$ ass
   2. $\exists y \forall x\, \alpha(x, y),\ \forall x\, \alpha(x, b) \vdash \forall x\, \alpha(x, b)$ ass
   3. $\exists y \forall x\, \alpha(x, y),\ \forall x\, \alpha(x, b) \vdash \alpha(a, b)$ $\forall$-elim 2
   4. $\exists y \forall x\, \alpha(x, y),\ \forall x\, \alpha(x, b) \vdash \exists y\, \alpha(a, y)$ $\exists$-intro 3
   5. $\exists y \forall x\, \alpha(x, y) \vdash \exists y\, \alpha(a, y)$ $\exists$-elim 1, 4
   6. $\exists y \forall x\, \alpha(x, y) \vdash \forall x \exists y\, \alpha(x, y)$ $\forall$-intro 5

Note that neither of the eigenvariable conditions was broken during this proof; this may be contrasted with the examples of unsound deductions below.

4. A proof of $P(0),\ \forall x(P(x) \rightarrow P(s(x))) \vdash \exists y P(s(s(y)))$

   1. $P(0),\ \forall x(P(x) \rightarrow P(s(x))) \vdash P(0)$ ass
   2. $P(0),\ \forall x(P(x) \rightarrow P(s(x))) \vdash \forall x(P(x) \rightarrow P(s(x)))$ ass
   3. $P(0),\ \forall x(P(x) \rightarrow P(s(x))) \vdash P(0) \rightarrow P(s(0))$ $\forall$-elim 2
   4. $P(0),\ \forall x(P(x) \rightarrow P(s(x))) \vdash P(s(0))$ $\rightarrow$-elim 1, 3
   5. $P(0),\ \forall x(P(x) \rightarrow P(s(x))) \vdash P(s(0)) \rightarrow P(s(s(0)))$ $\forall$-elim 2
   6. $P(0),\ \forall x(P(x) \rightarrow P(s(x))) \vdash P(s(s(0)))$ $\rightarrow$-elim 4, 5
   7. $P(0),\ \forall x(P(x) \rightarrow P(s(x))) \vdash \exists y P(s(s(y)))$ $\exists$-intro 6

Note that $\forall x P(x)$ is not a consequence of the given assumptions, in contrast to what may have been expected. Any attempted proof of this theorem will be blocked by the eigenvariable condition. It may have been felt that since, according to the axioms of the antecedent, P holds for 0 and if it holds for x then it holds for $s(x)$ (which may be taken to denote $x + 1$), it must hold for all x, and hence $\forall x P(x)$ should be a consequence. However, while $P(n)$ may be shown to hold for each n of the form $s(s(...s(0)...))$, analogously to the proof of $P(s(s(0)))$ above, it does not follow that $\forall x P(x)$ holds, for this is only an *inductive* consequence of the axioms; that is, it is *true* only in the *standard* interpretation of the axioms. This point will be clarified when induction is studied in later chapters.

5. An unsound deduction of the non-theorem $\exists x\, \alpha(x) \vdash \forall x\, \alpha(x)$

   1. $\exists x\, \alpha(x) \vdash \exists x\, \alpha(x)$ ass
   2. $\exists x\, \alpha(x),\ \alpha(a) \vdash \alpha(a)$ ass
   3. $\exists x\, \alpha(x) \vdash \alpha(a)$ $\exists$-elim 1, 2
   4. $\exists x\, \alpha(x) \vdash \forall x\, \alpha(x)$ $\forall$-intro

The unsound step in this "proof" is the deduction of line 3 from lines 1 and 2 by $\exists$-elim; the constant a occurs in the conclusion of line 2 as well as the antecedent and hence is not the "arbitrary constant" required for the application of $\exists$-elim.

6. An unsound deduction of the non-theorem $\forall x \exists y\, \alpha(x, y) \vdash \exists y\, \alpha(y, y)$

   1. $\forall x \exists y\, \alpha(x, y) \vdash \forall x \exists y\, \alpha(x, y)$ ass
   2. $\forall x \exists y\, \alpha(x, y) \vdash \exists y\, \alpha(y, y)$ $\forall$-elim

The application of $\forall$-elim is unsound because the substituted term y has become bound by the quantifier $\exists y$.

7. A proof of $\forall x \forall y(x = y \rightarrow y = x)$

   1. $a = b \vdash a = b$ ass
   2. $a = b \vdash a = a \rightarrow b = a$ =-elim
   3. $a = b \vdash a = a$ =-intro

4. $a = b \vdash b = a$ $\rightarrow$-elim 2, 3
5. $\vdash a = b \rightarrow b = a$ $\rightarrow$-intro 4
6. $\vdash \forall y(a = y \rightarrow y = a)$ $\forall$-intro 5
7. $\vdash \forall x \forall y(x = y \rightarrow y = x)$ $\forall$-intro 6

This theorem may alternatively have been expressed (and proved) in the schematic form $s = t \vdash t = s$, where s and t are term-schemas; the proof would correspond to steps 1-4 of the above deduction.

It is of interest, and of practical importance, to note the manner in which each of the proofs was performed in the above examples. With careful inspection, it may be seen that (except for the deduction of $\alpha \vee \neg\alpha$) a pattern emerges from these proofs: no formula is first introduced into a judgement by an introduction rule and then eliminated by an elimination rule. There is, in fact, a general result concerning natural deduction proofs due to D. Prawitz [Pr65] which states that all proofs of theorems not requiring application of $\neg\neg$-elim may be developed in this way. These theorems correspond, in fact, to the formulae valid in intuitionistic logic [Du77]. As a consequence of this style of deduction, all proofs for intuitionistic logic satisfy a "subformula property", expressed as follows.

Subformula Property: A proof of a judgement $\Gamma \vdash \alpha$ is said to satisfy the subformula property if every judgement $\Sigma \vdash \beta$ involved in the deduction of $\Gamma \vdash \alpha$ has the following property: the formula β and each formula occurring in Σ are *instances* of subformulae of either α or formulae in Γ.

The term *instance* is a generalisation of the term *ground instance* of Chapter 2; it will be defined formally in the section on resolution. This subformula property holds for each of the (intuitionistic) examples above. This style of proof is referred to as a proof in *normal form*. (More generally, a proof in a certain calculus is said to be in normal form if it cannot be reduced ("simplified") by a given set of transformation rules for "simplifying" proofs in the calculus [Du77]; cf. Chapter 7.) The importance of the subformula property for performing proofs in a "systematic" manner will become apparent later, in the discussion of the limitations of natural deduction systems in Section 3.1.3, and more so in the discussion of sequent systems in Section 3.2.

As already noted, the deduction of $\alpha \vee \neg\alpha$ does not fall into the same pattern as the intuitionistic deductions, for the formula $\neg\neg(\alpha \vee \neg\alpha)$ is first introduced by application of $\neg$-intro and then eliminated by application of $\neg\neg$-elim. Correspondingly, $\neg\neg(\alpha \vee \neg\alpha)$ is not a subformula of the formula of the deduced sequent, that is, $\vdash \alpha \vee \neg\alpha$. There is, in fact, no normal deduction of this classical theorem in the above system (see [Pr65]). However, in the sequent calculus of the next section it will be seen that all classical proofs are normal form proofs and thus exhibit a related subformula property.

Exercise 3.1:

1. Prove $(P \vee R) \wedge (Q \vee \neg R), (P \vee Q) \rightarrow S \vdash S$, the basis for the resolution method of Section 3.3.

2. Prove $\forall x(\alpha(x) \wedge \beta(x)) \vdash \forall x\,\alpha(x) \wedge \forall x\,\beta(x)$.

3. Using Example 3 as a guide, devise a general strategy for proving a judgement of the form $P(0), \forall x(P(x) \to P(s(x))) \vdash P(s(...s(0)...))$.
4. Show that there are proofs of the non-theorems $\forall y\,\alpha(y, y) \vdash \exists x \forall y\,\alpha(x, y)$ and $\forall x \exists y\,\alpha(x, y) \vdash \exists y \forall x\,\alpha(x, y)$ in the system, if the provisos on the quantifier rules are lifted.
5. Prove $s = t, t = r \vdash s = r$.

3.1.2.3 Alternative Representations

In the system described above, the rules are expressed in terms of judgements and proofs are presented as linear sequences. Also, each line of a proof either is an assumption axiom (i.e. a "valid formula") or follows from earlier lines of the proof according to the rules of inference. This representation of a natural deduction system will serve to bring out the relationship to other approaches to proof to be discussed later, but there are variations that may be said to be more "natural", and it is worthwhile discussing these here.

First consider the third point raised, the construction of proofs from assumption axioms. It is not difficult to show that this is unnecessary: any set of judgements may be taken as given (non-logical) axioms from which the required theorems are deduced. In other words, the above system is not only assertion complete, but is also deductively complete in the following sense: there is a deduction of the judgement $\Gamma \vdash \alpha$ from the "non-logical axioms" $\Gamma_1 \vdash \alpha_1,..., \Gamma_n \vdash \alpha_n$, iff the logical implication

$$\Gamma_1^c \to \alpha_1,..., \Gamma_n^c \to \alpha_n \models \Gamma^c \to \alpha$$

holds, where Γ^c denotes the conjunction of the elements of Γ, and similarly for the Γ_i^c.

Example: The deduction of $P \vdash R$ from the assumption $P \vee Q \vdash R$ may be performed as follows:

1. $P \vee Q \vdash R$ given
2. $\vdash (P \vee Q) \to R$ $\to$-intro 1
3. $P \vdash (P \vee Q) \to R$ air 2
4. $P \vdash P$ ass
5. $P \vdash P \vee Q$ $\vee$-intro 4
6. $P \vdash R$ $\to$-elim 3, 5

This corresponds to the logical consequence statement $(P \vee Q) \to R \models P \to R$.

Exercise 3.2: Deduce $\Gamma, \alpha \vee \beta \vdash \gamma$ from the axioms $\Gamma, \alpha \vdash \gamma$ and $\Gamma, \beta \vdash \gamma$.

Note the application of the assumption introduction rule in the above example of a deduction. While this rule is *redundant* (never required) for performing assertion proofs, it is required for the deductive completeness of the system. The reason for this is simply that whereas assertion proofs always begin with a set of assumption axioms in which all required formulae may be included, in deductive proofs, as illustrated in the example, it may be necessary to expand the antecedents of some of the (non-logical) axioms so that all of the premises of an inference have the same antecedents—as required by the rules with more than one premiss. It is easy to avoid this problem merely by re-expressing such inference rules so that the antecedents of their premises may be different from each other (e.g. ¬-elim would become, say, the sound rule 'from $\Gamma \vdash \alpha$ and $\Sigma \vdash \neg\alpha$ infer $\Gamma, \Sigma \vdash \beta$'). However, as noted, this is unnecessary for assertion proofs, and, more importantly, would cause problems in the case of "backward proofs" to be discussed later.

While it is not difficult to show that the deductive completeness of the above system follows naturally from its assertion completeness (cf. Section 3.2.5), there is a constraint that must be applied to deductions in the first-order case to ensure that proofs are sound. This is an extension of the eigenvariable condition: in the application of ∀-intro and ∃-elim to a judgement J, the constant "c" must not occur in any of the non-logical axioms from which J has been deduced. The need for this stronger eigenvariable condition is illustrated in the following example.

Example: Consider the non-theorem $P(a), \forall x(P(x) \to Q(x)) \models \forall x\, Q(x)$. With this re-expressed in terms of judgements, an unsound deduction may be constructed as follows:

1.	$\vdash P(a)$	given
2.	$\vdash \forall x(P(x) \to Q(x))$	given
3.	$\vdash P(a) \to Q(a)$	∀-elim 2
4.	$\vdash Q(a)$	→-elim 1, 3
5.	$\vdash \forall x\, Q(x)$	∀-intro 4

The unsound step in this example is the application of ∀-intro to $\vdash Q(a)$, since the supposedly "arbitrary constant" a occurs in one of the "given" judgements $\vdash P(a)$. The fact that this deduction is unsound may be clarified by attempting an assertion proof of the same theorem: the proof will be blocked by the original eigenvariable condition.

This style of proof is used throughout by Gries in [Gr81]. It is also related to the way in which new rules are derived, as in [Ma74], which will be discussed later. However, while the system above is deductively complete, and is sound with the additional proviso on the quantifier rules, the judgement construct has become almost redundant. The original motivation for using judgements was to keep track of the assumptions at each stage of the proof, but this applies only in the case of assertion proofs, not deductive proofs. For the purposes of deductive proofs, an alternative characterisation of a natural deduction system in which judgements are not involved would be preferable.

A problem with regard to the restatement of the above system without the use of judgements is that, in some of the rules of the judgement system, certain of the antecedents of the premises no longer appear as antecedents in the conclusion: they are either dismissed altogether or are moved to the consequent. These formulae are said to be *discharged assumptions*; they are formulae that are required as additional assumptions for the proof but not as assumptions in the deduced judgements. The rules with this form in the above system are ¬-intro, ∨-elim, →-intro and ∃-elim. To replace the above system by an alternative judgement-free system, a mechanism is required to express the *discharge of assumptions*. This mechanism is illustrated in the following rules for → and ∨ of a judgement-free calculus of natural deduction. The rules on the left are the introduction rules, while those on the right are the elimination rules.

$$[\alpha]$$

$$\vdots$$

$$\frac{\beta}{\alpha \to \beta} \qquad\qquad \frac{\alpha,\ \alpha \to \beta}{\beta}$$

$$[\alpha] \quad [\beta]$$

$$\vdots \quad \vdots$$

$$\frac{\alpha}{\alpha \vee \beta} \qquad \frac{\beta}{\alpha \vee \beta} \qquad\qquad \frac{\alpha \vee \beta \quad \gamma \quad \gamma}{\gamma}$$

The $\to$-elim and $\vee$-intro rules are quite straightforward, but the other two rules require further explanation. In the $\to$-intro and $\vee$-elim rules, the dots represent any sequence of inferences, while the square brackets around certain of the formulae express the *discharge* of these as assumptions. For instance, the idea behind the $\vee$-elim rule is that if γ may be shown to hold under the assumption that α holds and also under the assumption that β holds, then γ may be deduced if also $\alpha \vee \beta$ holds; in other words, γ must hold without the assumption of either α or β.

Example: To prove $\alpha \vee \beta \models \beta \vee \alpha$, the system first applies the $\vee$-intro rules to derive $\beta \vee \alpha$ from α and also from β, and then applies the $\vee$-elim rule to derive $\beta \vee \alpha$ from $\alpha \vee \beta$ without the assumption of either α or β.

The expression of these new rules of inference in the structured manner illustrated above leads naturally to a corresponding structure (usually referred to as a tree) for the presentation of proofs. This style of proof is illustrated in the following example.

Example: A deduction of $P \to (R \vee S)$ from $\{P \to (Q \vee R), P \to (Q \to S)\}$

$$\frac{\dfrac{[P]\ \ P \to (Q \to S)}{\dfrac{Q \to S \qquad [Q]}{\dfrac{S}{R \vee S}}}\qquad \dfrac{[R]}{R \vee S}}{\dfrac{R \vee S}{P \to (R \vee S)}}$$

$$\frac{[P]\ \ P \to (Q \vee R)}{Q \vee R}$$

In this format the formulae at the tips of the "branches" of the tree are the set of assumptions of the proof, while those formulae enclosed in square brackets are the discharged assumptions. For instance, it may be seen that, in the above example, $P, Q, R, P \to (Q \vee R)$ and $P \to (Q \to S)$ were taken as the initial assumptions, and that P, Q and R were discharged before the final deduction of $P \to (R \vee S)$. The formulae Q and R were discharged in the deduction of $R \vee S$, and then both assumptions of P were discharged in the deduction of $P \to (R \vee S)$.

Exercise 3.3: Construct a deduction of $P \to R$ from $(P \vee Q) \to R$, using as a guide its deduction in the judgement system in the example given earlier.

The above example illustrates an important point regarding the expression of a proof as a tree, namely the requirement that certain assumptions be duplicated in different parts of the tree. Sometimes it may even be necessary to duplicate certain deductions in different parts of a tree. This contrasts with the expression of a proof as a linear sequence, in which any line of the sequence may be used in a subsequent deduction. The advantage of the tree format as compared to the linear sequence is that it gives a structure to the proof, and thus should make the proof more readable. In interactive theorem provers the tree format is usually preferable.

Naturally, the representation of a proof as a tree is not limited to this style of natural deduction system, and is applicable to virtually any proof system. In particular, the proofs of the judgement system above could just as easily be expressed as a tree, and generally are (e.g. [Kl62]). In the judgement system this format is particularly suitable for the backward development of proofs. In the case of "backward proofs" (to be discussed in detail in Section 3.2), conjectures are decomposed into subgoals which are in turn decomposed, and so on, until axioms are derived. The expression of this decomposition as a (upside down) tree gives a clarifying structure to a proof (see, for instance, [Ri87] or [Tr90]).

It is not difficult to see the close connection between the new rules and the corresponding judgement rules. A straightforward translation allows each of the rules of the judgement system to be re-expressed as a rule of the judgement-free system, as illustrated by the above four rules. For the purposes of the translation it is assumed that the premises of the judgement rules do not require each judgement to have the same antecedents, as discussed previously. Hence, the assumption introduction rule is not required in the new system. The translation requires a minor re-expression of the eigenvariable condition again (see, for example, [Pr65]), but the details are not difficult and are left to the reader. The inverse translation from the alternative system to the original system is just as straightforward.

Considered from one point of view, the judgement rules may be seen as statements about the alternative system, with the symbol ⊢ taken to denote deduction in the new system. For instance, the →-intro rule in judgement form may be read exactly as indicated for the Hilbert system previously, but this time for the alternative natural deduction system. While it is a non-trivial task to prove the "deduction theorem" (→-intro) for Hilbert calculi, the theorem follows automatically for the natural deduction system.

From another point of view, the deductions of the alternative calculus may be viewed as abbreviations for the corresponding assertion proofs involving judgements: while the judgement proofs carry around the assumptions throughout the proof, in the judgement-free system the assumptions may be found at the tips of the tree. The problem with the judgement-free approach, and the usual reason for the use of judgements in a natural deduction calculus, is that it can be difficult to determine which assumptions may be discharged, particularly in those cases where they have been used in several parts of the deduction, as in the above example.

Regardless of the practical advantages and disadvantages of the distinct representations of a natural deduction calculus, the most important reason for expressing the main system of this section in terms of judgements is that it more clearly brings out the relationship to the sequent calculi of Section 3.2. It will be seen in that section that, while sequent systems use a similar basic construct to the judgement, these calculi usually cannot be transformed into "judgement-free" systems as for the natural deduction system.

3.1.3 Constructing Proofs

Natural deduction systems are not designed for the purpose of developing proofs in an efficient manner, but for displaying them in a "natural" form once they have been found. The current concern is to highlight some of the difficulties involved in developing proofs in the natural deduction system of Section 3.1.2.1, thus providing motivation for the later discussion of other more efficient approaches to proof, particularly the sequent calculi of the next section.

The first point of concern is the length and complexity of certain proofs, such as the proof of $\neg\alpha \vee \alpha$ in Section 3.1.2.2. This problem may be alleviated substantially by the derivation of new rules of inference. Essentially, these are rules that correspond to the deduction of a (schematic) judgement from assumed (schematic) judgements. For example, the deduction of the schema $\Gamma, \alpha \vee \beta \vdash \gamma$ from the schemas $\Gamma, \alpha \vdash \gamma$ and $\Gamma, \beta \vdash \gamma$ in Exercise 3.2 clearly may be applied as a new inference rule, allowing $\Gamma, \alpha \vee \beta \vdash \gamma$ to be inferred from $\Gamma, \alpha \vdash \gamma$ and $\Gamma, \beta \vdash \gamma$. In fact, this is one of the rules of a sequent calculus. As another example, the rule $\neg\neg$-elim is in fact derivable from the rules of ass, air and $\neg$-intro.

These derived rules thus combine several inference steps of the basic system into one "higher" inference step. They may also be viewed as (schematic) lemmas, that is, as proven theorems that may be applied in subsequent proofs. This is just a formalisation of the idea of using lemmas in mathematics. However, there is a distinction between deductions and the derivation of new rules at the first-order level. While the additional eigenvariable condition is required for deductions, as discussed in Section 3.1.2.3, it is not required in deriving new rules. This is simply because a derived rule need not correspond to a logical consequence, but is required merely to preserve validity. To illustrate this point, simply consider the application of the $\forall$-intro rule to the judgement $\Gamma \vdash \alpha(a)$—where a does not occur in Γ—to produce the judgement $\Gamma \vdash \forall x\, \alpha(x)$. The corresponding "derived" rule of inference is the $\forall$-intro rule itself, and thus it preserves validity, but this application of $\forall$-intro is not sound if it is meant to correspond to a deduction. The same idea holds for $\exists$-elim, of course. Less trivially, it will later be seen that the corresponding rules of a sequent calculus may be derived in this way. Apart from this issue, deductions and the derivation of new rules of inference are identical.

Of course, the degree to which such derived rules are applied may detract from the "naturalness" of the constructed proof, but once the proof has been constructed with the help of the "higher" rules it is a simple matter to expand out the steps where the derived rules have been applied. This idea will be discussed further in the next section on sequent calculi.

Another straightforward way of simplifying proofs is to treat some of the connectives and quantifiers as being predefined in terms of others. The most obvious example is $\alpha \leftrightarrow \beta$. This may be defined to be $(\alpha \rightarrow \beta) \wedge (\beta \rightarrow \alpha)$. For this reason $\leftrightarrow$ will generally be taken to be a defined symbol in the rest of this text. As another example, $\neg\neg\alpha$ may be defined to be α, since α and $\neg\neg\alpha$ are logically equivalent. For other examples of such equivalences see Section 3.3.1.

Even with the introduction of derived rules and definitions, the bottom-up style of proof described above clearly is not the most appropriate approach to the development of proofs in *any* system. In the natural deduction system, in particular, it entails that the appropriate instances of the axiom schema be found. Though there is only one axiom schema in the given system, choosing the right instance of this schema for a particular proof is a difficult task. In essence, it is necessary to enumerate all possible deductions (in the language chosen) until the required proof is generated (the British Museum or the One Million Monkeys method [NS63]). The easiest and most obvious way to overcome this difficulty is to perform the proof backwards, as will be discussed in detail in the section on sequent calculi.

Another problem is associated with the rules whose premiss and conclusion contain different formula schemas (e.g. ¬-elim and ∨-elim). The difficulty is that of choosing appropriate formulae as (part of) the inferred formula when applying such rules either forwards or backwards. For example, when applying the first ∧-elim rule it is necessary to find a formula to take the place of β which is relevant to the proof being performed. As already noted, however, for the intuitionistic subsystem it is assured that a proof of any theorem may always be found in which each formula involved in the deduction is a subformula of one of the formulae occurring in the theorem being proved. This is the importance of "normal form theorems" for systematic proof development alluded to earlier. This idea may be developed a step further by constructing a proof system each rule of which has at least the property that the formula schemas that occur in the premisses also occur in the conclusion. Sequent calculi have this form.

Even when a normal form theorem holds for a given proof system, there is still the problem of deciding which rule should be chosen to be applied at each step. Even the rules of a sequent calculus may have a critical "non-determinism" associated with their application: the application of a particular rule may lead the proof astray. Of course, the straightforward way to cater for this is to try all applicable rules at each step of the proof (giving an enumeration of proof attempts), but the sequent calculus to be described in the next section has the property that no matter in which order the rules are applied a proof will always be found.

Finally, a major problem is determining what term should be substituted for the quantified variable when the ∀-elim rule is applied in a proof. This question will be returned to in Chapter 4 following a discussion of the notion of "unification" in Section 3.3; see also the outline proof of the completeness of sequent calculi in Section 3.2.6.

3.2 SEQUENTZEN SYSTEMS

Sequent calculi are proof systems similar in style to the natural deduction system presented in the previous section and are also derived from the work of Gentzen (see [Kl62]). It was in realising the limitations of his natural deduction calculus for developing proofs that Gentzen was motivated to design the alternative sequentzen. What he wanted to show is that proofs can be performed in a "direct" way, by starting with axiom sequents and successively introducing connectives and quantifiers until the required theorem is derived. The backward application of these rules then corresponds to a decomposition strategy, reducing (or decomposing) the conjecture into subgoals which are then further decomposed until, if the given conjecture is a theorem, axiom sequents are derived.

Because of this direct style of proof inherent in sequent systems they lend themselves naturally to efficient implementation. In fact, most Gentzen-style systems that have been implemented on a computer for automatic theorem proving have been sequentzen systems—see, for example, [Wa60], [Ka63] and [Bo82] (and also [Pr60]). Furthermore, it seems that, in some way or other, all other proof systems that have been designed principally for the purpose of efficient proof development have a natural relationship to sequent calculi. For instance, Beth-tableaux, in their more efficient formulations (see [Sm68], [Wa85]), essentially correspond to the backward application of the rules of a sequent calculus. Also, in this book, the relationships between the different proof methods to be discussed will be brought out, in part, by reinterpreting each approach in terms of the sequent system to be described in this section.

3.2.1 Sequents and Their Semantics

A sequent is an expression of the form $\Gamma \vdash \Delta$ where both Γ and Δ are (possibly empty) finite sets of formulae. In the case where Γ and Δ are non-empty the meaning of such an expression is that at least one element of Δ is "entailed" by Γ, in the sense discussed for judgements earlier. In other words,

$$\{\alpha_1,..., \alpha_m\} \vdash \{\beta_1,..., \beta_n\} \quad \text{iff} \quad (\alpha_1 \wedge ... \wedge \alpha_m) \to (\beta_1 \vee ... \vee \beta_n) \text{ is valid.}$$

It may be seen that the judgement is just a special case of the sequent. If Γ is empty then it is the "empty conjunction", or the empty set of formulae, and hence is valid, while if Δ is empty then it is the "empty disjunction", which is unsatisfiable. Hence the correspondence between sequents and formulae may be extended to the case where Δ is empty by specifying

$$\{\alpha_1,..., \alpha_m\} \vdash \varnothing \quad \text{iff} \quad \alpha_1 \wedge ... \wedge \alpha_m \text{ is unsatisfiable,}$$

and analogously for the case where Γ is empty.

The major difference between sequent and natural deduction calculi lies not with the use of the more general sequent as opposed to the judgement, but with style of the inference rules. Whereas natural deduction systems have introduction and elimination rules, sequent systems essentially retain the introduction rules but replace the elimination rules by rules for introducing the connectives, quantifiers and equality into the antecedent of sequents.

3.2.2 The Underlying Calculus

The system to be described is a standard characterisation of a sequent calculus designed principally for backward proof. Almost identical versions of this system for the connectives and quantifiers may be found in the literature (e.g. [Sm68], [Bo82] and [Ro79]). An efficient mechanism for treating equality will be discussed in Chapter 4. The rules of the basic system are the following.

Basic Axiom and Rule

Sequent axiom: $\dfrac{}{\Gamma, \alpha \vdash \Delta, \alpha}$

Cut rule: $\dfrac{\Gamma, \alpha \vdash \Delta \text{ and } \Sigma \vdash T, \alpha}{\Gamma, \Sigma \vdash \Delta, T}$

Antecedent and Consequent Rules

	Antecedent	**Consequent**

$\neg$ _reductio_ $\left(\dfrac{\Gamma \vdash \Delta, \alpha}{\Gamma, \neg\alpha \vdash \Delta}\right)$ _inference_ $\qquad\qquad\qquad \dfrac{\Gamma, \alpha \vdash \Delta}{\Gamma \vdash \Delta, \neg\alpha}$

$\vee \qquad \dfrac{\Gamma, \alpha \vdash \Delta \text{ and } \Gamma, \beta \vdash \Delta}{\Gamma, \alpha \vee \beta \vdash \Delta} \qquad\qquad \dfrac{\Gamma \vdash \Delta, \alpha, \beta}{\Gamma \vdash \Delta, \alpha \vee \beta}$

$\wedge \qquad \dfrac{\Gamma, \alpha, \beta \vdash \Delta}{\Gamma, \alpha \wedge \beta \vdash \Delta} \qquad\qquad \dfrac{\Gamma \vdash \Delta, \alpha \text{ and } \Gamma \vdash \Delta, \beta}{\Gamma \vdash \Delta, \alpha \wedge \beta}$

$\rightarrow \qquad \dfrac{\Gamma \vdash \Delta, \alpha \text{ and } \Gamma, \beta \vdash \Delta}{\Gamma, \alpha \rightarrow \beta \vdash \Delta} \qquad\qquad \dfrac{\Gamma, \alpha \vdash \Delta, \beta}{\Gamma \vdash \Delta, \alpha \rightarrow \beta}$

$\forall \qquad \dfrac{\Gamma, \forall x \alpha(x), \alpha(t) \vdash \Delta}{\Gamma, \forall x \alpha(x) \vdash \Delta} \qquad\qquad \dfrac{\Gamma \vdash \Delta, \alpha(c)}{\Gamma \vdash \Delta, \forall x \alpha(x)}$

where t is free for x in $\alpha(x)$　　　　　where c does not occur in Γ or Δ

$\exists \qquad \dfrac{\Gamma, \alpha(c) \vdash \Delta}{\Gamma, \exists x \alpha(x) \vdash \Delta} \qquad\qquad \dfrac{\Gamma \vdash \Delta, \exists x \alpha(x), \alpha(t)}{\Gamma \vdash \Delta, \exists x \alpha(x)}$

where c does not occur in Γ or Δ　　　　　where t is free for x in $\alpha(x)$

Reference to a rule for one of the operators, *op*, will be denoted by either $\vdash op$ or $op\vdash$ depending on whether the rule is, respectively, the consequent or antecedent rule for this operator. With the view of a sequent as an abbreviation for the corresponding formula, there is little difficulty in showing that these rules are sound. The $\forall\vdash$ and $\vdash\exists$ rules may be opaque at first sight because the "introduced" formula already occurs in the premiss, but it will be seen below that this is required for the completeness of the system without the cut rule. The only problems with regard to the soundness of the system concern the $\vdash\forall$ and $\exists\vdash$ rules. These rules are closely related to the $\forall$-intro and $\exists$-elim rules, and have corresponding soundness issues. The details are not difficult to work out given the earlier discussion of the natural deduction rules.

Proofs in a sequent calculus may be expressed analogously to the proofs in the judgement system of the previous section, that is, as a sequence or tree of sequents built up from axiom sequents. Furthermore, the calculus above (including the cut rule) is deductively complete for deducing sequents from given (assumed) sequents. In fact, in [Ro79] it is shown that all of the rules apart from the cut rule may be replaced by corresponding axioms, and the system would still be deductively complete. On the other hand, the system above *without* the cut rule is only assertion complete. Naturally, assertion completeness is sufficient for the purposes of theorem proving, and hence the cut rule is, for practical purposes, *redundant*. This will be discussed further in the next two subsections.

Since the cut is redundant for theorem proving in a sequent calculus, the term "sequent calculus" will generally be used in the rest of the text to refer specifically to the cut-free version, and the qualifying term "cut-free" will be used only on those occasions where confusion may arise. On the other hand, while the cut rule is essentially redundant, it will take an important rôle in this book in bringing out the connections between the different proof systems. In particular, the resolution principle to be discussed in the next section will be seen to be closely related to the cut rule.

3.2.3 Normal and Non-normal Form Proofs

Gentzen included the cut rule in his original system because it allowed a very simple proof of the completeness of the system, assuming the completeness of the Hilbert calculus (or the natural deduction system). The proof simply involves showing that all the rules of the Hilbert (or natural deduction) system may be derived from the sequent calculus; see Section 3.2.5 below. The original intention of Gentzen was, in fact, to show that his system is complete using the cut rule and then to prove that this rule is redundant. A non-constructive way to show this is simply to prove the (assertion) completeness of the underlying sequent calculus in the standard way by referring to the underlying semantics of the logic (see Section 3.2.6), but Gentzen took the much more difficult approach of giving a constructive "syntactic" proof which showed how a proof using the cut rule may be transformed into a proof not using this rule. A detailed version of Gentzen's proof may be found in [Kl62], while an outline proof for an intuitionistic sequent calculus may be found in [Du77]; see also [Sm68]. Originally it was believed that this result was peculiar to sequent calculi, but, as has already been noted, it was later shown by Prawitz in [Pr65] that a corresponding result holds for the usual formulations of natural deduction systems.

The result proved by Gentzen corresponds to a normal form theorem for sequent calculi, since all proofs not involving the cut rule will clearly have the corresponding subformula property for sequents that normal natural deduction proofs have for judgements. This follows automatically from the fact that the premiss of each rule other than the cut contains only those formula schemas also contained in the conclusion. The significance of these normal form theorems, as hinted at in Section 3.1, is that they express the fact that proofs may be performed in a very "direct" way, without the detours inherent in the application of such devices as the cut rule. The following example illustrates this point.

Example: Consider the theorem $\vdash (\alpha \vee \neg\alpha)$, proved with the natural deduction calculus in Section 3.1.2.2. A similarly circuitous proof of this theorem in the sequent calculus may be performed (in tree form) as follows:

$$
\frac{
  \frac{
    \dfrac{\alpha \vdash \alpha, \neg\alpha}{\alpha \vdash \alpha \vee \neg\alpha}
  }{\vdash (\alpha \vee \neg\alpha), \neg\alpha}
  \qquad
  \frac{\neg\alpha \vdash \alpha, \neg\alpha}{\neg\alpha \vdash \alpha \vee \neg\alpha}
}{\vdash \alpha \vee \neg\alpha}
$$

The cut rule has been applied in the last step of this deduction, the "cut formula" being $\neg\alpha$. While this is an assertion proof, it is clearly "indirect". A much more direct and substantially simpler proof may be constructed without application of the cut, as follows:

$$
\frac{\dfrac{\alpha \vdash \alpha}{\vdash \alpha, \neg\alpha}}{\vdash \alpha \vee \neg\alpha}
$$

The first proof in this example should be compared with the proof of the same theorem in the natural deduction calculus. In the natural deduction proof, *modus ponens* ($\rightarrow$-elim) took the place of the cut rule, while the formula $\neg\neg(\alpha \vee \neg\alpha)$ took the place of $\neg\alpha$ as the cut formula. This illustrates the relationship between normal form proofs in the two calculi. The above example indicates the importance of the idea of normal form proofs, demonstrating the indirectness of non-normal proofs, but the real significance of normal proofs becomes apparent only when proofs are performed "backwards", as discussed in the next subsection.

3.2.4 The Backward Development of Proofs

Though expressed as sets of inference rules, implying that proofs are to be developed in a bottom-up manner, sequent calculi are designed principally for *backward proofs*. In this style of "proof", a given conjecture is "decomposed" into subgoals by matching the conclusion of one of the inference rules against the conjecture and then attempting to prove the corresponding instances of the premises. If the subgoals are theorems, then it is assured that the original conjecture is a theorem, by the soundness of the inference rules. The subgoals may in turn be reduced to further subgoals, and so on, until axiom sequents are derived.

Example: Let the conjecture be $P, P \rightarrow Q \vdash Q$. The only rule whose conclusion matches this conjecture is $\rightarrow\vdash$. The corresponding instances of the premises are $P \vdash P, Q$ and $P, Q \vdash Q$. These are subgoals, the proof of which would ensure that the original conjecture is a theorem. Both of these subgoals are instances of the axiom sequent, and hence the conjecture is a theorem.

Of course, strictly speaking, a "backward proof" is not a proof at all in the sense defined in Chapter 2, but is simply a demonstration that there exists a proof. The actual proof may be found simply by inverting the "backward proof". It will be seen in later chapters that many proof systems are concerned with showing that proofs exist rather than with developing them. These are the "recognition calculi" referred to in Chapter 2. The reason they are referred to as "calculi" is that usually they may be viewed as sets of inference rules in their own right, designed for recognition rather than deduction. In particular, the above sequent calculus may be re-expressed as a recognition calculus. This may be done merely by re-expressing sequents as formulae, re-expressing the premiss of each inference rule as a conjunction of formulae, and then inverting the derived rule. For instance, the inversion of the transformed →⊢ rule would be:

$$\text{from } (\Gamma \wedge \alpha \wedge \beta) \to \Delta \quad \text{infer} \quad ((\Gamma \wedge \alpha) \to \Delta) \wedge ((\Gamma \wedge \beta) \to \Delta),$$

where Γ and Δ are, in this instance, taken to be, respectively, a conjunction and a disjunction of formulae. This new rule, as is easily shown, is sound. In fact, the same result holds for each of the inference rules of the sequent calculus: they are all invertible. Thus, a *proof* may now be developed by applying these new rules to a given conjecture until a conjunction of formulae corresponding to axiom sequents is derived; at this point the conjecture is proven. (Note that, in this approach, the $\wedge\vdash$ and $\vdash\vee$ rules are redundant, for when re-expressed in the appropriate form their application will have no effect.)

Example: In this new calculus, the theorem $P, P \to Q \vdash Q$ from the previous example would be expressed in the form $(P \wedge (P \to Q)) \to Q$. By application of the corresponding inverted sequent rules, this may be decomposed into the single subgoal $(P \to (P \vee Q)) \wedge ((P \wedge Q) \to Q)$. This is a conjunction of formulae corresponding to axiom sequents, and hence the conjecture is proven.

The preceding discussion essentially captures the idea behind the Beth-tableaux approach to proof (see [Sm68]). Furthermore, it almost describes the connection-matrix method (see Chapter 5), though it will be seen that that method goes a few steps further to achieve greater efficiency in the development of proofs. More generally, it will be seen, as the book proceeds, that this style of proof using sequent calculi will serve to bring out the relationships between the distinct approaches to proof to be discussed. With this background as motivation some notation and definitions will now be introduced regarding the backward development of proofs.

Tactic: For any inference rule R, there is an associated tactic, referred to as the R-tactic, that transforms any instance of the conclusion of the rule into the corresponding instances of the premisses of the rule.

Example: The $\vee\vdash$-tactic transforms any sequent of the form $\Gamma, \alpha \vee \beta \vdash \Delta$ into sequents of the corresponding form $\Gamma, \alpha \vdash \Delta$ and $\Gamma, \beta \vdash \Delta$.

Thus a tactic generates from a conjecture a set of subgoals (cf. [Au79]). A tactic for a rule R will also be referred to as the *reversal* of rule R, as in [Bo82].

Decomposition Tactic: A tactic is said to be a decomposition tactic if it is the reversal of an inference rule in which the formula schemas occurring in the premiss of the rule are instances of subformulae occurring in the conclusion.

The term "decomposition tactic" is used as opposed to, say, "reduction" or "rewrite rule" for two reasons. The first is that these terms will be used in a more general context later (though with a very similar meaning to "decomposition"). The second reason is that, in the case of the quantifier rules, while in a strong sense the conjecture is decomposed into subgoals by the reversal of these rules, because of the duplications involved, the premiss of the rule is no "simpler" than the conclusion.

A tactic is said to be *sound* if it is the reversal of a sound inference rule. For instance, the decomposition tactic that transforms $\alpha \vee \beta$ to α is sound. A tactic is said to *preserve validity* if (whenever it applies) it transforms any valid formula to a set of valid formulae; it is thus the reversal of an invertible rule. It is clear from the example just given that a sound decomposition tactic need not preserve validity, for $\alpha \vee \beta$ may be valid even when α is not. When viewed as a set of inference rules, a set of decomposition tactics each of which preserves validity is referred to as an *analytic calculus* by R. Smullyan in [Sm68]. The motivation for this term (and this type of proof system) is that conjectures are "analysed" into their "components". This use of the term "analytic" is just a special case of its use in mathematics to refer to backwards reasoning in general. The term *analytic proof* will be used in this book, in a similar sense to Smullyan, to refer to "backward proofs" using decomposition tactics.

If each of a set of tactics preserves validity then it is clear that irrespective of the order in which they are applied an analytic proof will never be led astray. That is, an invalid subgoal will never be derived from a valid conjecture. Thus, it will never be necessary to "backtrack" during an attempted proof, that is, to undo some of the steps and to try a different sequence of tactic applications. For this reason, such a collection of tactics will be said to be *deterministic*. As a particular example, it has already been indicated that the tactics corresponding to the sequent calculus above are deterministic. This is not a property that necessarily holds for any sequent calculus (contrast the system of Kleene [Kl62]), but it is of immense advantage in developing efficient proof procedures. In [Bo82] K. Bowen shows that the current system has an even stronger property. He shows that for any two of the tactics, T and T', derived from this sequent calculus, $T(T'(S))$ is identical to $T'(T(S))$ (where $T(S)$ denotes the application of a tactic T to a sequent S). This is a special case of a "confluence" property to be discussed in Chapter 7. The term "confluent" is also sometimes used (e.g. [Bi87]) to refer to sets of tactics (or rules) that merely preserve validity, but the term "deterministic" is preferred here to avoid confusion with the different (though related) meaning of confluent to be used in Chapter 7.

Even though the sequent calculus presented in this chapter has these important properties, there is still a fundamental problem involved in its mechanisation: no systematic process has been proposed for finding the appropriate terms required in the applications of the quantifier rules. In the final subsection below, one straightforward procedure based on the enumeration of the ground instances is presented, but this is not a particularly efficient approach. A much more powerful mechanism will be discussed in Chapter 4, which is based on the concept of "unification", to be described in the Section 3.3 on resolution. For the moment, the appropriate terms will simply be introduced without explanation of their derivation.

For the purposes of describing analytic proofs, some simple notation will be introduced. The application of a tactic to an expression (conjecture) E, to produce a set of expressions (subgoals) E', will be denoted $E \longrightarrow E'$, which may be read informally as "E rewrites to E'". Also the subgoals of E' will be combined with the symbol &, to denote the fact that each must be proved in order to prove E. Furthermore, derived axiom sequents, and other sequents previously specified to be *true*, will automatically be deleted from the set of subgoals in the following step of the proof. With this notation, some example proofs will now be presented.

Examples:
1. Consider, once again, the conjecture $\neg\alpha \vee \beta \vdash \alpha \rightarrow \beta$. An analytic proof of this might proceed as follows:

$$\neg\alpha \vee \beta \vdash \alpha \rightarrow \beta \xrightarrow{\supset R} \neg\alpha \vee \beta, \alpha \vdash \beta \xrightarrow{\neg \vdash} \neg\alpha, \alpha \vdash \beta \ \& \ \beta, \alpha \vdash \beta$$
$$\longrightarrow \alpha \vdash \alpha, \beta.$$

2. The proof of the converse is now just as simple:

$$\alpha \rightarrow \beta \vdash \neg\alpha \vee \beta \longrightarrow \alpha \rightarrow \beta \vdash \neg\alpha, \beta \longrightarrow \beta \vdash \neg\alpha, \beta \ \& \ \vdash \neg\alpha, \beta, \alpha$$
$$\longrightarrow \alpha \vdash \beta, \alpha.$$

3. An analytic proof of $\vdash \exists x(P(x) \rightarrow \forall x P(x))$:

$$\vdash \exists x(P(x) \rightarrow \forall x P(x)) \longrightarrow \ \vdash P(a) \rightarrow \forall x P(x), \exists x(P(x) \rightarrow \forall x P(x)) \longrightarrow$$
$$P(a) \vdash \forall x P(x), \exists x(P(x) \rightarrow \forall x P(x)) \longrightarrow P(a) \vdash P(b), \exists x(P(x) \rightarrow \forall x P(x))$$
$$\longrightarrow P(a) \vdash P(b), P(b) \rightarrow \forall x P(x) \longrightarrow P(a), P(b) \vdash P(b), \forall x P(x).$$

Note the necessity of the duplication involved in the third example. Since the constant a had already been introduced in the first application of $\vdash\exists$, it could not then be introduced in the application of $\vdash\forall$ because of the eigenvariable condition. However, the duplication of $\exists x(P(x) \rightarrow \forall x P(x))$ allowed the second application of $\vdash\exists$ in which the required substitution of b for the variable was made.

Exercise 3.4: Construct analytic proofs of the following theorems:
$(P \vee R) \wedge (Q \vee \neg R), (P \vee Q) \rightarrow S \vdash S$ and $P(0), \forall x(P(x) \rightarrow P(s(x))) \vdash P(s(s(0)))$.

Because the reversals of the sequent rules described here are decomposition tactics that preserve validity, they may also be applied to disproofs to a certain extent. For instance, it is clear that in the propositional subsystem the application of the tactics to any sequent will always terminate irrespective of whether the sequent is a theorem or not. If the conjecture is not a theorem, then eventually a sequent will be derived that contains only atomic formulae (an *atomic sequent*) and which is not an axiom sequent. For such an atomic sequent an interpretation may be found in which the proposition letters of the consequent are *false* and those in the antecedent *true*. In this event, since the rules preserve validity, it is assured that the original conjecture is not a theorem—see the final subsection. Thus the given rules may be applied as a decision procedure for truth in propositional logic. For example, the sequent $R, P \rightarrow Q \vdash Q$ is not a theorem, as may be proved by decomposing it into the two atomic sequents $R \vdash P$ and $R, Q \vdash Q$; the second subgoal is valid, but for the first, R may be assigned the value **T** and P the value **F** in an interpretation. This result fails, in general, for first-order sequents simply because of the duplication of formulae required for completeness. Even in this case however, additional reasoning may sometimes be applied to ensure that any duplications performed will not lead to a proof. An example of such a mechanism is the purity principle which will be discussed in the context of resolution refinements in Chapter 4.

3.2.5 Connection to Natural Deduction Systems

As pointed out by Prawitz in [Pr65], a proof performed in a sequent calculus may be viewed as a "recipe" for a proof of the same theorem in a natural deduction system. This follows from the fact that the rules of a sequent calculus may essentially be derived from a natural system. This is certainly true for the usual intuitionistic subsystems of sequent calculi, since these generally do not allow more than one formula to occur in the consequent of a sequent. In the classical system above, however, there is a problem in this respect in that the consequents of sequents may involve more than one formula, in contrast to judgements. Perhaps the easiest way to overcome this problem is simply to treat the comma in the consequent of any sequent as '$\vee$'. It is not too difficult to show how the sequent rules may then be derived from the natural calculus, when the consequent of each sequent is non-empty—though these derivations will involve applications of $\vdash \neg\neg$, and hence will generally correspond to non-normal proofs. (For sequents with empty consequents some *false* formula such as $P \wedge \neg P$ may be inserted into the consequent in the sequent system, before performing the derivation.)

Example: For a non-empty consequent, the $\vdash\neg$ rule now becomes $\dfrac{\Gamma, \alpha \vdash \beta}{\Gamma \vdash \neg\alpha \vee \beta}$.
This may be derived from the natural deduction system in the following way:

$\Gamma, \alpha \vdash \beta \quad \vdash_N \quad \Gamma, \alpha \vdash \neg\alpha \vee \beta \quad \vdash_N \quad \Gamma, \alpha, \neg(\neg\alpha \vee \beta) \vdash \neg\alpha \vee \beta;$

$\Gamma, \alpha, \neg(\neg\alpha \vee \beta) \vdash \neg\alpha \vee \beta$ and $\Gamma, \alpha, \neg(\neg\alpha \vee \beta) \vdash \neg(\neg\alpha \vee \beta)$

$\quad \vdash_N \quad \Gamma, \neg(\neg\alpha \vee \beta) \vdash \neg\alpha \quad \vdash_N \quad \Gamma, \neg(\neg\alpha \vee \beta) \vdash \neg\alpha \vee \beta;$

$\Gamma, \neg(\neg\alpha \vee \beta) \vdash \neg\alpha \vee \beta$ and $\Gamma, \neg(\neg\alpha \vee \beta) \vdash \neg(\neg\alpha \vee \beta)$

$\quad \vdash_N \quad \Gamma \vdash \neg\neg(\neg\alpha \vee \beta) \quad \vdash_N \quad \Gamma \vdash \neg\alpha \vee \beta.$

Here $\vdash_N$ denotes deduction in the natural deduction system, and each line ending with a semi-colon (or full-stop) represents a particular sequence of inferences. With this derivation the sequentzen proof of the theorem $\vdash \neg\alpha \vee \alpha$ may be transformed into the natural deduction proof displayed in Section 3.1.2.2. (For a premiss with an empty consequent, the original $\vdash\neg$ rule must be replaced by, say, the new rule 'from $\Gamma, \alpha \vdash P \wedge \neg P$ infer $\Gamma \vdash \neg\alpha$' before the derivation is performed.)

In general, any application of the inference rule $\vdash\neg$ (to a sequent with a non-empty consequent) may be expanded into the corresponding sequence of inferences of a natural deduction system by means of the above derivation. The same idea may also be applied to the other rules. Whether this transformation is always desirable is another matter. For instance, the sequent rule for $\wedge\vdash$ is, in many ways, more natural than the corresponding natural deduction rules, since it stipulates (when applied backwards) simply that any conjunction of formulae in the antecedent of a sequent should be decomposed into its constituents—a very natural strategy. For this reason it might be preferable first to develop an alternative natural calculus that includes aspects of the sequent calculus, before attempting derivations. In this regard, it is worth mentioning that in [An80] a transformation from "connection proofs" (which are closely related to sequent-calculus proofs—see Chapter 5) to a very different natural system is described. Finally, it should be said that, as also noted by Prawitz in [Pr65], while natural deduction proofs may be derived from sequent proofs, these are not necessarily always the most natural or straightforward proofs that may be found in the natural calculus for a particular theorem. This is illustrated in the example of the following exercise.

Exercise 3.5: By deriving the rule for $\neg\vdash$, transform a sequent deduction of the theorem $\alpha \vdash \neg\neg\alpha$ into a natural deduction proof, and then compare this with the straightforward natural deduction proof.

An important point that has been glossed over in the above discussion is the completeness of the modified sequent calculus. Fortunately, for the purposes of completeness it is sufficient to express in the system the commutativity and associativity of $\vee$, which were implicit in the use of a comma in the original system. Given the completeness of the original system, is easy to see that the following rules are sufficient:

$$\frac{\Gamma \vdash \alpha \vee \beta}{\Gamma \vdash \beta \vee \alpha} \qquad\qquad \frac{\Gamma \vdash \alpha \vee (\beta \vee \gamma)}{\Gamma \vdash (\alpha \vee \beta) \vee \gamma}$$

These may also be shown to be derived rules of the natural deduction system; the commutativity of $\vee$ was proved for the judgement-free natural calculus in Section 3.1.2.3. While these are sufficient, further such rules are necessary to achieve the efficiency of the reasoning in the original calculus.

Given the soundness of the natural deduction system, the derivations of the rules of the sequent calculus ensure that this also is sound. Similarly, the reverse derivations ensure the completeness of the sequent system, given the completeness of the natural calculus. Unfortunately, it turns out that not all these derivations are possible to construct in the cut-free system. For instance, while it is easy to prove the theorem $\alpha, \alpha \rightarrow \beta \vdash \beta$, it is not possible to derive $\Gamma \vdash \beta$ from the assumed judgements $\Gamma \vdash \alpha$ and $\Gamma \vdash \alpha \rightarrow \beta$. With the cut rule this derivation is straightforward: prove $\Gamma, \alpha, \alpha \rightarrow \beta \vdash \beta$, and then transform this, via the cut rule, into $\Gamma, \alpha \rightarrow \beta \vdash \beta$ and then $\Gamma \vdash \beta$ using the assumed judgements. The same idea may be applied to all of the rules apart from $\forall$-intro and $\exists$-elim (which do not have associated theorems as for the other rules); $\forall$-intro is, however, trivial, while $\exists$-elim may be derived with an application of cut. The main point to note about this is the way in which theorems are transformed into inference rules via application of the cut rule. The same idea also applies to natural deduction systems, though a combination of the $\rightarrow$ elimination and introduction rules takes the place of the cut rule in this case; the straightforward details of this are left to the reader. This principle brings out the relationship between the use of the cut rule and the use of lemmas as discussed in the final subsection on natural deduction.

Having proved the completeness of sequent calculi in respect of natural deduction via the cut rule, the next task is to show that the cut is redundant for the purposes of performing assertion proofs. This, as already noted, is exactly what Gentzen did.

Alternatively, the completeness of sequent calculi may be proved by referring to an underlying model; this approach is outlined in the next section.

3.2.6 Completeness of Sequent Calculi

Because of the structure of the inference rules of the sequent calculus described above it is possible to give a quite straightforward proof of the completeness of the system. The simplicity of the proof lies in the fact that the reversals of the rules preserve validity. In particular, this allows a very simple proof of the completeness of the propositional subsystem, which, with a little more work, may be extended to the first-order system. Furthermore, a proof of the completeness of the sequent calculus will serve as proof of the completeness of the natural deduction calculus, since the sequent rules are derived rules of this system (together with the sound cut rule) as indicated above; also, later discussions of the completeness of other proof systems will depend upon the assumed completeness of the sequent calculus.

In the propositional case it has already been noted that the backward application of the rules to any given sequent will always terminate. Since the corresponding tactic also preserves validity, it follows automatically that any sequent is valid iff it may be decomposed into axiom sequents. For consider the decomposition of any conjectural sequent into a set of sequents involving only atomic formulae (proposition letters). If each such derived sequent is an axiom, then by the soundness of the rules, the conjecture must be a theorem. On the other hand, if at least one of these derived sequents is not an axiom, then an interpretation may be found in which it is *false*, simply by assigning **T** to each proposition letter in the antecedent and **F** to each one in the consequent. An example of this was described in Section 3.2.4 above. Now, since the rules preserve validity, it is easy to see that the original conjecture must be *false*. Thus the propositional sequent system is complete: a propositional conjecture is a theorem iff it may be decomposed into a set of axiom sequents by the backward application of the rules (and hence may be deduced from a set of axiom sequents by the forward application of the rules).

The above proof may be extended to the quantifiers, with a little effort. The idea behind this extension is similar to the idea behind the proof of Herbrand's theorem (Chapter 2), and, in fact, Herbrand's theorem may be seen as a special case. In outline this extension proceeds as follows (cf. [Sm68], [Bo82], [Ro79]). As for the propositional connectives, the tactics corresponding to the quantifier rules preserve validity. However, as already noted, the backward application of the rules $\forall\vdash$ and $\vdash\exists$ does not simplify sequents in the same way as the tactics for the connectives; there is not even any guarantee that the application of these quantifier tactics will terminate. Because of this an unsuitable proof procedure imposed on the quantifier tactics may be incomplete even if the underlying calculus is complete. This is not possible in the propositional case because each subgoal derived in an analytic proof is *decomposed* into a set of valid and "syntactically simpler" subgoals; thus an analytic proof can never be led astray. In contrast, a procedure for the application of the quantifier tactics may, for instance, apply the problematic $\forall\vdash$ and $\vdash\exists$ tactics repeatedly to each derived subgoal without ever applying the other rules, or the same set of terms may be repeatedly introduced in their application.

To avoid such possibilities, a sufficiently constrained proof procedure must be constructed. A first constraint is required to ensure that the applications of the problematic quantifier rules do not overwhelm the applications of the other rules, as suggested above. This may be done simply by ensuring that all the other rules are applied to any subgoal before $\forall\vdash$ and $\vdash\exists$ are applied (cf. [Ro79]). To overcome the possibility of inappropriate terms being introduced repeatedly requires more work. One quite natural solution is to introduce systematically the terms from the "Herbrand universe" when applying the two problematic rules. The term "Herbrand universe" was previously defined only for sentences in Skolem normal form, but the definition may be extended to the current context in the following manner. At each stage of an analytic proof, the Herbrand universe for a subgoal sequent consists of all those terms that may be constructed from the function symbols in the original conjecture (with a constant c if there is none in the conjecture) together with the constants occurring in that sequent due to earlier application of the rules $\exists\vdash$ and $\vdash\forall$. Now a simple modification of the two problematic quantifier rules to account for this specialisation will serve to assure completeness [Bo82]. For $\forall\vdash$ the modified rule is

$$\frac{\Gamma, \forall x\,\alpha(x), \alpha(t_1),..., \alpha(t_n) \vdash \Delta}{\Gamma, \forall x\,\alpha(x) \vdash \Delta},$$

where the sequent $\forall x\,\alpha(x) \vdash \Delta$ is n steps (that is, n tactic applications) from the original conjecture, and $t_1,..., t_n$ are the first n terms of (an enumeration of) the Herbrand universe for this sequent. The modified rule for $\vdash\exists$ is analogous.

It may be shown that, if a proof procedure is constructed according to these constraints, and if each subgoal derived from the original conjecture is not ultimately reduced to a set of axiom sequents after a finite number of steps, then the original conjecture is not a theorem ([Sm68], [Bo82]). Rather than give the technical proof of this final claim, the whole process will be illustrated with a simple example.

Example: Consider the theorem $\vdash \exists x(P(x) \to \forall y\,P(f(y)))$. The Herbrand universe for this sentence is the set $\{a, f(a), f(f(a)),...\}$. According to the procedure outlined above, the steps of an analytic proof may proceed as follows:

$\vdash \exists x(P(x) \to \forall y\,P(f(y))), P(a) \to \forall y\,P(f(y))$ reversal of new rule for $\vdash\exists$

$P(a) \vdash \exists x(P(x) \to \forall y\,P(f(y))), \forall y\,P(f(y))$ reversal of $\vdash\to$

$P(a) \vdash \exists x(P(x) \to \forall y\,P(f(y))), P(f(b))$ reversal of $\vdash\forall$

The Herbrand universe for this subgoal is the set $\{a, b, f(a), f(b),...\}$, and the next subgoal(s) are four steps away from the original conjecture. Thus, applying the reversal of the $\vdash\exists$ rule again, and abbreviating $P(x) \to \forall y\,P(f(y))$ to $\alpha(x)$, produces the subgoal

$P(a) \vdash \exists x\,\alpha(x), P(f(b)), \alpha(a), \alpha(f(a)), \alpha(b), \alpha(f(b))$.

Applying the reversals of $\vdash\to$ and $\vdash\forall$ to the sentence $\alpha(f(b))$ — which represents $P(f(b)) \to \forall y\,P(f(y))$ — reduces this subgoal to

$P(a), P(f(b)) \vdash \exists x\,\alpha(x), P(f(b)), \alpha(a), \alpha(f(a)), \alpha(b), \forall y\,P(f(y))$.

This is an axiom, and hence the theorem is proved.

3.3 RESOLUTION

The resolution principle was originally proposed by J. A. Robinson in the early 1960s [Ro65]. The motivation for developing the principle was to improve on the efficiency of earlier proof methods. It is admitted by Robinson in [Ro65] that the single inference rule of his calculus does not necessarily lead to proofs that are easy to comprehend, but he contended that all that is required of any set of inference rules to be employed on a machine is that they be sound and *effective* (that is, recursive). It turns out that his single inference rule also constitutes a (refutation) complete calculus for first-order logic without equality. (See Section 3.3.7 for a more detailed discussion of the equality relation.)

Although Robinson's original rule is complete by itself, it has since been separated into two rules which constitute a complete calculus. Not only does this make the rule easier to understand, but it has been found that the two rules may be more efficiently implemented, and also that it is easier to impose search strategies (see Chapter 4) on the two-rule system ([Lo78], [WO84]). Only the two-rule system will be described here.

Although the two rules are easier to understand in themselves, their use does not immediately give rise to proofs that are easy to understand. The main problem is to extract from a proof by resolution the steps of the proof that are truly necessary. This problem is partly solved by the imposition of search strategies, which totally avoid some steps whilst retaining completeness. The problem of extracting proof steps will not be explicitly considered here but the idea will become clear.

Recall that in classical logic proving that $\Gamma \models \alpha$ is equivalent to proving that $\Gamma \cup \{\neg\alpha\}$ is unsatisfiable (see Chapter 2). This fact is the basis for the *refutation procedures* to be discussed in this and the following chapters.

3.3.1 Clausal Form

Resolution is applied only to formulae (sentences, in fact) essentially in "clausal form". This "normal form" for formulae was originally advocated by Davis and Putnam in [DP60] as a useful form for automatic theorem proving, and has subsequently been used in most theorem-proving systems. In this section the concepts directly relevant to the "clausal form" of formulae will be defined, and a set of rules for transforming any sentence into a set of clauses will be described.

Negation: The negation of a formula α is $\neg\alpha$.

Literal: An atom is a literal, and the negation of an atom is a literal.

Clause: A clause is a disjunction of a (finite) set of literals with no literal appearing twice (that is, no duplicates). A clause with no literals is the *empty clause*, denoted $\emptyset$.

Example: $P(x, y) \vee \neg Q(y) \vee R(a, y) \vee \neg P(a, b)$ is a clause.

Note that the empty clause is an empty disjunction, and hence is unsatisfiable; it should be distinguished from the *empty set* of clauses, which is satisfiable. The variables of a clause are implicitly universally quantified. For example, the above clause should have the prefix $\forall x \forall y$. Any formula α may be converted into a conjunction of a (finite) set of clauses Σ such that

$$\alpha \text{ is satisfiable} \quad \text{iff} \quad \Sigma \text{ is satisfiable.}$$

It will be shown below how this transformation may be performed. The formula (the conjunction) derived is said to be in *clausal form*. The conjunction symbols within Σ are normally removed and left implicit. Equivalently, the transformation may be viewed as producing from the original formula a finite set of clauses. Resolution is applied to a (perhaps infinite) set of sentences each in clausal form. In this book only finite sets of clauses will be of concern.

The following five rules, when applied in the order they are given, are sufficient to convert any sentence σ into a conjunction of a set of clauses Σ such that the equivalence above is satisfied. Rules 1, 2 and 5 are to be applied by transforming a formula whose structure matches the schema on the left-hand side of the 'iff' to the corresponding formula whose structure matches the schema on the right.

1. Eliminate $\leftrightarrow$ and $\rightarrow$ using the equivalences

$$\alpha \leftrightarrow \beta \quad \text{iff} \quad \alpha \rightarrow \beta \wedge \beta \rightarrow \alpha, \quad \alpha \rightarrow \beta \quad \text{iff} \quad \neg\alpha \vee \beta.$$

2. Move $\neg$ inwards using the equivalences

$$\neg\neg\alpha \text{ iff } \alpha, \quad \neg(\alpha \vee \beta) \text{ iff } \neg\alpha \wedge \neg\beta, \quad \neg(\alpha \wedge \beta) \text{ iff } \neg\alpha \vee \neg\beta$$
$$\neg\forall x\,\alpha \text{ iff } \exists x\neg\alpha, \quad \neg\exists x\,\alpha \text{ iff } \forall x\neg\alpha$$

(so the scope of each occurrence of $\neg$ is now an atom).

3. Rename variables: if two quantifiers have the same bound variable name x (say), then choose one of the quantifiers and rename all the free occurrences of x in the scope of that quantifier. (For example $\forall x(P(x) \vee \exists x Q(x, x))$ would become, say, $\forall x(P(x) \vee \exists y Q(y, y))$.)

4. Eliminate existential quantifiers using Skolem functions as described in Section 2.2.3.4, and then move the universal quantifiers to the left.

5. Transform the matrix of the sentence to a conjunction of disjunctions of literals (that is, to *conjunctive normal form*—*cnf*) using the equivalences

$$\alpha \vee (\beta \wedge \gamma) \quad \text{iff} \quad (\alpha \vee \beta) \wedge (\alpha \vee \gamma), \quad (\beta \wedge \gamma) \vee \alpha \quad \text{iff} \quad (\beta \vee \alpha) \wedge (\gamma \vee \alpha),$$

and then remove duplicate literals from the disjunctions.

Note that Skolemisation is performed, in rule 4, before the quantifiers are moved to the left. As indicated in Chapter 2, this often serves to reduce the required arities of the Skolem functions introduced. This, in turn, may serve to simplify the proceeding proof of unsatisfiability. This is illustrated in the following exercise.

Exercise 3.6: Show that $\exists y \forall x P(x, y) \wedge \neg\forall x \exists y P(x, y)$ has as a Skolemised (prenex) form the sentence $\forall x \forall z (P(x, a) \wedge \neg P(b, z))$, according to the rules above, and then compare the Herbrand universe of this Skolem form with the one for the Skolemisation of $\exists y \forall x \exists u \forall v (P(x, a) \wedge \neg P(u, v))$ in Exercise 2.11.

In order to reduce the number of arguments of the Skolem functions introduced in rule 4, further rules may be added; see [Lo78]. The renaming of literals in rule 4 is necessary to allow the universal quantifiers to be moved left. If the initially given formula (to be proved unsatisfiable) contains free variables, then it is necessary to form its existential closure before the above rules are applied (see Exercise 2.6).

Application of the rules above will ultimately produce the final form

$$\forall x_1 \forall x_2 \ldots \forall x_m (C_1 \wedge \ldots \wedge C_n),$$

where $C_1, \ldots, C_n$ are clauses and $x_1, \ldots, x_m$ are the only variables appearing in these clauses. The quantifiers are then removed and left implicit. However, it should be noted that it is possible to distribute the quantifiers over $\wedge$ to give

$$\forall x_1 \forall x_2 \ldots \forall x_m C_1 \wedge \ldots \wedge \forall x_1 \forall x_2 \ldots \forall x_m C_n,$$

and then to remove redundant quantifiers from before each clause. Thus each clause may be thought of as being prefixed by its own set of quantifiers.

These conversion rules may be viewed either as transformation rules on logical formulae or as inference rules that are applied only in the preprocessing stage. As has been indicated, each of them preserves equivalence in classical logic, apart from Skolemisation. However, Skolemisation preserves satisfiability, which suffices. It also worth noting that every interpretation that satisfies the Skolemised sentence must also satisfy the original sentence; thus the transformation corresponds to a restriction on the models of the sentences.

Example (EX): This example will show how a particular conjecture would be converted into clausal form ready for application of resolution. Also it will serve to illustrate various points and proof techniques in the following chapters. For this purpose the example will be called, simply, EX. The conjecture is the following:

$$\exists y \forall x \forall z (P(x, z) \vee ((Q(x) \rightarrow R(x, y)) \wedge Q(x))), \ \forall x \forall y (P(x, y) \rightarrow \exists y R(x, y))$$
$$\vdash \forall y \exists x ((R(y, x) \rightarrow S(x)) \rightarrow S(x)).$$

The consequent $\forall y \exists x ((R(y, x) \rightarrow S(x)) \rightarrow S(x))$, in the context of resolution, is commonly referred to as the **goal** (cf. Chapter 6 on Prolog). It is negated, and then each of the sentences is converted into clausal form. The details for the antecedents are as follows:

first:
$\exists y \forall x \forall z (P(x, z) \vee ((Q(x) \rightarrow R(x, y)) \wedge Q(x)))$
$\exists y \forall x \forall z (P(x, z) \vee ((\neg Q(x) \vee R(x, y)) \wedge Q(x)))$
$\forall x \forall z (P(x, z) \vee ((\neg Q(x) \vee R(x, a)) \wedge Q(x)))$
$(P(x, z) \vee \neg Q(x) \vee R(x, a)) \wedge (P(x, z) \vee Q(x))$
$P(x, z) \vee \neg Q(x) \vee R(x, a)$ and $P(x, z) \vee Q(x)$

second:
$\forall x \forall y (P(x, y) \rightarrow \exists y R(x, y))$
$\forall x \forall y (\neg P(x, y) \vee \exists y R(x, y))$
$\forall x \forall y (\neg P(x, y) \vee \exists z R(x, z))$
$\forall x (\forall y \neg P(x, y) \vee R(x, f(x)))$
$\neg P(x, y) \vee R(x, f(x))$

Exercise 3.7: Transform the negated consequent into clauses.

The clauses produced are

$$\{P(x, z) \vee \neg Q(x) \vee R(x, a), \quad P(x, z) \vee Q(x), \quad \neg P(x, y) \vee R(x, f(x)),$$
$$\neg R(b, x) \vee S(x), \quad \neg S(x)\},$$

the first three clauses corresponding to the antecedents, while the fourth and fifth are the clauses of the negation of the consequent. This set of clauses may now be tested for unsatisfiability by means of resolution.

3.3.2 Ground Resolution

Ground (or propositional) resolution is applied only to ground (or propositional) clauses. While ground resolution was not claimed to be more efficient than its predecessor, the Davis-Putnam method of [DP60], it was shown by Robinson in [Ro65] that it leads naturally to a general principle of resolution for first-order clauses. It is thus natural to introduce (first-order) resolution by expressing the rule at the simpler ground level.

Complementary Literals: A pair of literals are complementary if one is the negation of the other, that is, one is an atom and the other is its negation.

Ground Resolvent: Let C and D be the (ground) clauses $C_1 \vee L \vee C_2$ and $D_1 \vee L' \vee D_2$, where L and L' are complementary (ground) literals. The clause

$$C_1 \vee C_2 \vee D_1 \vee D_2$$

(with any ensuing duplicates removed) is said to be a ground resolvent of C and D. Also, C and D are the clauses *resolved*, while L and L' are the literals *resolved upon*.

Ground Resolution: The ground resolution of two clauses is the derivation (i.e. deduction) of a ground resolvent from them (if one exists).

Example: Applying ground resolution to the clauses $\neg Q(c) \vee P(a, b) \vee R(a)$ and $R(a) \vee \neg P(a, b)$ produces the (only possible) ground resolvent $\neg Q(c) \vee R(a)$.

The preceding example may alternatively have been expressed at the propositional level as the deduction of $\neg Q \vee R$ from the clauses $\neg Q \vee P \vee R$ and $R \vee \neg P$. Throughout the rest of the text this propositional form will generally be used, as opposed to the explicit ground form.

The intention behind the application of ground resolution is to deduce the empty clause from a set of ground clauses, proving the inconsistency of the set; this then proves the unsatisfiability of the set, given that ground resolution is sound. Note that unless $\varnothing$ appears in the original Σ it will be produced by resolving two unit clauses A and $\neg A$ (where A is some atom). The deduction of the empty clause from a set of clauses Σ is called a *refutation* of Σ; a proof procedure designed to perform refutations is called a *refutation procedure*.

Example: A ground resolution refutation of the unsatisfiable set $\{P, \neg P \vee Q, \neg P \vee \neg Q\}$ may be constructed as follows: resolving P and $\neg P \vee Q$ produces Q; resolving Q and $\neg P \vee \neg Q$ produces $\neg P$; resolving $\neg P$ and P produces $\varnothing$.

Ground resolution is not deductively complete for propositional logic. For example, in the case of the *true* sequent $P \vdash P \vee Q$, clearly $P \vee Q$ cannot be deduced from P via ground resolution. However, ground resolution is refutation complete (see Chapter 2). For example, the set $\{P, \neg P, Q\}$, the clausal form of the above sequent (with negated consequent), can trivially be proved unsatisfiable by resolution. One explanation for resolution being refutation complete but not deductively complete is that it may be unable to deduce a particular clausal consequence, but is always assured to deduce a clause that implies this clause. (For example, P implies $P \vee Q$.) An alternative viewpoint on this issue may be found in Section 3.3.5.

The soundness and refutation completeness of ground resolution is just a special case of the corresponding result for first-order resolution, which will be discussed below. However, in contrast to first-order resolution, ground resolution procedures will always terminate (provided that steps are taken to ensure that the same resolvents are not generated repeatedly). Hence they constitute decision procedures for propositional logic; that is, a propositional formula is satisfiable if and only if the process stops without producing $\emptyset$.

To prove general (i.e. non-ground) clauses by means of ground resolution, an enumeration procedure for the Herbrand universe is required as in the case of the Davis-Putnam method. Though the ground resolution procedure will terminate for each finite subset of the enumeration, if the original clause set is satisfiable then the enumeration will, in general, go on *ad infinitum*.

3.3.3 Unification

The innovation that separated general resolution from earlier methods was the idea of the "most general unifier" of expressions and the corresponding unification algorithm. The mechanism of unification removes the need to generate the Herbrand universe, which hindered earlier proof methods. Unification had been at least hinted at in much earlier work on the mechanisation of proofs (such as, for example, by D. Prawitz in [Pr60]—see also [Pr69] and [Ro67] for a discussion of this earlier work), but it was in [Ro65] that an algorithm for computing an essentially unique representative of all possible "unifiers" for expressions was first introduced and incorporated into a one-rule system.

Since then, as will become apparent in the chapters to follow, unification has become universal in automated theorem proving, being used in both resolution and non-resolution systems, and in many other areas such as logic programming (see Chapter 6) and term rewriting systems (see Chapter 7). It has also been extended to provide special treatment for functions that are, for example, associative and commutative (cf. Sections 4.2.8 and 7.2.4), and to handle expressions of higher-order logic. In [Kn89] a review of unification is presented which looks at the history, computational complexity, applications, and, most importantly, extensions of the idea. In this section only the basic case will be discussed.

3.3.3.1 Definitions

Unification of expressions is simply the process of replacing the variables in the expressions by terms to make the modified expressions identical to each other. The replacement of variables by terms is formally expressed in the next few definitions.

Substitution: A substitution is an assignment of terms to variables. It may be viewed as a finite set of ordered pairs:

$$\{(x_1, t_1), (x_2, t_2),..., (x_n, t_n)\},$$

where $x_i \neq x_j$ for any i, j ($i \neq j$), and $x_i \neq t_i$ for any i. The empty substitution is denoted by ε. Each of the pairs (x_i, t_i) will be referred to as an *assignment*.

A preferable notation for substitutions is

$$\{x_1 \rightarrow t_1, x_2 \rightarrow t_2,..., x_n \rightarrow t_n\},$$

since the intention is that x_i is replaced by t_i in a formula/term in which x_i appears. This is the notation that will generally be used in this book.

Note that it is *not* stipulated as part of the definition of substitution that the variables $x_1,..., x_n$ must not occur in any of the t_i. However, it will later be seen that the unifiers constructed for expressions will always have this additional property. In [Bi87] such substitutions are referred to as idempotent.

Idempotent Substitutions: A substitution $\{x_1 \rightarrow t_1, x_2 \rightarrow t_2,..., x_n \rightarrow t_n\}$ is said to be idempotent if, for $i, j \in \{1,..., n\}$, x_i does not occur in t_j.

Instantiation: If θ is the substitution $\{x_1 \rightarrow t_1, x_2 \rightarrow t_2,..., x_n \rightarrow t_n\}$, and E is some expression, then the instantiation of E by θ, or the *application of* θ to E, is the replacement of each free occurrence of x_i ($1 \leq i \leq n$) by the term t_i. This expression is denoted $E\theta$, and is said to be an *instance* of E.

In a similar way, for a given set S of expressions, the instantiation of S by a substitution θ is defined by $S\theta = \{E\theta : E \in S\}$.

Example: If θ is the idempotent substitution $\{x \rightarrow g(y), z \rightarrow f(a)\}$, and if E is $P(x, w, g(z), f(x)) \vee Q(z)$, then $E\theta = P(g(y), w, g(f(a)), f(g(y))) \vee Q(f(a))$.

To "build up" substitutions, a mechanism is required for adding new assignments to given substitutions. This mechanism is required to have the property that an idempotent substitution will be expanded to another idempotent substitution. The following characterisation serves this purpose, under the assumption that, for the added assignment, x_{n+1} does not occur in t_{n+1}.

Adding Assignments: If $\{x_1 \rightarrow t_1, x_2 \rightarrow t_2,..., x_n \rightarrow t_n\}$ is a substitution, then the addition of a new assignment $x_{n+1} \rightarrow t_{n+1}$ produces the set

$$\{x_1 \rightarrow t_1\rho, x_2 \rightarrow t_2\rho,..., x_n \rightarrow t_n\rho, x_{n+1} \rightarrow t_{n+1}\},$$

where ρ is $\{x_{n+1} \rightarrow t_{n+1}\}$, and any assignment such that $x_i = t_i\rho$ is deleted.

Example: Adding the assignment $z \rightarrow x$ to $\{x \rightarrow z, y \rightarrow g(z)\}$ produces

$$\{y \rightarrow g(x), z \rightarrow x\}.$$

Note that if an attempt is made to add a new assignment $x_j \to t_j$ to a substitution in which x_j is already assigned a term, then the new substitution is merely discarded, and the original substitution unaffected [CL73]. However, this case will never have to be considered for the purposes of the algorithm about to be described in Section 3.3.3.2. Naturally, it is also possible to generalise the above definition of the addition of an assignment so that, in general, any two substitution sets may be combined. This also will not be required for the algorithm, and is left as an exercise to the reader.

Exercise 3.8: Define the *composition* $\theta.\upsilon$ of two substitutions θ and υ, so that, for any expression E, $(E\theta)\upsilon = E(\theta.\upsilon)$. Show that, with respect to this definition, composition is associative (that is, $\theta.(\upsilon.\omega) = (\theta.\upsilon).\omega$), but not commutative.

Unification: For expressions E_1 and E_2, if $E_1\theta = E_2\theta$ for some θ, then E_1 and E_2 are said to be be *unifiable* (or to *unify*), and θ is said to be a *unifier* for them. The computation of θ is called *unification* of E_1 and E_2.

Note that if quantifier-free formulae are taken to be implicitly universally closed, then the unification of two (or more) corresponds to the deduction of a single formula that is a consequence of each of them. The "most general unifier", now to be defined, produces the most general such consequence.

Most General Unifier: Suppose that $E_1\theta = E_2\theta$, and that for any other unifier θ' for E_1 and E_2, $E_1\theta'$ is an instance of $E_1\theta$; then θ is the most general unifier (mgu) for E_1 and E_2

Example: Let $E_1 = P(x, a)$, $E_2 = P(y, a)$, $\theta = \{y \to x\}$ and $\theta' = \{x \to b; y \to b\}$. Then $E_1\theta = E_2\theta = P(x, a)$, while $E_1\theta' = E_2\theta' = P(b, a)$. Clearly $E_1\theta'$ is an instance of $E_1\theta$ and for any other unifier θ'' of E_1 and E_2, $E_1\theta''$ would also be an instance of $E_1\theta$. Hence θ is a mgu for E_1 and E_2. Note, however, that $\{x \to y\}$ is also a mgu for E_1 and E_2.

In [Lo78] it is proved that if for two expressions there exists a mgu then it is essentially unique. If θ and θ' are different mgus for a pair of expressions then an appropriate renaming of the variables in $E_1\theta'$ will give $E_1\theta$. Thus $E_1\theta$ is an instance of $E_1\theta'$ and vice-versa. They are said to be **alphabetic variants** of each other. Such alphabetic variants may be ignored.

3.3.3.2 A Unification Algorithm

In [Ro65] an algorithm was presented for calculating the mgu of a set of expressions (rather than just a pair) and was shown to satisfy the required properties: it terminates on all input, and it computes the mgu of a pair of expressions whenever the mgu exists. Here an informal (and very inefficient) algorithm will be given for calculating the mgu of a pair of expressions which also has these properties. The following straightforward notion of a match will be used in the description.

Match: If a symbol s occurs in the nth symbol position (counting from left to right) of both of the expressions E_1 and E_2, then the two occurrences of s are said to match.

Algorithm: Let E_1 and E_2 be two simple expressions with no variables in common, and let ε be the initial (empty) substitution. To unify E_1 and E_2 proceed as follows:

1. If E_1 and E_2 are identical then stop with the current substitution.

2. Let n be the leftmost position at which the symbols of E_1 and E_2 do not match, and let s_1 and s_2 be, respectively, the symbols at this position in E_1 and E_2. If neither s_1 nor s_2 is a variable then stop with failure. Otherwise, if s_1 is a variable then let it be x and let t be the term whose first symbol is s_2, else let s_2 (which must thus be a variable) be x and let t be the term whose first symbol is s_1.

3. If x occurs in t then stop with failure. Otherwise, apply the substitution $\{x \to t\}$ to E_1 and E_2, add $x \to t$ to the current substitution, and then return to step 1.

The main step in the algorithm is step 3. In this step it is stipulated that x must not appear in t. This is called the **occurs check**. To see its significance consider the following pair of expressions:

$$E_1 = P(x, x), \quad E_2 = P(y, f(y)).$$

These two expressions cannot be unified because there is no substitution θ such that $E_1\theta = E_2\theta$. Without the occurs check, the above algorithm would loop indefinitely in trying to unify them, as it would proceed as follows.

The first place at which E_1 and E_2 do not match is the third position. The substitution $\{y \to x\}$, say, would be applied to E_1 and E_2 to give $P(x, x)$ and $P(x, f(x))$. Now x and f do not match, and the substitution $\{x \to f(x)\}$ would be applied to these two new expressions to give $P(f(x), f(x))$ and $P(f(x), f(f(x)))$. Now x and f would not match and once again the substitution $\{x \to f(x)\}$ would be applied, and so on.

Another algorithm—one that did not return to a previously checked position—might, without the occurs check, manage to unify incorrectly two expressions that are not unifiable; however, any attempt to find out what term had been substituted for x would lead to an infinite loop.

3.3.4 The Resolution Principle

By means of unification, ground resolution may be "lifted" to the first-order level.

Potentially Complementary Literals: Let L and L' be literals. If there is a substitution θ such that $L\theta$ is complementary to $L'\theta$ then L and L' are said to be potentially complementary.

Resolvent: Let C and D be the clauses $C_1 \vee L \vee C_2$ and $D_1 \vee L' \vee D_2$, where L and L' are literals. Suppose that C and D have no variables in common and that L and L' are potentially complementary. Let θ be the mgu for the atomic subexpressions of L and L' (of course, either L or L' will itself be an atom). Then the clause

$$(C_1 \vee C_2 \vee D_1 \vee D_2)\theta$$

with any ensuing duplicates removed is said to be a resolvent of C and D. Also, C and D are the clauses *resolved*, while L and L' are the literals *resolved upon*.

Resolution: The resolution of two clauses is the deduction of a resolvent from them (if one exists).

Note that in the definition of resolvent, C and D are required to have no variables in common. This creates no problem, because if they do have variables in common then the variables in one may be renamed, since $\forall x\, \alpha$ is logically equivalent to $\forall y\, \alpha'$ where α' is the same as α except that all free occurrences of x have been replaced by y. As a special case, if the two clauses happen to be the same clause, then after variable-renaming they would become alphabetic variants of each other.

The soundness of the resolution rule is easily shown [CL73]: If C and D are valid in some interpretation then so is any instance of them. Hence $(C_1 \vee L \vee C_2)\theta$ and $(D_1 \vee L' \vee D_2)\theta$ are valid in any interpretation in which C and D are valid. But $L\theta$ and $L'\theta$ cannot be valid in the same interpretation since they contradict each other, and so $(C_1 \vee C_2 \vee D_1 \vee D_2)\theta$ must be valid in any interpretation in which C and D are. Hence the resolvent of a pair of clauses follows from those clauses.

Example: Let C be the clause $P(x, y) \vee \neg Q(x, z) \vee R(b)$ and let D be the clause $\neg P(a, u) \vee \neg R(u)$. Resolving upon $P(x, y)$ and $\neg P(a, u)$ gives

$$(\neg Q(x, z) \vee R(b) \vee \neg R(v))\{x \to a, u \to y\}, \quad \text{i.e. } \neg Q(a, z) \vee R(b) \vee \neg R(y).$$

Resolving upon $R(b)$ and $\neg R(u)$ gives

$$(P(x, y) \vee \neg P(a, u) \vee \neg Q(x, z))\{u \to b\}, \quad \text{i.e. } P(x, y) \vee \neg P(a, b) \vee \neg Q(x, z).$$

As described, the resolution rule does not constitute a refutation-complete calculus by itself. For this purpose an extra rule, that of *factoring*, is required.

Factoring: Let C be a clause. Suppose that there is a pair of literals L and L' in C, for which there is a mgu θ (i.e. $L\theta = L'\theta$). Then apply θ to C and remove any duplicates. This produces a factor of C.

For simplicity, a factor of a factor of a clause C may be taken to be a factor of C, as is usual (e.g. [Lo78]). The important point to note is that the variables of the unified literals are not renamed when a clause is factored.

Example: The only factor of the clause $P(x) \vee P(f(x)) \vee \neg Q(x, a) \vee \neg Q(f(y), z)$ is $P(f(y)) \vee P(f(f(y))) \vee \neg Q(f(y), a)$.

Factoring is simply a generalisation of the deletion of duplicates at the propositional level (though, in general, a clause is not implied by its factors, and thus cannot always be replaced by its factors without loss of completeness). Its necessity for resolution refutations is illustrated in the following example.

Example: Consider the following unsatisfiable set of clauses

$$\{P(u) \vee P(f(u)), \neg P(v) \vee P(w), \neg P(x) \vee \neg P(f(y))\},$$

numbered respectively as 1, 2 and 3. Here is a refutation of this set:

4. $P(u) \vee P(w)$ resolvent of 1 and 2, upon $P(f(u))$ and $\neg P(v)$
5. $P(u)$ factor of 4
6. $\neg P(f(y))$ resolvent of 3 and 5, upon $P(u)$ and $\neg P(x)$
7. $P(u)$ resolvent of 1 and 6, upon $P(f(u))$ and $\neg P(f(u))$
8. $\varnothing$ resolvent of 6 and 7.

Exercise 3.9: Why is it clear that these clauses have no resolution refutation without factoring?

The next task is to devise a complete search procedure for applying resolution. This is not required to be efficient for the moment, but only to provide a basis for the proof of the completeness of resolution.

Resolution Set: Let Σ be a set of clauses. The resolution set of Σ, denoted $R(\Sigma)$, comprises the set of all members of Σ together with all ground resolvents of the members of Σ.

Factor Set: If Σ is a set of clauses, the factor set of Σ, denoted $F(\Sigma)$, is the set of all members of Σ together with all factors of the clauses of Σ.

Nth Resolution Set: The nth resolution set $\mathcal{R}^n(\Sigma)$ of a set of clauses Σ is given by the recursive equations

$$\mathcal{R}^0(\Sigma) = \Sigma, \qquad \mathcal{R}^{n+1}(\Sigma) = R(F(\mathcal{R}^n(\Sigma))).$$

In [Lo78], this simplistic enumeration process is referred to as a **saturation search procedure** for developing resolution refutations. The procedure leads to much redundancy, because not only are the members of $\mathcal{R}^n(\Sigma)$ resolved "against each other" each time a successive $\mathcal{R}^m(\Sigma)$ $(m > n)$ is produced, but also both the resolvent of the clauses C and D and the equivalent resolvents of the clauses D and C are computed. However, the procedure clearly ensures that all possible resolvents of each successive set of clauses is enumerated, and for the initial theoretical considerations this is all that is important. When examples of such enumerations are given these extra clauses will be ignored. Based on this enumeration process the following theorem expresses the refutation completeness of resolution:

$$\Sigma \text{ is unsatisfiable} \quad \text{iff} \quad \mathcal{R}^n(\Sigma) \text{ contains } \varnothing, \text{ for some } n;$$

its proof may be found in [Ro65], [CL73], and also [Lo78] (cf. Section 3.3.6).

For practical purposes, in this simplistic enumeration process both the repeated resolution of the same sets of clauses against each other and the resolution of the same pairs of clauses on the same pairs of literals twice should, of course, be avoided. This may be done without difficulty, but, on the other hand, avoiding the generation of resolvents inconsequential to the proof being performed is a much more difficult problem that cannot be solved in general; that is, there is no proof procedure that will always avoid all inference steps not relevant to a proof [Ko79]. However, regardless of this, the next step is to impose on the resolution calculus *search* strategies that will, in general, speed up the search for a proof. Such strategies will be looked at in the next chapter. The final three sections of this chapter will be concerned with, respectively, an alternative view of resolution, an informal completeness proof, and an extension to include the equality relation.

3.3.5 Relationship to the Cut Rule

It would seem, at first sight, that there is a very straightforward relationship between the cut rule of a sequent calculus and the resolution principle, particularly at the propositional level. Recall that the cut rule takes the form

$$\text{from}\quad \Gamma, \alpha \vdash \Delta \quad \text{and} \quad \Sigma \vdash \Psi, \alpha \quad \text{infer} \quad \Gamma, \Sigma \vdash \Delta, \Psi.$$

Re-expressed at the level of formulae rather than sequents, this becomes

$$\text{from}\quad (\Gamma \wedge \alpha) \to \Delta \quad \text{and} \quad \Sigma \to (\Psi \vee \alpha) \quad \text{infer} \quad (\Gamma \wedge \Sigma) \to (\Delta \vee \Psi).$$

This is equivalent to

$$\text{from}\quad \neg\Gamma \vee \neg\alpha \vee \Delta \quad \text{and} \quad \neg\Sigma \vee \alpha \vee \Psi \quad \text{infer} \quad \neg\Gamma \vee \neg\Sigma \vee \Delta \vee \Psi,$$

which is simply an application of resolution, if it is assumed that Γ and Σ are conjunctions of atomic formulae, that Δ and Ψ are disjunctions of atomic formulae, and that α is an atom.

This view of the relationship between the cut and resolution is the one usually assumed. However, as pointed out by Bibel in his book [Bi87], this correspondence is somewhat artificial, since the cut rule is applied in a deductive calculus, whereas resolution is applied in a refutation calculus. This is an important distinction, and indicates that there is some disparity between the view of resolution as an inference rule, and its application as a "recognition" type calculus. To overcome this disparity Bibel relates resolution to his own recognition calculus, the "matrix method" (cf. Chapter 5). A simpler way of overcoming the disparity is to view resolution not as an inference rule, but as a tactic, that is, as the backward application of an inference rule.

Recall that the aim of resolution is to deduce a contradiction. Expressed in terms of sequents again, the aim is to show that $\Sigma \vdash \varnothing$ (where Σ is a set of clauses), by deriving resolvents of the members of Σ until $\varnothing$ is "deduced". Viewed in this way, resolution may be seen, at the propositional level, as the reversal of a special case of the following sound rule of inference:

$$\frac{\Sigma, C \vee D \vdash \Delta}{\Sigma, C \vee P, D \vee \neg P \vdash \Delta},$$

where C and D are clauses. To generalise this to first-order clauses it is sufficient to add the universal quantifier rule $\forall \vdash$; for purposes of efficiency the application of this rule is implemented as unification, as before. Since resolution is not refutation complete without factoring, the additional rule

$$\text{from } \Sigma, Q \vdash \Delta \text{ infer } \Sigma, Q \vee Q \vdash \Delta$$

is required. This additional rule combined with $\forall \vdash$ corresponds to the factoring rule when applied backwards. The sequent axiom for this system is $\Sigma, P, \neg P \vdash \varnothing$.

The calculus just outlined constitutes an assertion (as opposed to refutation) complete calculus, if the assertion is taken to be the sequent $\Sigma \vdash \varnothing$. This representation of resolution may be clarified by considering the "dual" of the resolution rule, namely, the "affirmation-resolution" rule: 'from $(C \wedge P) \vee (D \wedge \neg P)$ infer $C \wedge D$'. This rule is unsound as it stands, but may be re-expressed in its usual sound formulation as the rule:

$$\text{from } (C \wedge P) \vee (D \wedge \neg P) \quad \text{infer} \quad (C \wedge P) \vee (D \wedge \neg P) \vee (C \wedge D).$$

The dual of this rule is then the re-expression of resolution as

$$\text{from } (C \vee P) \wedge (D \vee \neg P) \quad \text{infer} \quad (C \vee P) \wedge (D \vee \neg P) \wedge (C \vee D).$$

This is how Bibel expresses them both in [Bi87], with the motivation that even for resolution the duplication of the premiss in the conclusion is required for the completeness of the rule. Thus, in principle, affirmation resolution may be treated as a (sound) inference rule. However, the ultimate justification for its application is that if the empty conjunction is deduced then it is known that the original disjunction of conjunctions is valid. For this reason, the view of it as the tactic for the sound rule

$$\text{from } C \wedge D \text{ infer } (C \wedge P) \vee (D \wedge \neg P)$$

rather than a "deductive inference rule" seems more natural. It is then reasonable to claim that it is natural to view classical resolution as a tactic in the same way.

This then gives an alternative characterisation of the resolution principle as the backward application of inference rules. It also provides an alternative view as to why resolution is not deductively complete, since, in this interpretation, it is in fact not a deductive rule. However, while resolution may be viewed in this way as a tactic, it cannot be said to be a decomposition tactic as for the tactics of a cut-free sequent calculus. It is still merely the application of cut, and for this reason is, in principle, an indirect method of proof. To clarify this point, compare resolution with the rules of a sequent calculus for the propositional case: while their backward application decomposes formulae into simpler subgoals, resolution does not.

On the other hand, as Bibel shows in [Bi87], it is possible to find a correlation between resolution proofs and proofs in his own "cut-free" system; in Section 3.3.6 a similar correlation between resolution and a cut-free sequent system will be outlined. Furthermore, it turns out that resolution may be transformed into a decomposition strategy, as opposed to a cut-rule strategy, if a goal-directed strategy for its application is taken. This is the case for what are usually referred to as "linear resolution" strategies. Such a strategy is applied in the Prolog programming language, and this issue will be discussed further in the chapter on Prolog. Finally, while resolution may be given this alternative representation, the more common characterisation of resolution as an inference rule will be used throughout the rest of this book, except where explicitly indicated otherwise.

3.3.6 Completeness of Resolution

Now that resolution has been expressed in terms of the deduction of valid sequents in Section 3.3.5, it is worth building on this relationship to give an informal proof of the completeness of resolution. This will be done by connecting affirmation-resolution proofs to proofs in the (complete) sequent calculus of Section 3.2. (For brevity, a conjunction of literals will be referred to as a "clause" here.)

It may be seen that for deducing a valid disjunction of clauses, the only sequent calculus rules required are the axiom schema in the form '$\vdash \Delta, P, \neg P$' and the $\vdash\wedge$ rule restricted to clauses C and D:

$$\text{from} \quad \vdash \Delta, C \ \text{ and } \ \vdash \Delta, D \quad \text{infer} \quad \vdash \Delta, C \wedge D.$$

Example: To prove the clausal sequent $\vdash \neg P, \neg Q, P \wedge Q$, take $\vdash \neg P, \neg Q, P$ and $\vdash \neg P, \neg Q, Q$ as the axiom sequents and combine them according to the rule.

Assuming that this subsystem of a sequent calculus is complete for deducing valid disjunctions of propositional clauses, it follows that any such disjunction may be derived from instances of the axiom schema by application of the inference rule. Thus, the completeness of the "affirmation-resolution" rule described in Section 3.3.5 is assured if it can be shown that there is a resolution proof of any instance of the axiom, and that if there are resolution proofs of the sequents $\vdash \Delta, C$ and $\vdash \Delta, D$ then there is a resolution proof of $\vdash \Delta, C \wedge D$.

That there is an affirmation-resolution proof of the axiom sequent is clear (just resolve P and $\neg P$), while the second step is proven if it can be shown how any resolution proof of $\vdash \Delta, C$ and $\vdash \Delta, D$ may be transformed into a resolution proof of $\vdash \Delta, C \wedge D$. This is almost straightforward, but requires a little thought regarding duplications. There are two cases to consider:

- Δ has a resolution proof alone
- C and D are involved in the resolution proofs of Δ, C and Δ, D.

In the first case it is trivial that $\vdash \Delta, C \wedge D$ also has a resolution proof. In the second case, since C and D are involved in the proof, it must be the case that C and D are successively "expanded" and "contracted" (by addition and removal of literals) in the process of being resolved with other clauses, until they are both reduced to the (valid) empty clause. It would appear then that the resolvents of Δ with C and Δ with D may be obtained separately even when C and D are conjoined, and thus once C and D have been reduced to the empty clause separately their conjunction is reduced to $\varnothing \wedge \varnothing$ (which automatically reduces to $\varnothing$, completing the combined proofs). However, this holds only if duplicates may be removed from clauses, the problem being that each time C, in the clause $C \wedge D$, is resolved against another clause, the elements of D will be duplicated. Thus, while the sets (or disjunctions) $\Delta \cup \{C\}$ and $\Delta \cup \{D\}$ may have resolution proofs without the removal duplicates, this does not necessarily hold for $\Delta \cup \{C \wedge D\}$, as is illustrated in the following example.

Example: The sequent $\vdash P, \neg P \wedge \neg P$ clearly has a resolution proof without the need to remove duplicates. For resolving P against $\neg P \wedge \neg P$ produces $\neg P$ which may be further reduced to the empty clause by resolving with P. However, taking two of these sequents and combining them according to $\vdash \wedge$ produces the sequent $\vdash P \wedge P, \neg P \wedge \neg P$, which does not have a resolution proof without the removal of duplicates; for performing the same resolvents again on the first P of the clause $P \wedge P$ successively produces $P \wedge \neg P$ and then $P \wedge P$, and the latter is simply the original clause reproduced.

However, the removal of duplicates overcomes this problem, and thus it follows that resolution proofs of $\Delta \cup \{C\}$ and $\Delta \cup \{D\}$ may be combined into a resolution proof of $\Delta \cup \{C \wedge D\}$. Thus the completeness of resolution is proven.

This informal proof brings out a correspondence between resolution proofs and proofs in a sequent calculus, showing that any (analytic) sequentzen proof may be transformed into a resolution proof (cf. Chapter 5). It also explains why the removal of duplicates is required at the ground level and why factoring is required at the first-order level. The above proof may be "lifted" to first-order clauses by means of the standard "lifting lemma" explained in [Lo78]. This lemma states that for any ground instances of clauses C and D each of their resolvents (if there are any) are instances of some resolvent of (a factor of) C and (a factor of) D. Since, according to Herbrand's theorem, a set of clauses is unsatisfiable iff there is a set of ground instances of them that is unsatisfiable, the lifting lemma assures that the use of the most general unifier is sufficient to achieve completeness. An alternative mechanism to the lifting lemma for "lifting" the propositional proof of completeness to the first-order level may be found in [Bi87].

3.3.7 Building-in Equality

In the previous sections resolution has been defined for first-order logic without the equality relation. For purely theoretical purposes, the axioms for equality described in Chapter 2 may easily be converted into (Horn) clauses (see [Lo78] or [RW69]), and then resolution may be applied in the normal way. Naturally, however, an efficient and natural extension of resolution to treat equality is desirable. For this reason, a variety of inference rules have been proposed, designed to incorporate the meaning of the equality axioms into the resolution framework. One such rule, which is to be looked at here, is paramodulation.

The reasons for discussing only paramodulation as opposed to the many other inference rules devised for equality are that

a. Paramodulation is a simple rule that extends resolution to include equality in a natural way.

b. Most, though not all, other rules are based upon paramodulation.

c. Paramodulation is closely related to the critical pair process used in the Knuth-Bendix completion procedure to be discussed in Chapter 7.

Paramodulation: Let C be a clause (possibly involving $=$), and let D be the clause $D_1 \vee t_1 = t_2 \vee D_2$. Suppose that C and D have no variables in common, and suppose that a term t in C unifies with the term t_1 (or t_2) with mgu θ. Replace (one occurrence of) $t\theta$ in $C\theta$ by $t_2\theta$ (or $t_1\theta$) to give C', and infer $C' \vee (D_1 \vee D_2)\theta$.

The inferred clause is called a *paramodulant* of C and D; the deduction of this clause is referred to as paramodulation.

Examples:

1. Let C and D be, respectively, the (unit) clauses $w * (x * y) = (w * x) * y$ and $z * 1 = z$.

    a. Unifying the term $z * 1$ with the term $x * y$ produces the paramodulant $w * z = (w * z) * 1$.

    b. Unifying $z * 1$ with $w * x$ produces the paramodulant $z * (1 * y) = z * y$.

    c. Unifying z (the right-hand side of D) with $x * y$ produces $w * ((x * y) * 1) = (w * x) * y)$.

    d. Unifying $z * 1$ with $(w * x) * y$ (with mgu $\{z \rightarrow w * x, y \rightarrow 1\}$) produces $w * (x * 1) = w * x$.

These simple examples illustrate the similarities and the differences between paramodulation and the "critical-pair" process used in Knuth-Bendix completion (see Chapter 7). In particular, in the critical-pair process, paramodulation steps may be performed only between the left-hand sides of oriented equations (i.e. rewrite rules), and both of the terms involved in the paramodulation step must be non-variables (in contrast to Example 1c above).

2. For the clauses $P(x, f(g(x), h(y))) \lor Q(h(y))$ and $R(w, z) \lor f(z, h(z)) = k(z, z)$, unifying $f(g(x), h(y))$ with $f(z, h(z))$ produces the (only possible) paramodulant $P(x, k(g(x), g(x))) \lor Q(h(g(x)))$.

Paramodulation takes the place of the function axioms and predicate axioms described in Section 2.2.3.5; for completeness the axiom $x = x$ must be retained (see [Lo78]). Examples of the combined application of paramodulation and resolution may be found in [WO84] and [Lo78]. In the next chapter search strategies for resolution will be discussed; their application to systems involving paramodulation is treated in [Lo78]. A particular difficulty with regard to the imposition of strategies on the paramodulation rule concerns the necessity for what are referred to as the "function-reflexivity axioms". These are of the form $f(x) = f(x)$, where f is an n-ary function symbol and x is a sequence of n variables. It may be thought that such equations are superfluous because they are implied (subsumed) by the reflexivity axiom for equality, but it turns out that for most search strategies (including one of the simplest, the "set-of-support strategy" to be discussed in Chapter 4) it is necessary to include such an axiom for each function symbol in the language of the proposed set of axioms in order to preserve the completeness of the calculus. (The idea of a strategy preserving completeness will be explained further in Chapter 4.) This issue is discussed further by Loveland in [Lo78].

Another inference rule for equality that is closely related to paramodulation is E-resolution [Mo69]. This may be viewed as a strategy for the application of paramodulation rather than as a separate inference rule. Essentially, paramodulation is applied to atoms of literals only when an attempt to unify a pair of literals in a normal resolution step fails. There were in fact two rules described for E-resolution in [Mo69], but it has been found that the original formulation is not refutation complete. It transpires that paramodulation has to be applied to the terms of literals during a resolution step even when it is possible to unify the literals in the normal way. A complete variation of E-resolution is described in Loveland's book [Lo78].

In [DH86] "RUE-resolution" inference rules for equality are described, which are intended, on the one hand, to retain the essence of E-resolution, but on the other hand, to avoid totally the principle of paramodulation. In [Re87] a similar approach is described in the context of the Beth-tableaux method. Unfortunately, this does not use unification, and thus assumes that all variables have already been appropriately instantiated (with ground terms). However, in Chapter 4 an approach will be described which is based on the main ideas in [Re87], but which does include a unification component.

CHAPTER 4

SEARCH STRATEGIES

As far as theoretical considerations are concerned the problems of proving theorems in first-order logic on the computer are solved. Any of the three systems described in the previous chapter—the natural deduction calculus, the resolution principle or the sequent system—suffice because they are both sound and (refutation) complete and they may be implemented on a computer. However, the efficiency problems associated with them (particularly in time) are massive. Search strategies must be imposed on them that avoid the redundancy involved in simply performing all possible deduction sequences. In this chapter complete and heuristic search strategies that have been imposed on natural deduction and resolution-based calculi will be described. These will be discussed under the separate headings of "resolution" and "natural" strategies.

4.1 RESOLUTION STRATEGIES

There are many search strategies that have been created specifically for resolution. Only a few will be considered here, but these are some of the most effective. The strategies will be separated into three types: simplification, refinement and ordering strategies. Essentially, a simplification strategy is a principle for removing redundant clauses (or terms); a refinement determines those clauses to which resolution should be applied and those to which it should not; and an ordering strategy simply determines the order in which a set of clauses should have resolution applied to them. In [Lo78] refinement strategies are broken down further, and many more are treated than will be considered here.

Since these strategies have been devised for resolution, it is natural that they should be expressed in terms of resolution. However, the methods presented here are also applicable to other theorem-proving techniques. Of particular importance in this respect are the simplification strategies, which may be applied, sometimes with constraints, to clauses in most theorem-proving contexts.

4.1.1 Simplification Strategies

The first three simplification strategies allow certain clauses to be deleted, while the fourth is intended to "simplify" clauses at the term level. The principles to be expressed in this section are virtually self-explanatory, though often their effect on the completeness (and the soundness) of the underlying calculus is not so obvious, as will be indicated. Applications of each of these simplification strategies (except for the pure-literal principle) may be found in [WO84].

4.1.1.1 The Purity Principle

The purity principle was first noticed by Robinson [Ro65]. It allows clauses to be removed if they contain *pure literals*, defined as follows.

Pure Literals: Let L be a literal in some clause C of a set of clauses Σ. If L is not potentially complementary (see Section 3.3.4) to any literal appearing in any clause of $\Sigma - \{C\}$, then C is said to be *pure* in Σ.

If L is pure in Σ, then the clause C in which L appears may be removed without affecting the satisfiability of Σ. Intuitively, this is because L cannot be removed from C by resolution, and hence it is not possible to derive from C a unit clause that might contradict another unit clause.

A nice example is given in [Ro65]. Consider the set of clauses

$$\Sigma = \{P(0),\ \neg P(x) \vee P(s(x))\}.$$

The following sequence of resolvents would be produced from Σ:

$$P(s(0)),\quad P(s(s(0))),\quad P(s(s(s(0)))),...$$

—that is, a representation of the sequence of positive numbers. No other form of resolvent is possible and so no contradiction may be produced. The resolution principle as described previously would continue searching for a contradiction in these clauses *ad infinitum*, but the purity principle reduces Σ to the empty (satisfiable) set as follows. The literal $P(s(x))$ is not potentially complementary to any literal in the set $\Sigma - \{\neg P(x) \vee P(s(x))\}$, and hence the clause in which it appears may be removed. Now the literal $P(0)$ is not potentially complementary to any literal in the remaining clause set, and hence may also be removed. This leaves the empty set of clauses, which is satisfiable. This, in turn, means that the original set of clauses is satisfiable. (The purity principle forms the basis for the connection-graph proof procedure to be described in the next chapter.)

4.1.1.2 Removal of Tautologies

A tautology is defined as a valid propositional formula. This definition is usually extended, however, to include also formulae that are special cases of propositional tautologies.

Example: The formula $(\forall x P(x) \wedge (\forall x P(x) \rightarrow \exists y Q(y, z))) \rightarrow \exists y Q(y, z)$ is just a special case of the valid propositional formula $(P \wedge (P \rightarrow Q)) \rightarrow Q$.

Put another way, a tautology is a special case of a schematic theorem (as discussed in Section 3.1 on natural deduction) whose proof requires inference rules only for the connectives and not for the quantifiers. For instance, the propositional formula in the example may have been re-expressed as the schema $(\alpha \wedge (\alpha \rightarrow \beta)) \rightarrow \beta$, the proof of which clearly would not require quantifier rules. Special attention is given to this sort of valid formula because propositional logic is decidable, and hence tautologies may always be found with a finite search. In the more restricted setting of clauses, in particular, there is a very simple test to detect tautologies, for they will have the form expressed in the following definition.

Tautology: If both an atom A and its negation $\neg A$ appear in a clause then the clause is called a tautology.

With respect to this definition it should be recalled that a formula is valid iff its universal closure is valid (Exercise 2.6), and thus the validity of an unquantified clause ensures the validity of its closure.

Tautologous clauses clearly may be removed without affecting the satisfiability of the clause set. It follows from this that, usually, these clauses may be removed without affecting the completeness of the underlying calculus. This holds, in particular, for the unconstrained resolution principle, that is, the resolution principle with a saturation search procedure. However, for some resolution strategies, such as "locking" (to be discussed below), the removal of tautologies may affect their completeness. The reasons for this will become apparent when the relevant strategies are discussed.

4.1.1.3 Subsumption of Clauses

Essentially, a clause is said to be subsumed by some other clause if it is a logical consequence of that clause. However, this definition is too powerful for practical purposes, and hence it is usual to take a more restrictive and decidable characterisation (sometimes referred to as θ-subsumption, e.g. [Lo78]), proposed originally by Robinson [Ro65]:

Subsumption: A clause C subsumes a clause D if there is a substitution θ such that every literal in $C\theta$ appears in D.

Examples: $P(x)$ subsumes $P(y) \vee Q(z)$, and $P(a, x) \vee P(y, b)$ subsumes $P(a, b)$.

If a clause is subsumed then generally it is beneficial to remove it. On the other hand, in those cases where a clause is subsumed by a clause "longer" than itself, as in the second example above, the removal of the subsumed clause is often deemed to be detrimental rather than helpful to shortening a proof (see the unit preference strategy below). In [Lo78] subsumption is defined to allow a clause to subsume only clauses longer than itself. Regardless of this issue, it can be proved that if Σ is a set of clauses and if C is a clause in Σ that is subsumed by another clause in Σ, then

$$\Sigma \text{ is unsatisfiable} \quad \text{iff} \quad \Sigma - \{C\} \text{ is unsatisfiable}$$

(see [Ro65]).

Unfortunately, once again, the fact that the removal of subsumed clauses does not affect the satisfiability of a set of clauses does not mean that they may automatically be removed without affecting the completeness of the calculus. In fact, this is true even for the unconstrained resolution method. The problem that arises in this case is that, as already pointed out, the resolution calculus is not complete without the factoring rule, but, since clauses subsume their own factors, deleting all subsumed clauses as soon as they are generated would entail deleting all factors as soon as they are generated. For unconstrained resolution this problem may be overcome merely by applying subsumed clause removal immediately after the set $\mathcal{R}^n(\Sigma)$ has been computed, before the set $\mathcal{R}^{n+1}(\Sigma)$ is computed (see [CL73] or [Lo78]). Naturally, this means that subsumed clauses may always be deleted from the originally given set, since this is simply $\mathcal{R}^0(\Sigma)$. An example of the removal of subsumed clauses will be given in the discussion of *hyper-resolution* below.

4.1.1.4 Demodulation

Formal definition of demodulation would be superfluous here, since there are several different versions and it is only the basic idea that is important. As originally defined in [WR67] (see also [WO84]), demodulation is the application of equations as "destructive rewrite rules" to replace certain terms by others. The "rewrite rules" (oriented equations), in this context, are called *demodulators*, and the clause to which a demodulator is applied is said to be *demodulated*. A demodulator is applied to a clause by replacing any instance of one (previously designated) side of the demodulator occurring in the clause by the corresponding instance of the other side of the demodulator, and then removing the demodulated clause from the given set (hence the destructive nature of the process). A demodulator $t = t'$ may be denoted $t \rightarrow t'$ to indicate that instances of t may be replaced by instances of t' but not vice-versa. This form of demodulation does not provide a complete strategy, but is simply intended as a heuristic simplification principle.

Example: The set of clauses $\{P(a), \neg P(f(x)), f(x) = a\}$ is unsatisfiable, but the two clauses involving P cannot be resolved. However, with the application of the equation $f(x) = a$ as the demodulator $f(x) \rightarrow a$ to the other clauses, the new set $\{P(a), \neg P(a), f(x) = a\}$ is produced (the demodulated clause $\neg P(f(x))$ having been removed). Resolution may now be applied to $P(a)$ and $\neg P(a)$ to produce the empty clause. On the other hand, with only the slight modification of replacing $f(x) = a$ by $f(b) = a$, there is no longer a refutation of the resultant clauses (which are unsatisfiable) if only simple demodulation is allowed.

As defined in [Lo78] demodulation becomes a special case of paramodulation. In this version, a demodulator $t \rightarrow t'$ may be involved in a full paramodulation step, but again only instances of t may be replaced.

Example: In the case of the clauses $\{P(a), \neg P(f(x)), f(b) \rightarrow a\}$, demodulation may be applied by instantiating the negative clause to $\neg P(f(b))$ and then applying the demodulator as before.

It is pointed out in [Lo78] that a complete strategy may be determined in which this form of demodulation is employed, by allowing the demodulators to be applied before general paramodulation is performed, but eventually performing all possible paramodulations. This would constitute a strategy similar to the *unit preference strategy* (see Section 4.1.3 on ordering strategies below). However, this means that the demodulators may also be "applied" in the opposite direction to that originally designated; completeness may be lost if they are not applied in this way.

Example: The set of clauses $\{P(b), \neg P(c), a \to b, a \to c\}$ is clearly unsatisfiable but no demodulation steps are possible according to the stipulated orientation of the demodulators. In this case the demodulators have to be applied "backwards" to complete the proof.

On the other hand, it turns out that Loveland's version of demodulation, with the demodulators applied in only one direction, does preserve the completeness of the resolution calculus under certain conditions on the demodulators. The demodulators of the above example do not satisfy these extra conditions, but the set of demodulators $\{a \to b, c \to a\}$, which have exactly the same logical consequences, do satisfy the conditions, and the proof of the above theorem clearly may be completed by applying these demodulators in the stipulated direction. These conditions will be discussed in detail in Chapter 7.

4.1.2 Refinements

The following discussion is intended to outline a wide range of ideas concerning refinements, but not to encapsulate all known work. Deeper study of these and other strategies may be found in the books [Lo78] and [CL73].

4.1.2.1 The Set-of-Support Strategy

The set-of-support strategy of [WC65] was one of the early attempts to bring a degree of "goal-directedness" into the resolution framework. Essentially, in this strategy a set of clauses is taken as the "goal" and resolvents are derived from these clauses and then from the resolvents themselves (and so on) until the empty clause is produced. This strategy was later to be subsumed by the "linear strategies" (see Chapter 6), which are truly goal-directed resolution refinements, but it expresses the main idea behind the improved approaches.

Set of Support: If Σ is a set of clauses, then any subset T of Σ may be designated to be a set of support.

Supported Clause: A clause is said to have support if it is (a factor of) a clause in the designated set-of-support T or is (a factor of) a resolvent of two clauses one of which has support.

Set-of-Support Strategy: According to this strategy, every application of the resolution principle must be to clauses at least one of which has support.

It can be proved that if (for $T \subseteq \Sigma$) $\Sigma - T$ is satisfiable then the set-of-support strategy is refutation complete (see [Lo78] and also [WO84]). That is, if Σ is an unsatisfiable set of clauses then it may be proved to be so using this strategy. The most reasonable choice for T is the set of clauses that constitute the negation of the conclusion of the theorem to be proved. This choice would thus be based on semantic criteria depending on the user's understanding of the problem. A choice for T based upon a merely syntactic criterion would be to let T be the set of all negative clauses. This would make $\Sigma - T$ satisfiable, because if all the positive literals are assigned the truth value **T**, then every clause in $\Sigma - T$ would be *true*, since each contains at least one positive literal [WO84]. The limitation of the set-of-support strategy is that it tends to lose its effect as the set of supported clauses increases at each level of the saturation search proof.

Example: Let Σ be the set of clauses in EX of Section 3.3.1, namely

1. $P(x, z) \vee \neg Q(x) \vee R(x, a)$,   2. $P(x, z) \vee Q(x)$,   3. $\neg P(x, z) \vee R(x, f(x))$
4. $\neg R(b, x) \vee S(x)$,   5. $\neg S(x)$.

The first criterion for the choice of a set of support would make T be the clauses 4 and 5, while the second would make T be 5. If T is taken to be 5, the first level $\mathcal{R}^1(\Sigma)$ of the level-saturation proof will be the single clause:

6. $\neg R(b, x)$ 4 and 5.

Now the elements of T are expanded to the set comprising 5 and 6. At the next level $\mathcal{R}^2(\Sigma)$ the following two clauses are produced:

7. $\neg P(b, z)$ 6 and 3,
8. $P(b, z) \vee \neg Q(b)$ 6 and 1.

The next sequence of resolvents produces:

9. $\neg Q(b) \vee R(b, a)$ 7 and 1,
10. $Q(b)$ 7 and 2,
11. $P(b, z)$ 8 and 2,
12. $\neg Q(b)$ 7 and 8.

At the next level 10 and 12 are resolved to produce the empty clause.

Exercise 4.1: Prove that the set of clauses $\{P(0), \neg P(x) \vee P(s(x)), \neg P(s(s(0)))\}$ is unsatisfiable using the set-of-support strategy, taking $\{\neg P(s(s(0)))\}$ as the set of support. Compare this with the proof of the same theorem performed via the "goal-oriented methods" of natural deduction and sequent calculi.

4.1.2.2 Hyper-Resolution

Hyper-resolution is an inference rule whose underlying principle is to perform standard resolution only on certain clauses in a certain order. However it may be treated as a new inference rule that combines several resolution steps into one. More importantly, since it is a complete calculus in itself, and since its basic principle is to restrict the application of basic resolution, it not only combines several resolution steps, but avoids certain resolution steps totally. The clauses to which the rule is applied must consist of a single *negative* or *mixed* clause together with a set of *positive* clauses.

Positive, Negative Literals: An atom is a positive literal, and the negation of an atom is a negative literal.

Positive, Negative, Mixed Clauses: A clause is a positive clause if it contains only positive literals; negative clause is defined analogously. A clause is a mixed clause if it contains both positive and negative literals.

Hyper-Resolvent: Let $C_1,..., C_n$ be a set of n (> 0), not necessarily distinct, positive clauses, and let D be a negative or mixed clause containing exactly n negative literals. Suppose that there is a substitution μ such that, after application of μ to the $n + 1$ clauses, each negative literal in D is complementary to a literal in one of the C_i. The clause produced by applying the mgu θ of the atoms of these literals to the $n + 1$ clauses, removing the ensuing complementary literals from each of the clauses, and then forming the disjunction of the remaining literals is referred to as a hyper-resolvent of the $n + 1$ clauses.

Example: From the mixed clause $\neg P \vee \neg Q \vee R$ and the positive clauses $P \vee S$ and $Q \vee R \vee T$, the hyper-resolvent $R \vee S \vee T$ may be produced by deleting the pair-wise complementary literals $P, \neg P$ and $Q, \neg Q$ from each of the clauses, and then forming the disjunction of the remaining literals (deleting duplicates as usual).

Hyper-Resolution: The hyper-resolution of $n + 1$ clauses is the deduction of a hyper-resolvent from them (if one exists).

The main step of the application of this rule involves an attempt to unify simultaneously each pairing of potentially complementary literals in the resolved clauses (see [Ro67] and also [Lo78]), thus constructing a single most general unifier. Note also that hyper-resolvents are always positive clauses. It is proved in [Lo78] that hyper-resolution is a refutation-complete inference rule.

Example: In the clauses of the EX example, the only positive clause is clause 2, namely $P(x, z) \vee Q(x)$, and hence the first set of hyper-resolvents in $\mathcal{R}^1(\Sigma)$ will each involve this clause. They are all standard resolvents in this case:

   6. $P(x, z) \vee P(x, z') \vee R(x, a)$ 2 and 1
   7. $Q(x) \vee R(x, f(x))$ 2 and 3

Now there are two additional positive clauses 6 and 7, and these are involved in the next sequence of hyper-resolvents $\mathcal{R}^2(\Sigma)$:

   8. $P(x, z) \vee R(x, a)$ factor of 6
   9. $P(x, z) \vee R(x, f(x)) \vee R(x, a)$ 7 and 1
 10. $P(x, z') \vee R(x, f(x)) \vee R(x, a)$ 6 and 1 on $P(x, z)$ and $\neg P(x, y)$
 11. $P(x, z) \vee R(x, f(x)) \vee R(x, a)$ 6 and 1 on $P(x, z')$ and $\neg P(x, y)$
 12. $P(x, z) \vee P(x, z') \vee S(a)$ 6 and 4
 13. $R(x, a) \vee R(x, f(x))$ 8 and 3

All of these are positive clauses, but fortunately 8 subsumes 9, 10 and 11, so that only three more clauses, 8, 12 and 13, need to be added to the set. Clause 8 also subsumes clauses 1 and 6, and hence these may be removed also. (Clause 6 also subsumes clause 8, but it is preferable to retain the clause with fewer literals.) At the next level 8 and 4 are resolved to produce $S(a)$, and at the next level $S(a)$ and $\neg S(x)$ may be resolved to produce the empty clause, completing the refutation. The other details of the third stage are left to the reader.

Exercise 4.2: Using hyper-resolution, show that the following set of clauses is unsatisfiable: $\{P \vee \neg Q \vee \neg R, Q \vee S, R \vee S, \neg P \vee \neg Q, \neg S\}$.

As an aside, note that owing to the appearance of variants of the original resolution inference rule (such as hyper-resolution) the original rule (as it is described in the previous chapter) is sometimes referred to as *binary resolution*. It is important to note that both of the refinements described above may be viewed as examples of "model-based" strategies. This is because a certain satisfiable set of clauses is distinguished, such that each application of resolution must be to clauses at least one of which is not in this set. For the set-of-support strategy this set is $\Sigma - T$, while for hyper-resolution it is the set of mixed clauses. Thus, in each case a model may be chosen that satisfies the distinguished clauses. Much more on "model" strategies may be found in [Lo78] (called *setting refinements* there).

4.1.2.3 Lock Resolution

Lock resolution is a simple though surprising rule, and is an example of a strategy that is based upon a purely syntactic principle that seems to have no semantic underpinnings. For a given set of clauses, an arbitrary number (or index) is associated with each literal in each clause. From then on, any application of resolution must be upon only literals of the least index in each clause. In addition, the literals of the resolvent inherit the index of the literals of which they are an instance in the resolved clauses; when duplicates are removed those literals of the highest index are the ones to be deleted. Similarly, when a clause is factored the literals of the factor inherit the index from the literal of which they are an instance, and duplicates are removed according to the size of their index as above.

Example: Consider the set of indexed clauses,

   1. $P^1 \vee Q^2$,   2. $\neg P^1 \vee \neg Q^2$,   3. $\neg P^2 \vee Q^1$,   4. $P^2 \vee \neg Q^1$.

A lock resolution of this set may proceed as follows:

5. $Q^2 \vee \neg Q^2$	resolving 1 and 2
6. $P^2 \vee \neg Q^2$	resolving 4 and 5
7. P^1	resolving 1 and 6 (deleting P^2 from the resolvent)
8. $\neg Q^2$	resolving 7 and 2
9. $\neg P^2$	resolving 3 and 8
10. $\varnothing$	resolving 7 and 9

Exercise 4.3: Show that a refutation via lock resolution of the following set of clauses, according to the indicated indexing of the literals, is essentially identical to a hyper-resolution refutation of the same clauses:

$$\{P^2 \vee \neg Q^1 \vee \neg R^1, Q^1 \vee S^2, R^1 \vee S^2, \neg P^1 \vee \neg Q^2, \neg S^1\}.$$

This strategy, which might also be referred to as "index resolution", is, perhaps surprisingly, a complete refinement of resolution. However, it must be noted that it is not compatible with most other refinements, in the sense that soundness or at least completeness may be lost [Lo78]. For instance, it is clear from the preceding example that tautology deletion may destroy completeness (depending, of course, upon the choice of indices), for if in the example clause 5 had been deleted as soon as it was generated then there would have been no other possible resolvents and the attempted refutation would have failed. Naturally, if all the indices are chosen to be the same then the strategy would be complete even with tautology deletion, but this would, of course, defeat the purpose of the refinement.

Fortunately, lock resolution is very powerful alone, as is illustrated by the above example. A different formulation of this rule is presented in [Lo78], which relates it to model-based refinements of resolution. It is pointed out that this formulation subsumes most of the other setting refinements discussed in [Lo78], such as hyper-resolution, apart from the fact that tautologies may not always be removed in the case of lock resolution. The mechanism underlying lock resolution is also related to the idea behind *ordered clause* resolution refinements. These refinements do not use an explicit indexing scheme, but instead use the ordering on the literals of the clauses, allowing only the "left-most" literal of a clause (as the literals are input) to be resolved upon. They are discussed in detail by Loveland in [Lo78]. The SLD-resolution rule used in the Prolog language, to be discussed in Chapter 6, uses the idea of ordered clause deductions.

4.1.2.4 Theory Resolution

As defined in Chapter 2, the theory generated by a set of axioms is the set of all theorems of them (with respect to a given calculus). In Section 4.2.8 the idea of designing special reasoning procedures for particular theories will be discussed. A problem associated with such procedures is that of incorporating them into a more general theorem-proving system in an efficiency-oriented manner whilst retaining completeness. The theory-resolution principle described by M.E. Stickel in [St85] proposes a solution to this problem which is applicable to decidable theories. As in [St85] this will be described at the ground level, since treatment of the general level simply requires the inclusion of the relevant substitutions.

Let Σ be a set of clauses and let T be some set of formulae with an associated decision procedure. Here it is relevant to think of T as a (non-equational) formal specification for which a decision procedure has been constructed. The present task is to show that $\Sigma \cup T$ is unsatisfiable.

Theory Resolution: Let $C_1,..., C_m$ be the clauses $D_1 \vee E_1,..., D_m \vee E_m$ of Σ, where each of the D_i consists of at least one literal, and let $U_1,..., U_n$ be any unit clauses. If $T \cup \{D_1,..., D_m, U_1,..., U_n\}$ is unsatisfiable then the clause

$$E_1 \vee ... \vee E_m \vee \neg U_1 \vee ... \vee \neg U_n$$

is a T-resolvent of the clauses $C_1,..., C_m$. The theory resolution of two clauses is the derivation of a T-resolvent from them (if one exists).

In particular, if $n = 0$ and the D_i are single literals then $E_1 \vee ... \vee E_m$ is called a *total narrow* T-*resolvent* of $C_1,..., C_m$. It is shown in [St85] that if the set $\Sigma \cup T$ is unsatisfiable then there is a total narrow theory-resolution refutation of Σ using T. However, it is pointed out that total narrow theory resolution is not compatible with tautology deletion.

It is worthwhile illustrating the soundness of (and thus the intuition behind) the theory-resolution principle with a simple case. Suppose that the set $T \cup \{D, U\}$ is unsatisfiable; then $T \cup \{D\} \models \neg U$; thus $T \cup \{D \vee E\} \models E \vee \neg U$. A more specific illustration, taken from [St85], is given in the next example:

Example: Let $T = \{\neg x < x, (x < y \wedge y < z) \rightarrow x < z\}$. Then $P \vee Q$ is a total narrow resolvent of the clauses $a < b \vee P$ and $b < a \vee Q$, since the set $T \cup \{a < b, b < a\}$ is unsatisfiable.

Exercise 4.4: Given the same T as in the example, determine the total narrow theory resolvent of the set of clauses $\{a < b \vee P, b < c \vee Q, c < a \vee R\}$.

It is pointed out by Stickel that theory resolution is very closely related to other refinements such as hyper-resolution. In particular, in the case of (propositional) hyper-resolution, a clause $E_1 \vee ... \vee E_m \vee U$ is derived from a set of positive clauses $D_1 \vee E_1,..., D_m \vee E_m$ together with the clause $\neg D_1 \vee ... \vee \neg D_m \vee U$. There is an analogy to theory resolution in this inference if T is taken to be a set of formulae such that $\neg D_1 \vee ... \vee \neg D_m \vee U$ is a logical consequence.

It is particularly important to note that with respect to theory resolution the reasoning procedure associated with T simply becomes a "black box" the contents of which are not relevant as long as it is a reasoning procedure for T. Thus the most efficient procedure may be used without any worry about incorporating it into the overall system. A development of theory resolution is described in the report [ON86], where it is incorporated into a "semantic-clause-graph procedure" based on Kowalski's "connection-graph proof procedure" (to be discussed in Chapter 5).

A major omission in the discussion of refinements in this section is the treatment of the class of "linear refinements" (see [CL73], [Lo78]). There are two reasons for this. The first is that such a refinement will be discussed in Chapter 6 on Prolog, and this application to "logic programming" should provide additional motivation for its study. The second reason is that, while these strategies were originally developed as refinements of resolution, generally they may just as easily be expressed in terms of cut-free sequent calculi. It will be seen later that, as a consequence, the strategies are also naturally related to the matrix-connection method of Chapter 5, and hence it is preferable to leave discussion of them until after this alternative to resolution has been presented. Another resolution refinement, the connection-graph proof procedure, which is based upon a very different perspective on the resolution method, will be described in Chapter 5.

4.1.3 Ordering Strategies

Perhaps the most well-known ordering strategies are the depth-first and breadth-first procedures associated with general search problems. These will be discussed further in Chapter 6 on Prolog. In this section a very different approach will be discussed.

4.1.3.1 The Unit Preference Strategy

A **unit clause** is simply a clause with exactly one literal. In principle, the unit preference strategy requires that all applications of resolution be to pairs of clauses at least one of which is a unit clause. However, this very restrictive strategy is not complete for general clauses. (If it were then it would be more appropriate to view it as a complete refinement rather than as an ordering strategy.) For example, the unsatisfiable set of clauses given in the example illustrating lock resolution above clearly does not have a unit clause refutation because the initial set of clauses contains no unit clauses.

Exercise 4.5: Explain why the proof of completeness of resolution presented in Section 3.3.6 does not carry over to the unit preference strategy.

The unit preference strategy becomes an ordering strategy when it is stipulated that resolution be applied to pairs of clauses one of which is a unit clause before it is applied to more general clauses. In fact, the following ordering strategy clearly evolves from the unit preference strategy.

When applying resolution to a particular set of clauses, proceed as follows:
1. If the set is not empty, then choose a clause with the fewest number of literals of all those clauses not previously chosen.
2. Apply resolution to the clause chosen in 1 and each clause with which it has not previously been resolved, in increasing order of the number of literals. If the empty clause is not deduced then return to 1.

This is quite clearly a complete procedure for forming the set of all resolvents of a particular set of clauses, since it merely places an ordering on the resolutions performed: it does not disallow any. The idea behind the procedure is that the aim in a resolution proof is to deduce contradictory unit clauses; these should more speedily be found by resolving clauses involving the fewest literals. The degree of its effect, however, will depend upon which set of clauses it is applied to at each stage of an attempted refutation. If, in particular, it is applied merely to each set $\mathcal{R}^i(\Sigma)$ of a saturation search procedure, then its effect will be quite limited. A better method of application is described in [Lo78] (p.98), where each $\mathcal{R}^i(\Sigma)$ up to a bound k (for i) is processed before proceeding to $k + 1$.

An important point to make about the unit preference strategy is that the basic strategy (where at least one clause in each application of resolution must be a unit clause) is complete for Horn-clauses, defined as follows:

Horn-clause: A clause with at most one positive literal is called a Horn-clause.

This means that if the initial set of clauses involves only Horn-clauses, which is obviously mechanically checkable, then a proof of unsatisfiability, if there is any, may be found by applying resolution only to clauses at least one of which is a unit clause. It is also the case that no factoring is required. This was originally proved in [HW74], and is further extended in [Lo78]. The reason for mentioning this fact is that Horn-clauses will be the main topic in Chapter 6 on Prolog.

Example: A unit refutation of the set of Horn-clauses

$$\{P \vee \neg Q \vee \neg R, Q \vee \neg S, R \vee \neg S, \neg P \vee \neg Q, S\}$$

is given by the following sequence of resolvents: $R, Q, P \vee \neg Q, P, \neg Q, \varnothing$.

Exercise 4.6: Show that there is also a unit refutation of the set of clauses of Exercise 4.2, and of the clauses of EX, though neither is a set of Horn-clauses.

As already noted, two other ordering strategies, that of depth-first and breadth-first search, will also be discussed in Chapter 6 on Prolog.

4.2 NATURAL STRATEGIES

This section is concerned with strategies for proof development usually associated with natural deduction or sequentzen proof systems. These strategies are generally intended to capture some aspect of human reasoning, but not necessarily to be limited to human capabilities. Usually, they correspond to an efficient realisation of a principle used by humans, analogously to the way an efficient algorithm may be designed to improve on human methods of carrying out arithmetic problems.

Whereas in the discussion of resolution strategies the completeness problems associated with the different strategies were of major concern, these are not considered important in the study of "natural" strategies presented here. The reasons for this are considered in the next subsection. Following that, a general "characterisation" of natural systems will be presented in Section 4.2.2, and then some powerful natural strategies that have been developed will be discussed in the following subsections. This discussion in many respects follows [Bl77], but here more details and explanation will be given.

4.2.1 The Problem With Complete Strategies

Although, as indicated in Section 4.1, some very powerful complete search strategies were (and are) being developed for resolution (and other proof systems), many people soon began to feel that these alone would never be adequate to prove any but the most "simple" theorems. This view was prompted by a recognition of the vast search spaces inherent in the proof of complex theorems via strategies that are required to be complete for all of first-order logic.

As a simple illustration of this problem, consider the task of solving a pair of simultaneous equations, such as $x + y = 5$ and $x + 3 = y$. The theorem-proving methods discussed previously would have little difficulty showing that solutions to this problem exist (and possibly finding them), but the important point to note is that in doing so they would essentially have to check possible combinations of x and y until a solution is found. For example, the system Prolog, to be described later, would proceed by finding values of x and y that satisfy $x + y = 5$ and then checking whether they satisfy $x + 3 = y$. Though, in this case, solutions may be found very quickly (depending on how "+" is defined), it is easily seen that this is not an appropriate way to solve this type of problem, in general. Of course, there exist much quicker methods to solve equations such as the above. (On the other hand, if the simultaneous equations involve arbitrary functions then there may not exist any straightforward methods for finding solutions.) In this case the problem may be resolved, whilst retaining completeness, by incorporating special decision procedures within the theorem prover (see Section 4.2.8 for more on this), but the example should be sufficient to illustrate the general problem.

In an attempt to overcome this general problem, two very different (though not incompatible) directions have been taken. One is to give the user more scope for interaction with the theorem prover—either to direct it, or to give advice or to supply information that would be difficult (or impossible) for the theorem prover to find for itself. The other approach is to incorporate into the system heuristics and strategies that are intended to be relevant to some application rather than to general purpose theorem proving. Both of these ideas have led many people back to the natural deduction (or sequentzen) systems of Gentzen, and have given rise to the idea of "natural systems" as opposed to, say, resolution. Since this book is concerned with mechanical theorem-proving techniques it will be the ideas of natural systems and heuristic techniques that will be discussed in this chapter, rather than interactive theorem provers.

4.2.2 Natural Systems

The term "natural" is difficult to define, but here it is intended to evoke the picture of natural deduction systems as previously described, with the following provisos.

- Existential quantifiers may be removed in favour of Skolem functions.
- Proofs may be performed backwards or using a combination of backwards and forwards reasoning.
- Proof by contradiction may be dominant; thus the systems need only be refutation complete.
- Heuristic techniques that are sound (but possibly not complete) may be applied to "simplify" formulae.

In [Bl77]—a review of "natural" systems—it is contended that one of the main differences between natural and other types of theorem provers, in particular resolution theorem provers, is the greater ease with which heuristics, particularly those of a semantic nature, may be incorporated into natural systems. However, the main requirement of any natural system is that each step in a proof should be intuitively clear to any user, at least if the user has a basic understanding of the methods being used. There is no restriction that any application of a rule must be to only one part of a formula in each step of a proof. This would more likely lead to tedium rather than to understanding. In fact, on most occasions it would be preferable for a rule to be applied to all parts of a formula before proceeding to the next step. The main aim is for the user to get an overall feel for how the proof is being performed. For this purpose it is useful if a mechanisation of the method includes a component that describes the steps of the proof. The Boyer-Moore theorem prover (to be discussed in Chapter 8) is a very good example of this.

4.2.3 Reductions and Opening Up Definitions

A *reduction* or *rewrite rule* is a rule for replacing any instance of one expression by the corresponding instance of another expression. For example, in the proof system PROVER described in [Bl71], any instance of the expression $x \in (y \cap z)$ would be replaced by the corresponding instance of $x \in y \land x \in z$ using one of the rules— though the converse replacement would never be performed using the same rule.

Another example is the replacement of $\alpha \wedge \alpha$ by α. These are rewrite rules based on universally closed equivalences between formulae. Equations (universally closed equality atoms) may be treated in a similar manner. For example, if the equation $\forall x\, x + 0 = x$ is an axiom of the given system then it may be applied as a rewrite rule to replace any term of the form $t + 0$ by t.

Note that the choice of these rules depends on semantic considerations, and not merely on their syntactic form [Bl77]. If instances of the expression E are to be replaced by instances of E', then not only must E and E' be either equivalent (if they are formulae) or equal (if they are terms) according to the current set of axioms, but the choice of this replacement should be guided by the user's understanding of the problem. For instance, the replacement is likely to lead to a proof if the concepts expressed in E' are, in some sense, "less complex" than those expressed in E. This is particularly apparent if the rewrite rule corresponds to a definition of E. Opening up (or *expanding*) definitions is simply a special case of applying reductions. For example, suppose a binary predicate *Gparentof* is defined by

$$\forall x \forall y (Gparentof(x, y) \leftrightarrow \exists z(Parentof(x, z) \wedge Parentof(z, y))).$$

Then if, say, the formula $\exists x Gparentof(x, jane)$ occurs in a formula, it may be replaced by $\exists x \exists z(Parentof(x, z) \wedge Parentof(z, jane))$. Here, one expression is replaced by a "syntactically larger" but semantically "more primitive" expression. On the other hand, in some cases it may be preferable to use purely "syntactic" criteria for deciding to replace one expression by another. For example, such a choice may be assured to lead to the simplification of any conjecture, or perhaps may even give rise to a decision procedure for a certain theory. This possibility will be studied in more detail in Chapter 7, where "complete" sets of reductions will be discussed.

While applying reductions and expanding definitions may lead to simplification of a conjecture, there are also problems associated with their use. One problem is that if all reductions are applied then this will often lead to an excessive amount of new symbols and subexpressions. This not only makes the formulae difficult to read by a human user, but it may also hamper the theorem prover. In the context of definition expansion, the following heuristics might be applied to solve this problem, when provided with a conjecture of the form $\alpha \rightarrow \beta$.

1. If, on opening up one of the definitions in the hypothesis α, the new subgoal $(\alpha_1 \wedge \alpha_2 \wedge ... \wedge \alpha_n) \rightarrow \beta$ is derived, where one of the α_i is an atomic formula whose predicate symbol appears in the conclusion β, then retain the new formula and discard the previous version, else discard the new formula.

2. Open up the definition of the "main" predicate in the conclusion β.

3. Open up the definition of any symbol in the hypothesis that does not also occur in the conclusion.

4. If all else fails, open up any definition in the conclusion.

Similar heuristics may, of course, be applied for reductions in general. The reasoning behind the heuristics 1 and 3 is that if the hypothesis can be converted into a form which, at the very least, resembles the conclusion, then a proof of the given implication will more readily be found. The reasoning behind the heuristics 2 and 4 is that, especially if heuristics 1 and 3 have failed, the predicates involved in the conclusion may be defined in terms of a conjunction of formulae that occur in the hypotheses. The first rule above is also the essence of the heuristics for opening up definitions used in the Boyer-Moore system.

An extension of the idea expressed in heuristic 1 is proposed by D. Plummer in [Pl88]. In this extension a series of definition expansions may be performed if it is known that, ultimately, both the conclusion and hypothesis of the conjecture will be reduced to formulae involving the same predicates. For example, in a proof of the implication $x = y \rightarrow x \subseteq y$ (where x and y denote sets), the system would expand both $x = y$ and $x \subseteq y$ to their defining formulae involving the predicate $\in$. To be certain that the expansion of the definitions involved will produce formulae involving common symbols, initially each predicate is associated with the more "primitive" predicates occurring in its definition. For example, both $=$ and $\subseteq$ would be associated with $\in$. In addition, other attributes of the formulae occurring in the hypothesis and conclusion may be taken into account, such as their polarity (see Chapter 5) or any occurrences of function symbols within them. An extension of Plummer's work is proposed by Giunchiglia and Walsh in [GW89b], based upon the abstraction principles they present in [GW89a] (see Section 4.2.10).

A much greater problem may arise when expanding definitions of predicates (or functions) that are recursively defined: opening up such a definition may result in an infinite sequence of such reductions. The problem of treating recursively defined predicates/functions will be considered in Chapter 8 on the Boyer-Moore theorem prover and also in Chapter 7 on Knuth-Bendix completion.

4.2.4 Forward and Backward Chaining

There are a few variations on the theme of chaining, but they each have the same basic intention, which is illustrated by the formulation given here. For the following two definitions let $\alpha \rightarrow \beta$ be an axiom or (previously proven) theorem and let γ be the current conjecture.

Backward Chaining: If $\beta\theta \rightarrow \gamma$ is a theorem for some substitution θ, then try to prove $\alpha\theta$.

Forward Chaining: If $\alpha\theta$ is a theorem for some θ, then try to prove $\beta\theta \rightarrow \gamma$.

These may be restated informally as:

> BC: In attempting to prove γ an attempt is made to prove an instance of the hypothesis of a lemma.

> FC: In trying to prove γ, a new hypothesis, which is known to be a theorem, is introduced which may help to simplify the proof of γ.

The most straightforward case of the application of BC is where the conjecture to be proved, γ, is an instance of β.

Example: Suppose it is a theorem (or an axiom) that

$$\forall x \forall y \forall z ((Parentof(x, y) \wedge Parentof(y, z)) \rightarrow Gparentof(x, z)),$$

and it is required to prove that $Gparentof(tom, jane)$. If it could be proved that $\forall y (Parentof(tom, y) \wedge Parentof(y, jane))$, then the conjecture would be proved.

This example illustrates another point regarding the use of the backward chaining rule. Intuitively, the formula $\forall y(Parentof(tom, y) \wedge Parentof(y, jane))$ would not be a theorem with respect to a normal axiomatisation of the predicate $Parentof$. The problem here is that y does not occur in the conclusion of the lemma and thus does not become instantiated when the lemma is applied to the conjecture. However, by the distribution rules for $\forall$ over $\rightarrow$, if a variable x_i does not occur in β in a sentence of the form $\forall x(\alpha \rightarrow \beta)$, then the sentence is equivalent to $\forall x'(\exists x_i \alpha \rightarrow \beta)$, where x' is x excluding x_i. For example, using a modified backward chaining rule, to prove $Gparentof(tom, jane)$ it should be proved (if possible) that

$$\exists y(Parentof(tom, y) \wedge Parentof(y, jane))$$

is a theorem.

The first explicit formulations of backward and forward chaining seem to be those in [NS63], but these were for only the propositional case. Variations closer to the ones described above were used in the systems of Bledsoe et al (BC: [Bl71], [BB71], and BC, FC: [BB74]). Backward chaining is also used by the Boyer-Moore theorem prover (see Chapter 8). The SLD-resolution rule used by Prolog also has similarities to backward chaining (see Chapter 6), and, in this sense, resolution may be viewed as combining backwards and forwards chaining (see [Ko79]). Further discussion of forward chaining may be found in [Bl77], where references are given for some theorem provers that incorporate this chaining rule.

Both forward and backward chaining can lead to infinite repetition in general. The following example, from [BM79], illustrates this problem in the case of backward chaining. Given the theorem $x < (y - 1) \rightarrow x < y$, suppose it is required to prove the sentence $u < v$. Backward chaining suggests trying to prove $u < (v - 1)$, but to prove this BC suggests trying to prove $u < ((y - 1) - 1)$, but to prove this.... To avoid such infinite repetitions, various constraints are usually applied. Examples of such constraints may be found in [BB74] and [BM79].

While, as indicated above, forward and backward chaining are generally related in the literature to resolution-style approaches to proof, when given a goal-oriented characterisation (as above) they may also be related to cut-free sequent calculi. In essence, both are special cases of the reversal of the following rule combining the rules $\rightarrow\vdash$ and $\forall\vdash$ of a sequent calculus:

$$\text{from } \Gamma \vdash \alpha\theta \text{ and } \Gamma, \beta\theta \vdash \gamma \text{ infer } \Gamma, \alpha \rightarrow \beta \vdash \gamma.$$

The distinction between the two chaining principles lies in the way they apply this sequent rule. In the case of forward chaining the rule may more accurately be expressed in the form

$$\text{from } \Gamma, \beta\theta \vdash \gamma \text{ infer } \Gamma, \alpha\theta, \alpha \rightarrow \beta \vdash \gamma,$$

for when it is applied backwards, $\alpha\theta$ is assumed and an attempt is made to prove $\beta\theta \rightarrow \gamma$. The difference between viewing backward chaining as an application of resolution and viewing it in terms of sequent calculi is that the sequent representation makes explicit the analytic nature of chaining, as follows from the fact that, in the above rule, the formulae of the premises are instances of subformulae of formulae in the conclusion. The same idea applies to the backward chaining rule above, as is required to be shown in the next exercise. This idea will be returned to in Chapter 6 on Prolog, which, as noted above, uses a form of backward chaining.

Exercise 4.7: Express the reversal of the backward chaining rule as a decomposition tactic.

4.2.5 Merging Natural Deduction and Resolution

There are many ways that aspects of resolution and natural deduction calculi might be combined or be said to be combined. For instance, as already indicated several times, goal-directed resolution-style calculi may often be reinterpreted as rules of a (cut-free) sequent calculus. Here another view will be considered which highlights some important issues. The theorem prover to be discussed is that of A.J. Nevins (described in [Ne74]), which was an early attempt to combine aspects of resolution and natural deduction. The system of Nevins relied on two principal ideas:

1. The inference rule of resolution should be split into several rules according to the form of the formulae to which it is applied. For example, one rule is

If A and $\beta \rightarrow B$ are valid and A and B have mgu θ then infer $\neg\beta\theta$,

where A and B are atomic formulae.

2. If all other rules fail to prove the current conjecture, then a "splitting rule" should be applied to (implicitly universally quantified) sentences having the form $\alpha \vee \beta$. Such a sentence would be split into case α and case β.

Also, rather than requiring that all formulae be clauses (as in resolution), a number of the rules are intended effectively to reduce formulae to clausal form where required. For example, $\neg(\alpha \vee \beta)$ would be replaced by $\neg\alpha \wedge \neg\beta$. This, it is reasonable to suppose, serves to make the transformation more coherent to the human user, as opposed to simply converting all formulae to clausal form immediately; the latter, in general, tends to destroy totally the user's intuitive grasp of the meaning of the formulae. These ideas make Nevins' system more natural, but the style of the rules (apart from the splitting rule for $\alpha \vee \beta$) is clearly based upon the resolution principle.

The major difficulty involved in proofs in this system concerns treatment of the splitting rule. Since the formula $\alpha \vee \beta$ would be implicitly universally quantified and because universal quantifiers do not distribute over disjunctions (when their associated variable names occur in each of the disjoined formulae), it is necessary to take into account any variables that occur in both α and β. If they have no variables in common then there is no problem, but otherwise it is necessary to ensure that instantiations of common variables are *compatible*. In other words, the instantiating terms should unify. After several applications of the splitting rule it clearly becomes a complicated matter to treat these variables (see [Ne74], [Bi87]).

4.2.6 Incorporating Unification Into Sequentzen

It was noted in Section 3.2 on sequent calculi that a major problem involved in developing proofs in such a system is finding appropriate terms to substitute for the variables when applying the reversals of the quantifier rules. One way to overcome this problem is to introduce unification. The main obstacle in doing this is accounting for the eigenvariable condition on the other quantifier rules. The first attempt to resolve this difficulty seems to be that of S. Kanger in [Ka63], though his method is more closely related to the earlier work of Prawitz [Pr60] than to unification. More recently, K.A. Bowen [Bo82] has described a simpler approach intended to overcome some of the limitations of Kanger's method, but there seem to be problems with Bowen's approach also. While the underlying sequent calculus may be "deterministic" in nature, Bowen's method does not seem to be adequate to retain this important property. Fortunately, a simple modification of the quantifier rules is adequate to overcome this defect.

The basic idea behind the introduction of unification is very simple: on applying the rules $\forall\vdash$ and $\vdash\exists$ backwards, rather than trying to determine immediately what term to introduce, the system initially replaces the bound variables by new *dummy variables* which may then, at any successive stage of the proof, be instantiated by particular terms. As the proof develops, attempts are made to find a substitution for these dummy variables that unifies formulae in the antecedent of subgoal sequents with those in the consequent, thereby deriving assumption axioms. Thus these dummy variables take the place of the "implicitly bound" variables of resolution. For example, to prove the sequent $\forall x\,\alpha(x) \vdash \forall x\,\alpha(f(x))$ the universal quantifiers on both sides may be eliminated to produce the quasi-subgoal $\alpha(xd) \vdash \alpha(f(c))$, where xd is a dummy variable, and then $\alpha(xd)$ may be unified with $\alpha(f(c))$ by means of the unifying substitution $\{xd \rightarrow f(c)\}$; this subgoal is thus solved. Of course, in solving this subgoal in this way xd becomes instantiated to $f(c)$ wherever else it occurs in the other subgoals of the current conjecture; thus the same substitution of terms for variables must be universally applied to all subgoals.

Exercise 4.8: Prove $P(0), \forall x(P(x) \rightarrow P(s(x))) \vdash \exists y P(s(s(y)))$ using unification.

Recall, however, that there is the eigenvariable condition on the other quantifier rules, and it has to be ensured that this is not implicitly broken when unification is applied. For instance, in the above simple example, if $\forall\vdash$ had been applied before $\vdash\forall$ then the unification step would, in principle, have been unsound. This is simply because once $f(c)$ has been introduced as the term for the xd in the antecedent, it would violate the eigenvariable condition to introduce c as the constant replacing x for the application of $\vdash\forall$. On the other hand, it is quite clear that the appropriate choice of order in applying the quantifier rules (that is, exactly the opposite choice to the one just suggested) would have ensured that the unification performed was sound. Thus, the problem in general is that the order in which the rules are applied affects the soundness of the unification steps. Therefore, simply adding the usual eigenvariable test, as Bowen seems to do, would entail all different possible decomposition sequences being applied until one is found under which all assignments applied are sound. It would clearly be preferable if an additional mechanism could be found that ensured that, irrespective of the order in which the quantifier rules are applied, if a unification step is allowed then there is a suitable order of application of the rules under which this substitution would not violate the eigenvariable condition. Fortunately, it turns out that there are several such mechanisms.

One solution to the eigenvariable problem is to introduce Skolemisation. However, rather than Skolemising beforehand, which would be unnatural in a sequent calculus and would require preprocessing of the formulae within the sequent, it is preferable to Skolemise "as required". This is perhaps best explained by presenting revised versions of the rules for $\exists\vdash$ and $\vdash\forall$:

$$\frac{\Gamma,\,\alpha(f(yd_1,...,\,yd_n))\vdash\Delta}{\Gamma,\,\exists x\,\alpha(x)\vdash\Delta}\qquad\frac{\Gamma\vdash\alpha(f(yd_1,...,\,yd_n)),\,\Delta}{\Gamma\vdash\forall x\,\alpha(x),\,\Delta}\,,$$

where, in each rule, f is a new function symbol and $yd_1,...,\,yd_n$ are the dummy variables already occurring in α. Note that the universal quantifiers are Skolemised in the consequent of the sequent while the existential quantifiers are Skolemised in the antecedent. This is in keeping with the point made in Chapter 2 that to prove the unsatisfiability of a set of formulae the existential quantifiers are Skolemised, while to prove their validity it is the universal quantifiers that are Skolemised. The idea behind these rules is that the Skolemisation will cause there to be an occurs-check clash in the sequent calculus with unification where there would have been an eigenvariable clash in the standard calculus. To illustrate this, consider the non-theorem $\forall x\exists y\,P(x,\,y)\to\exists y\forall x\,P(x,\,y)$. If these new rules are applied (backwards), then the attempted proof would fail as follows:

$$\begin{array}{ll}
\forall x\exists y\,P(x,\,y)\vdash\exists y\forall x\,P(x,\,y) & \to\vdash\\
\exists y\,P(xd,\,y)\vdash\exists y\forall x\,P(x,\,y) & \forall\vdash\\
P(xd,\,a(xd))\vdash\exists y\forall x\,P(x,\,y) & \exists\vdash\\
P(xd,\,a(xd))\vdash\forall x\,P(x,\,yd) & \vdash\exists\\
P(xd,\,a(xd))\vdash P(b(\,yd),\,yd) & \vdash\forall
\end{array}$$

attempted unification fails because of occurs check

It should be noted that Skolemisation serves exactly the same purpose in the resolution calculus.

An alternative approach to Skolemising has been proposed by Bibel (see [Bi87]), and described in the full sequent (or, more accurately, Beth-tableaux) framework by L. Wallen [Wa85]. This approach is based on the idea that to ensure that a suitable sequence of applications of the quantifier rules is found, it simply has to be ensured that there are no "cycles" amongst the substitutions. To illustrate, consider the previous example again. It may be seen that no matter in what order the quantifiers are removed it must be the case that either $\forall\vdash$ has to be applied before $\vdash\forall$ or that $\vdash\exists$ has to be applied before $\exists\vdash$. If $\forall\vdash$ is applied before $\vdash\forall$ then the substitution $\{xd\to b\}$ would violate the eigenvariable condition, and similarly if $\exists\vdash$ is applied before $\vdash\exists$ the substitution $\{yd\to b\}$ would do the same. Rather than Skolemising (introducing $a(xd)$ for a and $b(\,yd)$ for b) suppose that the corresponding orderings $xd>a$ and $yd>b$ are placed on the expressions. Then the unifying substitutions $\{xd\to b\}$ and $\{yd\to a\}$ would mean that, after instantiation of the orderings according to these substitutions, a cycle would be produced: $b>a$ and $a>b$. This cycle violates the condition on the ordering ">" and thus disbars the proof, exactly as the occurs-check clash did. Further details of this process may be found in either [Bi87] or [Wa85].

As Bibel points out in [Bi87], this mechanism is more direct than Skolemising and applying the occurs check (as in resolution), and hence gives rise to a more efficient implementation. It seems to be particularly suitable in the context of his own matrix method (see Chapter 5), and is perhaps a useful alternative to Skolemising in a sequent calculus if efficiency is a major concern. On the other hand, if clarity is also required in the development of proofs then Skolemising "as required" may be a useful compromise between pre-Skolemising and applying the method Bibel proposes. Alternatively, Bibel's mechanism could be applied internally and then the user presented with the Skolemised version. It is worth mentioning, in this respect, that Bibel points out a strong analogy between his approach and recent proposals for very efficient unification algorithms in which cycle tests are introduced for the purposes of an occurs-check test.

4.2.7 Efficient Equational Reasoning in Sequentzen

With unification built into a sequent calculus (as described in the preceding section) it is not too difficult to extend equational reasoning to treat dummy variables in an efficient and natural manner. The set of rules proposed by Reeves [Re87], designed to extend Beth-tableaux to include equality in a more efficient way than earlier approaches, may be used as the basis for this development. The two rules of his system are concerned with the decomposition of atomic formulae. Expressed in terms of sequents, they are:

$$\frac{\Gamma \vdash \Delta, s_1 = t_1 \text{ and } ... \text{ and } \Gamma \vdash \Delta, s_n = t_n}{\Gamma, P(s_1,..., s_n) \vdash \Delta, P(t_1,..., t_n)},$$

$$\frac{\Gamma \vdash \Delta, s_1 = t_1 \text{ and } ... \text{ and } \Gamma \vdash \Delta, s_n = t_n}{\Gamma \vdash \Delta, f(s_1,..., s_n) = f(t_1,..., t_n)}.$$

These rules will be referred to as, respectively, the P-product and f-product rules for equality (cf. [Re87]). A slightly more efficient version of the P-product rule for the case when it is applied specifically to the equality predicate (that is, P is =) may be found in [DS88]. These rules were applied by Reeves only to ground atomic formulae, but it is not too difficult to apply them also to formulae involving dummy variables, as will become apparent. The first point to note regarding these rules is that they may be applied to the classical unification problem. The unification of two terms, t and t', may be viewed as the task of solving the equation $t = t'$, that is, the task of finding terms to replace the dummy variables in t and t' to make this equation an identity. Expressed in this way, the f-product rule may be applied to the problem according to the following algorithm:

1. Let E be the current set of equations, and select an equation $t = t'$ from this set for processing, such that t and t' are not identical.

2. If possible, apply the f-product rule to $t = t'$ to produce the set of equations $\hat{E}$, then let $E := E - \{t = t'\} \cup \hat{E}$ and return to step 1. Otherwise, go to step 3.

3. If neither t nor t' is a dummy variable then stop with failure. If one of the terms is a dummy variable xd (say) and it does not occur in the other term, then let $E := (E - \{t = t'\})\{xd \rightarrow s\}$, where s is the other term, and then go to step 1. Otherwise the unification fails.

Example: To unify the terms $f(a, g(xd))$ and $f(yd, g(b))$, the f-product rule may be applied essentially as follows:

$$\{f(a, g(xd)) = f(yd, g(yd))\} \longrightarrow \{a = yd, g(xd) = g(yd)\} \longrightarrow \{g(xd) = g(a)\}$$
$$\longrightarrow \{xd = a\}.$$

Thus the solution to the unification is the substitution $\{xd \to a, yd \to a\}$.

This algorithm is slightly more efficient than the one described in the section on resolution in the previous chapter, but its efficiency may be improved further by treating equations that equate dummy variables and terms very differently from the manner in which they are treated in step 3 of the above algorithm. In particular, this is where a "cycle test" (mentioned in the previous subsection) is introduced as an occurs check in more efficient formulations; see [Ra88] and [Bi87]. To unify two atomic expressions, one in the antecedent of a sequent and the other in the consequent (as discussed for more general expressions in the previous subsection), first the P-product rule may be applied to reduce this pair of atoms to a set of equations, and then the f-product rule may be applied as in the above algorithm to solve these equations simultaneously.

To apply the above rules to the more general task of reasoning about equations, it is necessary to account for the symmetry and transitivity properties of equality. The latter is accounted for by allowing the P-product rule to be applied repeatedly to solve equations, as may be deduced from the solution to the following exercise.

Exercise 4.9: Show that with the reflexivity rule (that is, the equality axiom) and the P-product rule, it is possible to prove

$$t_1 = t_2, t_2 = t_3 \vdash t_1 = t_3.$$

The symmetry property is slightly more problematic: the above rules are not adequate to prove the sequent $a = b \vdash b = a$. Thus the symmetry of equality is not provable in the cut-free sequent calculus together with only the above rules for equality, since clearly none of the other sequent rules apply. The cut rule applies, however, and with it symmetry is provable, as follows from the next exercise.

Exercise 4.10: Show that $t = t' \vdash t' = t$ (for arbitrary t and t') is provable with reflexivity and the P-product rule together with the new rule 'from $\Gamma, t = t \vdash \Delta$ infer $\Gamma \vdash \Delta$' (and hence together with the cut rule).

However, since the reversal of neither the cut rule nor the simpler rule is a decomposition tactic, a much preferable solution is simply to build symmetry into the P-product rule when it is applied to equalities: $t = t'$ may be replaced by $t' = t$ where necessary.

For ground equations it is not difficult to see that the above rules are sufficient for proofs (cf. [Re87]), since all of the properties of equality are provable. However, a problem arises when dummy variables are allowed: certain subgoals, though valid, are unsolvable. These are goals in which the equality to be solved equates a dummy variable and a term in which this variable occurs. In standard unification the derivation of such an equation means that the process must necessarily fail, but in general equational reasoning the equation may be solvable with the replacement of the term in which the dummy variable occurs by an equal term not involving this variable. For example, the sequent $f(yd) = a \vdash f(xd) = xd$ clearly may be solved with the substitution $\{xd \to a, yd \to a\}$.

The difficulty that arises in general with this sort of equation is that it may be impossible for any of the above rules to apply to it in the normal way. In the preceding example, the P-product rule applies and the generated subgoals are solvable, but the proposed rules are not sufficient (when applied in the normal way) to prove the theorem $f(g(a)) = a \vdash g(f(xd)) = xd$. The required instantiation of xd to solve this goal is $g(vd)$ (for any new dummy vd). This instantiation reduces the theorem to the subgoal $f(g(a)) = a \vdash g(f(g(vd))) = g(vd)$. Applying the f-product rule to this reduces it to $f(g(a)) = a \vdash f(g(vd)) = vd$, which is solvable in a similar manner to the goal in the example above. To achieve this instantiation of xd automatically with the proposed rules, their normal application as decomposition tactics has to be modified, as pointed out in [DS88]. While the conclusion of the f-product rule does not "match" the equation $g(f(xd)) = xd$, it may be "unified" with this equation as follows. With the s_i and t_i terms in the f-product rule replaced by variables, it becomes, for the current application,

$$\text{from } \Gamma \vdash \Delta, ud = vd \text{ infer } \Gamma \vdash \Delta, g(ud) = g(vd).$$

The conclusion of this rule is now unifiable with the goal $g(f(xd)) = xd$ with the unifying substitution $\{xd \rightarrow g(vd), ud \rightarrow f(g(vd))\}$. The unifying instance of the goal, $g(f(g(vd))) = g(vd)$, is then decomposed into $f(g(vd)) = vd$ as the corresponding instance of the hypothesis of the f-product rule. This subgoal is then solvable in the normal way, as already noted.

While there is little difficulty in implementing this process (see [DS88]), it is quite a drastic extension of the usual approach to applying sequent calculi. Fortunately, it need only be applied to equations that correspond to the "occurs check" in classical unification. As an alternative, there are other approaches to this problem which do not involve unification and which are perhaps more in keeping with the spirit of sequent calculi (see [DS88]). Nevertheless, the point has been brought out as to why Reeves' approach to equality reasoning may be applied to ground expressions but not to expressions involving variables, and it has been indicated how this limitation may be overcome.

Describing proofs of non-trivial theorems using these rules for equality is rather tedious because the standard unification process is built into the equality rules, as indicated above. This means that in a proof every step of the classical unification process must be included. To overcome this difficulty, the normal unification of terms may be performed as an "external activity". For this purpose, the equality axiom may be expressed in the form $\Gamma \vdash \Delta, xd = xd$. This axiom, which will be denoted by $\vdash xd$, applies as follows: suppose a subgoal of the form $\Gamma \vdash \Delta, t = t'$ is generated during a proof; then the expression $xd = xd$ will unify with $t = t'$ if t and t' unify, and in so doing the most general unifier of t and t' will be constructed. This mechanism, together with the application of the equality rules, will now be illustrated with a more general example.

Example: The theorem to be proved is the sequent:

$$g(xd) = a \lor xd = b, \ P(g(a), b) \vdash g(g(yd)) = yd, P(b, b).$$

Applying the rule $\lor\vdash$ backwards produces the two subgoals

1. $g(xd) = a, \ P(g(a), b) \vdash g(g(yd)) = yd, P(b, b)$, and
2. $xd = b, P(g(a), b) \vdash g(g(yd)) = yd, P(b, b)$.

With Γ denoting $\{g(xd) = a, P(g(a), b)\}$, subgoal 1 may be reduced, by application of the reversal of the P-product rule to $=$, to the two new subgoals

$\Gamma \vdash g(xd) = g(g(yd)), P(b, b)$ and $\Gamma \vdash a = yd, P(b, b)$.

These two subgoals are valid according to $\vdash xd$, and they produce the corresponding variable substitution $\{xd \to g(a), yd \to a\}$. This substitution is passed to the second subgoal, which is then solved as follows: the instantiated subgoal, that is,

$g(a) = b, \; P(g(a), b) \; \vdash \; g(g(a)) = a, P(b, b)$

is reduced by the reversal of the P-product rule to the two subgoals

$g(a) = b, P(g(a), b) \vdash g(g(a)) = a, g(a) = b$ and
$g(a) = b, P(g(a), g(b)) \vdash g(g(a)) = a, b = b$.

These are valid by, respectively, the sequent axiom and $\vdash xd$.

In the case where the equalities involved in a proof are given equations (as opposed to being part of larger formulae, as in the preceding example), the process of equality reasoning is commonly referred to as *equational unification*. This term expresses the fact that formulae are unified *modulo* an equational theory. For example, the atomic formulae $P(x + y)$ and $P(0)$ are unifiable modulo the equational axiom $z + 0 = z$, by means of the equational reasoning process described above, with the unifier $\{x \to 0, y \to 0\}$. If this reasoning is further restricted so that the symmetry property of equations may not be applied, then the process simulates the demodulation principle of Loveland described in the previous section; this is more commonly referred to as *narrowing* (as in [DS88]). As indicated in the discussion of demodulation in the previous section, the more restrictive narrowing process is complete only under certain constraints on the equations (see Chapter 7).

4.2.8 Building-in Theories and Models

In this context, building-in theories means incorporating special inference rules or procedures that take the place of sets of axioms for certain theories. For example, in Section 4.2.7 rules for building-in equational theories have been described. The idea of building-in decidable theories has also been mentioned. In general, particular theories are "built-in" because they are special in some respect. This will often be because the theorem provers into which they are incorporated are special application provers rather than general purpose.

One of the most important of the decidable theories (particularly in the context of program verification) is "Presburger arithmetic". This is the set of all formulae involving only the functions "0", "successor" and "+", and the predicate "<". Any such formula may be proved or disproved in a finite amount of time. An efficient algorithm for full Presburger arithmetic is described in [Co72] by D. C. Cooper. This was intended essentially as a "stand alone" theorem prover, rather than as a method to be incorporated into a more general system, and has often been cited as being unsuitable for incorporation into a larger system (e.g. [Sh79], [BM85]). However, there seems to be no reason why it could not be used in powerful combination with theory resolution.

Certain subsets of Presburger arithmetic are also considered important because of their relevance to program verification. In particular, algorithms for Presburger formulae that are universally quantified but which involve no other quantifiers are discussed in [Sh77], and an extension to include arbitrary function symbols is described in [Sh79]. Combining decision procedures for different theories is another important problem. As an example, suppose that separate decision procedures are provided for Presburger arithmetic and for reasoning about a theory concerning the "data-type" of "lists". Some mechanism for combining these procedures is required to solve problems involving functions from both theories. For example, if the theory of lists includes the axiom $car(cons(x, y)) = x$ (where, as in LISP, $cons$ is the constructor for lists and car selects the first element of such a list), then the mechanism should be able to prove the theorem $\exists x(1 + car(x) = 3)$ —which has as one solution $x = cons(2, nil)$. Possible solutions to the problem of deciding formulae in combinations of theories have been proposed by Nelson and Oppen in [NO80] for quantifier-free theories (that is, sets of implicitly universally closed quantifier-free formulae), and by Shostak in [Sh84] for special equational theories.

Apart from theories that are decidable, much effort has been applied to treat special classes of axioms such as those for sets, for partial and total orderings, and for functions that are commutative and/or associative. In [Sl72] a general method is described for finding complete sets of inference rules for certain theories, and, as examples, rules for equality (essentially paramodulation), sets, and partial orderings are derived. The idea of giving special treatment to associative and commutative functions first came to full prominence when it was found to be necessary for the inclusion of such functions in the Knuth-Bendix completion procedure (see Chapter 7), but earlier work by Plotkin in [Pl72] on such functions for general theorem proving formed the basis for this work.

The idea of building-in equational theories has also been seen as being of major importance. This idea also originated with Plotkin's work in [Pl72] and was later developed by Slagle in [Sl74]. Later it was realised that combining their ideas with Knuth-Bendix completion led to much more powerful methods. In [Hs85] the incorporation of such theories into a theorem prover which itself is based on Knuth-Bendix completion is discussed. These mechanisms for reasoning about equational theories will be discussed in a little more detail in Chapter 7.

A very different aspect of the idea of building-in theories is the use of models. If M is a model for a set of formulae Γ, a formula α could not possibly be a logical consequence of Γ if it is not also satisfied by M. The use of models in this manner to disprove conjectures or to eliminate subgoals is common in mathematics, and has also been used to a certain extent in mechanical theorem proving. A particular system that uses this idea as basis is described in [Re71] by R. Reiter. The following rule of his twelve-rule system explains the principal idea:

Suppose the theorem to be proved is $\Gamma \vdash \sigma_1 \vee \sigma_2$, where σ_1 and σ_2 are sentences, and suppose that M is a model of Γ. Then

- if M is not a model of σ_1 try to prove $\Gamma, \neg\sigma_1 \vdash \sigma_2$
- if M is not a model of σ_2 try to prove $\Gamma, \neg\sigma_2 \vdash \sigma_1$
- otherwise, try to prove $\Gamma \vdash \sigma_1$ or $\Gamma \vdash \sigma_2$.

A method for constructing models for sets of clauses is described in [WO84]. They show how such model generation was used to derive a counterexample to a previously unsolved conjecture concerning the independence of a set of axioms. By the construction of a model that satisfied all but one of the axioms it was shown that the unsatisfied axiom was independent (that is, not a consequence of the others).

4.2.9 Proof by Induction

Proving theorems by induction is well known to be important in mathematics, but is perhaps of even greater importance in computer science. The reason for this is that the data structures used in programs (for example, numbers, lists, queues, stacks, trees) are inductively (or constructively) defined, and because "recursively defined" functions are so fundamental. It is shown by Reynolds and Yeh in [RY76] that any system designed to reason about programs must involve a component for proving inductive theorems, simply because of the direct relationship that exists between induction and recursion.

The need for a mechanism for induction for reasoning about certain theories may seem to contradict the known fact that basic proof systems such as sequent calculi are already complete, but this is not the case. The inductive theory associated with any set of axioms is, in fact, an extension of the set of logical consequences, given by adding extra axioms to the set. To illustrate, consider the example in Section 3.1 on natural deduction. It was pointed out there that $\forall x P(x)$ does not follow from the axioms $\{P(0), \forall x(P(x) \rightarrow P(s(x)))\}$, but, on the other hand, it clearly does follow from these axioms when they are augmented with the following "axiom of induction" for P: $(P(0) \wedge (\forall x(P(x) \rightarrow P(s(x))))) \rightarrow \forall x P(x)$. This additional axiom for P restricts the class of models of the original axioms to those desired for the inductive theory. In general, a schema may be added to any set of axioms to capture the associated inductive theory for properties expressible by first-order formulae:

$$(\alpha(0) \wedge \forall x(\alpha(x) \rightarrow \alpha(s(x)))) \rightarrow \forall x \alpha(x).$$

For any particular given set of axioms, this schema may be replaced by a recursive set of "induction axioms", one for each formula in the language of the axioms. Strangely enough, this additional set of induction axioms is not powerful enough to capture the full power of induction (see [En72]), but it is powerful enough to achieve most of the results normally associated with proof by induction. This is illustrated in the following exercise.

Exercise 4.11: Let the function *sum* be defined by the equations

$$sum(0) = 0 \text{ and } sum(s(x)) = s(x) + sum(x),$$

and let the conjecture be $sum(x) + sum(x) = x * s(x)$. Specify the induction schema for this conjecture, and then prove the hypothesis of this schema using the definition of *sum*, thus proving that the conjecture is an inductive theorem.

With the set of axioms of induction expressed as a schema, it is then natural to re-express this schema as a rule of inference:

from $\Gamma \vdash \alpha(0)$ and $\Gamma, \alpha(x) \vdash \alpha(s(x))$ infer $\Gamma \vdash \forall x \alpha(x)$

(with the proviso that x is not free in Γ). This is the manner in which induction is normally presented. It is then usually applied as a tactic: a goal $\Gamma \vdash \forall x \alpha(x)$ is reduced to a set of subgoals that are the corresponding instances of the premises. This is the way the Boyer-Moore theorem prover applies such a rule (as will be explained in Chapter 8). Incorporating special procedures for induction might also be viewed as an example of the process of building-in theories, but in the case of induction the main concern is not to replace a set of axioms by an inference rule, but instead is to find the most appropriate application of the induction principle for any given conjecture.

Chapters 7 and 8 of this book will be concerned almost entirely with proof by induction. Two very different approaches to the mechanisation of this important aspect of theorem proving will be described in these chapters, the first based upon the idea of *Knuth-Bendix completion* and the second on the standard techniques used in mathematics.

4.2.10 Proof by Analogy and Abstraction

For a given conjecture α, there may be similarities between α (and the concepts involved in the statement of α) and some previously proved theorem. If so, then a human might note the analogy and proceed along similar lines to the first proof in an attempt to produce a proof of α. Similarly, it is often the case that some of the specific details of a theorem may be ignored and a more general framework for the purposes of constructing a proof be found; this is the principle underlying the use of abstraction in mathematics, where concepts involved in many disparate subject areas are brought together to form an "abstract theory". Perhaps the most familiar example of such abstraction is the set of axioms for a group (see Chapter 1).

Incorporating the use of such techniques into a mechanical theorem prover in a powerful way is clearly a difficult task, and it seems that the idea has been ignored for the most part. It is most likely that this is because of the difficulty of giving a useful formal definition of what is meant by analogy. However, some attempts have been made.

The first system to use proof by analogy was that described by R.E. Kling in [Kl71]. This, for example, proved that 'the intersection of two commutative rings is a commutative ring' using analogies with the theorem 'the intersection of two abelian groups is an abelian group'. Here an analogy is viewed essentially as being a mapping between predicates, atoms and so on.

More recently, complete and heuristic methods for using a form of abstraction (particularly in a resolution environment) have been described by D.A. Plaisted in [Pl81]. These "abstractions" involve removing certain of the information inherent in the clauses. For example, the simplest of the "abstractions" discussed is the replacement of atomic formulae in the formulae of some theorem by their predicate symbols, thus producing a conjecture of propositional logic (cf. Section 3.1). One of the requirements of Plaisted's abstractions is that if the conjecture is unsatisfiable then its abstraction must also be unsatisfiable (though the converse need not hold). In [GW89a], Plaisted's work has been extended by Giunchiglia and Walsh to characterise abstraction in a context more general than resolution. They present different forms of abstraction, each depending on the relationship required between the original conjecture and its abstraction.

4.3 CONCLUSIONS

In this chapter search strategies have been described that are intended to improve the efficiency (in time) and/or the "naturalness" of the reasoning of theorem-proving systems. These strategies impose constraints on the application of the underlying inference rules of a given calculus with the aim of avoiding certain inferences or of guiding the proof in a human-oriented manner.

The success of these and other such strategies has been quite significant. This will be illustrated to some extent in the third part of this book, where three special-purpose proof systems will be looked at which apply particular inference rules and strategies related to those discussed in this and the preceding chapter. These three systems have each been very successful in different ways according to their intended purpose, and are commonly felt to be important examples of "special application theorem provers".

On the other hand, although there is much work still being done on creating new strategies and combining old ones, there remains the problem of choosing the most appropriate strategies in any particular instance. Furthermore, logics other than that treated here are often found to be more appropriate for certain purposes, and much work is going into the revamping of the inference systems and strategies used in classical first-order logic for these systems. However, these issues are outside the scope of this book (though see the penultimate remarks in the conclusions section of Chapter 9).

CHAPTER 5

CONNECTION METHODS

In this chapter two proof methods will be described, both of which use the links (or connections) between formulae, determined by the unification of their literals, in a more explicit and powerful manner than the resolution-based methods described previously. They use these links in two very different ways, but it should become clear why both methods come under the title "connection methods".

5.1 THE CONNECTION-GRAPH PROCEDURE

The connection-graph method was introduced by Robert Kowalski in [Ko75]. It is perhaps the most widely known method apart from resolution and natural deduction because an account of it appears in Kowalski's well-read book [Ko79]. Before a full description of the procedure in terms of graphs is presented, its relationship to the resolution principle will be made more apparent.

5.1.1 The Basic Principle

The method is based upon the purity principle of J. Robinson, described in Section 4.1.1.1. For initial purposes this notion is redefined slightly as follows: if any clause in a set of clauses contains a literal that is not potentially complementary to any other literal in the set, then that clause may be removed without affecting the satisfiability of the set. The relevant literal is said to be *pure*. This principle is certainly not complete in itself but is extended as follows.

Consider a set of clauses in which all the factors of each clause appear. This set is processed as follows:

1. If the empty clause is in the set then stop with success.

2. If a literal is pure then remove the clause in which it appears. If any other literals then become pure remove their clauses also.

3. Generate the resolvent of two (not necessarily distinct) clauses and add its factors to the clause set in the standard way, but noting which two literals were resolved upon. Stipulate that any instances of these two literals are no longer potentially complementary. That is, no matter where any instance of them may appear later in the proof they may not be resolved upon together again. Return to step 1.

Given the soundness and completeness of the resolution principle, the soundness and completeness of the above procedure hinges on whether, once two literals have been resolved upon together, they need ever be resolved upon together again. If not, then, by the purity principle, if one of the literals is otherwise pure in the set then the clause in which it appears may be removed from the set.

Example: The set of clauses
1. $P \vee Q$
2. $\neg P \vee R$
3. $\neg Q \vee R$
4. $\neg R$

is unsatisfiable. It is, in fact, the clausal form of the negation of the simple theorem $((P \vee Q) \wedge (P \rightarrow R) \wedge (Q \rightarrow R)) \rightarrow R$. The following is a "saturation search" proof of this theorem via the procedure described above. The number before each clause is the number of that clause; the numbers following each clause are the numbers of the clauses resolved to produce that clause; and the remove statements indicate which clauses may be removed according to the extended purity principle.

$\mathfrak{R}^1(\Sigma)$:	5.	$Q \vee R$	1, 2	remove 1, 2
	6.	$\neg Q$	3, 4	remove 3
$\mathfrak{R}^2(\Sigma)$:	7.	Q	4, 5	remove 4, 5
$\mathfrak{R}^3(\Sigma)$:	8.	$\varnothing$	6, 7	

An analogous saturation search proof using unconstrained resolution would also be completed in $\mathfrak{R}^3$, but would require the generation of about twelve clauses as compared to four for the above method. This is because, by removing clauses, certain (unnecessary) applications of resolution are avoided. This gives an idea of the significance of the removal of pure literals. Comparison of the connection-graph procedure (described more accurately below) with major refinements of resolution such as hyper-resolution and SL-resolution (see Chapter 4) is performed in [Ko75].

Exercise 5.1: Using the method described above, prove that the set of clauses

$$\{P \vee \neg Q \vee \neg R, Q \vee S, R \vee S, \neg P \vee \neg Q, \neg S\}$$

is unsatisfiable.

5.1.2 Representation in Terms of Graphs

For a given initial set of clauses a "graph" is constructed with each node of the graph labelled by one of the literals of the set (and with the disjunction symbols between the literals of clauses omitted, for brevity). This is done as follows.

- Add the factors of each clause to the clause set.
- If two literals of distinct clauses are potentially complementary then join them by a "link" (or "arc") labelled with the most general unifier of their atoms (renaming variables of clauses where necessary).

Such a graph is now processed as follows:

1. If any literal does not have a link attached then remove the clause in which it appears and all the links that were attached to literals appearing in that clause. If in doing so any other literals become pure in the graph (i.e. lose all their links) then remove their clauses and all the associated links. If the empty set of clauses is produced then stop with failure—the set is satisfiable. Otherwise go to step 2.

2. Choose a link. Remove it and generate the corresponding resolvent, that is, the resolvent of the two clauses that contain the literals that were originally linked. If the empty clause is produced then stop with success, else go to step 3.

3. Add the resolvent and its factors to the graph and create links between the literals of the new clauses and the rest of the graph. Return to step 1.

Example: For the simple example above the initial graph and the graphs following the first three steps of the proof would be, respectively,

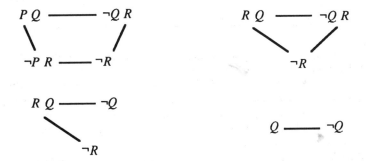

Finally, resolving Q and $\neg Q$ produces the empty clause, $\varnothing$. In this example the substitutions associated with each complementary pair were omitted since they are empty; a more general example will be given below.

Exercise 5.2: Construct the graphs corresponding to the refutation of the clauses of the previous exercise.

The main advantage of the use of graphs is that once the graph has been created at the start of the proof there is no need to search it each time a resolution step is performed, in order to create the new links between the resolvent and the rest of the graph. These new links may be found by inspecting the links connecting the literals in the resolved clauses. This is apparent from the example above, for when $P \vee Q$ and $\neg P \vee R$ are resolved at the start, $Q \vee R$ is added to the graph—in this case, the two original clauses are then removed—and then the new link between Q in the resolvent and $\neg Q$ is formed; this link may be found without search simply by noting the link between the Q in the resolved clause $P \vee Q$ and $\neg Q$ in the original graph. The same idea applies for the new link between R and $\neg R$. This also means that there is less search involved in finding new clauses to resolve, since all possible resolvents are represented by the links in the graph [Ko75]. Other advantages of the graph representation are discussed in [ON86] and [Ko79].

The main disadvantage of this representation, noted in [ON86], is the amount of space required to store the graphs. Dealing with 200 or so clauses is considered to be unfeasible.

Example: Consider again the set of clauses of EX. The representation in terms of a graph of the clauses in this example, with variables renamed appropriately, is

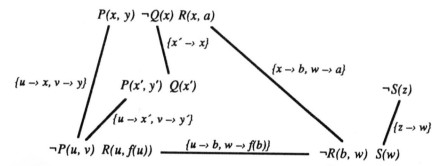

If $S(w)$ and $\neg S(z)$ are resolved upon then the corresponding resolvent $R(b, w)$ is added to the graph and the clauses $\neg R(b, w) \vee S(w)$ and $\neg S(z)$ are removed. The outcome is simply the removal of $S(w)$ and $\neg S(z)$. Suppose next that $\neg Q(x)$ and $Q(x')$ are resolved upon. The resolvent $P(x, y) \vee P(x, y') \vee R(x, a)$ is produced. This resolvent is logically equivalent to its factor $P(x, y) \vee R(x, a)$, and hence may be replaced by it. The factor is added to the graph and the two clauses that were resolved are removed, since both now have pure literals.

After these two resolution steps the graph is reduced quite dramatically to

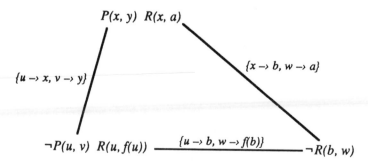

Suppose that $P(x, y)$ and $\neg P(u, v)$ are now resolved upon. Their associated clauses may be removed and the resolvent $R(x, f(x)) \vee R(x, a)$ is added to the graph:

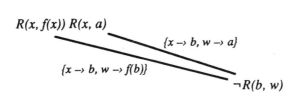

Resolving upon $R(x, f(x))$ and $\neg R(b, w)$ produces

$$R(x, a) \quad \underline{\quad \{x \rightarrow b, w \rightarrow a\} \quad} \quad \neg R(b, w)$$

Finally, resolving these unit clauses produces the empty clause $\varnothing$.

5.1.3 Pseudo-Links

It is often possible that a clause may be resolved with a copy of itself with re-named variables (i.e. an alphabetic variant). The clause $P(x) \vee Q(y) \vee \neg P(f(x))$, for instance, may be resolved with alphabetic variants of itself. In such cases, rather than explicitly duplicating the clause and adding the corresponding link between the potentially complementary literals, a "pseudo-link" may be added to a single copy of the clause, as in the following diagram:

$$P(x) \vee Q(x) \vee \neg P(f(x))$$

The interest in pseudo-links stems from the possibility of removing clauses that contain literals having only pseudo-links attached to them [Ko79]. If a literal has only pseudo-links then these links will not contribute to a refutation, and hence the literal is effectively pure. For this reason the clause in which the literal occurs may be deleted from the set without affecting satisfiability (see [Ko79]). For example, if the only clause in the set is the one above, namely $P(x) \vee Q(y) \vee \neg P(f(x))$, then there is clearly no contradiction, and hence the empty clause cannot be deduced. This holds despite the fact that there is a possible pseudo-link between $P(x)$ and $\neg P(f(x))$ as shown.

5.1.4 Soundness and Completeness Issues

The soundness of the connection-graph proof procedure (for performing refutations) follows from the soundness of the resolution principle. On the other hand, proving the refutation completeness of the procedure turned out to be a difficult task; proofs did not appear in the original publication [Ko75], nor in Kowalski's much less formal book [Ko79]. In [Bi81] Bibel gives a proof for the ground case, using the relationship he obtains between the graph method and the "matrix method" (to be discussed in Section 5.2). This proof is "lifted" to the general case in [Bi87]. Other proofs have been presented elsewhere (see [Ei87]).

Determining the completeness of refinements of the procedure has been found to be even more problematic. Of particular concern are the difficulties associated with factoring, removal of subsumed clauses, and elimination of tautologies. Although factoring is necessary for completeness, its excessive use can lead to redundancy; it is uncertain, however, what restrictions may be placed upon its use. On the other hand, the removal of subsumed clauses and the removal of tautologies (see [Ko79]) are not necessary, but are simple and useful simplification strategies, as for standard resolution, but once again there are problems with their application.

In the main, it seems that with minor restrictions the "most popular" resolution strategies do preserve refutation completeness when applied to the connection-graph procedure, as indicated by Eisinger in [Ei87]. However, the procedure has thrown up new issues regarding completeness that in other approaches to theorem proving either have no significance (as in standard resolution), or have a simple solution (as in sequent calculi). The most fundamental of these is the confluence property. In essence, a proof system is confluent if, irrespective of the order in which the inference rules of the system are applied, a proof may always be found for any theorem without having to undo any inference steps (that is, backtrack). Such a calculus was referred to as "deterministic" in the section on sequent calculi.

It was shown in the section on sequent calculi that the system presented there is deterministic, while it is clear that there is a "critical non-determinism" associated with the natural deduction system described in Section 3.1. In the case of unconstrained resolution, on the other hand, confluence is trivially achieved, since no clauses are removed during a proof and hence any necessary resolution steps may always be carried out. This does not automatically carry over to connection-graph resolution simply because clauses are deleted during most proofs. A potential problem is that a clause may be removed which is crucial to the refutation. In this way the set of clauses may be "collapsed" into the (satisfiable) empty set, though the original set is unsatisfiable. This does not affect the soundness of the procedure for refutations (a refutation still implies unsatisfiability), and, in theory, nor does it affect refutation completeness, but it is quite clearly of fundamental practical importance for efficient proof development. Having to try every possible sequence of inference steps from the initial set of clauses to be assured that there is no possible refutation would be an overwhelming disadvantage of the connection-graph method.

Fortunately, it turns out that the unconstrained connection-graph procedure is confluent, although the imposition of strategies may destroy this property [Ei87]. For instance, the main "linear strategies", such as SL-resolution (see Chapter 7), while preserving refutation completeness, do not preserve confluence. On the other hand, the set-of-support strategy, even when combined with restrictions on factoring, does preserve confluence. In general, it would seem that for each possible strategy that may be imposed, a proof of confluence as well as completeness is a necessary undertaking.

Further problems regarding the "practical completeness" of connection-graph resolution can arise. One difficulty concerns the termination issue: will all sequences of inferences always terminate. This is not possible for any calculus for first-order clauses/formulae, because of the undecidability problem (see Chapter 2), but, as has already been indicated, both resolution and sequent calculi (when the rules are applied backwards) are assured to terminate in a finite time for any set of propositional clauses. Hence the latter constitute decision procedures for this logic. On the other hand, it is necessary to be much more careful with regard to the application of connection-graph resolution to assure termination for propositional logic. This and other important "completeness" issues are discussed further in [Ei87].

5.1.5 Extensions for Equality

It seems that the first successful attempt to extend the connection-graph proof procedure to include equality was that described in [SW80]. In this approach the initial connection-graph is constructed by connecting potentially complementary literals with *R-links* (resolution links) exactly as above, and connecting unifiable terms, at least one of which is the left- or right-hand side of an equality literal, with *P-links* ("paramodulation links"). As before there is no necessity to search the graph each time one of the inference rules is applied since the links are inherited. Another method, proposed more recently, is discussed in [Bl86] and [ON86]. This method is based upon RUE-resolution rules of [DH86] mentioned previously, rather than paramodulation.

5.2 THE CONNECTION-MATRIX METHOD

The idea of proving theorems by showing that each path through a matrix of clauses contains a pair of complementary literals was first put forward by Dag Prawitz in [Pr69]. There the method was described in terms of Prawitz's earlier procedure for determining a minimal set of instances that make a set of clauses unsatisfiable. This earlier method is also fully explained in [Pr69] (see also [He79]).

In contrast to all the proof methods described earlier in this book, the present method does not constitute a deductive system in that no new formulae are deduced (though for the non-ground case it is necessary, in general, to add clauses to the matrix to ensure completeness). This "non-deductive" nature means that much of the redundancy of other proof methods is eliminated, for in deductive systems it is the derivation of formulae inconsequential to the proof that leads the theorem prover astray. As might be expected this new method has its own associated problems, some of which will come to light as the discussion proceeds.

Though the method initially received little attention, Prawitz's ideas have been developed and extended more recently by, in particular, W. Bibel and P.B. Andrews. The papers [Bi81] and [An81] are of most concern here (see also [An86], [Bi87]). In [Bi81] Bibel describes the extended method only for the ground level, but in [An81] a more general procedure is described using unification. Both show that the method is not restricted to clausal representations. This means that formulae may be left in a more natural form, as for the "natural" systems described earlier.

This section is divided into three main subsections. The first describes the basic connection-matrix method, the second studies its relationship to other approaches to proof, while the third briefly outlines some developments of the basic method.

5.2.1 The Basic Calculus

The description of the method will be separated into three stages:
1. A decision procedure for propositional logic with formulae in disjunctive normal form.
2. A decision procedure for a less restrictive normal form.
3. A complete extension to first-order formulae.

This separation quite naturally follows the historical development of the method, and will also serve to bring out the simplicity of the main ideas. It will also allow a simpler comparison with the other approaches to proof previously discussed. Stages 1 and 3 will bring out the relationship to resolution, while stages 1 and 2 will bring out different aspects of the relationship to sequent calculi; these comparisons will be studied in detail in Section 5.2.2 following the main discussion.

5.2.1.1 The Method for Propositional Clauses

In presenting a set of clauses, the disjunction symbol between the literals of clauses may be left implicit, and the set viewed as a matrix. The set of clauses will then have the form

$$
\begin{array}{cccc}
L_{11} & L_{12} & \ldots & L_{1m_1} \\
L_{21} & L_{22} & \ldots & L_{2m_2} \\
\vdots & \vdots & & \\
\vdots & \vdots & & \\
L_{n1} & L_{n2} & \ldots & L_{nm_n}
\end{array}
$$

where each L_{ij} is a literal. This is referred to as a *matrix of clauses* or a *clause matrix*. In describing the matrix method it is natural to use this abbreviated form for clauses. In the following let M be the above matrix of clauses.

Vertical Path: If one literal is chosen from each horizontal line of the matrix M to construct the set $\{L_{1k_1}, L_{2k_2}, \ldots, L_{nk_n}\}$, then this set constitutes a vertical path (or just a *path*) through the matrix.

If along each possible vertical path through the matrix there are at least two complementary literals, then the formula represented by the matrix is unsatisfiable. The converse is also true. In [Bi81] this is restated as follows.

Complementary Path: If a path contains at least one pair of complementary literals then the path is complementary.

Complementary Matrix: If every path through a matrix is complementary then the matrix is complementary.

If the matrix M represents the formula α, then

$$\alpha \text{ is unsatisfiable} \quad \text{iff} \quad M \text{ is complementary},$$

as will now be proved. As pointed out in [Pr69], the matrix method implicitly transforms the original formula in conjunctive normal form into a formula in disjunctive normal form (dnf), and then tests the conjunction of literals in each disjunction for satisfiability. From this viewpoint, the proof of the correctness of the method is straightforward, and will give an intuitive feel for the next two stages.

Proof: "⇐" Suppose that the matrix is complementary. Then each vertical path is complementary. Thus each path (a conjunction of literals) is unsatisfiable, since it contains a proposition letter and its negation. Therefore the disjunction of paths (the dnf of α) is unsatisfiable, and hence so is α.

"⇒" Suppose that M is not complementary. Then there is a vertical path that is not complementary. Hence it is possible to assign the value **T** to each literal of that path. Therefore each clause may be assigned the value **T**, since at least one literal of each clause may be assigned the value **T**. Therefore the set of clauses is satisfiable.

Example: Consider again the clauses of Section 5.1, now viewed as a matrix:

$$
\begin{array}{ll}
P & Q \\
\neg P & R \\
\neg Q & R \\
\neg R &
\end{array}
$$

There are eight paths through this matrix:

$$\{P\text{-}\neg P\text{-}\neg Q\text{-}\neg R,\ P\text{-}\neg P\text{-}R\text{-}\neg R,\ P\text{-}R\text{-}\neg Q\text{-}\neg R,\ P\text{-}R\text{-}R\text{-}\neg R,\ Q\text{-}\neg P\text{-}\neg Q\text{-}\neg R,$$
$$Q\text{-}\neg P\text{-}R\text{-}\neg R,\ Q\text{-}R\text{-}\neg Q\text{-}\neg R,\ Q\text{-}R\text{-}R\text{-}\neg R\}.$$

Clearly there is at least one pair of complementary literals in each path, providing another proof that the corresponding set of clauses is unsatisfiable.

From the statement preceding the proof, it might be asked why the formula was not converted into disjunctive normal form in the first place. The reason is that the space required to store the disjunctive normal form of an arbitrary formula will, in general, be too great for practical purposes. In contrast, with the matrix method there is no need to store the complete dnf of the formula at any one time [Pr69].

What also comes to light is the fact that it is not necessary to check every path through the matrix. This is because, once a particular path has been found to contain a pair of complementary literals, any other path that passes through those literals will also be complementary and hence need not be checked. This gives rise to the matrix reduction method of Prawitz [Pr69].

Exercise 5.3: Show that every path through the matrix

$$
\begin{array}{lll}
P & \neg Q & \neg R \\
Q & S & \\
R & S & \\
\neg P & \neg Q & \\
\neg S & &
\end{array}
$$

is complementary, thus proving that the corresponding formula is unsatisfiable.

5.2.1.2 Extension to Negation Normal Form

Now suppose the formula to be tested is converted into a form involving only ¬, ∧ and ∨, and in which the scope of each occurrence of ¬ is an atom. Such a formula is said to be in *negation normal form* (*nnf*). Conversion to this form is clearly possible by the rules that produce clausal form, presented in Chapter 3.

Example: $(P \vee (\neg Q \wedge R)) \wedge \neg R$ is in negation normal form.

This form is converted into a pictorial "matrix" in an analogous manner to clauses by writing disjoined formulae horizontally and conjoined formulae vertically.

Example: The formula above would be written

$$
\begin{matrix}
P & \begin{matrix} \neg Q \\ R \end{matrix} \\
\neg R &
\end{matrix}
$$

Exercise 5.4: Convert the formula

$$(\neg Q \vee ((P \vee \neg R) \wedge \neg P)) \wedge (S \vee (Q \wedge R)) \wedge \neg S$$

into a matrix.

Vertical Path: A path through a formula matrix is now defined as follows.

- If α is a single literal then there is a path through α.
- If α has the form $\beta \vee \gamma$, then there is no path that passes through some literal in β and another in γ.
- If α has the form $\beta \wedge \gamma$, then every path that passes through a literal in β (γ) must also pass through some literal in γ (β).

In terms of the matrix representation this may be expressed informally as

there is a path through L and L' iff L is "above" L', or L' is "above" L,

where L and L' are literals. For this new definition of path, it may be proved that

α is unsatisfiable   iff   all paths through α are complementary

(see [An81], [Bi87]).

Example: Through the matrix of the previous example there are only two paths:

$$\{P\text{-}\neg R, \quad \neg Q\text{-}R\text{-}\neg R\}.$$

Hence the formula the matrix represents is satisfiable.

It is of importance to note the redundancy involved, in general, in using the matrix method only on formulae in clausal form, as opposed to the less restrictive form. The use of clausal form will generally increase drastically the number of paths to check for complementarity.

Example: Consider again the formula above. In clausal form this has the matrix

$$
\begin{matrix}
P & \neg Q \\
P & R \\
\neg R &
\end{matrix}
$$

Now there are four paths rather than only two, and yet, of course, the new paths are inconsequential to the attempted refutation.

Exercise 5.5: Show that all the paths through the matrix constructed in the previous exercise are complementary.

5.2.1.3 An Extension to First-Order Formulae

The normal form for formulae of first-order logic is that used in Section 5.2.1.2, with the addition of Skolem functions for existentially quantified variables. As in [An81], unification may be applied to "lift" the method to the first-order level. The reasoning behind this development is as follows.

Let σ be a sentence and M be the matrix form of σ. If there is a matrix M' that is a complementary instance of M, then σ is unsatisfiable. However, if there is no such instance of M then this does not necessarily imply that σ is satisfiable. It is possible that several copies of the subformulae occurring in σ are required to allow a complementary instance of the derived matrix to be constructed. To deal with this eventuality, a subformula of σ of the form $\forall x \, \alpha$ (if one exists) may be replaced by $\forall x \, \alpha \wedge \forall x \, \alpha$ (called quantifier duplication) to produce a new sentence σ'; the matrix of σ' may then be generated and an attempt made to find a complementary instance of this matrix. This process may be repeated until, if the original sentence is unsatisfiable, a complementary matrix is found. The problem then becomes that of finding a complementary instance of a matrix, if one exists.

These ideas will now be clarified and formalised, and the problem of finding a complementary instance considered. The first three of the following definitions are essentially those given in [An81].

Quantifier Duplication: The process of replacing a subformula of the form $\forall x \, \beta$ by $\forall x \, \beta \wedge \forall x \, \beta$ in a formula is referred to as quantifier duplication. If α_1 and α_n are formulae and there is a sequence of formulae $\alpha_1, \alpha_2, ..., \alpha_n$ such that α_{i+1} ($i < n$) is produced from α_i by quantifier duplication, then α_n is said to have been produced from α_1 by a *sequence of quantifier duplications*.

Renamed Form: If the variables in a formula α are renamed so that no variable has occurrences that are bound by distinct quantifiers, then the new formula is a renamed form of α.

Amplification: Let σ be a Skolemised sentence in negation normal form. Suppose that σ' is obtained from σ by a sequence of quantifier duplications, that σ'' is a renamed form of σ', and that M is the matrix produced by the removal of universal quantifiers. Then M is said to be an amplification of σ.

In particular, if σ is in clausal form, then, effectively, an amplification of σ is produced by duplication of clauses (perhaps more than once for some of the clauses) followed by appropriate renaming of the variables in the new clauses. The next two definitions are based upon the ideas presented in [Pr69], [Bi81] and [An81].

Potentially Complementary Path: A path is potentially complementary if there is at least one pair of potentially complementary literals on it.

Thus, a path Π is potentially complementary if there is some substitution θ such that (with a slight abuse of notation) $\Pi\theta$ is complementary.

Refutable Matrix: A matrix is refutable if
- each path is potentially complementary, and
- the mgu of at least one pair of potentially complementary literals on each path is compatible with the substitutions computed for all other paths.

By "compatible" it is meant that if a variable appears on several paths the same overall substitution must be applied to it on each path (cf. Section 4.2.5).

Clearly, a matrix M is refutable iff there is a substitution θ such that $M\theta$ is complementary. The definition merely hints at an algorithm for determining such a substitution if it exists. First check each path to find out whether it is potentially complementary, at the same time ensuring that the mgu found for any path is compatible with each of the substitutions previously computed for other paths. If no such substitution can be found for a particular path then return ("backtrack") to a path that has been checked previously but which has another pair of potentially complementary literals on it not already tried; discard all the substitutions that were not performed before that path was previously tested, and compute the new mgu for the new pair of literals. Then proceed again to the next path. Repeat this process until a complementary matrix has been found or until all possible potentially complementary pairs of literals on all the paths have been checked without success. In the case of failure, a quantifier duplication must be performed if possible and the process of checking for complementarity repeated for the newly derived matrix.

Slight variations of the following theorem are proved in [An81]:

> a sentence σ is unsatisfiable   iff   some amplification of σ is refutable.

It is clear that a full search procedure for the method would involve, in part, a way of performing quantifier duplications systematically. The problem of choosing the order in which to apply the quantifier duplications and a procedure for developing refutations using the matrix method are discussed at length in [An81].

Example: Consider once again the example EX. In Skolemised negation normal form this becomes

$$\forall x \forall z (P(x, z) \vee ((\neg Q(x) \vee R(x, a)) \wedge Q(x)) \wedge$$
$$\forall x \forall y (\neg P(x, y) \vee R(x, f(x))) \wedge$$
$$\forall x (((\neg R(b, x) \vee S(x)) \wedge \neg S(x))$$

(which can be derived via a subset of the transformation steps used in Section 3.3.1 to convert EX to clausal form). The occurrence of $\forall x$ in the third line may now be distributed over $\wedge$ to reduce its scope. Then the matrix format of the sentence is

$$
\begin{array}{ll}
P(x, y) & \begin{array}{ll}\neg Q(x) & R(x, a)\\ Q(x) & \end{array}\\
\neg P(u, v) & R(u, f(u))\\
\neg R(b, w) & S(w)\\
\neg S(z) &
\end{array}
$$

There is no substitution that will make this matrix complementary. For consider the paths

$\{P(x, y)-\neg R(u, f(u))-\neg R(b, w)-\neg S(z)\}$ and $\{R(x, a)-Q(x)-\neg P(u, v)-\neg R(b, w)-\neg S(z)\}$.

On the first path $R(u, f(u))$ and $\neg R(b, w)$ are potentially complementary, as are $R(x, a)$ and $\neg R(b,w)$ on the second path (and no other pair of literals is potentially complementary on either path), but there is no substitution such that these two pairings of literals may be unified simultaneously. That is, the substitutions for w are not compatible. Therefore, a quantifier duplication must be performed.

It is intuitively clear in this case that the quantifier duplication should be applied to $\forall x(\neg R(b, x) \vee S(x))$. This gives (after variables are renamed)

$$
\begin{array}{ll}
P(x, y) & \begin{array}{ll} \neg Q(x) & R(x, a) \\ Q(x) \end{array} \\
\neg P(u, v) & R(u, f(u)) \\
\neg R(b, w) & S(w) \\
\neg R(b, w') & S(w') \\
\neg S(z)
\end{array}
$$

However there is still no substitution that will make this matrix complementary. It is necessary to duplicate $\neg S(z)$, which produces

$$
\begin{array}{ll}
P(x, y) & \begin{array}{ll} \neg Q(x) & R(x, a) \\ Q(x) \end{array} \\
\neg P(u, v) & R(u, f(u)) \\
\neg R(b, w) & S(w) \\
\neg R(b, w') & S(w') \\
\neg S(z) \\
\neg S(z')
\end{array}
$$

Finally, there is a substitution instance of this matrix that is complementary:

$$
\begin{array}{ll}
P(b, y) & \begin{array}{ll} \neg Q(b) & R(b, a) \\ Q(b) \end{array} \\
\neg P(b, y) & R(b, f(b)) \\
\neg R(b, a) & S(a) \\
\neg R(b, f(b)) & S(f(b)) \\
\neg S(a) \\
\neg S(f(b))
\end{array}
$$

This completes the proof that the original formula is unsatisfiable.

Exercise 5.6: Using the matrix method and then resolution, show that the set $\{P(a, x) \vee \neg P(x, b), \neg P(a, a), P(b, b)\}$ is unsatisfiable; compare the refutations.

5.2.2 Relationships to Other Calculi

It is shown in the first subsection here that the connection method is related in a very natural way to the cut-free sequent calculus of Chapter 3. It is then indicated in the next subsection that matrix calculus proofs and resolution proofs are virtually interchangeable, at which point the differences between the two approaches are studied from a more pragmatic point of view. Finally, the problem of providing a more natural interpretation of connection calculus proofs, for the purpose of human understanding, is outlined in the third subsection.

5.2.2.1 Relationship to Sequent Calculi

It may have been noticed that there is some similarity between the definition of a path for formulae in negation normal form and the inference rules for $\wedge$ and $\vee$ in the sequent calculus of Chapter 3. This analogy may be developed to bring out the relationship between the matrix-connection method and sequent calculi. It turns out that the connection method is essentially nothing more than an efficient mechanism for applying the reversals of the rules of a sequent calculus. This point is made by L. Wallen in [Wa87], where he expresses it in terms of Beth tableaux.

This relationship may be determined as follows. Suppose that the formulae of a given sequent are in negation normal form. A path through the sequent is then defined as follows.

- If α is a literal then there is a path through α.

- If α has the form $\beta \vee \gamma$ and is in the antecedent, or has the form $\beta \wedge \gamma$ and is in the consequent, then there is no path that passes through both a literal in β and a literal in γ.

- If α has the form $\beta \wedge \gamma$ and is in the antecedent, or has the form $\beta \vee \gamma$ and is in the consequent, then every path that passes through a literal in β (γ) must also pass through some literal in γ (β).

The difference between these "path rules" and the rules of a sequent calculus (when applied backwards as decomposition tactics) is simply that, while the sequent rules are applied to only the main connectives in a formula, the path rules apply also to the connectives of the subformulae of any formula. It is possible to reduce this disparity between the two systems by extending the rules of a sequent calculus so that they may apply to subformulae of negation-normal-form formulae. For example, the rule for $\vee\vdash$ would be extended to

$$\frac{\Gamma, \alpha[\beta]_i \vdash \Delta \quad \text{and} \quad \Gamma, \alpha[\gamma]_i \vdash \Delta}{\Gamma, \alpha[\beta \vee \gamma]_i \vdash \Delta},$$

where the notation $\alpha[\delta]_i$ denotes that δ is a subformula of α, and that δ occurs at some specific position within α indicated by the index i (formulae may be indexed according to their structure; cf. [Hu80]). For example, by the application of the reversal of this rule, the theorem $\neg Q, P \wedge (Q \vee R) \vdash R$ would be decomposed into the subgoals $\neg Q, P \wedge Q \vdash R$ and $\neg Q, P \wedge R \vdash R$, both of which are valid. It may now be seen that the connection method is simply a more efficient mechanism for applying such rules.

It should be noted, however, that the rule specified for $\vee\vdash$ and the above definition of a path are appropriate only for negation-normal-form formulae. To illustrate the type of problem that may arise if they are applied to general propositional formulae, consider the sequent $P, \neg(P \vee Q) \vdash Q$. Applying the above rule for $\vee\vdash$ produces the subgoals $P, \neg P \vdash Q$ and $P, \neg Q \vdash Q$, the second of which is invalid; but the original sequent is in fact valid. The problem that arose is that the negated *disjunction* occurring in the original sequent, $\neg(P \vee Q)$, corresponds to a *conjunction* of negated formulae, $\neg P \wedge \neg Q$, when transformed to negation normal form.

Thus, the sequent $P, \neg(P \vee Q) \vdash Q$ should be decomposed into the single subgoal $P, \neg P, \neg Q \vdash Q$. One way to overcome this problem is to determine the "polarity" of a subformula [Mu82] before applying the corresponding sequent rule.

Polarity: Suppose all formulae of the form $\beta \rightarrow \gamma$ are represented as $\neg \beta \vee \gamma$. A subformula α of a formula in the antecedent of a sequent has positive (negative) polarity if α is in the scope of an even (odd) number of negations. The converse applies to formulae in the consequent of a sequent.

For example, in the sequent $P, \neg(P \vee Q) \vdash Q$, the formula $P \vee Q$ has negative polarity, as do its two subformulae P and Q, while the first occurrence of P and the second occurrence of Q in the sequent have, respectively, positive and negative polarity (since both are in the scope of an even (0) number of negations). If the formulae occurring in a sequent are indexed with either '+' or '−' according to their polarity, then all occurrences of the negation symbol may be eliminated since they have become redundant, and the concept of a path may then be redefined once again, this time by simply exchanging "in the antecedent" for "has positive polarity" and exchanging "in the consequent" for "has negative polarity" in the previous definition of path. The details are left to the reader (cf. [Wa87]).

Exercise 5.7: Find a refutation for the sequent $P, \neg(P \wedge \neg(\neg P \vee Q)) \vdash Q$, by indexing the subformulae with either '+' or '−' according to their polarity, deleting the then redundant negation symbols, and then showing that every path through the sequent is complementary (that is, has positive and negative occurrences of some atom). Compare this with an analytic sequent calculus proof of the same theorem.

It should be noted that the idea of the polarity of formulae was originally proposed to extend resolution to treat non-clausal formulae (see [Mu82], [MW80]) before it was applied to the matrix method.

The final problem is to extend the above discussion to treat the quantifiers. If the formulae are in Skolemised negation normal form (existential quantifiers Skolemised in the antecedent and universal quantifiers Skolemised in the consequent), then extension involves merely adding unification and quantifier duplications (existential quantifiers in the consequent and universal quantifiers in the antecedent). For arbitrary formulae, apart from the addition of polarity, a mechanism is required to test that the eigenvariable conditions are not violated, as discussed in Section 4.2.6. In [Wa87] Wallen applies Bibel's alternative to Skolemisation to the problem.

5.2.2.2 Connection to Resolution

Given the relationship between resolution and sequent calculi discussed in Section 3.3.5, and the relationship between sequent calculi and the matrix calculus as just described, it should not come as a surprise that there is a natural correspondence between resolution proofs and matrix proofs. This is developed by Bibel in [Bi87], where he uses it to give an alternative proof of both the soundness and the completeness of resolution by showing how a resolution proof may be reinterpreted as a matrix proof. In fact, this idea was already implicit in the V-resolution rule of Chang some years earlier (see [CL73]).

The idea behind V-resolution is that, rather than checking the paths through a

matrix of clauses as Prawitz had suggested [Pr69], the system should attempt a
"ground" resolution refutation of the matrix, treating the variables as constants.
Bibel, in turn, takes this idea one step further by showing how each resolution step
may be translated into a connection in the matrix calculus and vice-versa.

Given this ability to transform resolution proofs naturally into matrix proofs and
vice-versa, the question arises again as to the difference (if there is any) between the
two approaches. As pointed out by Bibel, the major distinction lies in the fact that
while resolution is a "localised" strategy according to which proofs proceed in steps
by the successive derivation of clauses, the matrix calculus is a "global" strategy
that simply exhibits a refutation as a set of connections with no transference from
one connection to another.

This distinction has important consequences for both the practical and theoretical
applications of these two approaches. It is quite clear that resolution, in proceeding
according to inferred steps, is the more intuitive mechanism for proof, and, for this
reason, is still the more popular approach at the moment. On the other hand, there
is certainly a conceptual simplicity in the matrix method when viewed from a theoretical point of view, which contrasts sharply with resolution in the same light.
This claim is promoted by the ease with which the matrix method was proved to
be complete for propositional clauses in Section 5.2.1.1 as compared to the usual
proofs for the resolution method, which do not seem so intuitively straightforward.
The importance of this conceptual simplicity is that improvements and refinements
of the basic approach should more readily be found for the matrix calculus (as
maintained by Bibel in [Bi81] and [BE83]; see Section 5.2.3.1 below).

5.2.2.3 Reinterpreting Matrix Calculus Proofs

The difficulty of conceptualising proofs performed in the matrix calculus is, of
course, a severe hurdle to its practical application and popularity. The major problem in this respect is that, as already mentioned, there are no inference steps as in
other proof methods such as resolution and natural deduction. This is important
because part of the "naturalness" of natural deduction systems comes from the simplicity of each of the inference steps and the easy conceptualisation of a sequence of
applications of the inference rules.

There are various ways in which this problem may be overcome. For instance,
an algorithm for the matrix method described by Bibel in [Bi82] allows a simulation of "linear resolution" methods (see Chapter 6 on Prolog). Such a strategy
expresses a transference from one connection to another, thus solving, to a certain
extent, the "static" nature of the calculus. A preferable solution, perhaps, is to map
each connection into the corresponding inference step of a sequent calculus using
the natural relationship between the two. In a similar vein, Andrews shows, in
[An80], how a proof performed with the matrix method (or, more accurately, with
his "matings calculus") may be transformed into a natural deduction proof for the
purposes of reading and understanding by a human.

5.2.3 Developments

This subsection notes some strategies for developing proofs in the connection-
matrix calculus and outlines a possible extension for equality.

5.2.3.1 Refinements

It is shown in [Bi81], for the ground case, that all the simplification rules designed for resolution apply also to the connection-matrix method when it is restricted to clause matrices. Also described are some simplification techniques derived from a study of the matrix method itself. In [BE83] further powerful strategies are discussed which apply to sentences in negation normal form. These include a method for "dynamically" factoring the "clauses" of the matrix during the proof process, and an extension of the pure-literal principle. Furthermore, with regard to efficiency in time, Bibel (in [Bi82]) describes a strategy for the (ground) matrix method which he compares favourably with the connection-graph proof procedure, perhaps the most efficient resolution refinement known. With respect to space considerations, it is shown that the matrix method is a drastic improvement over the connection-graph method. These issues are also discussed in Bibel's book [Bi87].

5.2.3.2 Extension for Equality

In Chapter V of [Bi87] Bibel outlines an extension of the matrix method to include treatment of the equality relation. This involves finding an appropriate substitution instance of some amplification of the given conjecture and then performing equality replacements along each path to produce a matrix with the property that each path is either complementary or contains an inequality between identical terms; the resulting instance of the matrix is said to be E-complementary. This idea is closely related to the E-resolution procedure mentioned in Section 3.3.7.

A fundamental difficulty involved in this approach is finding an appropriate instance of the amplification; an analogous difficulty arose in the work of Digricoli and Harrison to develop a reformulation of E-resolution [DH86] (as pointed out by Bibel). At the simplest level one possible solution to the problem in the current context is simply to apply the equality rules for sequentzen described in Section 4.2.7. The idea is that since each path through a matrix corresponds to the application of the reversal of a sequent rule, the problem of finding an appropriate instance of a matrix reduces to the task of solving simultaneously each of a set of sequents. This is illustrated in the following simple example.

Example: Consider the example used to illustrate equational reasoning in Chapter 4. After the consequent of the conjectural sequent is negated, the matrix form of the theorem is

$$\begin{aligned}
g(x) &= a \quad x = b \\
P(g(a), b) \\
\neg g(g(y)) &= y \\
\neg P(b, b)
\end{aligned}$$

There are two paths through this matrix, given by

$g(x) = a - P(g(a), b) - \neg g(g(y)) = y - \neg P(b, b)$, and
$x = b - P(g(a), b) - \neg g(g(y)) = y - \neg P(b, b)$.

Finding a complementary instance of these two paths is equivalent to solving simultaneously the two subgoal sequents

$g(x) = a, \ P(g(a), b) \ \vdash \ g(g(y)) = y, P(b, b),$ and
$x = b, P(g(a), b) \ \vdash g(g(y)) = y, P(b, b),$

where x and y are "dummy variables". These two subgoals were solved in Chapter 4 with the substitution $\{x \to g(a), y \to a\}$. The application of this substitution to the original matrix produces the required E-complementary instance

$$g(g(a)) = a \quad g(a) = b$$
$$P(g(a), b)$$
$$\neg g(g(a)) = a$$
$$\neg P(b, b)$$

Hence the proof of unsatisfiability is completed.

PART 3

SPECIAL PURPOSE
THEOREM PROVERS

CHAPTER 6

PROLOG

6.1 INTRODUCTION

Prolog (**Programming in Logic**) is a programming language originally developed by Alain Colmerauer and Phillipe Roussel and their associates in Marseilles during the early 1970s. Since then there have been many implementations and much theoretical work aimed at improving the quality of Prolog and developing the area of logic programming in general. Here the discussion will centre around one particular implementation of Prolog, that of C-Prolog (see [Pe83]), which is a subsystem of DEC-10 Prolog described in [CM87]—though the main aim is to cover the general details of Prolog, not to describe the particular nuances of C-Prolog.

The inspiration for Prolog was Robinson's resolution principle, and thus Prolog is more closely related to automatic theorem proving than to standard programming languages. In Prolog a computational problem is stated as a theorem that stipulates the existence of some object satisfying certain constraints. A "constructive proof" of the theorem then finds such an object and hence solves the problem. Of course, it could be claimed that any computation performed in any programming language may be considered as a proof in at least a trivial sense. For example, if a correct Pascal program computes the factorial of 3 then it "proves" that the answer is 6. The difference is that whereas in the case of Pascal programs it is the programmer who develops the necessary algorithm to solve the given problem, in the case of Prolog it is the machine on which the program is run (the interpreter) that develops the algorithm using the constructive nature of unification. The important advantage Prolog has over the "classical" programming languages is summed up in the words "describe rather than command" [Col85]. This means that the programmer is not required to provide a sequence of instructions, but only to describe the object to be computed, leaving the details of the computation to the interpreter.

However, this theoretical viewpoint is not strictly accurate as regards the standard Prolog languages and the interpreters built for them. Problems arise because, in order to make Prolog as efficient and practical as typical programming languages, an incomplete search strategy is used and "impure" (or "non-logical") features have been introduced. It is pointed out in [Col85] that while the close link to logic was helpful initially it became, in some ways, more of a hindrance than an asset.

This chapter will be concerned, in the main, with the basic theory of Prolog, and the logical problems with some of the added features. Also, the examples given, though simple, will make it clear how a "theorem prover" may be used as a programming system.

6.2 THE BASIC THEORY

In this section the syntax of Prolog programs and the computation strategy of Prolog interpreters will be described.

6.2.1 Clause Sets as Programs

The first task is to show how a set of clauses may be interpreted as a program. For this purpose a slightly different syntax for clauses will be introduced, and then a "procedural interpretation" given to sets of clauses in this form.

6.2.1.1 Syntax

Prolog programs essentially consist of a set of Horn-clauses. This term was defined in Chapter 4, but, to reiterate, a clause is a Horn-clause if it has at most one positive literal. In fact, the Horn-clauses of a program must each contain exactly one positive literal. A query to be processed by a program consists of a Horn-clause with no positive literals. In most Prolog systems the notation for clauses differs from that used in Chapter 3. This section will describe the new syntax and explain its relation to the previously described form.

Program Clause: This is any expression of the form

$$A :- B_1, B_2,..., B_n.,$$

where A and the B_i are atomic formulae. If there is no B_i then the clause $A :-.$ is written simply $A.$, for brevity.

Head: A is referred to as the head of the clause.

Tail: The sequence $B_1, B_2,..., B_n$ is referred to as the tail of the clause.

Query: A query takes the form

$$?- A_1, A_2,..., A_m.,$$

where the A_i are, once again, atomic formulae.

To clarify the relationship of this format to the earlier clausal form, note that the symbols ':-', ',' and '?-' have respectively the same meanings as the symbols '←', '∧' and '¬', and that '$\beta \leftarrow \alpha$' is equivalent to '$\alpha \to \beta$'. Hence a program clause may be written in the form

$$A \leftarrow (B_1 \wedge B_2 \wedge ... \wedge B_n),$$

which, in turn, is logically equivalent to

$$A \vee \neg B_1 \vee \neg B_2 \vee ... \vee \neg B_n.$$

Similarly, a query may be written in the form

$$\neg(A_1 \wedge A_2 \wedge ... \wedge A_m),$$

which is equivalent to

$$\neg A_1 \vee \neg A_2 \vee ... \vee \neg A_m.$$

As for clauses defined earlier, program clauses and queries are implicitly prefixed by universal quantifiers. In particular if $x_1,..., x_k$ are the variables appearing in a query then the query should be written, say,

$$\forall x_1 ... \forall x_k(\neg A_1 \vee \neg A_2 \vee ... \vee \neg A_m),$$

which is equivalent to

$$\forall x_1 ... \forall x_k \neg(A_1 \wedge A_2 \wedge ... \wedge A_m),$$

which is also equivalent to

$$\neg(\exists x_1 ... \exists x_k(A_1 \wedge A_2 \wedge ... \wedge A_m)).$$

Thus, the important point to note is that a query is the negation of an existence theorem converted to Prolog clausal form.

In C-Prolog there are also changes to the notation used for atoms, namely, the symbols for predicates and functions must begin with a lower-case letter and the variable symbols must begin with an upper-case letter. This is very non-standard but will be used for programs in this chapter. It is also possible to specify unary symbols to be prefix or postfix, and binary symbols to be infix. This entails also stating the precedence and associativity of the symbol; for the details see [CM87] or [Pe83]. Predicates and functions built into the system are generally defined to have their usual pre-, post- or infix symbols. Some of these will be looked at later. The major difference between Prolog atoms and those described previously is that equality atoms are not usually allowed in Prolog. In most implementations of Prolog no special mechanisms are built in for dealing with equality.

Example: The following is a program for addition and multiplication.

```
plus(X, 0, X).
plus(X, s(Y), s(Z)) :- plus(X, Y, Z).
times(X, 0, 0).
times(X, s(Y), Z) :- times(X, Y, Z1), plus(X, Z1, Z).
```

In the intended interpretation of these clauses, the domain is the natural numbers, s is to be assigned the successor function, and **plus** and **times** are to be assigned the predicates

$$x + y = z \quad \text{and} \quad x * y = z,$$

respectively. Thus, intuitively, the procedures for **times** may be read as

$$x * 0 = 0, \text{ and}$$

$x * (y + 1) = z$ if $x * y = z1$ and $x + z1 = z$;

similarly for **plus**. To compute $2 * 3$ the user would supply the query

   ?- times(s(s(0)), s(s(s(0))), X)..

However, many other more interesting types of query may be posed such as

   ?- times(s(s(0)), Y, Z).,

which would generate all multiples of 2 as solutions, and

   ?- plus(s(s(0)), Y, Z), times(Y, Z, s(s(s(0)))).,

which would generate as solution the values of y and z that satisfy the simultaneous equations $2 + y = z$ and $y * z = 3$.

From these last two examples the advantage of a theorem prover over a typical programming language is immediately apparent. Normally a detailed and complex algorithm would be required to solve arbitrary queries such as these, while for the Prolog system all that is required is that the definitions of *plus* and *times* be given.

However, counter to this is the fact that to solve such queries, Prolog simply searches through possible pairings of values for **Y** and **Z** until suitable values are found. This, as pointed out previously, is disastrous as far as mechanical theorem proving is concerned. Seemingly worse, in the case of Prolog, solutions to some problems may never be found owing to its incomplete search strategy. However the loss of some possible solutions to some problems is perhaps more than made up for by the speed with which solutions to other problems are found, especially as far as the practical programmer is concerned.

Exercise 6.1: Define the exponentiation function for **N**, informally given by

$$x^y = x * x * \cdots * x \quad (y \text{ times}),$$

as a Prolog program, and express the query for the problem $2^x = 8$.

6.2.1.2 The Procedural Interpretation

The procedural interpretation of Horn-clauses originally described by R. Kowalski was the innovation that first brought the Prolog language to the attention of the general programming community. In this interpretation program clauses are viewed as procedures for performing some task in the style of standard programming languages. The following definitions which promote this view are based upon those in [Ho84] (see Chapter II) and [Ko79] (see Chapter 5).

If $A :- B_1, B_2,..., B_n$. is a program clause and the predicate symbol of A is **pred**, say, then the clause is said to be a *procedure for* **pred**. The B_i are then *procedure calls* which are processed by calling an appropriate procedure. If **pred** is the predicate symbol of the head of each of a set of clauses then that set of clauses is said to be a *procedure set for* **pred** (or, as in [Ll87], a *definition of* **pred**). The parameters of the head of a program clause are referred to as the *formal parameters* while those of the procedure calls in the tail of a program clause are called *actual parameters*. This is analogous to the definition of formal and actual parameters for functions and procedures in languages such as Ada (see [McG82], p. 146). As might be expected, the atoms occurring in a query are also viewed as procedure calls. The processing of these calls, as will be explained below, is then called a *computation*.

6.2.2 The Computation Strategy

Each step of a computation is either an application of the SLD-resolution rule (to be defined in Section 6.2.2.2) or the undoing of an application of this rule (that is, "backtracking"). The definitions and ideas to be explained in this section may be more easily understood in terms of the "computation tree" for a program and goal.

6.2.2.1 The Computation Tree

The computation tree represents all possible sequences of deductions from the initial set of clauses according to the inference rules. Each node of the tree, apart from the "failure nodes", is an inferred formula, referred to as a *goal*, consisting of a set of *subgoals* to be solved.

Goal: A goal is the negation of the conjunction of a set of atoms. All goals will be written in the form

$$?\text{-} A_1, A_2,..., A_n.,$$

where $A_1, A_2,..., A_n$ are the atoms occurring in the goal. (Thus a query is a goal, but it is not the only type of goal.)

Subgoal: Each atom occurring in a goal is a subgoal of that goal.

Computation Tree: If P is a program and G a goal then the resolution computation tree for $P \cup \{G\}$ is defined as follows:
1. Each node in the tree is a goal.
2. Each branch of the tree denotes a possible sequence of applications of resolution.
3. The initial goal (or *root node*) is G.
4. If N is a node other than the root node, then it is a resolvent of the goal immediately preceding it on the same branch and some program clause.

It is also useful to introduce the following definitions.

Predecessor/Successor Node: If N' is a node that is the resolvent of the node N and a program clause then N is the predecessor node of N'. If a node N is the predecessor node of a node N' then N' is a successor node of N.

A node may have any number of successor nodes (including none), but at most one predecessor node (only the root node has none). A branch may be either finite or infinite.

Terminal Node: If a node has no successor nodes then it is a terminal node (of a finite branch).

Success/Failure Branch: A finite branch whose terminal node is the empty goal $\varnothing$ is a success branch. A finite branch whose terminal node is not the empty goal is a failure branch; such a branch will be terminated with the "failed goal", denoted $\bullet$.

The tree is normally drawn "growing downwards" rather than "upwards", and this form will be used here.

Example: Let **G** be the query **?- p,q.**, and let **P** be the program

$$\{p., \quad q :- r., \quad q.\}.$$

The tree for **P** ∪ {**G**} is

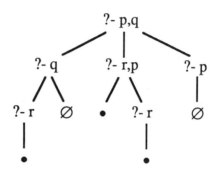

This computation tree represents the "resolution computation space"; for instance, the node 'r,p' gives rise either to a failure goal or to the resolvent 'r', depending upon the order in which resolution is applied. In fact, the Prolog interpreter does not attempt to search (or, more accurately, create) the whole tree but only a subtree determined by the SLD-resolution inference rule to be defined below.

Exercise 6.2: Let **G** be the goal **?- p.** and **P** be the program

$$\{p :- q., \quad q :- p., \quad q :- r, s., \quad p., \quad s.\}.$$

Give a finite representation for the (infinite) resolution computation tree for the set **P** ∪ {**G**}.

6.2.2.2 SLD-Resolution

The name "SLD-resolution" is an abbreviation for *Linear resolution* with *Selector function* for *Definite clauses*, where a definite clause is a Horn-clause with exactly one positive literal. SL-resolution, which applies to general clauses, is described in [Lo78]. Informally, the SLD-resolution rule is a refinement of resolution that, in each inference step, chooses some subgoal from the current goal and unifies this with the head of a program clause to produce a resolvent (with the literals ordered in a specific way), which then becomes the new goal. The following more formal definition of SLD-resolution is based upon the definition in [Ll87].

Computation Rule: A computation rule (or *selector function*) is a rule that, given some goal, selects a subgoal from the goal.

Derivation Via R: Let G_i be the goal ?- $A_1,..., A_i,..., A_m.$, let **C** be a program clause $A :- B_1,..., B_n.$, and let **R** be a computation rule. If **R** selects the subgoal A_i

from G_i, if A_i and A unify with mgu θ, and if the goal G_{i+1}, where

$$G_{i+1} = ?\text{-} (A_1,..., A_{i-1}, B_1,..., B_n, A_{i+1},..., A_m).\theta,$$

is inferred from G_i and C, then G_{i+1} is said to be derived from G_i and C via R.

SLD-Resolution: Let P be a program, G_0 be a goal, and R be a computation rule. If $G_0, G_1, G_2,...$ is a (possibly infinite) sequence of goals such that G_{i+1} is derived from G_i and some program clause via rule R, then the sequence is an SLD-derivation of $P \cup \{G_0\}$ via R. The goal G_i $(i > 0)$ is said to be derived from G_0 using SLD-resolution via R.

SLD-resolution determines a subtree of the resolution computation tree. It is proved in [Ll87] that all the solutions to a given program and query that occur in the whole tree may also be found in this subtree. It is also proven that this fact is independent of the computation rule chosen. This means that the computation rule may be chosen and fixed before the computation (proof) is performed.

The Standard Computation Rule: The rule that selects the left-most subgoal of each goal (as they are input) is built into most Prolog interpreters. This is commonly called the standard computation rule.

Example: Consider the previous example. The subtree of the whole tree determined by SLD-resolution using the standard computation strategy will be:

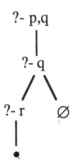

In this subtree there are only two branches, one for each procedure that is called by the ?- **q**. goal.

Exercise 6.3: Construct the SLD-resolution tree for this example, supposing that the computation rule chooses the right-most subgoal from each goal.

How this subtree is searched (created) will determine a SLD-refutation procedure, which may or may not be complete. The two most basic methods for searching such a tree are *breadth-first* and *depth-first* search ([Ko79] pp. 61-62).

Breadth-first Search: This requires that the first n nodes of all the branches be created (if possible) before proceeding to the $(n + 1)$th node.

Depth-first Search: This requires that one branch of the tree be created before any other is created.

If each branch of the tree is finite then all solutions will be found irrespective of whether breadth-first or depth-first search is used. However, if one of the branches is infinite then, though both methods of search, unless constrained, would create this infinite branch, the depth-first strategy may be trapped into the computation of this branch before finding all possible solutions. Thus, depth-first search does not constitute a complete search strategy.

On the other hand, in contrast to breadth-first search, depth-first search may be implemented very efficiently. For this reason it is the strategy used in most Prolog interpreters, since it is contended that Prolog is intended to be a programming language rather than a theorem prover. Another way to view the two rules is as, respectively, complete and heuristic strategies to solve the same problem.

For both search strategies the order in which the branches of the tree are created is determined by an *ordering rule*. This determines the order in which program clauses, whose heads unify with the selected subgoal, are tried. For breadth-first search the ordering rule chosen is almost totally inconsequential, but conversely depth-first search is virtually inseparable from the choice of ordering rule.

The Standard Ordering Rule: The rule that selects the "top-most" program clause, the head of which unifies with the selected subgoal, is built in to most Prolog interpreters.

6.2.2.3 Backtracking

If a computation tree is developed depth-first then it is natural, and usual, to backtrack from terminal nodes in order to create further possible branches. Backtracking, with respect to the computation tree, entails returning from a terminal node of a finite branch, whether successful or failed, to a previously generated node on the same branch from which other branches may be developed.

To clarify, recall that a branch of a computation tree represents a sequence of goals each of which is produced as a resolvent of the last goal generated and some program clause. Backtracking entails finding a goal in this sequence that may be resolved with a program clause with which it has not previously been resolved. For example, in the tree above, backtracking would occur at the terminal node labelled by the failure goal • until the goal ?- q. were found, and at this point a new branch would be created, which leads to the solution of the problem.

Exercise 6.4: Using the standard computation and ordering rules and the backtracking mechanism show that the set $P \cup \{G\}$ is unsatisfiable, where P and G are as in Exercise 6.2.

6.2.2.4 An Intuitionistic Sequent Calculus Interpretation

The description of SLD-resolution in the previous section is the standard presentation in terms of resolution. Alternatively, this rule may be described in terms of a cut-free sequent calculus. In particular, it may be interpreted as a strategy for the application of the $\rightarrow\vdash$ rule.

Consider a program **P** together with a goal ?- **G**. As pointed out earlier, '?-' represents '¬', and thus ?- **G** is equivalent to $\neg g_1 \vee ... \vee \neg g_n$, where the g_i are the subgoals of **G**. In terms of sequents, the task is to show $\Sigma, \neg g_1 \vee ... \vee \neg g_n \vdash \varnothing$, where Σ is **P** viewed as a set of clauses. This may alternatively be expressed as $\Sigma \vdash g_1 \wedge ... \wedge g_n$. Now, to solve a subgoal g_i, the interpreter matches it against the head of one of the clauses in Σ, and then treats the tail of this clause as a new goal to be solved. This may be expressed—in terms of the standard computation rule, for simplicity—as the following rule at the propositional level:

$$\frac{\Sigma \vdash g_2 \wedge ... \wedge g_n \wedge h_1 \wedge ... \wedge h_m}{\Sigma, h_1 \wedge ... \wedge h_m \rightarrow g_1 \vdash g_1 \wedge g_2 \wedge ... \wedge g_n}$$

This rule is clearly sound, and it may be seen that it is very closely related to the sequent rule $\rightarrow\vdash$. As it stands, however, it captures only the basic idea behind the SLD-resolution rule and is not complete. Two further eventualities have to be accounted for. One is that the clause $h_1 \wedge ... \wedge h_m \rightarrow g_1$ may be involved in several steps of the proof, and thus cannot be deleted after a single step as the above rule suggests. For this reason it should also occur as an antecedent in the premiss of the above rule. Another possibility not accounted for is that $g_1 \wedge g_2 \wedge ... \wedge g_n$ may follow from Σ alone. To allow for this the extra hypothesis $\Sigma \vdash g_1 \wedge g_2 \wedge ... \wedge g_n$ should also be included in the above rule "disjoined" from the other hypothesis. This is the case accounted for by backtracking in Prolog implementations. These two additional components are expressed more precisely in the following exercise, the result of which essentially proves the soundness and completeness of the SLD-resolution rule for Horn-clauses (assuming the adequacy of sequent calculi).

Exercise 6.5: Show that the "disjunction" of sequents

$$\Sigma \vdash g \wedge G \text{ or } \Sigma, H \rightarrow g \vdash G \wedge H$$

is equivalent to the "conjunction"

$$\Sigma \vdash g \wedge G, H \text{ and } \Sigma, g \vdash G.$$

It is not difficult to show that the sequent inference rule just outlined is also valid for intuitionistic logic. Thus, SLD-resolution may just as easily be viewed as the reversal of an inference rule of a cut-free intuitionistic sequent calculus. In fact, it might be claimed that this is the way in which the SLD-resolution rule should be presented, as opposed to expressing it as a refinement of resolution. This interpretation gives a better insight into the true nature of Prolog: an intuitionistic logic implemented by a cut-free calculus. In particular, it explains why Prolog is constructive in that it not only "proves theorems", but also finds the instances for which they are valid. This contrasts with general resolution which may derive only a disjunction of possible solutions (cf. the "classical" example in Section 1.3.2).

Though the general SL-resolution principle is, of course, not an intuitionistic calculus, it may also be interpreted in terms of cut-free sequent calculi. In general, this seems to be true for all linear-resolution strategies (cf. [Bi87]), and is probably true for all goal-directed resolution strategies.

6.2.2.5 The Binding History

In order to extract from the computation the values that satisfy the given query, it is necessary to keep track of the unifying substitutions that are applied. In this context, the substitution of terms for program variables is also referred to as the *binding* of terms to variables. The set of all assignments applied during a computation is then called the *binding history*. The answer-extraction process using the binding history is, of course, important for the purposes of programming with Prolog, but is not of further concern here. The details may be found in [Ho84].

6.3 ASPECTS OF PROGRAMMING IN PROLOG

This section discusses some aspects of computation and the statement of problems in Prolog. The first subsection is concerned with "pure" Prolog, while the second outlines some of the "impure" features that have been added to improve Prolog's expressiveness from a practical point of view.

6.3.1 The Pure Language

The "pure" language of Prolog is simply the Horn-clause subset described above. This language is expressive enough to compute any relation computable by any other known programming language (see [Ho84] Chapter VIII). Furthermore, pure Prolog is a "declarative" language in that the meaning of a program is dependent only upon the underlying logical semantics and is independent of the strategy of computation employed by the underlying interpreter/compiler. These two properties of Prolog are illustrated in the following subsections.

6.3.1.1 Reordering Subgoals and Procedures

According to the logical semantics of Prolog programs, the second procedure for **times** may be altered to

   times(X, s(Y), Z) :- plus(X, Z1, Z), times(X, Y, Z1).

without changing the meaning of the procedure. Clearly, the ordering of program clauses may also be changed without affecting the meaning of a program. This is in contrast to most programming languages where the ordering of the statements can have a dramatic effect on the meaning of a program. This is because for most languages the semantics of programs is bound up with the way in which they are processed. A particular example is that of variable assignment statements, the ordering of which is normally crucial to the operation of a program.

On the other hand, for Prolog, though the reordering of subgoals and procedures does not alter the meaning of a program, it will have an effect on the interpreter's processing of the program. The major difficulties that arise concern the inefficiency with which computations are performed, and also the possibility that some or all solutions to a problem may not be found.

Example: Consider again the example used to illustrate the purity principle in Chapter 4 (written as Prolog clauses):

program clauses: $p(0)$. and $p(s(X))$:- $p(X)$.; goal: ?- $p(Y)$..
If the program clauses are ordered with $p(0)$. "at the top", then the infinite set of solutions $\{0, s(0),...\}$ will be enumerated. But if the order is reversed then the interpreter will loop forever on the first clause and will thus produce no solutions.

Exercise 6.6: Let **P** and **G** be as in the previous exercise. Assuming, for simplicity, that the standard computation and ordering rules are built into the interpreter, show that the order in which both the program's clauses and subgoals are ordered in **P** may have an effect on whether **G** is solved (and also on the number of steps required in its solution).

6.3.1.2 Iteration

There are no iterative constructs in Prolog such as the "WHILE" and "DO"-loop of other languages, but it is possible to write programs that simulate such behaviour, as explained in [Ho84] and [Ko79]. In [Ho84] iterative procedures are defined to be any sets of clauses of the form A :- A'. or A :- $B_1,..., B_n, A'$., where A and A' have identical predicate names distinct from those of the B_i. Also, at least one unit clause with the same predicate symbol as A (the "base case(s)") is required, which should ensure termination of the "iteration" for all appropriate input.

For example, the definition of **times** in Section 6.3.1.1 above may be viewed as an "iterative procedure". Of course, such procedures are simply special types of recursive procedures, but in many cases the analogy with iteration is very natural. Consider the iterative procedure

```
hensel(X, Y, P, N, N).
hensel(X, Y, P, N, K) :-
        K < N, prime(P), Z is P^K, polyfn(X, Y1),
        diffpoly(Y, Y2),
        X2 is X − ((((P mod Y2) * (Y1 / Z)) mod P) * Z),
        K2 is K + 1, hensel(X2, Y, P, N, K2).,
```

based upon a theorem due to K. Hensel. Here some inbuilt arithmetic operators (see Section 6.3.2.4 below) have been used, and it has been assumed that **prime** (which checks whether a number is prime), **polyfn** (which evaluates a given polynomial *fn* for parameter X—returning the answer Y) and **diffpoly** (which evaluates the derivative of *fn* for parameter Y—returning the answer $Y2$) have previously been appropriately defined. Given a goal ?- **hensel**$(s, s, p, n, 1)$., the program computes a solution to the problem '$fn(x) \equiv 0 \bmod p^n$', where *fn* is a polynomial (in one variable) with integer coefficients, p is a prime, and s is a solution to the simpler problem '$fn(x) \equiv 0 \bmod p$, such that $fn'(x) \bmod p$ is not equal to 0' (where $fn'(x)$ denotes the derivative of *fn*). The predicate **hensel** itself simply creates a loop in which the solution to the problem is found.

Example: Let *fn* be $x^3 - 2$, p be 5 and n be 3. Since $3^3 - 2 \equiv 0 \bmod 5$, and the value of $fn'(x)$ (i.e. $3x^2$) for $x = 3$ is $3 * 3^2 = 27$ ($\equiv 2 \bmod 5$), the task is to solve the query ?-**hensel(3, 3, 5, 3, 1)**. In the first execution of the loop the subgoal ?-**hensel(3, 3, 5, 3, 2)**. is derived, and in the second execution the subgoal ?-**hensel(53, 3, 5, 3, 3)**. is derived. The "base case" now terminates the process, returning the solution 53 for X; that is, $53^3 - 2 \equiv 0 \bmod 125$.

For large n, the above program solves the proposed problem more efficiently than simply testing all x from 1 to p^n, but it requires the derivative of the given polynomial to be provided by the user.

As an aside, the format of the **hensel** program above was derived in a straightforward manner from a more constructive version of the proof given on page 96 of [HW54] of an existence theorem which the author believes was originally due to Hensel. The problem of proving this theorem in a constructive manner, such that a program (such as the above) may be derived from the proof, seems to pose quite an interesting and difficult task for a mechanical theorem prover.

6.3.1.3 Renaming Predicates

In theory, any problem that may be expressed as a set of clauses may also be expressed as a set of Horn-clauses [Ko79]. However, to the author's knowledge, there is no set of straightforward transformation rules that will perform this task as there was for transforming arbitrary formulae into clauses. In some cases, however, the idea of renaming predicates, as explained in [Ko79], may be used. For example, the clause $Happy(x) \vee Sad(x)$ may be converted into one of the Prolog clauses

happy(X) :- notsad(X). or sad(X) :- unhappy(X).,

which, effectively, have the same meaning (though they introduce an asymmetry).

Exercise 6.7: Show that the clauses of EX in Section 3.3.1 can be converted into Horn-clauses in this way.

However, this strategy for transforming sets of clauses into Horn-clauses will not always be successful, for otherwise the unit preference strategy would be complete; this follows from a result described in [Lo78] which essentially states that a set of clauses has a unit refutation iff it is renamable into a set of Horn-clauses. An example of a set of clauses that cannot be renamed as Horn-clauses may be found in [Ko79].

The idea of renaming predicates was first proposed by B. Meltzer in [Me66] as a means of generalising the hyper-resolution principle (see also [Lo78]). It was also shown that the concept of renaming could be used as a decision procedure for the propositional calculus, and a proposal was made that it might be extended to a complete strategy for first-order logic. To the author's knowledge, up to now there have been no further advances on this proposal.

6.3.2 Impure Features of Prolog Implementations

Partly due to the lack of expressiveness of Horn-clauses for practical purposes and partly due to the inefficiency associated with treating Prolog as a complete theorem prover (for Horn-clauses), various "impure" (or "non-logical") features have been introduced. Following their introduction much theoretical work has been put into explaining formally the nature of some of these changes with respect to the semantics of logic. This section will point out the most prominent of these additions, without going too far into the associated theory, which has little relation to the subject of this book.

6.3.2.1 The Occurs Check

The occurs check, explained in Chapter 3, is omitted from most implementations of Prolog for reasons of efficiency. It is pointed out in [Pe83] that whereas the time-complexity for performing unification without the occurs check is linear in the size of the smallest expression (that is, the time required is $ax + b$, where x is the size), with the occurs check it is at best linear in the size of both expressions.

Quite recently Colmerauer (see [Co82]) and others have advocated an extension of the theory of Prolog to include unification without the occurs check, by allowing infinitely long terms that have a circular structure (called infinite trees) in their logic. There is a well-developed theory concerning infinite trees, but as has been pointed out in, for example, [St84], it does not comply with the logic underlying mechanical theorem proving. In particular, many non-theorems may be "proved" when the occurs check is omitted (cf. Section 4.2.6).

Exercise 6.8: Show that the non-theorem $\forall x \exists y P(x, y) \rightarrow \exists y \forall x P(x, y)$ may be proved if the occurs check is omitted (following conversion to clausal form).

6.3.2.2 Negation by Failure

The prefix "connective" **not**, which is built into C-Prolog (and DEC-10), takes an atom as argument and succeeds iff an attempt to solve the given atom fails. This is commonly referred to as *negation by failure*. For example, according to the simple program

happy(X) :- not sad(X).
sad(john).,

the query **?-happy(jane).** will succeed, but the query **?-happy(john).** will fail. Also the query **?-happy(X).** will fail since **?-sad(X).** succeeds with the solution X = john. Clearly **not** is distinct in meaning from '¬', and much work has gone into determining the relationship between the two. In [Ll87] a theoretical discussion of negation by failure may be found, especially in relation to its use in Prolog databases.

As an aside, note that unlike the inference rules associated with the logical connectives used in this book, the rule of negation by failure is *non-monotonic*. This means that the addition of new axioms may decrease the set of theorems. This is in contrast to "standard" logic where the addition of independent axioms will always increase the set of theorems. As pointed out in [Ho84] standard logic and negation by failure have variously been attacked as being, respectively, monotonic and non-monotonic by different authors.

6.3.2.3 Cut and Fail

The cut, written **!** in C-Prolog, is a built-in "predicate" that enables a programmer to stop certain parts of the program tree from being searched. When **!** appears in the tail of a program clause then the first time an attempt is made to solve it during a computation it immediately succeeds, but if the computation ever backtracks to this call of **!**, then it fails and thus any part of the tree that "lay beyond" that call of **!** may not be searched. The predicate **fail**, on the other hand, as its name suggests, always fails, and is also used to "prune" the search tree.

To illustrate these predicates, suppose that, as is the case in C-Prolog, there is also a built-in predicate **call** that takes an atom as argument and simply calls a procedure whose head unifies with this atom; then it is possible to define **not** in terms of these three predicates:

    not(X) :- call(X), !, fail.
    not(X).

Suppose that a call of **not**(*A*) is made, where *A* is some atom. Then an attempt will be made to call a procedure that unifies with *A*. If one is found then ! will succeed, but **fail** will not. On backtracking to the subgoal !, this time it will fail and allow no further backtracking, causing the original call of **not** to fail. On the other hand, if **call**(*A*) fails then the second procedure for **not** will be tried and will succeed.

In favour of the cut, it is commonly pointed out that its use does not obscure the logical meaning of a program because, in this sense, it may simply be ignored. On the other hand, it clearly affects the computational meaning of the program, and as pointed out by Lloyd in [Ll87] may in some contexts transform a declaratively incorrect program into a correct implementation of the desired relation.

Exercise 6.9: Consider the following program defining the factorial function for the natural numbers:

    pred(0, 0).
    pred(s(X), X).
    fact(0, 1) :- !.
    fact(X, Y) :- pred(X, X1), fact(X1, Y1), times(X, Y1, Y).,

where **pred(X, Y)** means that Y is X−1 (or 0 if X is 0). Show that according to this program the query ?- **fact(0, Y)**. has two possible solutions (for Y) if ! is omitted from the first clause for **fact**.

The specification of **fact** in this exercise characterises the relation *factorial*(*x*) = *y* procedurally, but, declaratively, defines a very different relation for *x* = 0. Opponents to the use of cut generally claim that beginner programmers are encouraged to use the cut too much and that this leads to "sloppy" programming.

6.3.2.4 Arithmetic Functions and Predicates

The predicate **fact** may be defined in C-Prolog by

    fact(0, 1) :- !.
    fact(X, Y) :- X1 is X−1, fact(X1, Y1), Y is X∗Y1.

Though, perhaps, not as clear in meaning as an analogous definition in terms of the successor function and the predicate **times**, this version is more efficient. The major problem associated with the inbuilt arithmetic functions in C-Prolog is that they may be used only in combination with the built-in predicate **is**. For example, the term X−1 may not occur within **fact** above without the function '−' losing its predefined meaning. Even more problematic is the fact that **is** is analogous to the assignment expression of other languages and thus requires that its right-hand side be an arithmetical expression containing no uninstantiated variables. This means that the order in which the subgoals are solved becomes important not simply with respect to efficiency, but also with respect to the meaning of the program.

Exercise 6.10: Express the exponentiation function of Exercise 6.1 as a Prolog program using the built-in functions occurring in the definition of **fact** above.

6.3.2.5 Setof

The **setof** predicate built into C-Prolog was proposed as a useful extension to Prolog by D.H.D Warren in [Wa82]. The predicate has the form **setof**(t, H, S), where t is some term, H a Horn-clause, S a set of terms represented as a list with no duplicate elements, and the variables in t appear in H. To solve such a call of **setof**, an attempt is made to find a solution to H for each instance of t, and the set of instances of t such that H has a solution are collected in the set S. This allows the user to ask questions concerning the set of known solutions to certain goals. In [Wa82] the problems of making **setof** "backtrackable", and allowing variables to appear in H which do not also appear in t are discussed (see also [Pe83]).

6.3.2.6 Assert

Once some subgoal is solved, it may then be asserted as a new (bodiless) clause by means of the command **assert**. It thus becomes a lemma which may be used at a later stage of the computation ("proof"). This seems a reasonable and useful device, but there are problems associated with the use of **assert** statements, perhaps the most important of which concerns backtracking over them. For more discussion of these problems see [Ho84].

6.4 CONCLUSIONS

This chapter has discussed Prolog, a particular example of the application of automated theorem proving to programming. This language comes under the more general heading of "logic programming", a style of programming that is based directly upon the syntactical structures and concepts used in ("computational") logic. In particular, Prolog is based upon unification and the resolution principle.

Perhaps the major contribution of Prolog to computer science is that it has brought the paradigm of logic programming to a wide audience via the procedural interpretation of Kowalski (see Section 6.2.2). It may also be said to be a very good example of logic programming, as attested to by its popularity amongst computer scientists. Perhaps its major drawback is that (as J.A. Robinson claims in [Ro83]) to many people certain of the features of Prolog implementations have become synonymous with logic programming. He cites the standard computation rule (see Section 6.2.2.2) and the cut (see Section 6.3.2.3) as examples. This claim is furthered by the fact that most of the work done by the "logic programming community" seems to have been directed towards improving Prolog rather than developing new approaches, perhaps because new approaches have generally not had the success of Prolog.

Finally, it should also be noted that apart from extensions of Prolog to increase its expressiveness and "programming power" (see [Coh85]), there has also been some work on developing the techniques employed in Prolog for the purposes of producing an efficient complete theorem prover for first-order logic. In [St84] M. Stickel describes some ideas for extending Prolog in this sense. His major contention is that, rather than using factoring to treat general clauses, Prolog should employ a method related to D.W. Loveland's model-elimination procedure (see [Lo78]). However this requires that the *contrapositives* of each program clause (see [Lo78]) be added to the program. Other work in this area is discussed by Reed and Loveland in [RL89].

CHAPTER 7

KNUTH-BENDIX COMPLETION

7.1 INTRODUCTION

In total contrast to the previous chapter the concern here is almost entirely with the equality relation. In 1970 Donald E. Knuth and Peter B. Bendix introduced a procedure for deciding the equality of terms with respect to (special classes of) sets of equations [KB70]. Since then the number and diversity of the applications found for the procedure have been considerable (see [De83]). In this chapter the main concern is with the application of the procedure to proof by induction ("inductionless induction"). Applications to other aspects of theorem proving will also be looked at, but in much less detail. The reasons for paying special attention to inductive theorem proving are its importance within computer science (see Chapter 4) and because looking at one application will allow a more detailed study of the strengths and weaknesses of Knuth-Bendix completion when applied to areas for which it was not originally designed.

The practical experiments performed by the author were done on the REVE rewriting system generator [Le83], which includes special mechanisms for applying the induction method of Huet and Hullot [HH82]. The examples given in this chapter will be based on these experiments.

7.1.1 Motivation

By the semantics of universal quantification and the equality predicate it is sound to treat an equation as a "rewrite rule", as discussed in Chapter 4. For example, the equation $x+s(y) = s(x+y)$ may be oriented into the rule $x+s(y) \rightarrow s(x+y)$ and thus used to rewrite the term $(x+0)+s(x+y)$ to $s((x+0)+(x+y))$. In this way it is sometimes possible to prove that a certain equation is a consequence of other equations. For example, the rule above together with the rule $x+0 \rightarrow x$ may be used to prove

$$\{x+0 = x, x+s(y) = s(x+y)\} \implies (x+0) + s(x+y) = x+(x+s(y)),$$

simply by rewriting both sides of the equation of the conclusion until the identity $s(x+(x+y)) = s(x+(x+y))$ is derived.

This style of proof using equations is quite efficient, but there are two major problems with it, in general. One is that, for some given starting term, it may be possible to apply the rewrite rules indefinitely. (As a trivial example, consider the application of the rule $a \rightarrow f(a)$ to the term a: the infinite sequence $f(a), f(f(a)),...$ would be produced.) The second is that the final terms produced when application of the rules necessarily terminates (that is, when no more rules may be applied to the term produced) may depend upon the order in which the rules are applied. On the other hand, if neither of these eventualities is possible, then the rules act as a decision procedure for the equational consequences of the set of equations that are being treated as rewrite rules. This means that, apart from being able to prove all equational consequences, if two terms are not equal as a consequence of the equations then the decision procedure can prove that they are distinct. For instance, the two rules above act as a decision procedure for the equational consequences of the corresponding equations.

The two properties of concern are referred to as the termination and confluence properties of the rules (see next section). Termination of a set of rewrite rules is shown in [De85] to be undecidable in general; also, it is well known that confluence is undecidable (see [HO80]). However, under the supposition of termination (which may be proved in many cases), the Knuth-Bendix completion procedure acts as a decision procedure for confluence, and, in some cases, may also transform a set of rules that is not confluent into a logically equivalent confluent set of rules. Furthermore, it has been found that this procedure has applications to many, surprisingly diverse, problems. Of most interest here are the areas of theorem proving to which it has been applied. This chapter will concentrate on inductive theorem proving, but other areas of application will be highlighted.

The ideas regarding inductive theorem proving have generally been discussed in the framework of the development of abstract data-types (ADTs) in the literature. This is because the properties required of a set of equations for the purposes of "inductionless induction" are commonly naturally applicable to ADT specifications. For this reason the discussion here will also be directed along these lines, and many of the examples will be relevant to this subject. However, considerations of "signatures" and "typing" and other fine points of algebraic specifications will be avoided. This is reasonable because extensions of most of the ideas presented to treat a typed syntax seem to be straightforward (see [HO80], [Go80], [KM87]). (An introduction to the specification of abstract data-types may be found in [McG82] Chapter 10.) In the current context an algebraic specification will be viewed simply as a set of Horn-clauses of the following form.

Conditional Equation: A Horn-clause in which the positive literal (the head) is an equality atom is referred to as a conditional equation. If there are no conditions then the expression is called simply an *equation*.

In this chapter only equations will be treated in any detail; this will serve to simplify the discussion greatly. For the rest of this chapter the symbols '$\rightarrow$' and '$\Rightarrow$' will be stripped of their previous meanings and given new meanings.

7.2 THE COMPLETION PROCEDURE

This section will describe the main aspects of the Knuth-Bendix completion procedure, in the light of its application to proving equational consequences.

7.2.1 Termination and Confluence

As noted, the fundamental properties of concern are termination and confluence. These may be expressed in purely abstract terms as properties of arbitrary relations (see [Hu80]), but, for simplicity, are here expressed in terms of equational rewrite rules.

Rewrite Rule: A rewrite rule over a language L is a directed equation having the form $l \rightarrow r$ where l and r are terms of L and the variables occurring in r are a subset of the variables in l. A rewrite rule $l \rightarrow r$ (over L) applies to a term t of L if there is a subterm t' of t and a substitution θ such that $l\theta = t'$. The rule is applied by replacing t' by $r\theta$ in t.

Example: The rewrite rule $x + f(y) \rightarrow x + c$ applies to the term $(d + f(f(z))) * y$ to produce $(d + c) * y$, but does not apply to $w + z$; nor also to $a + c$, since it cannot be applied backwards like an equation.

Term Rewriting System (TRS): A set of rewrite rules over a language L is called a term rewriting system (TRS) over L.

If a member of a TRS R is applied to a term t_1 to produce a term t_2 then this is written $t_1 \Rightarrow_R t_2$, or simply $t_1 \Rightarrow t_2$ if R is understood from context.

Reduction: If $t_1 \Rightarrow_R ... \Rightarrow_R t_n$ (in possibly zero steps, i.e. $t_1 = t_n$, or one step, i.e. $t_1 \Rightarrow_R t_n$) then this is written $t_1 *\Rightarrow_R t_n$ (or simply $t_1 *\Rightarrow t_n$ if R is understood from context), and t_1 is said to reduce to t_n with respect to R.

Also the notation $t_1 \Downarrow t_2$ will be used (as in [Hu80]) to signify that there is some term t such that $t_1 *\Rightarrow t$ and $t_2 *\Rightarrow t$.

Irreducible Term: If no member of R applies to a term t then t is said to be irreducible with respect to R. In other words, there is no t' such that $t \Rightarrow t'$; but note that $t *\Rightarrow t$, even if t is irreducible.

Normal Form: If $t_1 *\Rightarrow_R t_n$ and t_n is irreducible (with respect to R) then t_n is said to be a normal form of t_1 (w.r.t. R). The notation $t!$ will denote any normal form of the term t.

Termination: A TRS R is said to be terminating (or Noetherian) if there is no infinite sequence of terms $t_1, t_2, t_3,...$ of L such that

$$t_1 \Rightarrow_R t_2 \Rightarrow_R t_3 \Rightarrow_R ....$$

Example: The one-rule TRS $\{x + y \to y + x\}$ is not terminating, since the term $a + b$ has the following infinite sequence of reductions:

$$a + b, b + a, a + b, ...$$

The TRS $\{a \to b, b \to a\}$ is also non-terminating since $a \Rightarrow b \Rightarrow a$ ..., though each of the two rules, by itself, constitutes a terminating system.

Exercise 7.1: Show, by informal reasoning, that the system $\{x + 0 \to 0 + x\}$ is non-terminating, but that the system $\{s(x) + 0 \to 0 + s(x)\}$ is terminating.

Confluence: A TRS is said to be confluent if when

$$t_1 \ast \Rightarrow t_2 \text{ and } t_1 \ast \Rightarrow t_3$$

there is a term t_4 such that

$$t_2 \ast \Rightarrow t_4 \text{ and } t_3 \ast \Rightarrow t_4,$$

that is, $t_2 \Downarrow t_3$.

Example: Though not terminating, both of the TRS of the previous example are confluent. The following TRS is also non-terminating but confluent:

$$\{a \to b, a \to c, c \to a\},$$

since a, b and c all have the single normal form b, though a and c also have an infinite reduction sequence: $a \Rightarrow c \Rightarrow a$ ...

Exercise 7.2: Show that the (terminating) one-rule system $\{f(g(f(x))) \to g(x)\}$ is not confluent, by finding a term that has two distinct normal forms.

It is worth noting that, technically, it is in fact the relation $\Rightarrow_R$ that is defined in terms of R that should be said to be terminating, confluent, and so on, and not R itself (see [Hu80]). This relates Noetherian TRS to other Noetherian (and well-founded) relations to be discussed below.

Quite clearly, as a consequence of the confluence of a TRS R every term must have at most one normal form with respect to R. Some, or all, of the terms may have no normal form, as in the examples just given. The importance of the confluence of a TRS lies, of course, in its relationship to equational reasoning, and the next step is to determine this relationship.

The general result for any set of rewrite rules is the following. Let the notation $t \Leftrightarrow t'$ denote the fact that either t rewrites in one step to t' or vice-versa, and then let the notation $t \ast \Leftrightarrow t'$ denote a (possibly empty) sequence of such rewrites:

$$t \Leftrightarrow t_1 \Leftrightarrow ... \Leftrightarrow t_n \Leftrightarrow t'.$$

Now if the set of equations E is re-expressed as the set of rules R, then for any equation $t = t'$ the equivalence $E \models t = t'$ iff $t \ast \Leftrightarrow_R t'$ holds (see [HO80]).

Example: The equation $a = e$ is a consequence of the rules $\{a \to b, c \to b, c \to d, d \to e\}$, as the following sequence of rewrites shows:

$$a \Rightarrow b \Leftarrow c \Rightarrow d \Rightarrow e,$$

where $t \Leftarrow t'$ means the same as $t' \Rightarrow t$. This proof may be read as: a and c rewrite to b, and c also rewrites to e, and hence a and e must be equal.

This result assures the completeness of rewriting with a very general strategy for the application of the rules, but a much more restrictive strategy is desirable. Equational reasoning by rewriting would be much more efficient if it could be assured that $t \Downarrow t'$ whenever $t = t'$; in other words, if t and t' are equal then they may always be rewritten to the same term t''. This does not hold for the rules of the previous example since a and e do not rewrite to the same term though they are equal. For this property to hold the rules must be confluent, as is expressed in the following result: if a set of equations may be converted into a confluent set of rewrite rules, then any two terms equal as a consequence of the given equations must have the same normal form with respect to R ([KB70], [HO80]).

In outline, this result follows from the following considerations. As noted, if a set of equations E is re-expressed as a set of rewrite rules R, then an equation $t = t'$ is a consequence of E iff $t *\Leftrightarrow_R t'$. Thus to achieve the desired result it is sufficient to show that if t has the normal form p and $t *\Leftrightarrow_R t'$, then t' must also have the normal form p. This may be shown by induction on the length of the sequence of rewrites, as expressed in the following exercise.

Exercise 7.3: Show that for a confluent set of rules R, if $s \Leftrightarrow_R s'$ (a one-step reduction) and s has normal form q, then s' must have normal form q. Deduce that if $t \Leftrightarrow ... \Leftrightarrow t'$ in a sequence of $n + 1$ steps, and t has normal form p, then t' must have normal form p.

Naturally, if t rewrites to t' in 0 steps then they are identical and hence the result holds trivially in this case. Hence the result holds in general. Note, in particular, that it holds without the supposition of termination; this property is required for the next important result below.

The only problem that remains is whether a given set of equations may be converted into a confluent set of rewrite rules. It is clear that if the equations of the set are such that the variables occurring in one side of each equation are a subset of the variables occurring in the other side, then the equations may all be converted into rewrite rules. However, if an equation in the set equates two terms t_1 and t_2 each of which contains variables not occurring in the other, then it is necessary to treat this equation as two rewrite rules by introducing a new function symbol f (say) and adding the rules $t_1 \rightarrow f(x_1,..., x_n)$ and $t_2 \rightarrow f(x_1,..., x_n)$, where $x_1,..., x_n$ are the variables occurring in both terms.

Example: The equation $x + z = g(y, z)$ may be re-expressed as the pair of rewrite rules $x + z \rightarrow f(z)$ and $g(y, z) \rightarrow f(z)$.

This technique allows any set of equations E to be converted into a set of rewrite rules R such that for all terms, t and t', in the language of E, the equivalence $E \models t = t'$ iff $t *\Leftrightarrow t'$ holds (see [HO80]). Counter to this the confluence of a set of rewrite rules is undecidable in general [HO80]; but under the condition that the

TRS is terminating, confluence is decidable via the notion of local confluence.

Local Confluence: A TRS R is said to be locally confluent if whenever

$$t_1 \Rightarrow_R t_2 \text{ and } t_1 \Rightarrow_R t_3$$

there is a term t_4 such that

$$t_2 \;^*\!\!\Rightarrow_R t_4 \text{ and } t_3 \;^*\!\!\Rightarrow_R t_4.$$

The important relationship between confluence and local confluence is the following: if R is a terminating TRS then

$$R \text{ is confluent} \quad \text{iff} \quad R \text{ is locally confluent.}$$

A proof of this theorem, which is commonly referred to as Newman's lemma, may be found in [Hu80]. That local confluence does not ensure confluence in general is illustrated in the following example (to be found in [Hu80]).

Example: The non-terminating system $\{a \to b, b \to a, a \to c, b \to d\}$ is locally confluent but not confluent. For instance, $a \Rightarrow b$ and $a \Rightarrow c$, and there is a term, c, such that $a \;^*\!\!\Rightarrow c$ and $b \;^*\!\!\Rightarrow c$, but $a \Rightarrow c$ and $a \Rightarrow b \Rightarrow d$ (i.e. $a \;^*\!\!\Rightarrow d$), though c and d do not reduce to some common term.

The importance of the equivalence of the two forms of confluence for terminating systems is that there is a decision procedure for determining whether a TRS (with a finite number of rules) is locally confluent [KB70]. This algorithm is based upon the idea of critical pairs.

Critical Pair: Let $l \to r$ and $l' \to r'$ be two rewrite rules of a TRS R. Then l *overlaps* l' if there is a non-variable subterm t of l', such that l and t have mgu θ. In this case a critical pair is formed as follows: $t\theta$ is replaced by $r\theta$ in $l'\theta$ to produce the term l'', and then the pair l'' and $r'\theta$ is a critical pair, denoted $<l'', r'\theta>$, of the two rewrite rules.

In other words, if l overlaps l' then both the rules $l \to r$ and $l' \to r'$ must apply to the term $l'\theta$. The first will produce l'' while the second will produce $r'\theta$ (thus giving $l'\theta \Rightarrow_R l''$ and $l'\theta \Rightarrow_R r'\theta$), and $<l'', r'\theta>$ is said to be a critical pair.

Example: The rule $x + c \to c$ overlaps the rule $(a + y) + z \to y + z$ at two separate subterms, $(a + y)$ and $(a + y) + z$, to give rise to the two critical pairs $<c + z, c + z>$ and $<c, y + c>$. The completion procedure forms the first critical pair by unifying $x + c$ with $a + y$ to produce the instance $(a + c) + z \to c + z$ of the second rule, and then reducing the left-hand side of this new rule to $c + z$ by applying the first rule. It derives the second pair in a similar manner, by unifying $x + c$ with $(a + y) + z$ to produce the instance $(a + y) + c \to y + c$ of the second rule, and then reducing the left-hand side of this rule to c.

Exercise 7.4: Show that there is a critical pair between the rule $f(g(f(x))) \to g(x)$ and (an alphabetic variant of) itself.

If R is finite there can be only finitely many critical pairs, and hence the following theorem given by Huet in [Hu80], based on [KB70], gives rise to a decision procedure for the local confluence of R:

R is locally confluent iff $p \Downarrow q$ for every critical pair $<p, q>$ of R.

This means that if both elements of each critical pair can be reduced to the same term by the rules of the TRS then the TRS is locally confluent. It should be clear that the left to right direction of this theorem is trivial.

Examples:
1. The TRS $\{0 + x \rightarrow x, x + s(y) \rightarrow s(x + y)\}$ is locally confluent since the only critical pair is $<s(y), s(0 + y)>$ and $s(0 + y)$ reduces to $s(y)$ via the first rule of the TRS. The TRS is also terminating and hence is confluent.

2. $\{f(g(x, a)) \rightarrow x, g(a, y) \rightarrow h(y)\}$, although terminating, is not locally confluent, since the critical pair is $<f(h(a)), a>$. It is thus not confluent.

Exercise 7.5: Using the above result, show that the non-terminating system $\{a \rightarrow b, a \rightarrow c, c \rightarrow a\}$ is locally confluent.

Canonical: A TRS is said to be canonical if it is both terminating and locally confluent.

Note that if a TRS is canonical then every term has exactly one normal form. Knuth and Bendix called a canonical TRS "complete", but it is preferable not to use this term because it has so many different meanings in logic.

Although termination and local confluence together provide sufficient conditions for confluence, termination is clearly not necessary (that is, it is stronger than is required). In [Hu80] G. Huet shows that, in particular, if the variables occurring in each rule occur only once in the left-hand side of the rule (called a left-linear rule), and if there are no critical pairs between the rules then the TRS is confluent even if it is non-terminating. This result applies, in particular, to equations that constitute "primitive-recursive definitions" of functions (see [Pe67]); cf. the three "specifications" in Section 7.3.2.

7.2.2 Extension to a Canonical Set

In the preceding subsection it has been indicated that it is decidable whether a terminating rewriting system is confluent, and hence canonical; suppose, however, that a given TRS is not canonical. The question arises: is it possible to transform a set of rewrite rules into a logically equivalent but canonical (and thus confluent) set of rules?

In fact, the "completion procedure" of Knuth and Bendix, which provides a partial solution to this problem, follows directly from the above discussion. The idea is that the initial set of equations is (if possible) converted into a terminating set of rules such that the left- and right-hand sides of each rule are irreducible with respect to the rest of the rules. Then, if a critical pair $<p, q>$ is found such that $p! \neq q!$ (recall $p!$ denotes a normal form of p), either the rule $p! \rightarrow q!$ or the rule

$q! \rightarrow p!$ is added to the system and a check made that the new TRS is terminating. Once a rule is added in this way the left- and right-hand sides of other rules may become reducible with respect to the new TRS (ignoring the application of a rule to the left-hand side of itself). If so, any rule whose left- or right-hand side may be reduced by the other rules is so reduced, and the pair of normal forms produced are added as a new rewrite rule with a subsequent test, once again, for termination. This process of finding and treating critical pairs continues until no more are left such that their normal forms differ. For a more precise description of a very similar completion procedure the reader is referred to [HO80].

Adding a critical pair to the set of equations does not extend the equational theory because each such pair must be a logical consequence of the initial equations (as with the application of the paramodulation rule, which is very similar). Thus, apart from the termination problem, which will be further discussed below, the only other question is whether the procedure described above will ever halt with a canonical set. Although, in general, it will not do so, in some cases it may. Obviously, this is possible only in those cases where the equality of terms with respect to the initial equations is decidable. The most commonly cited example is that described originally by Knuth and Bendix themselves in [KB70], wherein the three equational axioms for a group are converted into a canonical TRS consisting of ten rules. (See [KB70] or [HO80] for this set.) In the "non-confluent" second example near the end of Section 7.2.1, if the critical pair is added as the rewrite rule $f(h(a)) \rightarrow a$, then the new set is both terminating and locally confluent.

It has also been proved by G. Huet [Hu81] that, not too surprisingly, even in the case where the procedure described above does not terminate, if two terms are equal as a consequence of the initial equations then after a finite number of "steps" enough rules will be generated to reduce the terms to the same normal form. Of course, sometimes rules will be generated for which orientation (that is, expression as rewrite rules) is impossible because the termination property of the TRS will automatically be lost; on these occasions the implemented procedure will usually abort. It will also often happen that a derived equation cannot be oriented simply because there is no known (or implemented) method to prove that the TRS will terminate; in this case the system may either abort or continue regardless (under the assumption that the rewriting system does terminate).

As an important aside, note that a characterisation of the completion process very different from those of Knuth and Bendix and of Huet has recently been proposed by, in particular, L. Bachmair [Ba87]. Rather than express the completion process as a procedure, he represents each step of the process as the application of an inference rule. In this way he shows that it is possible to reason about completion procedures and their soundness at a more abstract and general level, without worrying about the nuances of any particular implementation. This means that a single set of results captures a more general class of implementations.

7.2.3 Termination of a Term Rewriting System

There have been many tests proposed for determining whether a TRS terminates, but, although the subject is important, it does not seem in keeping with the scope of this book to go into detail about them. In any case, two very extensive reviews of termination tests have already been given by Huet and Oppen in [HO80] and more recently by N. Dershowitz in [De85]. However it seems worthwhile to cite the theorem of Manna and Ness [MN70] which gives sufficient and necessary conditions for a TRS to be terminating, and thus illustrates the basic principles.

A relation > on a set S is said to be a **partial ordering** of S if it is
- *irreflexive*: $s > s$ for no $s \in S$, and
- *transitive*: $s_1 > s_2$ and $s_2 > s_3$ implies $s_1 > s_3$ for all $s_1, s_2, s_3 \in S$

(> is a *total ordering* if also $s > s'$ or $s' > s$ for all $s, s' \in S$ with $s \neq s'$).

A partial ordering > of a set S is said to be **well-founded** if there is no infinite sequence of elements $s_1, s_2, s_3,...$ of S such that $s_1 > s_2 > s_3 > ....$ (Thus a well-founded relation is a transitive Noetherian relation, since Noetherian relations must be irreflexive.)

Let > be a partial ordering of the ground terms of a language L; then > is said to be **monotonic** on the ground terms of L if for all such terms t_1 and t_2

$$t_1 > t_2 \text{ implies } f(t, t_1, t') > f(t, t_2, t'),$$

where $f \in L$ and t and t' are sequences of ground terms of L.

Theorem (Manna and Ness [MN70]): A TRS R over a language L is terminating iff there is a monotonic well-founded ordering > on the set of ground terms of L such that for each rule $l \rightarrow r$ of R, $l\phi > r\phi$ for every substitution ϕ such that $l\phi$ and $r\phi$ are ground terms of L.

A difficulty with the practical application of this theorem is the need to show that the ordering holds for all ground instances. Fortunately, in some cases the ordering may be "lifted" to non-ground terms ([De85], [HO80]). In other words, an ordering >> on terms with variables may be constructed such that $t >> t'$ implies $t\phi > t'\phi$ for every substitution ϕ such that $l\phi$ and $r\phi$ are ground. For instance, if the variables of a term t' are a proper subset of those in a term t, then clearly for any well-founded ordering on ground terms it must be the case that $t\phi > t'\phi$; thus >> may be defined so that $t >> t'$.

Note also that, in the theorem, the associated meanings of the function symbols are irrelevant: the orderings are purely "syntactic" in nature. This contrasts with the "semantic" orderings used in the definition principle of Boyer and Moore (see the next chapter). On the other hand, it sometimes simplifies matters in the construction of a syntactic ordering if the problem is re-expressed in terms of a semantic ordering. For this purpose a function f is constructed that maps the ground terms into some set of values, say the natural numbers $\mathbb{N}$, with a known well-founded ordering, say $>_\mathbb{N}$. It is then checked that this ordering preserves the monotonicity condition, and that for each rewrite rule $l \rightarrow r$ in the system, $f(l\phi) >_\mathbb{N} f(r\phi)$ for all substitutions ϕ such that $l\phi$ and $r\phi$ are ground. This process is illustrated in the following example taken from [De85].

Example: An example of a terminating set of rules that is particularly relevant in the current context is the set of rules for transforming (propositional) formulae into conjunctive normal form, given in Chapter 3. These may be expressed in terms of equational rewrite rules as follows:

$$\sim\sim x \rightarrow x, \quad \sim(x \mid y) \rightarrow \sim x \And \sim y, \quad \sim(x \And y) \rightarrow \sim x \mid \sim y$$
$$x \mid (y \And z) \rightarrow (x \mid y) \And (x \mid z), \quad (y \And z) \mid x \rightarrow (y \mid x) \And (z \mid x).$$

Previously, these rules were simply assumed to terminate for all input formulae, but now they may be proved to do so. Consider the following function "| |" which maps every "propositional formula" into a numeric value:

$$|\sim x| = 2^{|x|}, \quad |x \mid y| = |x| * |y|, \quad |x \And y| = |x| + |y| + 1, \quad |a| = 2,$$

where a is a constant. It is clear that $|x| >_N |y|$ implies $|\sim x| >_N |\sim y|$, and similarly for the other connectives, thus ensuring that monotonicity is preserved. It is also not difficult to show that the following orderings on the natural numbers are satisfied for any $m, n, p, q \geq 2$:

$$2^{(2^n)} >_N n, \quad 2^{m*n} >_N 2^m + 2^n + 1, \quad 2^{m+n+1} >_N 2^m * 2^n,$$
$$m * (p + q + 1) >_N (m * p) + (m * q) + 1,$$
$$(p + q + 1) * m >_N (p * m) + (q * m) + 1.$$

Each of the rewrite rules above "maps into" one of the inequalities, and thus the termination of the rules is proven.

Exercise 7.6: Show that the reverse application of each of the rules of the previous example, apart from the first rule, will also always terminate.

7.2.4 Extensions of the Completion Procedure

Many proposals have been made to extend the procedure described above to treat more general classes of equations. Particular emphasis has been placed on treating equations that describe the commutativity and/or the associativity of functions, and also conditional equations.

Commutative functions are problematic because it is not possible to orient an equation such as $x + y = y + x$ as a rule without automatically losing the termination property. The need for special treatment for associative functions is due to their common occurrence (in important theories) and the fact that when combined with some sets of rules a rule expressing the associativity of some function will lead to the generation of an infinite set of critical pairs no matter in which direction the equation is oriented (see the example in [PS81]). To account for such functions, the concept of "canonical" is extended to "canonical modulo associativity and/or commutativity". The propositional sequent system of Chapter 3, when the rules are applied backwards, is an example of a rewriting system that is canonical modulo associativity and commutativity. In other words, every propositional sequent may be decomposed in a finite time into a set of "atomic sequents" that are unique apart from the order in which the atoms are written.

More generally, extensions of the procedure have been proposed to treat either special classes of equations, or special types of rules with any equations. In both approaches the equations are separated into sets of rules and unoriented equations; these then comprise what is generally referred to as "equational TRS". Peterson and Stickel in [PS81] follow the first approach and use the mechanism of unification with respect to theories, as in Plotkin [Pl72], where two terms are unified under the supposition that some of the functions have special properties (see also [HO80] and [Si86]), and they require that there be a "finite and complete unification algorithm" for the theories of interest. Huet in [Hu80], on the other hand, follows the second approach and requires that each rule be left-linear. Both of these approaches have been unified by J.-P. Jouannaud, as described in [JK84], and incorporated into the REVEUR3 rewriting system (see [KK84]). A major problem associated with each of these approaches is showing that the combined system satisfies new termination criteria (see [Hu80] and [De85]), but in [JK83] conditions are given under which termination is not required (see also [Ba87]).

It seems that extending the procedure to deal with conditional equations has been found problematic and no particular approaches have been found to be most appropriate. The papers [ZR85] and [Ga87] discuss the problems and describe possible approaches to the solution.

7.3 INDUCTIVE THEOREM PROVING

It is now possible to turn to the main discussion, that is, proofs of inductive theorems via Knuth-Bendix completion, and, more generally, via consistency checks. (Such an approach to proof by induction was originally proposed by D.R. Musser in [Mu80].) For the purpose of illustration and motivation for the ideas in this section the following three examples of "algebraic specifications" will be used:

SPEC1 $\quad \sim T = F$ $\qquad\qquad$ SPEC2 $\quad x + 0 = x$

$\qquad\qquad \sim F = T$ $\qquad\qquad\qquad\qquad\qquad x + s(y) = s(x + y)$

$\qquad\qquad x \,\&\, F = F$

$\qquad\qquad x \,\&\, T = x$

SPEC3 $\quad reverse(nil) = nil$

$\qquad\qquad reverse(make(x)) = make(x)$

$\qquad\qquad reverse(append(x, y)) = append(reverse(y), reverse(x)).$

In the intended models of these specifications, SPEC1 is concerned with Boolean valued functions, SPEC2 with addition on **N**, and SPEC3 with the manipulation of lists (*make* denoting a function that converts an object into a one-element list).

7.3.1 Proof by Induction

First, the idea of an inductive theorem will be formalised for equations.

Axiom of Induction: Let E be a set of equations and let $t = t'$ be a particular equation of the same language. Then $t = t'$ is an inductive theorem of E if every ground ("Herbrand") instance of $t = t'$ is a theorem of E.

Examples:

1. Every ground instance of the equation $0 + x = x$ is a theorem of SPEC2.

2. Every ground instance of the equation $reverse(reverse(x)) = x$ is a theorem of SPEC3.

In neither of these examples is the inductive theorem also a theorem. Even if the domain of interpretation is taken to be **N** for SPEC2 it is not necessarily the case that $0 + x = x$ is valid in the interpretation. To see this, consider the following interpretation of the axioms for $\{0, s, +\}$ in SPEC2:

$$\{D = \mathbf{N}, 0 \to 0, s \to \text{identity function}, + \to --\},$$

where the "identity function" I (say) is defined by $I(x) = x$, and '--' is defined by

$$x -- y = \begin{cases} 0 & \text{if } y > x \\ x - y & \text{otherwise,} \end{cases}$$

where '$-$' and '$>$' have their standard meanings. This is a model, since both of the equations have the value **T** under the chosen interpretation of the symbols, but it is clear that $0 + x = x$ is not *true* in this model.

The very general definition of inductive theorem above is, however, not meaningful for all sets of equations. Consider, for example, the set of axioms for groups given in Chapter 1. The "inductive model" of these axioms turns out to be a trivial interpretation with a domain of one element (corresponding to the value assigned to e). The reason for this is that according to the given axioms every ground term is equal to e. In particular, $-e = e$ and $e * e = e$. Thus, while the ideas to be presented in this section may be applied to the equations of a group (especially given that these axioms may be transformed into a canonical rewriting system), the set of inductive consequences of these axioms is uninteresting.

The motivation behind this "axiom of induction" is the fact that computations performed in most programming languages are on ground objects (as opposed to objects containing variables, as in languages such as Prolog). Thus, in the context of algebraic specification the above definition of inductive theorem is meaningful because such specifications are intended to capture "computational structures", and these structures (or "data-types") may be represented by ground terms. For example, a programmer who writes a program to reverse a list will not be concerned with the properties of this definition of *reverse* when acting on arbitrary objects in arbitrary interpretations, but only with how it acts on lists—and these may be represented by the ground terms built from, say, the functions *nil* and *cons* (as in LISP) or the functions *nil*, *make* and *append* as in the definition of *reverse* above. In general, "data-types" such as the natural numbers and lists may be represented by the ground terms of some language.

A difficulty with the general notion of inductive theorem given above is that, in general, an infinite number of theorems would have to be proved. To avoid this it is necessary to derive rules such as "structural" and "Noetherian" induction on the ground terms. These derived inference rules depend upon the structure of the ground terms. For example, the principle of structural induction relies upon each ground term being equivalent to a term that may be constructed from a set of "constructor functions", while the more powerful rule of Noetherian induction, which is perhaps the most powerful rule for induction known, relies on there being a specified well-founded ordering on the ground terms. To illustrate the relationship between the statement of induction above and more common formulations, consider the statement of the principle of (structural) induction over the natural numbers, where '0', '1' and '+' have their standard meanings (cf. Chapter 4):

$$\frac{\alpha(0) \text{ and } \forall x(\alpha(x) \to \alpha(x+1))}{\forall x \alpha(x)}$$

In other words, if the conjecture is a theorem for $x = 0$ and under the assumption that it is true for x it may be proved to be true for the successor of x, then it is true for all x. By means of this principle, it is easily proved that $0 + x = x$ is an inductive theorem of the axioms of SPEC2 above, under the supposition that the constant 0 is associated with 0 and $s(x)$ with $x+1$. This ensures that every ground instance of the equation $0 + x = x$ is a theorem: it proves that for every x of the form $s^n(0)$, $0 + x = x$ is a consequence of the axioms of SPEC2, and it is the case that every ground term is equal to $s^n(0)$ for some n (corresponding to the fact that in the standard interpretation every expression involving '+' and elements of N is equal to some (unique) element of N). An exactly analogous idea may be applied to the treatment of the *reverse* example (see also [Go80]).

To provide an intuitive understanding of how Knuth-Bendix completion may be applied to inductive proofs an example will first be given. In [La80] (and [La81]) D. Lankford introduced the name "inductionless induction" for this type of proof.

Example: Here is a proof using the Knuth-Bendix completion procedure that the equation *reverse(reverse(x))* = x is an inductive theorem of the equation set SPEC3.

Orient initial equations:

Rule 1: *reverse(nil)* $\to$ *nil*,
Rule 2: *reverse(make(x))* $\to$ *make(x)*,
Rule 3: *reverse(append(x, y))* $\to$ *append(reverse(y), reverse(x))*.

These are terminating and easily seen to be locally confluent (since there are no critical pairs). Orient conjecture into

Rule 4: *reverse(reverse(x))* $\to x$.

There is one critical pair between rule 4 and each of the rules 1, 2 and 3. These are respectively

<reverse(nil), nil>,
<reverse(make(x)), make(x)>, and
<reverse(append(reverse(y), reverse(x))), append(x, y)>.

It is easily seen that for the first two critical pairs derived the normal forms of their elements with respect to the TRS (1-4) are the same. The third pair also has this property:

- The application of rule 3 to *reverse(append(reverse(y), reverse(x)))* produces *append(reverse(reverse(y)), reverse(reverse(x)))*.
- Applying rule 4 to *reverse(reverse(y))* and also to *reverse(reverse(x))* gives respectively, y and x.
- Thus, if R denotes the set of rules 1-4,

$$reverse(append(reverse(y), reverse(x))) \Rightarrow_R append(x, y),$$

and hence, *reverse(append(reverse(y), reverse(x)))!* = *append(x, y)!*.

There are also two critical pairs between rule 4 and itself, namely

$<x, x>$ and *<reverse(x), reverse(x)>*,

but these are trivial.

Intuitively, the computation of the first three critical pairs in this example and their reductions to normal form correspond to a standard proof by induction (in fact, the analogy is surprising). The fourth and fifth critical pairs are superfluous to the inductive proof but are required in order to show that R is confluent.

Following this example two questions arise:

- What are the conditions under which confluence tests are acceptable as inductive proofs?
- Are there inductive theorems that can be proved by standard induction methods that cannot be proved by confluence tests (or vice-versa)?

These questions will be discussed in the next two subsections. In Section 7.3.2 a very general and abstract view is taken where "inductionless induction" is expressed in terms of consistency tests, giving very general conditions under which it may be applied. In Section 7.3.3 the main limitations of the completion-based approach are discussed and a more classical interpretation is given which relates the underlying mechanism applied by the Knuth-Bendix procedure to the standard approach to proof by induction.

7.3.2 Underlying Theory

From a very general viewpoint "inductionless induction" may be justified according to a very simple underlying principle: an equation e is an inductive theorem (in the sense defined above) of a set of equations E iff for all ground equations $t = t'$,

$$E \cup \{e\} \models t = t' \quad \text{implies} \quad E \models t = t'.$$

In other words, e is an inductive theorem of E iff $E \cup \{e\}$ does not equate more ground terms than E. This is quite clear, for if $E \cup \{e\}$ does equate more ground terms than E then e must extend the ground consequences of E and hence cannot be an inductive theorem, while, for the converse, if e is not an inductive theorem then there is some ground instance of e that does not follow from E but which obviously does follow from $E \cup \{e\}$.

To express the fact that the set of equations $E \cup \{e\}$ does not equate more ground terms than the set E, it is generally said that $E \cup \{e\}$ is a *conservative extension* of E (e.g. [Pa89a]). It is also said that $E \cup \{e\}$ is "consistent" (e.g. [JK85], [KM87]). At first sight it may seem that this use of the term consistent is different from its use previously in this book, but the two are, in fact, the same, as will be shown presently. Because of the relationship to consistency, Kapur and Musser referred to the whole approach of inductionless induction, when considered from an abstract view, as "proof by consistency". However, in using this term they applied it to a more general conceptualisation of inductive theorem than that used in earlier work on the subject. While the earlier work was principally concerned with what is referred to as the "initial model" of a specification, Kapur and Musser were concerned with what is referred to as the "final model". Informally expressed, a conjecture is *true* in the initial model if it follows from the specification, while it is *true* in the final model if its negation does not follow from the specification. To express the relationship between inductionless induction and "proof by consistency" and to compare the two views (initial and final models) the concept of a *specification system* [KM87] will be used.

Specification System: A specification system is a triple (L,C,E), where L is a set of function symbols, C is a subset of the ground terms of L, and E is a set of equations between terms of L.

The set C is to be viewed as a set of terms that are required to be distinct in any interpretation. It will usually be determined by specifying "constructors" for the objects of interest (e.g. '0' and 's' for the natural numbers). The symbols c and d will be used to denote elements of C; these should not be confused with the constant symbols.

The set of inequalities (i.e. negated equality atoms) that express the fact that the elements of C are distinct will be denoted by C*. The set E ∪ C* is satisfiable iff c = d is not a consequence of E whenever ¬c = d is in C* (as follows from a result in Chapter 24 of [BJ89]). With regard to algebraic specifications, it is useful to introduce a notion of consistency [KM87] which is based upon this principle of satisfiability; for this purpose, it is assumed that a complete proof system for equational reasoning is given.

Consistency: A specification system (L,C,E) is said to be consistent if there is no distinct pair of terms c and d in C such that c = d is a theorem of E; otherwise it is said to be *inconsistent*.

Based upon this notion of consistency, 'proof by consistency' reduces to addressing the following question: under what conditions on a specification system (L,C,E) does the equivalence

$t = t'$ is an inductive theorem of E   iff   (L,C,E ∪ {$t = t'$}) is consistent

hold for any equation $t = t'$? The required conditions correspond to a form of "completeness" for algebraic specifications; the specification is complete in the sense that the required "data-type" (such as 'natural numbers' or 'lists') is completely characterised by the axioms. An example of such a completeness condition is the *sufficient completeness* of Guttag and Horning [GH78], which stipulates that every ground term must be equal to a ground term from some "primitive set" as a consequence of the equations of the specification. In the current context a condition similar to sufficient completeness is required that takes C as the primitive set. Naturally, this condition depends upon which characterisation of inductive theorem is assumed. In the following two subsections two very different conditions will be discussed, the first, *containment*, designed for reasoning about the initial model, and the second, *unambiguity*, designed for reasoning about the final model.

7.3.2.1 Containment

For the initial model a characterisation of completeness closely related to the principle of sufficient completeness is generally assumed as the basis for inductionless induction (e.g. [De85]). In its most general form this may be expressed as follows.

Containment: If every ground term in the language of the specification system (L,C,E) is equal to at least one ground term in C with respect to E then the system is said to be contained ("in C").

Examples: The system $(\{a, b\}, \{a, b\}, \{a = b\})$ is an example of a system that is contained but not consistent, while the system $(\{a, b, c\}, \{b, c\}, \{\})$, for example, is consistent, but not contained.

Convergence: If a specification system (L,C,E) is both contained and consistent then it will be said to be convergent ("on C").

In other words, if (L,C,E) is convergent then C contains a single element from each equivalence class generated by E on the ground terms of L (i.e. each ground term of L is equal (w.r.t. E) to a unique element of C). Straightforward consequences of this are that for any given L and E there always exists a C such that (L,C,E) is convergent, and that C will be unique iff E is empty. Convergence and non-uniqueness are illustrated with the very simple systems

$$(\{a, b, c\}, \{a, c\}, \{a = b\}) \text{ and } (\{a, b, c\}, \{b, c\}, \{a = b\}),$$

both of which are convergent. Sufficient completeness is, however, undecidable [KN87], and it follows that containment is also; on the other hand, decidability is assured under some quite weak conditions (see [KN87]).

The motivation for these definitions will now be clarified with respect to the specifications above. In the case of SPEC1 the specification system $(\{T,F,\sim,\&\}, \{T,F\}, \text{SPEC1})$ is convergent, and thus every ground term of SPEC1 is equal to either T or F, and $T = F$ is not a consequence of the equations. For SPEC2, the system $(\{0,s,+\}, \{0,s(0),s(s(0)),...\}, \text{SPEC2})$ is convergent, which means that every ground term is equal to a unique element of the form $s(...(s(0))...)$, as would be hoped. Similarly, for SPEC3, if C is taken to be the set of all ground terms involving only the symbols *nil, make* and *append* then the corresponding system is convergent.

The condition of containment is sufficient for proof by induction to be reduced to proof by consistency, as is expressed in the following exercise:

Exercise 7.7: Show that if (L,C,E) is contained and consistent, and t_1 and t_2 are terms of L, then

$$t_1 = t_2 \text{ is an inductive theorem of } E \quad \text{iff} \quad (L,C,E \cup \{t_1 = t_2\}) \text{ is consistent.}$$

As in Dershowitz's formulation in [De83], this principle can be expressed directly in terms of canonical rewriting systems by taking E to be a canonical set of rewrite rules and C to be the corresponding normal forms of the ground terms of L.

Example: If R is the TRS $\{x + 0 \to 0, s(x) + y \to s(x + y)\}$ for the corresponding equations E, then R is canonical and hence the specification system $(\{0,s,+\}, \text{irr}g_R(\{0,s,+\}), E)$ must be convergent (where $\text{irr}g_R(L)$ denotes the set of irreducible ground terms of the language L). Note, however, that $\text{irr}g_R(\{0,s,+\})$ is not just the set $\{0, s(0),...\}$ since, for instance, the term $0 + s(0)$ is irreducible.

Now the main theorem may be derived, connecting the Knuth-Bendix completion procedure to proof by induction. In Dershowitz's formulation this is as follows: with the proviso that the procedure does not abort with an unorientable equation, if the completion procedure is run with a canonical set of rules R together with a rule $t \rightarrow t'$, then $t = t'$ is an inductive theorem of the equations from which R was derived iff under the given ordering no rule is produced during the completion process whose left-hand side has a ground instance irreducible with respect to R.

This is not too difficult to prove using the theorem of the previous exercise. Letting G denote the set of irreducible ground terms with respect to R, suppose first that the completion procedure terminates with a canonical set R' and show that the specification system (L,G,R') is consistent (and thus $t = t'$ is an inductive theorem of R) iff no member of G is reducible with respect to R'. Then extend the reasoning to the case where the procedure does not necessarily terminate with a canonical set (but does not abort); see [De83].

This theorem indicates that what is required is a mechanism on top of the Knuth-Bendix procedure which is able to test whether a term has an irreducible ground instance. This, in fact, turns out to be a decidable property. Jouannaud and Kounalis originally showed this for left-linear systems in [JK85], where they introduced the concept of "quasi-reducibility" (later referred to as "inductive reducibility").

Inductive Reducibility: A term t is said to be inductively (or quasi-) reducible by a set of rules R if every ground instance of t is reducible by R.

Example: With respect to the canonical TRS $\{s(s(0)) \rightarrow 0\}$, corresponding to an axiom for modulo 2 arithmetic, the term $s(s(x))$ is inductively reducible while the term $s(x)$ is not (for it has the irreducible instance $s(0)$).

While inductive reducibility has been shown by various people (proposing different tests) to be decidable (see [KN87]), these tests are usually complex (both conceptually and computationally), and much simpler tests have been devised based on a "principle of definition" for functions, originally proposed by Huet and Hullot in [HH82] (cf. the definition principle of Boyer and Moore in the next chapter). This principle may be expressed in the following way.

Well-Defined Function: If R is a canonical TRS, an n-ary ($n \geq 0$) function symbol f is said to be (or, more accurately, to name) a well-defined function if every ground term of the form $f(t_1,..., t_n)$ is reducible by R.

Examples: Suppose that the equations of SPEC2 are oriented as the set of rules $\{x + 0 \rightarrow x, x + s(y) \rightarrow s(x + y)\}$; then this set of rules is canonical and every ground instance of $x + y$ is reducible by it. Thus '+' is a well-defined function according to these rules. Similar results hold for '~', '&' and '*reverse*' in SPEC1 and SPEC3.

Clearly, an n-ary function f is well-defined if $f(x_1,..., x_n)$ is quasi-reducible, and thus well-definedness is decidable. However, this concept gives rise to simpler algorithms. For this purpose, a much stronger condition is usually placed on the TRS of interest, as in [HH82]: it must be possible to divide the function symbols occurring in the TRS into two disjoint sets, *constructors* and *defined functions*, such that the left-hand sides of all the rules are of the form $f(c_1,..., c_n)$, where f is an n-ary defined-function symbol and the c_i involve only constructors and variables.

For example, the specifications described above are of this form, when oriented as rewrite rules in the appropriate direction: the constructors are, respectively, $\{T, F\}$, $\{0, s\}$ and $\{nil, make, append\}$, while the defined functions are $\{\sim, \&\}$, $\{+\}$ and $\{reverse\}$. Huet and Hullot proposed an algorithm to test that their principle of definition is satisfied which requires the stronger condition on the TRS that the rules be left-linear. Improved algorithms for more general TRS have since been proposed by, for instance, J.J. Thiel [Th84] and E. Kounalis [Ko85]. The basic idea behind these algorithms is that an n-ary function f is well-defined by a terminating TRS if every ground expression of the form $f(r_1,..., r_n)$, where the r_i involve only constructors, is an instance of the left-hand side of one of the rewrite rules.

7.3.2.2 Unambiguity

Convergence is a natural condition to impose on a specification system, and it leads to decidable conditions for testing the consistency of a specification system that is "enriched" by new equations. On the other hand, it is not a necessary condition for a specification system to satisfy for the purposes of proof by consistency in the initial model, as is illustrated in the following exercise.

Exercise 7.8: Consider the (ground) specification system

$$(\{0, s\}, \{0, s(0), s(s(0))\}, \{s(s(s(s(0)))) = 0\}),$$

which forms the basis for arithmetic modulo 4. Show that it is not convergent, but that if an independent ground equation (that is, one that is not a consequence of the given axiom) is added then the system will become inconsistent.

In [KM87] Kapur and Musser extend this idea even further, and, in so doing, generalise the concept of inductive theorem beyond the initial model. While the main discussion of induction in this book will be with regard to the initial model, it is worth outlining the ideas behind Kapur and Musser's proposal to clarify the relationship to the previous work. They propose a condition (which they refer to as the *unambiguity* of a specification system) for performing inductive proofs by consistency checks. They define this condition in terms of what they call **S**-*congruence* relations. Here a slightly different formulation of their notion of an **S**-congruence will be given and unambiguity will be defined in terms of this. It is hoped that this formulation will give a more intuitive understanding of what is intended. Rather than use **S**-congruence relations, **S**-equation-sets (or **S**E-sets for short) will be used.

SE-sets: Let **S** be a specification system (L,C,E). An **S**E-set is a set of equations **S**E between terms of L which has the two properties

- E is a subset of **S**E, and
- c = d is not a consequence of **S**E for any distinct terms c and d in C.

Two **S**E-sets are, quite naturally, considered to be the same if they have an identical set of consequences, since it is in fact the consequences that are of interest.

Maximal S E-sets: An **S**E-set **S**E is said to be maximal if there is no pair of ground terms, t and t', of L, such that **S**E $\cup$ $\{t = t'\}$ is a distinct **S**E-set.

It should be clear that a system S will normally have (infinitely) many SE-sets. It is also possible for it to have more than one maximal SE-set, as illustrated in the following example.

Example: Let S be the "ground system" $(\{T, F, \sim\}, \{T, F\}, \{\sim T = F\})$. The set $E = \{\sim T = F, \sim F = T\}$ is an SE-set. Also E is maximal since it is not possible to add any independent ground equation (that is, an equation that is not a consequence of E) without introducing inconsistency. The set $\{\sim T = F, \sim F = F\}$ is also a maximal SE-set and is clearly distinct from E. Thus S has at least two maximal SE-sets.

This leads to the definition of *unambiguity*.

Unambiguous System: A specification system is said to be unambiguous if it has only one maximal SE-set.

For example, the system $S = (\{T, F, \sim\}; \{T, F\}, \{\sim T = F\}, \{\sim F = T\})$ is, of course, unambiguous since its "E" is a maximal SE-set. It is shown in [KM87] that the unambiguity of a specification system is less restrictive than sufficient completeness in the sense that 'consistency + sufficient completeness' entails unambiguity. This is also true for the definition of containment given above. A proof of this will serve to pinpoint the disparity between requiring that a system be contained (and consistent) and requiring, on the other hand, only that it be unambiguous.

Suppose that the system (L,C,E) is convergent. Then to show that (L,C,E) is unambiguous it is necessary to show that it is not possible to add an independent ground equation $t = t'$ to E. However, if $t = t'$ is not a consequence of E, then t and t' must be equal to distinct elements of C, since the system is convergent. Hence E is a maximal (L,C,E)-set, and thus (L,C,E) is unambiguous.

That unambiguity does not entail containment is illustrated by an example given in [KM87]. Consider the following specification system

$$(\{a, f\}, \{a, f(a)\}, \{f(f(f(f(a)))) = a\}),$$

where a is nullary and f is unary. This system is clearly not contained but is very easily shown to be unambiguous.

Based upon the concept of an unambiguous specification system a principle of 'proof by consistency' may be derived automatically according to the following straightforward result: if a specification system $S = (L,C,E)$ is unambiguous and SE is its SE-set, then for any ground equation $t_1 = t_2$

$$SE \models t_1 = t_2 \quad \text{iff} \quad (L,C,E \cup \{t_1 = t_2\}) \text{ is consistent.}$$

(In Kapur and Musser's formulation $SE \models t_1 = t_2$ becomes $t_1 \equiv t_2$.) Furthermore, according to the definition of inductive theorem proposed in [KM87], if every ground instance of an equation $t = t'$ is a theorem of SE, then $t = t'$ is an "inductive theorem" of S. This is a generalisation of the definition given at the beginning of Section 7.3.1 because, for example, the equation $f(f(a)) = a$ is an inductive theorem of the system of the previous example according to Kapur and Musser's definition, though it is a ground equation that is clearly not a consequence of the equation in this system. Note, on the other hand, that for a system $S = (L,C,E)$ the two notions of inductive theorem coincide if the system has the property that E is its SE-set; for then an equation is an inductive theorem (in both senses) iff every ground instance is a consequence of E.

No algorithms are provided to test specifications for ambiguity in [KM87], but different formulations of the concept of ambiguity are presented which may lead to such tests. The most important of these, and in fact the motivation for the ideas expressed in Kapur and Musser's paper, is the following: a specification system (L,C,E) is unambiguous iff the binary relation $\sim$ on L defined by

$$t_1 \sim t_2 \quad \text{iff} \quad (L,C,E \cup \{t_1 = t_2\}) \text{ is consistent}$$

is transitive.

7.3.3 Limitations and Developments

From the discussion in Section 7.3.2.1 it may be seen how a sound procedure for proving inductive theorems based on the completion procedure may be constructed. First the initial equations are transformed into a canonical set of rewrite rules (if possible), and then the conjecture is added to the set as a new rewrite rule and the completion procedure run again on the combined set of rules. If the conjecture is not an inductive theorem, and if the procedure does not abort with an unorientable equation, then it is assured that the process will terminate with "disproof" after a finite time, having derived a rule whose left-hand side has a ground instance that is irreducible. Otherwise, if the process terminates without deducing an "inconsistent equation" then the theorem is proved.

The soundness of completion-based inductive proofs is guaranteed according to the above considerations. However, it was not long before it was found that such a procedure would be inadequate except in rather exceptional circumstances. The principal drawback with the use of the Knuth-Bendix procedure for inductive proofs is that, even when it is possible to derive a canonical set of rewrite rules for the given axioms, too often it happens that when the conjecture is added the procedure will produce critical pairs indefinitely, thus neither proving nor disproving the conjecture. Naturally, in those cases where the procedure continues processing the rules indefinitely without deducing an "inconsistent" critical pair, it is assured that the conjecture is in fact a theorem; but, of course, in such cases there is no general way of telling after a finite amount of time whether the procedure will terminate or not. This problem is illustrated with the following very simple example, taken from [Fr86].

Example: Suppose it is required to prove that $(x + y) + z = x + (y + z)$ is an inductive theorem of SPEC2. Orienting all three equations as rules from left to right, the corresponding system is terminating. The initial rules are:
1. $x + 0 \to x$.
2. $x + s(y) \to s(x + y)$.
3. $(x + y) + z \to x + (y + z)$.

When run on these rules, the completion procedure will continue *ad infinitum* generating critical pairs. This is because the completion procedure does more than is required for the inductive proof in order to construct a confluent system for 1-3.

To clarify this example, consider a classical proof by induction. Such a proof would involve choosing one of the variables of 3, y, say, and then applying the rule of structural induction given previously, with this variable in the place of x. The variable y is then said to be the variable "inducted upon". In this example the "correct" choice of variable is z since this leads to a simple proof, while any other choice will not even lead to a simplification of the problem. In attempting to construct a confluent set of rewrite rules for 1-3, however, the completion procedure must attempt the inductions on both z and y (though not the one on x), and the induction on y simply leads to further inductions. For this reason, unless lemmas are supplied, the procedure will never terminate.

To solve this problem, various proposals have been made, which have usually been based upon the idea of ground confluence. Ground confluence is defined exactly as for general confluence, except that "for every term t_1" is replaced by "for every ground term t_1". Often it happens that a rewriting system is canonical on ground terms, but not canonical on terms in general. For example, this is true for the set of rules of the last example. Naturally, ground confluence is sufficient for inductive proofs because only the ground instances of equations are of concern; it is not difficult to see that the earlier results, particularly Dershowitz's theorem, still hold for ground confluent systems. Consequently, it also becomes clear that a restriction of the Knuth-Bendix procedure is required which tests (and "completes") only for the ground confluence of a set of equations. Such restrictions have been proposed by L. Fribourg in [Fr86] and R. Göbel in [Gö87]. Both of these approaches can cope, in particular, with the associativity of addition in the example above.

The major limitation of these approaches is the requirement that the conjecture be oriented into a (terminating) rewrite rule. This restriction can often obstruct the proof, because the conjecture cannot always be oriented into a rewrite rule without losing the termination property, and also there are occasions when, for the proof to be completed, it is necessary that the conjecture be applied in the direction opposite to the one originally stipulated. Also, the expression of the principles involved in terms of procedures for manipulating equations in Fribourg's and Göbel's papers tends to obscure the main results. Recently, the author has proposed a principle of induction which takes many of its ideas from the completion-based approach, but which overcomes the main limitations of the earlier methods (see [Du89a]). This principle is not explicitly characterised in terms of the confluence and termination properties of term rewriting systems, but the relationship to the earlier approaches is sufficiently close to allow, for example, a very simple proof of the correctness of Fribourg's procedure; the original proof in [Fr86] required a couple of pages of detailed reasoning. On the other hand, its explicit expression as a principle of induction brings out the relationship to the classical approach (to be discussed further in the next chapter). It is worth outlining the main ideas behind this principle, as it will provide another view of "inductionless induction".

As indicated, it is possible to describe the induction principle independently of the confluence and termination properties of a rewriting system, but for the current discussion it will be assumed that the axioms form a ground canonical rewriting system. There are two reasons for making this assumption. The first is that for the practical application of the principle it is essentially required that the initial system be ground confluent. The second is that a quite straightforward characterisation of the method may be given if the axioms are assumed to form a ground canonical rewriting system.

To express the principle, some notation and definitions will be introduced. The most fundamental of these definitions is the concept of a *minimal covering*, which is essentially a re-expression of the notion of inductive reducibility introduced in Section 7.3.2.1.

Minimal Covering: With respect to a canonical rewriting system R, a conjecture $t = t'$ is said to be minimally covered by a set of equations $\hat{E}$ if $\hat{E}$ is a set of instances of $t = t'$ and every ground instance of the conjecture reduces to an instance of one of the equations in $\hat{E}$.

Example: In the preceding example concerning the associativity of addition, the conjecture is minimally covered by the following pair of equations

$$(u + v) + 0 = u + (v + 0) \text{ and } (u + v) + s(w) = u + (v + s(w)).$$

For example, the ground instance

$$((s(0) + 0) + s(0)) + (s(0) + s(0)) = (s(0) + 0) + (s(0) + (s(0) + s(0)))$$

of the conjecture may be reduced to $(s(0) + s(0)) + s(s(0)) = s(0) + (s(0) + s(s(0)))$, which is an instance of the second equation of the covering.

It is not difficult to show that the concept of a minimal covering is essentially equivalent to inductive reducibility. The former is defined for equations, while the latter was defined above only for terms, but this distinction may be overcome simply by viewing an equation as a term with main "function" symbol '='. With this in mind, the relationship between the two concepts may be expressed as follows: a conjecture is inductively reducible iff a minimal covering for the conjecture may be constructed by computing critical pairs with the axioms. This will be illustrated in the examples below.

If a set of equations $\hat{E}$ minimally cover a conjecture $t = t'$, then it is clear that a proof of $t = t'$ may be transferred to a proof of the equations in $\hat{E}$. Intuitively, $\hat{E}$ then corresponds to a set of subgoals. Usually, these subgoals will be no less difficult to prove than the original conjecture, but the motivation for their construction is that during an attempt to prove them instances of the conjecture may be assumed that are "smaller" according to the syntactic ordering on the original rewriting system; these instances correspond to "inductive hypotheses". In this way, the set $\hat{E}$ may be divided into "base cases" and "induction cases".

Base Case: Let R be a set of rewrite rules that terminates according to the ordering >, and let $t = t'$ be a conjecture containing the sequence of n variables x. If $\hat{E}$ is a minimal covering of $t = t'$, then an equation $t\theta = t'\theta$ in $\hat{E}$ is said to be a base case if there is no instance $t\upsilon = t'\upsilon$ of $t = t'$ such that $g(x)\theta > g(x)\upsilon$ (where g is any n-ary function symbol).

Induction Case: An equation in the covering set $\hat{E}$ is said to be an induction case (or an *induction conclusion*) if it is not a base case.

Induction Hypothesis: If, within $\hat{E}$, an instance $t\theta = t'\theta$ of the conjecture $t = t'$ is an induction case, then an instance $t\upsilon = t'\upsilon$ of the conjecture is said to be an induction hypothesis for $t\theta = t'\theta$ if $g(x)\theta > g(x)\upsilon$.

Example: In the minimal covering described in the previous example the first equation $(u + v) + 0 = u + (v + 0)$ is the base case, since there is no substitution υ such that $g(u, v, 0) > g(x, y, z)\upsilon$ (where $>$ is the ordering on the given rewrite system), while the second equation is the induction case. An example of a corresponding induction hypothesis is the equation $(u + v) + w = u + (v + w)$, since $g(u, v, s(w)) > g(u, v, w)$.

Principle of Induction: Suppose that R is a canonical set of rewrite rules that terminates according to the ordering $>$, that $t = t'$ is the current conjecture which contains the sequence of variables x, and that $\hat{E}$ is a minimal covering of $t = t'$. Then to prove that $t = t'$ is an inductive theorem of R it is sufficient to prove

- base cases: each base case in $\hat{E}$ is an inductive theorem, and
- induction steps: for each induction case $s = s'$ in $\hat{E}$, if the hypotheses for this case are inductive theorems, then $s = s'$ is an inductive theorem.

A proof of the soundness of this rule may be found in [Du89a]. The proof is not difficult since it follows the pattern of the usual proof of the soundness of classical induction: assume that there is a "minimal" instance of the conjecture that is not true and show that this assumption leads to a contradiction. The next few examples will illustrate the application of this principle and will also serve to clarify its relationship both to the earlier approaches to inductionless induction and to classical induction principles.

Examples:
1. Consider again the example of the associativity of addition discussed above. In the original discussion of this problem it was noted that to prove the theorem it is sufficient to induct on the variable z, while the completion procedure implicitly attempts both the induction on z and also the induction on y. Thus it may be deduced that only those critical pairs corresponding to the "induction" on z need to be considered for the purposes of the proof; this is the idea behind Fribourg's approach in [Fr86]. This may be expressed more precisely with the principle of induction described above, as follows.

According to the principle of induction, to prove the associativity of '+' it is sufficient to prove

- $(u + v) + 0 = u + (v + 0)$,
- $(u + v) + s(w) = u + (v + s(w))$ assuming that there is a proof of the hypothesis $(u + v) + w = u + (v + w)$.

The base case may be proved directly from the axioms for + simply by reducing it to $u + v = u + v$. The induction case, on the other hand, may be reduced by the axioms only to the new subgoal $s((u + v) + w) = s(u + (v + w))$. However, it is clear that this subgoal is *true* if the equation $(u + v) + w = u + (v + w)$ holds—but this holds by assumption, so the conjecture is proven.

This proof is, of course, identical to the usual classical proof of the same theorem; less trivial applications of the current induction principle will be considered below. At this point the intention is simply to bring out the analogy between the completion-based and classical approaches. It should be noted that the instances of the conjecture referred to as the "base case" and "induction case" correspond exactly to two critical pairs between the axioms for + and the conjecture, namely,

$$<u + v, u + (v + 0)> \text{ and } <s((u + v) + w), u + (v + s(w))>.$$

Furthermore, the second of these critical pairs reduces first to $s((u + v) + w) = s(u + (v + w))$ by the axioms for +, and then to $s(u + (v + w)) = s(u + (v + w))$ by application of the conjecture as the rewrite rule $(x + y) + z \rightarrow x + (y + z)$ to the term $(u + v) + w$. Thus it may be seen that the completion process could perform exactly the same proof if the correct choice is made of the critical pairs to process. This idea forms the basis for Fribourg's restriction of the completion procedure for inductive proofs (in [Fr86]).

2. Let the function # be defined by the following rewriting system

$$\{x \# 0 \rightarrow 0, x \# s(y) \rightarrow y \# x\},$$

and let the conjecture be $x \# y = 0$. It may be shown that $x \# y = 0$ is minimally covered by the equations

$$u \# 0 = 0 \quad \text{and} \quad u \# s(v) = 0.$$

By the definition of #, the first case, the base, clearly reduces to the identity $0 = 0$, while the induction case reduces to $v \# u = 0$. Now, since the ordering may be constructed so that $u \# s(v) > v \# u$, an instance of the conjecture may be applied, as the hypothesis, producing $0 = 0$. Thus the conjecture has been proven.

Note that, in contrast, the "natural" induction step, $u \# v = 0 \Rightarrow u \# s(v) = 0$, would have failed in this case. To achieve the proof of this theorem using a classical induction principle some mechanism such as the "measure functions" of Boyer and Moore (to be described in the next chapter) would have to be used.

3. Consider the simple rewriting system $\{s(s(0)) \rightarrow 0\}$ used to illustrate inductive reducibility in Section 7.3.2.1. It was noted there that the term $s(s(x))$ is inductively reducible according to this rewriting system, while the term $s(x)$ is not. These two facts may be used as a basis for proving the conjecture $s(s(x)) = x$ and disproving the conjecture $s(x) = x$. In the case of $s(s(x)) = x$, the equations $s(s(0)) = 0$ and $s(s(s(0))) = s(0)$ form a minimal covering, and these may be reduced, by the rule $s(s(0)) \rightarrow 0$, to the identities $0 = 0$ and $s(0) = s(0)$, respectively; thus this conjecture is proven. On the other hand, $s(x) = x$ may be oriented into the rule $s(x) \rightarrow x$ without losing the termination property, but $s(x)$ is not inductively reducible, and thus it follows automatically that $s(x) = x$ cannot be an inductive theorem. This provides a simple illustration of the generality of the induction principle described above, and the way in which it may be applied to disproofs as well as to proofs.

On the same theme (modulo arithmetic), suppose that the current one-rule system is combined with the rules for + above, and that the conjecture $x + x = 0$ is posed. A minimal covering of this conjecture is provided by the pair of equations

$$0 + 0 = 0 \text{ and } s(u) + s(u) = 0.$$

The base case is trivial, while the induction case may be reduced to $s(s(u) + u) = 0$. With the additional "lemma" $s(x) + y \rightarrow s(x + y)$, which may be proved from the axioms for $+$, the induction case may be further reduced to $s(s(u + u)) = 0$. Now since $g(s(u)) > g(u)$, the induction hypothesis $u + u = 0$ may be applied to this subgoal to give $s(s(0)) = 0$, which is true by the "modulo 2" axiom.

The point of this example, apart from illustrating the use of lemmas to complete proofs, is to clarify the distinction between the induction principle described above and classical rules. Essentially, in this proof the theorem was assumed for x and shown for $s(x)$. This follows the classical approach and thus seems to be justifiable in the usual way. However, as indicated by an example of an unsound deduction in [ZK88], this justification is incorrect because of the axiom $s(s(0)) = 0$. To illustrate the potential problem that can arise, consider the alternative *false* conjecture $x + x = s(0)$. This is covered (though not minimally covered) by the single instance $s(u) + s(u) = s(0)$ since, according to the axioms, every ground term is equal to $s(u)$ for some u. This covering instance reduces to $s(s(u + u)) = s(0)$, and this subgoal may be further reduced to $s(s(s(0))) = s(0)$, the conjecture being assumed *true* for u. But now this subgoal is *true* by the axiom $s(s(0)) = 0$, and thus the conjecture seems to be proven. The reason why this deduction is unsound is that, even though $0 < s(0)$, in the proof that the conjecture holds for 0 it is assumed that it holds for $s(0)$; this is simply because $0 + 0 = s(0)$ is equivalent to the instance $s(s(0)) + s(s(0)) = s(0)$ of the covering (by the axiom $s(s(0)) = 0$) and in the proof of this instance of the covering it is assumed that $s(0) + s(0) = 0$.

Thus the justification for the choice of the induction hypothesis in the original example proof is not as straightforward as may seem at first sight; the assumption that the covering is minimal is extremely important. If the minimal covering used in the proof of $x + x = 0$ had been used in the attempted proof of $x + x = s(0)$ also, then the proof would have broken down in the base case (i.e. $0 + 0 = s(0)$): the *false* subgoal $0 = s(0)$ would have been derived.

Exercise 7.9: Let the function $*$ (denoting multiplication) be defined by the rules

$$x * 0 \rightarrow 0 \text{ and } x * s(y) \rightarrow x + (x * y).$$

(The function $*$ is thus well-defined.) Assuming the axioms for $+$ and "modulo 2" used in Examples 1 and 3 above, and assuming the lemma $x + x = 0$ and any of the usual properties of $+$ and $*$ (for example, commutativity and associativity) required to complete the proof, prove the theorem $x * x = x$.

Each of the example proofs (and disproofs) just described could be performed not only by both Fribourg's and Göbel's methods, but even by the original completion procedure with the addition of a test for inductive reducibility; furthermore, the proofs would be almost identical. The aim of these examples was merely to outline the main principles involved in the "inductionless" approach, not to show how the principle described here improves over the earlier methods. Examples on which the current rule succeeds while the other approaches fail may be found in [Du89a]; the most important factor in this respect is the removal of the restriction that the conjecture be oriented as a rewrite rule.

On the other hand, it should not be thought that the principle of induction described above captures all aspects of "proof by consistency" as it is performed by the completion procedures of, for instance, Huet and Hullot [HH82] and Göbel

[Gö87]. Often, during the completion process performed by these systems, critical pairs are generated which may lead to a proof, but which do not correspond to part of a minimal covering. This is illustrated by the "inductionless" proof of the theorem *reverse(reverse(x))* = *x* in [HH82] for a definition of *reverse* in terms of the "LISP-constructors" for lists, *nil* and *cons*: in this case a critical pair, formed between the conjecture and a subgoal, subsequently eliminates all other subgoals, producing a completed (and consistent) rewriting system, and thus a proof of the theorem. (Boyer and Moore prove this theorem using a very different approach, as will be discussed in the next chapter.) However, it seems that, on the one hand, these critical pairs produced by the usual completion procedures may be viewed as "heuristics" on top of the underlying induction principle described above, and, on the other hand, this induction principle may itself be used as the basis for a completion procedure both for proving the ground confluence of rewriting systems and for completing non-confluent systems into ground confluent systems. These issues are, however, outside the scope of this book.

It should be noted that the principle described above may be viewed as being, essentially, a special case of the "cover-set" induction principle of Zhang et al [ZK88]. However, the more restrictive principle presented here more clearly reveals the relationship to the inductionless approach, which is not so apparent from the description of cover-set induction in [ZK88]. It also applies naturally to disproofs as indicated above, in contrast to the more general cover-set principle. On the other hand, cover-set induction is truly more powerful in that it applies to non-canonical (as well as canonical) systems.

Recently, E. Kounalis and M. Rusinowitch have proposed a principle of induction in [KR90] that is closely related to the one described here. They express their principle in a slightly different way from [Du89a] which makes comparison difficult, but they point out that the major idea is that any instance of the conjecture may be assumed during the proof whenever it is smaller (according to the ordering on the given rewriting system) than the subgoal currently being treated; this is, of course, the idea behind the principle described above. In [KR90], on the other hand, the method is extended to apply also to conditional equations, a topic that is not treated at all in [Du89a]. The main difficulty in extending the approach to the conditional case is the fact that inductive reducibility (and hence the minimal covering property) is undecidable for conditional equations; as a partial solution, Kounalis and Rusinowitch describe a testing procedure for a restriction of (their version of) the concept of a minimal covering.

7.4 OTHER APPLICATIONS

Without going into details, this section will describe some other applications of the Knuth-Bendix procedure to theorem proving.

7.4.1 Program Synthesis

In [De85] N. Dershowitz shows how the completion procedure may be applied to the task of synthesizing a program from its specification. He expresses the process as a transformational task, analogous to the methods of Burstall and Darlington [BD77], where, essentially, a specification is transformed by equational reasoning into the desired program. To illustrate the main ideas a very simple example synthesis, based upon an example in [Bi88], will be developed.

Expressed as a conjecture, the problem has the specification $\forall x \forall y \exists z \, z + y = x$. The required values of z are intended to correspond to the "difference" of x and y. For the purpose of the synthesis using the Knuth-Bendix procedure, this conjecture is re-expressed as the rewrite rule $eq(z + y, x) \rightarrow diff(x, y, z)$, where $diff(x, y, z)$ should be read as "the difference of x and y is z". Notice that no explicit distinction is made between the quantification of the variables in this rewrite rule: they are all taken to be implicitly universally quantified.

To achieve the desired synthesis, to this specification of $diff$ are added the following "transformation rules":

$$\{eq(u + 0, u) \rightarrow T, \ eq(u + s(v), 0) \rightarrow F, \ eq(u + s(v), s(w)) \rightarrow eq(u + v, w)\}.$$

These three rules characterize completely the equality (denoted by eq) of terms involving 0, s and +. For simplicity, two different data-types have been used in these equations, "natural numbers" and "boolean values", but this may be avoided if it is preferred by replacing T by $s(0)$ and F by 0, say. Regardless of this, all three are logical consequences of the axioms for + in SPEC2 augmented by the following axioms for eq defined as equality on the natural numbers:

$$\{eq(x, x) = T, \ eq(0, s(x)) = F, \ eq(s(x), 0) = F, \ eq(s(x), s(y)) = eq(x, y)\}.$$

The synthesis now proceeds by the overlapping of the transformation rules on the rule corresponding to the original conjecture. This produces three critical pairs:

$$<diff(x, 0, x), T>, \ <diff(0, s(y), z), F>, \ <diff(s(x), s(y), z), eq(z + y, x)>.$$

The third of these reduces to the new pair $<diff(s(x), s(y), z), diff(x, y, z)>$, by application of the original rule for $diff$. (Note the analogy to the application of an induction hypothesis in inductive proofs.) This completes the synthesis, for these derived equations may be re-expressed as a Prolog-style program for $diff$ as follows:

```
diff(X, 0, X).
diff(0, s(Y), Z) :- fail.
diff(s(X), s(Y), Z) :- diff(X, Y, Z).
```

Alternatively, it is not difficult to see that they may be re-expressed as an "equational program" for $diff$ as follows:

$$diff(x, 0) = x, \ diff(0, s(y)) = \text{undefined}, \ diff(s(x), s(y)) = diff(x, y).$$

If preferred, some numerical value, say 0, may be returned for $diff(0, s(y))$ rather than "undefined".

It may be seen that the choice of the transformation rules to apply in this synthesis was not simply fortuitous: it required an understanding of the problem on the part of the developer. In general, the need to find the appropriate transformations to apply in synthesis and program transformation tasks (commonly referred to as "eureka" steps, as in [BD77]) is a fundamental hurdle to automation. In the paper [Bi88] from which the above problem was taken the need for a eureka step was overcome to a certain degree by the choice of the initial specification of the problem: the required "cases" of the program were naturally derived by application of the axioms in the same way that the transformation rules above were applied.

However, the problem remains of choosing the appropriate axiomatisation. Further discussion on this issue may be found in the recent paper of Bundy et al [BS90].

A more important concern in the current context is to bring out the relationship between the "transformational" approach to program synthesis illustrated above and the "deductive" approach of, for instance, Manna and Waldinger in [MW80]. From a methodological point of view these two approaches to synthesis seem to be very different, for the former involves only equational reasoning, while the latter uses an explicit application of proof by induction. On the other hand, while the synthesis above was expressed as a transformational task, it could just as easily have been expressed as an application of the induction principle described in the previous section. This follows from the comment made in the description of the synthesis that one of the steps corresponds to the application of an induction hypothesis. In this way, the transformational approach may be seen as an implicit application of induction, or, more accurately, as an application of "inductionless induction". Thus, in practice, there seems to be very little difference between the transformational and deductive approaches to program synthesis.

7.4.2 Refutation Theorem Proving

It has been shown by, for example, Hsiang in [Hs85] and Kapur and Narendran in [KN85] how the completion procedure may be used for "refutation-style" theorem proving. Both approaches use "exclusive-or" in the place of "or" and try to derive the equality $T = F$. However, while Hsiang relies upon a canonical set of rules for Boolean algebra with an associative-commutative unification algorithm, Kapur and Narendran treat formulae as polynomials (with "ex-or" as "addition" and "and" as "multiplication"), and compute what is generally referred to as the "Gröbner basis" of the rewrite system. (See also [Bu85] for a discussion of the relationship between "Gröbner-basis" algorithms and Knuth-Bendix completion.)

As an aside, it is worth noting that the correctness of Hsiang's approach to refutation theorem proving may be justified by referring to the principles involved in the application of the Knuth-Bendix procedure to proof by induction, as pointed out by Dershowitz in [De85]. This follows from the fact that Hsiang's approach is based upon the use of a canonical rewriting system according to which the only irreducible ground terms are the constants T and F. Essentially, the idea is that if a formula is unsatisfiable then it is *not* an "inductive consequence" of the rewriting system for Boolean algebra, and thus $T = F$ will eventually be generated by the completion procedure.

7.4.3 Building-in Equational Theories

The ideas of Plotkin [Pl72] and Slagle [Sl72] have already been mentioned in Section 4.2.8, and also their extension using the Knuth-Bendix completion procedure. In [Hs85] Hsiang shows that building-in equational theories by simply rewriting with a canonical set of rewrite rules does not give a complete strategy. Instead, during the proof it is necessary to perform full unification between the left-hand sides of rules and the terms appearing in the formulae of the conjecture. Hsiang describes an algorithm that allows the incorporation of this principle into his own refutation theorem-proving system.

Similarly, the completion procedure may be applied to the equational-unification problem. For a theory T, generated by a set of formulae Γ, a T-unifier for a pair of expressions E_1 and E_2 is a substitution θ such that $\Gamma \models E_1\theta = E_2\theta$ (or, in other words, $E_1\theta = E_2\theta$ is in T). A pair of expressions may have no, several or infinitely many T-unifiers. If T is empty then T-unification is simply standard unification. Unification algorithms for theories, which have been mentioned previously, are algorithms that compute, for a given theory T, *complete* sets of T-unifiers for expressions (see [HO80]). Normally it is also required that the algorithm compute *minimal* sets of unifiers for expressions, where by a minimal set it is meant that there should not be two unifiers in the set such that when both are applied to any term one simply produces an instance of the term the other produces.

In [HO80] and [De83] it is shown how the completion procedure may be used to compute T-unifiers for terms in an equational theory T. In particular, Dershowitz shows that, provided the completion procedure does not abort, two terms t_1 and t_2 are T-unifiable iff adding the two rules $eq(x, x) \to T$ and $eq(t_1, t_2) \to F$ to a set of equations E that generates T causes the procedure to produce $T = F$. If a canonical set of rules may be derived initially from E then a solution is guaranteed. The actual unifiers may be found by including the variables of the terms as arguments of F. However, it is pointed out in [HO80] that the procedure cannot be depended upon to produce minimal sets of unifiers unless some adequate restriction can be found. Thus, for instance, Plotkin's algorithm for "associative unifiers" in [Pl72] is more appropriate in practice.

CHAPTER 8

THE BOYER-MOORE THEOREM PROVER

8.1 INTRODUCTION

The system developed by R.S. Boyer and J.S Moore (referred to as BM from here on) is designed for proving inductive theorems in the standard mathematical style. If its simplification techniques fail to prove a conjecture presented to it, then the theorem prover will invent an induction argument based on the axioms defining the types of objects possible (numbers, lists, and so on) and on the recursively defined functions appearing in the conjecture. Hence there is no onus on the user to invent the correct induction schema or to assume the correctness of "axioms" or "lemmas" on which the theorem prover should depend. Apart from its principle of induction and its simplification mechanisms, the system also depends on various heuristics designed to convert formulae to a form for which an appropriate induction schema may more effectively be produced.

There were various motivations behind the development of the system, but it seems that the main aim was to automate the proof process as far as possible. In [BM79] Boyer and Moore say that they are interested in how people go about proving theorems by induction. This gives rise to their many heuristics for inventing inductions, for removing undesirable or irrelevant elements from conjectures, and for generalising formulae by replacing certain terms by variables. Most of these ideas will be described here.

The language of the theorem prover is their own version of (pure) LISP. Originally the system was built with the intention of proving theorems about recursive functions defined on lists (see [BM75]), and hence LISP was a natural language to choose. One problem with this choice is that some of the reasoning mechanisms of BM are closely bound up with the underlying language and thus do not always transfer easily to other proof systems. Another problem is the difficulty of reading the LISP-like prefix notation. However, the language of (pure) LISP is to a great extent declarative and hence it is quite easy to understand the meaning of statements. It will be found that little knowledge of LISP is required, especially since only recursive "programs" are allowed on BM; that is, variable assignments, loops, and so on, are not allowed. Not surprisingly most implementations of the system have also been in various versions of LISP. Here the adaptation to Franz LISP on the Vax by J. Nagle will be looked at.

The chapter will consist of four main parts. The first section will describe the basic theory; the second, the heuristic techniques; the third will discuss the level of interaction and guidance that the user is allowed by the system; the fourth will be concerned with recent developments and improvements of the methods employed in the system.

8.2 THE UNDERLYING THEORY

Since there are only functions in the language of BM, the syntax and semantics of the system are slightly different from that used in the preceding chapters; the first two subsections will clarify these differences. The rest of the section will then be concerned with the way in which new structures are introduced into the system, and with the system's basic reasoning principles.

8.2.1 The Syntax and Assumed Functions

All function symbols consist of a string of letters and digits starting with a letter. There are no predicate symbols, as will be explained below. The system does not distinguish between upper and lower case letters, but all output is written in normal text. Expressions are written using a LISP-like prefix notation. In particular, a constant c would be written (c) rather than $c()$ or just c. For built-in constants such as T, F and 0, 1, 2,..., which have special meaning (are simply abbreviations, in fact) brackets are omitted. Variables also have no enclosing brackets. For example,

$plus(times(a, x), 3)$ would be written   (PLUS (TIMES (A) X) 3)

To improve readability here, this notation will often be abused to include the use of prefix and infix symbols.

There are no formulae as previously defined. The "connectives" and "predicates" introduced are defined as functions. Thus the only expression is the term, which is defined essentially as before. The four basic functions of the system are the distinguished constants T and F which assume the role of truth values, the "predicate" EQUAL of two arguments and the function IF of three arguments. The operators EQUAL and IF are defined by

$$(\text{EQUAL X Y}) = \begin{cases} \text{T} & \text{if } X = Y \\ \text{F} & \text{if } X \neq Y, \end{cases}$$

$$(\text{IF X Y Z}) = \begin{cases} Z & \text{if } X = F \\ Y & \text{if } X \neq F. \end{cases}$$

The "connectives" are defined in terms of IF. For example, AND and IMPLIES are defined by the following equations:

(AND X Y) = (IF X (IF Y T F) F), and
(IMPLIES X Y) = (IF X (IF Y T F) T).

Note also that when new types of objects are introduced into the system, as will be explained in Section 8.2.2, new axioms for EQUAL are generated.

Since there are no formulae it becomes natural to treat certain terms as such. For example, the "theorem" (EQUAL (PLUS X Y) (PLUS Y X)) is in fact a term and hence cannot be a theorem since theorems are formulae. In this case it should be thought of as (EQUAL (PLUS X Y) (PLUS Y X)) ≠ F.

8.2.2 Introducing Inductively Defined Objects

As mentioned previously, an early version of the system, described in [BM75], was concerned purely with functions defined on lists. Since then a general method has been introduced for defining inductively constructed objects such as natural numbers, lists, stacks, and so on. Of course, normally when new types are axiomatised questions arise such as: is the type fully specified, and are there any inconsistencies? To avoid such problems, a very specific method of defining types has been implemented, referred to as the **shell principle**.

The user is allowed to specify the following:

	EXAMPLES	
	for N	**for "lists"**
A constructor of n arguments	ADD1	CONS
A (nullary) bottom object	ZERO	
A recogniser for the type	NUMBERP	LISTP
n (unary) accessors	SUB1	CAR, CDR
n type restrictions	NUMBERP	
n default values	ZERO	

These "parameters", input by the user, constitute a "shorthand" for the required axioms which are then generated by the system. In the table, examples are given of the relevant "parameters" for the natural numbers and ordered pairs (where ADD1, ZERO, SUB1 and NUMBERP represent, respectively, the "successor" function, 0, the "predecessor" function, and a "predicate" that recognises numbers, and where, as in LISP, the pair (x, y) is represented as the term (CONS X Y), the functions CAR and CDR access (or select), respectively, the left and right element of a pair, and the "predicate" LISTP recognises pairs or "lists"). Already axiomatised in this manner are the natural numbers, literal atoms ("litatoms"), ordered pairs (or "lists") and negative integers. The details of this specification mechanism may be found in [BM79]. Most importantly it should be noted that axioms are introduced that ensure that the built-in "relation" LESSP is well-founded on the "size" of the objects introduced (as determined by the function COUNT). The following example shows how a new type would be introduced on the Vax version of BM, and outlines the main features of the defined type.

Example: The following input introduces the new type "sequence" to the system.

(ADD-SHELL INSERT E-SEQ SEQP ((HEAD (NONE-OF) ZERO)
                                       (TAIL (ONE-OF SEQP) E-SEQ)))

In this "specification", INSERT is a "constructor" for the objects of type sequence, E-SEQ is the "empty sequence" (i.e. the "bottom object"), the "predicate" SEQP is a recogniser for sequences which returns T for objects of type "sequence" and F otherwise, and HEAD and TAIL are unary functions that select, respectively, the first element of a sequence and the rest of a sequence other than the first element. The comment NONE-OF indicates that there are no constraints on the type of objects that may appear as an item in the sequence, while ONE-OF SEQP indicates that the tail of a sequence must also be a sequence. The objects defined thus have the form

$$(\text{INSERT } item_1 \text{ (INSERT ... (INSERT } item_n \text{ E-SEQ)...))},$$

where the "*items*" may be objects of any type (possibly sequences). In addition, the "default value" ZERO (i.e. 0) is returned if HEAD is supplied with an object other than a sequence, while TAIL returns E-SEQ for such an object. Finally, the size or COUNT of a sequence is essentially given by

$$(\text{COUNT } seq) = \begin{cases} 0 & \text{if (E-SEQP } seq) \\ 1 + (\text{COUNT (TAIL } seq)) & \text{otherwise,} \end{cases}$$

where (E-SEQP X) is defined to be $(X = \text{E-SEQ}) \vee \neg(\text{SEQP X})$, and the corresponding well-founded ordering > for sequences is then given by

$$seq > seq' \quad \text{if (LESSP (COUNT } seq') \text{ (COUNT } seq)).$$

Hence the ordering on sequences is reduced to the usual ordering on N.

8.2.3 Defining New Functions

It is possible to add axioms that define new functions on the system. However, for these axioms to be acceptable it is necessary that certain constraints be complied with. These constraints are intended to ensure that the function introduced is "well-defined" (cf. Chapter 7).

Since the function definitions of (pure) LISP and hence the Boyer-Moore system have a totally different format from those defined by rewrite rules as on REVE, the techniques mentioned in the previous chapter cannot be applied. To illustrate this, consider the following definition of PLUS:

$$(\text{PLUS X Y}) = (\text{IF (ZEROP X) Y (ADD1 (PLUS (SUB1 X) Y)))},$$

where (ZEROP X) is defined to be $(X = \text{ZERO}) \vee \neg(\text{NUMBERP X})$. The problem here is not simply the introduction of conditionals, but the fact that there is no well-founded monotonic ordering < on terms such that

$$(\text{ADD1 (PLUS (SUB1 X) Y)}) < (\text{PLUS X Y}).$$

Thus, there is no purely syntactic method of ensuring that such functions will terminate for all input. To solve this problem, Boyer and Moore employ a "principle of definition" that depends upon the meaning of the function symbols rather than simply their syntactic form.

If the specific syntax is ignored (see Section 8.4 below) a definition of a function FN would take the form

$$(FN \ X_1 \ X_2 \ ... \ X_n) = DEFN,$$

where $X_1 \ X_2 \ ... \ X_n$ are variables and DEFN is a term. There are four constraints that such a definition must satisfy. The first three, which are merely syntactic, are

1. FN is a function symbol new to the system,
2. $X_1, X_2,..., X_n$ are distinct variables, and
3. DEFN is a term that involves no variables other than $X_1, X_2, ..., X_n$.

These are sufficient to ensure that any "simple" function (corresponding merely to an abbreviation) is well-defined. For example, the function SQUARE defined by

$$(SQUARE \ X) = (TIMES \ X \ X)$$

would be accepted by the system. A fourth condition accounts for "recursively defined" functions, that is, functions whose definition includes occurrences of their own name in their DEFN part (e.g. PLUS above). (The term "recursively defined" should be distinguished from the term "recursive", since all (Turing-) computable functions are recursive in the mathematical sense.) To describe the fourth condition, the following definition is required.

Governing Term: Let a subterm of a term t have the form (IF $t_1 \ t_2 \ t_3$). Then t_1 is said to govern each subterm of t_2 in t, and (NOT t_1) is said to govern each subterm of t_3.

The fourth condition may now be stated:

4. Suppose
   a. that, for terms $s_1, s_2,..., s_n$, a subterm of the form (FN $s_1 \ s_2 \ ... \ s_n$) occurs in DEFN (called a *recursive call* of FN),
   b. that this term is governed by the terms $t_1, t_2,..., t_m$, and
   c. that FN does not occur in any one of $t_1, t_2,..., t_m$.

Then for FN to be accepted under the definition principle, the "recursion lemma"

$$(t_1 \wedge t_2 \wedge ... \wedge t_m) \rightarrow (LESSP \ (f \ s_1 \ s_2 \ ... \ s_n) \ (f \ x_1 \ x_2 \ ... \ x_n)),$$

(where f is some ("measure") function of n arguments) must be a theorem.

It is proved in [BM79] that these conditions ensure that every function accepted "exists" and is "unique", which means that it terminates for all input and returns a single value for each input. Note that, in fact, it is not strictly necessary that f be of n arguments since if f is of $k < n$ arguments then a function f' of n arguments may be defined which is equal to f. The k variables of FN that do occur as the arguments of f on the right-hand side of LESSP in the required theorem are said to be a **measured subset** of FN.

Examples:
The definition of PLUS above is accepted since the implication

$$(NOT \ (ZEROP \ X)) \rightarrow (LESSP \ (COUNT \ (SUB1 \ X)) \ (COUNT \ X)),$$

where COUNT is a predefined function that calculates the "size" of an object (see [BM79]), is a theorem (or, in fact, an axiom).

The definition

(APPEND X Y) = (IF (LISTP X) (CONS (CAR X) (APPEND (CDR X) Y)) Y)

is accepted because it is an axiom that

(LISTP X) $\rightarrow$ (LESSP (COUNT (CDR X)) (COUNT X)).

In other words, the right element of a pair is smaller than the pair itself.

A more complex example is MC-FLATTEN (due to J. McCarthy [BM79]):

(MC-FLATTEN X Y) =
    (IF (LISTP X)
       (MC-FLATTEN (CAR X) (MC-FLATTEN (CDR X) Y))
       (CONS X Y)).

This is accepted even though (MC-FLATTEN (CDR X) Y) is the second argument of the first occurrence of MC-FLATTEN in the "DEFN" part. This is because the first argument of MC-FLATTEN (in both calls) is "decreasing" and hence the second argument is superfluous to deciding whether the function is accepted.

The unusual definition of the "factorial" function
(FACTORIAL X Y) =
        (IF (LESSP Y X) (TIMES Y (FACTORIAL X (ADD1 Y))) 1)

is accepted given the theorem

(LESSP X Y) $\rightarrow$ (LESSP (DIFFERENCE Y (ADD1 X)) (DIFFERENCE Y X)),

where DIFFERENCE has the obvious meaning (but is defined only for the natural numbers, e.g. (DIFFERENCE 3 5) = 0).

Exercise 8.1: Find a measure function and lemma which ensure that the following purposeless function is "well-defined":

(G X Y) = (IF (ZEROP Y) 0 (G (SUB1 Y) X)).

(This may be compared with the function "#" of the previous chapter.)

The justifications of each of the function definitions above used the fact that, in each case, the same arguments "decreased" in each recursive call; in the case of MC-FLATTEN it was the first argument, and in the case of FACTORIAL both. It is also possible to account for functions for which different arguments decrease in separate recursive calls, using "lexicographic relations", defined as follows.

Lexicographic Relations: If $>$ is any relation on the set S, then the binary lexicographic relation $>_2$ on S, based on $>$, is defined by

$$(s, t) >_2 (s', t') \text{ iff } s > s' \text{ or } (s = s' \text{ and } t > t').$$

If $>$ is well-founded then so is $>_2$ (see [Ma74]). Naturally, this idea may be extended to produce lexicographic relations on n-tuples of objects. The same relation is used to order words in a dictionary; hence the name. The well-foundedness of lexicographic relations should be contrasted with the simpler ordering $(s, t) \gg (s', t')$ iff $s > s'$ or $t > t'$. This is not well-founded even if $>$ is, since, for instance, one possible "infinite descending sequence" according to this ordering is:

$$(1, 0) \gg (0, 1) \gg (1, 0)....$$

Lexicographic relations are built into BM, and hence it is possible to justify the definitions of functions in which different arguments decrease in different calls, as in the following example. The definition

```
(EUCLID X Y Q R) =    (IF (ZEROP Y) T
                      (IF (EQUAL (PLUS (TIMES Y Q) R) X) T
                      (IF (NOT (LESSP Q X)) F
                      (IF (LESSP R Y) (EUCLID X Y Q (ADD1 R))
                      (EUCLID X Y (ADD1 Q) 0)))))
```

is accepted by the system according to the predefined lexicographic relation LEX2. However, for the system to discover this, a hint needed to be added by the user at the end of the definition, the hint being

(LEX2 (LIST (DIFFERENCE X Q) (DIFFERENCE Y R))).

It is perhaps also worth noting that binary lexicographic relations allow the proof of termination of a more general class of functions than do unary relations. The function EUCLID above is equivalent to a simpler function which may be proved to terminate using the normal ordering on the natural numbers, but, for instance, the well-known "Ackermann's function" may be proved to terminate using a lexicographic relation, but not using a unary relation on the natural numbers (see [Pe67]). The reason lexicographic relations are more powerful is that while there is a one-to-one correspondence between sets of pairs of natural numbers and the natural numbers, the well-founded lexicographic ordering on the pairs cannot be preserved in the mapping. For instance, the function *pair* defined by

$$pair(m, n) = (\frac{1}{2} * (m + n) * (m + n + 1)) + m$$

is a correspondence from $\mathbb{N}^2$ to $\mathbb{N}$, but it does not preserve the well-founded ordering, for $pair(1, 0) = 2 < 5 = pair(0, 2)$. This result is expressed in general in the following exercise.

Exercise 8.2: Show that for any one-to-one correspondence $pr(m, n)$ from $\mathbb{N}^2$ to $\mathbb{N}$ there is a number k such that $pr(0, k) > pr(1, 0)$, and hence no pr can preserve the lexicographic ordering.

8.2.4 The Principle of Induction

For the purposes of proving inductive theorems, a restricted form of the principle of Noetherian induction is used (commonly referred to as structural induction in computer science). Noetherian induction is dependent on there being a given well-founded relation on the objects of a given set, and also on the *minimal elements* of the set with respect to this relation.

Minimal Element: Let $<$ be a well-founded relation on a set S. An element s of S is said to be minimal if there is no element s' of S such that $s' < s$.

Noetherian Induction: Let $\alpha(x)$ be the given conjecture and let "$<$" be a well-founded relation on a set S. Then to prove that $\alpha(x)$ is a theorem for all x in S, it is sufficient to show the following:

- base case: $\alpha(s)$ is a theorem for each minimal s in S, and
- induction step: if $\alpha(s')$ is a theorem for all s' such that $s' < s$, then $\alpha(s)$ is a theorem.

The base case may, in fact, be omitted from this definition, since it is subsumed by the induction step: if s is minimal then there is no s' such that $s' < s$ and hence the induction step requires that $\alpha(s)$ be proved alone in any case.

On the Boyer-Moore system this principle becomes, in its simplest form: if the implication $\beta \rightarrow f(x) < x$ is a theorem, then to prove α it is sufficient to prove

- base case: $\neg\beta \rightarrow \alpha$, and
- induction step: $(\beta \wedge \alpha(f(x))) \rightarrow \alpha(x)$.

Example: To prove (PLUS X 0) = X it is sufficient to prove

- base case: (ZEROP X) $\rightarrow$ (PLUS X 0) = X, and
- induction step:
  $(\neg(\text{ZEROP X}) \wedge (\text{PLUS (SUB1 X) 0}) = 0) \rightarrow (\text{PLUS X 0}) = X.$

In the implementation of BM this principle is further restricted by the condition that the ordering $<$ is either the usual ordering on $\mathbf{N}$ or is the corresponding lexico-graphic ordering; Noetherian induction allows arbitrary well-founded orderings. For practical improvement, however, the function f involved in the ordering condition is allowed to be of any arity, and there may be more than one base and induction step to be proved. To express this generalised principle of induction formally it is perhaps simplest to use the idea of a "covering", closely related to the concept of a "minimal covering" discussed in the previous chapter. This characterisation is in fact a development of BM's version, and hence further discussion of it will be left to the final section on extensions of the system.

The principle of induction is applied as a tactic: a goal is decomposed into a set of subgoals. (In fact, all the steps of a proof in BM correspond to application of tactics on a natural deduction style proof system: the aim is to reduce a conjecture to "*true*".) To invent inductions that satisfy the principle, the system depends upon the structure of any recursively defined functions appearing in the given conjecture. The generalised principle indicated above (where f may be of any arity) is, in fact, directly related to the principle of definition; essentially, each recursive call in a function definition corresponds to a step in an inductive proof. For this reason further discussion of the inductive reasoning mechanisms will be left to the section on heuristics below.

8.2.5 Types and Internal Representation

The theorem prover is able to determine the possible types of objects that may be returned by terms in a conjecture, and it will use this type information implicitly when attempting to prove the conjecture. For example, if both (NUMBERP t_1) and (LISTP t_2) were theorems (or axioms) then the term (EQUAL t_1 t_2) would be immediately reducible to F if it appeared in a conjecture.

This ability to determine the types of terms is based upon the type axioms and lemmas that the system already has at its disposal. These may have been introduced in various ways: as axioms produced by the adding of a new shell type, or as axioms/lemmas explicitly introduced by the user, or as consequences of acceptable function definitions.

In the case of function definitions, immediately following the acceptance of a function a theorem regarding the types of objects that may occur in the range of the function will be deduced. The details of this, though interesting, are not of great importance for the present purposes and may be found in [BM79]. All that need be commented on here is the fact that often the type of the range of a function cannot be fixed completely. This happens whenever the function must return one of its arguments. The function APPEND above is such a function since it must return its second argument whenever its first argument is not a list. To account for this, the "definition type" [BM79] of a function must consist of a set of "types", which are the types of the objects that may be returned, and a set of variables, which are those variables occurring in the definition of the function (its *formal arguments*), instances of which must be returned whenever certain arguments are supplied to the function. For example, it is a theorem that

(LISTP (APPEND X Y)) ∨ (EQUAL (APPEND X Y) Y).

Other examples of type theorems deduced from function definitions may be found in Section 8.4. Note that because type information is used so extensively by the prover it rarely informs the user of such use.

It should also be noted that internally all formulae are converted into a disjunction of literals. Boyer and Moore point out that this was to overcome the problems associated with the asymmetry of conditional statements (see [BM79]). However, for the most part, this representation is not of concern.

8.3 THE HEURISTICS

One of the most difficult tasks in proving inductive theorems is finding the most appropriate induction schema for a particular conjecture. This involves choosing the most suitable variable(s) upon which to induct, and the most suitable base and induction cases. As illustrated already, in the discussion of inductionless induction in the preceding chapter, merely the wrong choice of induction variable can lead the proof astray.

For this reason, Boyer and Moore have designed a series of heuristics for developing inductive proofs, based upon a study of the way people normally perform such proofs. As well as choosing inductions, heuristics are applied to "simplify" a given conjecture (subgoal) in various ways. This may involve simply the replacing of a particular term by an (inductively) equivalent term, or may, in fact, involve the "generalisation" of the conjecture to a more general theorem which happens to be easier to prove. This subsection will be concerned with describing and indicating the importance of the main heuristics built into the system.

8.3.1 Deriving Induction Schemas

Possible inductions are derived from terms in the given conjecture. For a term to "suggest" an induction it must be a *recursive term*, that is, it must be of the form (FN $t_1 \ldots t_n$), where FN is the function symbol of a recursively defined function. Furthermore, the t_i occurring in at least one measured subset of FN must be distinct variables, except in the case where one or more of the variables in the measured subset remain unchanged in the recursive calls of FN (e.g. FACTORIAL and EUCLID), in which case the t_i in those places may be any terms not involving the other variables of the measured subset. For example, the recursive term (FACTORIAL (SUB1 X) Y) suggests an induction, but if X is replaced by Y then no inductions are suggested. The idea is that all possible cases of the conjecture must be covered by the induction steps derived from the function definitions—this principle is expressed explicitly by the concept of a covering, to be discussed in the final section.

The induction that is derived is based upon the recursion lemma that the system has used to ensure that the measured subset "decreases"—see condition 4 in Section 8.2.3. For example, the recursive term (PLUS X t) (for any term t) occurring in a conjecture α suggests the induction (schema)

base case: (ZEROP X) $\rightarrow$ (α X Y),
induction step: ($\neg$(ZEROP X) $\wedge$ (α (SUB1 X) Y)) $\rightarrow$ (α X Y),
    where Y is the set of variables appearing in α other than X.

The variables of the measured subset that forms the basis for the induction are said to be the *induction variables* of the associated induction schema. For instance, the variable X is the induction variable in the preceding induction schema.

Exercise 8.3: What induction is suggested by the term (G X Y), where G is the function of Exercise 8.1 above, and what is (or are) the induction variable(s)? (Cf. Chapter 7.)

If it happens that several terms in a conjecture suggest possible induction schemas, the problem then becomes that of either choosing the most appropriate or combining several into one induction and then choosing the most appropriate from the set of possible combinations. For this purpose various powerful heuristics have been built into the system.

8.3.1.1 Merging and Subsumption

It is sometimes possible to "merge" several induction schemas into one. For example, the conjecture

$$((\text{LESSP X Y}) \wedge (\text{LESSP Y Z})) \rightarrow (\text{LESSP X Z})$$

suggests six inductions (see [BM79]), none of which is more appropriate than any other. In this case they all merge into one induction with induction step

($\neg$(ZEROP X) $\wedge$ $\neg$(ZEROP Y) $\wedge$ $\neg$(ZEROP Z) $\wedge$
    (α (SUB1 X) (SUB1 Y) (SUB1 Z))) $\rightarrow$ (α X Y Z).

Intuitively, this is because none of the inductions is any better than the others and so the "best of all possible worlds" is taken.

In other cases, one suggested induction may be just a special case of another. For example, with EVEN defined by

(EVEN X) = (IF (ZEROP X) T
                 (IF (ZEROP (SUB1 X)) F (EVEN (SUB1 (SUB1 X)))))),

if a conjecture involves PLUS and EVEN, the induction suggested by PLUS will usually be ignored in favour of the induction for EVEN (which will include an induction step with X replaced by (SUB1 (SUB1 X)) in the hypothesis). This is because, on opening up (PLUS X Y) twice, a term will be produced that involves (SUB1 (SUB1 X)) and no other occurrences of (SUB1 X); thus both (PLUS X Y) and (EVEN X) may be transformed into terms that involve (SUB1 (SUB1 X)). This is clearly helpful in the course of a proof because it produces a formula that involves as many like terms as possible (see the heuristics for opening up functions below). In this case, the induction suggested by EVEN is said to "subsume" that of PLUS.

The idea behind these merging and subsumption mechanisms will become more apparent when the heuristics for opening up definitions and applying equality hypotheses are discussed below. The underlying motivation will be returned to in the final subsection, where a more detailed explanation of the BM's mechanisms will be given, together with a discussion of some possible extensions.

8.3.1.2 Flawed Inductions

If a variable x appears in terms t and t' in a conjecture, and if these terms suggest induction schemas s and s', respectively, then s is said to be *flawed* if either x is an induction variable in both schemas but is instantiated differently in the hypotheses of each schema (in which case s' is also flawed), or x is an induction variable of only the schema s. More generally, the schema resulting from a merge of several inductions is flawed if one of the inductions from which it was derived was flawed. Whenever possible, flawed inductions are not used because they tend to instantiate variables in such a way that the application of the induction hypotheses is blocked. This is illustrated in the following example from [BM79].

Example: Let the function APPEND be defined as in Section 8.2.3, and consider the inductive theorem

(APPEND (APPEND X Y) Z) = (APPEND X (APPEND Y Z)).

There are three inductions suggested by the four recursive terms in the conjecture, two on the variable X, and one on Y. However, the induction on Y is flawed since the other occurrence of Y is a non-induction variable of the induction suggested by (APPEND X Y). If the induction on Y in (APPEND Y Z) were to be performed, then the corresponding induction hypothesis would be

(APPEND (APPEND X (CDR Y)) Z) = (APPEND X (APPEND (CDR Y) Z)).

The difficulty with this hypothesis is that the occurrence of (CDR Y) in the left-hand side is likely to block any attempt to apply the hypothesis to the induction conclusion. This is because the second parameter is unchanged in the definition of APPEND, and thus the term (APPEND X Y) in the conclusion of the induction step cannot be reduced to (APPEND X (CDR Y)) simply by "expanding" the definition of APPEND (cf. Section 8.3.2 below).

8.3.1.3 Nasty Functions

A function is said to be *nasty* if the recursive calls in its definition involve functions other than itself and "shell accessors" (Section 8.2.2). The FACTORIAL function above is an example of a nasty function. Inductions involving nasty functions are applied first in an attempt to derive formulae with nasty functions appearing in the hypothesis and conclusion and thus, hopefully, to remove them at an early stage using equality reasoning and generalisation (see below).

8.3.2 Opening Up Definitions

The major concern associated with expanding functions is the expansion of recursively defined functions. This can lead to indefinite expansions. For example, if PLUS is defined as above then expanding a call of PLUS such as (PLUS Z *t*) may lead to expansion of (PLUS (SUB1 Z) *t*) which may, in turn, lead to expansion of (PLUS (SUB1 (SUB1 Z)) *t*), and so on. Though Boyer and Moore acknowledge the problem of expanding all function calls in a conjecture even if none of the calls are of recursively defined functions (see Chapter 4), they choose to ignore this issue and centre their heuristics for opening up calls around the problem of recursive definitions. Their heuristics are thus essentially the following: a call is expanded if

1. the call is not of a recursively defined function,

2. on opening up the call, no further calls of the function are met (for example, if the call is (PLUS 0 Z) then Z will be returned on expansion),

3. opening up the call introduces more ground terms than occur in the call itself,

4. the number of function symbols occurring in some measured subset decreases (e.g. (LESSP X (ADD1 Y)) would be expanded to (LESSP (SUB1 X) Y)),

5. (the most powerful heuristic) some of the arguments of the call do not already appear in the conjecture and on opening up the call each of the arguments of the new call do appear elsewhere in the conjecture.

The fifth heuristic is not only useful for avoiding infinite expansions, but it is also the basis for BM's choice of induction schemas. A possible induction suggested by a recursive term is considered to have potential if it is likely to lead to simplification of the conjecture via application of this fifth heuristic. The idea is that if, on expanding the definition of a function, the same terms occur in both the hypothesis and conclusion of the induction step, then it should be possible either to apply the hypothesis to the conclusion (cf. Section 8.3.4) or (if that fails) at least to "generalise" the conjecture with a reasonable chance of deriving a subgoal that is a theorem (see Section 8.3.6). Examples of the application of the fifth heuristic may be found in Section 8.4 below.

8.3.3 Rewriting Terms

If an axiom or a lemma has the form (EQUAL l r), where l and r are terms, then it may be used to replace any instance of l appearing in a conjecture by the corresponding instance of r. It is also possible to treat expressions such as (NOT t) as rewrite rules, since it may be viewed as (EQUAL t F).

More generally, if an axiom/lemma has the form (IMPLIES h (EQUAL l r)), then it may be used as a rewrite rule in the following obvious manner. If an instance $l\theta$ of l occurs in a conjecture then an attempt is made to reduce the corresponding instance of the hypotheses, $h\theta$, to T (backwards chaining), and if this can be done then $l\theta$ is replaced by $r\theta$.

There are three main problems with the use of such rules, as already discussed:

- orienting rewrite rules so that all applications of them will terminate—in particular treating *permutative rules* such as commutativity,

- infinite backwards chaining,

- different rewrite rules may apply to the same term, and the corresponding normal forms may differ.

To solve the problem of permutative rules (i.e. rules in which the two sides contain the same symbols) BM uses a lexicographic ordering on the terms to which the rewrite is to be applied. It is required that, when a permutative rule is applied, no term should be moved to the left of a term "alphabetically smaller" than itself. For example, (PLUS Y X) may be rewritten to (PLUS X Y) but not vice-versa.

Boyer and Moore's solution to the second problem is to retain a list of the (negation of) hypotheses that need to be proved and to check that a newly derived hypothesis is not the same as or an *elaboration* of a previously derived hypothesis. Essentially, H is an elaboration of H' if (1) either H' occurs in H or an argument of H' occurs in the term in the corresponding argument position of H, and the converse is not also true, and (2) H does not contain any ground term built only from shell functions in an argument position in which H' also contains such a term. See the example in Section 4.2.4.

The third problem is "solved" simply by applying rules in the order that they were introduced to the system. In [Gl80] a complex example is described where this treatment of rewrite rules causes problems. In [GL80], following from the experiment in [Gl80], a method was described for solving such problems which differs from the Knuth-Bendix approach in that critical pairs are generated "dynamically" during the application of a set of rewrite rules, rather than beforehand. (See also the comments and example on pages 232-5 of [Bi87], which compares Knuth-Bendix completion to standard equational reasoning principles for proving the equality of terms.)

8.3.4 Using Equality Hypotheses

If an equality of the form (EQUAL t_1 t_2) appears in the hypothesis of a goal, where t_2 is a term not constructed entirely from constructors, bottom objects and variables, then the equality may be "used up" by replacing t_2 by t_1 wherever t_2

occurs elsewhere in the formula, and then deleting the equality. Similarly t_1 may be replaced by t_2. A single proviso to this is that when the conclusion of the formula is also an equality then only those occurrences of t_2 are replaced by t_1 (or t_1 by t_2) that are in the "right-hand side" of any un-negated equalities or in any negated equalities. This Boyer and Moore call **cross-fertilising**.

The motivation for using equality hypotheses to replace terms by others are:

1. It may lead to further applications of the other simplification rules.

2. If induction is required again (as will probably happen) a "stronger" inductive argument is likely to be generated once equality hypotheses have been removed. (This is the most important consideration as far as Boyer and Moore are concerned; see [BM79].)

3. Once occurrences of t_2 have been removed from the formula, hopefully some functions occurring within t_2 will be removed totally from the formula. This would clearly be useful for many reasons. In particular, if the function(s) are recursively defined and further inductions are required in an attempt to prove that the formula is a theorem then, in general, fewer possible inductions will be suggested by terms in the formula after the removal of t_2.

The third of these points makes the idea of cross-fertilising surprising, since it means that sometimes not all occurrences of t_2 will be removed, and hence a chance may be lost of removing completely from the formula some function occurring within t_2. However, it may be that situations such as those envisioned in 3 do not occur often enough for this issue to be of significance, especially since in most cases cross-fertilisation has exactly the same effect as general equality replacement (because the only terms replaceable are exactly those that are replaced by cross-fertilisation). An occasion when a non-trivial cross-fertilisation step is very successful is in the proof of the theorem (REVERSE (REVERSE X)) = X. In this case, one of the subgoals derived during the construction of the proof includes the hypothesis (REVERSE (REVERSE Y)) = Y. By an application of cross-fertilisation, Y is replaced by (REVERSE (REVERSE Y)) in only the right-hand side of the equality conclusion, leaving unchanged occurrences of Y in the rest of the formula. Partly because of this application of cross-fertilisation, no help was required from the user in order for the system to prove the theorem (which is non-trivial with the given definition of REVERSE); the full proof may be found in [BM79].

8.3.5 Destructors and Irrelevant Formulae

When new shells are introduced, axioms are generated by the system for replacing "destructors" in formulae by "constructors". For example, SUB1 would be removed in favour of ADD1, and CAR and CDR would be replaced by CONS using, respectively, the axioms

$\neg$(ZEROP X) $\rightarrow$ (ADD1 (SUB1 X)) = X, and

(LISTP X) $\rightarrow$ (CONS (CAR X) (CDR X)) = X.

The idea here is that it is often better to restate a formula with certain functions replaced by others. Thus it is considered preferable to treat a formula involving the constructor ADD1 rather than the destructor SUB1. The idea is intuitively understandable, because it is standard practice of mathematicians when proving theorems by induction to try to prove

$$P(X) \rightarrow P(X + 1) \quad \text{rather than} \quad P(X - 1) \rightarrow P(X).$$

Further justification may be found in [BM79]. It is also possible for the user to introduce elimination theorems such as

(NOT (ZEROP Y)) ∧ (NUMBERP X)
   → (EQUAL (PLUS (REMAINDER X Y) (TIMES Y (QUOTIENT X Y))) X).

This theorem would allow a formula involving REMAINDER and QUOTIENT (with obvious meanings) to be replaced by a formula involving only PLUS and TIMES, which are "simpler" functions. (See [BM79] for the definitions of all these functions.) In this case it is, of course, the user who decides which terms should be replaced by which. The format of "elimination" lemmas and the exact details of their application may be found in [BM79].

   Another example of the slight modification of goals to simplify their proof is the eliminating of "irrelevant" formulae. This is just a special case of the backward application of the assumption introduction rule; removing these formulae will not lead to possible proofs of non-theorems. The difficulty is merely deciding which formulae are *irrelevant*, in the sense that they will not contribute to the proof. Boyer and Moore propose one solution to this problem which depends upon the categorisation of formulae into groups. As stated earlier, all formulae are converted (internally to the system) into a disjunction of "literals". When attempting to eliminate "irrelevant" literals, the system first partitions the literals into sets with two literals placed in the same set if they involve at least one mutual variable. If one of these sets involves either no recursively defined functions or nothing but (possibly the negation of) a term of the form (FN $x_1 \ldots x_n$), where FN is a recursively defined function, then the literals in that set are removed from the formula. Examples of removal of irrelevant terms may be found in Section 8.4.

8.3.6 Generalisation

Generalisation is the backward application of the ∀-elim rule of a natural deduction calculus. It is a rather surprising tactic since it entails converting a conjecture to a more general conjecture by replacing certain terms by variables. To understand the reasoning behind the application of this operation in proofs by induction, consider the following two simple examples.

1. Conjecture: $0 * (x * y) = 0$. If '$*$' is defined by the equations

$$x * 0 = 0 \text{ and } x * s(y) = x + (x * y)$$

the "natural" induction step would be

$$0 * (x * y) = 0 \rightarrow 0 * (x * s(y)) = 0.$$

Opening up '$*$' in the conclusion gives

$$0 * (x * y) = 0 \rightarrow 0 * (x + (x * y)) = 0.$$

Here the derived induction step is no easier to prove than the original conjecture; in fact, it is more difficult. Essentially, the problem with the initial conjecture is that it was necessary to induct upon a variable that is not an "immediate subterm" of the main (or "outermost") function; that is, it is a subterm of a subterm (other than itself). This means that opening up the functions in the conclusion of the induction step does not immediately serve to reduce the conclusion to a term that can be simplified by the hypothesis. Thus the variables are too deeply "embedded" in the conjecture. However, generalising $x * y$ to z brings a variable to "the surface" and produces an easily proved, though more general, theorem. However, it is not to be supposed from this that generalisation is always necessary in cases where all the induction variables are not immediate subterms of the main function; for example the theorem $0 + (x + y) = x + y$ is easily proved.

2. Conjecture: $(y + y) + y = y + (y + y)$. The problem in trying to prove this is that on inducting on one occurrence of y, the other occurrences of y will become instantiated by any term that is substituted for the first y. This, once again, makes it difficult to reduce the conclusion of the induction step to a term to which the hypothesis may be applied. In this case (if '+' is defined as in Section 8.2.3) generalising the conjecture to the theorem $(x + y) + y = x + (y + y)$ serves to "separate" the important variables, and the proof may then be completed with a single induction on x.

In practice, the heuristics used by BM are quite simplistic, and tend very often to generalise theorems "too far", producing non-theorems. Apart from some simple constraints, the heuristics are: if the same term appears in both the conclusion and the hypothesis, or on both sides of an equality, then replace it by a variable. These heuristics clearly do not apply to the second example above (cf. Section 8.5.2.2).

As an added precaution when generalising a formula, if the term being replaced is known to be of one particular type (e.g. if (LISTP t) is a known theorem), then the system will constrain the variable introduced in the place of the term by a type predicate (e.g. (LISTP X)) which will be included in the hypothesis of the derived formula. This is quite important, because often a formula may be rejected as a theorem simply because its variables are not specified to be of a certain type; for example (PLUS 0 X) = X is not a theorem unless the hypothesis (NUMBERP X) is added, because, for instance, (PLUS 0 T) = 0. This is due to the lack of "strong typing" in BM.

8.3.7 Linear Arithmetic

The term *linear arithmetic* refers to formulae of Presburger arithmetic that are universally quantified but which contain no other quantifiers. In order both to improve the efficiency of the system and to avoid having to use induction to prove "simple" arithmetic theorems, a procedure for linear arithmetic has been built into BM recently [BM85]. This procedure allows the system to prove theorems like

$$(\text{DIFFERENCE (PLUS X Y) X}) = Y$$

without use of induction. The precise details of the procedure are quite complex and may be found in [BM85]. Here merely some important points will be made about it. The first is that, for the purposes of integrating the decision procedure into the system in a powerful manner, it was decided that the efficiency of the procedure as it stands alone is not paramount, since more important is the efficiency of the overall system. For this reason, the procedure of Cooper in [Co72] was not used.

The second point to make is that the basic procedure decides the unsatisfiability of formulae over the rational numbers, not over the natural numbers, because decision procedures for the rationals were felt to be simpler and also more commonly used in program verification systems. This means that the procedure is sound for unsatisfiability over N, but formulae that are unsatisfiable over the natural numbers but not the rational numbers may escape detection.

Thirdly, the procedure "co-operates" with the rewriting techniques in that they will call each other during an attempt to simplify formulae. Fourthly, it was felt that to ignore completely the properties of functions and relations other than those of Presburger arithmetic (i.e. 0, s, '+', '<' and '=') would be a disastrous blow to the usefulness of the procedure in the main system. For example, to prove the simple theorem

$$x \leq min(a) \rightarrow x < max(a) + 1$$

requires the knowledge that $min(a) \leq max(a)$. To deal with such examples as this the system will use previously proved theorems involving $\leq$ and the functions of interest, such as, in this case, $min(y) \leq max(y)$.

8.3.8 Notes on the Heuristics

In practice, the order of application of these heuristics is not as described above. Before the first induction, rewriting (which preserves validity) may be applied to "simplify" (or even prove) the conjecture, and the linear arithmetic algorithm may be used, but no other techniques. Following the first induction, rewriting, linear arithmetic and expanding definitions (which also preserves validity) may essentially be applied at any time, allowing for the constraint described below; the heuristic methods that do not generally preserve validity are performed in the order: destructor elimination, application of equality hypotheses, generalisation, then irrelevance elimination. All these methods are applied in a loop until the conjecture cannot be simplified any further, and then, unless proven or failed, another induction will be performed. The idea is, of course, that the more risky heuristics should be performed only after the other methods have failed.

If the function IF ever appears within a formula (such as, for example, after opening up some function call), then it will be pushed to the outside using distribution rules (see [BM79]).

Opening up definitions in combination with destructor elimination without constraints may produce loops. This occurs, for example, in opening (PLUS X t) to introduce (SUB1 X), and then eliminating SUB1 using destructor elimination. BM's solution to this is simply to disallow the elimination of any term that contains a variable that was introduced by a previous elimination, unless an induction has been performed in the meantime.

Under certain constraints, described in [BM79], destructor elimination preserves validity. For example, all elimination lemmas introduced by new shell definitions preserve validity.

8.4 INTERACTION

The only interaction possible in Prolog and REVE is the addition of further clauses or equations as "lemmas", and in the case of REVE some scope for aiding the directing of rules. BM, on the other hand, though it is not and was not intended as an interactive theorem prover, does allow the user to give some direction. For this reason this section will describe the user interaction and guidance afforded by the system.

The discussion will be based upon two examples of proofs performed by the author on the system. A discussion of these will illustrate some of the problems associated with the use of the theorem prover. For the purposes of abbreviation, in the descriptions of the formulae (other than definitions) input to and output from the system, the prefix symbol $\neg$ and the infix symbols $\vee$, $\wedge$, $\rightarrow$ and = will be used in place of the system's prefix symbols NOT, OR, AND, IMPLIES and EQUAL, respectively.

8.4.1 Example 1: An Example From Set Theory

Based upon the axiomatisation of the type "sequence" (with the ADD-SHELL command), as described in the example in Section 8.2.2, the theorem to be proved is

$$(SIZE\ (PRODUCT\ X\ Y)) = (TIMES\ (SIZE\ X)\ (SIZE\ Y)),$$

where PRODUCT specifies the "Cartesian product" of two sequences and SIZE computes the number of elements of a sequence. This is a well-known theorem of set theory, but it is not possible to axiomatise structures such as (even finite) sets (in a useful manner) on BM, and thus the type "sequence" (which has the relevant properties) is axiomatised. If the major objective was to implement finite sets as sequences then it would be necessary to "enrich" the specification in the style of [Br87], by adding, for example, a function that removes duplicate elements from a list. However, for the purposes of this example, it was not felt necessary to add complexity in this way.

After inputting the "specification" of the new type "sequence" the following definitions were introduced into the system:

(DEFN E-SEQP(S) (OR (EQUAL S E-SEQ) (NOT (SEQP S))))

(DEFN APP-SEQS(X Y) (IF (E-SEQP X) Y (INSERT (HEAD X)
                                               (APP-SEQS (TAIL X) Y))))

(DEFN SIZE(S) (IF (E-SEQP S) 0 (ADD1 (SIZE (TAIL S)))))

(DEFN PROD(X Y) (IF (E-SEQP Y) (E-SEQ)
                     (INSERT (CONS X (HEAD Y))
                              (PROD X (TAIL Y)))))

(DEFN PRODUCT(X Y) (IF (E-SEQP X) (E-SEQ)
                      (APP-SEQS (PROD (HEAD X) Y)
                                 (PRODUCT (TAIL X) Y))))

The function E-SEQP recognises empty sequences and objects distinct from sequences, the function APP-SEQS appends any two sequences, while PROD is simply a subfunction of the definition of PRODUCT; the meanings of the functions SIZE and PRODUCT have already been explained. Following the introduction of the definition of PRODUCT, the system pointed out to the user that it was able to prove the acceptability of the definition according to its "principle of definition" using the lemmas stating that the COUNT of the HEAD and TAIL of a list are smaller than the list itself according to the well-founded relation LESSP. It also noted that (SEQP (PRODUCT X Y)) is a theorem that follows from the definition. Similar comments were also made by the system after the introduction of each of the other definitions.

In the original attempt to prove the theorem the prover was then supplied with the conjecture, essentially as follows:

(PROVE-LEMMA PRODUCT-THM NIL (SIZE (PRODUCT X Y))
                        = (TIMES (SIZE X) (SIZE Y)))

where PRODUCT-THM is simply the name given to the conjecture for future reference and the comment NIL indicates that this conjecture (if proved) will not be required in the proof of any further theorems. The system is unable to prove this theorem by simplification and so proposes an induction schema:

$$((\text{E-SEQP X}) \rightarrow (\text{P X Y})) \wedge ((\neg(\text{E-SEQP X}) \wedge (\text{P (TAIL X) Y})) \rightarrow (\text{P X Y})),$$

where (P X Y) is a schematic representation of the conjecture. The base case is trivial, while the induction case is initially reduced to the subgoal

((SEQP Z) ∧ (SIZE (PRODUCT Z Y)) = (SIZE Z) * (SIZE Y)) →
   (SIZE (APP-SEQS (PROD V Y) (PRODUCT Z Y))) =
                        (SIZE Y) + (PRODUCT Z Y),

by opening up the definitions of the main functions. At this point the theorem prover uses the equality in the hypothesis to produce

(SEQP Z) → (SIZE (APP-SEQS (PROD V Y) (PRODUCT Z Y))) =
                        (SIZE Y) + (TIMES (SIZE Z) (SIZE Y)).

It then invents an induction for this new subgoal. Although this subgoal is a theorem there has been no simplification of the problem and, in fact, the theorem prover fails in this attempt to prove the conjecture. Monitoring the system's activities, the user has little difficulty seeing in this case that no progress has been made (though in general the LISP-style notation tends to hamper instantaneous checks). Once the user notices such a failure there is no recourse but to terminate the proof attempt, deduce the necessary lemmas from the system's output, have the system prove these additional lemmas, and then restart the main proof.

Deducing the appropriate lemmas is normally a very non-trivial and time-consuming task. This is partly due to the LISP notation, but is also due to the system sometimes using the lemma in an unexpected way and then being led totally along the wrong track. Even when the lemma is used in the manner anticipated the proof may still not be immediate and further lemmas may be required.

In this example, after some thought, it is apparent that both of the lemmas

(SIZE (PROD X Y)) = (SIZE Y) and
(SIZE (APP-SEQS X Y)) = (SIZE X) + (SIZE Y)

are necessary for the proof. These are input in almost the same manner as the original conjecture with the respective names SIZE-PROD and SIZE-APP, except that the comment REWRITE takes the place of NIL in both cases. The system was able to prove these two lemmas without help, and then with these was able to complete the proof of PRODUCT-THM without difficulty.

Though the theorem prover depends almost entirely on rewrite lemmas (see for example the appendix to [BM79]), in general the user may supply lemmas that are a subset of

{rewrite, elimination, generalise, meta}.

Rewrite and elimination lemmas have already been discussed. Generalisation lemmas are theorems that exhibit type information regarding some term, which is to be used in the event that the term is replaced by a variable in a generalisation step. For a discussion of meta-lemmas, which are felt to be outside the scope of this book, the reader is referred to [BM81]. Note that if the user states that a lemma is to be used as a rewrite rule, say, then that is exactly how it will be used wherever possible.

8.4.2 Example 2: Equivalence of Two Schemas

In this example the (inductive) equivalence of two "function schemas" is proved. Here a function schema is viewed simply as a function that is defined in terms of some function symbols that have not themselves been provided with definitions. These "undefined functions" may thus denote arbitrary functions, perhaps of some specific arity and perhaps compliant to certain other constraints (say, associativity). In this way, any theorem proved about the function schema must apply to any function that has the form of the schema (and satisfies the given constraints).

The two schemas of interest here are

(FN1 X) = (IF (R X) (C) (H (FN1 (K X)))), and
(FN2 X Y) = (IF (R X) Y (FN2 (K X) (H Y))),

where R, C, H and K are undefined functions, X denotes a sequence of variables and Y is a single variable (or a sequence of variables if FN1 and FN2 are procedures that may return a sequence of values). The intention is to prove that

(FN1 X) = (FN2 X (C)).

Thus (FN1 X) and (FN2 X (C)) may be construed to be "recursive" and "iterative" versions of the same operation.

Adding R, C, H and K as undefined functions is simple via the "declaration" command DCL, but there is clearly a problem associated with getting the theorem prover to accept FN1 and FN2 under the definition principle. To deal with this it is necessary to assume that some of the undefined functions have certain properties. In this case the axiom

$$(\text{NOT } (R\ X)) \rightarrow (\text{LESSP } (\text{COUNT } (K\ X))\ X)$$

was added as a rewrite rule with the name K-LESSP using the "axiom" command ADD-AXIOM. This was sufficient for the theorem prover to accept both FN1 and FN2 under the principle of definition.

The first *failed* attempt to prove the theorem will now be described. This is of interest because it illustrates a successful application of the generalisation heuristic. The reason for the theorem prover's failure is that after deriving an appropriate generalisation, it then, distressingly, chooses an inappropriate induction schema for the derived subgoal.

The induction schema derived for the conjecture is, unsurprisingly,

    base case: $(R\ X) \rightarrow (P\ X)$, and
    induction step: $(\neg(R\ X) \wedge (P\ (K\ X))) \rightarrow (P\ X)$.

The base case reduces trivially to T by the expansion of the definitions of FN1 and FN2. The induction step is initially simplified, again by expansion of the definitions, to the new goal

$$(\neg(R\ X) \wedge (\text{FN1 } (K\ X)) = (\text{FN2 } (K\ X)\ (C)))$$
$$\rightarrow (H\ (\text{FN1 } (K\ X))) = (\text{FN2 } (K\ X)\ (H\ (C))).$$

At this point the system uses the equality hypothesis by replacing (FN1 (K X)) by (FN2 (K X) (C)) to produce

$$\neg(R\ X) \rightarrow (H\ (\text{FN2 } (K\ X)\ (C))) = (\text{FN2 } (K\ X)\ (H\ (C))).$$

This goal is now generalised by the replacement of (K X) and (C) by the variables Y and Z, respectively. This produces the much more general conjecture

$$\neg(R\ X) \rightarrow (H\ (\text{FN2 } Y\ Z)) = (\text{FN2 } Y\ (H\ Z)).$$

This is further simplified by removing the now irrelevant hypothesis, to give

$$(H\ (\text{FN2 } Y\ Z)) = (\text{FN2 } Y\ (H\ Z)).$$

This new goal cannot be simplified further and thus the system calls it *1.1 and proceeds to derive an induction schema for its proof. Unfortunately, while this new conjecture is a theorem, the system invents an inappropriate induction schema for it. The problem lies not in the choice of the induction variable (since Y is the only possible choice), but in the instantiation of the other variable in the hypothesis of the induction step. The correct choice is the schema

    base case: $(R\ Y) \rightarrow (P\ Y\ Z)$, and
    induction step: $(\neg(R\ Y) \wedge (P\ (K\ Y)\ (H\ Z))) \rightarrow (P\ Y\ Z)$,

while the system opts for the more straightforward induction step

$$(\neg(R\ Y) \wedge (P\ (K\ Y)\ Z)) \rightarrow (P\ Y\ Z).$$

The only difference between the two is the instantiation of Z, the "non-induction" variable in the hypothesis. The choice of instantiating it to (H Z) is more appropriate because this corresponds to the definition of FN2 and thus is more likely to lead to simplification on expansion of the definition of FN2 during the proof.

The reason that it is sound to instantiate Z in the hypothesis in this way (or any other way) is that Z is not an induction variable and thus is essentially "existentially bound" in the hypothesis. To see this, consider some conjecture $\forall x \forall y\, \alpha(x, y)$

the proof of which involves an induction (over the natural numbers) on x alone. This gives rise to the schema

$$\forall y\, \alpha(0, y) \text{ and } \forall y\, \alpha(x, y) \to \forall y\, \alpha(s(x), y).$$

In particular, the occurrences of y in the hypothesis and conclusion of the induction step are bounded by different quantifiers. It follows from this fact that the induction step is equivalent to $\exists y(\alpha(x, y) \to \forall y\, \alpha(s(x), y))$, and thus any instances of y may be assumed in the hypothesis to complete the proof.

No guidance during a proof is possible and thus it is necessary to terminate, once again, at the point where the prover chooses the inappropriate induction. However, it is possible for the user to supply the derived theorem as a rewrite lemma together with a hint as to which induction to choose, using the command INDUCT. In this case the hint (INDUCT (FN2 X Y)) is appropriate.

Exercise 8.4: Complete the proof of (H (FN2 Y Z)) = (FN2 Y (H Z)) using the induction schema suggested.

Apart from suggested inductions, hints may also be supplied to guide the system to choose the relevant lemmas, to accept a function definition (as in the EUCLID example above), to ignore certain lemmas in the database, and also to include certain lemmas, with their variables instantiated appropriately, as extra hypotheses in a conjecture. Examples of important applications of the latter two possibilities may be found in [Ru85].

8.5 DEVELOPMENTS AND EXTENSIONS

Mainly based upon the early work of Boyer and Moore, there has been constant research into both the theory underlying the mechanisation of inductive proofs and the development of more powerful heuristics. Boyer and Moore themselves have since extended their theorem prover to treat more difficult problems, while others have implemented improved versions of Boyer and Moore's theory and heuristics in other environments. In other cases new ideas have been proposed which may be applied in BM without the introduction of any new theory or (program) code. In this section some of these developments will be outlined.

8.5.1 Characterising Proof by Induction

Several directions have been taken in the development of new induction principles which generalise the principle used in BM. On the one hand are the principles for general equational theories (which includes the work on inductionless induction), and on the other hand are the (first-order) rules designed for reasoning purely about (functional) programs. These will each be discussed in the next two subsections.

8.5.1.1 A Principle of Induction for Equational Theories

It is possible to express a much generalised version of Boyer and Moore's principle of induction in terms of the ideas of *coverings* and *semantic orderings*. A covering is a generalisation of the notion of a minimal covering defined in Chapter 7, while a semantic ordering is an ordering on expressions that is dependent, in part, on the equalities between terms (according to the given axioms). These two concepts are expressed more formally for equational theories in the next two definitions.

Covering: A set of equations $\hat{E}$ is said to cover an equation $t = t'$ with respect to a set of equations E if for every ground instance $t\phi = t'\phi$ of $t = t'$ there is an instance $s = s'$ of an equation in $\hat{E}$ such that $E \models t\phi = s$ and $E \models t'\phi = s'$.

Semantic Ordering: Let E be a set of equations of a language L and let G be some subset of the ground terms of L. Any ordering $>$ on G may be extended to a semantic ordering $>_s$ on all the terms of L as follows: for ground terms t and t', $t >_s t'$ if there are any terms c and d in G such that $E \models t = c$, $E \models t' = d$ and $c > d$; for general terms t and t', $t >_s t'$ if $t\phi >_s t'\phi$ for every ground instance $t\phi$ and $t'\phi$.

The ordering $>_s$ may be extended to an ordering on an n-ary sequence of terms in exactly the same way as Boyer and Moore construct orderings, by taking an n-ary measure function f and defining

$$(t_1,..., t_n) >_s (s_1,..., s_n) \text{ if } f(t_1,..., t_n) >_s f(s_1,..., s_n).$$

Variations of these two concepts (coverings and semantic orderings) have been used as the basis for "classical" induction principles by several researchers recently. In particular, P. Padawitz in [Pa89a] describes a quite general principle for conditional theories; see also [Du89a]. Padawitz also discusses in more detail methods for testing for and constructing appropriate coverings; see also [ZK88] and Section 8.5.2.1 below. The idea behind each of the principles is that with a given covering and a given well-founded semantic ordering, a principle of induction may be automatically derived. For equational theories this principle may take the same form as the principle of induction described in the preceding chapter. The derivation of this principle is left as an exercise.

Exercise 8.5: Using the expression of the principle of induction in Chapter 7 as a guide, substituting "covering" for "minimal covering" and "semantic ordering" for "syntactic ordering", derive another principle of induction.

The principle implemented in BM is a special case of the rule required in the exercise. BM always takes the conjecture itself as the covering (of course, any equation covers itself), while the LESSP ordering on the COUNT of the underlying data-types forms the basis for the required semantic ordering. For example, if the conjecture (PLUS X 0) = X is given, exactly the same induction schema as proposed in Section 8.2.4, that is,

(ZEROP X) → (PLUS X 0) = X
((NOT (ZEROP X)) ∧ (PLUS (SUB1 X) 0) = (SUB1 X)) → (PLUS X 0) = X,

may be applied as an instance of the application of the current principle. In this case the conjecture (PLUS X 0) = X covers itself, while the semantic ordering $>_s$ is defined in the following obvious manner. Each ground term representing a numerical value is equal either to 0 or to (ADD1 X) for some X, so the set G (in the definition of "semantic ordering") may be taken to be {0, (ADD1 0),...}, with the well-founded ordering given by the syntactic ordering (ADD1 X) > X. It follows from this that X $>_s$ (SUB1 X) for X ≠ 0, given the axioms (SUB1 0) = 0 and (SUB1 (ADD1 X)) = X. More examples of applications of the rule to functional programs may be found in [Pa89a] and [Pa89b].

The principle outlined above also applies naturally to other equational theories. For instance, it may be applied in the proof of x # y = 0 discussed in the previous chapter. In this proof the same ordering may be assumed as in the earlier proof of the theorem, and for the construction of the semantic ordering the measure function required in Exercise 8.1 may be used.

A problem to which the above principle does not apply is the modulo example discussed in the previous chapter. It fails on this example because, as indicated in Chapter 7, x is not smaller than $s(x)$ according to a semantic ordering (as defined above), since $s(s(0)) = 0$. Thus, while it is not restricted to "minimal coverings", the current principle does not completely subsume the principle described in Chapter 7: they are independent results. The next research task is to combine the ideas behind them into one principle; the principle of induction described in [ZK88] may be seen as a step in this direction.

8.5.1.2 Induction Principles for Functional Programs

As already explained, the underlying induction principle employed by the Boyer-Moore theorem prover is Noetherian induction. This principle requires that the application of an induction hypothesis be justified according to some well-founded ordering. In applying this principle BM uses the lemmas that justify the introduction of new recursively defined functions; these lemmas provide a suitable ordering according to which an induction may be performed. On the other hand, the idea behind the construction of appropriate induction schemas for conjectures is that any recursively defined function automatically gives rise to an induction schema, and that applying the relevant schema for a particular function occurring within the given conjecture will naturally lead to some "simplification" steps. This heuristic is not explicitly dependent upon the assumption that the function has been proven to be "well-defined". Using this fact, Morris and Wegbreit [MW77] proposed a principle of induction, called *subgoal induction*, that takes the heuristic as basic and discards the requirement for a well-founded ordering.

In this way, Boyer and Moore's reasoning mechanisms may be applied to non-terminating functions. For example, in the proof of the equivalence of two function schemas in the preceding section it was assumed as an additional axiom that (H X) is smaller than X according to some well-founded ordering (LESSP), and this was used as justification for the application of the induction hypothesis; but in fact this assumption is unnecessary for the equivalence to hold: according to the principle of subgoal induction, the proof could have been justified without this assumption.

To explain how the principle of subgoal induction works and why it is sound it will simplify matters to describe another, very straightforward, principle, *step induction*, defined by Padawitz in [Pa89b]. This rule allows both subgoal and computational induction (a "second-order" principle for reasoning about functional programs) to be reduced to simple induction on the natural numbers. The idea is that an index is associated with each recursive call of a function definition, and then induction is performed on this index. For example, consider the well-known "McCarthy's 91-function" described in [Ma74]:

$$mc(x) = \text{if } x > 100 \text{ then } x - 10 \text{ else } mc(mc(x + 11)).$$

This apparently complex "functional program" not only terminates for all input, but turns out to be equivalent to the very trivial function

$$\text{if } x > 100 \text{ then } x - 10 \text{ else } 91.$$

By means of Noetherian induction, it is possible to prove that mc terminates for all input (see [Ma74]), but the current concern is to prove its equivalence to the trivial function assuming termination. For this purpose a slightly different function will first be defined:

$$h(i, x) = \text{if } i = 0 \text{ then } 91 \text{ else if } x > 100 \text{ then } x - 10$$
$$\text{else } h(i - 1, h(i - 1, x + 11)).$$

The relationship between mc and h may be expressed as follows. Suppose that mc is applied to some number n; then the definition of mc will be entered j times (for some j) until $mc(n)$ is computed (if, that is, mc terminates for input n). For example, for the value $n = 100$, the definition of mc will be entered twice before the answer 91 is returned. It follows from this that if a sufficiently large value for i is chosen then $h(i, n)$ will terminate before "$i = 0$" is reached and thus will return exactly the same value as $mc(n)$. For example, the computation of $h(2, 100)$ will proceed as follows:

$$h(2, 100) \longrightarrow h(1, h(2, 111)) \longrightarrow h(1, 101) \longrightarrow 91.$$

On the other hand, if mc does not terminate for input n then no matter how large i is chosen to be, "$i = 0$" will be reached eventually and at this point the value 91 will be returned by h in any case. Suppose then that it could be proved that for all i

$$h(i, x) = \text{if } x > 100 \text{ then } x - 10 \text{ else } 91;$$

then it would follow that for any input n either mc does not terminate or it returns the value 91. The proof that $x \leq 100 \rightarrow h(i, x) = 91$ may be performed simply by inducting on i, and thus the proof of the original conjecture has been reduced to the task of performing a simple induction on the natural numbers.

Since the induction is on the variable i, any values for x may be assumed in the induction hypotheses. In outline, the proof of $x \leq 100 \rightarrow h(i, x) = 91$ proceeds as follows.

- The base case is $x \leq 100 \rightarrow h(0, x) = 91$. This is true since $h(0, x)$ is 91 by the "fortuitous" definition of h for $i = 0$.
- By expansion of the definition of h in $x \leq 100 \rightarrow h(i, x) = 91$, the subgoal
$$x \leq 100 \rightarrow (\text{if } i = 0 \text{ then } 91 \text{ else if } x > 100 \text{ then } x - 10$$
$$\text{else } h(i - 1, h(i - 1, x + 11))) = 91$$
  is derived. This simplifies to $x \leq 100 \rightarrow h(i - 1, h(i - 1, x + 11)) = 91$, for $i > 0$. Thus, with $i - 1$ omitted for brevity, the proof reduces to the task of proving the sequent
$$x + 11 \leq 100 \rightarrow h(x + 11) = 91, h(x + 11) \leq 100 \rightarrow h(h(x + 11)) = 91$$
$$\vdash x \leq 100 \rightarrow h(i, x) = 91,$$

where the antecedents are assumed induction hypotheses. The details of the proof of this sequent are left to the reader; for the purposes of the proof, some of the properties of the natural numbers must be assumed.

The proof of the theorem $x \leq 100 \rightarrow h(i, x) = 91$ using subgoal induction would follow exactly the same form as the induction case of the proof just outlined; that is, the hypotheses $x + 11 \leq 100 \rightarrow mc(x + 11) = 91$ and $mc(x + 11) \leq 100 \rightarrow mc(mc(x + 11)) = 91$ are assumed to hold and $x \leq 100 \rightarrow h(x) = 91$ is shown to follow. An identical proof, apart from the justification for the application of the hypotheses, could also be performed with computational induction (see [Ma74]). The base case, for $i = 0$, of the proof just given would, of course, not be part of either the subgoal or the computational induction proofs; for the step induction principle, the value that the indexed function (h above) returns for $i = 0$ must be chosen appropriately to ensure that the base case is trivial.

Step induction may also be applied to the task of proving the non-termination of functional programs, a task that computational induction is normally applied to. For this purpose, the indexed program may be defined such that it returns some arbitrary value for $i = 0$, and then shown to return this value for all input from the set on which the original program is to be proved to be non-terminating. This idea is illustrated in the following exercise.

Exercise 8.6: Show that the program

$$f(x) = \text{if } x = 0 \text{ then } 1 \text{ else } f(x + 1)$$

is non-terminating for all input from the set $\{1, 2,...\}$, by showing that, for all i, the program

$$h(i, x) = \text{if } i = 0 \text{ then } k \text{ else if } x = 0 \text{ then } 1 \text{ else } h(i - 1, x + 1)$$

returns the (predetermined) value k for all $x > 0$.

Step induction is essentially nothing more than a re-expression of computational induction, but it has the benefit of being a first-order principle. Furthermore, using the principle of step induction, Padawitz shows in [Pa89b] that some of the restrictions normally proposed for the sound application of computational induction may be lifted.

8.5.2 Improved Heuristics

In the developments of new heuristics, two issues have been of major concern to researchers: developing appropriate induction schemas for conjectures and finding suitable generalisations. Proposals for solving these two problems are discussed in this section.

8.5.2.1 Finding Appropriate Induction Schemas

The method of constructing induction schemas from the definitions of recursively defined functions occurring within a conjecture is a powerful heuristic that has been employed in many proof systems apart from the Boyer-Moore theorem prover. For instance, the "natural" systems of [Au79] and, more recently, [ZK88] and [Pa89a] explicitly use such a principle, while its use is implicit in the "inductionless" method of, for instance, [HH82] outlined in the preceding chapter. It has also directly formed the basis for principles of induction, as in the work of [MW77] discussed above.

Realising the limitations of this mechanism when applied alone, Boyer and Moore developed additional heuristics for combining and discarding inappropriate induction schemas. These are quite powerful strategies and have been very success-ful in practice. However, it has been pointed out by Stevens in [St88] that these too have defects, partly as a consequence of their rather ad hoc nature. By rational-ising the success of the Boyer-Moore heuristics, Stevens derives a more powerful expression of their techniques, with explicit motivation for each feature. The main aspects concern the merging and subsumption mechanisms and the flawed-function test. In the case of the flawed-function test, he considers the different cases under which the variable instantiations of two induction schemas clash, and discusses Boyer and Moore's choice of which induction to discard. In this respect he explains the reason for a failure case of their heuristics pointed out in their book. To explain Stevens' improvements to BM's merging heuristics it is necessary first to provide a more precise explanation of the idea behind them.

Essentially, BM's merging heuristics apply by unifying the equations of several coverings to produce a new covering. For example, suppose that the function $>$ is defined by the equations

$$\{0 > x = F, \ s(x) > 0 = T, \ s(x) > s(y) = x > y\},$$

and the conjecture is $(x > y \wedge y > z) \rightarrow x > z$. Three potentially suitable coverings are suggested by the recursive terms $x > y, y > z$ and $x > z$ occurring in this conjecture. These are given by the sets of variable substitutions

$$\{\{x \rightarrow 0, y \rightarrow v\}, \{x \rightarrow s(u), y \rightarrow 0\}, \{x \rightarrow s(u), y \rightarrow s(v)\},$$

$$\{\{y \rightarrow 0, z \rightarrow w\}, \{y \rightarrow s(v), z \rightarrow 0\}, \{y \rightarrow s(v), z \rightarrow s(w)\},$$

$$\{\{x \rightarrow 0, z \rightarrow w\}, \{x \rightarrow s(u), z \rightarrow 0\}, \{x \rightarrow s(u), z \rightarrow s(w)\}.$$

For instance, the induction case for the first set is

$$(s(u) > s(v) \wedge s(v) > w) \rightarrow s(u) > w.$$

None of these coverings is appropriate, however, for the induction case in each set cannot be simplified sufficiently to allow the application of an instance of the conjecture as the induction hypothesis. For example, the simplified induction case of the covering suggested by the term $x > y$ is $(u > v \wedge s(v) > w) \rightarrow s(u) > w$, which is no less difficult to prove than the original conjecture. However, if the induction case of the first set is unified with the induction case and second base case of the second set then the following pair of equations is derived:

$$(s(u) > s(v) \wedge s(v) > 0) \rightarrow s(u) > 0 \text{ and } (s(u) > s(v) \wedge s(v) > s(w)) \rightarrow s(u) > s(w).$$

This is a covering of the induction case of the first set, and thus may replace it. Hence a new induction schema is produced by adding these two equations to the first two equations of the first set. This increases the number of subgoals that have to be proved, but the proof of these is much less difficult. In particular, the new induction case $(s(u) > s(v) \wedge s(v) > s(w)) \rightarrow s(u) > s(w)$ may simplified, by an application of the axioms for >, to an instance of the conjecture, namely, the subgoal $(u > v \land v > w) \to u > w$.

From this example it may be seen that the motivation for combining coverings is that this will always lead to further simplification via application of the axioms. On the other hand, combining coverings is superfluous if none of the coverings combined have variables in common, for the same results could be achieved by applying the two schemas independently. In the above example, the two coverings combined had the variable v in common.

A similar process applies in the case of subsumption. The only difference in this case is that one of the covering sets (the subsumed set) will be eliminated during the unification.

Exercise 8.7: Let the function *half* be defined by the equations

$$half(0) = 0, \quad half(s(0)) = 0, \quad half(s(s(x))) = s(half(x)),$$

and let + be defined as in SPEC2 in Chapter 7. Construct the inductions suggested by + and *half* for the theorem $half(y) < 0 + y$ and then show that each case of the schema for *half* is either identical to or is an instance of the schema for +. Use this fact to explain the justification for discarding the schema for +.

With this alternative explanation and justification of Boyer and Moore's merging and subsumption heuristics in mind, the limitations pointed out by Stevens can be described. A very simple example will indicate the potential difficulties. Let *half* and > be defined as above, and consider the theorem $half(x) > y \to x > y$. In this conjecture the term $x > y$ suggests inducting on both x and y with induction case $half(s(x)) > s(y) \to s(x) > s(y)$, while the term $half(x)$ suggests inducting on x alone with induction case $half(s(s(x))) > y \to s(s(x)) > y$. It is not difficult to see that neither of these cases is appropriate: in the first, the term $half(s(x))$ is irreducible, while in the second the term $s(s(x)) > y$ is irreducible. Merging these two induction cases via unification produces the new induction case $half(s(s(x))) > s(y) \to s(s(x)) > s(y)$, but this reduces only to $half(x) > y \to s(x) > y$, and thus is no more suitable. One way to overcome this problem is first to expand the induction case suggested by > to the two new cases $half(s(x)) > s(0) \to s(x) > s(0)$ and $half(s(x)) > s(s(y)) \to s(x) > s(s(y))$, and then to perform the merge. This produces the induction case $half(s(s(x))) > s(s(y)) \to s(s(x)) > s(s(y))$, which simplifies to $half(x) > y \to x > y$, which, in turn, is identical to the conjecture, thereby completing the proof of this case. Based on this idea, Stevens presents a general algorithm for iteratively building up induction cases until the most appropriate possible merge may be constructed. The subsumption mechanism then becomes merely a special case of his "iterated merging" operation.

With regard to the problem of constructing suitable coverings, the very distinctive approach of Göbel [Gö87] is worth mentioning. He was principally concerned with constructing a test for ground confluence, but, as already noted in the preceding chapter, such tests may be applied also to inductive theorem proving.

8.5.2.2 Generalisation

As indicated in Section 8.3.6, the generalisation heuristics of BM are very simple and correspondingly not very powerful. A more subtle approach was proposed by

R. Aubin in [Au79], based upon the symbolic evaluation of functions. The idea is that a term occurrence is a good candidate for generalisation if each of its *super-terms* (i.e. terms of which it is a subterm—including itself) either is a component of an atomic formula or occurs in the argument position of a measured subset of a (recursively defined) function. Since a generalisation may produce a non-theorem, Aubin's system attempts to refute each potential generalisation, by finding a false ground instance, before accepting it. As an additional simplifying heuristic, as in BM, only those terms that have occurrences on both sides of an equation or an implication are considered for generalisation.

Example: Consider the theorem

$$append(x, append(x, x)) = append(append(x, x), x),$$

where *append* is defined as in Section 8.2.3. While BM's simple generalisation method would derive the invalid conjecture $append(x, y) = append(y, x)$ for this theorem, Aubin's system correctly determines that an optimal choice of generalisation is $append(y, append(x, x)) = append(append(y, x), x)$ by the following reasoning. The only term occurrences that satisfy all the constraints are the first and fourth occurrences of x and the second occurrence of $append(x, x)$. For example, the first occurrence of x is in the first argument position (the only measured subset) of *append*, and its only other superterm is the left-hand component of the equation. However, with regard to the second occurrence of $append(x, x)$, not only does the other (the first) occurrence of this term violate the constraints, but the generalisation derived after replacing the two occurrences of $append(x, x)$ by a new variable is the falsifiable subgoal $append(x, y) = append(y, x)$ that would be derived by BM. Thus the only acceptable generalisation is the one indicated.

Aubin also proposed a second generalisation mechanism. This was specifically designed for treating conjectures involving functions corresponding to iterative programs. The idea is expressed in the following example.

Example: Let the function FLATTEN be defined as

```
(FLATTEN X) = (IF (NLISTP X)   (CONS X NIL)
                               (APPEND   (FLATTEN (CAR X))
                                         (FLATTEN (CDR X))))),
```

and suppose it is required to prove the theorem

$$(FLATTEN\ X) = (MC\text{-}FLATTEN\ X\ NIL).$$

The difficulty in proving this theorem without first generalising it arises from the occurrence of the constant NIL: the attempt to complete the induction step by matching the hypotheses against the conclusion is blocked by this constant. While some simplification may be made in the first induction step of an attempted proof —by the replacement of instances of the term (FLATTEN X) by the corresponding instances of (MC-FLATTEN X NIL)—at the next induction no simplification at all is possible because of the occurrences of NIL. To overcome this problem it is necessary to generalise the constant NIL to a variable. Unfortunately, NIL does not occur on both sides of the conjecture and thus generalising it in this way leads to a non-theorem. To overcome this second difficulty it is necessary somehow to introduce the constant NIL into the left-hand side. This may be done by applying the lemma (APPEND X NIL) = X. With this lemma, the left-hand side of the conjecture may be replaced by the term (APPEND (FLATTEN X) NIL), and then the two occurrences of NIL may be replaced by a new variable Y. This produces the new, more general, conjecture

$$\text{(APPEND (FLATTEN X) Y)} = \text{(MC-FLATTEN X Y)}.$$

This new goal turns out to be a theorem, and its proof is not too difficult; Boyer and Moore describe the proof of exactly this theorem in their book [BM79].

It may be noticed that in the attempt to prove the initial theorem in this example, the main difficulty was the inability to match the induction hypotheses against the subgoal derived in the induction step. While this difficulty is the implicit motivation behind Aubin's generalisation technique, it has been shown by others that it may be used explicitly as the basis for a generalisation mechanism. The idea is that if the induction hypotheses cannot be matched against a derived subgoal in the induction step, then the places where the matching clashes occur indicate precisely where new variables should be introduced to provide a suitable generalisation. As in the example above, where APPEND and NIL are introduced, this method may involve first introducing extra function symbols into one of the terms of the conjecture.

This idea of using the matching process for deriving generalisations of conjectures has been used, for instance, in the synthesis system of Manna and Waldinger [MW80]. However, in their paper the mechanism is explained only by example and no general procedure is presented for applying it. In more recent work, such as [AK82], [Ca85] and [JT88], the same idea has been developed to a more precise level, and explicit procedures have been provided for performing the process. The paper [AK82] is concerned with the problem of transforming programs, and, in particular, of overcoming the requirement for "eureka" steps (as in the system of Burstall and Darlington, mentioned in Chapter 7); the generalisation method described therein is thus restricted to this domain. On the other hand, the work in [Ca85] (based upon Aubin's work rather than Manna and Waldinger's) is concerned with the more general task of proving inductive theorems, while [JT88] is concerned with the closely related task of solving the "divergence" problem in Knuth-Bendix completion (that is, the generation of infinite sets of critical pairs). Since the motivation in these papers is different and the procedures described are slightly different in their details, comparison is not trivial, but it seems that the general approach presented in [Ca85] is the more powerful; for example, it is shown that it applies also to the *append* example above (the first and fourth occurrences of x are again chosen for replacement by new variables); this problem does not seem to be directly solvable by any of the other approaches mentioned.

PART 4

CONCLUSIONS

CHAPTER 9

REVIEW AND CONCLUSIONS

The overall purpose of this book has been to describe methods of mechanising mathematical proofs with special regards to

- efficiency and naturalness,
- treating special theories and relations
  - e.g. decidable theories and the equality relation,
- mechanising mathematical induction,

and (as an aside)

- applications
  - formal methods (reasoning about specifications)
  - programming (in particular, the Prolog language)
  - synthesis of programs.

The preceding chapters have thus covered a wide range of issues in automated theorem proving. In successive chapters new techniques have been introduced and have (generally) been related to concepts described previously. It will have been noticed that the most important ideas have cropped up repeatedly in various contexts, and that there are certain underlying themes in all of the approaches. However, as new ideas have been introduced the overall structure of the subject and the most prominent issues may have become blurred. The purpose of this chapter is to provide a sketch, in a series of notes, of the major principles that have been introduced, and then to draw some conclusions.

PROOFS

The underlying structure for proofs is provided by the "formal axiomatic method". As a generalisation of this method, "top-down" proof and "strategies" may also be included. Thus, in outline, proofs take the following form.

Initially a calculus is given, comprising a set of
- axioms:
    - formal axioms ("logical truths", e.g. $P \rightarrow P$),
    - non-formal axioms (assumed truths, e.g. $x + 0 = x$),
- inference rules: these map valid formulae to valid formulae.

On the calculus is imposed the method of proof:
- Bottom-up proof (synthesis):
    - start with axioms,
    - apply inference rules until the goal (theorem) is deduced.
- Top-down proof (analysis):
    - start with conjecture,
    - apply inference rules backwards until axioms are derived,
    - reverse derivation for actual proof.
Sometimes a combination of synthesis and analysis may be used.

On the proof method is imposed a strategy. This determines which rules to apply and where to apply them. It may also include special (e.g. decision) procedures for dealing with subtasks.

APPROACHES TO MECHANISATION

Each system described may be divided into two components: a reasoning procedure for the propositional connectives, and an extension of this procedure for the first-order quantifiers.

The Propositional Case
For the propositional connectives the different systems described operate essentially as follows.

Natural Deduction: In the proof of a *judgement*

$$\gamma_1, ..., \gamma_n \vdash \alpha$$

the rules (in the main) eliminate and introduce the connectives on the right-hand side (the *consequent*). These systems are designed to express proofs in a natural form rather than to ease proof construction.

Sequent Calculi: In the proof of a *sequent*

$$\gamma_1, ..., \gamma_n \vdash \alpha_1, ..., \alpha_n$$

the rules introduce the connectives into both the *antecedent* (that is, the left-hand side) and the *consequent*. These systems are a development of natural deduction calculi designed for more efficient (and "direct") proof construction. It is natural to apply them backwards, thus eliminating the connectives until axioms are derived.

Resolution: This is a single inference rule

$$\neg P \vee C \text{ and } P \vee D \Rightarrow C \vee D$$

designed to deduce a contradiction from a set of *clauses*. This calculus essentially combines bottom-up with top-down reasoning, working backwards from the conjecture and forwards from the axioms at the same time.

Matrix Method: This is a "non-deductive" method which involves showing that each line through a matrix (of clauses) contains a contradiction, P and $\neg P$, for some P. It was shown in Chapter 5 that the matrix method has a very natural relationship to sequentzen, and, in fact, the construction of a line through a matrix may be reinterpreted as the application of the reversals of the inference rules of a sequent calculus.

The First-Order Case
At the first-order level, rules are required to treat the universal and existential quantifiers. In the standard natural deduction and sequent calculi, quite simplistic rules are introduced for this purpose, which tend to be difficult to apply in an efficient manner. To overcome this inefficiency in the context of the resolution principle, the mechanism of unification was introduced. This mechanism may also be applied to the rules of $\forall \vdash$ and $\vdash \exists$ in sequent calculi, but an additional test is required to ensure that the *eigenvariable condition* on the other quantifier rules, $\exists \vdash$ and $\vdash \forall$, is not violated. This may be done by means of Skolemisation, as in resolution.

Skolemisation (illustrated in the following example): Replace the assumption $\forall x \exists y \, Parent(y, x)$ by the Skolemised assumption $\forall x \, Parent(father\_of(x), x)$, say, where *father_of* is some new function symbol.

In sequentzen, Skolemisation (if it is used) must also be applied to the universal quantifiers occurring in the consequent of a sequent. In resolution, the formulae are preprocessed before Skolemisation is applied. To avoid the need to preprocess a sequent in sequent calculus proofs, Skolemisation may be applied "as required" (Chapter 4). As an alternative to Skolemising, Bibel's "term ordering" mechanism may be employed (briefly described in Chapter 4). Once the eigenvariable conditions have been accounted for, unification may be introduced.

Unification: This involves finding a common instance of several formulae, e.g.

$$P(g(x), f(y)) \text{ and } P(g(a), z) \Rightarrow P(g(a), f(y)).$$

AN EXAMPLE PROOF
To provide an outline of the main mechanisms for proof that have been discussed, it will be shown how the example theorem given in the introduction may be proved using the different approaches. It will be recalled that the theorem to be proved was the following:

$$\neg R(a), R(exp(exp(a, a), a)) \models \exists x \exists y (\neg R(x) \wedge \neg R(y) \wedge R(exp(x, y))),$$

where, in the intended interpretation, R represents the property "rational", $exp(x, y)$ represents the exponentiation of x to y, and a denotes the square root of 2. First, a proof using a sequent calculus (Section 3.2) will be performed.

A Sequent Calculus Proof: The task is to prove the sequent

$$\neg R(a), R(exp(exp(a, a), a)) \vdash \exists x \exists y (\neg R(x) \wedge \neg R(y) \wedge R(exp(x, y))).$$

An analytic proof of this theorem is as follows. First the (reversal of) the $\vdash \exists$ rule is applied, "decomposing" the consequent of the conjecture to

$$\exists x \exists y (\neg R(x) \wedge \neg R(y) \wedge R(exp(x, y))), \neg R(xd) \wedge \neg R(yd) \wedge R(exp(xd, yd)).$$

Note that, whereas, in classical sequentzen proofs, terms are introduced for the existentially quantified variables, in this proof "dummy variables" (Chapter 4) have been introduced instead. This takes into account the fact that, at this point, it is unknown what terms are appropriate to complete the proof; the dummy variables will later become instantiated by the relevant terms via the "unification" mechanism. (Since there are no existentially quantified variables in the antecedent nor universally quantified variables in the consequent of the current conjecture, there is no possibility in this case that the unification process could violate the eigen-variable conditions associated with the $\exists \vdash$ and $\vdash \forall$ rules during the proof.) Note also the duplication of the original consequent; several instances of the consequent may be required to complete the proof.

At the next step the $\vdash \wedge$ rule is applied twice to reduce the newly derived sequent to three further subgoals (where δ denotes $\exists x \exists y (\neg R(x) \wedge \neg R(y) \wedge R(exp(x, y)))$):

$$\neg R(a), R(exp(exp(a, a), a)) \vdash \delta, \neg R(xd),$$
$$\neg R(a), R(exp(exp(a, a), a)) \vdash \delta, \neg R(yd),$$
$$\neg R(a), R(exp(exp(a, a), a)) \vdash \delta, R(exp(xd, yd)).$$

In the first two subgoals it is now possible to "unify" one of the formulae in the consequent with a formula in the antecedent: $\neg R(xd)$ may be unified with $\neg R(a)$ in the first subgoal via the unifier $\{xd \rightarrow a\}$ (i.e. x is replaced by a), and $\neg R(yd)$ may be unified with $\neg R(a)$ in the second subgoal via the unifier $\{yd \rightarrow a\}$. These two subgoals are thus solved, and the third subgoal is reduced to

$$\neg R(a), R(exp(exp(a, a), a)) \vdash \exists x \exists y (\neg R(x) \wedge \neg R(y) \wedge R(exp(x, y))), R(exp(a, a)).$$

To complete the proof it is necessary to apply the $\vdash \exists$ rule again (as was antici-pated). This produces the same consequent as the original application of $\vdash \exists$ except for the addition of the new formula $R(exp(a, a))$. With δ denoting the formula $\exists x \exists y (\neg R(x) \wedge \neg R(y) \wedge R(exp(x, y)))$ as above, the subgoal after this step is

$$\neg R(a), R(exp(exp(a, a), a)) \vdash \delta, \neg R(ud) \wedge \neg R(vd) \wedge R(exp(ud, vd)), R(exp(a, a)),$$

where ud and vd are new dummies. After two more applications of the $\vdash \wedge$ rule, three new subgoals are derived:

$$\neg R(a), R(exp(exp(a, a), a)) \vdash \neg R(ud), R(exp(a, a))$$
$$\neg R(a), R(exp(exp(a, a), a)) \vdash \neg R(vd), R(exp(a, a))$$
$$\neg R(a), R(exp(exp(a, a), a)) \vdash R(exp(ud, vd)), R(exp(a, a)).$$

The second of these subgoals may be solved by instantiating vd to a, but for the first subgoal, rather than perform the same substitution for ud, it is appropriate to apply first the $\vdash \neg$ rule to this subgoal. This produces the further subgoal

$$\neg R(a), R(exp(exp(a, a), a)), R(ud) \vdash R(exp(a, a)).$$

This subgoal may now be solved by instantiating *ud* with $exp(a, a)$, thus reducing the third subgoal above to

$$\neg R(a), R(exp(exp(a, a), a)) \vdash R(exp(exp(a, a), a)), R(exp(a, a)).$$

This sequent is *true* since $R(exp(exp(a, a), a))$ appears in both the antecedent and the consequent, and thus all subgoals have been solved. The original conjecture has therefore been proven. (The classical "synthetic" proof of this theorem using a sequent calculus may be derived simply by inverting the above "analytic" proof.)

In this analytic proof several inference rules could have been applied to each derived subgoal. To achieve a proof in a reasonable (in fact, seemingly the smallest possible) number of steps, a **strategy** was imposed on the calculus to determine the most appropriate rule to apply at each step. This proof was performed by the author using the classical proof (given in the Introduction) as a guide. Whether a mechanical proof system would find precisely this proof or would instead derive some useless subgoals depends upon the power of its strategies. It may be noted that if the "Herbrand-style" procedure outlined in Section 3.2.6 had been used then the proof would have been a little longer, if only because it then would have been necessary to apply the connective rules (in particular, the negation rules in the example) before applying the quantifier rules.

As an additional point of interest, it may be asked why the above proof required a duplication of an existentially quantified formula for its completion, whereas the original classical proof described in Chapter 1 did not. The reason for this is simply that in the classical proof the (informal equivalent) of the non-logical axiom $\neg R(exp(a, a)) \vee R(exp(a, a))$ was included as an additional assumption together with the non-logical axioms. If this logical axiom had been added to the antecedent of the conjectural sequent above, then the duplication of the existentially quantified formula would have been unnecessary (cf. the second natural deduction proof of the current conjecture below). In fact, such duplications may always be avoided by adding the appropriate logical axioms of the form $\neg P \vee P$ to the antecedent of the conjecture. The important point to note is that sequentzen are complete systems for proof, and thus the addition of any logical axioms is unnecessary.

With the above analytic sequent proof as a guide, the theorem was proved in the other calculi. These proofs are described next.

Natural Deduction Proof: A bottom-up proof of this theorem (based upon the above sequentzen proof) is as follows.

For brevity, let $\Gamma = \{\neg R(a), \neg R(exp(a, a)), R(exp(exp(a, a), a))\}$,

$\Gamma' = \{\neg R(a), R(exp(exp(a, a), a))\}$, and

$\alpha = \exists x \exists y (\neg R(x) \wedge \neg R(y) \wedge R(exp(x, y)))$.

1. $\Gamma \vdash \neg R(exp(a, a))$	ass
2. $\Gamma \vdash \neg R(a)$	ass
3. $\Gamma \vdash R(exp(exp(a, a), a))$	ass
4. $\Gamma \vdash \neg R(exp(a, a)) \wedge \neg R(a) \wedge R(exp(exp(a, a), a))$	$\wedge$-intro (twice) 1, 2 and 3
5. $\Gamma \vdash \exists x \exists y (\neg R(x) \wedge \neg R(y) \wedge R(exp(x, y)))$	$\exists$-intro (twice) 4
6. $\Gamma, \neg\alpha \vdash \alpha$	air 5
7. $\Gamma, \neg\alpha \vdash \neg\alpha$	ass

8. $\Gamma - \{\neg R(exp(a, a))\}, \neg\alpha \vdash R(exp(a, a))$ $\neg$-elim 6, 7

9. $\Gamma', \neg\alpha \vdash \neg R(a)$ ass

10. $\Gamma', \neg\alpha \vdash \neg R(a) \wedge \neg R(a) \wedge R(exp(a, a))$ $\wedge$-intro (twice) 9, 9 and 8

11. $\Gamma', \neg\alpha \vdash \alpha$ $\exists$-intro (twice) 10

12. $\Gamma', \neg\alpha \vdash \neg\alpha$ ass

13. $\Gamma' \vdash \neg\neg\alpha$ $\neg$-elim 11, 12

14. $\Gamma' \vdash \alpha$ $\neg\neg$-elim 13

Line 14 is the required result and thus the theorem is proven. If this bottom-up proof is read backwards, then the relationship to the sequentzen proof above will become more apparent. An alternative natural deduction proof of the theorem, which is almost identical to the informal proof given in Chapter 1, may be constructed using a "derived rule of inference" (Section 3.1.3). The bottom-up version of this proof is as follows.

For brevity, let $\Gamma = \{\neg R(a), R(exp(a, a)), R(exp(exp(a, a), a))\}$ and
$$\Gamma' = \{\neg R(a), \neg R(exp(a, a)), R(exp(exp(a, a), a))\}.$$

1. $\Gamma \vdash \neg R(a)$ ass

2. $\Gamma \vdash R(exp(a, a))$ ass

3. $\Gamma \vdash \neg R(a) \wedge \neg R(a) \wedge R(exp(a, a))$ $\wedge$-intro (twice) 1, 1, 2

4. $\Gamma \vdash \exists x \exists y (\neg R(x) \wedge \neg R(y) \wedge R(exp(x, y)))$ $\exists$-intro (twice) 3

5. $\Gamma' \vdash \neg R(a)$ ass

6. $\Gamma' \vdash \neg R(exp(a, a))$ ass

7. $\Gamma' \vdash R(exp(exp(a, a), a))$ ass

8. $\Gamma' \vdash \neg R(exp(a, a)) \wedge \neg R(a) \wedge R(exp(exp(a, a), a))$ $\wedge$-intro (twice) 5, 6, 7

9. $\Gamma' \vdash \exists x \exists y (\neg R(x) \wedge \neg R(y) \wedge R(exp(x, y)))$ $\exists$-intro (twice) 8

Now with the rule

$$\text{from } \Gamma, \alpha \vdash \beta \text{ and } \Gamma, \neg\alpha \vdash \beta \text{ infer } \Gamma \vdash \beta$$

(which may be derived from the other rules), the required result, namely,

$$\neg R(a), R(exp(a, a)) \vdash \exists x \exists y (\neg R(x) \wedge \neg R(y) \wedge R(exp(x, y))),$$

may be inferred from lines 4 and 9. It is not difficult to see that the proof of this theorem given in Chapter 1 is the informal analytic version of the above deduction.

A Resolution Refutation: For resolution, the conjecture may be re-expressed as follows:

$$\neg R(a), R(exp(exp(a, a), a)), [\forall x \forall y] R(x) \vee R(y) \vee \neg R(exp(x, y)) \vdash \varnothing.$$

A refutation:

1. $\neg R(exp(a, a))$ resolvent of $R(x) \vee R(y) \vee \neg R(exp(x, y))$ and $\neg R(a)$, on $R(x)$ and then on $R(y)$

2. $R(y) \vee \neg R(exp(exp(a, a), y))$ resolvent of $R(x) \vee R(y) \vee \neg R(exp(x, y))$ with the newly derived clause $\neg R(exp(a, a))$

3. $\neg R(exp(exp(a, a), y))$ resolvent of clause 2 with $\neg R(a)$

4. $\varnothing$ resolvent of clause 3 with $R(exp(exp(a, a), a))$.

A careful analysis of this proof will reveal that for each step there is an exactly analogous step in the analytic sequentzen proof above.

A Matrix Calculus Refutation: The conjecture may be represented as for resolution, and then the refutation proceeds by showing that the following matrix is complementary:

$\neg R(a)$

$R(exp(exp(a, a), a))$

$R(a)\ R(a)\ \neg R(exp(a, a))$

$R(exp(a, a))\ R(a)\ \neg R(exp(exp(a, a), a))$.

(The last two clauses in this matrix are the required instances of the conjecture.) It may be seen that every vertical path through this matrix is complementary, and thus the refutation is completed. The analogy to the sequentzen proof should be even more apparent in this matrix calculus refutation.

TREATING SPECIAL RELATIONS AND THEORIES

In this book three specialised reasoning mechanisms were studied in detail.

Equational Reasoning
Apart from the simplistic axiomatisation approach discussed in Chapter 2, and the unimaginative rules employed in the natural deduction system of Chapter 3, the equational reasoning procedures discussed correspond essentially to developments of classical unification to treat the equality relation. In their simplest form these procedures may be broken down into three components:

rewriting: $a = b$ and $f(a) = c\ \Rightarrow\ f(b) = c$,

matching and rewriting: $f(x) = g(x)$ and $f(h(a)) = c\ \Rightarrow\ g(h(a)) = c$,

unification and rewriting: $f(x, a) = g(x)$ and $f(b, y) = h(y)\ \Rightarrow\ g(b) = h(a)$.

In Chapter 4, these processes were re-expressed in terms of decomposition tactics of a sequent calculus. In particular, it was shown how classical unification could be treated as a specialised application of sequent rules for equality.

These general equality rules allow equations to be applied (to "rewrite") in both directions; that is, the symmetry property of the equality relation may be utilised. This, however, can lead to highly inefficient proof construction; to avoid this, the "completion procedure" (Chapter 7) attempts to derive sufficient consequences of a set of equational axioms such that all subsequent proofs may be performed with rewriting in one direction. The process of unification and rewriting with the "rewrite rules" derived by the completion procedure in this way is then referred to as *narrowing* (Chapter 4).

Programming
In logic programming, programs are just special types of theories, that is, sets of non-logical axioms that correspond to computational procedures. The meaning of these programs is given by the semantics of the logic, while the computation strategy is provided by a specialised calculus of proof which allows easy reinter-

pretation as a procedure-invoking mechanism. The Prolog language (Chapter 6) was taken as an example of the application of automated theorem proving to programming. It was shown that the Horn-clauses used in Prolog have a natural re-interpretation as procedures when expressed in the form

$$P \leftarrow Q_1, Q_2,...., Q_n,$$

namely, P declares the name and formal parameters of the procedure, while the sequence of Q_i is the procedure body. It was also shown that the computation strategy of Prolog has a natural relationship to the resolution principle of Section 3.3 and may also be expressed in terms of the cut-free sequent calculi of Section 3.2. On the other hand, it was indicated that the depth-first search strategy used by most Prolog implementations is incomplete for the purposes of a general theorem prover, and that the lack of an "occurs check" (Section 3.3.3.2) makes the language unsound for logical deduction in classical logic.

Induction
Two approaches to proof by induction were described:

Classical approach (Chapter 8):
  • uses an inference rule for induction
  • applies rules backwards
  • uses heuristic simplification and generalisation techniques.

Proof by consistency, inductionless induction (Chapter 7):
  • shows that for sentences Σ and σ, the set $\Sigma \cup \{\sigma\}$ is consistent
  • then deduces, under certain conditions on Σ, that σ is an inductive theorem of Σ (the conditions being expressed only for equational Σ in this book)
  • generally uses completion method; in practice proofs are virtually identical to classical proofs.

CONCLUSIONS

It seems that sequent calculi are the most appropriate proof systems for combining naturalness with efficiency. To increase efficiency further, an additional mechanism for proof may be applied internally, while the user of the system is presented with the sequent calculus version externally. The matrix calculus is perhaps the most appropriate for this purpose, since it has a direct relationship to sequent systems. In addition, the efficient search strategies devised in the context of resolution generally may be applied to the matrix calculus. This is particularly true of the linear resolution strategies (such as SLD-resolution described in Chapter 7) which generally may be reinterpreted in terms of a sequent calculus, and thus in terms of the matrix method—for further discussion of this see [Bi87]. If sequentzen proofs are not considered to be sufficiently natural for a particular application (for example, where natural language proofs are to be derived from a computer proof), they may first be transformed into natural deduction proofs via the procedure outlined in Section 3.2.5. On the other hand, natural deduction proofs derived in this way often tend to be more complicated than is necessary, and it may be worthwhile devising further "transformation" strategies for replacing complicated sequentzen deductions by simpler natural deductions (as in Exercise 3.5); cf. [An80].

With regard to equational reasoning, the new completion-based approaches (developments of the Knuth-Bendix procedure) are of especial interest. In particular, if a canonical set of rules may be derived for a set of equations, then further proofs are simplified considerably. Based upon the work of Dershowitz and Sivakumar [DS88], it was also indicated in Section 4.2.7 how the "narrowing" process— where paramodulation (Section 3.3.7) is applied to only the left-hand sides of the rewrite rules of a canonical set—may be simulated in a sequent calculus.

The Knuth-Bendix completion procedure is also of importance for its diversity of applications to other areas of computer science, such as in logic programming, program synthesis and induction [De83]. In particular, its application to proof by induction in "inductionless induction" (discussed in detail in Chapter 7 of this book) could lead to methods of proof more powerful than the classical approaches —current research already provides examples of inductive theorems to which the completion-based inductionless induction applies naturally, where the "classical" approaches require much more work (see Chapter 7). However, it seems that three important developments of this approach to induction are required before it can truly be said to subsume the classical approach: extension to non-canonical rewrite systems, extension to general clauses (and first-order formulae), and incorporation into sequent (or natural deduction) calculi. The recent work concerned with the re-expression of the main ideas in inductionless induction in terms of inference rules in [Du89a] and [KR90], as discussed in Chapter 7, and the related work of Zhang et al [ZK88], may be seen as a step towards achieving these goals.

The application of Knuth-Bendix completion to the task of program synthesis was also briefly discussed in Chapter 7. The important point to note about the example synthesis described is its implicit use of induction. The view may be taken that the synthesis performed corresponds to a failed top-down "proof" in which the failure nodes (of the proof tree) provide the desired program. With this viewpoint, it seems that any system involving a component for induction may be applied to synthesis and transformation tasks. This includes even the Boyer-Moore theorem prover (Chapter 8). This system is commonly cited as being useless for synthesis tasks (e.g. [MW80]), because it does not allow existential quantifiers; however, the completion procedure does not allow these quantifiers either, and yet may still be applied to program synthesis.

The main difficulty in the case of BM lies in its method of deriving induction schemas only from functions appearing in the conjecture. Since in synthesis tasks the definition of the most important function (the one being synthesized) is not given, BM has little chance of deriving the correct schema. On the other hand, if the user can construct a function with the right structure, then the system can be advised to induct according to this definition, and in this way will be forced to derive the required function—this process was applied by the author in [Du88] to guide BM to perform a non-trivial program transformation. The problem with this approach is that the user is required to perform most of the work, which is what automated synthesis is intended to avoid. Recent work by Bundy et al [Bu90] has been concerned with extending the methods used in the Boyer-Moore system to treat synthesis problems. The main mechanism they use has a direct relationship to the narrowing-style process used by the completion procedure: the left-hand sides of a given set of transformation rules are unified with the conjecture to provide the required cases of the function being synthesized. It may be recalled that the completion-based synthesis in Chapter 7 performed exactly this operation—many other systems, including that of Manna and Waldinger [MW80], have also used such a mechanism.

This book has concentrated on theorem proving in classical first-order logic. Thus, work on many other interesting logics such as second-order, modal and intuitionistic logic has been omitted. On the other hand, recent work has shown that very often the methods used for classical first-order logic may be extended to treat these other logics. For instance, a first-order theorem prover may be "lifted" to treat second-order formulae via the incorporation of second-order unification (see [Kn89]). The process of unification also is used by L. Wallen to extend the matrix calculus to treat the modal operators (see [Wa87]). In a study note for PROSPEC-TRA [Du89b] the author showed how Wallen's method may also be applied quite straightforwardly to propositional intuitionistic logic. (The quantifiers may also be dealt with, but the main ideas can be expressed at the propositional level.) However, a major problem with Wallen's approach is that, although a proof is assured for any theorem (since the method is complete), the proofs derived are in a classical format, and thus do not naturally correspond to proofs in the intended logic. On the other hand, it seems that once the proof has been derived, an algorithm may be applied to construct a proof in the original calculus—such an algorithm is proposed for intuitionistic logic in [Du89b]. (As an aside, it may be noted that for intuitionistic logic, efficient proof derivation is perhaps not a principal concern amongst researchers, who are more concerned with its semantics and application to program synthesis.) An alternative approach to extend first-order theorem provers to treat non-classical logics, called "reification", is described in [Ra88]. Essentially, in this approach the modal operators are defined by classical first-order formulae, thus making modal logic simply a theory in classical logic; this approach may be applied also to intuitionistic logic.

Even disregarding proof methods for other logics, this text has certainly not covered every issue in automated theorem proving. At most it has discussed the basic ideas. On the other hand, a proof system that combined the main principles described in this book would be a good starting point for the development of a truly powerful theorem prover. Following the discussion above, this system would be a sequentzen-based prover utilising efficient reasoning mechanisms internally, would provide efficient equational reasoning (including simulation of narrowing for canonical theories), and perhaps would combine the most important features of the inductionless and classical approaches to proof by induction (and then perhaps would also incorporate a mechanism for performing program synthesis). On top of this basic procedure may be built a mechanism for reinterpreting each proof in natural deduction style and describing the steps in a limited natural language. More ambitious projects than this have already been undertaken by various research groups.

OUTLINE SOLUTIONS TO
SELECTED EXERCISES

The solutions provided here are mainly for those exercises whose solution requires more than mere bookwork. In some cases references are given for texts where the solution may be found.

2.1 The question supposes that an algorithm is given for S and that procedures are given for S' and $S - S'$. The decidability of S', and thus also $S - S'$, may be derived as follows. Since S is decidable, it is possible to determine whether or not any given object e is in S. Thus all that is required is a procedure **P** that alternates between running the given procedure for S' and running the given procedure for $S - S'$, spending a finite time (say 10 seconds) on one before swapping to the other. Since e must be in either S' or $S - S'$, ultimately the procedure for one of them will return the answer "yes", and at that point **P** will return the answer "yes" or "no" depending on whether e is or is not in S'. Thus S' is decidable.

2.2 For $\neg\alpha$, $\forall u\,\alpha$ and $\exists u\,\alpha$ to be well-formed formulae, α must be a well-formed formula. Thus $\neg\neg\forall x\neg\forall y(\exists z P(x, z) \to Q(y))$ is unambiguous because it can have only one possible "decomposition" into well-formed subformulae. For example, the only well-formed subformulae of $\neg\forall y(\exists z P(x, z) \to Q(y))$ are itself and the set

$$\{\forall y(\exists z P(x, z) \to Q(y)), (\exists z P(x, z) \to Q(y)), \exists z P(x, z), Q(y), P(x, z)\}.$$

2.3 If the set of unary functions is enumerable, then the function f must be in the enumeration, and thus must correspond to f_j for some j. But then what is the value of $f(j)$? It must be equal to both $f_j(j)$ and $f_j(j) + 1$, which is impossible. Thus f cannot be in the enumeration, and hence the set cannot be enumerable.

2.4 The formula $\forall x\exists y P(x, y) \to \exists y\forall x P(x, y)$ is *true* if P is assigned the relation $\geq$ on the domain **N**, for then $\exists y\forall x P(x, y)$ is *true* (choose $y = 0$); however, it is *false* if P is assigned the relation $\leq$ on **N**, for then $\forall x\exists y P(x, y)$ is *true* while $\exists y\forall x P(x, y)$ is *false*.

2.6 The solutions for the different cases are as follows.

- α is valid in $\mathbf{I}$ iff α is *true* in $\mathbf{I}$ for every assignment of values to its free variables, and thus iff $\forall x\,\alpha$ is valid in $\mathbf{I}$.
- The second statement follows.
- If α is *true* in some interpretation then $\neg\alpha$ must be *false* in that interpretation, and thus the required conclusion follows.
- $\mathbf{I}(\exists x\alpha)[d] = \mathbf{T}$ (for some interpretation $\mathbf{I}$ and sequence of values d of the domain of $\mathbf{I}$) iff $\mathbf{I}(\alpha)[d, d] = \mathbf{T}$ for some d in the domain of $\mathbf{I}$, iff α is satisfiable. The corresponding unsatisfiability result follows by means of the propositional theorem $\beta \leftrightarrow \gamma \Rightarrow \neg\beta \leftrightarrow \neg\gamma$.

2.7 $\Gamma \models \alpha$ iff α is *true* (in an interpretation) whenever Γ is *true* (in that interpretation), iff $\neg\alpha$ is *false* whenever Γ is *true*, iff $\Gamma \cup \{\neg\alpha\}$ is unsatisfiable.

2.8 The rule 'from $\exists x P(x)$ infer $P(x)$' preserves satisfiability, but is unsound.

2.9 Solutions to the two parts of this question are as follows. First, a proof that the completeness theorem implies the consistency theorem:

Γ is unsatisfiable iff there is some α such that $\Gamma \models \alpha$ and $\Gamma \models \neg\alpha$ (as may easily be shown), iff for the same α, $\Gamma \vdash \alpha$ and $\Gamma \vdash \neg\alpha$ (by the completeness theorem), iff Γ is inconsistent (by the definition of consistency).

Secondly, a proof that the consistency theorem implies the completeness theorem under the stipulated condition:

It may be assumed, by Exercise 2.7, that $\Gamma \models \alpha$ iff $\Gamma \cup \{\neg\alpha\}$ is unsatisfiable. Then, with '$\Gamma \models \alpha$' denoted by P, '$\Gamma \vdash \alpha$' by Q, '$\Gamma \cup \{\neg\alpha\}$ is satisfiable' by R, and '$\Gamma \cup \{\neg\alpha\}$ is consistent' by S, the problem reduces to the task of proving the propositional theorem

$$((R \leftrightarrow S) \wedge (Q \leftrightarrow \neg S) \wedge (P \leftrightarrow \neg R)) \rightarrow (P \leftrightarrow Q).$$

Perhaps the easiest way to prove this is to treat the first two equivalences as "rewrite rules". In this way $P \leftrightarrow \neg R$ becomes $P \leftrightarrow \neg S$, and then $P \leftrightarrow Q$.

2.10 By Exercise 2.7, α is valid iff $\neg\alpha$ is unsatisfiable, and thus it follows automatically that if unsatisfiability were decidable then validity would be also. Furthermore, since unsatisfiability is semi-decidable, satisfiablity cannot be, for otherwise unsatisfiability would be decidable by Exercise 2.1.

2.12 According to the axioms for $\approx$, it may be inferred (by substitution of $\approx$ for P) that $x \approx y \rightarrow (x \approx x \rightarrow y \approx x)$. This is equivalent to $(x \approx y \wedge x \approx x) \rightarrow y \approx x$, and since $x \approx x$ is true by the reflexivity axiom it may be eliminated from the hypothesis. Thus symmetry is derived. The proof of transitivity is easier: substituting $\approx$ for P in the second axiom for a binary P gives $y \approx z \rightarrow (x \approx y \rightarrow x \approx z)$, and this, in turn, is equivalent to transitivity $(x \approx y \wedge y \approx z) \rightarrow x \approx z$.

3.1(3) A strategy for proving a judgement of the form $P(0), \forall x(P(x) \rightarrow P(s(x))) \vdash P(s(...(s(0))...))$ —where $P(s(...(s(0))...))$ is taken to include the case of $P(0)$ —is as follows:

- show that $P(0)$ holds (using the assumption axiom, as indicated in the example preceding the exercise), and
- derive a proof of $P(s^{n+1}(0))$ from a proof of $P(s^n(0))$, as follows:

1. $P(0), \forall x(P(x) \rightarrow P(s(x))) \vdash \forall x(P(x) \rightarrow P(s(x)))$ ass
2. $P(0), \forall x(P(x) \rightarrow P(s(x))) \vdash P(s^n(0))$ lemma
3. $P(0), \forall x(P(x) \rightarrow P(s(x))) \vdash P(s^n(0)) \rightarrow P(s^{n+1}(0))$ $\forall$-elim 1
4. $P(0), \forall x(P(x) \rightarrow P(s(x))) \vdash P(s^{n+1}(0))$ $\rightarrow$-elim 2, 3

It may be noted that this corresponds to an *inductive proof* of $\forall x\, P(x)$.

3.8 See [CL73] for a solution to this problem.

3.9 That the clauses do not have a resolution refutation without factoring is clear because resolution can only derive a unit clause from a pair of non-unit clauses if the corresponding resolvent contains two (or more) identical literals, and this will never happen in this case (as the reader may verify). Thus resolution will never produce both a unit clause and its negation from these clauses and therefore will not prove the unsatisfiability of the clause set.

4.4 Since $T \cup \{a < b, b < c, c < a\}$ is unsatisfiable, the clause $P \lor Q \lor R$ is a total narrow theory resolvent of the given clauses.

4.5 To apply the completeness proof of resolution to the unit preference strategy it would be necessary to show that unit refutations of two sets of clauses $\Sigma \cup \{C\}$ and $\Sigma \cup \{D\}$ may always be transformed into a unit refutation of the new set $\Sigma \cup \{C \lor D\}$. However, this is not generally possible since, for example, C and D may be the only unit clauses (making $\Sigma \cup \{C \lor D\}$ a set of non-unit clauses).

4.7 One expression of the reversal of the backward chaining rule as a decomposition tactic is 'from $\Gamma, \alpha\theta \vdash \gamma$ infer $\Gamma, \alpha \rightarrow \beta, \beta\theta \rightarrow \gamma \vdash \gamma'$.

4.9 A simple analytic proof of $t_1 = t_2, t_2 = t_3 \vdash t_1 = t_3$ is as follows:

$t_1 = t_2, t_2 = t_3 \vdash t_1 = t_3 \quad \longrightarrow$
$\qquad t_1 = t_2, t_2 = t_3 \vdash t_1 = t_1 \;\&\; t_1 = t_2, t_2 = t_3 \vdash t_2 = t_3.$

4.10 An analytic proof of $t = t' \vdash t' = t$ which uses the P-product rule together with the new rule 'from $\Gamma, t = t \vdash \Delta$ infer $\Gamma \vdash \Delta$' is as follows:

$t = t' \vdash t' = t \quad \longrightarrow \quad t = t', t = t \vdash t' = t$
$\qquad \longrightarrow \quad t = t', t = t \vdash t = t' \;\&\; t = t', t = t \vdash t = t.$

To use the cut rule instead of the new rule simply take $t = t$ as the "cut" formula, and apply the reflexivity axiom.

4.11 The hypothesis of the induction schema for the conjecture is

$sum(0) + sum(0) = 0 * s(0) \land$
$\qquad \forall x(sum(x) + sum(x) = x * s(x) \rightarrow sum(s(x)) + sum(s(x)) = x * s(s(x))).$

(The conclusion is $\forall x(sum(x) + sum(x) = x * s(x)).$) By the definition of *sum*, the first hypothesis $sum(0) + sum(0) = 0 * s(0)$ may be reduced to the identity $0 = 0$, while the second hypothesis (the induction step) may initially be simplified to

$\forall x(sum(x) + sum(x) = x * s(x) \rightarrow s(x) + sum(x) + s(x) + sum(x) = x * s(s(x)))$,
and then (with the assumed commutativity of addition) to
$\forall x(sum(x) + sum(x) = x * s(x) \rightarrow s(x) + s(x) + sum(x) + sum(x) = x * s(s(x)))$.
The hypothesis of this subgoal may now be applied to the conclusion (to replace
the term $sum(x) + sum(x)$ by the term $x * s(x)$), and then discarded, to produce the
new subgoal $\forall x(s(x) + s(x) + (x * s(x)) = x * s(s(x)))$. This is *true* (according to
the usual definitions of $+$ and $*$) and thus the two hypotheses of the induction
schema have been proven. It therefore follows from the full induction schema that
$\forall x(sum(x) + sum(x) = x * s(x))$ holds.

5.6 The indexed sequent, after all occurrences of the negation symbol have been
deleted, is

$$P^+, P^- \wedge^- (P^- \vee^+ Q^+) \vdash Q^-,$$

where the sign next to each symbol is the index for the subformula of which the
symbol is the "main" operator (e.g. the $+$ in $\vee^+$ is the index of the subformula
$P \vee Q$). There are three paths through this indexed sequent, given by

$P^+\text{-} P^-\text{-} Q^-, \quad P^+\text{-} P^-\text{-} Q^-, \quad P^+\text{-} Q^+\text{-} Q^-$.

Each of these paths has occurrences of some literal with both positive and negative
indices and thus the sequent is complementary.

6.1 One definition of the exponentiation function for **N** is
    exp(X, 0, s(0)).
    exp(X, s(Y), Z) :- exp(X, Y, Z1), times(X, Z1, Z)..

6.5 With the view of a sequent as an abbreviation for the corresponding formula,
and with 'or', 'and' and 'iff' taken to represent $\vee$, $\wedge$ and $\leftrightarrow$, respectively, the
problem reduces to the task of proving the propositional theorem
    $((\Sigma \rightarrow (g \wedge G)) \vee ((\Sigma \wedge (H \rightarrow g)) \rightarrow (G \wedge H))) \leftrightarrow$
      $((\Sigma \rightarrow ((g \wedge G) \vee H)) \wedge ((\Sigma \wedge g) \rightarrow G))$.
The proof of this is left to the reader.

6.7 A renamed Horn-clause form of the clauses of EX is
$\{\neg nP(x, z) \vee \neg Q(x) \vee \neg nR(x, a), \quad \neg nP(x, z) \vee Q(x), \quad nP(x, y) \vee \neg nR(x, f(x)),$
    $nR(b, x) \vee \neg nS(x), \quad nS(x)\}$.

6.9 If **!** is omitted from the first clause for **fact** in the program, then the query
?- fact(0, Y). has two possible solutions for **Y**, namely **Y** = 0 and **Y** = 1.

7.1 The system $\{x + 0 \rightarrow 0 + x\}$ is non-terminating since the term $0 + 0$ has the
infinite reduction sequence $0 + 0 \Rightarrow 0 + 0 \Rightarrow$ .... On the other hand, the system
$\{s(x) + 0 \rightarrow 0 + s(x)\}$ is terminating because whenever it applies to some term it
always moves occurrences of 0 as the right argument of $+$ to the left argument of $+$
and never vice-versa; thus after a finite time the term will be rewritten to a form to
which the rule can no longer apply because there is no remaining subterm of the
form $s(t) + 0$.

7.2 The term $f(g(f(g(f(x)))))$ has the two normal forms $f(g(g(x)))$ and $g(g(f(x)))$ according to the system $\{f(g(f(x))) \to g(x)\}$.

7.3 First, let s have normal form q; then if $s' \Rightarrow_R s$ clearly s' must have normal form q, while if $s \Rightarrow_R s'$ then (by the confluence of R) s' must have normal form q. Next, consider the $n+1$ sequence of rewrites $t \leftrightarrow t_2 \leftrightarrow ... \leftrightarrow t_n \leftrightarrow t'$. Under the assumption that if $t! = p$ then $t_n! = p$, it follows (by the previous result) that if $t! = p$ then $t'! = p$.

7.4 The (only) critical pair between the rule $f(g(f(x))) \to g(x)$ and itself is the pair $<f(g(g(x))), g(g(f(x)))>$; cf. the solution to Exercise 7.2.

7.5 The only critical pair in the system $\{a \to b, a \to c, c \to a\}$ is $<b, c>$ (derived from the rules $a \to b$ and $a \to c$). Since $c \Rightarrow a \Rightarrow b$, it follows that the system is locally confluent (but this does not assure its confluence, though this also happens to hold, as shown earlier in the text).

7.7 If $t_1 = t_2$ is an inductive theorem of **E**, and (**L,C,E**) is consistent, then clearly (**L,C,E** $\cup$ $\{t_1 = t_2\}$) is consistent. For the converse, if $t_1 = t_2$ is not an inductive theorem of **E**, then there is some ground instance $t_1\phi = t_2\phi$ of $t_1 = t_2$ that does not follow from **E**; but since (**L,C,E**) is contained there are terms **c** and **d** in **C** such that $\mathbf{E} \models t_1\phi = \mathbf{c}$ and $\mathbf{E} \models t_1\phi = \mathbf{d}$, which means that (**L,C,E** $\cup$ $\{t_1 = t_2\}$) is inconsistent.

7.8 The ground specification system

$$(\{0, s\}, \{0, s(0), s(s(0))\}, \{s(s(s(s(0)))) = 0\})$$

is not contained since the term $s(s(s(0)))$ is not equal to any member of the set $\{0, s(0), s(s(0))\}$. That no independent equations may be added to the system without introducing inconsistency may be shown as follows. Since, according to the axiom $s(s(s(s(0)))) = 0$, every ground term is equal to one of the terms in the set $S = \{0, s(0), s(s(0)), s(s(s(0)))\}$, adding an independent equation $t = t'$ to the system would mean that two terms in S would become equal with respect to the set of axioms thus extended. Since the terms in the set $\{0, s(0), s(s(0))\}$ are not allowed to be equal, one of t or t' must be equal to $s(s(s(0)))$, while the other must be equal to either 0, $s(0)$ or $s(s(0))$ (since $t = t'$ is not a consequence of $s(s(s(s(0)))) = 0$). Thus, adding $t = t'$ to the system is equivalent to adding the equation $s(s(s(0))) = k$, where k is 0, $s(0)$ or $s(s(0))$; but then from the set $\{s(s(s(s(0)))) = 0, s(s(s(0))) = k\}$ it follows that either $s(0) = 0$ or that $s(s(0)) = 0$ (as may easily be shown). Therefore, adding an independent equation to the specification system would make the system inconsistent.

7.9 A proof of $x * x = x$.

Base case: $0 * 0 = 0$—true by definition of $*$.
Induction case: assume that $y * y = y$ and try to show that $s(y) * s(y) = s(y)$; expanding out $s(y) * s(y) = s(y)$, with the usual properties of $+$ and $*$, produces the subgoal

$$(y * y) + y + y + s(0) = s(y);$$

then applying the hypothesis and the lemma $x + x = 0$ reduces this subgoal to $y + s(0) = s(y)$, which is true by the definition of $+$.

Alternatively, it may simply be shown that $x * x = x$ holds for both 0 and $s(0)$; this is sufficient because every ground term is equal to either 0 or $s(0)$. However, the more complicated proof above forms the basis for a proof of a generalisation of the theorem (due to Fermat): $x^p \equiv x \bmod p$, for any prime p.

8.1 A suitable measure function is PLUS, with the lemma ensuring that the function G is well-defined being

$\neg$(ZEROP Y) $\rightarrow$ (LESSP (PLUS (SUB1 Y) X) (PLUS X Y)).

8.2 If pr is a one-to-one correspondence from $\mathbf{N}^2$ to $\mathbf{N}$, then every pair in the sequence $(0, 0), (0, 1), (0, 2),...$ must be mapped onto a distinct value by pr. Thus for any number m there is some n such that $pr(0, n) > m$. Since $pr(1, 0)$ must take some specific value, it follows that there is a k such that $pr(0, k) > pr(1, 0)$; thus no pr can preserve the ordering on the natural numbers. In other words, the problem lies in the fact that while there are no infinite "descending" sequences, between some (in fact, infinitely many) of the elements in the set of pairs there are infinite "ascending" sequences; in particular, $(1, 0) >_2 (0, 0)$, but between them is the infinite ascending sequence $(0, 1) <_2 (0, 2) <_2 (0, 3) <_2 ....$

8.3 Suggested induction for conjecture α: show $\alpha(X, 0, Z)$, and show $\alpha(X, Y, Z)$ assuming $\alpha((SUB1\ Y), X, Z)$. The induction variables are X and Y.

8.5 Each of the papers referred to in the preceding text essentially provides a solution to this problem.

8.6 A proof of $h(i, x) = k$ for all i and $x > 0$.

Base case: $h(0, x) = k$, which is true by the definition of h.

Induction case: $h(i, x) = h(i - 1, x + 1)$ for $i \neq 0$ and $x > 0$; and by the induction hypothesis $h(i - 1, x + 1) = k$ (since $x + 1 > 0$ for all x).

As k is arbitrary the original function f cannot return k for any input, and thus the above proof shows that f must be non-terminating for all $x > 0$.

8.7 The induction schema suggested by $+$ is

$\{half(0) < 0 + 0, half(y) < 0 + y \rightarrow half(s(y)) < 0 + s(y)\}$,

while the schema suggested by $half$ is

$\{half(0) < 0 + 0, half(s(0)) < 0 + s(0),$
$\quad half(y) < 0 + y \rightarrow half(s(s(y))) < 0 + s(s(y))\}.$

The cases of the first schema are $half(0) < 0 + 0$ and $half(s(y)) < 0 + s(y)$, while the cases for the second schema are $half(0) < 0 + 0$, $half(s(0)) < 0 + s(0)$ and $half(s(s(y))) < 0 + s(s(y))$. It may be seen that each of the cases of the second schema is an instance of a case in the first schema. The justification for discarding the first schema is that if it may be simplified by application of the axioms then so too may the second schema, while the converse does not hold.

REFERENCES

Abbreviations

AAAI: American Association for Artificial Intelligence.
AI: Artificial Intelligence.
CACM: Communications of the Association for Computing Machinery.
CADE: Conference on Automated Deduction.
EATCS: European Association for Theoretical Computer Science.
ECAI: European Conference on Artificial Intelligence.
ICALP: International Colloquium on Automata, Languages and Programming.
IEEE: Institute of Electrical and Electronic Engineers.
IJCAI: International Joint Conference on Artificial Intelligence.
JACM: Journal for the Association for Computing Machinery.
JAR: Journal of Automated Reasoning.
JCSS: Journal of Computer and System Sciences.
LNCS: Lecture Notes in Computer Science.
MI: Machine Intelligence.
POPL: Principles of Programming Languages.
RTA: Rewriting Techniques and Applications.
TCS: Theoretical Computer Science.
TOPLAS: Transactions on Programming Languages and Systems.

Most of the early papers on automated theorem proving (1957-70) may be found in [SW83a, b]. Many of the early papers on the foundations of logic, some of which have a bearing on ATP (such as Herbrand's thesis, Skolem's papers on logic and arithmetic, and Gödel's papers on both his completeness and incompleteness theorems), may be found in [He67].

[An80] P.B. Andrews. Transforming Matings into Natural Deduction Proofs. CADE-5, LNCS, Eds. W. Bibel, R. Kowalski. Springer Verlag, 1980, 281-292.

[An81] P.B. Andrews. Theorem Proving Via General Matings. JACM 28, 2, 1981, 193-214.

[An86] P.B. Andrews. An Introduction to Mathematical Logic and Type Theory: To Truth Through Proof. Academic Press, 1986.

[AH76] K. Appel, W. Haken. Every Planar Map is Four-Colorable. Bull. Amer. Math. Soc. 1976, 711-712.

[AK82] J. Arsac, Y. Kodratoff. Some Techniques for Removing Recursion from Recursive Programs. ACM TOPLAS 4, 2, 1982, 295-322.

[Au79] R. Aubin. Mechanising Structural Induction. TCS 9, 1979, 329-362.

[Ba87] L. Bachmair. Proof Methods for Equational Theories. PhD Thesis, University of Illinois, 1987.

[Ba77] J. Barwise. An Introduction to First-Order Logic. Handbook of Mathematical Logic, Ed. J. Barwise, 1977, 5-46.

[BM86] F.L. Bauer, B. Moller, H. Partsch. An Overview of the Munich Project CIP: Computer-Aided, Intuition-Guided Programming. Institut für Informatik, Technische Universität Munchen, 1986.

[Bi81] W. Bibel. On Matrices with Connections. JACM 28, 4, 1981, 633-645.

[Bi82] W. Bibel. A Comparative Study of Several Proof Procedures. AI 18, 1982, 269-293.

[Bi87] W. Bibel. Automated Theorem Proving 2nd ed. Vieweg, 1987.

[BE83] W. Bibel, E. Eder, B. Fronhoefer. Towards An Advanced Implementation of the Connection Method. IJCAI, 1983, 920-922.

[Bi88] S. Biundo. Automated Synthesis of Recursive Algorithms as a Theorem Proving Tool. Proc. ECAI, Pitman, 1988, 553-558.

[Bl86] K-H. Blasius. Construction of Equality Graphs. Fachbereich Informatik, Universität Kaiserslautern, 1986.

[Bl71] W.W. Bledsoe. Splitting and Reduction Heuristics in Automatic Theorem Proving. AI 2, 1971, 55-77.

[Bl77] W.W. Bledsoe. Non-Resolution Theorem Proving. AI 9, 1977, 1-35.

[BB71] W.W. Bledsoe, R.S. Boyer, W.H. Henneman. Computer Proofs of Limit Theorems. IJCAI, 1971, 586-600.

[BB74] W.W. Bledsoe, P. Bruell. A Man-Machine Theorem-Proving System. AI 5, 1974, 51-72.

[BJ89] G.S. Boolos, R.C. Jeffrey. Computability and Logic, 3rd ed. Cambridge University Press, 1989.

[Bo82] K.A. Bowen. Programming with Full First-Order Logic. MI 10, 1982, 421-440.

[BM75] R.S. Boyer, J.S. Moore. Proving Theorems About LISP Functions. JACM 22, 1, 1975, 129-144.

[BM79] R.S. Boyer, J.S. Moore. A Computational Logic. Academic Press, 1979.

[BM81] R.S. Boyer, J.S. Moore. Metafunctions: Proving Them Correct and Using Them Efficiently as New Proof Procedures. The Correctness Problem in Computer Science, Eds. R.S. Boyer, J.S. Moore. Academic Press, 1981, 103-185.

[BM85] R.S. Boyer, J.S. Moore. Integrating Decision Procedures into Heuristic Theorem Provers: A Case Study in Linear Arithmetic. Artificial Intelligence Dept., University of Texas at Austin, 1985.

[Br87] M. Broy. A Short Study in the Correctness Proof of Algebraic Specifications. Technical Report, Fakultät für Mathematik und Informatik, Universität Passau, 1987.

[Bu85] B. Buchberger. Basic Features and Development of the Critical-Pair/Completion Procedure. RTA 1985, LNCS, 1-45.

[BS90] A. Bundy, A. Smaill, J. Hesketh. Turning Eureka Steps into Computations in Automatic Program Synthesis. UK Information Technology Conf., 1990, 221-226.

[BD77] R.M. Burstall, J. Darlington. A Transformation System for Developing Recursive Programs. JACM 24, 1, 1977, 44-67.

[Ca85] J. Castaing. How to Facilitate the Proof of Theorems by Using Induction-Matching and by Generalisation. IJCAI, 1985, 1208-1213.

[CL73] C.L. Chang, R.C.T. Lee. Symbolic Logic and Mechanical Theorem Proving. Academic Press, 1973.

[CM87] W.F. Clocksin, C.S. Mellish. Programming in Prolog, 3rd ed. Springer Verlag, 1987.

[Coh85] J. Cohen. Describing Prolog by Its Interpretation and Compilation. CACM 28, 12, 1985, 1311-1324.

[Co82] A. Colmerauer. Prolog and Infinite Trees. Logic Programming, Eds. K.L. Clark, S-A. Tarnlund. Academic Press, 1982.

[Col85] A. Colmerauer. Prolog in 10 Figures. CACM 28, 12, 1985, 1296-1310.

[Co72] D.C. Cooper. Theorem Proving in Arithmetic without Multiplication. MI 7, 1972, 91-99.

[DP60] M. Davis, H. Putnam. A Computing Procedure for Quantification Theory. JACM 7, 1960, 201-215.

[De70] H. Delong. A Profile of Mathematical Logic. Addison-Wesley, 1970.

[De83] N. Dershowitz. Applications of the Knuth-Bendix Completion Procedure. Technical Report ATR-83(8478)-2, Office of Laboratory Operations, The Aerospace Corporation, 1983.

[De85] N. Dershowitz. Termination. RTA 1985, LNCS, 180-224.

[DS88] N. Dershowitz, G. Sivakumar. Goal-Directed Equation Solving. Proc. AAAI 7th National Conf. on Artificial Intelligence, 1988, 166-170.

[DH86] V.J. Digricoli, M.C. Harrison. Equality-Based Binary Resolution. JACM 33, 2, 1986, 253-289.

[Du88] D. A. Duffy. A Program Transformation by Induction and Completion. PROSPECTRA Report S.3.4-SN-13.0. University of Strathclyde, 1988.

[Du89a] D. A. Duffy. A General Principle of Inductionless Induction. Internal Report. University of Strathclyde, 1989.

[Du89b] D. A. Duffy. An Alternative To an Abstract Syntax for Proofs. PROSPECTRA Report S.3.4-SN-18.0. University of Strathclyde, 1989.

[Du77] M. Dummet. Elements of Intuitionism. Clarendon Press, 1977.

[EM85] H. Ehrig, B. Mahr. Fundamentals of Algebraic Specification I: Equations and Initial Semantics. EATCS Monographs on Theoretical Computer Science. Springer, 1985.

[Ei87] N. Eisinger. What You Always Wanted to Know About Clause Graph Resolution. CADE-8, 1986, 316-336.

[En72] H.B. Enderton. A Mathematical Introduction to Logic. Academic Press, 1972.

[Fr86] L. Fribourg. A Strong Restriction of the Inductive Completion Procedure. Proc. ICALP, 1986, 105-115.

[Ga87] H. Ganzinger. A Completion Procedure for Conditional Equations. Conditional Term Rewriting Systems, Eds. S. Kaplan, J.-P. Jouannaud. LNCS, Springer Verlag, 1987, 62-83.

[Ge69] G. Gentzen. Investigations into Logical Deduction. The Collected Papers of Gerhard Gentzen, Ed. M. E. Szabo. North Holland, 1969, 68-131.

[GW89a] F. Giunchiglia, T. Walsh. Abstract Theorem Proving. Proc. IJCAI, 1989, 372-377.

[GW89b] F. Giunchiglia, T. Walsh. Theorem Proving with Definitions. Research Report. Dept. of AI, University of Edinburgh, 1989.

[Gl80] P.Y. Gloess. An Experiment with the Boyer-Moore Theorem Prover: A Proof of the Correctness of a Simple Parser of Expressions. CADE-5, Eds. W. Bibel, R. Kowalski. Springer Verlag, 1980, 154-169.

[GL80] P.Y. Gloess, J.-P.H. Laurent. Adding Dynamic Paramodulation to Rewrite Algorithms. CADE-5, Eds. W. Bibel, R. Kowalski. Springer Verlag, 1980, 195-207.

[Gö87] R. Göbel. Ground Confluence. Proc. 2nd Conf. RTA, Ed. P. Lescanne. LNCS, Springer Verlag, 1987, 156-167.

[Go80] J.A. Goguen. How to Prove Inductive Hypotheses without Induction. CADE-5, Eds. W. Bibel, R. Kowalski. Springer Verlag, 1980, 356-372.

[Gr81] D. Gries. The Science of Programming. LNCS, Springer Verlag, 1981.

[GH78] J.V. Guttag, J.J. Horning. The Algebraic Specification of Abstract Data Types. Acta Informatica 10, 1978, 27-52.

[HW54] G.H. Hardy, E.M. Wright. An Introduction to the Theory of Numbers, 3rd ed. Oxford University Press, 1954.

[He67] J. v. Heijenoort (Ed.). From Frege to Gödel: A Source Book in Mathematical Logic, 1879-1931. Harvard University Press, 1967.

[He79] L.J. Henschen. Theorem Proving By Covering Expressions. JACM 26, 3, 1979, 385-400.

[HW74] L. Henschen, L. Wos. Unit Refutations and Horn Sets. JACM 21, 4, 1974, 590-605.

[Ho84] C.J. Hogger. Introduction to Logic Programming. Academic Press, 1984.

[Hs85] J. Hsiang. Refutational Theorem Proving Using Term Rewriting Systems. AI 25, 1985, 255-300.

[Hu80] G. Huet. Confluent Reductions: Abstract Properties and Applications to Term Rewriting Systems. JACM 27, 4, 1980, 797-821.

[Hu81] G. Huet. A Complete Proof of Correctness of the Knuth-Bendix Completion Algorithm. JCSS 23, 1981, 11-21.

[HH82] G. Huet, J.M. Hullot. Proofs By Induction in Equational Theories with Constructors. JCSS 25, 2, 1982, 239-266.

[HO80] G. Huet, D. Oppen. Equations and Rewrite Rules: A Survey. Formal Languages: Perspectives and Open Problems, Ed. R. Book. Academic Press, 1980, 349-400.

[JT88] K. P. Jantke, M. Thomas. Inductive Inference for Solving Divergence in Knuth-Bendix Completion. Internal Report. University of Glasgow, 1988.

[JK83] J.-P. Jouannaud, H. Kirchner, J-L. Remy. Church-Rosser Properties of Weakly Terminating Term Rewriting Systems. IJCAI, 1983, 909-915.

[JK84] J.-P. Jouannaud, H. Kirchner. Completion of A Set of Rules Modulo a Set of Equations. Proc. 11th Symp. on POPL, 1984, 83-92.

[JK85] J.-P. Jouannaud, E. Kounalis. Proofs by Induction in Equational Theories Without Constructors. Bull. Assoc. Theor. Comput. Sci. 27, 1985, 49-55.

[Ka63] S. Kanger. A Simplified Proof Method for Elementary Logic. Computer Programming and Formal Systems, Eds. P. Braffort, D. Hirshberg. North Holland, 1963, 87-94.

[KM87] D. Kapur, D.R. Musser. Proof by Consistency. AI 31, 1987, 125-157.

[KN85] D. Kapur, P. Narendran. An Equational Approach to Theorem Proving in First-Order Predicate Calculus. IJCAI, 1985, 1146-1153.

[KN87] D. Kapur, P. Narendran, H. Zhang. On Sufficient Completeness and Related Properties of Term Rewriting Systems. Acta Informatica 24, 1987, 395-415.

[KK84] C. Kirchner, H. Kirchner. New Applications of the REVE System. Centre de Recherche en Informatique de Nancy, 1984.

[Kl62] S.C. Kleene. Introduction to Meta-Mathematics. North Holland, 1962.

[Kl71] R.E. Kling. A Paradigm for Reasoning by Analogy. IJCAI, 1971, 568-585.

[Kn89] K. Knight. Unification: A Multi-Disciplinary Survey. ACM Comput. Surveys 21, 1, 1989, 93-124.

[KB70] D. Knuth, P.B. Bendix. Simple Word Problems in Universal Algebras. Computational Problems in Abstract Algebra, Ed. J. Leech. Pergamon Press, 1970, 263-297.

[Ko85] E. Kounalis. Completeness in Data Type Specifications. Proc. EUROCAL Conf., ed. B. Buchberger. LNCS, Springer Verlag, 1985, 348-362.

[KR90] E. Kounalis, M. Rusinowitch. Mechanising Inductive Reasoning. Bull. EATCS 41, 1990, 216-226.

[Ko75] R. Kowalski. A Proof Procedure Using Connection Graphs. JACM 22, 4, 1975, 572-595.

[Ko79] R. Kowalski. Logic for Problem Solving. North Holland, 1979.

[Kr85] B. Krieg-Bruckner. A Little Example of PROgram Development by SPECification and TRAnsformation. FB Mathematik und Informatik, Universität Bremen, 1985.

[Kr87] B. Krieg-Bruckner. Integration of Program Construction and Verification: the PROSPECTRA Methodology and Support System. FB Mathematik und Informatik, Universität Bremen, 1987.

[Kr90] B. Krieg-Bruckner et al. PROSPECTRA, ESPRIT Project 390. LNCS, Springer Verlag, To Appear.

[La90] C.W.H. Lam. How Reliable is a Computer-Based Proof? Mathematical Intelligencer 12, 1, 1990.

[La80] D. Lankford. Some Remarks About Inductionless Induction. Research Report, Louisiana Tech. University, 1980.

[La81] D. Lankford. A Simple Explanation of Inductionless Induction. Research Report, Louisiana Tech. University, 1981.

[Le83] P. Lescanne. Computer Experiments with the REVE Term Rewriting System Generator. Proc. 10th POPL Conf., 1983, 99-108.

[Ll87] J. Lloyd. Foundations of Logic Programming. Springer Verlag, 1987.

[Lo78] D.W. Loveland. Automated Theorem Proving: A Logical Basis. North

Holland, 1978.

[Ma74] Z. Manna. Mathematical Theory of Computation. McGraw-Hill, 1974.

[MN70] Z. Manna, S. Ness. On the Termination of Markov Algorithms. Proc Int. Conf. on System Science, 1970, 789-792.

[MW80] Z. Manna, R. Waldinger. A Deductive Approach to Program Synthesis. ACM TOPLAS 2, 1, 1980, 90-121.

[McG82] A.D. McGettrick. Program Verification Using Ada. Cambridge University Press, 1982.

[Me66] B. Meltzer. Theorem-Proving for Computers: Some Results on Resolution and Renaming. Computer J. 8, 4, 1966, 341-343.

[Mo69] J.B. Morris. E-Resolution: Extension of Resolution to Include the Equality Relation. IJCAI, 1969, 287-294.

[MW77] J.H. Morris, B. Wegbreit. Subgoal Induction. CACM 20, 4, 1977, 209-222.

[Mu82] N.V. Murray. Completely Non-Clausal Theorem Proving. AI 18, 1, 1982, 67-85.

[Mu80] D.R. Musser. On Proving Inductive Properties of Abstract Data Types. Proc. 7th POPL Conf., 1980.

[NO80] G. Nelson, D.C. Oppen. Fast Decision Procedures Based on Congruence Closure. JACM 27, 2, 1980, 356-364.

[Ne74] A.J. Nevins. A Human-Oriented Logic for Automatic Theorem-Proving. JACM 21, 4, 1974, 606-621.

[NS63] A. Newell, J.C. Shaw, H.A. Simon. Empirical Explorations with the Logic Theory Machine: A Case Study in Heuristics. Reproduced in Computers and Thought, Eds. Feigenham and Feldman. McGraw-Hill, 1963, 109-133.

[ON86] H.J. Ohlbach, A. Nonnengart. A Deductive Tool Kit for Verification Tasks: An Informal Synopsis of the MKRP-System. Report for ESPRIT Project 1033, University of Kaiserslautern, 1986.

[Pa89a] P. Padawitz. Inductive Proofs by Resolution and Paramodulation. Internal Report, Universität Passau, 1989.

[Pa89b] P. Padawitz. Inductive Expansion. Internal Report, Universität Passau, 1989.

[Pe83] F. Pereira, D. Warren, D. Bowen, L. Byrd, L. Pereira. C-Prolog's User's Manual Version 1.2. SRI International, 1983.

[Pe67] R. Peter. Recursive Functions. Academic Press, 1967.

[PS81] G.E. Peterson, M.E. Stickel. Complete Sets of Reductions for Some Equational Theories. JACM 28, 2, 1981, 233-264.

[Pl81] D.A. Plaisted. Theorem Proving with Abstraction. AI 16, 1981, 47-108.

[Pl72] G.D. Plotkin. Building-in Equational Theories. MI 7, 1972, 73-90.

[Pl88] D. Plummer. Gazing: Controlling the Use of Rewrite Rules. Research Report, Dept. of AI, University of Edinburgh, 1988.

[Pr60] D. Prawitz. An Improved Proof Procedure. Theoria 26, 1960, 102-139.

[Pr65] D. Prawitz. Natural Deduction: A Proof Theoretical Study. Almqvist and Wiksell, 1965.

[Pr69] D. Prawitz. Advances and Problems in Mechanical Proof Procedures. MI 4, 1969, 59-71.

[Ra88] A. Ramsay. Formal Methods in Artificial Intelligence. Cambridge University Press, 1988.

[RL89] D.W. Reed, D.W. Loveland. A Comparison of Three Prolog Extensions. Computer Science Technical Report, Duke University, 1989.

[Re87] S.V. Reeves. Adding Equality to Semantic Tableaux. JAR 3, 1987, 225-246.

[Re71] R. Reiter. A Semantically Guided Deductive System for Automatic Theorem Proving. IJCAI, 1971, 41-46.

[RY76] C. Reynolds, R.T. Yeh. Induction as the Basis for Program Verification. IEEE Trans. Software Eng. SE-2, 4, 1976, 244-252.

[Ri87] B. Ritchie. Design and Implementation of an Interactive Proof Editor. PhD Thesis, University of Edinburgh, 1987.

[Ro69] J.W. Robbin. Mathematical Logic: A First Course. W.A. Benjamin, 1969.

[RW69] G. Robinson, L. Wos. Paramodulation and Theorem-Proving in First-Order Logic with Equality. MI 4, 1969, 135-150.

[Ro65] J.A. Robinson. A Machine-Oriented Logic Based on the Resolution Principle. JACM 12, 1, 1965, 23-41.

[Ro67] J.A. Robinson. A Review of Automatic Theorem Proving. Annual Symp. in Applied Mathematics XIX, Amer. Math. Soc., 1967, 1-18.

[Ro79] J. A. Robinson. Logic: Form and Function—The Mechanisation of Deductive Reasoning. Edinburgh University Press, 1979.

[Ro83] J. A. Robinson. Logic Programming—Past, Present and Future. New Generation Computing, 1983, 107-124.

[Ru85] D.M. Russinof. An Experiment With the Boyer-Moore Theorem Prover: A Proof of Wilson's Theorem. JAR 1, 2, 1985, 121-139.

[Sh77] R.E. Shostak. On the SUB-INF Method for Proving Presburger Formulas. JACM 77, 4, 1977, 529-543.

[Sh79] R.E. Shostak. A Practical Decision Procedure for Arithmetic with Function Symbols. JACM 26, 2, 1979, 351-360.

[Sh84] R.E. Shostak. Deciding Combinations of Theories. JACM 31, 1, 1984, 1-12.

[Si86] J.H. Siekmann. Unification Theory. Proc. 7th ECAI, vi-xxxv.

[SW80] J. Siekmann, G. Wrightson. Paramodulated Connection Graphs. Acta Informatica 1980, 67-86.

[SW83a] J. Siekmann, G. Wrightson. Automation of Reasoning, Part 1: Classical Papers on Computational Logic 1957-1966. Springer Verlag, 1983.

[SW83b] J. Siekmann, G. Wrightson. Automation of Reasoning, Part 2: Classical Papers on Computational Logic 1967-1970. Springer Verlag, 1983.

[Sl72] J.R. Slagle. Automatic Theorem Proving with Built-in Theories Including Equality, Partial Orderings and Sets. JACM 19, 1, 1972, 120-135.

[Sl74] J. R. Slagle. Automatic Theorem-Proving for Theories with Simplifiers, Commutativity, and Associativity. JACM 21, 4, 1974, 622-642.

[Sm68] R.M. Smullyan. First-Order Logic. Springer-Verlag, 1968.

[St88] A. Stevens. A Rational Reconstruction of Boyer and Moore's Techniques for Constructing Induction Formulas. Proc. ECAI, Pitman, 1988, 565-570.

[St84] M.E. Stickel. A Prolog Technology Theorem Prover. Proc. Int. IEEE Conf. on Logic Programming, 1984, 371-383.

[St85] M. E. Stickel. Automated Deduction By Theory Resolution. IJCAI, 1985, 1181-1186.

[Th84] J.J. Thiel. Stop Losing Sleep over Incomplete Data Type Specifications. 11th Annual ACM Symp. on POPL, 1984.

[Tr90] O. Traynor. The Design, Implementation and Integration of a Proof System for a Transformational Programming Environment. PhD Thesis, University of Strathclyde, 1990.

[Wa85] L. Wallen. Generating Connection Calculi from Tableaux and Sequent Based Proof Systems. Artificial Intelligence and its Applications, Eds. A.G. Cohn, J.R. Thomas, 35-50.

[Wa87] L. Wallen. Matrix Methods for Modal Logics. Proc. 10th IJCAI, 1987, 916-923.

[Wa60] H. Wang. Toward Mechanical Mathematics. IBM J. Res. Dev. 4, 1960, 2-22.

[Wa82] D.H.D. Warren. Higher-Order Extensions of Prolog: Are They Needed? MI 10, 1982, 441-454.

[WC65] L. Wos, D. Carson, G. Robinson. Efficiency and Completeness of the Set-of-Support Strategy in Theorem Proving. JACM 12, 1965, 536-541.

[WO84] L. Wos, R. Overbeek, E. Lusk, J. Boyle. Automated Reasoning: Introduction and Applications. Prentice-Hall, 1984.

[WR67] L. Wos, G. Robinson, D. Carson, L. Shalla. The Concept of Demodulation in Theorem Proving. JACM 14, 4, 1967, 698-709.

[ZK88] H. Zhang, D. Kapur, M. S. Krishnamoorthy. A Mechanizable Induction Principle for Equational Specifications. Proc. CADE-9, 1988, 162-181.

[ZR85] H. Zhang, J.L. Remy. Contextual Rewriting. RTA 1985, LNCS, 46-62.

INDEX

Discourses of War and Peace

Edited by Adam Hodges

OXFORD
UNIVERSITY PRESS

Oxford University Press is a department of the University of Oxford.
It furthers the University's objective of excellence in research,
scholarship, and education by publishing worldwide.

Oxford   New York
Auckland   Cape Town   Dar es Salaam   Hong Kong   Karachi
Kuala Lumpur   Madrid   Melbourne   Mexico City   Nairobi
New Delhi   Shanghai   Taipei   Toronto

With offices in
Argentina   Austria   Brazil   Chile   Czech Republic   France   Greece
Guatemala   Hungary   Italy   Japan   Poland   Portugal   Singapore
South Korea   Switzerland   Thailand   Turkey   Ukraine   Vietnam

Oxford is a registered trade mark of Oxford University Press
in the UK and certain other countries.

Published in the United States of America by
Oxford University Press
198 Madison Avenue, New York, NY 10016

Library of Congress Cataloging-in-Publication Data
Discourses of war and peace / edited by Adam Hodges.
   p.   cm.—(Oxford studies of sociolinguistics)
Includes bibliographical references and index.
ISBN 978-0-19-993727-1 (alk. paper)
1. Discourse analysis—Political aspects. 2. Political science. I. Hodges, Adam.
P302.77.D566   2013
401'.47—dc23   2012028433

9 8 7 6 5 4 3 2 1

Printed in the United States of America
on acid-free paper

In memory of Susan L. Swartz Knight who embodied peace in her everyday actions

CONTENTS

ACKNOWLEDGMENTS

This volume would not have taken shape without the input, feedback and support of numerous individuals. I owe an immense debt to Nikolas Coupland and Adam Jaworski who helped plant the seed for the volume. They were instrumental in its early conceptualization and together acted as a vital sounding board as I formulated ideas for the project.

The work on the volume was helped along by the generous support of the A.W. Mellon Foundation, as well as the English Department and the Dietrich College of Humanities and Social Sciences at Carnegie Mellon University. These institutions provided the fellowship funding that allowed me to spend two academic years teaching at Carnegie Mellon University. While there, I had the great fortune to interact with numerous colleagues and students who had various influences on this book and my scholarly pursuits more generally. In particular, I am grateful to Barbara Johnstone and all the participants in the Social Meaning in Language reading group from the University of Pittsburgh and Carnegie Mellon University, including Soudi Abdesalam, Mariana Achugar, Laura Brown, Scott Kiesling, Thomas Mitchell, and Mark Thompson. In addition, I thank all my colleagues at Carnegie Mellon University, including Christine Neuwirth, John Oddo, and Christopher Warren, for providing a stimulating intellectual environment in which to pursue my scholarly interests.

I thank Jennifer Andrus and Thomas Huckin for organizing a conference at the University of Utah in 2011 where I had the opportunity to lead a roundtable on politics and war and discuss some of the ideas found in the introductory chapter to this volume. Many thanks to the participants in that roundtable, including Karen Adams, Patricia Dunmire, and Sandra Silberstein. I am forever grateful to Kira Hall as well as to Barbara Fox, Chad Nilep, and Karen Tracy for the substantial impact they have had (and continue to have) on my career as a scholar. I owe special thanks and gratitude to my partner, Sarah Vieweg, for her love, support, and intellectual insight. I thank my parents for their unswerving support in everything I undertake, and for teaching me about love and empathy.

I have dedicated the book to Susan L. Swartz Knight, a beloved family member who passed away as I readied the book for production. Although her life and career in law was cut short by multiple sclerosis, the caring attitude she brought to all the roles she played in her short life—daughter, sister, aunt, mother, wife, friend, lawyer—demonstrates the embodiment of peace in everyday living. Her life is a testament to the way small, positive actions can have a big impact on the lives of others. She will be missed, but never forgotten.

Discourses of War and Peace

Introduction

1

War, Discourse, and Peace

Adam Hodges

War

Humans never engage in war[1] without the mediating force of discourse. From the rhetorical saber rattling that precedes conflict through the diplomatic overtures that sue for peace, discourse plays an integral role in the outbreak, conduct, and disputation of armed political conflict around the world. Warfare as an undertaking relies upon the organizational capacity of discourse to mobilize forces, direct resources, and legitimize actions. The creation of enemies requires the discursive process of constructing an out-group and distancing that group from the humanity of the in-group. Moreover, the realities of war are magnified or minimized, remembered or forgotten through the discursive processes humans use to give them meaning. The integral relationship between discourse and war is evidenced by the dedicated genre of "war stories" that form a familiar place in our world, operating to variously detail, celebrate, explain, glorify, mythologize, grieve, caution against, prepare for, cope with, and generally talk about war. From historical and literary accounts stretching back to Thucydides' documentation of the Peloponnesian War through the numerous Hollywood action films about wars past and present, war holds a privileged yet troubled place in the popular imagination.

Given the ubiquity of war from our current historical perspective, it is easy to see why war is commonly viewed as an inevitable aspect of the human condition. This popular view has even been helped along by prominent intellectuals, including the psychologist William McDougall (1920) and psychoanalyst Sigmund Freud (1921), who argued that warfare was the result of a primitive instinct or innate propensity toward aggression and destruction. Biologically based theories of war have remained with us into the twenty-first century despite a growing body of anthropological evidence that contradicts innatist claims. As a discipline dedicated to understanding what it means to be human,

---

[1] Ferguson (1984) defines war as "organized, purposeful group action, directed against another group . . . involving the actual or potential application of lethal force" (5; 1990: 26).

anthropology since Franz Boas has placed a primary importance on culture as the distinguishing feature between humans and other animals. Given that much of human development occurs after birth and is subject to the powerful process of enculturation—achieved to a large extent, as sociocultural linguists recognize, through linguistic socialization—Clifford Geertz (1973) suggests "that there is no such thing as a human nature independent of culture" (49). To simply explain war as the result of human nature erases the complexity of culture and human behavior from the explanatory equation; and it risks mistaking culturally shaped practices for human universals.

Since war is often taken as a given, it is worth exploring the anthropology of war in some detail here. One of the leading researchers on this topic is R. Brian Ferguson whose three decades of research engages with archaeological, biological, cultural, and primatological studies on war. Ferguson (2008) collapses his findings into ten key points, beginning with the point that "no work has demonstrated that non-pathological humans have an inborn propensity to violence" (34).

If anything, as social animals, humans are more endowed with empathy and compassion than a drive to kill. As discussed by Hourcade et al. (2011), historical studies of firing rates on the front lines of war support such a view. Brigadier General S. L. A. Marshall's survey during World War II points to a firing rate of 15 percent for an average infantry company on an average day of battle, with that figure rising to only 25 percent under the most intense circumstances for the most aggressive infantry companies (Marshall 1947; see also Grossman 1996). Marshall set out to overcome this perceived "problem" (i.e., a lack of killer instinct) through training methods that better desensitized soldiers to the task of killing. Through more effective training practices, firing rates indeed rose substantially to 90 percent or more during the Vietnam War. As anthropologists emphasize, humans are an adaptable species and we are well equipped to learn how to kill if socialized into such practices.[2] Yet we are equally capable of being socialized into practices that promote peace.

If war were an inescapable aspect of social life, one would expect to find evidence of war throughout the archaeological record. Ferguson (2006, 2008, inter alia) points to empirical evidence from early archaeological remains to argue that war is a relatively recent phenomenon (in archaeological terms). Instead of warfare being an inescapable aspect of human nature, several preconditions must be in place for it to arise, and he notes that "the preconditions that made war likely were lacking for most of humanity's really ancient history" (Ferguson 2006: 470). War is not wired into human brains, but rather exists as a culturally contingent phenomenon.

---

[2] This does not mean, of course, that learning to kill through desensitization to our humanity does not come without consequence. One need only note the psychological problems such as post-traumatic stress disorder that follow many soldiers home from war.

Ferguson (2008: 36) provides a model to explain the practice of war based on a nested hierarchy of material, institutional, and ideological constraints. In material terms alone, it is staggering to consider the resources dedicated to warfare in the international system. According to figures provided by the Stockholm International Peace Research Institute, world military expenditures in 2009 reached $1.5 trillion, which represents a 49 percent increase in global spending over the first nine years of the twenty-first century. "The 10 largest military spenders in 2009 accounted for 75 percent of world military spending, with the USA alone accounting for 43 percent" (Stockholm 2010). Within the United States, according to the budget analysis of the Friends Committee on National Legislation, 39 percent of 2010 income taxes went toward Pentagon spending for current and past wars. In contrast, 2 percent went toward diplomacy, development, and war prevention (FCNL 2010).[3] Such figures underscore the material foundations for the culture of war that currently grips our world, led by American military hegemony as it manifests itself in Iraq, Afghanistan, and elsewhere around the globe.

While Ferguson (2008: 38) argues that from an etic perspective, materialistic self-interests on the part of decision makers can explain the impetus for actual wars, he acknowledges that leaders typically do not conceptualize or talk about war through such a materialistic framework. Instead, through the rhetoric that paves the road to war (such as the call to arms speeches examined in the first part of this volume), advocates convert practical self-interests into "moral rights and duties" so that war "becomes the 'right' thing to do" (Ferguson 2008: 38). As a result, even those who benefit the most from war come to see moral values as the overriding rationale for entering into conflict. Importantly, discursive practices constitute a central means by which culturally specific systems of meaning—including the moral values important in a given society—are brought into existence.

Moreover, once symbolic processes help instantiate war and realize the institutions that support it, the presence and practice of war in turn shapes society. Ferguson (1994) has compared war to an addiction. "Once a given society is internally adapted for war, making war becomes much easier—a necessity, even, for the reproduction of existing social relations" (Ferguson 2008: 40). The famous words of warning uttered by President Dwight D. Eisenhower in his farewell address cautioned Americans against just this type of internal adaptation for war. As foreseen, the influence of the military-industrial complex[4] has

---

[3] "FCNL calculations based on estimated expenditures reported by the White House Office of Management and Budget. This analysis covers the $2,844,461 million 'federal fund' budget, which is the spending supported by income taxes, estate taxes, and other general revenues. Not included are trust funds, such as Social Security and Medicare, which are supported by dedicated revenues" (FCNL 2010).

[4] More accurately, one should speak of the military-industrial-congressional complex, a term that was shortened to military-industrial complex in the final draft of Eisenhower's speech. Despite deleting the congressional aspect from the term, the role of Congress in the political economy of war holds just as much import as the role played by the armaments industry.

effectively institutionalized war in American society with ramifications for the global system as a whole. Crucially, the effects of war are not restricted to the societies involved in fighting each other. Ferguson notes that the contexts for war come in layers so that overarching zones of conflict, such as dueling superpowers on the global stage, impact local groups and actors in complex ways.

The division of humanity into groups draws from the need to organize and categorize the world around us, but during times of war this process becomes exaggerated to produce invidious distinctions with deadly consequences. "Many biologically oriented theories postulate that war is, in some way, an expression of an innate tendency to in-group amity and out-group enmity. In these views, the existence of the group generates the conflict" (Ferguson 2008: 42). However, as widely recognized by sociocultural linguists and other social scientists, group divisions are created rather than found; and discourse plays a central role in the construction of in-group and out-group identities (Bucholtz and Hall 2004, 2005, inter alia). Moreover, Ferguson (2008) notes that it "is unusual, if not rare, for war to involve two preexisting groups, and only them. In actual practice, it is the conflict that firms up the opposed groups" (42). As seen in conflicts around the world, groupings vary in composition and duration. Alliances are formed, broken, and realigned according to the exigencies of the conflict. The contingent nature of Us versus Them is illustrated when one compares the binaries established for the current wars in Iraq and Afghanistan: "them" in Iraq is different from "them" in Afghanistan despite the discursive work done within Bush's narrative about those wars to conflate disparate entities—namely, the Taliban, al Qaeda, Saddam Hussein—into one overarching enemy—that is, "terrorists" (Hodges 2011). The realities on the ground expose such constructions for what they are when looked at more closely.

Although war is often conceived of and viewed as a struggle between Us and Them—namely, as a relation between two or more nation-states—domestic politics are as central to war as are international relations. "It is the nature of war that its politics are internal as well as external" (Ferguson 2008: 43; see also, Ferguson 1990, 1995, 1999; Ferguson and Whitehead 1992). Not only are there different interests, ideas, and arguments within a polity over the course of action that should be taken to counter outside threats, but such moves impact the play for power within the polity as well. While political leaders are not always in favor of war and their political interests are often better served by avoiding it, "war has several general consequences that can be used to enhance a leader's position" (Ferguson 2008: 45). Namely, the unity that typically arises when a nation enters into war tends to consolidate public support for the leader and the leader's policies. "It leads to the acceptance of certain situations— heightened aggression in war leaders and acquiescence to their directives—that would not be tolerated if there were no lethal enemy" (Ferguson 2008: 45). Consider how the stature and popularity of George W. Bush dramatically rose in American society immediately after the acts of foreign terrorism in the

United States on September 11, 2001. Arguably, President Bush was able to gain overwhelming congressional support for the PATRIOT Act (legislation that curtailed many civil liberties) as well as the Iraq War Resolution (legislation that gave him authority to invade Iraq) because of his status as a "wartime president."

In general terms, Ferguson sketches out the process of internal political machinations in a manner that sounds all too familiar to analysts involved in critical dissections of the political rhetoric employed to justify war:

> To build a following, they construct narratives and histories to define "us" and demonize "them." They speak to local cultural understandings and fears, invoke potent symbols, and offer plausible—even if false—explanations of recent miseries (al-Zarqawi's letter to bin Laden is a textbook illustration of such a militarized construction of history, invocation of sacred values, and demonization of the other). Many leap to the cause, providing a hard core of followers to command. Thus empowered, the leaders foster polarization and fear, and start the killing. With the die cast, it becomes a situation of "follow the leader." (Ferguson 2008: 45)

It is the construction of such discourses that justify and support, in addition to the discourses that respond to and contest war, that this volume aims to address.

Discourse

As Elshtain (1985) emphasizes, it is important to recognize "the ways in which received doctrines, 'war stories,' may lull our critical faculties to sleep, blinding us to possibilities that lie within our reach" (55). With this in mind, this volume sets out to provide empirical analyses that examine discourses of war and peace in an effort to better understand the socially constructed and culturally contingent nature of these aspects of the human condition. Contributors, who come from backgrounds in linguistics, anthropology, rhetoric, and communication studies, draw from discourse analytic and/or ethnographic methods to examine the discourse used by politicians and social actors in societies that include the United States, Canada, the United Kingdom, Morocco, Ireland, the Palestinian territories, and Japan. The book is divided into four sections that foreground the political effects of discourse on issues of war and peace, including the way discourse is harnessed to justify war (part I), negotiate military deployment (part II), respond to armed conflict (part III), and promote peace (part IV).

Before providing an overview of the book's contents, it is important to note that *discourse* in this volume is broadly conceived as more than just language-in-use (although it certainly is that, too). Discourse is taken to encompass "all forms of meaningful semiotic human activity seen in connection with social, cultural, and historical patterns and developments of use" (Blommaert 2005: 3). Chapters in the book deal with spoken language, written texts, and even the use of silence as a semiotic activity as authors examine political speeches, national security documents, public inquiries and hearings, press reports, family interactions, activists' discussions, political protests, and sightseeing tours. In several chapters, narrative figures prominently into the way discourse organizes cultural understandings—whether they are understandings about the future, the nature of Us and Them, or historical lessons from past conflicts. In addition, the volume as a whole is concerned with the discourses (in the Foucauldian sense of the term) that are representative of the ways of thinking about war and peace in the world today.

Part I, "Justifying War," features four chapters that address the use of discursive resources that allow leaders to legitimize foreign policy and military ventures. In chapter 2, "'New World Coming': Narratives of the Future in US Post–Cold War National Security Discourse," Patricia Dunmire analyzes the reports put out by the US Commission on National Security/21st Century. The reports consist of assessments of the international security environment in the first quarter of the twenty-first century, the role the United States should play in that environment, and the political, economic, and military challenges and opportunities the environment presents to the United States. These assessments of the future security environment, in turn, serve as the foundation for various economic, political, and military policies that are to be enacted in the near term. The discourse revolves around the premise that the future is both knowable and controllable, and seeks to tamp down the uncertainty inherent in moments of significant social change through policies and actions designed to shape the future in such a way as to maintain the status quo and, hence, the privileged status of the United States. Through the examination of the narratives of the future that are present in these documents, the chapter illustrates how those narratives serve to legitimize US global supremacy as a military power.

Also dealing with political narrative, chapter 3, "The Generic US Presidential War Narrative: Justifying Military Force and Imagining the Nation," examines the generic elements of the war narrative told by American presidents from Woodrow Wilson through George W. Bush. Each new president draws from a remarkably similar generic schema to make the case for entering into war. The tradition and history bound up in the narrative about America's involvement in war, which closely aligns with the tenets of Just War Theory's *jus ad bellum*, instills each new call to arms with tradition and authority. Through this rhetorical process, American national identity is constructed and reaffirmed across presidencies. The rehearsal of the narrative draws upon familiar patriotic imaginings that eclipse debate and demand uncritical public support for the war effort. Through the dissection of the war narrative, the chapter attempts to provide a critical understanding of this process in an effort to challenge what is all too often taken as familiar and accepted.

Continuing with the thread of underlying similarities in call to arms speeches, in chapter 4, "The Discursive Battlefield of the 'War on Terror': Enabling Strategies for Garnering Public Support in the Rhetoric of George W. Bush and Osama bin Laden," Anna Podvornaia provides a comparative analysis of the "call to arms" rhetoric used by both the Bush administration and al Qaeda to drum up support for their respective sides in the "war on terror." Bin Laden issued his call to arms in the form of religious decrees that urged and sanctioned attacks against Western targets, eventually leading to the events of 9/11 in 2001. Bush's call to arms comes in the form of an address before the US Congress in the wake of those attacks. The chapter contends that the division between the Self and the Other is achieved in "call to arms" discourse through two simultaneous processes: unifying the members of an in-group by reinforcing their similarities, and condemning the behavior of the out-group by amplifying the differences that distinguish Us from Them. The outcome is the delegitimization of the enemy's cause and the justification of any retaliatory action. The juxtaposition of Bush and bin Laden illustrates the haunting similarity of these processes used by leaders irrespective of political allegiances.

In chapter 5, "World of the Impolitic: A Critical Study of the British WMD Dossier," Aditi Bhatia provides a look at the decision to invade Iraq in 2003 from the perspective of the British government led by Prime Minister Tony Blair. During the lead-up to the war, the Blair administration compiled the Weapons of Mass Destruction Dossier, a fifty-page document that detailed Iraq's history of use, planning, and possession of WMDs, in addition to its breach of UN resolutions, and current plans to resume its prohibited WMD program. The dossier constructed Iraq as a threat to international security and thereby allowed the government to justify taking military action to remove Saddam Hussein from power. In the chapter, Bhatia analyzes the rhetorical processes used in the dossier to present evidence in a light favorable to gaining domestic and international support for the decision to go to war. These processes positioned Saddam Hussein's Iraq as an inevitable threat, drawing on a discourse of historicity to connect the past, present, and future as well the discourse of legal authority to represent the case in an authoritative voice. Bhatia argues that such rhetorical processes serve to heighten the impact of the dossier's arguments, creating a sense of urgency in the call for war. As a whole, these four chapters underscore that discourse is the sine qua non of war. Discourse is crucial to the process of legitimizing policy and leading polities into war—whether democratic or autocratic, nation-states or non-state groups.

Part II, "Negotiating Military Deployment," features two chapters that examine the domestic political struggles over how, whether, and where militaries should be deployed during times of war as well as peace. In chapter 6,

"Culture Clash: Framing Peacekeeping and Its Role in a Canadian Context," Janis Goldie examines the different visions of peacekeeping that arose out of a Canadian commission of inquiry into the torture and death of a Somali teenager by members of the Canadian Airborne Regiment while serving in Somalia. Tackling the largest military scandal in Canadian history, the commission produced thousands of pages of documents, held hundreds of hours of public hearing testimony, and ran until it was forced to produce its final report on June 30, 1997. The chapter displays how peace and conflict are constructed in very different ways by those associated with a "civilian" perspective (as represented by the commissioners and lawyers) versus a "military" perspective (as represented by the military witnesses and bureaucrats). Throughout the commission discourse, differing norm systems are evident as is the significant battle over the definitions of peacekeeping, conflict, and the appropriate role for the military in Canada's foreign policy.

In chapter 7, "Promising without Speaking: Military Realignment and Political Promising in Japan," Chad Nilep provides a different take on military deployment. In this case, at issue are domestic politics and the debate in Japan over the presence of the US military in Okinawa. His analysis of Japanese newspaper coverage during the administration of Yukio Hatoyama shows that discourses of "political promising" may develop in complexes of interaction in which the politician held responsible for the promise exerts relatively little control. Hatoyama became prime minister when his Democratic Party of Japan (DPJ) won an August 2009 lower-house election, wresting control of the Japanese government from the Liberal Democratic Party (LDP) for only the second time since the end of World War II. In June of 2010 Hatoyama resigned the post amid plummeting approval ratings. Newspaper editorials cited Hatoyama's failure to deliver on a promise of removing the US military from the Futenma base in Okinawa as a key reason for his declining popularity. This analysis suggests that in Japan, as in the United States, "promising" can be a dangerous act. Furthermore, this act need not be grounded in any specific locution by the promiser. Both Nilep and Goldie underscore the importance of political discourse in negotiating allowable uses and installations of military forces.

Part III, "Responding to Armed Conflict," features two chapters that examine how citizens outside of governmental positions discuss, debate responses to, and negotiate understandings of armed conflicts. In chapter 8, "'Everyone Has Their Particular Part to Play': Commensuration in the Northern Irish and Palestinian Victims' Rights Movements," Candler Hallman explores how the blockade of Gaza impacts commensuration between the Irish and Palestinian victims' rights movements, as activists link their narratives and cast the insurgency in Palestine as the current day instantiation of past resistance in Ireland. On the one hand, in the wake of violence by the Israeli Defense Forces, Palestinian activists argue that, much like the past insurgency in Northern Ireland, violence must be used to prevent further rights abuse. However, the

Irish activists represent political violence as a past "necessary evil" that is less effective than present-day peaceful rights advocacy. This leads to a situation in which Irish and Palestinian victims' rights advocacy are positioned as relatively incommensurate, which may indicate a post-9/11 unease with supporting political violence among Western audiences. This incommensurability may affect the ability of Palestinian advocates to lobby international audiences, and thus has implications for the formation of transnational victims' rights networks.

Chapter 9 shifts the scene to Morocco and the use of language by families to construct understandings of violence. In "Reasonable Affects: Moroccan Family Responses to Mediated Violence," Becky Schulthies provides an ethnographic account of the interactions that take place within the homes of Moroccan families as they collaboratively construct affect in response to mediated violence, often using the same linguistic resource both to express emotion and assess propositions. News and talk programs provide almost daily accounts of conflict within the region: the Abu Ghraib scandal; bombings of Shiite pilgrims in Kerbala, Iraq; Al Qaeda attacks in Saudi Arabia; and Israeli targeted assassinations in Gaza, in addition to reports of clashes between insurgents, soldiers, police, and civilians. Schulthies shows that as families collaboratively evaluate these images and accounts, they pair emotional responses with reasoning of who was involved and how it could happen, at times challenging official narratives. In fact, both of the chapters in this section hold implications for the way new narratives are constructed outside the framework of officially recognized discourses.

Finally, Part IV, "Promoting Peace," features two chapters that examine the way discourse can be harnessed to promote peace. In chapter 10, "Performing Peace: The Framing of Silence in a Quaker Vigil," Anna Marie Trester draws from her ongoing ethnographic participation with a Quaker vigil for peace held weekly on the lawn of the US Capitol in Washington, DC. Her analysis explores this silent event against the ever-shifting background of US involvement in Iraq. Specifically, she analyzes how this group's use of silence is repackaged as a means for performing peace. She considers the objects, activities, and rituals used to organize the silence, including how participants employ intertextual biblical links on a banner as part of the construction of individual and group identity. She examines flyers distributed at the event that state the goals and purpose (and later history) of the vigil; and she tracks changes in reference and perlocutionary force resulting in changing relationships with audience(s) of this performance. Additionally, she considers how these shifts are tracked semiotically in changes to the banner and emplacement of the event itself, which serves to interrupt the visual field of the Washington Mall for would-be photographers and passers-by. While such silent and symbolic engagement with institutions of power may have varying levels of success in generating public discourse, ultimately, regardless of speaker or setting, such performance is staged for consumption by multiple audiences and is capable of embodying shifting responses to, experiences of alienation from, and disagreement with the institutions and structures of power.

Chapter 11 also holds important implications for how discourse can be employed in the service of peace. In "Narrating War and Peace at Battle Ruins: Okinawan Tourism-Activism Discourses," Taku Suzuki explores the narratives told at Okinawan World War II memorial sites by, on the one hand, sightseeing guides for tourist groups, and, on the other hand, peace activists guiding educational tours for Japanese schoolchildren. Okinawa was the site of a brutal ground battle in World War II, which killed more than 240,000 combatants and noncombatants in the spring of 1945. As evidenced in Nilep's chapter, it has remained a highly militarized land with the majority of the US military facilities in Japan located there. Suzuki juxtaposes ethnographic portrayals of the tour guiding narrations by these two types of guides, showing how the former advocate a "sentimentalist" conceptualization of peace that leads to a depoliticized view of the past, while the latter adopt an approach that challenges tourists to consider how the past might have been otherwise, cultivating a critical ethos to inform present stances toward militarization. As other chapters have emphasized, narrative plays a primary role in shaping understandings and promoting social action. Thus, the way peace is narrated in these tours has important implications for the effectiveness of peace-building projects. Suzuki argues that, in contrast to the sentimental and depoliticized tours of the sightseeing guides, the peace activists leading educational tours are more effective in challenging tourists to critically consider the past within the context of the present.

Beyond the empirical investigations into specific sites of discursive interaction provided by each of these chapters, the volume as a whole aims to inform a broader conversation about how peace might be more productively conceived.

Peace

In the last of his ten points about war, Ferguson (2008) echoes a key critique waged by feminist theorists regarding the way we conceptualize peace. As poststructuralists point out, any binary opposition establishes a hierarchy so that one term in the binary moves into a privileged position over the other. In the war/peace binary, war provides the dominant conceptual framework through which both terms come to be defined, conceptually subordinating peace to war. *Peace* therefore becomes the "absence of war" (rather than a concept defined on its own terms), perpetuating a militaristic framework for thinking about peace. In warist terms, peace comes to be viewed as a "strategic stability" (Cohn 1987: 708) between the outbreak of hostilities—or, the continuation of war by other means (Arendt 1970: 9). Moreover, attempts to reposition or reimagine conflict resolution outside the overarching framework of war come to be viewed as weak, unrealistic, or "soft-headed" (Cohn 1987: 708). Consequently, movement toward peaceful resolution of conflict becomes all the more difficult to achieve in a culture where warist thinking takes precedence. Through the analyses provided in this volume, we can gain a better understanding of the way different discourses conceptualize *war* and/or *peace* (implicitly or otherwise). Although the enterprises of discourse analysis and ethnographic analysis are largely descriptive in nature, the knowledge gained holds important implications for informing the creation of alternative discourses.

In discussing peace, it is worth pointing out that the number of international conflicts since the 1950s has actually declined, according to the *Human Security Report 2009/2010*, suggesting a positive shift away from war. In addition, deaths associated with conflicts have trended downward (HSRP 2011: 11). Indeed, the figures for the number of worldwide battle-deaths since the 1950s is quite striking: from 600,000 in 1950 (the first year of the Korean War) to 300,000 in 1972 (the deadliest year of the Vietnam War) to 270,000 in 1982 (the height of the Iran-Iraq War) to 130,000 in 1999 (the time of wars between Ethiopia and Eritrea) to 27,000 in 2008 (amid the US-led wars in Afghanistan and Iraq). As the *Report* argues, "the demise of colonialism and the Cold War removed two important causes of war from the international system" (HSRP 2011: 13). Risks of large conflicts have been further reduced due to an increase in global economic interdependence, the number of democracies, and "an emerging norm of war-averseness" (HSRP 2011: 13). As international affairs scholar Andrew Bacevich (2010b) emphasizes, as we move further into the twenty-first century, "the prospect of Big Wars solving Big Problems is probably gone for good." Yet the discourse of big wars solving big problems is giving way to a new way of thinking about war—the discourse of permanent mobilization, or "semiwar" (Bacevich 2010a: 27). It is important to understand this new war discourse if an alternative discourse of peace is to compete with it.

In chapter 2, Dunmire illustrates this shift in the way of thinking about war. Entailed in the narrative forwarded by the US Commission on National Security/21st Century is a new conception of peace as a form of permanent militarization in the service of "global stability." Indeed, not since World War II has the US Congress made an official declaration of war. Yet, as we know, the US has been involved in numerous military "operations." As Dunmire's analysis illustrates, this reconceptualization of war leads to a highly militarized foreign policy that allows the president to use force without congressional approval as part of a business as usual approach to international affairs (e.g., Obama's commitment of military resources in Libya in 2011). Peace is thereby further conceptualized, in warist terms, as maintaining "stability" and "the international order" (compare to Cohn's "strategic stability" noted earlier).

Despite the shift toward "semiwar," or permanent "militarization," the discursive strategies used to legitimize military operations still draw from familiar tropes and make use of other well-established war discourses. The generic presidential war narrative dissected in chapter 3 draws from canonical images of past wars (e.g., World War II) to justify military operations of all sizes, including ventures in Grenada, Panama, and Kosovo. In addition, the narrative crucially builds upon the ethical framework of Just War Theory—itself an established way of thinking about war that perpetuates the use of military action as a viable (if limited) option for conflict resolution. Despite its moral underpinnings, Just War Theory does little to forward the notion of peace as anything other than the absence of war. In the presidential narrative, as well as in the Bush and bin Laden speeches examined by Podvornaia in chapter 4, war is additionally conceived as a necessity forced upon one side by an uncultivated "other." Through the discourse of "otherness," the enemy is stripped of its humanity, foreclosing alternative possibilities to conflict resolution. Faced with a dehumanized enemy, peace is then viewed as the eradication of the "other." The tension with Just War Theory's limits on the use of force becomes apparent here, and this tension underscores that the boundaries around what is considered just fluctuate as these different discourses of war collide and impinge upon political debates. As Bhatia illustrates in chapter 5, justificatory discourses—such as the one found in the British WMD Dossier—can sometimes shift what is viewed as acceptable by using technical and logical-sounding language to legitimize the process of decision making.

Dominant conceptions of war not only subordinate peace and define it in terms of war (i.e., the "absence of war"), but such conceptions have infected our politics as well. In *On War*, Carl von Clausewitz famously noted that war is politics by other means; but Foucault (2003) points out that it is more appropriate to invert this dictum to "say that politics is the continuation of war by other means" (2003: 15). That is to say, politics "has been conceived as a continuation, if not exactly and directly of war, at least of the military model as a fundamental means of preventing civil disorder" (Foucault 1977: 168–69). As Hannah Arendt (1970) discusses in *On Violence*, this model conflates power with violence so that collective violence is viewed as the ultimate exercise of power. To heed Arendt's call "to rescue politics from war" (Elshtain 1985: 48) requires replacing the view of power-as-domination, or *power-over* with the view of power as a productive and empowering force, or *power-to* (Allen 1998: 33; Wartenberg 1990: 85). Instead of being predicated upon the exercise of power qua domination (through force, if needed), politics is thereby defined as individuals acting together in concert (Arendt 1970: 44; Arendt 1958: 200).

Arendt's conception of politics as people acting together is on display in the remaining chapters of the volume. The different visions of peacekeeping that are discussed and debated in the Canadian hearings examined by Goldie in chapter 6 illustrate the way new visions of peace and war arise out of the political process—even as that process is filled with discord. As Nilep emphasizes through his examination of Japanese politics in chapter 7, discord is part and parcel of the political process—a process that requires ongoing active engagement among different factions. Yet what is the best way to engage across lines of deep division? This question becomes central in chapter 8 as Hallman examines the way Palestinian-rights activists discuss and debate the best course of action for challenging the blockade of Gaza. Hallman's analysis blurs what is often taken to be a clear-cut distinction between violent and peaceful methods of resistance for achieving conflict resolution, illustrating how established narratives are opened up for scrutiny. Importantly, revisions of official narratives do not only take place within overtly political contexts. Schulthies's focus in chapter 9 on the way family members recontextualize television coverage within the home speaks to the role everyday social interaction plays in the way cultures are revised through dialogue. It is this type of dialogic revision that the project of peace building requires.

Established war discourses—including the realist approach to international relations that emphasizes "peace through strength" as well as the tenets of Just War Theory that attempt to justify when and how collective violence can legitimately be used—require revision if we are to disassociate violence from the exercise of power, as Arendt (1970) argues is necessary. The actions taken to promote peace by the Quakers studied by Trester in chapter 10, as well as the educational tour guides studied by Suzuki in chapter 11, reflect conscious attempts to expunge collective violence from the diagram of power. For the Quakers, the vigil they hold on the lawn of the US Capitol seeks to convey a decidedly pro-peace (rather than anti-war) message. For them, peace is a lifestyle that informs every decision a person makes. For the educational tour guides, peace exists as an ongoing political struggle that seeks to shatter the myth that past wars are an inevitable tragedy.

In fact, identifying and dismantling discourses that position war as an inevitable aspect of the human condition is a key aim this volume pursues. In support of that project, the anthropological evidence on war cannot be overemphasized in a world where "the language and imperatives of war become a permanent rhetorical condition" and thereby does "much of our thinking for us" (Elshtain 1985: 50). Equally as dangerous as specious biological explanations is the view that warfare's enduring presence in modern cultural systems makes it nearly as inescapable as if it were hard-wired into human brains. After all, "the concepts through which we think about war, peace, and politics get repeated endlessly, shaping debates, constraining consideration of alternatives, often reassuring us that things cannot really be much different than they are" (Elshtain 1985: 54). But, as we know, "cultures are continuously produced, reproduced, and revised in dialogues among their members" (Mannheim and Tedlock 1995: 2). It is through dialogue—individuals coming together to speak and hence act in concert—that new systems of thought arise. This is what humans do. We speak and act together; and that discursive action enables war as well as peace.

Crucially, to most effectively enable peace requires developing an *ethos of peace* that is not subordinate to war. Too often, the discourse of war displaces concrete human considerations with the abstract considerations of strategic planning—even to the extent that "weapons themselves" can become the fundamental reference point around which all thinking revolves (Cohn 1987: 711). A discourse of peace requires that humans be positioned as the central reference point. The costs that war inflicts on humanity—in the form of lives lost, destroyed, or ruptured—must be placed into sharp focus. In addition, an ethos of peace recognizes that "factors leading to peaceful conflict resolution are quite distinct from those that lead to war. Peace has its own dynamic, including behavior patterns, social and political institutions, and value systems that foster equitable treatment and the rejection of violence as acceptable means to an end" (Ferguson 2008: 46; see also, Sponsel 1994, Ury 1999, Fry 2006).

So what is *peace* in positive terms of its own? To begin with, instead of the inert absence of the action-filled undertaking of war, peace must be turned into an activity in its own right. To reimagine peace begins by viewing it as a practice. It is a practice that is fundamentally an "enterprise of justice" (Segers 1985: 627). To practice peace involves promoting education, democracy, and equality. It involves fostering cross-cultural connections that emphasize our common humanity. Whereas to wage war involves increasing social distance and decreasing compassion, to wage peace involves decreasing social distance and increasing compassion. Through its concern with justice, peace works to reverse economic decline, environmental stress, social and economic inequality, and the incentives for war. In short, peace "must be actively constructed on the basis of central human values: truth, justice, freedom, love" (Segers 1985: 627).

Shifting away from old discourses of war toward new discourses of peace requires active engagement—the type of engagement Arendt characterizes in her definition of politics. To be certain, such engagement requires work, but no more work than it took to construct the discourses of war that currently grip the world. As Ackermann (2003: 345) describes, the creation of new norms occurs in three stages. The first stage involves advocacy and raising awareness; next comes acceptance and institutionalization, and finally internationalization of the norms (see also Finnemore and Sikkink 1998). New norms around conflict prevention are in the first stage, and the contributions in this volume aim to provide additional momentum to that stage of development.

Conclusion

To work toward peace requires understanding the conditions that make war possible in our current world, including the way discourse operates to construct cultural understandings and to perpetuate ideological frameworks that reproduce the culture of war. It is through the disruption of taken-for-granted representations of the social world that discourse scholars can contribute to this endeavor. By exposing the ideologies and discourses that underlie the rhetoric of war, the accepted image of *the world as it is* can shift toward reimagining *the world as it can be*. Through the examination of specific contexts in which discourse operates in the service of war, we can gain insight into the symbolic conditions that make war possible across human societies as well as the culturally specific values that allow particular societies to engage in war and to engage in peace.

As a collective whole, these chapters highlight the concept that projects of war and peace both involve substantial amounts of discursive work. Indeed, as the anthropological approach to war shows us, war is not an inevitable aspect of the human condition. It is a cultural achievement that is situated, defined, and produced within particular sites of sociopolitical interaction undergirded by semiotic activity. Likewise, for projects of peace to proliferate as past wars have done in human history, a discourse of peace building needs to be sown and cultivated to reap fruitful results. Scholars involved in unpacking the discursive underpinnings of war are well positioned to inform projects of peace building. Although the reach of academic treatments of the topic may have little direct impact on popular discourses, greater knowledge of the phenomenon can only benefit future action. Raising a critical awareness of the discursive processes and historical underpinnings that lead to war is a valuable step in the promotion of peace, as Suzuki illustrates in the final chapter of the volume. These findings are echoed by Ferguson's (1988) comment that "working to strengthen the ideas and organizations of those who mobilize popular opposition to militarism [are] likely to have some positive impact, however slight" (2). Thus, this volume is a type of cultural project in its own right, one that attempts to further understandings of the discourses of war and peace in an effort to inform public discussions on these issues that are so vital to humanity's future.

References

Ackermann, Alice. 2003. "The Idea and Practice of Conflict Prevention." *Journal of Peace Research* 40(3): 339–47.

Allen, Amy. 1998. "Rethinking Power." *Hypatia* 13(1): 21–40.

Arendt, Hannah. 1958. *The Human Condition*. Chicago: University of Chicago Press.

Arendt, Hannah. 1970. *On Violence*. New York: Harcourt Brace.

Bacevich, Andrew. 2010a. *Washington Rules: America's Path to Permanent War*. New York: Metropolitan Books.

Bacevich, Andrew. 2010b. "The Western Way of War Has Run Its Course." CBS News website; retrieved: August 4, 2010. www.cbsnews.com/stories/2010/08/04/opinion/main6742001.shtml.

Blommaert, Jan. 2005. *Discourse: A Critical Introduction*. Cambridge: Cambridge University Press.

Bucholtz, Mary and Kira Hall. 2004. "Language and Identity." In *A Companion to Linguistic Anthropology*, Alessandro Duranti (ed.), 369–94. Malden, MA: Blackwell.

Bucholtz, Mary and Kira Hall. 2005. "Identity and Interaction: A Sociocultural Linguistic Approach." *Discourse Studies* 7(4–5): 585–614.

Cohn, Carol. 1987. "Sex and Death in the Rational World of Defense Intellectuals." *Signs* 12(4): 687–718.

Elshtain, Jean Bethke. 1985. "Reflections on War and Political Discourse: Realism, Just War, and Feminism in a Nuclear Age." *Political Theory* 13(1): 39–57.

FCNL. 2010. Friends Committee on National Legislation: A Quaker Lobby in the Public Interest. www.fcnl.org/budget/.

Ferguson, R. Brian. 1984. "Introduction: Studying War." In *Warfare, Culture and Environment*, R. Brian Ferguson (ed.), 1–81. Orlando, FL: Academic Press.

Ferguson, R. Brian. 1988. "How Can Anthropologists Promote Peace?" *Anthropology Today* 4(3): 1–3.

Ferguson, R. Brian. 1990. "Explaining War." In *The Anthropology of War*, J. Haas (ed.), 22–50. New York: Cambridge University Press.

Ferguson, R. Brian. 1994. "The General Consequences of War: An Amazonian Perspective." In *Studying War*, S. Reyna and R. E. Downs (eds.), 85–111. Langhorne, PA: Gordon and Breach.

Ferguson, R. Brian. 1995. *Yanomami Warfare: A Political History*. Santa Fe, NM: School of American Research.

Ferguson, R. Brian. 1999. "A Paradigm for the Study of War and Society." In *War and Society in the Ancient and Medieval Worlds: Asia, the Mediterranean, Europe, and Mesoamerica*, K. Raaflaub and N. Rosenstein (eds.), 409–58. Cambridge, MA: Center for Hellenic Studies, Harvard University Press.

Ferguson, R. Brian. 2006. "Archaeology, Cultural Anthropology, and the Origins and Intensification of War." In *The Archaeology of Warfare: Prehistories of Raiding and Conquest*, Elizabeth N. Arkush and Mark W. Allen (eds.), 469–523. Gainesville: University Press of Florida.

Ferguson, R. Brian. 2008. "Ten Points on War." *Social Analysis* 52(2): 32–49.

Ferguson, R. Brian and Neil L. Whitehead. 1992. *War in the Tribal Zone; Expanding States and Indigenous Warfare*. Santa Fe, NM: School of American Research Press.

Finnemore, Marth and Kathryn Sikkink. 1988. "International Norm Dynamics and Political Change." *International Organization* 52(4): 887–91.

Foucault, Michel. 1977. *Discipline and Punish: The Birth of the Prison*. New York: Random House.

Foucault, Michel. 2003. *"Society Must Be Defended": Lectures at the Collège de France, 1975–1976*, Mauro Bertani and Alessandro Fontana (eds.), David Macey (trans.). New York: Picador.

Freud, Sigmund. 1921. *Massenpsychologie und Ich-Analyse*. Leipzig-Vienna-Zürich: Internationaler Psychoanalytischer Verlag.

Fry, Douglas. 2006. *The Human Potential for Peace: An Anthropological Challenge to Assumptions about War and Violence*. New York: Oxford University Press.

Geertz, Clifford. 1973. *The Interpretations of Cultures*. New York: Basic Books.

Grossman, Dave. 1996. *On Killing: The Psychological Cost of Learning to Kill in War and Society*. Boston: Back Bay Books.

Hodges, Adam. 2011. *The "War on Terror" Narrative: Discourse and Intertextuality in the Construction and Contestation of Sociopolitical Reality*. New York: Oxford University Press.

Hourcade, Juan Pablo and Natasha E. Bullock-Rest. 2011. "HCI for Peace: A Call for Constructive Action." In Proceedings of ACM CHI 2011, 443–52.

HSRP—Human Security Report Project.

Human Security Report Project. 2011. *Human Security Report 2009/2010: The Causes of Peace and the Shrinking Costs of War*. Oxford: Oxford University Press.

Mannheim, Bruce and Dennis Tedlock. 1995. "Introduction." In *The Dialogic Emergence of Culture*, Dennis Tedlock and Bruce Mannheim (eds.), 1–32. Urbana: University of Illinois Press.

Marshall, S. L. A. 1947. *Men against Fire: The Problem of Battle Command in Future War*. Washington, DC: Combat Forces Press.

McDougall, William. 1920. *The Group Mind*. Cambridge: Cambridge University Press.

Segers, Mary C. 1985. "The Catholic Bishops' Pastoral Letter on War and Peace: A Feminist Perspective." *Feminist Studies* 11(3): 619–47.

Sponsel, Leslie. 1994. "The Mutual Relevance of Anthropology and Peace Studies." In *The Anthropology of Peace and Nonviolence*, L. Sponsel and T. Gregor (eds.), 1–36. Boulder, CO: Lynne Reiner.

Stockholm International Peace Research Institute. 2010. *SPIRI Yearbook 2010: Armaments, Disarmament and International Security*. New York: Oxford University Press. www.sipri.org/yearbook/2010/05.

Ury, William. 1999. *Getting to Peace: Transforming Conflict at Home, at Work, and in the World*. New York: Viking.

Von Clausewitz, Carl. 1976. *On War*. M. Howard and P. Paret (eds.). Princeton: Princeton University Press.

Wartenberg, Thomas. 1990. *The Forms of Power: From Domination to Transformation*. Philadelphia: Temple University Press.

PART ONE

Justifying War

2

"New World Coming"

NARRATIVES OF THE FUTURE IN US POST–COLD WAR
NATIONAL SECURITY DISCOURSE

Patricia L. Dunmire

Introduction

This chapter is concerned with the discourse of "peace" that has characterized
the post–Cold War era. I focus specifically on the narratives of the future that
have circulated in US national security policy documents in the aftermath of
the Cold War. Such narratives merit study because of the role they play in legitimating the highly militarized approach the United States has taken to national
security and foreign policy since the demise of the Soviet Union. Moreover,
they help shed light on how peace has been conceptualized and practiced in the
aftermath of the Cold War. In short, to understand the post–Cold War "peace,"
we have to complicate the *peace as the absence of war* conception that underlies
conventional understandings of peace and war (Galtung 1964). This conception, which Galtung (1964) terms "negative peace," does not adequately capture the complexity of how policy makers, politicians, and military leaders have
viewed peace for, at least, the past couple of decades (2).[1]

The first complication stems from the fact that during the post–Cold War
period the absence of war, as well as the absence of the threat of war between two
global superpowers, has not translated into the absence of a highly sophisticated
and lethal US global military presence. Indeed, as Bacevich (2010) explains, the
United States has insisted that "unambiguous and perpetual global military supremacy" is essential to its post–Cold War global leadership role, a role deemed
necessary for securing the post–Cold War peace (14). Rather, the peacetime
policy of the United States has been geared toward a "condition of permanent

---

[1] According to Layne (2006), the "grand strategy" for US national security that has been attributed to the post–Cold War era was actually in place well before the Cold War. He argues that, in fact,
the foundations for the strategy were put into place during World War II and that the Cold War was
merely used to rationalize and legitimate the strategy (12).

national security crisis," or "semiwar" (Bacevich 2010: 27).² This condition is justified by a "presumption of enmity" (Doyle 1986: 1161) according to which

> great dangers always threaten the United States and will continue doing so into the indefinite future. When not actively engaged in hostilities, the nation faces the prospect of hostilities beginning at any moment, with little or no warning. (Bacevich 2010: 27–28)

In sum, the post–Cold War peace has been a highly and extensively militarized peace aimed at ensuring US global hegemony and the stability of the international order.

The other significant qualification of post–Cold War peace is captured in the phrase "democratic peace" which posits that democratic nations typically do not wage war against each other.³ Democratic peace is rooted in the Enlightenment vision of "perpetual peace" championed by Immanuel Kant at the end of the eighteenth century.⁴ For Kant, "perpetual peace" was not to be a temporary peace created through a peace treaty but rather an eternal peace that would "seek to end *all* wars for good" and that would nullify "all existing reasons for a future war" (Kant 1991: 104, 93; emphasis in the original). A condition of perpetual peace, in Kant's view, would end the "general warlike condition within which pretexts can always be found for a new war" (104). It would also mean the end to the ruling class ordering "people to immolate themselves for a cause that does not truly concern them" (103). Indeed, to attach the adjective "perpetual" to "peace" is, Kant insisted, "suspiciously close to pleonasm" (93).

It is important to note, however, that both "perpetual peace" and "democratic peace" offer qualified conceptions of peace as their calls for and recognition of a state of peace concerns specific types of governments and nations: republican/democratic governments versus monarchical/autocratic governments; first world/developed nations versus third world/developing nations. That is, perpetual peace was conceived as a condition that would exist between states that adopted a republican form of government; democratic peace designates peace between democratic nations. States subscribing to other forms of governance are not included within either conception of peace.⁵ Since the

---

² The term "semiwar" was coined by James Forrestal, the nation's first secretary of defense (Bacevich 2010: 27).

³ For divergent arguments concerning the claim that democratic nations "never or rarely" go to war with each other, see Doyle 1983a, b; Kinsella 2005; Layne 1994, 2006; Russert 1993a, 2005; Singer and Wildavsky 1993; Small and Singer 1976.

⁴ Kant's 1795 essay "Perpetual Peace" was preceded by James Madison's "Universal Peace," portions of which correspond to some of the articles underlying Kant's systematic program (Madison 1792).

⁵ It is important to note that Kant (1991) did envision a genuinely global perpetual peace. He explained that emerging from the "lawless condition of pure warfare" would require an "international state that would necessarily continue to grow until it embraced all the peoples of the earth" (105). He noted, however, that such a state was not "the will of the nations" and, thus, settled on the idea of "an enduring and gradually expanding *federation* likely to prevent war" (105; emphasis in original).

inception of republicanism during the Enlightenment, then, peace has been partial in terms of how it has been conceived, practiced, and experienced.

This partiality is crystallized in the post–Cold War conception of the "real world order" which divides the world into two wholly distinct parts: "zones of peace, wealth, and democracy" and "zones of turmoil, war, and development" (Singer and Wildavsky 1993: 3). The zones of peace hold "most of the power in the world" and, as such, do not "face a serious threat to their survival or freedom" (3). Moreover, war among the nations within this zone is highly unlikely because "modern democracies do not go to war with one another, do not even seriously imagine the possibility of being at war with one another" (3).[6] The reticence of democracies not to wage war against each other does not mean, however, that the democratic form of governance is inherently peaceful, and, thus, less war prone than other forms; nor does it mean that democracies are peaceful and non-aggressive in their relations with nondemocratic governments (Doyle 1983a; Kinsella 2004; Layne 1994, 2006; Risse-Kappen 1995; Rosato 2003; Russert 1993a, b; Small and Singer 1976).

Although a democratic peace may mean the absence of war among democratic nations, it does not entail the absolute absence of war or, even, the "absence of discriminatory and inegalitarian social structures and institutions," that is, the absence of structural violence (Wenden and Schäffner 1995: xiii). Galtung (1964) insists, however, that both forms of non-violence are necessary for achieving a "general and complete peace" (2). More specifically, some states "do not acquire the right to be free from foreign intervention" as maintaining and extending the zone of democratic peace, a key foreign policy initiative of the post–Cold War era, *does* require that modern democracies "imagine" war and conflict with other, less developed nations, nations occupying the "zones of turmoil" (Doyle 1983b: 325). Although the nations and actors comprising such zones do not represent existential threats to Western democracies, they are seen as threatening "global stability." As such, they are the perennial target of national security policies and aggressive operations designed to "dampen forces of global instability" so that the benefits of "freedom, security, and prosperity" of Americans and others can endure well into the future (USCNS/21st Century 2000: 6).[7]

Like *peace, stability* is only partial in its application and experience as the rhetoric of "global stability" translates into the practice of ensuring stability for some through policies and actions that create instability for others. Within

---

[6] The authors' language here presents a strong version of the democratic peace thesis. Other scholars offer more qualified versions, noting that "modern democracies" "almost never" or "rarely" wage war against each other. See note 3.

[7] To avoid repeating the rather cumbersome phrase "United States Commission on National Security/21st Century," I refer to the Commission's reports by the shorthand "USCNS/21st Century" in the in-text citations.

this dichotomized world, the rhetoric of "fighting for freedom," "eliminating tyranny," and "liberating the oppressed" represents a code designed to disguise the fundamental objective of national security: "safeguarding the American way of life" by forcing others to "conform to American values" (Bacevich 2010: 189; see also Doyle 1983b: 328, 334). Such a partial conception of peace is, according to Galtung (1964), inherently non-peaceful as it privileges the rights and well-being of some over the rights and well-being of others. In the analysis that follows, I examine the ways in which a particular narrative of the post–Cold War future legitimates, and, thus, helps realize, this partial, militarized conception of peace.

Securing the Modernist Future

I understand US national security, both its discourse and its practice, as a manifestation of and vehicle for a modernist conception of the future. Heller (1999) contends that a notable stage of modern historical consciousness is anchored in a "grand narrative" of a monolithic history of the human race which holds that the future is knowable and controllable and adheres to a model of "infinite progress" (3).[8] As a temporal domain that is free and open to human creativity, the modernist future is assumed to hold the promise of a qualitatively better world and way of life (8). This conception of the future serves both ideological and pragmatic functions as "high modernism legitimated modernity with . . . a distant future which is allegedly incipient in modernism itself from its gestation onward. . . . In the 'infinite' 'progressivist' story, it is the future that legitimates the present and its conflicts and sufferings" (8, 10). The modernist future is exemplified by the "modern futures movement"—"Futures Studies"—which began in earnest in the 1930s, accelerated in the latter half of the twentieth century, and continues to thrive today in various aspects of social, commercial, and political life (Bell 2005: xvii). Futures Studies seeks scientifically grounded insights into the future in order to shape it in accord with the needs and interests of particular social agents and institutions (Bell 2005; King 1975; Wells 1985). This deliberate shaping of the future is a normative enterprise concerned with "discovering or inventing, examining and evaluating, and proposing" possible, probable, and preferable futures (Bell 1997: 1).

Such projects are particularly important during moments of significant social change which offer, at least in theory, the possibility of a future that differs significantly from the present. The prospect of an open and uncertain future is viewed by those in power as a threat to their status (Inayatullah 1996; Sardar

---

[8] For an extended discussion and review of the modernist conception of the future, see Dunmire (2010, 2011).

1993, 1999). Dominant political and social actors, consequently, seek to contain the uncertainty inherent in such moments through policies and actions designed to shape the future in ways that will maintain the status quo. Futures research is typically oriented to the interests of dominant institutions, namely, corporations, military institutions, and governments (Bell 2005: 108; Slaughter 2002). During the Cold War, Futures Studies focused mainly on national security as governmental leaders, in their determination to "protect Americans from whatever dangers may come," became "perforce ardent students of futurism" (Cornish 1977: 84). The post–Cold War era has seen a similar proliferation of "future efforts" aimed at managing the uncertainties brought about by the demise of the Soviet Union.[9]

"The United States Commission on National Security/21st Century" (USCNS/21st Century) is such a project as it aimed to ensure the "conscious evolution of human society" by increasing control over "potential future social changes" ushered in by the new millennium and the end of the Cold War (Bell 2005: xxii, xx). The project represents "the most comprehensive and ambitious national security visioning effort" since the end of World War II (Bell 2005: xx). This "visioning" project took place from 1998 to 2001 and comprises three phases and corresponding reports. The Phase I report, "New World Coming: American Security in the 21st Century" (USCNS/21st Century 1999b), "describes" the evolution of the global security environment during the first quarter of the twenty-first century. The Phase II report, "Seeking a National Security: A Concert for Preserving Security and Promoting Freedom" (USCNS/21st Century 2000), presents policy prescriptions for the national security strategy needed to deal with this "new world." The Phase III report, "Road Map for National Security: Imperative for Change" (USCNS/21st Century 2001), outlines the institutional changes needed to "meet the challenges of 2025."

In the following analysis, I examine the narrative of the future embedded within and projected through the USCNS/21st Century reports and consider how this narrative legitimates the Commission's national security policy prescriptions. Simply put, USCNS/21st Century narrativizes the post–Cold War security environment so as to "evoke assumptions about the past, the future, and the agents who bring about possible negative outcomes" and those who bring about future benefits (Edelman 1988: 90).

Narrating Sociopolitical Practice

The importance and ubiquity of narrative as a social, cognitive, and cultural phenomenon has been well established by numerous scholars. As a fundamental "sense-making device," narrative mediates thought and serves as a "cultural

---

[9] USCNS/21st Century (1999d) provides an overview and synthesis of these "future efforts."

tool-kit" for representing and acting in the social world (Bruner 1991: 4; Ochs and Capp 1996: 19). Narratives reflect social and cultural ways of organizing knowledge and provide a key means by which institutions and communities socialize their members into their value system, solve problems, and instantiate social identities (Blommaert 2005: 84; Ochs 1997: 189, 201). An important means for conceptualizing and describing a culture, then, is through "the narrative models it makes available" for depicting various aspects of social life (Bruner 1987: 15). The essential function all narratives serve is to "depict a temporal transition from one state of affairs to another" (Ochs 1997: 189). Although they typically recount past events, narratives can have a past, present, or future temporal orientation (Ochs 1997: 189). The rhetorical impact of narratives derives, in part, from exploiting the phenomenon of "displacement" which renders events and people spatially and temporally remote from a narrator and audience as "uncommonly present" (Toolan 1988: 4, 1).

Like all narratives, those produced for political purposes serve a constructive function by shaping sociopolitical reality and organizing the collective experience of a particular constituency or an entire nation (Hodges 2007: 68; see also Hodges 2011 and this volume). A key aspect of this process is the construction of "the identities of individuals and groups that populate experience" (68). In fact, the capacity of narrative to "structure experience and construct social reality" is instrumental to creating the identities that "shape actions and interaction on a global scale" (84). And although a given narrative may be locally focused, it, nevertheless, plays a role in broader ideological struggles as a type of political action that carries "political and ideological freight" (Toolan 1988: 227). Indeed, to narrate a given event or happening is "to make a bid for a kind of power" (Toolan 1988: 3).

Of particular concern to the present project is the issue of "legitimacy" which Bruner (1991) has identified as a "central concern" of narrative (15). He explains that a narrative "pivots on a breach in legitimacy" which is seen as a familiar human plight (15, 12). When "conventional expectations" are breached, "Trouble," which furnishes "the engine for the drama," ensues (15, 16). In terms of USCNS/21st Century, the issue of legitimacy has to do with the superpower status of the United States in the aftermath of the Cold War and at the inception of the twenty-first century. That is, the demise of the Soviet Union raised questions concerning the need for and legitimacy of the United States as an active player on the global stage, particularly in a military capacity. The "conventional expectation" applied to the post–Cold War world was that the ending of a war, even a "cold" war, would be followed by a period of peace as citizens would no longer have to live in fear for their security and way of life. The "breach" of this expectation derives from the fact that, according to "those in the know," the post–Cold War world actually posed "an unprecedented range of threats and actors" that were not easily recognizable to the general public (USCNS/21st Century 1999c: 46). As such, despite their sense of safety and security, the future that lay ahead was one in which "Americans will become increasingly less secure and much less secure than they now imagine themselves to be" (USCNS/21st Century 1999b: 8).

This breach and the potential trouble it could lead to (e.g., a public unwilling to support an aggressive national security policy, a future determined and controlled by terrorists and tyrants) is the impetus behind the USCNS/21st Century narrative as it seeks to establish the legitimacy of an aggressive national security strategy in a period of "peace." In the Commission's words, "Since the fall of the Berlin Wall, our leaders have been searching for a unifying theme to provide a strategic framework appropriate to current and future circumstances" (USCNS/21st Century 2000: 5). As Edelman (1988) explains, a central function of many governmental agencies is to create and disseminate narratives concerning the threats and dangers that are remote from the public's daily experience (30). In articulating these threats and dangers, such narratives provide a rationale for the policies and actions of "intelligence organizations, national policy agencies, and departments of defense . . . through the spectacle of dramatic action they create" (30–31). Moreover, by creating such hostile actors and the "narrative plots that determine their place in history," political discourse legitimates "enmity" against them by narrativizing the past and future in particular ways (76). The plot of narratives that rationalize "draconian measures" is warranted by the assumption that "evil" must be destroyed in order "to save the social order" and, thereby, to secure a better future (76). In this way, narratives, which consist not only of stories and myths but also of "reasons for doing and not doing" something, function as legitimation devices (Bruner 1991: 4; van Dijk 1998: 255).

Analysis

EXPANDING NATIONAL SECURITY

The conception of national security advocated in USCNS/21st Century illustrates the call, as termed in the Clinton administration's national security strategy, for "enlarging" both the concept and practice of national security beyond mere national defense (United States National Security Council 1996). This policy of enlargement emerged in the wake of World War II as the United States sought to protect its global economic interests by projecting US military power abroad (Layne 2006: 8). This expansion of economic interests ultimately transformed the goal of US grand strategy from being oriented to national *defense* to being oriented to national *security*: from focusing on defending the physical territory of the United States to "defending the nation's core values, its organizing ideology, and its free political and economic institutions" (Leffler, as quoted in Layne 2006: 8–9). This conception of US strategy underlies the Commission's project as it explained that "We do not equate national security with 'defense'"; accordingly, the Commission outlined a strategy it deemed appropriate to both "the early 21st century *global* security environment" and "the nation's character" (USCNS/21st Century 2001: viii; USCNS/21st Century 1999a: 1; emphasis added). This conception includes "all key political, social, cultural, technological, and economic variables that bear on state power and behavior" (USCNS/21st Century 2001: v). Pursuing the nation's aims and objectives will ensure that security strategy focuses not only on the "threats" and "challenges" of the new century but also on its "opportunities":

> the essence of American strategy must compose a balance between two key aims. The first is to *reap the benefits of a more integrated world in order to expand freedom, security, and prosperity for Americans and for others*. But, second, American strategy must strive to *dampen the forces of global instability so that those benefits can endure*. (USCNS/21st Century 2000: 5–6; emphasis in the original).

Both the content and structure of the preceding excerpt provide a clue as to the future heralded by the onset of the twenty-first century. In specifying the "essence" of security policy aims, this statement embeds a vision of the future which comprises positive ("benefits") and negative ("instability") dimensions that stand in opposition to each other. This vision is one of conflict and tension as future global instability is rendered as a force that can limit the extent to which benefits of the post–Cold War era will endure for "Americans and others." The implication of this conflictual future is a security policy that consists of two interacting processes: ensuring the benefits of some by taking action against others and, correspondingly, tempering instability by constraining benefits. That is, the choice of the conjunction "but" rather than "and" sets up a relationship in which policy aims are not related temporally as conditions that can exist simultaneously (i.e., the policy will ensure benefits while, at the same time, dampening instability) but causally as conditions that have negative implications for each other. It is through this volatile relationship, and, more generally, through the Commission's expansive conception of national security, that Orwell's dictum "war is peace" comes to life in the contemporary world.

A TALE OF TWO FUTURES

The future hinted at in the Commission's conception of national security is explicated in the Phase I report, "New World Coming: American Security in the 21st Century," which opens by juxtaposing two future worlds that could come to define the twenty-first century. The future of "opportunity" is one in which "the spread of knowledge, the development of new technologies, and an increasing recognition of common global problems will present vast opportunities" (USCNS/21st Century 1999b: 1). This "promise of the next century" is by no means assured as "greater global connectedness can lead to an increased possibility of misfortune as well as benefit" (1). Indeed, "the future is one of rising stakes" as the failure of humanity to successfully carry out various political and humanitarian tasks "could produce calamity on a worldwide scale" (1). In this future of "challenges," "economic downturns . . . may become more systemic and fully global in their harmful effects," "isolated epidemics could metastasize into global pandemic," and "scientific discoveries . . . could become a tool of genocide on an unprecedented scale" (1). This introductory narrative is followed by the section "Our View of the Future" which lists the twelve key features the Commission "believes" will characterize the first quarter of the twenty-first century. These beliefs are rhetorically authorized, in part, by "factualizing grammatical forms" which "describe" particular future events and conditions (Ochs and Capps 1996: 33). Specifically, of the eighteen verb forms comprising the list, fifteen are coded through a modality of "will," which casts these statements as relatively certain and unequivocal. These "descriptions" subsequently serve to ground the policy prescriptions presented in the Phase II and Phase III reports.

These opening passages serve as the *orientation* of USCNS/21st Century's narrative of the future as they specify the characters and circumstances that define the narrative (Toolan 1988: 155). In sum, the Commission's characterization of post–Cold War global society subscribes to a fundamental strategy of political discourse: a binary depiction of the social world that embeds a superficial dichotomy between "Us" and "Them" (Cap 2008: 29; Chilton 2004: 202). Such depictions rely on the "ideological square" of "positive self-presentation" and "negative other-presentation" to legitimate various kinds of actions by members of the "in-group" against members of the "out-group" (van Dijk 1998: 267; van Dijk 1993).

As can be seen in table 2.1, the Commission designates the characters populating its narrative through noun phrases, motivations, and actions that categorize them as particular types of social actors. The table also shows that the circumstances in which these characters act to be a world divided into two antagonistic parts: the "zone of peace" and the "zone of turmoil." The characters populating these zones are categorized as one of two types of social actor, the "great powers" or the "disaffected," who are motivated by different goals and are pursuing different actions. The zone of peace includes Western powers seeking to spread freedom, democracy, and prosperity. The zone of turmoil includes actors seeking to undermine those efforts and, more generally, to spread strife and instability. While constituents of the former category are motivated by a desire to improve the plight of global society, constituents of the latter are motivated by their resentment of US global preeminence. The Commission notes, "Much of the world will resent and oppose [the United States], if not for the simple fact of our preeminence, then for the fact that others perceive the United States as exercising its power with arrogance and self-absorption"

TABLE 2.1
USCNS/21st Conception of the Global Actors

Zone	Actors	Actions	Motivations
Peace, wealth, democracy	The great powers: developed nations; mature democracies; agents of change; major powers; and powerful states	Not fighting with one another; guaranteeing global stability; providing reassurance; helping; expanding material abundance; eradicating poverty worldwide; realizing a positive future; preventing, mitigating, and responding to crises	A desire to extend peace, democracy, prosperity, and freedom throughout the world
Turmoil, war, under-development	The disaffected: forces of global instability; emerging threats; parts of the world beset by acute political conflict and brutish, nasty, and potentially genocidal conflict; authoritarian regimes; extreme nationalists; clever and determined adversaries; emerging powers; crazy states; psychologically aberrant, evil, or unglued leaders; other societies; subnational groups; unprincipled tribal or ethnic paramilitary groups; and governments and groups hostile to the United States	Posing major threats to peace and stability; resorting to extreme violence; surprising us; using science as a tool for unprecedented genocide; maximizing the violence and dangers of war; attacking; launching non-traditional and unannounced attacks; acquiring, using, and proliferating weapons of mass destructions; constraining US influence and countering its military advantage	Resentment of US preeminence and Western culture and values; perception of the United States as arrogant and self-absorbed

(USCNS/21st Century 1999b: 8). Consequently, the success of US efforts to improve global living conditions will depend on whether societies and peoples "embrace" American values and efforts. For the global constituency that "mocks our values, deflates our optimism, threatens our life and limb, and seems unresponsive to our best efforts to help," there is little the United States can do (USCNS/21st Century 1999c: 127–28).

USCNS/21st Century's construal of a bifurcated world represents the *function* level of the narrative's structure. Drawing from Barthes, Toolan (1988) explains that this level of structure serves to "drive" the narrative as it represents "the seed that it sows in the narrative, . . . an element that will come to fruition later" (Barthes, as quoted in Toolan 1988: 21). Function is what gives a narrative global coherence and orients it toward long-term goals (21). The dualistic world mapped out here articulates the "real hinge point" of risk when "things can go either way" depending on which of the "alternative path openings" are chosen (22, 25). This level of narrative structure is made explicit as the Commission considers the "elemental trajectory" by which the post–Cold War world could develop in the future (USCNS/21st Century 1999c: 146). Noting that "today's world is divided more or less between a zone of democratic peace and a zone of chronic trouble," the Commission considers the "alternative path openings" along which these zones could travel in the future, thereby situating its narrative at the "nexus of morally organized past, present, and possible experiences" (Ochs and Capps 1996: 22). It asks:

> Will many members of the former world fall away into the latter, or will many members of the latter find their way into the former? And what will be the relationship between the parts of such a divided world? Can a zone of prosperity and relative tranquility remain isolated from the pain, the heartbreak, the refugees, and possibly the diseases of the zone of hardship and turmoil? (USCNS/21st Century 1999c: 136–37)

In USCNS/21st Century's dichotomized world, people living in the zones of peace and in the zones of turmoil comprise oppositional identities. As Edelman (1988) explains, defining the Other in political narratives entails acts of self-definition that lend "passion to the whole transaction" (76; see also van Dijk 1998). More often than not these definitions are oppositional: to support some form of physical action against an enemy is to render oneself an "innocent hero"; "to define the people one hurts as evil is to define oneself as virtuous" (76). As the natural opposite of the Other, Western democracies are defined as "emerging from an innocent past" unconnected to the history, conditions, and experiences of those living in the zone of turmoil (76). Consequently, such nations are represented as "destined to bring about a brighter future world cleansed from the contamination"—from the pain, heartbreak, refugees, and diseases—embodied by the Other (76).

The Commission's construal of characters can be represented more specifically by Greimas's model for narrative character roles. Toolan (1988) explains that Greimas's model provides six roles, or "actants," that the characters can occupy in a given narrative (93). These general categories, which underlie all narratives, consist of three interacting pairs: giver/receiver, subject/object, and helper/opponent (93). The subject is the character who seeks an object to be bestowed upon any number of receivers. This quest is opposed, however, by some person, force, or entity that seeks to undermine the subject's efforts. As such, the subject often requires a "helper" who aids in the fight against the subject's opponent. Typically, the efforts of the subject and the helper are met with limited success and, thus, a "super helper," a person or force with extraordinary power, is needed to assure the success of the quest. In terms of the present narrative, the subject role is occupied by "western democracies" which seek a more democratic and peaceful future for all of global society. These efforts are opposed, however, by "forces of instability," "clever and determined adversaries," and "the disaffected." As we'll see, the United States occupies the "super helper" role as it is the only nation with the military, economic, and political power needed to lead the world to a future of democracy, freedom, and prosperity.

SHAPING THE GLOBAL FUTURE

The resolution of the tension in the Commission's narrative lies, ultimately, with who holds "rein on the future" (Kaufer and Butler 1996: 249), whether it be the "heroes" of the world order striving for peace and freedom or the "villains" seeking to undermine that order. Of course, the goal of the Commission's work is to ensure that the "great powers," the United States specifically, occupy this position. Echoing H. G. Wells's (1987: 90) admonition that modern man can no longer just "let the future happen," and, thus, must better anticipate potential consequences "before they hit us hard," the Commission stresses the need for US policy makers to get out ahead of the future "before Americans find themselves shocked by events they never anticipated" (USCNS/21st Century 2000: 5). Indeed, without such critical thinking and the attendant policy changes, "The U.S. will lose its capacity to shape history and instead will be shaped by it" (USCNS/21st Century 2001: viii). Getting rein on the future requires that the United States collaborate with allies "to shape the future of the international environment, using all the instruments of American diplomatic, economic, and military power" (USCNS/21st Century 1999b: 7). The United States will lead this effort as "its size, wealth, power, cultural sway, and diplomatic reputation render it inevitable that the U.S. will retain a significant role . . . in shaping the international security environment" (USCNS/21st Century 1999c: 3). As Bacevich (2010) notes, shaping the global future is no small order as "bending the arc of history necessarily entails vast exertions on a sustained basis" (19). Not only does it require the capacity to "discern the arc's proper shape" and "the possession of great power," shaping the future of the international environment requires "a willingness to expend that power so as to assure the accomplishment of history's purposes" (19). The willingness of the United States to make such exertions and its capacity to "know" the future warrant it as the super helper of the post–Cold War environment.

Indeed, such effort is essential if the United States is to realize its overriding national security goal: to protect and advance US interests. The Commission declares that "America must find its anchor in U.S. national interests, interests that must be both protected *and advanced* for the fundamental well-being of American society" (USCNS/21st Century 2000: 7; emphasis added). These interests fall into one of three categories, "survival," "critical," and "significant," and extend the concept and practice of national security well beyond the "near term integrity of national sovereignty and borders" (USCNS/21st Century 2000: 7; Betts, as quoted in Crawford 2003: 11).[10] With the expansion of national interests comes an expansion of the number and types of threats and enemies the United States will face. As Herring (2008) points out, "the more overseas interests [the nation] has, the more targets it presents to foes, and the more it has to lose" (10). Moreover, its extensive range of interests compels the United States to intervene anywhere around the world (Zenko 2010: 8; see also Layne 2006: 36; Russert 2005: 397).

The "trouble" for national security derives from the false sense of security the public feels in the aftermath of the Cold War (USCNS/21st Century 1999b: 8). What the public doesn't perceive and what it needs to be protected against is "a variety of complex threats" that are "more diffuse and harder to anticipate" than those of the past (USCNS/21st Century 1999b: 12, 8). As such, the Commission's professed security goals, however lofty, may not be incentive enough for the American public to support a "world role that requires much potential sacrifice and the mobilization of substantial national resources and will" (USCNS/21st Century 1999c: 130). Noting the lack of a "troublesome event" (Ochs 1997: 197) that typically galvanizes public support for military endeavors, the Commission asks whether such a global role can endure "very long with an America that does not feel threatened" (USCNS/21st Century 1999c: 130). It concludes that although citizens will not likely "sacrifice blood and treasure" over "indirect challenges" or what appear to be "abstract moral imperatives," they will do so if "they feel fundamental interests are imperiled" (USCNS/21st Century 1999c: 130). The "trouble" of the public's perception of and potential reaction to twenty-first-century threats poses a rhetorical and material exigency for USCNS/21st Century just as it did for others seeking to develop a post–Cold War security strategy (Dunmire 2009). The Commission's concern points to the role that readily identifiable

---

[10] See Layne (2006) and Mitchell and Newman (2006) for a discussion of the expansion of US national security interests during, respectively, the post–World War II and the Cold War periods.

hostile global actors have historically served in the international security arena as a means of manufacturing public consent to policy proposals or acts of intervention (Chomsky 2004: 349).

Notwithstanding the apparent "America 1st" orientation of USCNS/21st Century, the Commission casts its proposals and prescriptions as universal and as serving the "broader interests of global peace and security" (USCNS/21st Century 2000: 15). Indeed, the fundamental assumption held by the Commission is that the United States has always been the world's "super helper" as it has consistently acted as "a strong, secure, and persuasive force for freedom and progress in the world" (USCNS/21st Century 1999a). As "the first nation with fully global leadership responsibilities," the United States will continue to be this benevolent force in the new security era through a strategy designed "to consolidate and advance the peace, prosperity, democracy and cooperative order of a world now happily free from global totalitarian threats" (USCNS/21st Century 2000: 15, 8). The United States, of course, does not pose any sort of global threat because "leadership does not mean dominance" and, as the "the acknowledged dominant global power," it "seeks neither territory or political empire" (USCNS/21st Century 1999b: 2). Rather, the magnanimity and benevolence of "Pax Americana" derives from the universality of values and ideals which led to victory over the Soviet Union and which will lead to victory over the emerging threats of the post–Cold War era. Indeed, the "apparent global triumph of fundamental American ideals" has positioned the United States as a leader that provides benefits not only for the domestic population but for "most of the world" (USCNS/21st Century 1999c: 1). As such, American power will serve to "advance the values we hold to be universal in application" (USCNS/21st Century 1999c: 128). The exercise of this power will, in turn, help create a post–Cold War world that is "very much in the American interest" (USCNS/21st Century 1999c: 141).

The Commission's rendering of the post–Cold War world reveals the prefabricated nature of its narrative of the future. That is, a key aspect of narrative is *prefabrication*, the fact that specific narratives "often seem to have bits" of characters, actions, and plots that we've encountered before (Toolan 1988: 4). The individualized characters populating a narrative represent "tokens" of more enduring archetypes, and their actions "seem to repeat themselves over and over again—with important variations, of course" (Toolan 1988: 4; Bruner 1991: 7). Indeed, the "suggestiveness" of a given narrative derives from "the emblematic nature of its particulars" (Bruner 1991: 7). Moreover, prefabrication helps explain how narrative functions as a cultural tool "par excellence" for rendering "the exceptional comprehensive" and for articulating and sustaining "common understandings of what the culture deems ordinary" (Ochs 1997: 193; Bruner, as quoted in Ochs 1997).

Prefabrication manifests in USCNS/21st Century through representations of the nature and function of the United States' global role and status. This representation is an instance of the "institutionalized master storyline" (Ochs and Capps 1996: 33) of American Exceptionalism which, throughout the nation's history, has served to legitimate US global intervention through a rhetoric of "providence" and "destiny." According to this narrative, providence has chosen the United States to do "the world's work" of bringing the blessings of civilization to less developed nations and peoples (Herring 2008: 363–64). Leaders in the late nineteenth and early twentieth centuries, for example, insisted that "they had a God-given obligation to spread the blessings of their superior institutions to the less fortunate peoples of the world" (304). President Wilson declared that the United States had been providentially designated to show others "how they shall walk in the paths of liberty" (380). The nation's destiny, Wilson emphasized, demanded that the United States conduct its foreign policy "according to the necessities of the present and the prophecies of the future": it must accept "the great part in the world which was providentially cut out for her" (407).

Despite their grand visions of the nation's role in global society, the nation's leaders have consistently insisted that the United States seeks neither territory nor treasure. The foreign policy objective at the end of the Spanish-American War, for example, was "'not to conquer [the people of former Spanish colonies] . . . but to restore peace and order'" (Herring 2008: 394). This altruism is part of a "national mythology" whereby the acquisition of territory or global power is viewed as "accidental or aberrational, an ad hoc response to situations that had not been anticipated" (317).[11] Rather, America's intention lay in "regenerating" the world by spreading "American values, principles, and institutions" (358). Such a project was necessary and inevitable at the turn of the twentieth century as these principles, President Wilson averred, were "the principles of mankind and must prevail" (408). Within this framework "barbaric people" were seen as a threat to civilization and, as such, had to be forcibly kept in line. Such military interventions were right and true, Theodore Roosevelt insisted, because "warlike intervention by civilized powers would contribute directly to the peace of the world," to the spread of "American virtues," and, thus, to the "advance of civilization" (347).

In the history of empire and imperialism, then, the United States has represented a new breed of world power. Rather than seeking territory, wealth, and dominance, it has rightly pursued, according to policy makers and politicians, self-interests that are at one with freedom, peace, and security. At the dawn of the twenty-first century the United States must continue to "play a special international role into the future" as it has a "responsibility to itself and others to reinforce the international order" (USCNS/21st Century 2001: 5). The role of the United States is so important, the Commission insists, that

---

[11] Herring (2008) documents the deliberate and intentional nature of such acquisitions (317).

"the abrupt undermining of U.S. power and prestige is the worst thing that could happen to the structure of global peace in the next quarter century" (USCNS/21st Century 2001: 23).[12]

"PEACE IS OUR PROFESSION"

Despite[13] the lethality of future conflicts, the Commission is optimistic that the "New World Coming" in the twenty-first century will, nevertheless, be "amenable" to US interests. It does caution, however, that such a future "will not come into being by itself" (USCNS/21st Century 2000: 8). As such, USCNS/21st Century outlines the means by which the United States will engage its super helper role of shaping the future of the global environment.

The Commission, to be sure, pays due attention to the non-military means (diplomacy, economic policy, humanitarian measures) of shaping the global future. This focus is overshadowed, however, by the persistent emphasis of the military dimension of national security. For the Commission, ensuring a future of peace and stability will require not only continued military preeminence but also the *active display* of that preeminence. It notes that the United States "is likely to remain a primary . . . military force . . . through 2025, and will thus have a significant role to play in shaping the international environment" (USCNS/21st Century 1999b: 3). These forces must be characterized by "stealth, speed, range, accuracy, lethality, agility, sustainability, reliability . . . in order to deal effectively with the spectrum of symmetrical and asymmetrical threats" (USCNS/21st Century 2000: 14; USCNS/21st Century 1999b: 7).

With such a military force, the United States will be able to fulfill the "fundamental" need of national security strategy: "to *project U.S. power globally* with forces stationed in the U.S. and those stationed abroad and afloat in the *forward presence role*" (USCNS/21st Century 2000: 14; emphasis added). Through its military, the United States will be able to "stabilize those parts of the world still beset by acute political conflict" and to "tame the disintegrative forces spawned by an era of change" (USCNS/21st Century 2000: 8, 13). In sum, the "complex contingencies" of the future require a military force that can "deter wars, preclude crises from evolving into major conflicts . . . and provide *prolonged stability operations*" (USCNS/21st Century 2000: 15; emphasis added). USCNS/21st Century is quick to acknowledge that ideally "preventive diplomacy" would serve this "taming" function. Unfortunately, "diplomacy

---

[12] See Doyle (1983a) for a discussion of the military and economic impact that a decline in the United States' hegemonic status would have for liberal democracies.

[13] The term in the heading, "Peace Is Our Profession," is the official motto of the Strategic Air Command (Bacevich 2010: 54). The slogan also adorns the War Room in Stanley Kubrick's movie *Doctor Strangelove*.

will not always work" and, thus, the "United States should be prepared to act militarily" (USCNS/21st Century 2000: 13).

Consequently, fundamental to the post–Cold War strategy of enlarging and expanding the "zone of democratic peace" is a mission rooted in "power projection," "forward presence," and "stability operations." Taken together, these practices represent the requisite means by which "The Great Power" can fulfill its role as "super helper" and get rein on the future, directing it along the path preferred by other "great nations" and away from that preferred by the "disaffected." I will take each of these concepts in turn.

As explained in the Army Field Manual, "power projection" is "the ability of the U.S. to apply any combination of economic, diplomatic, informational, or military instruments of national power" to influence the international system and the security environment (Department of the Army 1995b).[14] "Military force projection," the "ability . . . to deploy . . . forces in any region of the world and sustain missions spanning the operational continuum," is a particularly important component of power projection capability because "military power translates directly into influence in the international system" (Department of the Army 1995b, 1995a). Such power projection requires the "rapid deployment of combat power and military operations designed to terminate conflicts as quickly as possible on terms that are favorable to the U.S. and its allies" (Department of the Army 1995b). This force must be "lethal," "expandable," and "sustainable" (Department of the Army 1995b). In short, the "peaceful employment of our military forces . . . demonstrates our capabilities, promotes stability, and contributes to our ability to influence international outcomes" (Department of the Army 1995a).

As USCNS/21st Century explains, effective power projection requires that military forces be situated in a "forward presence role": the proactive military posture of stationing forces abroad in order to influence foreign governments and shape the global environment (Fullenkamp 1994: ii). In a report to the Faculty of the Naval War College, Fullenkamp (1994) identifies forward presence as a preeminent aspect of post–Cold War national security strategy that will enable the United States to "seize" the new opportunities for expanding peace, democracy, and prosperity (ii, 1, 6). Although not new to the post–Cold War era, the conceptualization and practice of forward presence must change to keep pace with the "broadening of U.S. objectives" and interests. Moreover, such changes will "transmit the message" to the post–Cold War world that "the United States still cares" (6, 7). Like power projection, forward presence has non-military components; the military element, however, "offers much

---

[14] The Army Field Manuals referenced in this section do not include page numbers. The material from the 1995a document came from Chapter 6, "Force Projection"; the material from the 1995b document came from Chapter 1, "Power Projection."

promise to gain long-term peacetime influence in the accomplishment of national objectives" (ii).[15]

Finally, the future security environment will comprise "emerging nations discontented with the status quo" and will lack clear delineation of "the lines separating war and peace, enemy and friend" (Department of the Army 2008: Foreword). As such, it will require "prolonged stability operations" which integrate "the tools of statecraft with our military forces, international partners, humanitarian organizations, and the private sector" (Department of the Army 2008: Foreword). In an era of "persistent conflict," stability operations will draw upon the "unflagging bravery" of US soldiers and position them "to carry the banner of freedom, hope and opportunity to the people of the world" (Department of the Army 2008: Foreword). The essence of stability operations is to "provide the foundations of enduring peace and stability" through "various military missions, tasks, and activities conducted outside the U.S. in coordination with other instruments of national power" (vi).

In USCNS/21st Century's narrative of the future, then, living in peace requires living with war.[16] Or, if not full blown war, then, at the very least, it requires living with "Operations Other Than War" that require the active engagement of a highly sophisticated and highly lethal military force (Fullenkamp 1994: 8). In this scheme the military represents "but one institution among many attempting to temper the world's most grievous political and economic failures" and, in so doing, has come to represent "social work with guns" (Bacevich 2010: 200–201; see also Englehardt 2010). What we get with this type of "social work," Bacevich explains, is a "semblance of order replacing disorder and a semblance of stability replacing instability—with even this little achievement requiring many years of struggle" (207).[17]

What this "proactive" approach provides, moreover, is a security strategy based in a *preventive* rather than *defensive* military posture; indeed, "proactive means preemptive" (Fullenkamp 1994: 6).[18] And it is this preventive posture that provides the true power undergirding the United States' position as the world's super helper. Through the triple play of power projection, forward presence, and

---

[15] In the post-9/11 security environment, forward presence has been enabled by "an arc" of military bases—"lily pads"—that can serve as a "jumping-off point for future 'preventive wars' and military missions" (Sterngold 2004).

[16] According to Herring (2008) the phenomenon of preparing for peace by preparing for war dates back to 1890s (303).

[17] Herring (2008) provides an extensive history of how US efforts to stabilize particular regions actually led to rampant instability and, in many cases, damage to US interests. See also Blum (1995).

[18] The concept of "preemption" became a key component of post-9/11 national security strategy through the "Bush Doctrine," which sanctioned the right to take military action against a target prior to being attacked. Although the Bush administration labeled its policy "preemptive," it was, in fact, "preventive" as it claimed the right to take military action against "emerging threats" rather than "imminent threats." For a discussion of the difference between preemption and prevention, see Dunmire (2009) and Keller and Mitchell (2006).

stability operations, the United States uses its military power to "compel an *adversary* to accede to U.S. will" (Department of the Army 1995a; emphasis added). The use of "adversary" rather than "enemy" points to the preventive approach advocated by the Commission. In military parlance, an enemy is "a party identified as hostile against which the use of force is authorized" (Department of the Army 2008: Glossary). An adversary is akin to a "pre-enemy" as it represents "a party acknowledged as potentially hostile to a friendly party and against which the use of force *may be envisaged*" (Department of the Army 2008: Glossary; emphasis added). Consequently, a peacetime posture of preparing for war lends itself to a concern over "potential enemies" and "emerging threats" (Herring 2008: 303). Consequently, national security involves the "defense of American freedom even in places where the actual threat to American freedom is oblique or imaginary" (Bacevich 2010: 22). In the end, what Bacevich terms the "sacred trinity" of security and military policy—global military presence, global power projection, and global intervention—although relentlessly "touted as essential to peace," has actually "propelled the U.S. into a condition approximating perpetual war" (14, 16). Within this view, war and peace become virtually indistinguishable: War is peace is war.

Concluding Remarks

The generative quality of narratives stems, in part, from their capacity to express "what's possible" in a given culture, society, or community and to "provide new models, open up novel possibilities, for the shape of our lives to come" (Bruner 1987: 15; Ochs 1987: 191). All too often, however, the opportunity to narrate possibility is "asymmetrically allocated" with such opportunities falling more to some than to others (Ochs 1987: 191, 203). Consequently, rather than narratives of genuine possibility and potentiality, contemporary life is defined by "institutionalized master story lines" which serve to limit understandings, experiences, and relationships (Ochs 1987: 203). The producers of such narratives, when faced with "enigmatic or frustrating situations," tend to map out "one coherent, correct solution to a problem" (Ochs and Capps 1996: 32). Such has certainly been the case in the post–Cold War era as numerous national security documents have presented, each in their own terms, a narrative of the future similar to that of USCNS/21st Century in their efforts to maintain global stability and US hegemony into the twenty-first century (Dunmire 2009).

Such narratives serve to maintain the status quo as their authors seek to impose order and continuity between past, present, and future (Ochs and Capps 1996: 32). The stability they ostensibly create, however, is false and partial as such narratives help maintain a global system in which stability means stability for wealth and investment. In this system, "threats to stability" are those that call into question the "security of wealthy classes and investors" (Chomsky 2004: 721–22). As Layne (2006) puts it, "hegemonic power acts deliberately to establish and maintain the kind of stable international security order that is needed for economic interdependence. . . . Firms that engage in overseas trade and investment don't like instability" (124). The Commission admits as much when it declares that "America's political and economic commitments have cast it as the apparent guarantor of global stability" (USCNS/21st Century 1999c: 127). Such commitments mean that "When U.S. access to resources central to the global economic system is imperiled, U.S. interests are imperiled" (USCNS/21st Century 2000: 13). In such an environment, it is imperative that the United States play the role of "geopolitical stabilizer," a role based in unmatched global military supremacy (Layne 2006: 36).

So, what sort of future do such institutionalized narratives offer to those whose needs and interests are not served by the status quo? The "legacy of elitism" of narratives of the future promulgated by organizations like USCNS/21st Century clearly neglects and marginalizes the experiences, desires, and needs of the poor and disenfranchised (Slaughter 2002: 350). This legacy also denies narrative rights to such peoples, who are centrally involved in the projects such narratives promote, by characterizing their resistance to and critiques of the West as stemming from "resentment" and as representing nothing more than a "mocking" of Western values (Ochs and Capps 1996: 34). Rather, the future is conceived of as a "Western challenge and opportunity" and, as such, is shaped in the image of the West (Wyn Davies 1999: 234). In this Westernized future, the "third world's" future is predefined as "catch up with the first world" because the "backward" are deemed only to be recipients, not creators, of the future (Galtung and Jungk 1969: 368; Inayatullah 1999: 510). Moreover, it is a conception of the future that rationalizes brutality and oppression through the "gerund defense" (Easterly 2010: 38). By labeling countries as "developing" and "democratizing," policy makers legitimate their prescriptions by claiming that they serve people's "innate tendency" toward democracy and development (38). Indeed, mesmerized by its "appealing vision of perpetual peace," democratic peace theory has become the "lodestar" guiding US foreign policy (Layne 1994: 48, 45). Based on "excessive ideological zeal," this approach has led to the exporting of democracy to those outside the zone of democratic peace through "disastrous military interventions," a rather dangerous means for producing a "democratic world order" (Layne 1994: 46, 47; Russert 1993b: 280). Unfortunately for the alleged beneficiaries, the peace offered through such interventions is a "peace of illusion" (Layne 1994: 48).

In short, non-Western people, those living in the "zones of turmoil, war, and development," are there "to be futurised" rather than to "provide authentic alternatives to the global problematique" (Inayatullah 1999: 57). Unfortunately for such people, "if it is not to be peace foreseen and planned and established, then it will be disaster and death" (Wells 1987: 91). The question that needs to be asked, then, is whose "peace" and what sort of "peace" is to be foreseen and established? Answers to this question must recognize that "not every instance of non-war can be called peace" (Wenden and Schäffner 1995: xiii). This has certainly been the case in terms of the approach the United States has taken to the post–Cold War "peace" which, as Hodges points out in his introduction to this volume, has not led to formal declarations of war but certainly has not led to peace. Answers must also take seriously the distinction between "negative peace" as the "absence of violence, absence of war" and "positive peace" as the "integration of human society" (Galtung 1964: 2). Narratives of "peace" that divide the world into two distinct and mutually exclusive zones are not only antithetical to positive peace; they also serve to legitimate the structural violence that has been, and continues to be, endemic to the making and maintenance of the modern world (Mishra 2011: 12). Finally, answers must embrace the "audacious" project of "peace *search*" through which "new visions of new worlds" would be generated and ultimately actualized, visions of a future world that embrace the concept of a "general and complete peace" (Galtung 1964: 4, emphasis added).

References

Bacevich, Andrew. 2010. *Washington Rules: America's Path to Permanent War*. New York: Metropolitan Books.

Bell, Wendell. 1997. *Foundations of Futures Studies: Human Sciences for a New Era* (vol. 2: *Values, Objectivity, and the Good Society*). New Brunswick: Transaction Publishers.

Bell, Wendell. 2005. *Foundations of Futures Studies: Human Sciences for a New Era* (vol. 1, *History, Purposes, and Knowledge*; 2nd printing). New Brunswick: Transaction Publishers.

Blommaert, Jan. 2005. *Discourse: A Critical Introduction*. Cambridge: Cambridge University Press.

Blum, William. 1995. *Killing Hope: U.S. Military and CIA Interventions since World War II*. Monroe, ME: Common Courage Press.

Bruner, Jerome. 1987. "Life as Narrative." *Social Research* 54: 11–32.

Bruner, Jerome. 1991. "The Narrative Construction of Reality." *Critical Inquiry* 18(1): 1–21.

Cap, Piotr. 2008. "Towards the Proximization Model of the Analysis of Legitimization in Political Discourse." *Journal of Pragmatics* 40: 17–41.

Chilton, Paul. 2004. *Analyzing Political Discourse: Theory and Practice*. London: Routledge.

Chomsky, Noam. 2004. *Language and Politics*. Edinburgh: AK Press.

Cornish, Edward. 1977. *The Study of the Future: An Introduction to the Art and Science of Understanding and Shaping Tomorrow's World*. Washington, DC: World Future Society.

Crawford, Neta C. 2003. "The Best Defense: The Problem with Bush's 'Preemptive' War Doctrine." *Boston Review*. http://bostonreview.net/BR28.1/crawford.html.

Department of the Army. 1995a. "Force Projection." *Army Field Manual 100–7*. www. globalsecurity.org/military/library/policy/army/fm/100-7/f1007_11.htm#REF53h2.

Department of the Army. 1995b. "Power Projection." *Army Field Manual 100–10*. www. globalsecurity.org/military/library/policy/army/fm/100-10-1/ch1.htm.

Department of the Army. 2008. "Stability Operations." *Army Field Manual 3–07*. http:// usacac.army.mil/cac2/repository/FM307/FM3-07.pdf.

Doyle, Michael W. 1983a. "Kant, Liberal Legacies, and Foreign Affairs." *Philosophy and Public Affairs* 12(3): 205–35.

Doyle, Michael W. 1983b. "Kant, Liberal Legacies, and Foreign Affairs: Part 2." *Philosophy and Public Affairs* 12(4): 323–53.

Doyle, Michael W. 1986. "Liberalism and World Politics." *American Political Science Review* 80(4): 1151–69.

Dunmire, Patricia L. 2009. "'9/11 Changed Everything': An Intertextual Analysis of the Bush Doctrine." *Discourse and Society* 20(2): 195–222.

Dunmire, Patricia L. 2010. "Knowing and Controlling the Future: A Review of 'Futurology.'" *Prose Studies* 32(3): 240–63.

Dunmire, Patricia L. 2011. *Projecting the Future through Political Discourse: The Case of the Bush Doctrine*. Amsterdam: John Benjamins.

Easterly, William 2010. "Foreign Aid for Scoundrels." *New York Review of Books*, November 25. www.nybooks.com/articles/archives/2010/nov/25/foreign-aid-scoundrels/? pagination=false.

Edelman, Murray. 1988. *Constructing the Political Spectacle*. Chicago: University of Chicago Press.

Englehardt, Tom. 2010. *The American Way of War: How Bush's War Became Obama's*. Chicago: Haymarket Books.

Fullenkamp, Bernard. 1994. "Forward Presence and the Search for Peacetime Influence." Newport, RI: Naval War College. http://www.dtic.mil/cgi-bin/GetTRDoc?Location= U2&doc=GetTRDoc.pdf&AD=ADA283405.

Galtung, Johann. 1964. "An Editorial." *Journal of Peace Research* 1(1): 1–4.

Galtung, Johann and Robert Jungk. 1969. "Postscript: A Warning and a Hope." In *Mankind 2000*, Robert Jungk and Johann Galtung (eds.), 368. London: Allen and Unwin.

Heller, Agnes. 1999. *A Theory of Modernity*. London: Blackwell.

Herring, George C. 2008. *From Colony to Superpower: U.S. Foreign Relations since 1776*. Oxford: University of Oxford Press.

Hodges, Adam. 2007. "The Narrative Construction of Identity: The Adequation of Saddam Hussein and Osama bin Laden in the 'War on Terror.'" In *Discourse, War, and Terrorism*, Adam Hodges and Chad Nilep (eds.), 67–88. Amsterdam: John Benjamins.

Hodges, Adam. 2011. *The "War on Terror" Narrative: Discourse and Intertextuality in the Construction and Contestation of Sociopolitical Reality*. Oxford: Oxford University Press.

Inayatullah, Sohail. 1996. "What Futurists Think: Stories, Methods and Visions of the Future." *Futures* 28(6/7): 509–17.

Inayatullah, Sohail. 1999. "Reorienting Futures Studies." In *Rescuing All Our Futures*, Ziauddin Sadar (ed.), 49–60. Westport, CT: Praeger.

Kant, Immanuel. 1991. "Perpetual Peace." In *Kant: Political Writings*, H.S. Reiss (ed.), 93–130. Cambridge: Cambridge University Press.

Kaufer, David S. and Butler, Brian. 1996. *Rhetoric and the Arts of Design*. Mahwah, N.J.: Lawrence Erlbaum.

Keller, William W. and Gordon R. Mitchell, eds. 2006. *Hitting First: Preventive Force in U.S. Security Strategy*. Pittsburgh: University of Pittsburgh Press.

King, Alexander. 1975. "The Future of a Discipline and the Future of Disciplines." In *The Future as an Academic Discipline, Ciba Foundation Symposium* 36, 35–52. Amsterdam: Elselvier.

Kinsella, David. 2004. "No Rest for the Democratic Peace." *American Political Science Review* 99(3): 453–57.

Layne, Christopher. 1994. "Kant or Cant: The Myth of the Democratic Peace." *International Security* 19(2): 5–49.

Layne, Christopher. 2006. *The Peace of Illusions: American Grand Strategy from 1940 to the Present*. Ithaca: Cornell University Press.

Madison, James. 1792. "Universal Peace." *The National Gazette*, February 2. Retrieved: February 10, 2011. http://oll.libertyfund.org/?option=com_staticxtandstaticfile=show.php%3Ftitle=1941andItemid=27#a_07.

Mishra, Pankaj. 2011. "Watch this Man. Review of Niall Ferguson's Civilization: The West and the Rest." *London Review of Books* 33(21): 10–12.

Mitchell, Gordon and Robert Newman. 2006. "By 'Any Measures' Necessary: NSC—68 and Cold War Roots of the 2002 National Security Strategy." In *Hitting First: Preventive Force in U.S. Security Strategy*, William Keller and Gordon Mitchell (eds.),70–92. Pittsburgh: University of Pittsburgh Press.

Ochs, Elinor. 1997. "Narrative." In *Discourse as Structure and Process*, Teun van Dijk (ed.), 185–207. London: Sage.

Ochs, Elinor and Lisa Capps. 1996. "Narrating the Self." *Annual Review of Anthropology* 25: 19–43.

Risse-Kappen, Thomas. 1995. "Democratic Peace—War like Democracies? A Social Constructivist Interpretation of the Liberal Argument." *European Journal of International Relations* 1(4): 491–517.

Rosato, Sebastian. 2003. "The Flawed Logic of Democratic Peace Theory." *American Political Science Review* 97(4): 585–602.

Russert, Bruce. 1993a. *Grasping the Democratic Peace: Principles for a Post–Cold War World*. Princeton: Princeton University Press.

Russert, Bruce. 1993b. "Can a Democratic Peace Be Built?" *International Interactions* 18(3): 277–82.

Russert, Bruce. 2005. "Bushwacking the Democratic Peace." *International Studies Perspectives* 6: 395–408.

Sardar, Ziauddin. 1993. "Colonizing the Future: The 'Other' Dimension of Futures Studies." *Futures*, March, 197–87.

Sardar, Ziauddin, ed. 1999. *Rescuing All Our Futures: The Future of Future Studies*. Westport, CT: Praeger.

Singer, Max and Aaron Wildavsky. 1993. *The Real World Order: Zones of Peace/Zones of Turmoil*. Chatham, NJ: Chatham House Publishers.

Slaughter, Richard A. 2002. "Futures Studies as a Civilizational Catalyst." *Futures* 34: 349–63.

Small, Melvin and David J. Singer. 1976. "The War-proneness of Democratic Regimes, 1816–1965." *Jerusalem Journal of International Relations* 1(4): 50–69.

Sterngold, James. 2004. "After 9/11, U.S. Policy Built on World Bases." *San Francisco Chronicle*, March 21. http://www.articles.sfgate.com/2004-03-21/news/17417655_1_foreign-policy-military-missions-military-base.

Toolan, Michael J. 1988. *Narrative: A Critical Linguistic Introduction*. London: Routledge.

United States Commission on National Security/21st Century. 1999a. *Charter, September 15*. Washington, DC: US Government Printing Office.

United States Commission on National Security/21st Century. 1999b. *New World Coming: American Security in the 21st Century: Major Themes and Implications, September 15*. Washington, DC: US Government Printing Office.

United States Commission on National Security/21st Century. 1999c. *New World Coming: American Security in the 21st Century: Supporting Research and Analysis, September 15*. Washington, DC: US Government Printing Office.

United States Commission on National Security/21st Century. 1999d. *New World Coming: American Security in the 21st Century: Study Addendum, September 15*. Washington, DC: US Government Printing Office.

United States Commission on National Security/21st Century. 2000. *Seeking a National Security Strategy: A Concert for Preserving Security and Promoting Freedom, April 15*. DC: US Government Printing Office.

United States Commission on National Security/21st Century. 2001. *Road Map for National Security: Imperative for Change, February 15*. DC: US Government Printing Office.

United States National Security Council. 1996. A National Security Strategy of Engagement and Enlargment. www.fas.org/spp/military/docops/national/1996stra.htm.

Van Dijk, Teun A. 1993. *Elite Discourse and Racism*. Newbury Park, CA: Sage.

Van Dijk, Teun A. 1998. *Ideology: A Multidisciplinary Approach*. London: Sage.

Wells, Herbert G. 1985. "The Discovery of the Future." *Futures Research Quarterly*, 56–73.

Wells, Herbert G. 1987. "Wanted: Professors of Foresight!" *Futures Research Quarterly*, 89–91.

Wenden, Annita L. and Christina Schäffner, eds. 1995. "Introduction." In *Language and Peace*, Christina Schäffner and Anita Wenden (eds.), xi–xxi. Brookfield, VT: Dartmouth Publishing.

Wyn Davies, Merryl. 1999. "Other Futures Studies: A Bibliographic Essay." In *Rescuing All Our Futures*, Ziauddin Sadar (ed.), 234–47. London: Adamantine.

Zenko, Micah. 2010. *Between Threats and War: U.S. Discrete Military Operations in the Post–Cold War World*. Stanford, CA: Stanford University Press.

3

The Generic US Presidential War Narrative

JUSTIFYING MILITARY FORCE AND IMAGINING THE NATION

Adam Hodges

Introduction

In his 1795 essay on perpetual peace, Kant points out that in political systems where power rests with the people and their representatives, "the consent of the citizens is required to decide whether or not war is to be declared" (Kant 1991: 100). In theory, the necessity of obtaining the consent of citizens should help stave off unwarranted uses of the military because, as Kant explains, "it is very natural that they [the citizens] will have great hesitation in embarking on so dangerous an enterprise" (Kant 1991: 100). In other words, and more specific to the American context, given the need for presidents to gain public support for war, citizens and their representatives are supposed to act as a crucial curb to potential abuses of power that might lead to questionable uses of the military. Yet, when a president addresses the nation and makes a case for war—even in the absence of a direct invasion or an egregious threat—consent is typically granted on the part of the citizenry as a whole. Thus, a critical issue that Kant does not discuss is the topic taken up by many discourse scholars interested in war and peace—namely, how presidential rhetoric serves to convince citizens that military force is needed where hesitation and opposition should otherwise prevail. Or, in critical terms, how do presidents discursively manufacture consent for war?

Crucially, narrative plays a key role in justifying war. As Campbell and Jamieson (2008) point out in their study on presidential rhetoric, "The justification [for war] is embodied in a dramatic narrative from which, in turn, an argument is extracted" (224). The analysis that follows focuses on the generic elements of the American presidential war narrative that spans presidencies and conflicts. Each new president draws from this generic schema to narrate the need for the particular military engagement of the moment. The tradition and history bound up in the story about America's involvement in war instills each new call to arms with a sense of tradition and authority. Each new call also recreates the presidential war narrative in line with current needs, borrowing from the generic framework and remaking it in light of the current situation. In the process, the presidential war narrative (re)constructs the American national identity. That is, it plays a pivotal role in defining American values and in constituting the "national consciousness" of the "imagined community" of which Anderson (1983) speaks in his treatise on nationalism. Moreover, by drawing upon patriotic imaginings through the rehearsal of a common war narrative, presidential war rhetoric eclipses further debate. Where democracy demands critical consideration and careful weighing of evidence, presidential war rhetoric demands uncritical support. Presented through the (re)production of a widely recognized cultural narrative, presidential justifications for war therefore become difficult for many citizens—and the establishment press—to engage critically. This chapter, therefore, attempts to dissect the presidential war narrative in an effort to open it up to critical inspection.

Data come from speeches and messages delivered by American presidents stretching from Woodrow Wilson's request to Congress for a declaration of war against Germany in 1917 through George W. Bush's addresses to the nation at the onset of the invasion of Iraq in 2003. A full timeline of the conflicts and list of these materials is provided in table 3.1; complete transcripts can be found in the online database provided by *The American Presidency Project* at the University of California at Santa Barbara (Woolley and Peters 2010). The materials primarily include addresses delivered directly to the nation, as well as addresses delivered before Congress. They also include written messages to Congress provided by Harry Truman on the situation in Korea and by Lyndon Johnson on the Gulf of Tonkin incident. In addition to addresses delivered to the nation by George W. Bush at the very beginning of the US invasion of Iraq on March 19, 2003, I also include his address to the nation from Cincinnati on October 7, 2002. This latter speech marked a key rhetorical moment in the Bush administration's case for war against Iraq. The remaining speeches in the corpus come from addresses or messages delivered by presidents at the onset or immediately in the wake of conflicts that require the president to gain public support and congressional approval for military actions.

The delivery of presidential war rhetoric has evolved since the founding of the United States in the eighteenth century. While early presidents often sent written requests to Congress for declarations of war (for example, James Madison's message to Congress on June 1, 1812), delivering speeches in person to joint sessions of Congress became the norm in the twentieth century. Moreover, given the movement away from formal declarations of war by Congress after the two world wars,[1] plus the ability of modern communication

---

[1] War has been officially declared only three other times in addition to World War I and World War II: in 1812 for the War of 1812, in 1846 for the Mexican-American War, and in 1898 for the Spanish-American War.

TABLE 3.1

US Military Conflicts and Accompanying Presidential Rhetoric Used in the Analysis

Conflict	President	Date	Speech/message
World War I	Woodrow Wilson	April 2, 1917	Address to a Joint Session of Congress Requesting a Declaration of War against Germany
World War II	Franklin D. Roosevelt	December 8, 1941	Address to Congress Requesting a Declaration of War with Japan
Korea	Harry S. Truman	July 19, 1950a	Radio and Television Address to the American People on the Situation in Korea
		July 19, 1950b	Special Message to the Congress Reporting on the Situation in Korea
Vietnam	Lyndon B. Johnson	August 4, 1964a	Radio and Television Report to the American People Following Renewed Aggression in the Gulf of Tonkin
		August 5, 1964b	Remarks at Syracuse University on the Communist Challenge in Southeast Asia
		August 5, 1964c	Special Message to the Congress on US Policy in Southeast Asia
Grenada	Ronald Reagan	October 27, 1983	Address to the Nation on Events in Lebanon and Grenada
Panama	George H. W. Bush	December 20, 1989	Address to the Nation Announcing United States Military Action in Panama
Persian Gulf	George H. W. Bush	January 16, 1991	Address to the Nation Announcing Allied Military Action in the Persian Gulf
Kosovo	William J. Clinton	March 24, 1999	Address to the Nation on Airstrikes against Serbian Targets in the Federal Republic of Yugoslavia (Serbia and Montenegro)
Afghanistan	George W. Bush	October 7, 2001	Address to the Nation Announcing Strikes against Al Qaida Training Camps and Taliban Military Installations in Afghanistan
Iraq	George W. Bush	October 7, 2002	Address to the Nation on Iraq from Cincinnati, Ohio
		March 17, 2003a	Address to the Nation on Iraq
		March 19, 2003b	Address to the Nation on Iraq

technologies to allow presidents to speak directly to the nation through radio and television, modern presidents tend to deliver speeches directly to the American public at times of inchoate military conflicts. Even addresses before Congress or a local audience take into account and are aimed at the wider American public to which they are typically broadcast in whole or in part. Thus, the rhetorical act of justifying war is implicated in a national dialogue in the Bakhtinian sense of dialogism (Bakhtin 1981, 1986) where the president responds to and anticipates numerous possible objections to the use of military force. While the distinction between acceptable defensive measures to protect the nation and overreaching offensive uses of the military is subject to considerable debate, the successful implementation of the presidential war narrative erases any doubt about the situation under consideration.

Below, I first discuss the importance of narrative and outline the generic schema of the presidential war narrative. I then examine the elements of the narrative in detail, drawing examples from presidential speeches. Finally, I end with a general discussion of the role narrative plays in both justifying war and constructing the nation's image of itself.

The Power of Narrative and the Generic Presidential War Schema

The world in which we live is filled with events and happenings; but those events and happenings do not intrinsically contain their own meanings. Rather, we use narrative to imbue events with meaning. Through narrative, we name protagonists, ascribe motivations, and produce explanations. In short, narrative is a potent means for structuring and organizing our perceptual experience. In many ways, as Bruner (1991) discusses, narrative is a much more powerful device for achieving shared understandings than "logical and scientific procedures that can be weeded out by falsification" (3). Part of the power of narrative arises from our "tendency to view narratives as icons of events" (Bauman 1986: 5)—that is, as transparent representations of what happened. Any successful narrative erases the interpretive act that it is by conveying the impression that it simply presents the world "as found" rather than represents it from one among many potential viewpoints. In other words, any rhetorical justification of war by the president effectively constructs a reality rather than simply depicts a preexisting reality that somehow contains its own significance outside the discursive process that gives it meaning. Narrative is the means by which the social construction of reality takes place (Bruner 1991).

A prime means by which narrative limits "the hermeneutic task of making sense of human happenings" is through the use of genre (Bruner 1991: 14). Genres help to situate the *particulars* of narrated events[2] within conventional models or "orienting frameworks" (Hanks 1987: 670) for interpreting those particulars. In other words, a narrator uses a generic precedent to frame a story by mapping the particulars of the narrated events onto that framework. The genre thereby provides "conventional guidelines or schemas" (Bauman 2004: 5) for both the telling and interpretation of a new narrative. While the fit between the generic schema and a particular text is never exact—what Briggs and Bauman (1992) call the *intertextual gap*—the distance can be minimized to render

---

[2] Narrative scholars distinguish between *narrated events*, the events that narratives recount, and *narrative events*, the situations in which narratives are told (Jakobson 1971; Bakhtin 1981: 255; Bauman 1986: 2).

"the discourse maximally interpretable" (149). Elements common to the genre may be rehearsed in a manner that aligns the new situated telling with previous renditions of similar narratives in a consistently recognizable manner. Such consistency provides for *generic realism* (Chandler 2007: 67) whereby the narration of events in the current situation fit tightly with generic expectations for how characters should act and how events should unfold. This helps absorb us in the narrative where we fall into a "suspension of disbelief" so that alternative scenarios or interpretations fail to be considered or given adequate play.

The ability of presidents to discursively justify war stems in part from the rehearsal of a common presidential war narrative that builds upon multiple layers of precedent. In previous times of war, former presidents addressed the nation in a similar manner in similar settings marked by similar seals of presidential authority. Whether they spoke to a live audience from podiums adorned with the presidential seal, while sitting behind the presidential desk in the Oval Office, or from the lectern in front of a joint session of Congress, they drew upon the familiar trappings of presidential authority that provided them with "the *delegated power* of the spokesperson" (Bourdieu 1991: 107). With the authority to be heard and listened to, they contextualized the occasion with the degree of solemnity characteristic of the office and the task at hand, and they drew from a familiar cast of characters—familiar imaginings of the American character and the nature of the enemy—and a familiar plot of the nation at war.

Moreover, in narrating the onset of war, the president draws upon shared ethical understandings about the morality of war in certain situations, which derive from the philosophical tradition of Just War Theory. With roots stretching back to Aristotle, Cicero, and Augustine, as well as Thomas Aquinas (1948) in the thirteenth century, and contemporary scholars such as Michael Walzer (2000, 2004), Just War Theory deals with the right to enter into war (*jus ad bellum*), the ethical conduct of war (*jus in bello*), and the ethics of postwar peace agreements (*jus post bellum*). Of particular concern for presidents attempting to garner support for war are the six principles of *jus ad bellum*, which demand that a nation possesses (1) just cause, (2) right intention, (3) proper authority, that it enters into war (4) as a last resort (5) with a reasonable probability of success, and that (6) it uses means proportional to the ends (Mosley 2009; Orend 2005).

The generic presidential war narrative contains several common elements, which cohere around a particular topic or theme and build upon one another to form the narrative whole. Below, I outline these five components along with a concise rendition of the narrative in generic terms. Through this generic template, the narrative lays out the justification for war in line with the six tenets of *jus ad bellum*.

1. **Precipitating event /casus belli**
   An enemy committed a sudden and deliberate act of aggression against us (the United States or an ally) without justification. This act represents a threat to peace, freedom, democracy, and the interests of all humanity.

2. **Implication of and response to the precipitating event**

   We are therefore thrust into war against our will. We have no choice but to act militarily. All other options have been exhausted and are no longer practicable. The decision to go to war has been made only after thoughtful, deliberate, and careful consideration. Our military action is defensive in nature in contrast to our enemy's aggressive actions.

3. **Our motives and objectives**

   We have no selfish interests, no territorial ambitions. We have no quarrel with the citizens of the country we are fighting, only their government. Our response will be firm and steadfast. Our motives and objectives are to restore peace, to prevent a wider or more devastating war in the future, and to protect freedom, democracy, and the greater good of the world. We act for the good of all humanity.

4. **Identifying Us versus Them**

   We stand for and represent peace, freedom, and democracy. We possess legal authority, moral authority, resolve, and unity. In contrast, our enemy rules autocratically by force, practices aggression and deception, and disregards international law and agreements.

5. **Coda**

   Although we face a great challenge that requires sacrifice, we will stand together committed to the cause and will prevail in our fight.

Next, I further explicate this generic schema through an examination of how it plays out in specific renditions of the presidential war narrative.

Precipitating Event / *Casus Belli*

In their work on narrative, Labov and Waletzky (1967) invoke the concept of a "precipitating event," which acts as the starting point for a story. Bruner (1991) draws from this notion in his discussion of the way narrative highlights some type of break from the normalcy of everyday life to warrant its "tellability." Bruner (1991) explains that breaches of the canonical "are often highly conventional and are strongly influenced by narrative traditions. Such breaches are readily recognizable as familiar human plights" (12). One such familiar plight is that of a nation at war, which is readily assimilated into the presidential war narrative where the narrative's precipitating event corresponds with the *casus belli* of a military conflict. As seen in examples (1) through (8), presidents reference a specific date to mark the beginning of the war narrative.

1. Yesterday, December 7, 1941—a date which will live in infamy . . . (Roosevelt 1941)

2. On Sunday, June 25th, Communist forces attacked . . . (Truman 1950a)

3. On August 2 the United States destroyer Maddox was attacked . . . (Johnson 1964)
4. On October 12th, a small group in his militia seized . . . (Reagan 1983)
5. Last Friday, Noriega declared . . . (Bush 1989)
6. This conflict started August 2nd when the dictator of Iraq invaded . . . (Bush 1991)
7. In 1989 Serbia's leader . . . (Clinton 1999)
8. Since September 11 . . . (Bush 2001)

Reference to a precipitating event establishes the boundary to the narrative realm, dividing the world into a "before" and an "after." The time within the narrative realm is "human time" rather than merely "clock time" (Ricoeur 1984). As Bruner (1991) explains, "It is time whose significance is given by the meaning assigned to events within its compass" (6). For example, in George W. Bush's narrative about a "war on terror," history is split into a pre-9/11 world and a post-9/11 world, as referenced in (8). As I discuss elsewhere (Hodges 2011), this division serves the interpretive function of positioning events after September 2001—such as the 2003 invasion of Iraq—within the rubric of waging a single "war on terror" where Afghanistan and Iraq are seen as "fronts" rather than separate wars. In generic terms, reference to the precipitating event marks the beginning of a discrete war or military campaign.

In the presidential war narrative, the precipitating event invariably takes the form of an "act of aggression" committed by an enemy. According to Just War Theory, "war is only permissible if its purpose is to retaliate against a wrong already committed (for example, to pursue and punish an aggressor)" (Mosely 2009). Thus, the framing of the precipitating event as an "act of aggression" serves to fulfill the first tenet of *jus ad bellum:* just cause. Embedded in the naming of the precipitating event is an evaluation that variously emphasizes that the act came suddenly, without warning, without justification, yet with deliberate intent—descriptors that underscore the aggressive and unwarranted nature of the act. These descriptions can be seen in (9) through (15) where the lexical descriptors are marked in bold.

9. Vessels . . . have been ruthlessly sent to the bottom: **without warning** . . . (Wilson 1917)
10. . . . the United States of America was **suddenly** and **deliberately** attacked . . . (Roosevelt 1941)
11. That attack came **without provocation** and **without warning**. It was an **act of raw aggression, without** a shadow of **justification**. (Truman 1950a)
12. . . . the attack was naked, **deliberate, unprovoked aggression, without** a shadow of **justification**. (Truman 1950b)
13. The attacks were **deliberate**. The attacks were **unprovoked**. (Johnson1964b)
14. **Aggression—deliberate, willful**, and systematic **aggression** . . . (Johnson 1964b)
15. . . . bring **sudden** terror and suffering to America. (Bush 2002)

Note that these examples come from speeches that mark the onset of major wars—World War I, World War II, Korea, Vietnam, Afghanistan, Iraq—as opposed to the less involved (in terms of American commitment of forces, time, and lives) military actions of Grenada in 1983, Panama in 1989, the Persian Gulf in 1991, and Kosovo in 1999. In the latter cases, the precipitating event is often further removed from the time of the speech and requires a more elaborate account to explain the need to use military force. For example, the precipitating event for military action in Grenada in 1983 began four years earlier in 1979, according to Ronald Reagan's narrative seen in (16).

16. In 1979 trouble came to Grenada . . . (Reagan 1983)

Over the course of several concise lines, Reagan then recounts a series of events between that initial precipitating event and the more immediate *casus belli* in the days prior to the military action, presented in (17).

17. On October 12th [1983], a small group of his militia seized . . .
    (Reagan 1983)

Likewise, in Bill Clinton's address to the nation in 1999 on airstrikes against Serbia, he provides a condensed history lesson that begins in 1989, as illustrated in (18).

18. In 1989, Serbia's leader, Slobodan Milosevic . . . (Clinton 1999)

Clinton then takes listeners up to the present actions that constitute the more immediate *casus belli* presented in (19).

19. Now they've started moving from village to village, shelling and
    torching . . . (Clinton 1999)

Cases such as these make use of a two-part precipitating event to set up the war narrative. Alone, and without more grounding for an audience who may not be familiar with the history of the region being discussed, the more immediate precipitating event could easily fail to answer the question, "so what?" That is, as Labov and Waletzky (1967) point out, narrative must not only tell what happened but convey why it is worth telling. With regard to the presidential war narrative, the president must convey why the story is worth telling in a way that leads to the public's support for the commitment of American forces in a military venture. Delivering the mini-history lesson that begins with a more remote precipitating event provides context for instilling the immediate precipitating event with a sense of import and urgency. It also helps the narrator answer the question "why now?" by laying the ground upon which the figure of the immediate precipitating event can be contrasted.

Answering "why now?" can make use of an ultimatum to construct a striking figure against the (back)ground of the status quo up to that point. This may come in the form of a warning issued to an enemy that may also be backed by the institutional authority of the United Nations. This can be seen in (20) and (21).

20. Saddam was warned over and over again to comply with the will of the United Nations: Leave Kuwait, or be driven out. Saddam has arrogantly rejected all warnings. (Bush 1991)
21. More than 2 weeks ago, I gave Taliban leaders a series of clear and specific demands. . . . None of these demands were met. And now the Taliban will pay a price. (Bush 2001)

In (20), George H. W. Bush provides an answer to "why now?" after five months had passed between the invasion of Kuwait by Saddam Hussein and Bush's launch of the American-led war against Iraq in January 1991. Here, Bush invokes Saddam Hussein's rejection of UN Security Council resolutions and accompanying warnings that such a violation of international law would result in military action. Likewise, George W. Bush issued a pointed ultimatum to Afghanistan's Taliban government before the US invasion of that country in 2001, as alluded to in (21). From a critical perspective, the genuineness of such ultimatums in seeking to solve the issue without military involvement is highly dubious. That is, the issuance of a final ultimatum does more to manufacture consent with a domestic audience than to act as a serious diplomatic gesture to prevent war. Yet, in terms of the former, it provides a dramatic means for achieving its aims.

Implication of and Response to the Precipitating Event

The next major section of the presidential war narrative deals with the implication of and response to the precipitating event as *casus belli*. Across the board, the precipitating event is positioned as an offensive act of aggression committed by an enemy with the implication that the United States is thrust into war as a matter of self-defense with no choice but to respond militarily. Importantly, this defensive posture holds regardless of the type of situation. Even in US military ventures that could be construed as more "offensive," the actions are narrated as defensive in nature. In fact, the importance of constructing actions as defensive becomes all the more important in cases when public opinion is more sharply divided over which side of the line (offensive or defensive) proposed actions fall. For example, the discursive work done by Franklin D. Roosevelt in his speech after Pearl Harbor pales in comparison to the work done by George W. Bush to lay the groundwork for the invasion of Iraq. In the latter case, critics described the action as a "war of choice" and questioned its defensive nature. As Dunmire (2009) discusses, the Bush Doctrine, which laid the groundwork for the invasion of Iraq, effectively appropriated the terminology of "preemptive" actions—recognized as legitimate actions of self-defense in accord with Just

War Theory and international law³—as cover for a policy of "preventive" attacks (see also, Dunmire, this volume). In contrast, depicting the US entrance into World War II in terms of self-defense faced much less resistance among the public. Roosevelt's request to Congress for a declaration of war consisted of a mere 506 words compared to Bush's speech of 3,327 words in Cincinnati on October 7, 2002,⁴ a key rhetorical moment in the administration's push for war. In sum, the ideas of *jus ad bellum*—that is, the right to go to war—guide the rhetorical process all presidents follow in justifying military actions. Whether a war is primarily defensive in actual fact,⁵ the presidential war narrative must discursively present it as such to fulfill the *jus ad bellum* principles of just cause and right intention. This means positioning the war as defensive in nature through use of the lexeme "defense," as seen in (22) through (26).

22. . . . I have directed that all measures be taken for our **defense**. (Roosevelt 1941)
23. The free nations face a worldwide threat. It must be met with a worldwide **defense**. (Truman 1950a)
24. . . . **defense** of peace in southeast Asia. (Johnson 1964a)
25. . . . in **defense** of their fellow citizens, in **defense** of democracy. (Bush 1989)
26. . . . we will meet the responsibility of **defending** human liberty against violence and aggression. (Bush 2002)

It also involves emphasizing that the war has been thrust or forced upon us so there is no choice but to go to war, as illustrated in (27) through (31).

27. I advise that the Congress . . . formally accept the status of belligerent which has thus been thrust upon [the United States] . . . (Wilson 1917)
28. We enter this war only where we are clearly forced into it because there are no other means of defending our rights. (Wilson 1917)
29. I believe our government has a responsibility to go to the aid of its citizens, if their right to life and liberty is threatened. (Reagan 1983)
30. These countries had hoped the use of force could be avoided. Regrettably, we now believe that only force will make him leave. (Bush 1991)
31. We did not ask for this present challenge, but we accept it. (Bush 2002)

---

³ Notably, Article 51 of Chapter VII of the United Nations Charter ensures the "inherent right of individual or collective self-defense if an armed attack occurs against a Member of the United Nations" (Charter of the United Nations 1945).

⁴ It is no coincidence that this date falls on the one year anniversary of the invasion of Afghanistan. The scheduling of the speech on this date acts as another way human time enters into the significance of the narrating event.

⁵ Of course, characterizing the nature of military action (i.e., as defensive or offensive) is anything but clear-cut; and I do not mean to convey otherwise. To the contrary, I wish to underscore the inherent ambiguity in such determinations and emphasize, with Campbell and Jamieson (2008), that considerable "divisions of opinion arise over the line to be drawn between appropriate actions in defense of the nation and offensive use of the nation's military capabilities" (219).

This discursive move strategically shifts agency, and hence responsibility for the outbreak of hostilities, to the enemy. As seen in (27), this shift in agency can be accomplished through the use of passive voice so that *war has been thrust upon us*. By contrast, any actions that the United States may have done to contribute to the conflict are erased. Even the arguably more offensive uses of the nation's military in the cases of Grenada in (29) and Iraq in (31) are presented as defensive responses to acts of aggression carried out by enemies who initiated the conflicts. Furthermore, the agentive military actions that are taken by the United States are presented as moves of last resort, another crucial principle of *jus ad bellum*—that is, as actions taken only after all other options have been exhausted and are no longer practicable, as illustrated in (32) through (35).

32. I took this action only after reaching the conclusion that every other avenue was closed . . . (Bush 1989)
33. Now the 28 countries with forces in the Gulf area have exhausted all reasonable efforts . . . have no choice but to drive Saddam from Kuwait by force. (Bush 1991)
34. The United States, together with the United Nations, exhausted every means at our disposal to bring this crisis to a peaceful end. (Bush 1991)
35. Over the last few months we have done everything we possibly could to solve this problem peacefully. (Clinton 1999)

In one of their five key characteristics of war rhetoric, Campbell and Jamieson (2008) point out that "every element in it proclaims that the momentous decision to resort to force is deliberate, the product of thoughtful consideration" (221). The exhortations that war comes only as a last resort seen here are often accompanied by explicit commentary about the difficulty of making the final decision to engage American forces and the solemn responsibility it entails, as demonstrated in (36) through (39).

36. With a profound sense of the solemn and even tragical character of the step I am taking and of the grave responsibilities which it involves . . . (Wilson 1917)
37. It is a solemn responsibility to have to order even limited military action (Johnson 1964a)
38. No President can easily commit our sons and daughters to war. (Bush 1991)
39. Do our interests in Kosovo justify the dangers to our Armed Forces? I've thought long and hard about that question. (Clinton 1999)

Thus, appeals to the nation for support of war underline the deliberative process taken by the president and, crucially, position that deliberative process as having already taken place. Placing the deliberative process in the past, rather than leaving it open to continued public debate and consideration, allows the president to assume the "extraordinary, even near-dictatorial powers" (Campbell and Jamieson 2008: 243) associated with the office of commander-in-chief. If met with dissent or public skepticism, the issuance of a call to arms would be doomed to failure. Thus, the president overcomes the public's hesitation by using the narrative to emphasize the principles of just cause, right intention, and last resort.

America's Motives and Objectives

In the third major section of the presidential war narrative, the president outlines the motives and objectives of the nation's response to the enemy's act of aggression. Not only does this work to further allay concerns that the use of force is conducted without right intention, but it also begins to lay out a common set of values that define the national character. To these ends, one or more points may be emphasized. First, whereas objectionable uses of the military involve conquest or territorial expansion, the president emphasizes that the United States has no selfish interests or territorial ambitions, as seen in (40) through (43).

40. We have no selfish ends to serve. We desire no conquest, no dominion. (Wilson 1917)
41. I wish to state that the United States has no territorial ambitions . . . (Truman 1950b)
42. We have no military, political or territorial ambitions in the area. (Johnson 1964c)
43. We have no ambition in Iraq except to remove a threat and restore control of that country to its own people. (Bush 2003b)

Instead, underlying America's motives is a stated desire for peace; and war is therefore waged in the service of peace, as in (44) through (48).

44. . . . to fight thus for the ultimate peace of the world . . . (Wilson 1917)
45. . . . restore peace and security . . . (Truman 1950a)
46. . . . peace is the only purpose of the course that America pursues. (Johnson 1964b)
47. . . . the pursuit of peace (Reagan 1983)
48. . . . advancing the cause of peace. (Clinton 1999)

Moreover, accompanying the discourse of peace are the discourses of freedom and democracy, seen in (49) through (55).

49. The world must be made safe for democracy. (Wilson 1917)
50. This is not just a jungle war, but a struggle for freedom . . . (Johnson 1964c)

51. . . . keep freedom and maintain peace. (Reagan 1983)
52. . . . an affront to mankind and a challenge to the freedom of all. (Bush 1991)
53. . . . to save innocent lives and preserve peace, freedom, and stability in Europe. (Clinton 1999)
54. We defend not only our precious freedoms but also the freedom of people everywhere . . . (Bush 2001)
55. Now as before, we will secure our Nation, protect our freedom, and help others to find freedom of their own. (Bush 2002)

The concepts of peace, freedom, and democracy are sufficiently vague and positively valued so that they constitute a set of core values that all Americans agree upon.[6] When a call to war is presented as a fight for peace, freedom, and democracy, objections to war on those very terms would call into question the desire for peace or the value of freedom and democracy. Thus, regardless of the specific details of the impending conflict, the narrative presents the fight in general terms to which Americans would find little objection.

Moreover, the values of peace, freedom, and democracy are presented as universal values; and the United States is therefore positioned as representing the interests of the world as a whole and not just its own interests. Note the references, for example, to "the world" in (49), to "mankind" in (52), and to "people everywhere" in (54). The threat is therefore not just a threat to the United States but to the entire world. This makes the war at hand all the more urgent and pressing.

In addition, with the United States said to be fighting for the universal interests of everyone around the world, this can also include the citizens of the nation against which the United States is fighting, as demonstrated in (56) through (59).

56. We have no quarrel with the German people. We have no feeling towards them but one of sympathy and friendship. It was not upon their impulse that their government acted in entering this war. (Wilson 1917)
57. We have no argument with the people of Iraq. Indeed, for the innocents caught in this conflict, I pray for their safety. Our goal is not the conquest of Iraq. It is the liberation of Kuwait. (Bush 1991)
58. The United States of America is a friend to the Afghan people, and we are the friends of almost a billion worldwide who practice the Islamic faith. (Bush 2001)
59. We come to Iraq with respect for its citizens, for their great civilization, and for the religious faiths they practice. (Bush 2002)

---

[6] One could also think of these as "god-terms" (Burke 1945) or "ideographs" (McGee 1980).

This discursive befriending of the people against which one is about to wage war creates a distinction between the citizens of that nation—for example, "the German people" as in (56) or Iraqis as in (59)—and the government of that nation, which is typically embodied in the personage of a dictator (e.g., Adolph Hitler or Saddam Hussein). Importantly, this rhetorical move adheres to and reinforces the logic of the narrative in which the United States is said to be fighting for universal values. According to the presidential war narrative, the people of the nation the United States is fighting are threatened by their own government just as Americans are so threatened since universal values—and not solely American national security—are under attack. Within the framework of the narrative, the United States is positioned as a benevolent actor with everyone's best interests in mind. In this way, nationalistic interests can be couched inside "the claim that these actions are within the general moral order, and hence not justified only by partisan, self-serving grounds" (van Dijk 1998: 258). The motives and objectives are therefore presented as pure and untainted by selfish interests.

Identifying Us versus Them

The protagonist and antagonist in any given conflict are, in generic terms, quite similar from one rendition of the presidential war narrative to another. Although some versions of the narrative devote a particular section to explicitly define the enemy, the binary opposition between Us and Them nevertheless permeates the narrative from beginning to end. Making use of the common process of positive self-presentation and negative other-presentation discussed by van Dijk (1998: 267) and represented by the "ideological square" (depicted in table 3.2), presidents construct images of the American nation and its enemy through both explicit and implicit characterizations and evaluations embedded in the narrative. Since the suppression or de-emphasis of information that is negative about Us and positive about Them (the bottom line of the ideological square) typically manifests itself through absence rather than presence in discourse, I focus here on the top line of the ideological square where We are discursively positioned in positive terms and They in negative terms.

All wars require an antagonist with attributes and values antithetical to those of the protagonist. Statements about attributes and values possessed by

TABLE 3.2

Representing Us and Them Using the "Ideological Square"

	Us	Them
Express/emphasize information that is:	positive	negative
Suppress/de-emphasize information that is:	negative	positive

Us therefore implicate a set of oppositional ones possessed by Them, and vice versa. Table 3.3 summarizes the attributes, values, and activities characteristic of Us and Them in the presidential war narrative.

The distinction between the democratic nature of Us and the autocratic nature of Them is made explicit through references to the enemy's leader as "dictator" or "tyrant." The imagery associated with such lexical descriptors emphasizes the authoritarian nature of the enemy; but it also works to embody the enemy in a single personage—for example, Hitler, Noriega, Saddam, among others. This attributes individual agency to that person, and thereby works to endow the enemy as a whole with intentional states embodied in the consciousness of an individual actor. As Bruner (1991: 7) points out, the assignment of intentional states to protagonists underlies much of the explanatory power of narrative. As seen in the earlier discussion of (27) through (31), positioning the enemy as an intentional actor with agency works to assign responsibility to the enemy for the outbreak of war. This simultaneously absolves Us from having contributed to the outbreak of war, and thereby allows for a defensive posture in response to the enemy's "aggression—deliberate, willful, and systematic aggression" (Lyndon Johnson, excerpt 14).

The naming of a figurehead to personify the enemy also allows for the discursive move seen earlier in (56) through (59) where a subtle distinction is created between the government and the people of the nation against which the United States fights. This differentiation further highlights the autocratic nature of Them whereby the enemy rules over and hence works against the best interests of its own citizens. The image of an autocratic enemy that oppresses its own people reinforces the enemy's position as a threat not just to Our values but to universal values shared by all humanity. By implication, the United States takes on the role of defender of those universal values—peace, freedom, and democracy. These values are aligned with both US national security and the good of all humanity so that by fighting to defend itself the United States

TABLE 3.3

Characteristics of the Us versus Them Binary in the Presidential War Narrative

Us	Them
Free, civilized, democratic nation	Autocratic nation ruled by dictator/tyrant
Stand for peace, freedom, democracy, good of all	Stand for own selfish interests and ambitions
Defenders of universal values	Aggressors that threaten universal values
Engage in self-defense	Engage in aggression
Follow rule of law	Practice deception
Enforce international agreements	Break international agreements
Possess legal authority	Lack legal authority
Possess moral authority	Lack moral authority
Possess unity	Lack unity

in turn defends the universal interests of the world. This benevolence—which encompasses the moral and ethical duties to act with proportionality in line with *jus ad bellum*—stands in stark contrast to the malevolence of the enemy that practices aggression in pursuit of its own selfish ambitions and threatens Americans, its own people, and humanity as a whole. Moreover, emphasizing the democratic nature of Us and the autocratic nature of Them works to legitimate Our proper authority to wage war and delegitimate Their authority to do so, another key aspect of *jus ad bellum*.

In addition, the threat from the enemy initially manifests itself through what are described as deceptive practices, as in (60) through (63).

60. Cunningly contrived plans of deception or aggression . . . (Wilson 1917)
61. . . . the Japanese Government has deliberately sought to deceive the United States by false statements. (Roosevelt 1941)
62. Grenada, we were told, was a friendly island paradise for tourism. Well, it wasn't. It was a Soviet-Cuban colony, being readied as a major military bastion to export terror and undermine democracy. (Reagan 1983)
63. The entire world has witnessed Iraq's 11-year history of defiance, deception, and bad faith. (Bush 2002)

Whereas defenders of universal values follow the rule of law, the deception practiced by the enemy is carried out to circumvent international agreements and commitments, illustrated in (64) through (68).

64. International law . . . the German Government has swept aside . . . (Wilson 1917)
65. . . . with no heed to the resolution of the Security Council of the United Nations. (Truman 1950b)
66. The agreements of 1954 and 1962 were also signed by the government of North Viet-Nam. . . . That government of North Viet-Nam is now willfully and systematically violating those agreements of both 1954 and 1962. (Johnson 1964b)
67. Serbia stationed 40,000 troops in and around Kosovo in preparation for a major offensive—and in clear violation of the commitments they had made. (Clinton 1999)
68. Eleven years ago, as a condition for ending the Persian Gulf war, the Iraqi regime was required to destroy its weapons of mass destruction, to cease all development of such weapons, and to stop all support for terrorist groups. The Iraqi regime has violated all of those obligations. (Bush 2002)

By emphasizing the United Nations resolutions or other international agreements that the enemy violates, the presidential war narrative invokes a legal basis for America's military action. As a nation said to value the rule of law, the

United States therefore possesses legal authority to act as an enforcer of international law. Moral authority accompanies this legal authority as the narrative positions the United States in line with *jus ad bellum* and its own treaty commitments with its allies.

Central to the overarching Us versus Them binary featured in table 3.3 is the aggregation of attributes on each side of the divide so that these sets of attributes come into semiotic alignment. "The notion of semiotic alignment can be traced to Claude Lévi-Strauss's discussion of analogical relationships which generate systems of meaning within culture" (Chandler 2007: 101). Through analogical thought, a set of differences between one set of binary oppositions (e.g., raw vs. cooked) can be mapped onto the differences between another set of binary oppositions (e.g., nature vs. culture). Such alignments result in homologous oppositions so that, for example, *raw is to cooked as nature is to culture* (Lévi-Strauss 1969; compare also to Irvine and Gal's 2000 notion of *fractal recursivity*). In the scheme presented in table 3.3, each positive attribute of Us not only opposes a negative attribute of Them but also aligns with a cluster of other positive attributes that come to be associated with one another. Thus, reference to a democratic nation aligns with the values of peace, freedom, and democracy which in turn align with universal values. That democratic nations are associated with the rule of law implies adherence to international agreements and *jus ad bellum*; in turn, the use of military force is necessarily associated with self-defense, legal authority, and moral authority. Invoking one of these characteristics of Us implicates the others. Likewise, on the other side of the divide, numerous attributes align together to form an image of Them so that invoking one characteristic (e.g., autocratic ruler) indexes other characteristics in the cluster (e.g., self-serving uses of military force).

In Lévi-Straussian terms, such alignments result in a series of homologous oppositions so that, for example, *democratic nation is to autocratic nation as self-defense is to aggression*—or, *Us is to Them as universal values are to selfish interests*. The oppositions continue in this way to form composite images of Us and Them. These images provide the generic basis for the characters in the presidential war narrative. In this way, the enemies from different American wars appear nearly identical in generic terms. Any differences between America's various past enemies are viewed as superficial variations on an underlying structural theme. This allows, for example, George W. Bush to convey in his "war on terror" narrative the idea that fascists, Nazis, and Communists are interchangeable with one another and spawn today's terrorists as their "heirs" and "successors" (Hodges 2011).

Semioticians like Jakobson (1990: 165) warn that "we should be aware of allowing separate dichotomies to slip into unquestioned alignments" (Chandler 2007: 103). Although possessing legal authority is the antithesis of lacking legal authority, it does not necessarily follow that the former invariably aligns with Us while the latter always aligns with Them—and so on and so forth for the other homologous oppositions that result from the alignments in the binary. Yet within the presidential war narrative, such clusters of attributes invariably align and result in stock images of Us and Them. These taken-for-granted identities become part of the generic expectations of the narrative, and renditions of the narrative that adhere to these expectations instill the case for war with generic realism that adds to its persuasive power. Put another way, the discursive positioning of such attributes as "natural" and necessarily aligned rather than constructed and contingently linked makes them difficult to deconstruct at the very moment when inchoate war demands critical dissection of the issues presented to the nation in presidential war rhetoric. In sum, the process of creating the Us versus Them binary is one of the most potent means by which the presidential war narrative lays the groundwork for justifying war because it draws from deep-seated images ingrained in the national mythology.

The Narrative's Coda

Finally, war rhetoric characteristically exhorts the audience "to unanimity of purpose and total commitment" (Campbell and Jamieson 2008: 221). Such exhortations are particularly salient in the coda of the presidential war narrative. Here, the president underscores the challenges faced in the war and emphasizes America's resolve to persevere amid those challenges, as demonstrated in (69) and (70).

69. The hard facts of the present situation require relentless determination and firm action. (Truman 1950b)
70. We will not waver; we will not tire; we will not falter; and we will not fail. Peace and freedom will prevail. Thank you. May God continue to bless America. (Bush 2001)

A large component of this resolve stems from the discursive projection of unity among an otherwise diverse polity. In times of war, differences within the nation—whether racial, ethnic, religious, economic, or political (including dissenting voices opposed to war)—are backgrounded while the common element of shared citizenship is foregrounded. In other words, an *adequation* is achieved whereby "potentially salient differences are set aside in favor of perceived or asserted similarities that are taken to be more situationally relevant" (Bucholtz and Hall 2004: 383). The "united we stand" slogan in the aftermath of 9/11 is one example of the way semiotic resources are employed to achieve adequation and unity. Lyndon Johnson and Ronald Reagan exemplify this type of discursive work done in the presidential war narrative as seen in (71) and (72).

71. There are no parties and there is no partisanship when our peace or the peace of the world is imperiled by aggressors in any part of the world. We are one nation united and indivisible. (Johnson 1964b)

72. In this city, where political strife is so much a part of our lives, I've seen Democratic leaders in the Congress join their Republican colleagues, send a message to the world that we're all Americans before we're anything else, and when our country is threatened, we stand shoulder to shoulder in support of our men and women in the Armed Forces. (Reagan 1983)

In short, the coda ends the narrative by looking ahead to the future—namely, a future where America's resolve, unity, and commitment allow it to persevere amid the challenges it faces. The success that is projected works to fulfill the requirement of *jus ad bellum* that war should be waged only when there is a reasonable probability of success. It also works to mobilize the polity in an effort to ensure success. The coda thereby places a final exclamation point on the president's call to arms and bridges "the gap between the moment of time at the end of the narrative proper and the present" context in which the narrative is told (Labov 1972: 365).

Conclusion

In this chapter, I have illustrated the generic elements that comprise the common narrative told by American presidents at the onset of military ventures to win public consent for war. By drawing examples from presidential speeches spanning from Woodrow Wilson's call for entry into World War I through George W. Bush's marketing of the war in Iraq, we can see how the generic schema of the presidential war narrative frames entry into any conflict in a remarkably similar manner. Notably, the use of this generic schema not only works to justify war in line with *jus ad bellum*, but the cumulative rehearsals of the narrative across presidencies and conflicts also works to continually reconstruct America's national identity as an enduring image from one generation to the next. The formation of the "imagined community" of the nation-state—itself a cultural artifact, in Anderson's (1983: 4) terms—results from such ongoing cultural projects.

In justifying war to the American public, presidents effectively imagine the national community and lay out a set of understandings that Americans have about themselves and their nation's place in the world. Although such national imaginings are not unique to presidential rhetoric during wartime, war rhetoric does provide particularly penetrating insight into the identity of Us when it is viewed in sharp contrast to the foil of Them. In the narrative, We are presented as a benevolent, peace-loving nation ready to defend the interests of humanity as a whole. In contrast, They represent autocratic regimes that engage in acts of aggression for self-serving interests that threaten universal values of peace, freedom, and democracy.

Certainly, the idealization of Us invoked by such imaginings presents a positive image of right action and civic duty. Yet within the bounds of the presidential war narrative, these idealizations work to position American actions as beyond questioning, and obscure the various motives and complex array of issues in international affairs that lead nations to take up arms against one another. The American use of military force is invariably positioned as "self-defense" regardless of the nature of such actions in actual fact. Moreover, the wartime distinction between Us and Them exaggerates difference to the point that the resulting schismogenesis (Bateson 1972) necessitates conflict and thereby precludes any further attempt to productively communicate—whether within the group as part of the democratic process of deliberation or without in terms of diplomatic action. The presidential war narrative paves the way for war, not diplomacy, and it lends itself to rote patriotic fervor rather than nuanced consideration of the issues and consequences of war.

As it draws from powerful images in the national mythology, any implementation of the presidential war narrative erases doubt about the justness of the situation under consideration. As a result, citizens—the citizens that Kant describes as the stopgap to illicit or overreaching uses of the nation's military—face a difficult task if they rely on presidential pronouncements (and uncritical amplification of those pronouncements in the media) to accurately judge the need for war. The recent implementation of the generic presidential war schema by George W. Bush to justify the 2003 invasion of Iraq underscores the crucial role rhetoric plays in manufacturing consent for war where uncritical acceptance overcomes warranted hesitation. Although Kant didn't account for the power of discourse to impact this process, discourse scholars are well positioned to contribute to its examination. In my mind, a primary task for scholars and citizens alike is to develop the critical tools and ethos needed "to question over and over again what is postulated as self-evident" and "to dissipate what is familiar and accepted" (Foucault and Kritzman 1988: 265) so that discourses of peace can better compete with discourses of war in democratic practice.

Acknowledgments

I am grateful to the participants of the Social Meaning in Language reading group at Carnegie Mellon University and the University of Pittsburgh for our discussions of topics that helped shape this chapter. In particular, I owe special thanks to Barbara Johnstone, Scott Kiesling, Thomas Mitchell, and Mark Thompson for their feedback on an earlier version of this chapter. Any shortcomings that remain are, of course, my sole responsibility.

References

Anderson, Benedict. 1983. *Imagined Communities*. New York: Verso.

Aquinas, Thomas. 1948. *Summa Theologica*. Fathers of the English Dominican Province (trans.). New York: Benziger Bros.

Bakhtin, Mikhail. 1981. *The Dialogic Imagination: Four Essays*, Caryl Emerson and Michael Holquist (trans.), Michael Holquist (ed.). Austin: University of Texas Press.

Bakhtin, Mikhail. 1986. *Speech Genres and Other Late Essays*, Vern W. McGee (trans.), Caryl Emerson and Michael Holquist (eds.). Austin: University of Texas Press.

Bateson, Gregory. 1972. *Steps to an Ecology of Mind*. Chicago: University of Chicago Press.

Bauman, Richard. 1986. *Story, Performance, and Event: Contextual Studies of Oral Narrative*. Cambridge: Cambridge University Press.

Bauman, Richard. 2004. *A World of Others' Words: Cross-cultural Perspectives on Intertextuality*. Malden, MA: Blackwell.

Bourdieu, Pierre. 1991. *Language and Symbolic Power*, Gino Raymond and Matthew Adamson (trans.), John B. Thompson (ed.). Cambridge, MA: Harvard University Press.

Briggs, Charles and Richard Bauman. 1992. "Genre, Intertextuality, and Social Power." *Journal of Linguistic Anthropology* 2(2): 131–72.

Bruner, Jerome. 1991. "The Narrative Construction of Reality." *Critical Inquiry* 18: 1–24.

Bucholtz, Mary and Kira Hall. 2004. "Language and Identity." In *A Companion to Linguistic Anthropology*, Alessandro Duranti (ed.), 369–94. Malden, MA: Blackwell.

Burke, Kenneth. 1945. *A Grammar of Motives*. New York: Prentice-Hall.

Campbell, Karlyn Kohrs and Kathleen Hall Jamieson. 2008. *Presidents Creating the Presidency: Deeds Done in Words*. Chicago: University of Chicago Press.

Chandler, Daniel. 2007. *Semiotics*. New York: Routledge.

Charter of the United Nations. 1945. www.un.org/en/documents/charter/chapter7.shtml.

Dunmire, Patricia. 2009. "'9/11 Changed Everything': An Interxtextual Analysis of the Bush Doctrine." *Discourse & Society* 20(2): 195–222.

Foucault, Michel and Lawrence D. Kritzman. 1988. *Politics, Philosophy, Culture: Interviews and Other Writings, 1977–1984*. New York: Routledge.

Hanks, William F. 1987. "Discourse Genres in a Theory of Practice." *American Ethnologist* 14(4): 668–92.

Hodges, Adam. 2011. *The 'War on Terror' Narrative: Discourse and Intertextuality in the Construction and Contestation of Sociopolitical Reality*. New York: Oxford University Press.

Irvine, Judith and Susan Gal. 2000. "Language Ideology and Linguistic Differentiation." In *Regimes of Language*, Paul Kroskrity (ed.), 35–84. Santa Fe: School of American Research.

Jakobson, Roman. 1971 [1957]. "Shifters, Verbal Categories, and the Russian Verb." In *Roman Jakobson: Selected Writings*, vol. 2, 130–47. The Hague: Mouton.

Jakobson, Roman. 1990. "The Time Factor in Language." In *On Language*, Linda R. Waugh and Monique Monville-Burston (eds.), 164–75. Cambridge, MA: Harvard University Press.

Kant, Immanuel. 1991 [1795]. "Perpetual Peace." In *Kant: Political Writings*, H. S. Reiss (ed.), 93–130. Cambridge: Cambridge University Press.

Labov, William. 1972. "The Transformation of Experience in Narrative Syntax." In *Language in the Inner City: Studies in the Black English Vernacular*, William Labov (ed.), 354–96. Philadelphia: University of Pennsylvania Press.

Labov, William and Joshua Waletzky. 1967. "Narrative Analysis: Oral Versions of Personal Experience." In *Essays on the Verbal and Visual Arts*, J. Helm (ed.), 12–44. Seattle: University of Washington Press.

Lévi-Strauss, Claude. 1969. *The Raw and the Cooked*, John Weightman and Doreen Weightman (trans.). Chicago: University of Chicago Press.

McGee, Michael Calvin. 1980. "The 'Ideograph': A Link between Rhetoric and Ideology." *Quarterly Journal of Speech* 66(1): 1–16.

Mosley, Alexander. 2009. "Just War Theory." *Internet Encyclopedia of Philosophy*. www.iep.utm.edu/justwar/.

Orend, Brian. 2005. "War." *Stanford Encyclopedia of Philosophy*. http://plato.stanford.edu/entries/war/#2.1.

Ricoeur, Paul. 1984. *Time and Narrative*. Chicago: University of Chicago Press.

Van Dijk, Teun A. 1998. *Ideology*. London: Sage.

Walzer, Michael. 2000. *Just and Unjust Wars: A Moral Argument with Historical Illustrations*, 3rd ed. New York: Basic Books.

Walzer, Michael. 2004. *Arguing about War*. New Haven: Yale University Press.

Woolley, John T. and Gerhard Peters. 2010. The American Presidency Project [online]. Santa Barbara, CA. www.presidency.ucsb.edu/ws/?pid=65366.

4

The Discursive Battlefield of the "War on Terror"

ENABLING STRATEGIES FOR GARNERING PUBLIC
SUPPORT IN THE RHETORIC OF GEORGE W. BUSH
AND OSAMA BIN LADEN

Anna Podvornaia

Introduction

The terrorist attacks of September 11, 2001 (9/11), have produced an avalanche
of events that resulted in a shift in the balance of power among the US president, Congress, and interest groups. Beyond the American borders, the incident
was followed by an international acceptance of the US doctrine of so-called
preemption,[1] the war in Afghanistan in 2001, the invasion of Iraq in 2003, and
a dramatic increase in Islamist violence around the world. While it is difficult to
fully elucidate specific factors that effectuated these unexpected changes in the
global political climate, valuable insight can be gained from the political discourse surrounding the 9/11 attacks.

As an important medium of communication that enables common understanding of events, individuals, and concepts, language—and manipulation
thereof—has the potential to modify human behavior. This exhortatory power
of language is the driving force behind war discourse, which aims primarily to
unify an aggrieved collective against its perceived aggressor(s). Specifically,
"call to arms" rhetoric effectuates social cohesion by cultivating and reinforcing
the notion of a shared identity within discourse. This resulting sense of connection to a broader community—or social identity—implies accountability of
each member to the collective. Moreover, it creates the perception of anonymity
by diffusing responsibility across the group's membership. Studies in social psychology (Ellemers, Spears, and Doosje 2002; Grossman 1995; Tetlock 1992;
Zimbardo 1969) demonstrate that the notions of accountability and anonymity
perform an important function in rhetoric as the primary mobilizing force by

---

[1] For a discussion of how the Bush administration couched a policy of preventive intervention
within the framework of preemptive war, see Dunmire (2009).

rendering *personal* identity and ideology largely irrelevant in the audience's consideration of the course of action proposed by the orator.

Overall, the deployment of identity-building narratives allows the orator to (re)define national identity and to create and maintain the illusion of national integration. However, the corollary of enclosing the boundaries of one group is a natural exclusion of everything beyond its frontiers. This illusory unity consequently functions as a mobilizing force enabling violent action against participants who are perceived as threatening to the group's integrity: the outsiders, or the *Other*. "Call to arms" rhetoric therefore distorts meanings of identity, separating the world into two camps: "Us" and "Them" (Chilton 2004; Fairclough 2005; Silberstein 2002; van Dijk 2002). As James Der Derian (2009: 238) keenly points out, "people go to war because of how they see, perceive, picture, imagine, and speak of others: that is, how they construct the difference of others as well as the sameness of themselves through representations." We can therefore assert that the "call to arms" language that prevailed around the time of the 9/11 attacks was more than a mere commentary on the situation at hand. On a broader scale, it functioned as a tool to *recreate* the ongoing events, constructing a version of reality that provided grounds for a specific course of action for the purpose of advancing political goals.

The aim of this study is to discern the strategies of the "call to arms" discourse of President George W. Bush and Osama bin Laden that function as enablers to garnering public support for violent action. The analytical focus of this research is Bush's address to the nation in front of a joint session of Congress on September 20, 2001, and Osama bin Laden's declaration of jihad against the Jews and the Crusaders published three years prior on February 23, 1998. Drawing from work done in Critical Discourse Analysis (Chilton 2004; Chilton and Schäffner 2002; Fairclough 2005; van Dijk 1993; van Leeuwen 1993), I conduct a comparative study of the two texts with the goal of illustrating the parallels and diversions in the rhetorical framework of discourses produced in different social and cultural contexts.

Analytical Approach

Over the course of history, "call to arms" rhetoric has proven to be a powerful exhortatory tool used by political leaders as a means to rally a collection of disparate individuals to a violent cause peripheral to their personal interests (e.g., Graham, Keenan, and Dowd 2004). As such, this type of rhetoric exploits the psychological vulnerabilities exhibited by human beings in crisis situations that necessitate immediate action. The field of Critical Discourse Analysis is, accordingly, concerned with understanding *how* power is exhibited in discourse as well as pinpointing grammatical structures and lexical choices that endow language with affecting properties. In this respect, Critical Discourse Analysis is an effective tool for determining how dominance is expressed and legitimated in rhetoric and what consequences these structures have for the minds of recipients (van Dijk 1993; van Leeuwen 1993).

At its most basic level, the act of persuasion addresses an existing imbalance within a particular context with the intent of inducing the audience to move toward a new balance proposed in the rhetoric. Accordingly, the process by which that sense of disequilibrium is constructed in the communicative act becomes of special interest (White 1992). In "call to arms" rhetoric, the proposed resolution to a matter of concern necessarily involves public acceptance of conflict. For that reason, the primary objective of "call to arms" texts is to direct the audience to consume the rhetoric in a way that incites the individual to pick up arms for a cause external to his or her personal interests. As a result, this type of discourse carries linguistic features that cohere with the underlying psychological and cognitive processes that govern human decision making (Chilton and Schäffner 2002; Graham, Keenan, and Dowd 2004).

Research in the area of social psychology suggests that the discursive task of rallying the masses in "call to arms" rhetoric is met with a number of psychological inhibitors that form part of the resistance inherent in human beings to killing one of their own kind (Grossman 1995; Lorenz 1966). Therefore, at the lexico-grammatical level, "call to arms" texts seek to emulate the psychological mechanisms known to enable the act of aggression. This chapter will consequently examine how "call to arms" discourses influence social cognition, particularly focusing on the mechanisms responsible for determining psychological states and constructing subjective reality. As a whole, this study is undertaken not for interpretative purposes but as an investigation of the underlying workings of exhortative rhetoric. By illuminating the lexico-grammatical mechanisms at play in the "call to arms" texts in the context of the "war on terror," this study seeks to elucidate the enabling strategies at the core of all exhortatory rhetoric: that is, strategies that produce the necessary psychological conditions to effectuate a particular behavioral response in the target audience.

The perception of difference is critical to maintaining the collective identity of a group. Since the mental process of organizing experience is based on contrasts, the understanding of one's own identity is to a large degree achieved via the discursive articulation of an external "Other." Consequently, one of the main features of the "call to arms" genre is the positive representation of the orator's own group against the background of (or even implicitly resulting from) the negative representation of the Other (Graham, Keenan, and Dowd 2004; Jackson 2005, 2006; Lazar and Lazar 2004). This allows the orator to construct and reaffirm the identity of the in-group, to evoke among audience members a common mental state conducive to the desired behavioral response (i.e., a violent action of some sort), and to conceptualize an external "Other," who—as a result of his cultural, social, or moral deviance—presents an existential threat to the in-group, effectively justifying his excision. From a stylistic perspective, contemporary Western "call to arms" texts also tend to be packaged in euphemistic language, which constructs a virtual, sterile version of reality, conveying information and objectives in a way that inhibits a negative emotional response and resistance to the subject of discussion. As the subsequent analysis will demonstrate, five dominant discursive strategies can be identified in the discourses produced by Bush and bin Laden as part of the "war on terror" rhetoric:

1. construction and reaffirmation of the shared identity of the in-group;
2. evocation of a common mental state among audience members;
3. articulation of cultural and social distance;
4. articulation of moral distance;
5. articulation of mechanical distance.

Text 1: Address by President George W. Bush to the Joint Session of Congress, September 20, 2001

Following the 9/11 terrorist attacks on the World Trade Center and the Pentagon, in a historic address to the nation and joint session of Congress, President George W. Bush pledged to defend America's freedoms against the terrorist threat. Recognized as one of the defining speeches in the aftermath of 9/11, the address was a declaration of the "war on terror," rallying public support for military action, which ultimately took the form of counterterrorism and counterinsurgency operations in Afghanistan, Iraq, and other parts of the world in an effort to defeat al Qaeda and curb the threat of transnational terrorism.

CONSTRUCTION OF IDENTITY

At the lexico-grammatical level, the perception of national unity is realized in Bush's address via the deployment of pronouns. The personal pronoun "we" and its objective variant "us" are used a total of sixty times in the text (representing 38 percent of the overall use of personal pronouns). The possessive pronoun "our" appears forty-three times (43 percent) in such collocations as "our Union," "our country," "our National Anthem," "our freedoms," "our nation," "our way of life," "our principles," and "our mission." These collocations, intimately linked with the conception of American identity, are juxtaposed with the nominal group "our enemies," which allows the speaker to firmly establish the boundaries of the in-group vis-à-vis the existence of an out-group. The assertion that "this is the world's fight" enables Bush to extend the group's membership beyond national borders, thus instilling a sense of shared responsibility as well as strengthening the perception of anonymity among in-group members. This discursive technique works to relieve individual audience members of personal accountability for all future action undertaken under the banner of the "war on terror," thus effectively increasing the likelihood of the addressees' participation in any controversial activities that may be associated with the advocated campaign.

Throughout the speech, Bush maintains a tone of determination and vengeance, framing the crisis in terms of the values inherent in the in-group: freedom and justice. He places the notion of freedom in the foreground as a sacred value universal in scope. The word itself appears in the text a total of thirteen times in such collocations as "freedom and fear" and "enemies of freedom," thus discursively positioning this value as a target. This reinforcement of society's communal values allows the speaker to invoke a sense of collective identity, renewing the group's self-concept by clearly identifying the attributes that constitute its positive image (Kuypers 2007: 20). National identification is further strengthened vis-à-vis the enumeration of symbols inextricably linked to the identity of the in-group:

> All of America was touched on the evening of the tragedy to see *Republicans* and *Democrats* joined together on the steps of this *Capitol*, singing *"God Bless America."*

By employing recognizable symbols that hold great affective power, Bush develops cognitive associations with the greater collective, eliciting feelings of patriotism within the individual and, by extension, a sense of duty to the in-group (Cerulo 1995: 4).

One of the most significant themes in Bush's address is its well-developed victimhood narrative, which invokes a sense of innocence and moral worth embodied in the in-group. The speaker lexicalizes the concept of victimhood in such nominal constructions as "the victims of this tragedy" and "the victims of terror." At the implicit level, the theme is supported through the speaker's reiteration of the verbal groups "will remember" and "will never/not forget," which reflect the magnitude of the psychological impact of the event on its targets. Such repetitive lexical representations serve to facilitate the audience's internalization of the information presented in the discourse (Kuypers 2007: 11–12).

The notion of victimhood is also maintained in the text through repeated references to the injury sustained by the members of the in-group. The passive voice construction of the statement "great harm has been done to us" allows the speaker to remove the Actor (the perpetrator) from the clause, thereby foregrounding the Beneficiary (the victim) of the process. More powerfully, Bush refers to the events of 9/11 as a "wound" inflicted upon "our country," effectively personifying a geo-political entity by portraying the United States as a body besieged. His depiction of individual grief as a collective emotion enables Bush to strengthen even further the shared nature of the experience (Ferrari 2007: 615–16; Lazar and Lazar 2007: 232).

In addition, the speaker integrates into the theme of victimhood external participants who are located outside the physical borders of his own group. Once again employing a passive clause, Bush notes that, just like American citizens, "Afghanistan's people have been brutalized," thus insinuating that there are more victims trapped in the enemy territory. This discursive technique works to establish an affiliation among the perceived victims of the perpetrator responsible for the 9/11 attacks—an affiliation that transgresses national boundaries. The verb "brutalize" is an interesting lexical choice in this example, as it supplies contextual information, suggesting criminal activity and human rights violation attributed to the Taliban regime in Afghanistan. Bush goes on to depict in detail the repressive environment in which the people of Afghanistan lead their everyday lives, touching on such prominent issues as education, women's rights, property ownership, and religion, as a result adding a psychological dimension of shock to his argumentation. By providing dramatic examples of oppression that stand in sharp contrast to the freedoms enjoyed and taken for granted in the United States, Bush effectively concretizes the power imbalances that exist within the enemy territory, which, by implication, necessitates subdual (cf. Lazar and Lazar 2007: 232). The delegitimization of the Afghan government consequently enables the president to shift the response strategy from defensive to offensive posture.

Narrative convention creates an expectation that in the time of crisis a hero would intercede to save the victim, thus reestablishing a state of equilibrium (Pugsley 2006). In accordance with this convention, Bush develops the hero narrative in his address by concretizing participants and actions. He identifies specific individuals, whose brave deeds epitomize the meaning of selfless service, including "[Flight 93] passengers like an exceptional man named Todd Beamer" and "a man named George Howard, who died at the World Trade Center trying to save others." Heroism in Bush's speech is also exemplified by the target audience itself, particularly by "the endurance of rescuers, working past exhaustion" and the "loving and giving people who have made the grief of strangers their own." The speaker thus reinforces the virtuous qualities possessed by his own culture and implicitly extends hero status to the nation at large. This heroic nation is portrayed as selfless, driven by "patient justice"—as opposed to the primitive emotion of revenge—as the final reward. Ultimately, the US president transforms his in-group from a victim to a self-designated savior of mankind, unequivocally expressed in the statement: "Our nation—this generation—will lift a dark threat of violence from our people and our future."

EVOCATION OF A COMMON MENTAL STATE

As demonstrated in the previous section, the rhetoric of President Bush effectively responds to a crisis, effectuating communal understanding of the events. His discourse, however, is also characterized by its crisis-*creating* features, which ascertain the urgency of undertaking an action as well as the expediency of the proposed course of action in given circumstances. A closer examination of Bush's rhetoric gives insight into the three main features that determine the effectiveness of the fear appeal: (1) the perceived severity of the threat (crisis); (2) the perceived susceptibility of the in-group members to the threat (danger); and (3) the perception that the recommended course of action will eliminate the threat (Rogers 1975).

First, Bush articulates the existence of a "continuing threat" that "can threaten the stability of legitimate governments." The recurrent motif of a *shared* threat fosters a spirit of cooperation among in-group members. In addition, such nominal groups as "sudden national challenges" and "emergency" emphasize the sense of urgency surrounding present events. These lexical choices connote to the addressee the presence of immediate danger, thereby creating a requirement for a decisive, prompt intervention in order to counter the threat.

Second, a sense of urgency is invoked via an appeal to fear, which greatly amplifies the degree of danger posed to the target audience. Bush portrays the enemy as an entity that is to be *feared*, seeing that this entity threatens "*our* people," "*our* principles," "*our* nation," "*our* future," and "*our* way of life." The gravity of the situation is further inflated vis-à-vis the assertion that this enemy is in effect "threatening people *everywhere*." In addition to endangering the citizens' physical well-being, the enemy in fact presents a threat to the identity of the in-group as a whole:

[Al Qaeda's] goal is *remaking the world*—and *imposing its radical beliefs* on people everywhere.

By conceptualizing the threat in terms of a loss of group distinctiveness, the speaker effectively amplifies the sense of invasion within the target audience (Brewer 2001: 32–33). This image of incursion—both physical and intellectual—presents a justifiable cause for collective action both to American nationals and to citizens of other nations, who "understand that if this terror goes unpunished, their own cities . . . may be next."

The notion of encroachment on the in-group's turf paints the image of an omnipresent enemy, whose agents are "sent to hide in countries around the world to plot evil and destruction." The sense of uncertainty is intensified via allusions to the vulnerability of in-group members on home soil, as evidenced in the statement: "We are not immune from attack." By warning the audience that "there are thousands of these terrorists in more than sixty countries," the speaker signals to the addressees that the threat cannot be simply evaded and, therefore, it must be eliminated. The danger of terrorism is further amplified in Bush's speech by the dramatic claims with respect to the volume of participants involved ("there are thousands of these terrorists"), the enemy's aims ("the terrorists' directive commands them to kill Christians and Jews, to kill all

Americans"), his methods ("trained in the tactics of terror"), and his unpredictability ("surprise attacks") (Ferrari 2007: 617–18).[2]

Third, the urgency of the situation is intensified in the text by characterizing the status quo as a catastrophe of monumental proportions, which is effectively underscored in the very beginning of the speech with the formulaic "in the *normal* course of events." The semantic significance of this lexical choice is threefold; it signals to the audience (1) the abnormality of the situation at hand, (2) the necessity to return to the status quo, and (3) the requirement for special tools or approaches (relating back to the *ab*normal nature of the situation) to reestablish a state of balance. This conception of an anomalous threat is also achieved through such nominal groups as "an important time," "a different world," and, most evidently, through Bush's declaration that "freedom and fear are at war," which equates the existing situation to an epic struggle (Lazar and Lazar 2004: 230). These lexical choices sustain the perception of a potentially cataclysmic threat, which in turn supports the public's acceptance of *any* measure chosen by the government for the purposes of its removal (Jackson 2006: 168). This premise enables Bush to establish the parameters delineating the permissible proportion of the response as well as presents an endorsement of exploitation of new resources and tactics (Shafir, Brysk, and Wehrenfennig 2007: 178–79). From a strategic perspective, the US president interprets the events of 9/11 as "an act of war," by implication legitimizing the mobilization of the world's most powerful military against a poor Middle Eastern country on the basis of self-defense.[3] Furthermore, by issuing the ultimatum "Either you are with us, or you are with the terrorists," Bush makes it clear that the severity of the threat and the urgency of the situation preclude any debate, appealing to the audience for support, as opposed to a discussion on the issue (cf. Kuypers 2007: 2).

The idea of threat alone, however, cannot effectuate compliance of all members of the in-group. It is important to note that the act of compliance is motivated by two fundamental desires: avoidance of punishment and acquisition of rewards (Lewin 1935). As evidenced by Bush's ultimatum, the president applies coercion against defection, thus inculcating his authority in the minds of the people. The speaker also provides legal substantiation for the proposed course of action by invoking Article 5 of the NATO Charter: "An attack on one is an attack on all." Furthermore, by employing a series of questions throughout the speech, Bush reinforces his own quasi-divine status. The speaker

---

[2] For a similar discussion of discursive representation of the threat posed by an out-group, see van Dijk's analysis (2004) of a parliamentary debate in the British House of Commons on the topics of immigration, minorities, and the Muslim community.

[3] For additional discussion of implied inferences in political discourse, see Chilton (2004).

thus functions as an omniscient figure who is aware of the questions posed by his followers and who possesses all of the answers.[4] Interestingly, the orator's role fluctuates throughout the speech between that of an authoritarian leader giving a direct order to the enemy (realized via imperatives "release," "protect," "close," "hand over") and the role of a libertarian figure who appeals to in-group members for compliance as a personal favor, realized primarily via repeated usage of the grammatical metaphor "I ask"/ "I ask you" employed in the role of an imperative. The establishment of a personal connection between the leader and the audience is also achieved vis-à-vis the speaker's personalization of the same emotions that have been attributed to the addressees, thus presenting the president himself as one of the victims. By conveying the idea of affinity between the orator and the people, Bush successfully builds a sense of rapport with his audience (Stiff and Mongeau 2003: 120). His role as a victim becomes proof of personal involvement, thereby providing an affirmation to the listener that what is promised will in fact occur.

The success of the response yet to follow is rhetorically assured via quasi-prophetic language that foreshadows the future. This language is manifested mainly through the predominant usage of the future tense, as seen in the following extracts:

what you will do
what we will do together
this will not be an age of terror; this will be an age of liberty

In addition, by describing the perpetrators as "heirs of all the murderous ideologies of the twentieth century," Bush implicitly reminds his listeners that it was the United States that helped lay these ideologies "in history's unmarked grave of discarded lies" and, in so doing, strengthens the vision of a favorable outcome. As a discursive technique, foreshadowing allows Bush to elicit in his audience unconscious affective reactions to the context, which could in turn influence subsequent judgments. On the whole, affective priming functions to abate the potential psychological impact of the projected course of action by giving the audience the opportunity to experience the predicted event on the emotional level prior to its actual occurrence (Higdon 2009: 14–18).

The emotional dimension of the target audience is exploited to an even greater extent in the text via allusions to the various stages of the grieving process, including "grief," "anger," and "resolution." As a whole, the president's address conveys a strong sense of victimhood in the listener, encouraging blame—one of the coping mechanisms in the healing process—as an appropriate reaction to the given circumstances. Throughout the speech, Bush

---

[4] Dunmire (2007) provides a detailed analysis of how knowledge of the future is claimed in the political discourse of the Bush administration, legitimating the policy of preemptive war.

continuously revisits the sources of pain and grief, thus maintaining a mood of crisis (Gunn 2004: 14). He ultimately exploits this emotional state by advancing communal action as the most appropriate coping strategy for overcoming this trauma, most powerfully exemplified by the repeated proclamation "we will come together."

The prophetic language invoked in the text enables Bush to incorporate the divine appeal in his address, positioning himself as an intermediary between God and the people. The religious dimension is further elaborated by tapping into the instinctive association of public virtue in the Western culture with the idea of God; in other words, equating civic virtue with a responsibility to history and, by extension, a duty to God. Civil religion is formulated in the text via recognized symbols of democracy—infused with ethical significance, as they represent the ideals upheld by the in-group—including "tolerance and freedom," "progress and pluralism," "justice," "prosperity," and "legitimate governments." This emphasis on the principles endorsed by the collective effectively complements the underlying narrative depicting the in-group's glorious historical past, perilous present, and prosperous future, implicitly urging the audience to demonstrate commitment to these values through action (Menegatos 2007: 5).

ARTICULATION OF CULTURAL AND SOCIAL DISTANCE

The discourse of President Bush reflects Orientalist-driven attitudes, which subsequently shape the public's conception of the adversary. The speaker invokes the image of a fanatical, irrational enemy—the Terrorist—whose "goal is remaking the world—and imposing radical beliefs on people everywhere." From this perspective, the enemy presents "a threat to our way of life"; that is, an encroachment on America's cultural identity. The Terrorist, however, is decidedly disassociated from the Pious Muslim through discursive removal of the adversary from the collective in which he claims to hold membership, as evidenced in the following examples:

> The enemy of America is not our many Muslim friends; it is not our many Arab friends.

> The terrorists practice a fringe form of Islamic extremism

This alienation of the Other from his own in-group signals the notion that the enemy is in fact unworthy of belonging to any modern community (Stollznow 2008: 188).

The European connotation of the foreigner as barbarian has been historically applied to the portrayal of the Middle East and its people (Raines 1996; Said 1979). By presenting the out-group members as uncivilized brutes who "make no distinction among military and civilians, including women and children," Bush denigrates the adversary as a savage beast, effectively dehumanizing the Other. Thus, the Terrorist becomes a ruthless enemy opposing the archetypal hero of America. This enemy is primitive, "abandoning every value except the will to power," and deviant, employing "radical" methods. In addition, by associating the values of progress, pluralism, tolerance, and freedom with "civilization" and by aligning "civilization" with America, Bush conveys the notion that any individual who opposes these ideals and fails to support the United States in its efforts is in effect uncivilized.

Discursive criminalization of the enemy plays a vital role in the delegitimization of the opponent's actions and objectives. In his address, Bush favors the referent "terrorist"/"terrorists" (used 18 times in the speech)—a term associated with *unlawful* use of force in the US criminal justice system—which constructs criminal connotations. This allows the speaker to develop the concept of "terror as crime," as opposed to "terror as war," thus rallying the support of democratic nations. Bush also employs the term "murderers" to denote the opponent, specifically "the same murderers indicted for bombing American embassies in Tanzania and Kenya and responsible for bombing the USS Cole." By connecting the current state of affairs with past incidents of extreme and irrational violence, Bush is able to situate the events within a preexisting pattern, guiding the listener's emotional response as well as facilitating the identification of the perpetrator. Moreover, this approach allows the speaker to reintroduce an earlier state of disequilibrium, thus amplifying the existing emotional stress within the audience.

The narrative of victimhood discussed earlier also plays an important part in the discursive criminalization of the enemy. Semioticians (Derrida 1978; de Saussure 1966; Jakobson 1957; Lacan 1977) argue that meanings are not communicated exclusively through linguistic units and patterns but are also realized through the underlying binary structure of language itself, with one unit of a relational pair implying the existence of its complementary unit.[5] Accordingly, the concept of the victim foregrounded in Bush's rhetoric is naturally linked to the second constituent element of its binary set—the perpetrator. Thus, the speaker's pleas to his audience to "continue praying for the victims of terror" and "to continue to support the victims of this tragedy" also serve to implicitly evoke the agent responsible for the participants' identification as victims.

ARTICULATION OF MORAL DISTANCE

Discursive criminalization of the enemy is complemented with techniques used to vilify the adversary, thus forging a moral distance between the agent and his target. In his address, Bush explicitly classifies the opponent's actions as "evil" as well as inflates their scope by asserting that the enemy is targeting the entire global community, as opposed to selected individuals of some particular

---

[5] For a discussion of binary conceptualizations in political discourse, see Chilton (2004: 197–205).

affiliation. Moreover, in a powerful culmination, the speaker declares that "freedom and fear are at war," evoking the cosmic conflict between the forces of good and evil. Bush's narrative of evil effectively mystifies the enemy, denying him human characteristics. The in-group is in turn portrayed as a guardian angel of all that is righteous, thus transforming the heinous act of killing into an honorable enterprise aimed at eradicating sin. Dehumanization of the opponent is further reinforced through the deployment of a metaphor that likens the enemy to a weed—an uncultivated, undesired entity that seeks to crowd out others:

> the only way to defeat terrorism . . . is to stop it, eliminate it, and *destroy it where it grows.*

As a result, the enemy becomes disassociated from the emotions, impulses, and thoughts attributed to the human species. This strategy in turn serves to eliminate any guilt on the part of the audience that may be associated with the idea of endorsing a violent course of action against another human being (Stollznow 2008).

In order to strengthen his hold on the moral high ground, Bush actively delegitimizes the opponent's views and political claims. The speaker effectively undermines the enemy's claimed source of power (religion) by portraying members of the out-group as deceitful:

> We are not deceived by their *pretenses to piety.*

The opponent's duplicity and his scheming nature are further embellished with his ability to "hide" in plain sight and his secret agenda "to plot evil and destruction." These verbal processes evoke a sense of uncertainty about the enemy's subsequent actions, consequently reinforcing the image of an unpredictable supernatural entity. Further, by labeling the out-group members as "traitors to their own faith," Bush effectively disassociates the Other from any claims to righteousness.[6]

The illegitimate exploitation of religious doctrine by the enemy is also countered by a nonaggressive, respectful stance toward the ideology misappropriated by the opponent—Islam (Lazar and Lazar 2004: 238). In his address to the Muslim world, Bush pronounces: "We respect your faith. . . . Its teachings are good and peaceful"; the enemies, however, "commit evil in the name of Allah" and thus "blaspheme the name of Allah." America's rhetorical alignment with an ideology that upholds fundamental human values effectively reinforces the nation's own morality. The enemy's rhetoric is in turn construed as propaganda, intentionally skewed to pervade collective consciousness with the aim of furthering a deadly political agenda. The Other is thus reduced to a

---

[6] For a discussion of moral authority as a legitimizing strategy in political discourse, see Chilton (2004: 110–34).

"murderous ideology," which America—as it has done time and time again over the course of history—must put away.

ARTICULATION OF MECHANICAL DISTANCE

Metaphors and euphemisms are among the discursive techniques that aid Bush in establishing what Grossman (1995: 158–60) terms a "mechanical distance" between the in-group and the aggressor. This strategy mimics the modern technological means used in combat to distort soldiers' reality by reducing their visual perception of the enemy to a nonhuman target (Stollznow 2008: 188–89). The impending war is repeatedly described in the text as a "struggle," a term that carries positive associations with a physical and spiritual strife against a supernatural entity. The envisioned fate of the enemy is depicted in vague terms, with the speaker creating an associative link between the implied objective (physical liquidation of the enemy) and an accepted value (justice), thereby valorizing the act of killing:

> Whether we bring our enemies to justice, or bring justice to our enemies, justice will be done.

In another example, the metaphor "we'll meet violence with patient justice" is effectively used to ascribe a moral value to the US response strategy, suggesting that all future actions would be founded upon virtuous considerations (justice), undertaken solely for the purpose of eliminating vile acts (violence). Nominal groups such as "new measures," "means," "tools," and "instrument" sustain the ambiguity surrounding the methods that would be adopted as part of the justice enforcement process, thus allaying the sense of repugnancy associated with the various activities that would play a part in the attainment of the ultimate objective.

In anticipation of an imminent armed conflict, Bush prepares his audience for the casualties that will be likely sustained as part of the war. The idea of combat losses is introduced in the speech in a subtle manner by dissimilating future events from a known historical reference point—the Kosovo conflict. The president warns that "[the 'war on terror'] will not look like the air war above Kosovo two years ago, where no ground troops were used and not a single American was lost in combat." Yet, Bush fails to clarify strategic objectives or define parameters for measuring success, intentionally dispersing the blame among a number of different actors (al Qaeda, the Taliban, terrorists, countries harboring terrorism). As a result, the proposed response strategy lacks clearly defined boundaries, suggesting the desired final state to be the elimination of every last one of the terrorists and their supporters through military action.

Overall, the sanitizing language in Bush's rhetoric mirrors the effects of modern computerization of combat on the soldiers' perception of reality, reducing the gruesome phenomena of war to an abstraction. The president employs euphemistic language that maintains a cloak of ambiguity over his campaign strategy as well as legitimizes any future conduct that may be deemed reprehensible. Thus, the audience is presented with a "sanitized" version of reality that coheres to each listener's moral compass, while the actual scope of the response strategy remains largely obscured.

Text 2: Statement of the World Islamic Front, February 23, 1998

In 1996, Osama bin Laden, the leader of al Qaeda, asserted the claim of Western occupation of Islamic lands in a fatwa (a religious decree) that urged attacks on Western military targets in the Arabian Peninsula. Two years later, under the banner of the World Islamic Front, bin Laden, together with four other radical Islamist leaders, issued another fatwa, which sought to mobilize the Muslim community, sanctioning indiscriminate killing of all Western targets across the world. On September 11, 2001, bin Laden put his directive into action by orchestrating one of the most devastating terrorist attacks in modern history.

The 9/11 attacks were immediately condemned by a number of recognized religious authorities in Islam, including Sheikh Yusuf al-Qaradawi, who asserted that "Islam . . . considers the attack against innocent beings a grave sin" (quoted in Bukay 2008: 296).[7] Islamic scholar Safir Akhtar also disclaims bin Laden's authority in the Muslim world, arguing that "[Muslim] people think of [bin Laden] more as an adventurer than as an Islamic leader" (quoted in Burns 2002: para. 11). Nevertheless, bin Laden's rhetoric quickly gained widespread support around the world, as many Muslims endorsed al Qaeda's efforts to resist the status quo and, more important, its audaciousness to oppose the world's superpower.[8] As a result, in the aftermath of 9/11, al Qaeda—initially a small terrorist group—rapidly expanded into a vast, transnational network composed of a collection of loosely affiliated terrorist organizations, transforming Islamist struggle into a jihadist campaign transcending borders and continents—what could now be seen as a *global* insurgency (Rabasa et al. 2006: 8).

CONSTRUCTION OF IDENTITY

Bin Laden's statement, like the statement of President Bush, is marked by the predominant usage of the first-person pronoun "we." However, in contrast to the American discourse, the pronoun "we" in bin Laden's text is exclusive; that

---

[7] For a collection of statements issued by prominent Muslim figures and Islamic organizations around the world condemning the 9/11 attacks, see Kurzman (2010).

[8] For a detailed discussion of al Qaeda's influence on its intended audience, see Byman (2003).

is to say, it excludes the addressee as one of the referents, thereby disassociating the interlocutor from the decision-making process. The notion of active consent, however, plays a crucial part in the text and is achieved via a number of discursive strategies. Bin Laden's statement is an attempt to forge harmony among the many conflicting interests that exist within the diverse populace of the Arabian Peninsula, bringing about an intellectual and moral unity across the various social classes of the population and the many (at times overlapping) national, religious, ethnic, and dynastic identities (Clark 1997: 22; Gershoni and Jankowski 1997). Bin Laden signals to his audience that a collective agreement has already been reached on the issue at hand by asserting that "*all* people of the Arabian Peninsula have now acknowledged" the fact that their territories are unlawfully occupied by the US forces. It should be noted that, with communal issues, individuals tend to look to the conduct of other members of their in-group before committing to a course of action (Stiff and Mongeau 2003: 65). Bin Laden's rhetoric thus fosters assent by feeding the perception that a universal agreement among in-group members is already in effect.

Territorial dispute has been at the heart of intergroup conflict in the Middle East for centuries, and al Qaeda's rhetoric presents this issue as the central theme in the fatwa. Bin Laden foregrounds the narrative of Western occupation of the Arabian Peninsula and the consequent corruption of the territory and its people. He employs symbols of historical and religious significance that evoke the historical trauma of Islamic resistance to the European Crusades (Blanchard 2007). Such phrases as "the Islamic lands," "Muslim countries," and "the territory of Islam" forge a link between the Muslim religious universe and modern secular, geo-political concepts, as a result instilling within the minds of the target audience a sense of religious and geographical unity (Menegatos 2007).

The history of the deep-rooted conflict and victimization has formed parts of the in-group's collective cultural memory, which contributes directly to the contemporary sense of victimhood among its members. Bin Laden emphasizes the helplessness of his in-group at the hands of the perpetrator vis-à-vis such attributives as "powerless" and "oppressed." Furthermore, employing a passive voice construction, the author asserts that the present trauma was "inflicted upon" his in-group, thus placing emphasis on the involuntary nature of the affliction. Bin Laden builds upon the victimhood narrative, communicating the need for a heroic figure to deliver the innocent from the hand of the offender with his plea, "give us a protector and a helper," implicitly attributing the role of the protector to the interlocutor.

Echoing the approach observed in the US discourse, bin Laden appeals to a unifying moral force that is recognized to embody the ideals and moral values upheld by the in-group. This moral force is identified to be God in the opening sentence of the fatwa, which allows the author to employ the construct of religious duty as the foundational element of his call to arms. In the Quran, the concept of jihad—a struggle for faith—is presented as a religious duty of all Muslims. While Scripture lays greater emphasis on the inner moral struggle within the individual, as opposed to an armed conflict, through selective reporting bin Laden effectively manipulates verses of the Quran to fit his own definition of jihad (Bonner 2006; Gafoor and Noorani 2002; Marranci 2006). The following extract from the text demonstrates how the writers of the fatwa misrepresent a Quranic verse in order to mobilize the audience:

> When the forbidden months are over, wherever you find the polytheists, kill them, seize them, besiege them, ambush them.

The fatwa in fact omits a condition that modifies this call to arms in the original text: "but if they turn [to God], maintain the prayer, and pay the prescribed alms, let them go on their way, for God is most forgiving and merciful" (Lawrence 2005: 59). By reiterating the divine directive throughout the text and selectively withholding any information that could hinder the attainment of the established goal—mobilization of the collective—bin Laden successfully develops the theme of jihad as "an individual duty," thereby creating a legitimating factor and a moral obligation for the audience to comply with the order "to kill the Americans and their allies."

Evocation of a Common Mental State

In unison with the US rhetoric, al Qaeda's statement describes the status quo as unprecedented and urgent, thus establishing an atmosphere of crisis. Bin Laden places emphasis on the extraordinary nature of the circumstances, which functions as a mitigating factor that justifies the gravity of al Qaeda's methods. By presenting the attacks carried out against Muslims around the world as interconnected, systematic, and alarming (especially in terms of their toll), bin Laden effectively gains moral high ground (Shafir, Brysk, and Wehrenfennig 2007: 186). Unlike the relatively novel nature of the threat from the US perspective, in al Qaeda's case, foreign presence in the Middle East has been a source of anxiety for the indigenous populations for many decades. Bin Laden asserts that this historical threat has never actually disappeared, claiming that "the Americans are trying to repeat [their] horrific massacres," as a result fomenting a sense of insecurity and moral panic among audience members. Akin to the US strategy, this perception of danger allows bin Laden to justify the mobilization of his in-group on the grounds of self-defense. To inflate the scope of the threat even further, the author stresses its apocalyptic proportions. More specifically, he emphasizes the enemy's plans "to annihilate what is left of this people," "to destroy Iraq," and "fragment all the states in the region," all of which represent an existential threat to the in-group. The fatwa also evokes a strong affective response in the reader by exploiting past traumas via allusions to historical events, such as the Israeli-Palestinian conflict, thus communicating fear in visualizable terms (cf. Lazar and Lazar 2004: 232).

In hindsight, Iraq—one of the prominent topics in bin Laden's fatwa—proved to be a rather powerful argument in the anti-American discourse, as Iraq became a focal point of the US rhetoric following the 9/11 attacks, culminating in the launch of Operation Iraqi Freedom in 2003.[9] The paradox of Iraq's "liberation" strategy of "shock and awe," which failed to adhere to the principle of proportionality or show reverence for noncombatants, emphasized the incongruity of the US approach in a war for the hearts and minds of the local population. The most damning evidence of the disproportionality of the coalition's strategy in the Iraq War comes from a scientific study conducted in 2006, which estimates that the US-led military campaign has contributed the excess death toll of 655,000 Iraqis, which is equivalent to approximately 2.5 percent of Iraq's population (Burnham et al. 2006: 6). Thus, al Qaeda's claims that the United States was targeting Iraq ultimately proved to be an accurate assessment of the enemy's future course of action. The eventual invasion of Iraq five years later subsequently contributed to the erosion of US credibility and, by confirming bin Laden's warnings, indirectly served to legitimize al Qaeda's discourse.

The predominance of direct speech in the fatwa, referencing religious texts, enables the author to effectively pass on the directive by positioning himself in the role of a messenger. This role is reinforced by bin Laden's appeals to what is recognized as the highest authority among the in-group members. In addition, intertextuality supplies support for the views expressed in the text by demonstrating that a reputable authority figure (God) maintains the same beliefs. As a result, the author elicits a degree of confidence in the validity of his ideas, stemming from the perceived trustworthiness of the source (Stiff and Mongeau 2003: 111). In fact, all direct orders that are lexicalized via imperatives ("kill," "seize," "besiege," "ambush") are produced in the embedded texts. This allows the responsibility of issuing the order to be placed on the sanctioning agent, thus absolving the writer of liability. Consequently, bin Laden presents God as the agent of the deeds, positioning himself, the writer, as a middleman who neither planned nor executed violent acts (Leudar, Marsland, and Nekvapil 2004: 259). In other words, God emerges in the discourse as a virtual actor directly responsible for the acts that have been committed against the enemy. The moral power attributed to the idea of God works to disassociate from sin any acts that may appear immoral, thereby painting violent response as a justifiable—even virtuous—course of action.

---

[9] For a detailed discussion of how Bush incorporated the issue of Iraq into the "war on terror" discourse, see John, Domke, Coe, and Graham (2007).

In order to deter the audience from inaction, bin Laden formulates a retribution strategy that incorporates both rewards and sanctions. Positive reinforcement is used in the text to urge "everyone who believes in God and wants reward" to comply with the ruling, thus placing an emphasis on the idea that participation in jihad qualifies one for rewards. The author also warns his reader that in the event of inaction, "God will punish you severely," thus drawing attention to the punitive measures associated with noncompliance. This information effectively influences the appraisal process used by the audience members to assess the potential costs and benefits of the different courses of action at their disposal in order to determine the response that would yield the best results at a minimal cost.

Another discursive technique prominent in the text involves exploitation of the collective psyche of the Muslim community. In his statement, bin Laden invokes grievances and frustrations that have been a part of the collective memory for centuries through such lexical choices as "Crusader," "idolators," and "polytheists," all of which are recurrent themes in Islamic history (Ranstorp 1998: 324–25). Intertextual references also capitalize on the reader's religious beliefs by drawing an associative link between the reader's faith and potential outcomes of the proposed course of action, as evidenced by the affirmation "if you are true believers you will have the upper hand." Unlike Bush, bin Laden refrains from assuring his personal involvement in the advocated cause. However, intertextual references are effectively used in the discourse to demonstrate the commitment of the higher authority to address the situation through decisive action. Specifically, the embedded quotation of Prophet Muhammad—"I have been sent with a sword in my hands so that only God may be worshipped"—represents a personal pledge made by a recognized authority figure to take action, implicitly urging the devoted disciples to follow his lead.

ARTICULATION OF CULTURAL AND SOCIAL DISTANCE

From a sociocultural standpoint, Western rhetoric is once again mirrored in al Qaeda's text, as bin Laden develops the civilizational conflict narrative as the central theme in his discourse. As was already discussed, bin Laden forges a divide between "Us" and "Them" by framing his argument in historic-religious terms via repeated references to the Crusades, thereby weaving into his discourse a symbol of historical and religious significance that has been effectively used throughout history to justify actions of both Islamic extremists and Arab nationalists (Riley-Smith 2004). The author also expresses the primitiveness of the adversary's behavior by comparing the Western nations' aggression against Muslims to the uncultivated, almost feral, act of "fighting over a bowl of food." Bin Laden further denigrates the enemy's actions by portraying the opponent as ruthless through such attributes as "brutal" and "vicious." The author completes the image of the aberrant Other with the term "idolator," which conveys the idea that the enemy is driven by a depraved value system that has no place in the in-group's universe.

In congruence with the rhetoric of President Bush, bin Laden also relies on criminalization as one of the main discursive strategies in his text. This is achieved via an overtly criminal lexicon used to denote the enemy's actions, including "murder of Muslims," "horrific massacres," and "excessive aggression." The author also emphasizes the illegality of America's presence in the Arab territory, further criminalizing the adversary's behavior:

> America has occupied . . . the Arabian peninsula, plundering its wealth, dictating to its leaders, humiliating its people, terrorizing its neighbours.

As earlier analysis has shown, bin Laden (like President Bush) effectively ascribes to his in-group the role of a victim, which implicitly evokes the second constituent of the binary set *victim–perpetrator*. Thus, by identifying the out-group as the "oppressors," the author is able to further reinforce the sense of victimhood among the target audience members.

ARTICULATION OF MORAL DISTANCE

The "Us" versus "Them" dichotomy is constructed in bin Laden's statement primarily in religious terms. The fatwa is addressed to "all Muslims," who are in turn juxtaposed with the "Crusader hordes." Bin Laden vilifies the enemy by explicating the cataclysmic nature of his objectives, including "[the Americans'] eagerness to destroy Iraq . . . and their efforts to fragment all the states in the region." Theological formulations, such as "the soldiers of Satan" and "devil's supporters," invoke the supernatural forces of God and the Devil, thus constructing an evil, metaphysical enemy. Further reinforcing the divide between the in-group and the out-group, bin Laden asserts that his own collective has been chosen by God to carry out the higher mission for the sake of humanity. More specifically, al Qaeda's discourse suggests that the in-group has been selected as the "protector" of the "oppressed men, women, and children." The deployment of an insect metaphor comparing the enemy to "locusts" further degrades and dehumanizes the adversary, disassociating him from the category *human*.

Similar to the strategy observed in Bush's discourse, al Qaeda's fatwa brings the reader's attention to the opponent's duplicity. Bin Laden exposes the enemy's lies and corruption by claiming that the "wars [on the Arabian Peninsula] are being waged by the Americans for religious and economic purposes." The author thereby suggests that America's rhetoric—as that produced by pagans driven by economic greed and thirst for power—is not to be taken seriously. Bin Laden goes even further to deny legitimacy to the opponent by unveiling his cunning nature via the assertion that this enemy is "diverting attention from its occupation of Jerusalem." Thus, the case of Palestine becomes an affirmation of the enemy's true objectives in the Middle East.

ARTICULATION OF MECHANICAL DISTANCE

In a striking departure from the discursive construction of Western "call to arms" rhetoric, bin Laden refrains from using sanitizing language to forge a mechanical distance between the target audience and the enemy. The reality of violence on the Arabian Peninsula has plagued its population for generations, which could account for the brusqueness in the author's delivery style, on grounds that the routinization of violence resulted in people's desensitization to its sights (Gupta 2001: 137). Another explanation holds bin Laden's discursive crudeness as part of his allure: fundamentally, his rhetoric is based on the concepts of revenge as a justified punishment for unjustified crime, and, as such, it is overtly militant and violent by design. The appeal of bin Laden's language lies in its simplicity, expressiveness, and apparent sincerity, as these stylistic elements reinforce the affective power of the themes of victimhood, revenge, brutality, and the Manichean order. His narrative of self-pity, rage, and fear is effectively supplemented with blunt directives from the Quran as well as prominence of such themes as the Palestinian crisis, the Iraqi people, and Muslim persecution through history, which hold special significance in the emotional universe of the target audience, allowing the author to exploit the appeal of revenge as the most favorable response in the given circumstances (O'Shaughnessy 2004: 195–99).

Discussion and Conclusions

The analysis presented here demonstrates that the "war on terror" discourses produced by George W. Bush and Osama bin Laden contain corresponding lexico-grammatical features that coalesce into an overarching strategic framework guiding the audience's consumption of the rhetoric. This framework is governed by two simultaneous processes conducive to the mobilization of the target audience: (1) the unification of the members of the in-group through reinforcement of their similarities; and (2) the alienation of the members of the out-group through articulation and amplification of the differences—be those real or imagined—between the two groups. First, Bush and bin Laden reaffirm the identity of their respective in-groups via the deployment of recognizable symbols of historical or religious significance. In his speech, the US president relies on the unifying construct of nationhood, directing his persuasive rhetoric at the American citizens, who are united rhetorically through the perception of mutual grief and collective purpose. Bin Laden, on the other hand, employs the Quran as the source of his power, aspiring to mobilize his audience on the basis of their religion. Both leaders combine the idea of political well-being with spiritual vision, advocating social action as the process via which this vision can be realized. While the rhetoric of al Qaeda presents God as an agent, a driving force to action, Western discourse maintains God as a symbolic figure, likely due to the shift of the authority previously associated with the divine to the state and the modern individual (Graham, Keenan, and Dowd 2004; Meyer and Jepperson 2000).

Second, the discourses of the "war on terror" address the perceived differences between the in-group and the out-group. Both opponents depict their respective enemies as uncultivated, drawing on the long-standing traditions of Orientalism and Occidentalism, which play a crucial part in the interlocutor's interpretation of the adversary's attitudes and actions. These traditions have a debilitating effect on the audience's understanding of their enemy, as they exploit and encourage cultural assumptions. On the whole, both Bush and bin Laden construct an image of a Manichean struggle, where forces of Order confront forces of Chaos. Both leaders thus develop a dichotomous conception of the universe, which does not recognize neutrality or ambivalence. This dualist worldview creates an enemy so morally deviant that he appears alien to humankind—outside the human beings' sphere of existence—thereby justifying the target's excision without the burden of guilt.

From a macro perspective, it is evident that the statements of the United States and al Qaeda leadership mirror one another, employing identical discursive strategies to construct two contrasting versions of reality. In both exhortations, the speaker is presented as the righteous defender of sacred human values, seeking to unite an aggrieved collective against their perceived perpetrators. For his part, Bush frames his rhetoric in ethico-political terms as a campaign led by the civilized world against fanatical terrorists and the "rogue states" that support them. Bin Laden, on the other hand, construes the conflict as a holy war of the faithful against the nonbelievers. In their discursive battle, both sides hold the enemy accountable for the conflict, claiming their own rationality and righteousness by presenting their actions as unavoidable and honorable while delegitimizing the claims contended by the adversary.

As this study has demonstrated, crisis rhetoric is an integral part of the "call to arms" discourse, functioning as a unifying force that delineates the boundaries that define the in-group and consequently outcast the Other. Yet, from a political standpoint, the rhetoric of Bush and bin Laden is a case of mere counter-messaging rather than a meaningful dialogue. The "war on terror" discourse fails to address the underlying grievances motivating the adversary's behavior, thus functioning as nothing more than a conditioning tool meant to inspire individuals to act en masse without any objective understanding of the issue at hand. Certainly, dropping bombs on an abstract concept is easy. The real challenge, however, lies in accepting something held as foreign and incomprehensible, in engaging in a meaningful debate, and in recognizing the shared humanity of the opponent. It is, therefore, only by elucidating and addressing through rhetoric the collective cognitive conditions that breed animosity and perpetuate conflicts—rather than simply liquidating all those that stand against "Us"—that we will be able to develop a discourse that effectively negates aggressive impulses and alleviates negative attitudes among the intended recipients, cultivating intergroup awareness and positive interrelations.

References

Bin Laden, Osamah, Ayman al-Zawahiri, Rif'ai Ahmad Taha, Mir Hamzah, and Fazlur Rahman. 2005. "The World Islamic Front: February 23, 1998." In *Messages to the World*, James Howarth (trans.), Bruce Lawrence (ed.), 58–62. London: Verso.

Blanchard, Christopher M. 2007. *Al Qaeda: Statements and Evolving Ideology*. Washington, DC: Congressional Research Service. www.fas.org/sgp/crs/terror/.

Bonner, Michael D. 2006. *Jihad in Islamic History: Doctrines and Practice*. Princeton: Princeton University Press.

Brewer, Marilynn B. 2001. "Ingroup Identification and Intergroup Conflict: When Does Ingroup Love Become Outgroup Hate?" In *Social Identity, Intergroup Conflict, and Conflict Reduction*, Richard D. Ashmore, Lee J. Jussim, and David Wilder (eds.), 17–41. Oxford: Oxford University Press.

Bukay, David. 2008. *From Muhammad to Bin Laden: Religious and Ideological Sources of the Homicide Bombers Phenomenon*. New Brunswick, NJ: Transaction Publishers.

Burnham, Gilbert, Riyadh Lafta, Shannon Doocy, and Les Roberts. 2006. "Mortality after the 2003 Invasion in Iraq: A Cross-sectional Cluster Sample Survey." *Lancet* 368(9545): 1421–28. Accessed December 4, 2011. doi:10.1016/S0140-6736(06)69491-9.

Burns, John F. 2002. "A Nation Challenged: A Fighter's Tale; Bin Laden Stirs Struggle on Meaning of Jihad." *New York Times*, January 27. Accessed December 4, 2011. www.nytimes.com.

Bush, George W. "National Cathedral Address." Speech presented at the National Cathedral, Washington, DC, September 20, 2001.

Byman, Daniel L. 2003. "Al-Qaeda as an Adversary: Do We Understand Our Enemy?" *World Politics* 56:139–63.

Cerulo, Karen A. 1995. *Identity Designs: The Sights and Sounds of a Nation*. New Brunswick, NJ: Rutgers University Press.

Chilton, Paul. 2004. *Analysing Political Discourse: Theory and Practice*. New York: Routledge.

Chilton, Paul and Christina Schäffner. 2002. "Introduction: Themes and Principles in the Analysis of Political Discourse." In *Politics as Text and Talk: Themes and Principles in the Analysis of Political Discourse*, Paul Chilton and Christina Schäffner (eds.), 1–41. Philadelphia: John Benjamins.

Clark, Romy and Roz Ivanič. 1997. *The Politics of Writing*. London: Routledge.

De Saussure, Ferdinand. 1966. *Course in General Linguistics*. Wade Baskin (trans.). New York: McGraw-Hill.

Der Derian, James. 2009. *Virtuous War: Mapping the Military-Industrial-Media-Entertainment Network*. London: Taylor & Francis.

Derrida, Jacques. 1978. *Writing and Difference*. Alan Bass (trans.). London: Routledge and Kegan Paul.

Doran, Michael S. 2003. "Palestine, Iraq, and American Strategy." *Foreign Affairs* 82(1): 19–33.

Dunmire, Patricia L. 2007. "'Emerging Threats' and 'Coming Dangers': Claiming the Future for Preventive War." In *Discourse, War and Terrorism*, Adam Hodges and Chad Nilep (eds.), 19–43. Philadelphia: John Benjamins.

Dunmire, Patricia L. 2009. "'9/11 Changed Everything': An Intertextual Analysis of the Bush Doctrine." *Discourse & Society* 20:195–222.

Ellemers, Naomi, Russel Spears, and Bertjan Doosje. 2002. "Self and Social Identity." *Annual Review of Psychology* 53:161–86.

Fairclough, Norman. 2005. "Critical Discourse Analysis in Transdisciplinary Research." In *A New Agenda in (Critical) Discourse Analysis*, Ruth Wodak and Paul Chilton (eds.), 53–100. Philadelphia: John Benjamins.

Ferrari, Federica. 2007. "Metaphor at Work in the Analysis of Political Discourse: Investigating a 'Preventive War' Persuasion Strategy." *Discourse & Society* 18:603–25.

Gafoor, Abdul and Abdul M. Noorani. 2002. *Islam & Jihad: Prejudice versus Reality*. New York: Palgrave.

Gershoni, Israel and James Jankowski. 1997. "Introduction." In *Rethinking Nationalism in the Arab Middle East*, James Jankowski and Israel Gershoni (eds.), ix–xxvi. New York: Columbia University Press.

Graham, Phil, Thomas Keenan, and Anne-Maree Dowd. 2004. "A Call to Arms at the End of History: A Discourse—Historical Analysis of George W. Bush's Declaration of War on Terror." *Discourse & Society* 15:199–221.

Grossman, Dave. 1995. *On Killing: The Psychological Cost of Learning to Kill in War and Society*. Boston: Little, Brown.

Gunn, Joshua. 2004. "The Rhetoric of Exorcism: George W. Bush and the Return of Political Demonology." *Western Journal of Communication* 68:1–23.

Gupta, Dipak K. 2001. *Path to Collective Madness: A Study in Social Order and Political Pathology*. Westport, CT: Praeger.

Higdon, Michael J. 2009. "Something Judicious This Way Comes . . . The Use of Foreshadowing as a Persuasive Device in Judicial Narrative." Research Paper No. 74, University of Tennessee. Accessed December 4, 2011. http://ssrn.com/abstract=1454887.

Jackson, Richard. 2005. *Writing the War on Terrorism: Language, Politics and Counterterrorism*. New York: Manchester University Press.

Jackson, Richard. 2006. "Genealogy, Ideology, and Counter-terrorism: Writing Wars on Terrorism from Ronald Reagan to George W. Bush Jr." *Studies in Language & Capitalism* 1:163–93.

Jakobson, Roman. 1957. "Shifters, Verbal Categories, and the Russian Verb." In *Selected Writings*, Stephen Rudy (ed.), 130–47, vol. 3. The Hague: Mouton.

John, Sue L., David S. Domke, Kevin Coe, and Erica S. Graham. 2007. "Going Public, Crisis after Crisis: The Bush Administration and the Press from September 11 to Saddam." *Rhetoric & Public Affairs* 10:195–220.

Kurzman, Charles. 2010. "Islamic Statements against Terrorism." University of North Carolina at Chapel Hill. www.unc.edu/~kurzman/terror.htm.

Kuypers, Jim A. 2007. "From Chaos, Community: The Crisis Leadership of Virginia Tech President Charles W. Steger." *American Communication Journal* 9(1): 1–37.

Lacan, Jacques. 1977. *Écrits: A Selection*, Alan Sheridan (trans.). London: Tavistock/Routledge.

Lawrence, Bruce (ed.). 2005. *Messages to the World*. London: Verso.

Lazar, Annita and Michelle M. Lazar. 2004. "The Discourse of the New World Order: 'Out-casting' the Double Face of Threat." *Discourse & Society* 15: 223–42.

Lazar, Annita and Michelle M. Lazar. 2007. "Enforcing Justice, Justifying Force: America's Justification of Violence in the New World Order." In *Discourse, War and Terrorism*, Adam Hodges and Chad Nilep (eds.), 45–66. Philadelphia: John Benjamins.

Leudar, Ivan, Victoria Marsland, and Jiří Nekvapil. 2004. "On Membership Categorization: 'Us', 'Them' and 'Doing Violence' in Political Discourse." *Discourse & Society* 15: 243–66.

Lewin, Kurt. 1935. *A Dynamic Theory of Personality: Selected Papers*, Donald K. Adams and Karl E. Zener (trans.). New York: McGraw-Hill.

Lorenz, Konrad. 1966. *On Aggression*. New York: Bantam Books.

Marranci, Gabriele. 2006. *Jihad beyond Islam*. Oxford: Berg.

Menegatos, Lisa. 2007. "Using Religious Discourse to Construct Reality: How George W. Bush and Osama bin Laden United and Divided Nations." Paper presented at the 93rd Annual Convention of the National Communication Association, Chicago, IL, November. www.allacademic.com/meta/p193434_index.html.

Meyer, John W. and Ronald L. Jepperson. 2000. "The 'Actors' of Modern Society: The Cultural Construction of Social Agency." *Sociological Theory* 18: 100–120.

O'Shaughnessy, Nicholas J. 2004. *Politics and Propaganda: Weapons of Mass Seduction*. Ann Arbor: Manchester University Press.

Pugsley, Peter C. 2006. "Constructing the Hero: Nationalistic News Narratives in Contemporary China." *Westminster Papers in Communication and Culture* 3(1): 78–93.

Rabasa, Angel, Peter Chalk, Kim Cragin, Sara A. Daly, Heather S. Gregg, Theodore W. Karasik, Kevin A. O'Brien, and William Rosenau. 2006. *Beyond al-Qaeda. Part 1. The Global Jihadist Movement*. Santa Monica, CA: Rand.

Raines, John C. 1996. "The Politics of Religious Correctness: Islam and the West." *Crosscurrents* 46(1): 39–49.

Ranstorp, Magnus. 1998. "Interpreting the Broader Context and Meaning of bin-Laden's 'Fatwa.'" *Studies in Conflict & Terrorism* 21: 321–30.

Riley-Smith, Jonathan. 2004. "Jihad Crusaders: What an Osama bin Laden Means by 'Crusade.'" *National Review Online*, January 5. Accessed December 4, 2011. www.nationalreview.com.

Rogers, Ronald W. 1975. "A Protection Motivation Theory of Fear Appeals and Attitude Change." *Journal of Psychology* 91: 93–114.

Said, Edward. 1979. *Orientalism*. New York: Random House of Canada.

Shafir, Gershon, Alison Brysk, and Daniel Wehrenfennig. 2007. "Human Rights in Hard Times." In *National Insecurity and Human Rights: Democracies Debate Counterterrorism*, Alison Brysk and Gershon Shafir (eds.), 177–87. Berkeley: University of California Press.

Silberstein, Sandra. 2002. *War of Words: Language, Politics and 9/11*. New York: Routledge.

Stiff, James B. and Paul A. Mongeau. 2003. *Persuasive Communication*, 2nd ed. New York: Guilford Press.

Stollznow, Karen. 2008. "Dehumanisation in Language and Thought." *Journal of Language and Politics* 7: 177–200.

Tetlock, Philip E. 1992. "The Impact of Accountability on Judgment and Choice: Toward a Social Contingency Model. In *Advances in Experimental Social Psychology*, Mark P. Zanna (ed.), 331–76, vol. 25. New York: Academic Press.

Van Dijk, Teun A. 1993. "Principles of Critical Discourse Analysis." *Discourse & Society* 4: 249–83.

Van Dijk, Teun A. 2002. "Political Discourse and Political Cognition." In *Politics as Text and Talk: Analytical Approaches to Political Discourse*, Paul A. Chilton and Christina Schäffner (eds.), 204–36. Amsterdam: Benjamins.

Van Leeuwen, Theo. 1993. "Genre and Field in Critical Discourse Analysis: A Synopsis." *Discourse & Society* 4: 193–223.

White, Eugene E. 1992. *The Context of Human Discourse: A Configurational Criticism of Rhetoric*. Columbia: University of South Carolina Press.

Zimbardo, Philip G. 1969. "The Human Choice: Individuation, Reason, and Order versus Deindividuation, Impulse, and Chaos." *Nebraska Symposium on Motivation* 17: 237–307.

5

World of the Impolitic

A CRITICAL STUDY OF THE BRITISH WMD DOSSIER

Aditi Bhatia

Introduction

While much work has been conducted on the definitional construct of terrorism (Collins 2002; Bhatia 2007a, 2007b, 2008, 2009), its data drawn often from political speeches and press conferences, relatively fewer studies have explored the more macro consequences of political contention on a broader international platform, namely, war, of which terrorism is an integral element. One particular discourse that deserves further investigation is the British government's Weapons of Mass Destruction Dossier (WMDD) (2002). The dossier put forward by the British Intelligence Agency and endorsed by the country's government was intended as evidence in the case for war presented to the United Nations. Deviating at the time from George W. Bush's relatively more emotionalized stance on the need for an Iraqi invasion, the WMDD attempted to put forth a more studied, strategic, and rational justification for war. Analysis of the WMDD in this chapter reveals that war is conceptualized as a necessary step toward the creation of a possible world of peace. In line with what Ferguson (2008) refers to as the "right thing to do" (38), the discourse of the WMDD carves out a need for war, drawing on an urgency to rectify the threat posed by Iraq, in order to persuade audiences that war is the rational step toward the creation of peace. In this regard, peace might be understood as a desired state of being, a possible world that encompasses stability and justice, embracing a new world order, modeled by civilized nations who recognize the removal of "others" that threaten this potential state, as a means to achieving what boils down to be essentially a type of *political peace*.

There have been various studies in different fields conducted on the WMD Dossier (cf. Bluth 2004; Hartnett and Stengrim 2004; Aldrich 2005; Humphreys 2005), most of them, however, focusing on specific sections or aspects of the dossier (i.e., the infamous "45-minutes" claim or the prime minister's Foreword) and others analyzing the dossier in the context of various legal enquiries (i.e., Hutton Inquiry 2003). This chapter however, will attempt a more comprehensive look at the dossier, in order to identify as far as possible the rhetorical strategies employed in order to objectify what have turned out to be subjective perceptions and exaggerated assumptions to convince its audience of the factuality and truthfulness of its claims, and ultimately justify the case for war.

The analysis of data was conducted by employing a combination of elements borrowed from Critical Discourse Analysis (CDA) (Fairclough 1989) and Layder's (1993) historical analysis. These approaches were utilized since the WMD Dossier is a complex and intricately compiled piece of discourse full of sociopolitical implications, and as such it requires, in order to obtain depth and accuracy, analysis of text within context (Fairclough 1989). Like all discourses, the WMD Dossier is an intricate mesh of ideologies given meaning by the socio-cultural and political context within which it is embedded. The interpretation of any discourse, the way we make sense of it, interact with it, what motivates us to construct it in a particular way (cf. Fairclough 1989), is based on our subjective conceptualization of the world, thereby constructing this ideological reality within which we structure our experiences. It is of utmost importance therefore to recognize that historicity is a crucial part of discourse, which comes to mean various things to various people over various time periods. Therefore, borrowing inspiration from Layder (1993), social context, both the broader sociopolitical and the more immediate socio-institutional frames of context, and the historical context, which explores the influence of sociopolitical and cultural ideologies on discursive practices, was taken into consideration to provide a better view of how and why discursive manipulations take place.

Furthermore, political discourses engender many delineating categories and stereotypes resulting in the prioritization of one version of reality over another. More specifically, these categories are a result of a more powerful social group outcasting a less powerful minority group. Analysis of illusive membership categories can indicate to a certain degree the segregation such discourse engenders and the impact of it on sociopolitical relations, and particularly in the creation of "possible worlds" (Fairclough 2003), in addition to the relationship between different social groups, creators of discourses and their target audience. Here Fairclough employs the term "possible worlds" to explicate how discourses are "projective, imaginaries, representing possible worlds which are different from the actual world, and tied in to projects to change the world in particular directions" (124). Following this line of thinking, the WMDD attempts through its discourse to put forward a representation of a "possible world" (a state of threat-free peace) that may exist should a certain course of action (a necessary war) be followed, influencing other people's perceptions, and projecting "to change the world in particular directions," namely, the author's reconceptualizations of reality.

CDA (Fairclough 1989) proves to be a powerful tool for diffusing, to whatever extent possible, the complexity of power relations within relevant sociopolitical and institutional structures. CDA can help make relatively more comprehensible the complex mesh of power relations, which appear even more overwhelming when we begin to decipher the ideological intentions behind the construction of discourses such as those of power, war, and terrorism. It is thus essential to consider these relationships among text, context, and sociocultural practice, which produce ideological and power-laden discourses. CDA is about the discovering of social and linguistic reality, going into multifaceted discourses such as political discourses to explore the subjective conceptualizations of reality that they present, which are often prone to dynamic changes, engendering many linguistic and semiotic actions. The precedence of certain versions of reality, namely, those of powerful social groups, is implicative of the power struggles within society between social and political groups. In order to take a closer look at these conflicts it is important to take into account the different perspectives people have on the various reconceptualizations of any particular construct. A secondary set of data consisting of news, views, and reports from a variety of media sources in this sense provides alternate versions of realities, in contrast to the ones being studied within the primary data, which is the WMDD.

Weapons of Mass Destruction Dossier: The Assessment of the British Government

The WMDD published on September 24, 2002, by the British government is a fifty-page document that details Iraq's history of use, planning, and possession of WMDs, in addition to its breach of United Nations (UN) resolutions, and current plans to resume its prohibited WMD program. The dossier, as claimed on the front page, was the "Assessment of the British Government," making it possible to assume that the dossier was the result of the Blair government's conceptualization of reality since it was endorsed by them. The dossier is structured in three parts: the first part gives detailed information about the role of the Joint Intelligence Committee in the reviewing and gathering of data regarding Saddam Hussein's weapons activity; the second part reviews a history of Iraq's WMD programs between 1971 and 1998, its current position, and a history of United Nations' weapons inspections in Iraq; and the last part relays an account of Iraqi life under the rule of Saddam Hussein. The dossier could be considered an important governmental document since it lays ground for future actions, attempting to justify any future policy decisions. The dossier seems to be compiled by the Joint Intelligence Committee but the actual scripting of the dossier could have been by a team of skilled diplomats, speechwriters, and forensic experts. Although the dossier was endorsed by Tony Blair, the former British prime minister, there was also an element of detachment, as Blair claimed in a statement to Parliament,

> The dossier is based on the work of the British Joint Intelligence Committee. . . . Normally its work is secret. Unusually, because it is important we explain our concerns over Saddam to the British people, we have decided

to disclose these assessments. I am aware, of course, that people are going to have to take elements of this on the good faith of our intelligence services. But this is what they are telling me the British Prime Minister and my senior colleagues. The intelligence picture they paint is . . . extensive, detailed and authoritative. (Blair 2002, September 24)

The dossier takes a rather authoritative tone and employs in parts specialist language in order to exert its knowledge and authority over laymen. The WMDD, although it may not originally have been intended for the general public, was released to them; however, due to strong militaristic overtones, the language of the document remained relatively inaccessible to laymen.

Analysis of the WMDD

The proceeding sections focus on a closer, textual analysis of the WMDD, which aims to lay down grounds for an invasion of Iraq; as such, the underlying theme that runs through the document is that of war, which is reflected in the following rhetorical strategies: *inevitability of threat* aims at justifying the need for military invasion by reinforcing the probability of a WMD strike by Iraq through quantification; *historicity* makes a connection between past and future experiences emphasizing the length of the struggle against Iraq's WMD program; *attack versus self-defense* also serves to reiterate the inevitability of attack, this time through examples of Saddam's past behavior and the "type" of person he is and the regime he runs; and *appeal to "lawful" authority* serves to legitimize the West's show of authority and passing of judgment through the use of legal terminology. This discursive construction of the dossier can be viewed as an effort on the part of its authors to persuade audiences of the need for war through the objectification of the threat posed by Iraq. Based on Saddam Hussein's past actions, justifications for future actions are derived. The objectification of a certain conceptualization of reality that produces various sociopolitical agendas, working toward the creation of new and "possible worlds" (Fairclough 2003), imbricate in the text, exercising subliminal effects, seemingly naturalizing into social consciousness in order to gain collective consent. The attempt to create new, alternative worlds in order to create a demand for a desired state of being (peace) defines an abstract construct like war in terms of a rational step in the quest for a better world.

INEVITABILITY OF THREAT

The suggestion of military action against Iraq seemed a viable option only if Iraq was perceived as an immediate threat to international security. As part of the strategy of justification (Wodak et al. 1999) the repetition of expressions such as "current and serious threat," "increasingly alarmed by the evidence from inside Iraq," and "threat is serious and current" in the foreword by Blair presupposed the immediacy of the threat being faced. More effectively, the WMDD made use of figures in the form of temporality and quantities in order to illustrate the inevitably of an attack.

(Extract 1) And the document discloses that his military planning allows for *some of the WMD* to be ready *within 45 minutes* of an order to use them. (Weapons of Mass Destruction Dossier 2002: 4)

(Extract 2) *Some of these weapons* are *deployable* within 45 minutes of an order to use them. . . . (Weapons of Mass Destruction Dossier 2002: 5)

(Extract 3) . . . forces are able to use *chemical and biological weapons*. . . . The Iraqi military are able to *deploy these weapons* within 45 minutes of a decision to do so. . . . (Weapons of Mass Destruction Dossier 2002: 17)

(Extract 4) Intelligence indicates that the Iraqi military are able to *deploy chemical or biological weapons* within 45 minutes of an order to do so. (Weapons of Mass Destruction Dossier 2002: 19)

The most obvious feature of these extracts is their mechanical repetition, which dispels any illusions about the contemporariness of the dossier and instead reinforces what is possible to interpret as the militaristic, inflexible, and planned nature of the document. Repetition is seen as an important linguistic trope in the WMDD, often in the repeated use of favored collocations or rhetorical strategies, which serve sometimes to reinforce arguments without making them redundant and are employed at other times for the purpose of evasion. The precision of the time given ("45 minutes") not only made the danger posed immediate but the timescale more relatable to the ordinary layman. It is possible to say that "45 minutes" as a figure arouses more fear than perhaps one year or ten years. However, the use of "some" puts into use the strategy of vagueness (cf. Ricento 2003); raising questions such as "What weapons?," "How many are deployable within 45 minutes?" "Deployable to where within 45 minutes?" This relative depersonalization and passivization with regard to the agents who would "deploy" the weapons while keeping assertions vague also helped retain their warning of inevitability. Vagueness enables ideologically fueled, and often contested, representations of reality to be discoursed in a more persuasive manner, making up for a lack of factual evidence.

The use of the figure '45' has been criticised much by the media that claims:

Blair took Britain to war last year—against the majority of public opinion—on the basis of a now notorious dossier, released in September 2002, claiming Iraq was stockpiling weapons of mass destruction and that Saddam could have some weapons ready for use in 45 minutes. No such banned weapons have been found in Iraq and the 45-minute claim has been discredited. (*China Daily* 2004, July 8)

Former British ministry of defense expert, Brian Jones, indicated that the extracts quoted claiming that weapons were deployable within forty-five minutes should have instead been phrased thus:

A source has claimed some weapons may be deployable within 45 minutes of an order to use them, but the exact nature of the weapons, the agents involved and the context of their use is not clear . . . back in September 2002, had the executive summary been written in the way I suggest, it would have been much more difficult for the prime minister's foreword to make the positive assertions it did about Hussein's chemical and biological warfare capabilities and the threat they represented to Britain. (Jones 2004, July 13)

The rephrasal above converts the original forty-five minute claim, which made Iraq an almost imminent threat, into more a possibility than actuality. Similarly, BBC reporter Andrew Gilligan reiterated this flaw at his hearing during the Hutton Inquiry, saying that there were

inconsistencies in this document; and in all cases it was the harder—the firmer statement, that they actually had weapons, rather than just the ability to produce weapons or research and development facilities, actual weapons, that is the statement, that they had actual weapons deployable or ready within 45 minutes. Those are the statements that make it into the executive summary, into the Prime Minister's foreword. . . . On the 45 minutes specifically, I also saw that the language changed a bit. In the body of the dossier it says that weapons of mass destruction could be "deployed or deployable within 45 minutes." In the foreword it says they could be "ready within 45 minutes." It may be a semantic distinction but "ready" is a stronger word I think than "deployable." That is a slightly more debatable point, it is a semantic debate, but I think "ready" is a stronger word. "Deployable" just means moveable. (Gilligan 2003, August 12)

The use of manipulative language within political discourse is a universal practice, as Holly (1989: 124) points out, that is formulated in a manner in which any expression or statement chosen "conveys as much additional material as possible for propaganda purposes." He continues, "the most effective place for this material is not in the official focus of an utterance, nor in the obvious speech act or in the central predication, but in less obvious positions: for example referential expressions, presuppositions and implications" (124).

Other figures used in addition to temporal references include the quantities of weapons possessed, the geographic distances, and most important, dates. The use of numerals to denote quantities is eye-catching and more convincing than if words were to be used. They register a more immediate impact, in many cases the plentiful zeros giving the impression of excess weapons possessed by Iraq and hence, a greater danger. The use of figures such as "4,000 tonnes of agent," "19,000 litres of botulinum toxin," "8,500 litres of anthrax," "2,850 tonnes of mustard gas," "over 16,000 free-fall bombs," "over 30,000 special munitions," "over 20,000 artillery munitions," in conjunction with the adverb "over" and verb "continue" give the illusion of plentiful WMDs, ready and waiting for an order to be deployed. They perpetuate a reality that conceptualizes the dangerous existence of WMDs, although this representation of reality was disputed by many, thereby highlighting the manipulative nature of the discourse.

HISTORICITY

The use of temporal references and quantitative figures proves to be persuasive not only because they are visually arresting, and in some cases relatable to the reader in a much more immediate manner, but they also indicate temporality that helps reveal the historicity behind the recontextualization of events, providing a sense of continuity between past, present, and future frames of experience. Here the historicity of discourses is reflective also of the naturalization of subjective conceptualizations of reality into social consciousness, becoming ordinary commonsensical knowledge. Invocation of such constructs and concepts naturalized over time can be seen as relevant to audiences' thought processes because they are part of their habitus (Bourdieu 1990). It is on the basis of these past experiences that we define and frame new or complex constructs and experiences, of which the concept of war is a prime example.

Graham, Keenan, and Dowd (2004) argue that human history of discourses is not random or incoherent and the "process of historical *reconstruction*" is really an attempt "to grasp human history as a seamless, unbroken whole" (216). The changes over time in our perceptions of the world, and thus the influence of them on the discourses that we construct, do not contribute to a disjointed history of experiences but instead are the reason for constant growth and development in our process of the reconceptualization of social reality and our skills as communicators. Historical analysis helps reveal not only the cause of particular perspectives but if one digs deeper, also the root of the cause itself. Historicity acknowledges the cause and effect relationship of past experiences and future actions:

> (Extract 5) Iraq has been involved in chemical and biological warfare research for *over 30 years*. (Weapons of Mass Destruction Dossier 2002: 11)
>
> (Extract 6) In the *late 1970s* plans were made to build a large research and commercial-scale production facility. . . . (Weapons of Mass Destruction Dossier 2002: 11)
>
> (Extract 7) . . . in the *early 1980s*, the biological weapons programme was revived. (Weapons of Mass Destruction Dossier 2002:11)
>
> (Extract 8) Iraq's nuclear programme was established under the Iraqi Atomic Energy Commission *in the 1950s*. (Weapons of Mass Destruction Dossier 2002:13)

(Extract 9) *In mid-2000* the JIC (Joint Intelligence Committee) assessed that Iraq retained some chemical warfare agents, precursors, production equipment and weapons from before the Gulf War. (Weapons of Mass Destruction Dossier 2002:18)

(Extract 10) *Since 1998* Iraqi development of mass destruction weaponry had been helped by the absence of inspectors. . . . (Weapons of Mass Destruction Dossier 2002:18)

(Extract 11) *In 1997* UNSCOM (United Nations Special Commission) also examined some munitions which had been filled with mustard gas prior to 1991. . . . (Weapons of Mass Destruction Dossier 2002:19)

(Extract 12) . . . Iraq acknowledged to UNSCOM the deployment to two sites of free-fall bombs filled with biological agent *during 1990–91.* (Weapons of Mass Destruction Dossier 2002: 22)

The use of dates in conjunction with such subsection headings that make a reference to temporality, such as "The *Current* Position: 1998–2002," "Joint Intelligence Committee (JIC) Assessments: *1999–2001,*" "*History* of UN Weapons Inspections," and adjectives like "continuous," verbs like "continues," particles like "as well," and adverbs "repeatedly" and "since" bring about a sense of continuity. It can be interpreted that there is a synthesis of the past into the present reinforcing the strength of the argument. Such continuity can be seen to indicate that the issue or problem at hand is not a random occurrence but an ongoing process, or rather struggle. Temporality could be seen to present the Blair government's argument in a much more historical, and as a result, more persuasive manner; the threat was portrayed not as a random occurrence but as part of an ongoing historical process. It further gave the impression that all diplomatic options had been exhausted and that military action was the only option left.

Historicity and continuity were also conveyed through the use of time-related verbs, nouns, prepositions, and phrases such as "dated," "history," "during this period," "history dating," "were," and "was" while the evocation of past events and experiences built argument on the grounds of tumultuous history. In the following statement, "Iraq was also seeking to reverse-engineer the SCUD engine with a view to producing new missiles. *Recent intelligence* indicates that they may have succeeded *at that time*" (14), the juxtaposition of "recent intelligence" and "at the time" as part of the strategy of continuation (Wodak et al. 1999) connects the past with the present, laying ground for future action. There are also several references to the Iran-Iraq war, in addition to World War II. The first Gulf War is mentioned an estimated thirty-four times within the WMDD (2002), in statements such as these:

(Extract 13) Saddam has used chemical weapons, both against Iran and against his own people. *Following the Gulf War*, Iraq had to admit to all this. (Weapons of Mass Destruction Dossier 2002: 5)

(Extract 14) *By the time of the Gulf War* Iraq was producing very large quantities of chemical and biological agents. (Weapons of Mass Destruction Dossier 2002: 12)

(Extract 15) *Prior to the Gulf War*, Iraq had a well-developed ballistic missile industry.

Many of the missiles fired *in the Gulf War* were an Iraqi modified version of the SCUD missile, the al-Hussein, with an extended range of 650km. (Weapons of Mass Destruction Dossier 2002: 14)

(Extract 16) From Iraqi declarations to the UN *after the Gulf War* we know that *by 1991* Iraq had produced a variety of delivery means for chemical and biological agents. . . . (Weapons of Mass Destruction Dossier 2002: 15)

(Extract 17) *At the end of the Gulf War* the international community was determined that Iraq's arsenal of chemical and biological weapons and ballistic missiles should be dismantled. (Weapons of Mass Destruction Dossier 2002: 16)

(Extract 18) *During the Gulf War* a number of facilities which intelligence reporting indicated were directly or indirectly associated with Iraq's chemical weapons effort were attacked and damaged. (Weapons of Mass Destruction Dossier 2002: 19)

(Extract 19) Parts of the al-Qa'qa' chemical complex damaged *in the Gulf War* have also been repaired and are operational. (Weapons of Mass Destruction Dossier 2002: 20)

(Extract 20) Iraq has managed to rebuild much of the missile production infrastructure destroyed *in the Gulf War* and in Operation Desert Fox in 1998. . . . (Weapons of Mass Destruction Dossier 2002: 30)

In these extracts, the entire period before, during, and after is consulted and presented as evidence of the long-standing dilemma of Iraqi weapons of mass destruction, which is what Lazar and Lazar (2004: 231) refer to as "past actions," "habitual actions," and "projected actions" that "encompass a range of time frames, suggesting that the threat is an enduring one." Parallels were implicitly drawn between the Gulf War and possible global consequences, indicating the outcome if military action were not taken against Iraq. Extracts 13–17 demonstrate Iraq's willingness to use WMDs if given a chance, while extract 20 portrays Iraq as resilient, managing to rebuild its weapons facilities despite the fact they have been destabilized and destroyed (see extracts 18 and 19). Evocation of the Gulf War also served as a reminder of past promises and objectives that the government was now asking to be fulfilled. As Bishop and Jaworski (2003: 254) mention,

This invocation of past events . . . arguably constructs and legitimizes the reporting of the events in terms of a military conflict and perpetuates and naturalizes a collective engagement with such events in terms of 'wars' or 'battles.'

However, some parts of the dossier have been disputed more than others, as a former British ministry of defense expert argues, extract 13 should have been phrased instead as:

In the 1980s, it [Iraq] used chemical weapons against elements of its own population in Iraq, and against Iranian forces in its war against the country . . . Iraq responded to attacks against its cities by Iranian Scud missiles. . . . (italics in original; Jones 2004, July 13)

It can be assumed here that just simple rephrasing or even what can be understood as the recontextualization of events can shed a significantly different light on the social reality presented to us, creating new and alternative "possible worlds" (Fairclough 2003), shaping the world in agreement with a subjective perception of reality and toward a specific purpose, within which Saddam Hussein is transformed from a relentless murderer of innocent civilians to a leader who was defending his country against outside forces. This also serves as a reminder of the ideological nature of language, within which subjective conceptualizations of social realities are so imbibed and embedded. How true the offered representations of reality are we may never know, but the recognition that both are in fact ideologically stimulated *versions* of reality is important. The rhetorical strategy of historicity is prevalent throughout the data serving to legitimize conceptualizations of reality, reinforce categorizations, and emphasize struggle, among other purposes.

The evocation of past events leads to the development and design of the future. The Gulf War brought with it the era of a New World Order, as Freedman (1991: 195) states, "The idea that the Gulf crisis was a test case for a 'new world order' was introduced almost as the Iraqi tanks rolled into Kuwait on August 2, 1990." The term could be interpreted as officially becoming part of international politics, more specifically part of the American political agenda on September 11, 1990, in a speech by President George H. W. Bush to the Joint Session of the Congress:

We stand today at a unique and *extraordinary* moment. The crisis in the Persian Gulf, as grave as it is, also offers a rare opportunity to move toward an *historic* period of cooperation. Out of these troubled times, our fifth objective—*a new world order*—can emerge: *a new era*—freer from the *threat of terror*, stronger in the pursuit of justice, and more secure in the quest for peace. . . . A world where the *rule of law supplants the rule of the jungle. A world in which nations recognize the shared responsibility for freedom and justice.* A world *where the strong respect the rights of the weak.* (Bush 1990, September 11)

In this extract, a pledge is made, an obligation invoked, and an objective stated through a series of parallels that form "part of a Social Contract metaphor system that was, in turn, projected on to a New World Order metaphor system" (Charteris-Black 2005: 190). The use of terms such as "extraordinary" and "historic" provide context for a fifth political objective of "a new world order." A "new era" that will highlight the contrast between the "rule of law" and the "rule of jungle," where illustrated in a category-pair are nations that "recognize the shared responsibility for freedom and justice" and they are distinguished from barbarians who engage in the "threat of terror." In another category-pair, nations who are part of this new world order are "strong" who need to "respect the rights of the weak."

This speech was made exactly eleven years prior to the 9/11 attacks on the World Trade Towers in America. It is a fair possibility that evocation of the past, more specifically in context of the Gulf War, was a reminder to nations of the pledge made to protect the weak, and to fight against terror for justice and peace for all. Iraq was portrayed as a terrorist threat in the WMDD, following the very law of the jungle that the world pledged to fight eleven years earlier. A similar appeal, complementing the speech of then president George H. W. Bush, is made in the WMDD, which Freedman (1991: 198) recapitulates as

> . . . capacity for action depended on co-operation from three other groups of states: those in the region who were threatened by Iraq; Western states who shared the risks and responsibilities of taking action against Iraq; and states unwilling or unable to take direct action but who were crucial in ensuring the passage of UN Security Council resolutions, China and the Soviet Union being most important in this regard.

Evocation of history, however, can be and may be interpreted in this case as being partial. The Gulf War was depicted in the media as an epic event, in terms of heroes and warriors. A turn in the direction of the New World Order, the Gulf War was a hero's journey to battle for good against evil, succeeding in his conquest and returning home to glory. As Kanjirathinkal and Hickey (1992: 106) emphasize,

> . . . the elites used the media, particularly television, to transform the social consciousness of people from mundane concerns about territorial boundaries, jobs, and oil into a primal struggle between good and evil.

While the West viewed the Gulf War in terms of nominal definitions of good versus evil, victim versus aggressor, the Arab side of the world perceived the war as another intervention by the West to achieve global dominance rather than a truly new world order, and so the West "did not come into the Middle East with clean hands" (Draper 1992). Ideologies were seen relatively explicitly at work in the tone and context in which the history of the Gulf War was invoked in the WMDD. However, while the West claims Islamic radical terror ideology is barbaric, backward, and invasive with regard to the new world order, Gray (2003: 3) argues,

Like communism and Nazism, radical Islam is modern. Though it claims to be anti-western, it is shaped as much by western ideology as by Islamic traditions. Like Marxists and neo-liberals, radical Islamists see history as a prelude to a new world. *All are convinced they can remake the human condition. If there is a uniquely modern myth, this is it.*

The last sentence of this quote is evidence of the illusory nature of social and political discourse; each group perceives itself as capable of revolutionizing the new world order, while claiming the ideologies of the "other" will only prove destructive.

ATTACK VERSUS SELF-DEFENSE

The most predominant rhetorical strategy utilized within the WMDD is that of *attack versus self-defense*, which was used less as a tactic to reassure audiences that the administration was capable of defending itself and more as a signifier of the inevitability of a terrorist threat. The WMDD, although made available to the public, was in actuality targeting leaders of the international community and the United Nations (UN) as supporting evidence in a bid to gain allies in the US-led war on terror; thus constant reiteration of threat and Iraq's past actions create a need for defense on the part of the threatened nations.

Within the WMDD, "attack" was not counter-measured with the reassurance of self-defense, but rather the idea of attack was used to reiterate the inevitability of the Iraqi threat, not solely through the use of figures (as discussed earlier) but also through an appeal to Saddam Hussein's past, which was used to justify him as a current threat:

(Extract 21) Under Saddam Hussein Iraq developed chemical and biological weapons, acquired missiles allowing it *to attack neighbouring countries.* . . . (Weapons of Mass Destruction Dossier 2002: 5)

(Extract 22) Iraq used significant quantities of mustard, tabun and sarin during the war with Iran resulting in over 20,000 Iranian casualties. A month after *the attack on Halabja*, Iraqi troops used over 100 tonnes of sarin against Iranian troops on the al-Fao peninsula. (Weapons of Mass Destruction Dossier 2002: 15)

(Extract 23) During the Iran-Iraq war, Saddam appointed his cousin, Ali Hasan al-Majid, as his deputy in the north. In 1987–88, al-Majid led the *"Anfal" campaign of attacks on Kurdish villages.* (Weapons of Mass Destruction Dossier 2002: 44–5)

(Extract 24) *A massive chemical weapons attack on Kurds in Halabja* town in March 1988 killing 5000 and injuring 10,000 more. (Weapons of Mass Destruction Dossier 2002: 45)

These extracts illustrate more literally Saddam's supposed "penchant" for biological and chemical attacks. However, the attacks mentioned were concerned with the same incident that was instead multiplied in an effort to justify him as a current threat. Again, use of repetition is an effective tool in building an otherwise "flat" argument. The repetitive use of the word "attack" (both in nominal and verbal forms) can be interpreted as having an almost barbaric feel to it. Meanwhile, the use of the same word "attack" to describe actions by the West had warrior-like and relief-action connotations:

> (Extract 25) By the end of 1984 Iraq was self-sufficient in uranium ore. One of the reactors was *destroyed in an Israeli air attack* in June 1981 shortly before it was to become operational; the *other was never completed.* (Weapons of Mass Destruction Dossier 2002: 13)

> (Extract 26) During the Gulf War a number of facilities which *intelligence reporting* indicated were directly or indirectly associated with *Iraq's chemical weapons effort were attacked and damaged.* (Weapons of Mass Destruction Dossier 2002: 19)

> (Extract 27) . . . the Castor Oil Production Plant at Fallujah: *this was damaged in UK/US air attacks in 1998 (Operation Desert Fox) but has been rebuilt.* (Weapons of Mass Destruction Dossier 2002: 22)

> (Extract 28) *Recent intelligence confirms* that the Iraqi military have developed mobile facilities. These would help *Iraq conceal and protect biological agent production from military attack or UN inspection.* (Weapons of Mass Destruction Dossier 2002: 22)

Extract 25 gives the impression that the Israeli air attacks prevented Iraq's self-sufficiency from becoming too much of a threat, and that the attacks were not destructive as far as loss of resources was concerned since Iraq itself never completed its reactors. Extract 26 attempts to merit some justification for the US attacks by illustrating them as a countermeasure to Iraq's nuclear weapons facilities. Similarly, extract 27 also justifies "UK/US air attacks" by associating them with "Operation Desert Fox" which has less terrorist associations and more efficient and legal military connotations. Last, extract 28 provides a different kind of legitimacy for the concept of attack. First, a form of legal justification can be interpreted as being given for any future attack by the alignment of the West with an institution-sponsored "UN inspection." Second, the attacks would be in response to confirmed reporting about "mobile facilities," which "would help Iraq conceal and protect biological agent production" by an objective and higher source of authority—intelligence. One can interpret, therefore, that the concept of "attack" when invoked with regard to Saddam Hussein and Iraq was negative other-presentation, while in the context of the West it was raised in a more positive manner, in what can be referred to as the topos of difference (Wodak et al. 1999), whereby a presupposition of "us" being better, superior, to "them" was made.

Inevitability of threat was also reinforced through the attack versus self-defense antonym without the use of the word "attack" or evocation of past events:

(Extract 29) But the *threat from Iraq does not depend solely on the capabilities we have described. It arises also because of the violent and aggressive nature of Saddam Hussein's regime.* His record of internal repression and external aggression gives *rise to unique concerns about the threat he poses.* (Weapons of Mass Destruction Dossier 2002: 7)

(Extract 30) Saddam's *willingness to use chemical and biological weapons*: intelligence indicates that as part of Iraq's military planning *Saddam is willing* to use chemical and biological weapons, *including against his own Shia population.* (Weapons of Mass Destruction Dossier 2002: 19)

(Extract 31) Saddam practises *torture, execution and other forms of coercion against his enemies, real or suspected.* His targets are *not only those who have offended him, but also their families, friends or colleagues.* (Weapons of Mass Destruction Dossier 2002: 43–4)

(Extract 32) It is *routine for Saddam to take preemptive action against those who he believes might conspire against him.* (Weapons of Mass Destruction Dossier 2002: 44)

In these extracts Saddam's "willingness" (extract 30) to use chemical and biological weapons equals the imminence of the threat he poses. Fear is aroused in the topos of threat as part of the strategy of unification (cf. Ricento 2003) when the WMDD's intended audience is reminded that Saddam Hussein would not even spare his friends and colleagues let alone "his enemies, real or suspected" (extracts 30, 31, and 32). The immanency of the threat could be seen as leading the audience to infer the particular interpretative frame (Bednarek 2005) that allowed them to perceive the threat Saddam Hussein posed as "expected," invoking a memory data-structure that captured the "typical" features of an instance such as the one listed, thus legitimizing the argument of an immediate threat. A negative other-presentation was made of Saddam Hussein through the use of terms such as "violent" and "aggressive" (extract 29), and the threat he posed was not only imminent but also "unique" since it was "routine for Saddam to take preemptive action against those who he believes might conspire against him" (extract 35 and 40), and Western states could be interpreted as being top priorities considering the 9/11 attacks and the ensuing suspicions regarding Iraq. It is also important to recognize the irony here, of the West accusing Saddam Hussein of preemptive action, when America and Britain themselves were planning to invade Iraq in similar preemptive fashion. Persuasive language, especially the kind made use of frequently within the WMDD, therefore,

> to a large extent employs language material that is emotionally charged, the general trend is towards reduction, especially of intensity, which obviously results from hyperbolic language usage, i.e. from exaggeration in the use of evaluative lexical material. (Sornig 1989: 99)

Portrayal of the Iraqi regime as a danger and threat to the "stability of the world" (Weapons of Mass Destruction Dossier 2002: 3) could be seen as justification for military action:

> From the outset, the legitimacy of the invasion depended on making a case that regime change in Baghdad was necessary, as a matter of urgency in order to save the world from a grave danger. . . . Without this context, the invasion would have been almost impossible to sell to their domestic constituencies, let alone the rest of the world. (*South China Morning Post* 2004, January 14)

The rhetorical strategy of attack versus self-defense can thus be seen to lay down grounds for an impending invasion by arousing caution and fear; it reflects the general theme of war, and to do so successfully, employs a certain mix of lexico-syntactical and semantico-pragmatic tools.

APPEAL TO "LAWFUL" AUTHORITY

In order to convince audiences that the reality being presented to them is legitimate and objective, the elites of society presenting this truth needed authority on their side. Graham et al. (2004) mention that legitimate power and authority over time has been generated from the Christian God (eleventh century), the Church and Nation-State (sixteenth century), and the Democratic Nation-State (twentieth century). The authors of the WMDD emanated a certain appeal to authority bringing to attention their social and political status. The British government brought with it legal and political authority. Being a member or one of the leaders of the free world, a democratic state, and part of the West could be interpreted as institutionalizing Britain, authorizing it to pass moral judgment. In doing so, Britain not only served to reinforce the *us versus them* demarcation, but also the *lawful versus lawless* one. The use of legal terminology enhanced this division: "Security Council Resolutions," "sanctions and the policy of containment," "illicit," "illegal," "breach of international law," "in breach of its obligations under the Non-Proliferation Treaty," "in breach of UNSCR 687," "Non-Proliferation Treaty," "prohibited by UNSCR 687 and 715," "UN sanctions," "UN Security Council Resolution 1051," "violating the 1925 Geneva Convention banning the use of chemical weapons." Legal jargon could be seen as representative of two things: first, the dossier, although it had been released to the public, was clearly intended for a different audience; it was part of public discourse yet very much inaccessible to the layman. Barring certain professions, the everyday person would not necessarily be aware of what "UNSCR 687" or "UN Security Council Resolution 1051" is. As Fowler and Marshall (1985: 3) mention,

> Such jargon is common to technical registers, not particular to Nukespeak; its function is to give an air of technical or scientific authority while making

the concepts referred to inaccessible to non-specialists: it is thus mystifica-
tory in aim and power-building effect.

The knowledge distribution here is asymmetrical, with the British government being in the position of power, their expertise in matters of military, law,
and economics outweighing that of the general public, and this was not only
evident in the legal terminology used but also in the ability to connect this terminology to actual events both in the present and past. Individuals and groups
with expertise in one matter or the other are thus

> more likely to give an historical analysis, relying more heavily on past
> states, events, and goals in their explanations . . . and perhaps most impor-
> tant . . . political expertise . . . [is] accompanied by both the increased use
> of causal reasoning and one type of goal-based reasoning (i.e., initiating
> reasoning). . . . (Jones and Read 2005: 74)

This sort of power in the eyes of the public can often be understood as the
reason that many times when a representation of reality is put forward by the
government, or any other elitist group in society, it is accepted as the objective
truth by the masses. Jones and Read also make a valid point about "goal-based
reasoning," which is evident within the WMDD. The WMDD was presented as
supposed proof that Saddam Hussein was an active threat to the free world and
was an attempt to draw support for military action against Iraq. As a result it
is possible to say that the reality presented in the WMDD was molded to the
particular sociopolitical agenda mentioned earlier.

A second consequence of the repeated use of legal terminology is that Britain and its allies, especially America, always aligned themselves with the law.
This led to the negative other-presentation of Iraq as lawless. The WMDD
worked to criminalize Saddam Hussein in an attempt to outcast him from the
civilized world:

> (Extract 33) . . . *despite sanctions, despite the damage* done to his capability
> in the past, *despite the UN Security Council Resolutions* expressly *outlawing*
> it, and *despite his denials*, Saddam Hussein is *continuing to develop WMD*,
> and with them the *ability to inflict real damage* upon the region, and the
> *stability of the world.* (Weapons of Mass Destruction Dossier 2002: 3)

In this extract, the repeated use of the preposition "despite" is followed by
a list of three acts as an enhancer, serving as a reminder that diplomatic efforts
had been pursued before but to no avail. Furthermore, it implies that Saddam
Hussein continued to develop WMDs that were "outlawed," the verb categorizing Saddam Hussein as unlawful and criminal, and against the lawful nations. In quoting the UN Security Council Resolutions, again, Britain can be
seen as associating itself with a legal institution such as the United Nations.
There is a certain amount of certainty in the extract as it declares that Saddam

Hussein is in fact developing WMDs that can threaten "the stability of the world," which acts as an amplifier, whereby a local, regional, or maybe even an American threat is amplified and made into a global threat. However, many members of the international community have disputed this perspective of reality, as Robin Cook, former British foreign secretary, stated in a speech to Parliament,

> Iraq's military strength is now less than half its size than at the time of the last Gulf war. Ironically, it is only because Iraq's military forces are so weak that we can even contemplate its invasion. Some advocates of conflict claim that Saddam's forces are so weak, so demoralized and so badly equipped that the war will be over in a few days. We cannot base our military strategy on the assumption that Saddam is weak and at the same time justify pre-emptive action on the claim that he is a threat. Iraq probably has no weapons of mass destruction in the commonly understood sense of the term—namely a credible device capable of being delivered against a strategic city target. (Cook 2003, March 3)

Nonetheless, statements that emphasized Saddam Hussein as secretive, manipulative, and deceptive continued to further develop his image as a criminal:

> (Extract 34) . . . Iraq is *preparing to conceal evidence . . . incriminating* documents . . . despite sanctions and the policy of containment, Saddam has *continued to make progress* with his *illicit* weapons programmes. (Weapons of Mass Destruction Dossier 2002: 5)

> (Extract 35) . . . Iraq's *history of deception, intimidation and concealment* in its dealings with the UN inspectors. (Weapons of Mass Destruction Dossier 2002: 6)

> (Extract 36) . . . a *continuous* and sophisticated programme of harassment, *obstruction, deception and denial.* . . . (Weapons of Mass Destruction Dossier 2002: 16)

These statements in conjunction with words and phrases such as "flouted," "covertly," "discrepancies," "unable to establish the truth," "obstructive Iraqi activity," "practice of concealment," "cover up of its activities," "Iraqi obstruction and intimidation," "policy of deception," "hiding proscribed material," all emanated from a similar semantic field denoting illegitimacy and general "wrongdoing," thus categorizing Saddam Hussein as the enemy, a criminal who needed to be brought to justice. As mentioned before, the use of various time frames— "preparing to conceal," "continued to make progress," "history of deception"— illustrate Iraq's history, present, and future (cf. Lazar and Lazar 2004), and more important, became the basis for confirming presuppositions about Iraq's intentions as inevitable and actual threats. Saddam Hussein's history and past actions were transformed into part of his character, depicting him as a man not to be trusted (cf. Jayyusi 1984):

(Extract 37) . . . Iraq has *claimed* repeatedly that if it had retained any chemical agents from before the Gulf War they would have deteriorated sufficiently to render them harmless. (Weapons of Mass Destruction Dossier 2002: 19)

(Extract 38) Iraq has *claimed* that all its biological agents and weapons have been destroyed. (Weapons of Mass Destruction Dossier 2002: 19)

(Extract 39) . . . Iraq *claimed* that it had merely conducted a military biological research programme. (Weapons of Mass Destruction Dossier 2002: 38)

Here the asymmetrical category-pair of lawful versus lawless often denotes the lawful side as having the power to pronounce moral judgment on the lawless side, while the "other" side is denied any grounds for explanation, as is evident in the use of the verb "claimed" that implied plenty of doubt in the word of Saddam Hussein. Taking into account Fairclough's (2003) reality-rhetoric dichotomy, which explores the politics of the gaps between what is real and what is rhetorical, it seems as if the WMDD draws a very potent, discriminating, and illusive line between the "we" that aligns Britain, the United States, and other elite countries who were willing to bring Iraq to justice and punish Saddam Hussein for his criminal acts, against the rest of the world, perhaps even putting the "elite core" into a minority.

The public and the rest of the international community were assured of the sound legal basis for military action against Iraq, as the British broadsheet *The Guardian* noted,

> An unrepentant Tony Blair yesterday said that the case for war against Iraq remained intact even though it has emerged that Baghdad possessed no weapons of mass destruction prior to the invasion. The legal basis for war remained secure, the prime minister said, since the war had been triggered by Saddam Hussein's refusal to cooperate with UN weapons inspectors "in breach upon breach" of UN resolutions. (Wintour 2004)

However, despite British and American reassurances, many objected to the "legal basis" of the Iraq invasion, including Kofi Annan, former secretary-general of the UN, in an interview with BBC correspondent Owen Bennett-Jones (September 16, 2004):

> Bennett-Jones: I wanted to ask you that—do you think that the resolution that was passed on Iraq before the war did actually give legal authority to do what was done?
>
> Annan: Well, I'm one of those who believe that there *should have been a second resolution* because the Security Council indicated that if Iraq did not comply there will be consequences. But then *it was up to the Security Council to approve or determine what those consequences should be.*
>
> B-J: So you don't think there was legal authority for the war?
>
> . . .

A: Yes, I have indicated it is not in conformity with the UN Charter, from our point of view and *from the Charter point of view it was illegal.*

It can be understood here that the Iraq war was illegal from the point of view of the UN Charter since the draft resolution, sponsored by Britain and America, which initiated military action should Iraq not comply with the conditions set by the resolution, was not put to a vote at the UN Security Council. It was assumed the primary reason for this was the possible opposition that the resolution faced by other permanent, veto-power yielding nations like China and France, who objected to the clause sanctioning military action against Iraq (cf. Blix 2004). Weapons inspections were brought to a more or less halt so that a way for armed action could be paved, since for countries like America and Britain, who in the discourses of terrorism (see Bhatia 2009) have touted their affinity for the law and Iraq's disregard for it, "what was needed was a judgement, not inspection. The war was seen as certain and the adoption of the resolution endorsing it desirable but not indispensable" (Blix 2004: 216). This legal controversy could be described as an example of "double contrastive identity" (Leudar, Marsland, and Nekvapil 2004), whereby participants of particular categories played dual roles; in this case while the British were accusing Iraq of being unlawful, others felt it was the British whose activities were illegitimate. This is a common attribute when a contestation of social realities and perspectives occurs.

However, it is possible to interpret that persuasive discourses, such as the WMDD, often require the distortion and politicization of facts and truths, since they are ideological and subjective. Despite how objective and honest one may believe his or her version of reality to be, it is still in fact a particular *representation* of reality, which relies on the invocation of certain emotions and sociocultural traditions to be accepted by groups and individuals as legitimate, as such persuasion has

> nothing to do with science, but has all to do with politics and social action. . . . There is, inherent in politics, a need to persuade the other, the listener, the audience, the populace. And this persuasion—as opposed to inducement which does not rest on legitimate justification—can only be effected when both reason and rhetoric are put to work. (Biletzki 1997: 163)

The analysis of the data in this chapter reveals that the "emotionalization of facts" (Menz 1989) is not necessarily a result of lies, exaggeration, or even the intentional withholding of truth but is rather a product of an individual or group's subjective conceptualization of reality, especially in the case for justification of war. The governmental document analyzed in this chapter, that is the Weapons of Mass Destruction Dossier, puts forward a subjective conceptualization of reality, the objectivity of which has been questioned by many and at various points in time. The content of the dossier and the rhetorical processes that it employed are relatively less emotive and more factual. The WMDD drew upon various rhetorical processes that included inevitability of threat, which played on audiences' core weaknesses invoking fear; historicity that connected the past, present, and future to further amplify the threat being faced; and appeal to "lawful" authority which legitimized the Blair government's right to judgment. Such rhetorical processes served the purpose of heightening the impact of the arguments conveyed, creating an effective discourse of illusion, which engineered conditions for an urgent war against Iraq.

Conclusion

To conclude, what made the WMDD worthy of investigation was that at the time of its release the dossier differed significantly in terms of rhetorical strategy from other political discourses, often conveyed in the form of emotionalized political speeches and pleas, since it presented a justification for war in a more studied and strategic manner. War was conceptualized in the discourse not in terms of more traditionally entrenched concepts of chaos, violence, and collateral damage, but rather reconceptualized as a rational action to undertake in the quest for a more desired possible world of peace, drawing on what Ferguson (2008) refers to as the right moral choices to make. Peace thus is redrawn as an ideal state, something that is tangible in that it is "achievable" through the performance of certain actions (i.e., defending against threat and attack in the form of a preemptive war). The irony here, of course, lies in the "type" of peace this quest is for, which if one were to be persuaded by the discourse of the WMDD would involve a simple war to root out peace-threatening radicals. However, what seems to be really demanded of the audiences by this discourse is blind consent for a war to achieve not a perpetual peace in Kantian terms (what Dunmire elaborates on in her chapter in this volume), but a peace generating from a new world order modeled by Western nations, a *political peace*, which champions the possible worlds reconceptualized by hegemonic superpowers, and is likely to remain only as long as their version of reality is accepted unconditionally.

References

Aldrich, Richard. 2004. "Whitehall and the Iraq War: The UK's Four Intelligence Enquiries." *Irish Studies in International Affairs* 16: 73–88.
Bednarek, Monika A. "Frame Revisited—the Coherence-Inducing Function of Frames." *Journal of Pragmatics* 37: 685–705.

Bhatia, Aditi. 2007a. Discourse of Illusion: A Critical Study of the Discourses of Terrorism. PhD thesis, Macquarie University, Australia.

Bhatia, Aditi. 2007b. "Religious Metaphor in the Discourse of Illusion: George W. Bush and Osama bin Laden." *World Englishes* 26(4): 507–24.

Bhatia, Aditi. 2008. "Discursive Illusions in the American National Strategy for Combating Terrorism." *Journal of Language and Politics* 7(2): 201–27.

Bhatia, Aditi. 2009. "Discourses of Terrorism." *Journal of Pragmatics* 41(2): 279–89.

Biletzki, Anat. 1997. *Talking Wolves: Thomas Hobbes on the Language of Politics and the Politics of Language*. Netherlands: Kluwer Academic.

Bishop, Hywel and Adam Jaworski. 2003. "'We Beat 'Em': Nationalism and the Hegemony of Homogeneity in the British Press Reportage of Germany versus England during Euro 2000." *Discourse & Society* 14(3): 243–71.

Blix, Hans. 2004. *Disarming Iraq: The Search for Weapons of Mass Destruction*. London: Bloomsbury.

Bluth, Christoph. 2004. "The British Road to War: Blair, Bush and the Decision to Invade Iraq." International *Affairs* 80(5): 871–92.

Bourdieu, Pierre. 1990. *The Logic of Practice*. Cambridge: Polity Press.

Charteris-Black, Jonathon. 2005. *Politicians and Rhetoric: The Persuasive Power of Metaphor*. New York: Palgrave Macmillan.

China Daily. 2008. "UK Government's WMD 45-Claim 'Not Supported.'" www.chinadaily. net/english/doc/2004-07/08/content_346546.htm.

Collins, John. 2002. "Terrorism." In *Collateral Language: A User's Guide to America's New War*, John Collins and Ross Glover (eds.), 155–73. New York: New York University Press.

Cook, Robin. 2003. "Standing against the American and British Invasion of Iraq." http://articles.cnn.com/2003-03-18/world/sprj.irq.cook.speech_1_agreement-or-domestic-support-leader-inspections?_s=PM:WORLD.

Draper, Theodore H. 1992. "The Gulf War Reconsidered." *New York Review of Books* 39 (1&2).

Fairclough, Norman. 1989. *Language and Power*. New York: Longman.

Fairclough, Norman. 1998. "Political Discourse in the Media: An Analytical Framework." In *Approaches to Media Discourse*, Alan Bell and Peter Garrett (eds.), 142–62. Oxford: Blackwell.

Fairclough, Norman. 2000. *New Labour, New Language?* London: Routledge.

Fairclough, Norman. 2003. *Analysing Discourse: Textual Analysis for Social Research.* London: Routledge.

Fowler, Roger and Tim Marshall. 1985. "The War against Peace-mongering: Language and Ideology." In *Language and the Nuclear Arms Debate*, Paul Chilton (ed.), 4–22. London: Frances Pinter.

Freedman, Lawrence. 1991. "The Gulf War and the New World Order." *Survival* 33(3): 195–209.

Gilligan, Andrew. 2003. "Hutton Inquiry Hearing." www.the-hutton-inquiry.org.uk/content/hearing_trans.htm.

Graham, Phil, Thomas Kennan, and Anne-Maree Dowd. 2004. "A Call to Arms at the End of History: A Discourse—Historical Analysis of George W. Bush's Declaration of War on Terror." *Discourse & Society* 15(2–3): 199–221.

Gray, John. 2003. *Al Qaeda and What It Means to Be Modern*. New York: New Press.

Hartnett, Stephen J. and Laura A. Stengrim. 2004. "'The Whole Operation of Deception': Reconstructing President Bush's Rhetoric of Weapons of Mass Destruction." *Cultural Studies Critical Methodologies* 4(2): 152–97.

Hodges, Adam. 2011. *The "War on Terror" Narrative: Discourse and Intertextuality in the Construction and Contestation of Sociopolitical Reality*. New York: Oxford University Press.

Holly, Werner. 1989. "Credibility and Political Language." In *Language, Power and Ideology: Studies in Political Discourse*, Ruth Wodak (ed.), 115–35. Amsterdam: John Benjamins.

Humphreys, James. 2005. "The Iraq Dossier and the Meaning of Spin." *Parliamentary Affairs* 58(1): 156–70.

Jayyusi, Lena. 1984. *Categorization and the Moral Order*. Boston: Routledge & Kegan Paul.

Jones, Bennett. 2003. "Hutton Inquiry Hearing." www.the-hutton-inquiry.org.uk/content/hearing_trans.htm.

Jones, David K. and Stephen J. Read. 2005. "Expert-Novice Differences in the Understanding and Explanations of Complex Political Conflicts." *Discourse Processes* 39(1): 45–80.

Kanjirathinkal, Mathew and Joseph Hickey. 1992. "Media Framing and Myth: The Media's Portrayal of the Gulf War." *Critical Sociology* 19(1): 103–12.

Layder, David. 1993. *New Strategies in Social Research: An Introduction and Guide*. Cambridge: Polity Press.

Lazar, Annita and Michelle M. Lazar. 2004. "The Discourse of the New World Order: 'Out-casting' the Double Face of Threat." *Discourse & Society*, 15(2–3): 223–42.

Menz, Florian. 1989. "Manipulation Strategies in Newspapers: A Program for Critical Linguistics." In *Language, Power and Ideology: Studies in Political Discourse*, Ruth Wodak (ed.), 227–49. Amsterdam: John Benjamins.

Morales, Jorge. 2005. "Proliferation of Nuclear Weapons: Myth or Reality?" www.iaea.org (International Atomic Energy Agency).

Ricento, Thomas. 2003. "The Discursive Construction of Americanism." *Discourse & Society* 14(5): 611–37.

Silberstein, Sandra. 2002. *War of Words: Language, Politics and 9/11*. London: Routledge.

Sornig, Karl. 1989. "Some Remarks on Linguistic Strategies of Persuasion." In *Language, Power, Ideology: Studies in Political Discourse*, Ruth Wodak (ed.), 95–114. Amsterdam: John Benjamins.

South China Morning Post. 2005. "Closer to Midnight," Agenda, A11.

Wodak, Ruth, Rudolph de Cillia, and Martin Reisigl. 1999. *The Discursive Construction of National Identity*. Edinburgh: Edinburgh University Press.

PART TWO

Negotiating Military Deployment

6

Culture Clash

FRAMING PEACEKEEPING AND ITS ROLE IN A
CANADIAN CONTEXT

Janis L. Goldie

Introduction

The brutal torture and death of a Somali teenager by members of the Canadian Airborne Regiment (CAR) while serving on a peace-enforcement mission
in Somalia shocked the Canadian public in the spring of 1993. The death of
Shidane Arone, in addition to various reports of murder and questionable
behavior to other Somalis and members of the Canadian Forces that were later
uncovered, directly challenged Canadians' notions of themselves as racially tol-
erant people who are respectful of basic human rights the world over. Testing
important norms within Canada, the scandal of the Somalia Affair had a
lasting impact on the Canadian Forces and the nation more generally.

Following the uncovering of the affair over the next two years, the federal
government of Canada appointed a commission of inquiry to investigate the
events surrounding the scandal as well as its related military institutions such as
the Canadian Forces and its bureaucratic counterpart, the Department of National Defence. Tackling the largest military scandal in Canadian history, the
commission produced thousands of pages of documents, held hundreds of
hours of public hearings, and ran until it was forced to produce its final report
on June 30, 1997.

It is the discourse found within the Somalia commission that is of interest
for this chapter. Specifically, this chapter investigates the "culture clash"
between the military and civilian discursive communities around the issue of
peacekeeping and its role for Canadians. Utilizing frame analysis methodology
to investigate how the various commission participants framed the issues and
values around the Somalia Affair, this chapter displays how peacekeeping and
the role of Canadian soldiers were constructed in very different ways by two
discursive communities—a "civilian" discursive community (generally represented by the commissioners and the lawyers involved in the commission) in
contrast to a "military" discursive community (as represented generally by the

119

military witnesses and bureaucrats). The resulting significant discursive battle that became evident over the role, definition, and value of peacekeeping in Canada reveals important insights about the direction and discourse of the role of the Canadian military as well as how the myth of peacekeeping in Canada more generally gets constructed in institutional settings. In this way, this chapter elucidates the domestic discursive political struggles that sometimes occur around endeavors of conflict and peace for a nation. While this analysis focuses on discourse that occurred as a result of a nation's involvement in a conflict situation rather than discourse that occurred prior to decisions that led to military deployment (as in part 1 of the book, for example), it nonetheless speaks to issues of negotiation by national actors around military engagement. The commission discourse in this situation, then, works to illuminate the reflective discourse that occurred around the role of Canada, and Canadian soldiers more specifically, after engagement in a peace-enforcement mission like Somalia.

The Somalia Affair

Remaining the largest military scandal in Canadian history to date, the Somalia Affair consists of a number of separate but related events that took place over a four year period.[1] First, in the spring of 1993, the Canadian public learned that a Somali teenager had been brutally tortured to death at the hands of a few Canadian soldiers who were serving on a peace-enforcement mission there. Shidane Arone, the media later uncovered, had wandered into the Canadian camp and was taken prisoner. For three hours on the evening of March 16, 1993, Master Corporal Clayton Matchee allegedly punched and kicked Arone, beat him with a riot stick over a ration pack, struck him with an iron bar across the face and shins, and burned the soles of his feet with a cigarette butt while another soldier, Private Brown reportedly looked on. "Trophy shots" of Matchee and the half-dead Arone were taken and Arone, who was coming in and out of consciousness, was reported to scream, "Canada, Canada, Canada" over and over again. After approximately three hours of intermittent beating, Arone died. By that time, it was reported that at least eight members of the Canadian Forces had seen the beating taking place and did nothing to stop it or report it. Accusations later followed that many more either heard the abuse or knew that it was taking place. Matchee was eventually arrested on suspicion of murdering Arone, but his failed suicide attempt left him mentally unfit to face trial at a later date (Bercuson 1997; Government of Canada 1997).

---

[1] For detailed information on the Somalia Affair, see Bercuson (1997), Dawson (2007), Government of Canada (1997).

Shortly afterward, Major Barry Armstrong, a doctor who served in Somalia, went public with allegations that another Somali, killed on March 4, 1993, had been shot in a suspicious manner. On that day, one Somali had been injured and another killed, reportedly shot in the back after not heeding warning shots and fleeing from the compound. The Somali who was killed had sustained point-blank shots to the head and neck and it later was alleged that the Somalis had been "baited" with food and water to entice them to enter the compound to make an example of them for other would-be intruders.

Not too long after the convictions of those involved in the beating and torture of Arone, videotapes of brutal hazing rituals within the Canadian Airborne Regiment (the regiment that was stationed in Somalia) were run on Canadian news stations. The first tape, aired January 15, 1995, on CBC, showed members of Two Commando (three commando units made up the Canadian Airborne Regiment) drinking beer and making racist comments about Somalis such as "we ain't killed enough niggers yet" ("Rampant Racism in the Airborne Regiment" 1995). The second tape aired January 19, 1995, on CTV and showed members of One Commando engaged in initiation rites where drunken-troop members were forced to eat feces and urine-soaked bread and to imitate sex acts. Perhaps the most shocking image on the tape showed an African Canadian soldier with the letters "I love the KKK" smeared on his back and being led on all fours on a leash. The soldier was later tied to a tree and sprinkled with white flour, the act titled a "Michael Jackson" (Razack 2004).

The Canadian public was appalled and there was an outcry to put an end to the aggressive and seemingly racist behavior of the CAR. The Defence Minister at the time, David Collenette, responded to the calls, and announced on January 23, 1995, that the CAR would be disbanded. In addition, he appointed a Federal Commission of Inquiry on March 20, 1995, to investigate the happenings of the Somalia Affair, which produced its final report on June 30, 1997.

Commissions of Inquiry in Canada

Since its inception as a nation, Canada has frequently employed commissions of inquiry to investigate events of political scandal, accidents, and mishaps as well as to research and report on broad areas of policy interest such as health care or the status of women in Canada more generally.[2] Also referred to as public inquiries and task forces, commissions of inquiry are independent political bodies, often headed by a judicial chairperson (or chairpersons), usually mandated into existence and form by the government and tasked with the job

---

[2] For an excellent introduction to Commissions of Inquiry and all their varied issues, see Manson and Mullan (2003) and Pross, Innis, and Yogis (1990).

of investigating some topic or event, reporting on said topic or event and then making recommendations as to what the government should do next. Commissions of inquiry can be defined as "any body that is formally mandated by a government, either on an ad hoc basis or with reference to a specific problem, to conduct a process of fact-finding and to arrive at a body of recommendations" (Salter 1990: 175). With over 500 federal commissions appointed since confederation and no sign of their use slowing down, commissions of inquiry have played a crucial role in the economic, social, and political development of the country.

The Somalia Commission

The commission on the Somalia Affair, announced officially on March 21, 1995, was the first major public inquiry into the military in Canadian history (Desbarats 1997). The commission had a broad mandate and was charged to "inquire into and report generally on the chain of command system, leadership, discipline, operations, and decisions of the Canadian Forces, and on the actions and decisions of the Department of National Defence in respect of the Somalia operation" (Government of Canada 1997). In addition, the commissioners were required to look at specific matters in relation to pre-deployment, in-theater, and post-theater phases of the operation, such as the suitability of, and state of discipline within, the CAR, the extent to which cultural differences affected the conduct of operations and the manner in which the Canadian Joint Force Somalia (CJFS) responded to the operational, disciplinary, and administrative problems encountered in-theater, including allegations of cover-up and destruction of evidence, among other things.

After two years of operations—116 witnesses testified over 183 days of hearings, resulting in approximately 38,000 pages of testimony—the Canadian government announced it was terminating the inquiry, a notable and challenged break from tradition. After a frantic rush to completion, the final report of the commission was released to the public on July 2, 1997, with 160 recommendations in the five-volume report, which ran 1,600 pages. Both the media and the government were surprised by the harsh tone of the report, entitled "Dishonoured Legacy: The Lessons of the Somalia Affair" (Government of Canada 1997; Desbarats 1997).

Frame Analysis

In order to investigate the discourse of the Somalia Commission, frame analysis is an exceptionally useful methodology. Since Goffman (1974) introduced the concept, framing has become a valuable way to examine discourse, particularly in communication studies, sociology, and political science.[3] Defining frames as "schemata of interpretation" that help to classify and allow individuals to "locate, perceive, identify, and label a seemingly infinite number of concrete occurrences defined in its limits," Goffman's (1974) concept has frequently been employed in the examination of media texts as a way to investigate how events and issues are organized and made sense of by media professionals and their audiences (21).

Since Goffman, a number of useful definitions of the term frame have been created.[4] A particularly helpful one comes from Entman (1993), who describes a frame in the following way: "To frame is to select some aspects of a perceived reality and make them more salient in a communicating text, in such a way as to promote a particular problem definition, causal interpretation, moral evaluation, and/or treatment recommendation" (11). According to Entman (1993), salience can be emphasized by repetition, placement, or association with culturally familiar symbols. In addition, frames select by highlighting some features of reality while omitting others, and "the omission of potential problem definitions, explanations, evaluations and recommendations may be as critical as the inclusions" (Entman 1993: 54). In this way, frames define problems, diagnose causes, make moral judgments, and suggest remedies; they are powerful in their ability "to bring otherwise amorphous reality into a meaningful structure, making it more than the simple inclusion or exclusion of information. Thus, frames are active, information generating as well as screening devices" (Reese 2003: 11).

Framing research often asks "precisely how are issues constructed, discourse structured, and meanings developed?" (Reese 2003: 7). Frames are persistent over time as well as valuable for maintaining social order, and culture is permeated with them. While frames are relatively stable cultural structures, new frames are created and existing ones modified, replaced, or faded out. In essence, "frames provide the widely understood context for understanding new phenomena. When a topic is 'framed' its context is determined; its major tenets prescribed; individuals, groups and organizations are assigned the roles of protagonist, antagonist, or spectator; and the legitimacy of varied strategies for action is defined" (Hertog and McLeod 2003: 147).[5]

---

[3] Goffman (1974) attributes Bateson (1972) with originating the metaphor.

[4] For many other examples, see Iyengar (1991), Gamson and Modigliani (1989), Gitlin (1980), and Reese (2003).

[5] As Hertog and McLeod (2003) outline in their work, this chapter approaches frames as cultural rather than cognitive phenomena so that myths, narrative, and metaphors are understood to be at the basis of some of the most powerful frames because of the extensive meaning they carry to individuals. In addition, frames are viewed as content-based rather than format or structure-based in this chapter. While structure is certainly important in the creation of a content-based frame, formats themselves do not necessarily constitute a frame.

Despite the tendency for frame analysis research to be applied to media texts,[6] there has recently been a move beyond the media in its application. Importantly, Pan and Kosicki (2003) have moved framing from a focus on news discourse alone to argue that framing is an essential part of public deliberation. Defining public deliberation as "a process of collective and open reasoning, and discussion about the merits of public policy," the authors note that public deliberation is the essence of democracy and see political communication as being increasingly democratized so that opportunities for public participation are on the rise (36). Arguing that the discursive practice of framing can be done by all and is "not the exclusive province of political elites or media," Pan and Kosicki (2003) argue that people *construct* their understanding of issues "by tapping into the symbolic resources that are available to them in their everyday lives," such as via experiential knowledge, popular wisdom, and media discourse, and "combine such symbolic resources differently across varying situations . . . individuals *strategically* maneuver to "tame the information tide" and to communicate with others" (37, 39). Thus, individuals frame to make sense and to contest the frames of others.

Noting the conflict inherent in battles over framing, Pan and Kosicki (2003) refer to framing as an "ideological contest" over the scope of an issue as well as who is responsible or affected, which principles or values are relevant, and where the issue should be addressed. In this contest, "participants maneuver strategically to achieve their political and communicative objectives" (40). In addition, Pan and Kosicki (2003) note how framing is part of constructing a political spectacle in that it involves elite manipulations and performances, interpreting political activities and statements to construct the factuality of the political world so that in all, framing involves political drama and theater.

Interestingly for this paper, Pan and Kosicki (2003) also argue that frames create "discursive communities." In essence, discursive communities are created by those who share conventions and tacit rules of discourse so that "in framing an issue, each social aggregate "acts out" its discursive as well as sociological binding" (Pan and Kosicki 2003: 42). Examples of discursive communities that have been identified in previous framing research include political, strategic expert, scientific expert, and challenger discourses in a study on nuclear weapons public discourse (Meyer 1995) or specialist, official, and challenger discourses in the study of media nuclear discourse (Gamson and Modigliani 1989). According to Pan and Kosicki (2003), different individuals "develop their own frames of an issue based on their own ideological principles and institutionally specified roles" (43). In this way,

---

[6] Frame analysis is often associated with agenda-setting, or more broadly, media effects, research in that it claims that how a social problem is cast makes a big difference in how one responds to it (Reese 2003).

Framing not only frames an issue but also frames social groups. In other words, frames of an issue also frame framers. They define not only the categories of social groups. They shape not only the public discourse concerning an issue but also the discursive communities involved. Through framing, cultural categories are reproduced and enriched and the sociological boundaries of these physical units are also reinforced or remapped. It is in this sense that discourse helps construct the very social structure that serves as its physical support and political alignment that supports it. (Pan and Kosicki 2003: 44)

Paying attention to the discursive communities created within texts is imperative to the application of frame analysis. At the same time, it is important to recognize that social actors differ in their access to resources and their framing power. Here, resources are "the material, social structural, institutional, and cultural means that are available to an actor to promote his or her frame and to influence the language, context, and atmosphere of public deliberation concerning an issue" (Pan and Kosicki 2003: 44). Not surprisingly, different actors have access to different resources (so that elected officials have access to positions in the authority hierarchy while experts have academic standing resources, and public members can claim their voices as legitimate). And resources are clearly not equally distributed. By acknowledging the import of discursive communities in framing and access to resources, it becomes clear that framing is not a one-way street where elites manipulate the public. Instead, "framing is a multifaceted process in which influences travel in different directions" (Pan and Kosicki 2003: 45).

The Study

Applying frame analysis and its theoretical and analytical principles as outlined in the previous section, this paper works from Hertog and McLeod's (2003) suggestions on how to study frames.[7] The authors claim that the first step in a frame analysis is to identify the central concepts that make up varied frames, and that a common feature at the core of most frames is a basic conflict. Here, the choice of actors presenting information, ideas, and positions within a text is often an indicator of a central conflict. A second step in a frame analysis, in this approach, is to seek a master narrative or myth. As powerful organizing devices and efficient in making meaning, narratives and myths are "often widely shared and understood within a culture, and are especially prone to drawing in a wide

---

[7] Importantly, I differ from Hertog and McLeod's (2003) suggestions that deductively identifying frames is appropriate. The authors instruct readers to read widely in order to identify the various frames for the topic under study and thus, move deductively from the identification of the frame to the hypothesis to test the data. In this study, I move inductively from the data itself so that the frames are identified, or emerge, from the data.

array of additional beliefs, feelings, expectations, and values" (148). Interestingly, a challenge to frame analysis researchers in identifying myths or narratives is that they may not need to be mentioned often to have a profound effect in the process of framing and they may be difficult to identify within the discourse as a result. Finally, the authors note that each frame has its own vocabulary. However, identifying the repetition of certain adjectives, adverbs, verb tenses, and nouns may be less important than identifying the usage. For example, the use of *baby* versus *fetus* signals a very different approach to the topic of abortion. Vocabulary for Hertog and McLeod (2003) are similar to Miller and Riechert's (2003) call to identify frame terms. Following Entman's (1993) dictum that frames can be detected by probing for "the presence or absence of certain key words" (53), this study understands that while key words are not themselves the frames, key words are "indicative of perspectives, or points of view, by which issues and events can be discussed and interpreted" (Miller and Riechert 2003: 114). In this way, a researcher can qualitatively investigate the choice of words, figures of speech, pictures, catch phrases, and others used within a text. Noting issues such as salience and selection in a general sense (and not strictly in a quantifiable manner) is important to identifying frames.

With this approach to frame analysis in mind, an in-depth case study of the Somalia Affair and its commission was undertaken.[8] To investigate the frames being constructed within the commission on the Somalia Affair, primary documentary sources from the commission itself were utilized and an in-depth frame analysis on the data was performed; particular emphasis was put on the central concepts that made up the frames, myths, or master narratives being drawn upon as well as, most important, the vocabulary or frame terms being utilized to construct the framing process. In this way, the analysis was particularly sensitive to word use in the commission data. The sources included the commission documents such as the transcripts of the public hearings, the final report, written submissions, and research reports. In all, the documentary sources were many, and the analysis was undertaken on the almost 20,000 pages of data. Following such a detailed, qualitative, and inductive approach to data analysis allowed for a close examination of the framing work that was occurring within the commission in the Somalia Affair.

Findings

Upon analyzing the commission discourse, it became apparent that there were two very different frames of peacekeeping and its role in Canada being put forth by the participants. Most notably, it was the way that peacekeeping was defined,

---

[8] I followed the social constructivist case study approach outlined in Stark and Torrance (2006).

valued, and seen as an appropriate role for Canadians that was framed differently by two discursive communities identified from the commission data. The following section illustrates how peacekeeping and its related issues were constructed discursively in very different ways by those who could be seen to come from a "civilian" discursive community, such as the commissioners and the lawyers involved, and those in a "military" discursive community, as represented generally by the military witnesses and bureaucrats.[9] As I refer to it, this "culture clash" between the military and civilian discursive communities became very apparent upon detailed inspection, as were the unique frames these sides presented and the significant discursive battle that ensued in the commission discourse.

As I will illustrate, the framing work that can be identified within the discourse of the commission is found in varying places throughout the commission documents that I examined—in the transcripts of the public hearings (procedural hearings, pre-deployment hearings, and in-theater hearings), in the final report produced for the commission (executive summary as well as Volumes 1–5), and in the written submissions, the historical documents of the commission, and the research reports for the commission. In my analysis, I found that the transcripts of the public hearings and the final report were particularly fruitful for evidence of the framing process around peacekeeping. This will be apparent from the following discussion as I outline where evidence of the framing of peacekeeping occurred in the commission discourse.

Peacekeeping as a concept and its role for Canadians and their military was framed in very different terms by both the civilian and military discursive communities. Often, the civilian discursive community frames peacekeeping in terms of policing, mediating, and helping and assisting others, in contrast to soldiering, or military work, which is framed to include combat, force, or war. In contrast, the military discursive community frames peacekeeping and soldiering as one and the same, so that peacekeeping, from the military perspective, isn't distinguished from soldiering so that peacekeeping almost seems like an irrelevant term for the military discursive community. As the military discursive community frames it, peacekeeping involves combat, danger, and the use of force with casualties and carnage. In essence, while the civilian discursive community frames the issue of peacekeeping as a benevolent, assistive, and from this perspective, positive practice, the military discursive community tends to reject this frame

---

[9] The distinctions between the "civilian" and the "military" discursive communities arose from the analysis of the texts themselves. After much detailed analysis, it began to be clear that two very distinct constructions were being represented around the value of peacekeeping in a Canadian context. These differences were often represented discursively in a socially stratified way so that, generally speaking, the civilian perspective was often represented by people in the commission such as the commissioners, the commission counsel, and other civilian groups with standing. The military perspective was most often represented by people who were either in the Canadian Forces or the Department of National Defence. While these sociocultural differences cannot clearly be over-generalized, the tendency toward a culturally stereotypical representation was surprisingly palpable.

almost entirely as appropriate for their role, and presents their own frame of the practice of peacekeeping, thereby attempting to reframe peacekeeping and its role in Canada and for the Canadian military. Interestingly, peacekeeping did not appear to be as positive a frame for the military discursive community as it is for the civilian discursive community, as we will see.

The framing of peacekeeping by the civilian discursive community is often presented in terms of binary oppositions within the commission discourse, so that what is a peacekeeper, for instance, is presented as the opposite of the definition of a soldier; or peacekeeping is what Canadians do, not what Americans do, and so on. Most notably, the distinction made by the civilian discursive community in framing peacekeeping as directly opposed to soldiering was particularly interesting. We can see this at work in the final report, for example. After outlining the five characteristics that differentiate airborne forces like the CAR from more conventional forces (i.e., air mobility; quick reaction; flexibility in terms of tactical deployment; lightness of equipment; and suitability to low-intensity conflicts such as peacekeeping or peace enforcement), the report reads that "some would contend that there is a basic incompatibility between the elite parachutist's creed, including a commitment to fight on to the objective and never surrender, and the peacekeeper's constabulary ethic, which requires a commitment to the minimum use of force" (Final Report: 26). Here, the soldier who is trained to "never surrender" is put into a binary opposition with a peacekeeper who is required to have a commitment to the "minimum use of force" and a "constabulary ethic" (suggesting that a soldier is committed to more than the minimum use of force, for instance). This is particularly evidenced by the discursive move of the terms "basic incompatibility." Using the term "incompatibility" indicates that there is a major difference between these two ends so that they can't be seen as similar and can't be rejoined in some way. By opposing these concepts and related ideas behind peacekeeper and elite soldier, peacekeeping is being framed as entailing the opposite kind of work of the soldier, so that the two concepts or roles are seen as "incompatible" or entirely different. In this way, the concept of peacekeeper is being framed as the other extreme of the concept of soldier. Thus, the framing of peacekeeping in statements like this very often reflected the kind of extreme distinction outlined within the civilian discursive community between the two terms. This is notable for two reasons: first, because the framing of peacekeeping as opposed to soldiering is very typical of the civilian discursive community in this case; and second, because there is very little direct mention of who is to do the work of peacekeeping as framed in this manner, if not soldiers.[10]

---

[10] For the purposes of this analysis, I will refer to the authors of this report as the commissioners. While the commissioners themselves didn't pen every word in this report, the final report is understood to be "signed off" by the commissioners and is to represent their beliefs and opinions about the situation. That is, it is to represent their work. As a result, and to make the analysis more clear, I will discuss the report in terms of the commissioners' work.

Peacekeeping is also framed as "naturally" Canadian by the civilian discursive community and is tied into national values and identity issues within the commission discourse. For instance, the report notes that "peacekeeping has become a characteristic Canadian métier, a function distinguishing us from Americans and reinforcing our sovereignty and independence. Americans were seen to fight wars, but Canadians pictured themselves as working for peace" (Final Report: 198). This last statement is particularly telling in terms of the kind of framing work being done in the discourse of the commission. Here, peacekeeping, framed as "a characteristic Canadian métier" is held in contrast with fighting wars, and that of American behavior, while Canadians "work for peace" by the civilian discursive community. Extending the use of binary oppositions holds much symbolic power here so that the framing of peacekeeping by the civilian discursive community highlights the work of peace done by Canadians against the perceived warring of Americans. This kind of discursive construction also holds a potential great deal of power for Canadians, who, when pressed to define themselves, often claim to be "not American."

Many other similar statements are made throughout the final report, which work to represent the civilian discursive community's framing of peacekeeping. For instance, the following quote was directly inserted into the final report, taken from David Rudd's editorial in the *Ottawa Citizen* on February 12, 1995. Noting the role of the modern peacekeeper, it reads:

> The soldier of the 1990s must be flexible. He must be a diplomat, an aid worker, a policeman, as well as a warrior. He must exercise an unprecedented level of self-discipline by, in effect, programming himself to fit the prevailing situation. . . . The soldier of the 1990s must be better educated than ever before. He must be acquainted with the political, military and socio-cultural dynamics of the crisis area. . . . He must realize that as a representative of his country, his conduct will be held to extremely high standards. (Final Report: 559)

Here, the "soldier of the 1990s" is framed in terms associated with peacekeeping by the civilian discursive community. That is, soldiering is defined as work that entails "diplomacy," "aid," "policing," "self-discipline," and political, military and sociocultural education of the area. This is not generally the way that soldiering has been defined (i.e., as brave, patriotic, or involving battling, warring, fighting, combat, casualties, death, etc.). Instead, "the soldier of the 1990s" sounds a lot like the framing of peacekeeping that the civilian discursive community presents. Thus, while in many places the soldier is framed as doing the opposite kind of work as the peacekeeper by the civilian discursive community, at the same time, there is much discursive work to frame a peacekeeper as a soldier, so that soldier = peacekeeper in the civilian discursive frame. The framing of peacekeeping as being opposite to soldiering work, but at the same time, framing Canadian soldiers *as* peacekeepers, as being one and the same as peacekeepers, is an extremely interesting discursive move. In this way, today's "warrior" is not a warrior at all but a peacekeeper for the civilian discursive community. And this peacekeeper, beyond being a "representative of his country," is "held to extremely high standards." This kind of idealized language is also representative of the civilian discursive community's framing of peacekeeping and its role for Canadians.

Further evidence that the civilian discursive community constructs soldiers as peacekeepers in its framing can be found again in the final report when the importance of the Canadian Charter of Rights and Freedoms as guiding the Canadian Forces in terms of soldier development is noted. It reads:

> The values Canadians expect their soldiers to demonstrate in their actions and conduct abroad as makers and keepers of peace may be gleaned from the Charter. These values include fairness, decency, respect for human rights, compassion, and a strong sense of justice. We believe that the characteristics and values of the CF—founded on the traditional core values as reinforced through great sacrifice in waging war and securing peace—can and must be adapted to accommodate the evolving character of Canadian society. (Final Report: 1448)

This is very interesting discursive work in terms of what it suggests about the civilian framing of peacekeeping and its role for Canadians. First, the statement that "Canadians expect their soldiers . . . as makers and keepers of peace" directly connects the two terms again so that in the civilian discursive community's framing of peacekeeping, a Canadian soldier *is* a peacekeeper. Thus, here Canadian soldiers are defined as "makers and keepers of peace" first and foremost; and as makers and keepers of peace, they are expected to uphold the values of the Canadian Charter, so that "fairness," "decency," "respect for human rights," "compassion," and a "strong sense of justice" are understood as part of the job description for Canadian soldiers, framed as peacekeepers by this discursive community. The demand for Canadian soldiers to "adapt to accommodate the evolving character of Canadian society" appears to be noting the discrepancy between the framing work done by the civilian discursive community around peacekeeping and that followed or defined by the military. This works to establish proof of a frame battle occurring in the discourse, one that is interestingly noted by the participants themselves. In addition, by drawing on a major source of symbolic power in Canada, the Charter of Rights and Freedoms, the civilian discursive community is employing another myth in an effort to associate peacekeeping with positive connotations. Furthermore, in this example, there is very little leeway for a frame that includes combat, force, sacrifice, war, or even battle as part of the job description of Canadian soldiers. Instead, this frame presents soldiers as the very antithesis of what has traditionally been framed as military work—as makers and keepers of peace. In this way, the civilian discursive community is framing peacekeeping as Canadian soldiers' raison d'être in statements like this and by doing so, is relying or drawing on a powerful symbolic myth of Canadians as peacekeepers more generally.

This framing and the acknowledgment of a discursive battle is further evidenced when the civilian discursive community acknowledges that a frame different from that of the military discursive community exists. Within the report, the commissioners outline Canada's historical role as peacekeeper in Volume One, and claim:

> Despite Canada's distinguished role as peacekeeper, the Canadian military has been reluctant to embrace peacekeeping as a priority in defence policy. Its first priority remains the retention and advancement of its combat capabilities for the protection of Canadians and their interests and values at home and abroad, notwithstanding the fact that since the end of the Cold War, combat responsibilities have greatly diminished. (Final Report: 242)

We can see from this statement the civilian discursive community's framing of peacekeeping again. First, peacekeeping is framed as a "distinguished role" for Canadians. The positive connotations of the word "distinguished" (versus traditional, historical, or even notable, for example) imply that the commissioners believe this to be a positive and appropriate role. In contrast, however, the commissioners point out that the "Canadian military has been reluctant to embrace peacekeeping as a priority," thereby explicitly noting the differing frame on the issue. They continue that its "first priority" remains focused on its "combat capabilities." Again, we can see how peacekeeping is defined explicitly in opposition to combat within the civilian discursive community, which as we will see shortly, is not the way that peacekeeping is framed by the military discursive community. Furthermore, the commissioners, as representative of the civilian discursive community note their normative positioning and disapproval over this creation of priorities for the military when they state, "notwithstanding the fact that since the end of the Cold War, combat responsibilities have greatly diminished." This final sentence implies that the military's prioritization of their role and needs is out of line with the geo-political realities of today.

In contrast to the framing of peacekeeping that is presented in various ways throughout the commission discourse by the civilian discursive community, the military discursive community frames it in very different terms. This was most obvious in the public hearing transcripts rather than in the final report.[11] Throughout the public hearings, witnesses were often given ample room to

---

[11] This could be argued to speak to the issue of the resources available for discursive communities and their framing work so that the civilian discursive community was able to utilize the final report to elucidate their frame, while the military discursive community had the public hearings and transcripts as their major dissemination resource in this context.

postulate on their beliefs and opinions on everything from what occurred in Somalia, to the values that a good leader must have, to whether the CAR should have been disbanded. At one place in the public hearing transcripts, a participant, Colonel (Ret.) Joly, describes his experience with returning soldiers to Canada and frames peacekeeping in a way that is very different from the frame presented by the civilian discursive community. He states:

> And when I saw the repeated news reports of other Canadians who had been maimed and eventually saw them in NDMC [National Defence Medical Centre] when they returned to Canada and when I recognized the absolute horror in which—not horror, poor choice of words, but the terrible conditions under which we sent our troops to places like Yugoslavia where the warring factions did not allow them freedom of movement, where they use them for target practice, where they were tied to poles, where they expected air strikes to occur, where they were taken hostage by people who we were supposed to be trying to protect and support, I came to realize in my own mind that we should not be spilling Canadian blood in that ungrateful piece of soil that we have sent so many Canadians to and in which so many Canadians have died. And so I found it extremely difficult for me to be assembling contingents of young Canadian men and women who were my son's age to be sent to that country. And I found it extremely difficult to look at them when they came back and see the condition they were in, and recognize that nobody in Canada really gave a shit about what happened to them because they became a footnote in history. (Transcripts, Vol. 16, Wednesday, November 15, 1995, PG 3066)

This framing of peacekeeping is quite different from the often idealized or benevolent framing put forward by the civilian discursive community. Here, peacekeeping is associated with "repeated" "maim[ing]," "horror," and "terrible conditions." The people involved in the mission are cited as the "warring factions" (versus, for instance, participants, competing sides, or even civilians) who used the Canadians for "target practice," tied them to poles, put them on the receiving end of air strikes, took them hostage—these were "the people who we were supposed to be trying to protect and support." This latter statement is interesting in that the framing of peacekeeping by the military discursive community here privileges the act of protection and support as inherent to the concept, rather than the functions of diplomats, policemen, or aid workers as we saw in the civilian community's framing. While this may seem to be a very slight difference, the use of terms like "protect" particularly emphasize the role of "defending" or "guarding," "looking after" or "caring for" that the military discursive community framed as included in peacekeeping. Instead of "making and keeping peace" here, the military discursive community frames peacekeeping as keeping people from harm. In this example, then, the framing of peacekeeping is associated with what we traditionally understand to be a war situation—where danger and threat of death lurk around every corner and where death and violence and blood abound. Instead of highlighting the "helping" aspect of peacekeeping, Joly, as part of the military discursive community, frames peacekeeping as an activity where Canadian blood is spilled and Canadians have died, specifically in an "ungrateful piece of soil." Use of the term "ungrateful" is a very interesting discursive selection as it is in opposition to how peacekeeping is framed in the civilian discursive community—that the recipients of such a "helpful" action are usually grateful for the Canadians' assistance. Instead, within the military framing, peacekeeping is posited as a very fruitless effort that often ends in death. In all, this statement is a very telling one in the way it represents the kind of framing of peacekeeping the military perspective tends to provide within the commission discourse.

In a similar way, the peacekeeping that the Canadian soldiers did while in Somalia was framed in terms of a war context by quite a few of those from the military discursive community, particularly with the witnesses. In another excerpt, for example, a witness, Major Moreau, described the dangerous combat-type situation that they encountered in Somalia:

> So we had to assume, every time we left the camp, that everybody was a threat. . . . They favoured ambushed and sniping attacks because they knew the city very well. They knew the lay of the ground so they could maximize the use of buildings, small alleys to try to attract us into sideroads and ambush us. Other tactics that they were using, at one point, one of the warlords distributed toy guns to kids, now when you're patrolling late evening or early morning it's not always easy to make the difference between a toy gun and a real weapon. That was done deliberately in the hope that somebody from the Coalition would shoot a kid so we would get bad publicity. (Transcripts, Vol. 52, Monday, April 1, 1996, PG 10351)

Within this excerpt, the peacekeeping mission[12] that Canadian soldiers were on in Somalia is framed as fraught with "threat[s]" and danger where "ambush[es]" and "sniping attacks" were the favored method of attack. Using terms like "ambush" and "sniping attacks" to describe the situation they were in is an interesting discursive move as it highlights the high level of anxiety that the soldiers felt. Choosing to highlight the ambush and sniping actions draws attention to the high level of uncertainty and anxiety that the soldiers felt, as they never knew when they might be under attack, and thus, presumably felt as though they were *always potentially* under attack. Also, the framing of the peacekeeping situation is one in which the threat was strategic, so that they were

---

[12] While the Somalia mission was actually a peace-enforcement mission, it was most often understood and framed as a peacekeeping mission, both within the commission texts as well as within popular media representations of the events.

using "small alleys to try to attract [them] into sideroads and ambush [them.]" The "warlords" within the peacekeeping context ensured that the soldiers felt anxious by providing "toy guns," thereby increasing the possibility that a civilian child might be shot and "get bad publicity." All of these discursive choices around the mission in Somalia work to frame peacekeeping in a very different light from the one presented in the civilian context. Certainly, danger, threat, anxiety, and the strategic and manipulative nature of the enemy (the "warlords) in a combat-oriented situation are being privileged within the military discursive community's frame of peacekeeping as opposed to the diplomatic, assistive, and policing role that is emphasized in the civilian discursive community's frame.

The combat-focused and dangerous frame of peacekeeping in general, but the Somalia mission in particular, was evidenced in multiple places throughout the commission discourse by the military discursive community. For example,

> . . . I was trying to indicate that there was, in fact, some danger to these patrols. It wasn't just a matter of going downtown and walking around. From either this alley or one very similar just a little bit to the south of it, my patrol was fired on directly from this ally. Three shots were fired directly at my scouts who returned two shots into the ally and basically ended the firing right then. No casualties were found, but there was a requirement to carry weapons in the alert position particularly at night and be vigilant at all times because you never knew when something was going to happen. (Transcripts, Vol 54, Wednesday, April 3, 1996, PG 10713)

In this excerpt, as in the one previously, the military discursive community participants frame their experiences in peacekeeping as very different from the civilian discursive community's perspective presented prior, so that "it wasn't just a matter of going downtown and walking around" (which one may assume to be the case under the understanding of peacekeeping from a civilian discursive community framing), but that there was "some danger to these patrols." "Shots" were "fired" and "returned," and "weapons" were to be carried in the "alert" position and "vigilan[ce]" was required at all times. Again, we can see how the framing of peacekeeping is an experience fraught with danger, combat, and threat of death by members of the military discursive community.

For the civilian discursive community, peacekeeping is framed in contrast to war (unlike the military discursive community's frame as we saw earlier), and this is often tied to beliefs and statements about the appropriate kind of training for soldiers. For instance, when discussing the training used to prepare Canadian Forces personnel for missions, the commissioners make the statement that "peacekeeping, and even peace enforcement, differ fundamentally from the conduct of war" (Final Report: 28). The report continues to point out that General Purpose Combat Training (GPCT) is the "traditional method of preparing to wage war," which involves basic soldiering skills, including firing specific weapons, throwing grenades, achieving fitness standards, applying military first aid, performing individual fieldcraft, performing nuclear/biological/chemical defence, applying mind awareness, navigating using a map and compass, communicating using communications equipment, and identifying fighting vehicles and aircraft. (Final Report: 28)

The report, and thus the civilian discursive community, frames "basic soldiering skills including firing specific weapons, throwing grenades," and similar actions as "the traditional method of preparing to wage war" and thus, as naturally combat oriented via the use of terms like "defence," "fieldcraft," "fighting," "firing," and "weapons" (Final Report: 28). In contrast, the statement after this description of GPTC reads, "In the Canadian Forces, GPCT forms the basis for peacekeeping training" (Final Report: 28). By citing peacekeeping training directly after this list of combat-oriented training, the commissioners appear to be relying once again on a binary opposition between war and peacekeeping (while the military discursive community frames peacekeeping as equal in practice to war, or peacekeeping = war). The implied inappropriateness of this relationship between peace and combat, that peacekeeping should be non-combat-related, for the civilian discursive community at least, is made clearer later in the report when the commissioners state:

Today's soldiers must be more than avid warriors. They must exercise skills that fit more naturally within the realms of civilian policing, diplomacy and social service. . . . Suffice to say that a mix of generic and mission-specific training beyond GPCT seems to be required. Peacekeeping soldiers require an understanding of the peacekeeper's roles and responsibilities; they must learn advanced techniques of negotiation and conflict resolution to be effective; the diversity of their assignments demands sensitivity to issues of intercultural relations; they require an appreciation of the full gamut of UN procedures affecting such matters as the establishment of buffer zones, the supervision and monitoring of cease-fires, and the protection of humanitarian relief efforts. The modern peacekeeper must know how to establish and maintain law and order, impose crowd control, conduct searches, and handle detainees, while at the same time lending assistance to relief efforts and co-operating with humanitarian agencies. These general skills must be supplemented by an acquired knowledge of the language, culture, geography, history, and political background of the theatre of operations. (Final Report: 28)

This example is an excellent one to display the way that peacekeeping was framed by the civilian discursive community. In this way, peacekeepers are framed by the civilian discursive community as needing to be "more than avid warriors," and thereby distancing "today's soldiers" from a combat-related role.

In this way, it is no longer enough, in this framing, to be an avid warrior. Instead, "today's soldiers" must "exercise skills that fit more naturally within realms of civilian policing, diplomacy and social service." Here, the framing insinuates that being an avid warrior doesn't fit naturally into policing, diplomacy, and social service, and thus, draws on the binary opposition of war and peace once again. Furthermore, by drawing on this opposition, the discourse here frames combat-related activities, or "warrior" activities out of the role of the soldier altogether, thereby equating soldier = peacekeeper again. They are, in fact, termed "peacekeeping soldiers"; thus they are not differentiated as two separate entities but are seen as one and the same role so that soldiers in Canada *are* peacekeepers. By suggesting that the "peacekeeping soldiers" require more specific training to understand the "peacekeeper's roles and responsibilities" and that "they must learn advanced techniques of negotiation and conflict resolution to be effective," as well as be "sensitiv[e] to issues of intercultural relations," and so on, it is the peacekeeping role that is being emphasized over the soldier here. As the report notes that "establish[ing] buffer zones," "supervis[ing] and monitoring cease-fires," and "protect[ing] . . . humanitarian relief efforts" is their raison d'etre, the "soldier" role of the "peacekeeping soldier" eventually gets eradicated altogether by the end of this statement and framing work. In the excerpt, what was once the "soldier" and "avid warrior" becomes the "peacekeeping soldier," and finally "the modern peacekeeper" in the end. This is incredibly telling in terms of the framing of the role of Canadians within the definition of peacekeeping in the civilian discursive community's framing of the issues. The roles of the "peacekeeper," including "maintain[ing] law and order, impos[ing] crowd control, conduct[ing] searches, and handl[ing] detainees" becomes the work of "today's soldier." Thus, "today's soldier" *is* a peacekeeper within the civilian discursive frame.

In contrast to the commissioners and lawyers who can be seen to claim that Canadian soldiers should have received more specific peacekeeping training to prepare for Somalia, the military discursive community generally rejects this frame. One military witness, for instance, in response to a question about whether the military should have more specific peacekeeping (or mission) training, replied, "I believe that the army is trained for one thing and that is to fight a war" (Transcripts, Vol 4P, Wednesday, June 21, 1995, PG 645P). Again, the framing of soldiers = soldiers, and thus, rejecting the civilian frame of soldiers = peacekeepers, is being established here. While the civilian discursive frame attempts to distance the role of the soldier from combat, the military discursive frame emphatically embraces this as the first and foremost role. This is representative of the kind of framing work done by the military discursive community in regard to the use of force and the necessary training that the soldiers undergo in this respect. Here, it is evident that despite the civilian discursive community's framing of soldiers as peacekeepers (as presented in the definitional work, for instance), the military discursive community highlights the combat role. Differing frames, and thus norm systems, are being presented within the commission discourse in this way, evidenced by the debate within the commission around the framing of peacekeeping and its role for Canadians.

A related example of the "peacekeeping versus combat" frame occurs when a commissioner asks whether combat skills are translatable to peace-keeping operations. Here, the commissioner, as representative of the civilian discursive community, appears to equate combat as bad and peacekeeping as good. In response, a member of the military discursive community displays his difficulty with distinguishing between peacekeeping and soldiering so that soldiering is the only frame presented again:

> Lieutenant-General (Ret) Foster: I used to describe our shooting programs as shoot to live and you shoot to live. We're talking about survival. I wouldn't know any other way to describe this kind of training other than combat. Now the distinction between that and peacekeeping, those skills, the ability to do reconnaissance, the ability to assess troops that the UN is monitoring or watching or supervising, the ability to know where mortar fire is coming from, or the difference between mortar fire and artillery and what that means to you, the difference between a.50 caliber machine gun and a rifle, are all very useful peacekeeping skills and they come from learning to train for combat. (Transcripts, Vol. 3, Thursday, October 5, 1995, p. 484)

As we can see from this excerpt, there is a fundamental difference in values or perspectives here between the military discursive community and the civilian. The civilian community, as displayed by the commissioner's comment, is attempting to distinguish between peacekeeping and combat training, as these are framed differently from this perspective. In contrast, the military perspective appears to refuse this frame, and furthermore, to have a hard time understanding the frame the commissioner is presenting. For instance, the witness first describes their "shooting programs as shoot to live," indicating again the combat-oriented role of the soldier. Indicating that "survival" is the key to this kind of training, Foster also notes his difficulty with the contrary frame presented when he states, "I wouldn't know any other way to describe this kind of training as combat." In this way, Foster is clearly having difficulty making a distinction between combat and peacekeeping training. In the next statement, Foster is attempting to ap-proach the topic via the frame presented by the civilian discursive community when he states "the distinction between that and peacekeeping" and addresses the specific skills that he sees as relevant to peacekeeping, such as "ability to do reconnaissance, the ability to assess troops that the UN is monitoring or watch-ing or supervising, the ability to know where mortar fire is coming from," and so on. This is interesting in that Foster returns to a combat-based frame to describe the specific skills. By highlighting that "fire," "artillery," and "machine gun" training are "all very useful peacekeeping skills," he works to show how mem-bers of the military discursive community tend not to distinguish between combat and peacekeeping. This is a useful example to display the way that the civilian community and the military community framed their understandings and opinions from two very different perspectives, thereby often making the discussion around particular issues quite difficult.

Conclusion

As this chapter has demonstrated, the discourse within the Somalia commission was notable for the "culture clash" that arose between two discursive communities—the civilian and the military—around the framing of peacekeeping and its place for Canadians. While the differences in the framing work were often subtle, clear demarcation between the communities could be traced. I would like to summarize them here briefly before discussing the potential ramification of these findings. I've included a table to illuminate (table 6.1).

The framing work that the discursive communities performed around the issue of peacekeeping can be broken down into two broad categories—that of the practice of peacekeeping and the role of the Canadian military, although these categories often overlapped within the framing process in the discourse. As we saw, the civilian discursive community framed the practice of peacekeeping as distinct from, and even opposed to, the practice of soldiering. That is, while peacekeeping was framed in terms such as policing, mediating, helping, aid working, education, and so on, soldiering was framed in combative terms such as never surrendering, a commitment to fight, or to wage war. In addition, the practice of peacekeeping is framed as the preferred option within the discourse, thereby associating the practice of peacekeeping as the positive option and thus implicitly suggesting that soldiering has a negative connotation by omission (although this wasn't made explicit).

In contrast, the military discursive community frames peacekeeping and soldiering as the same practice, so that the distinction between the two is irrelevant or non-existent. In this way, when a member of the military discursive community frames "peacekeeping," he draws on what the civilian discursive community would consider a "soldiering" frame. In this way, when discussing the practice of peacekeeping, terms like "combat," "force," "weapons," "danger,"

TABLE 6.1

The Framing of "Peacekeeping" among the Civilian and Military Discursive Communities

	Civilian Discursive Community	Military Discursive Community
Practice of Peacekeeping	Peacekeeping ≠ Soldiering (Positive) (Negative)	Peacekeeping = Soldiering (Negative) (Positive)
Role of Canadian Military	Peacekeepers = Soldiers (Positive) (Negative)	Peacekeepers ≠ Soldiers (Negative) (Positive)

"casualties," "carnage," or "threat" are used by members of the military discursive community, thereby presenting a very different frame around the practice of peacekeeping from the one used by the civilian discursive community. The frame for peacekeeping, as presented by the military discursive community, is the same frame as that used to distinguish soldiering from peacekeeping by the civilian discursive community. However, the military discursive community doesn't see peacekeeping and soldiering as being distinct and thus frames peacekeeping *as equal to* soldiering. For the military discursive community, peacekeeping and soldiering are the same practice. Despite this, the practice of peacekeeping was associated with negative connotations for some of the members of the military discursive community, as we saw.

In terms of the role of the Canadian military, the distinctions between the frames become even more complex. For the civilian discursive community, despite the fact that this group frames the practice of peacekeeping as *not equal to* soldiering, they nonetheless frame peacekeepers *as equal to* soldiers when discussing the role of the Canadian military. Thus, when members of the civilian discursive community refer to peacekeepers, they equate peacekeepers to soldiers in Canada (i.e., "today's soldier," "peacekeeping soldiers," etc.) so that Canadian soldiers are framed as peacekeepers as their first and foremost role. In fact, soldiers are almost non-existent in this frame so that peacekeepers are all that Canadians have (versus soldiers). Again, the peacekeeper role is presented in positive connotations over the soldier role for Canadians by the civilian discursive community.

In contrast, the military discursive community frames the role of the Canadian military as soldiers first, and thus, as *not equal to* peacekeepers. Within the discourse, the military discursive community repeatedly framed the role of the military, in its training, practice, and history, as being first and foremost soldiers. When pressed to consider the military's role as peacekeepers by the civilian discursive community, the military discursive community members continued to frame their work in words associated with acting as soldiers (combat, force, weapons, threat, etc.) even when referring to peacekeeping explicitly. In this way, the members of the military discursive community seemed to have great difficulty seeing themselves as peacekeepers under the civilian discursive community's frame. For the military discursive community, soldiering and being soldiers are framed in positive terms.

In all, the culture clash in terms of the framing of peacekeeping is evident in this way—the civilian discursive community frames peacekeeping as distinct from soldiering, and yet sees Canadian soldiers to be peacekeepers as their primary or main role, while the military discursive community sees peacekeeping and soldiering as the same work (and thus, "peacekeeping" as a term is almost irrelevant) and sees soldiers as primarily soldiers, not peacekeepers. While the framing work within the military discursive community could be argued to be more consistent in this way (a soldier is a soldier is a soldier so that peacekeeping is irrelevant—and perhaps a buzzword thrown easily aside), the framing work within the civilian discursive community is fascinating for its inherent contradiction. In this way, while peacekeeping is distinguished from soldiering, with the two as polar opposite practices within this community's frame, this community nonetheless sees Canadian soldiers as its peacekeepers. Moving beyond the discourse, trying to rationalize this contradictory frame for Canadian soldiers is seemingly problematic, for how can Canadian soldiers be defined as soldiers (and thus practice combat, force, use weapons, participate in war, etc.) and at the same time be peacekeepers (who are flexible, diplomatic, educated, aid workers, etc.)?

Beyond the inherent contradiction within the civilian discursive community's framing of peacekeeping, these findings speak to some larger issues. First, these findings indicate that in places of public deliberation such as in a commission, frames do in fact also frame social groups as Pan and Kosicki (2003) suggested. Within the Somalia commission discourse, the cultural categories associated with a civilian framing and a military framing were reproduced, which works to construct social structure via institutional discourse. Second, the framing work was clearly done by more than social elites in the commission discourse. While political and social elites certainly had their opportunity to frame, and arguably had great access to resources (via the final report, for example), framing work was done by all. Both elite and populace alike had a chance to frame and to display their framing work within this public arena. Third, the framing work done by the civilian discursive community draws heavily on the Canadian myth of peacekeeping. Since the Suez Crisis in 1956, the image of Canadians as non-violent and peaceful, mainly through the image of the peacekeepers who help to make the world a better place, has been ingrained into the country's national construct. Canadians often purport to see themselves as peacekeeping, mediating, neutral, impartial, and non-aggressive actors—particularly on the world stage. This "core myth," traceable to Pearson's diplomatic efforts during the Suez Crisis and his ensuing Nobel Peace Prize, has come to represent an important piece of the Canadian national construct, and at the same time, it has allowed the governments of the day to strategically pursue Canada's political and economic interests. While it is impossible to go into great detail on this myth in the concluding pages of this chapter, it is important to note that evidence of this myth was clearly constructed and reproduced within the framing by the civilian discursive community. It was not as evident within the military discursive framing work, and this may help to explain the distinct frames that were presented therein. Finally, the distinct framing by the discursive communities on peacekeeping was never resolved in the commission discourse. That is, both the civilian discursive community and the military discursive community remained consistent in their contradictory framing of peacekeeping and its role for Canadians throughout the commission discourse. That this discursive battle occurred throughout the commission was referenced within the final report, as were indications that it was never resolved by the two communities. This may help to explain, in part, why the scandal of the Somalia Affair has continued to plague the Canadian military. When the military discursive community frames this issue in such a different manner as the civilian discursive community, resolution that can be agreed upon by both communities seems almost impossible.

In relation to what these findings suggest more broadly about discourses of war and peace, we can see how war and peace are, on one hand, defined in opposition to each other as Hodges suggests in the introduction to this book. However, in this case, the binary opposition around war and peace is framed around the action of peacekeeping, so that *peacekeeping as war* is put into opposition with *peacekeeping as peace*. In this way, it is actually the behavior of peacekeeping that is framed in opposition. *Peacekeeping as war*, as framed by the military discursive community, includes

- Combat
- Force
- Never surrendering
- Maiming
- Horror
- Terrible conditions
- Support
- Ungrateful recipients
- Threats
- Ambushes
- Sniper attacks
- Danger
- Shots
- Alert
- Vigilance
- Fighting
- Firing
- Weapons

In contrast, *peacekeeping as peace* is presented within the civilian discursive community in terms such as

- Policing/constabulary ethic
- Mediating
- Helpful
- Assistive/aiding
- Benevolent
- Commitment to minimum use of force
- Diplomacy
- Self-discipline

- ¤ Makers and keepers of peace
- ¤ Fair
- ¤ Decent
- ¤ Respectful of human rights
- ¤ Compassionate
- ¤ Strong sense of justice

These binary oppositions around the role of peacekeeping are certainly present within the discourse; what is particularly interesting about the commission case is that when examining which of the terms in binary opposition move into a privileged position depends on which discursive community you're referring to. And it depends upon context as well. For example, when considering which of the *peacekeeping as war/peacekeeping as peace* binary oppositions takes precedence within the civilian discursive community, it's clear that peace, via the preferred action of peacekeepers, is privileged generally. However, in a more complex way, the two terms are often conflated, rather than opposed, so that the actors who should be conducting the described peaceful actions (peacekeepers) are actually Canadian soldiers who are usually associated with warfare.

In contrast, when examining which term the military discursive community privileges, it is also quite clear that of the two, they posit *peacekeeping as war* to be in a privileged position. For this group, however, *peacekeeping as war* is also conflated with *peacekeeping as peace*, but in a very different way from that of the civilian discursive community. For the military discursive community, this opposition is conflated to such an extent that *peacekeeping as peace* almost seems non-existent, or impossible. Even when engaged in peacekeeping in this discursive context, the military discursive community see themselves as engaged in war and heightened conflict. In this way, the Canadian example may begin to illustrate that the war/peace dichotomy may not be complex enough to take into account the various ways that citizens and national actors utilize these discursive constructs. And while these examples show that traditional conceptions of peace as the end or absence of war may be evident within this discourse, they point more to the fact that discourses of war and peace are complex and nuanced. Even within a relatively stable discursive community, these terms can be drawn upon and used in very different ways to achieve different goals. It is this complexity that needs much more scholarly attention if we are to begin to untangle the intricate strands of discourses of war and peace.

References

Bateson, Gregory. 1972. *Steps to an Ecology of Mind: Collected Essays in Anthropology, Psychiatry, Evolution, and Epistemology*. New York: Ballantine.

Bercuson, David. 1997. *Significant Incident: Canada's Army, the Airborne, and the Murder in Somalia*. Toronto: McClelland and Stewart.

Cairns, Alan. 1990. "Reflections on Commission Research." In *Commissions of Inquiry*, Paul Pross, Innis Christie, and John Yogis (eds.), 87–108. Toronto: Carswell.

Dawson, Grant. 2007. *Here Is Hell: Canada's Engagement in Somalia*. Vancouver: UBC Press.

Desbarats, Peter. 1997. *Somalia Cover-Up: A Commissioner's Journal*. Toronto: McClelland and Stewart.

Entman, Robert. 1993. "Framing: Toward Clarification of a Fractured Paradigm." *Journal of Communication* 43(4): 51–58.

Gamson, William and Andre Modigliani. 1989. "Media Discourse and Public Opinion on Nuclear Power: A Constructionist Approach." *American Journal of Sociology* 95: 1–37.

Gitlin, Todd. 1980. *The Whole World Is Watching*. Berkeley: University of California Press.

Goffman, Erving. 1974. *Frame Analysis: An Essay on the Organization of Experience*. Boston: Northeastern University Press.

Government of Canada. 1997. *Dishonoured Legacy: The Lessons of the Somalia Affair. Report of the Commission of Inquiry into the Deployment of Canadian Forces to Somalia*. Ottawa: Canadian Government Publishing.

Gubrium, Jaber and James Holstein. 2003. "Analyzing Interpretive Practice." In *Strategies of Qualitative Inquiry*, Norman Denzin and Yvonna Lincoln (eds.), 214–48. London: Sage.

Hertog, James and Douglas McLeod. 2003. "A Multiperspectival Approach to Framing Analysis: A Field Guide." In *Framing Public Life: Perspectives on Media and Our Understanding of the Social World*, Stephen Reese, Oscar Gandy, and August Grant (eds.), 139–62. Mahwah, NJ: Lawrence Erlbaum.

Iyengar, Shanto. 1991. *Is Anyone Responsible? How Television Frames Political Issues*. Chicago: University of Chicago Press.

Manson, Allan and David Mullan (eds.). 2003. *Commissions of Inquiry: Praise or Reappraise?* Toronto: Irwin Law.

Maloney, Sean. 2005. "From Myth to Reality Check; From Peacekeeping to Stabilization." *Policy Options* September: 40–46.

Meyer, David. 1995. "Framing National Security: Elite Public Discourse on Nuclear Weapons during the Cold War." *Political Communication* 12: 173–92.

Miller, M. Mark and Bonnie Riechert. 2003. "The Spiral of Opportunity and Frame Resonance: Mapping the Issue Cycle in News and Public Discourse. In *Framing Public Life: Perspectives on Media and Our Understanding of the Social World*, Stephen Reese, Oscar Gandy, and August Grant (eds.), 107–22. Mahwah, NJ: Lawrence Erlbaum.

Pan, Zhongdang and Gerald Kosicki. 2003. "Framing as Strategic Action in Public Deliberation." In *Framing Public Life: Perspectives on Media and Our Understanding of the Social World*, Stephen Reese, Oscar Gandy, and August Grant (eds.), 35–66. Mahwah, NJ: Lawrence Erlbaum.

Potter, Jonathan. 2004. "Discourse Analysis." In *Handbook of Data Analysis*, Melissa Hardy and Alan Bryman (eds.), 607–24. London: Sage.

Potter, Jonathan and Margaret Wetherell. 1987. *Discourse and Social Psychology: Beyond Attitudes and Behavior*. London: Sage.

Pross, Paul, Innis Christie, and John Yogis (eds.). 1990. *Commissions of Inquiry*. Toronto: Carswell.

"Rampant Racism in the Airborne Regiment." 1995, January 15. CBC Digital Archives. www.cbc.ca/archives/categories/war-conflict/peacekeeping/the-somalia-affair/ rampant-racism-in-the-airborne-regiment.html.

Razack, Sherene. 2004. *Dark Threats and White Knights: The Somalia Affair, Peacekeeping, and the New Imperialism.* Toronto: University of Toronto Press.

Reese, Stephen. 2003. "Prologue—Framing Public Life: A Bridging Model for Media Research." In *Framing Public Life: Perspectives on Media and Our Understanding of the Social World*, Stephen Reese, Oscar Gandy, and August Grant (eds.), 7–31. Mahwah, NJ: Lawrence Erlbaum.

Salter, Liora. 1990. "The Two Contradictions in Public Inquiries." In *Commissions of Inquiry*, Paul Pross, Innis Christie, and John Yogis (eds.), 173–96. Toronto: Carswell.

Stark, Sheila and Harry Torrance. 2005. "Case Study." In *Research Methods in the Social Sciences*, Bridget Somekh and Cathy Lewin (eds.), 33–40. London: Sage.

Tonkiss, Fran. 2004. "Analyzing Text and Speech: Content and Discourse Analysis." In *Researching Society and Culture*, Clive Seale (ed.), 367–82. London: Sage.

Wood, Linda and Rolf Kroger. 2000. *Doing Discourse Analysis: Methods for Studying Action in Talk and Text.* London: Sage.

7

Promising without Speaking

MILITARY REALIGNMENT AND POLITICAL PROMISING IN JAPAN

Chad Nilep

Introduction

US Marine Corps Air Station Futenma, an American military base in Okinawa, Japan, has long been unpopular with local residents. This chapter discusses a plan to relocate the base and focuses particularly on charges that former Japanese Prime Minister Yukio Hatoyama failed to deliver on a promise to remove the base from Okinawa Prefecture in 2010. Data come primarily from news coverage and editorials during Hatoyama's election campaign and administration. I will argue that the promise of action came not from any particular speech by Mr. Hatoyama but was an interdiscursive achievement involving Hatoyama, members of his cabinet, the main opposition party, and the Japanese news media. I discuss the concept of a metaphorical promise, an expectation of future action created not through any specific speech act but through complexes of social interaction.

In 1945, during the Second World War, US Army and Marine divisions launched an attack on Okinawa and the Ryūkyū Islands in the south of Japan. The plan was to seize the islands in order to build a forward base from which to attack the main islands of the Japanese archipelago. Anticipating such an attack, the Japanese military had fortified Okinawa and the surrounding area, conscripting some 20,000 local men and boys in the process (Fisch 1987). In fierce fighting from April to June 1945, the US forces defeated the Japanese troops defending the islands. A US Marine Corps estimate suggests that more than 107,000 Japanese fighters were killed during the battle, while US losses included 38,000 killed, wounded, or missing in action, plus an additional 26,000 noncombat casualties (Nichols and Shaw 1955).

Following the Battle of Okinawa, the US Army established an administration to govern the islands while building bases from which to continue the war (Fisch 1987). In August of 1945, following the atomic bombings of Hiroshima and Nagasaki, Japan surrendered to the Allied Forces, ending the fighting. Japan was occupied by American and British Commonwealth forces from 1945 to 1952, during which time control of Okinawa and the surrounding Ryūkyū Islands was shifted from the Army to a US civil administration. In practice, however, policies and programs of the military and civilian administrations were largely unchanged (Fisch 1987). The Japanese Constitution, accepted in 1947, renounced war and committed the nation not to establish military forces.[1] US forces in Okinawa therefore continued to build bases to serve in place of Japanese forces. With the start of the Cold War and the establishment of a communist government in China, Okinawa's proximity to US interests in the Philippines, Taiwan, and Guam also made it a valuable staging ground for American forces (Fisch 1987).

Under the 1952 peace treaty that formally ended the war, administrative control of Okinawa was ceded to the United States (Treaty of Peace with Japan 1952). The islands were administered by the United States from 1952 until 1972, when they were returned to Japanese control. During this time dozens of Marine, Air Force, Navy, and Army bases were established in the islands that now comprise Okinawa Prefecture, and many remain there even after the islands' return to Japan.

While many Japanese people favor the presence of US troops, which are thought to deter aggression from neighboring states, the majority in Okinawa are less sanguine. Although Okinawa comprises less than 1 percent of Japan's land area, it hosts nearly 75 percent of US military installations in the country (Ministry of Defense 2006). The large military presence creates noise, land use conflicts, and safety issues, including occasional military accidents and frequent traffic incidents. US Marine Corps Air Station Futenma, an installation of more than 1,200 acres (500 hectares) in the middle of the city of Ginowan, has been a particular focus for Okinawans uneasy with the US military presence (Inoue 2007). Futenma came under increased criticism in 1995 when a twelve-year-old girl was abducted and raped by US Marines stationed there (*Economist* 2010). In 1996 Tokyo and Washington began negotiations to remove Air Station Futenma from Ginowan and to return the land and facilities to Japanese control (Inoue 2007).

Today, more than a decade after the start of negotiations and five years after Tokyo and Washington agreed on a realignment plan, Air Station Futenma remains in Ginowan. The 2006 realignment plan called for the Marines at Futenma to be split between locations in Guam and elsewhere in Okinawa. Press coverage in 2009 and 2010 suggested that then-prime minister Yukio Hatoyama had promised to remove the Marines from Okinawa entirely, a promise that he failed to deliver. Yet there is no single moment, no clear speech in which Hatoyama commits himself and his government to such a

---

[1] Japan today has a de facto military called the Self Defence Forces. The United States nonetheless commits to defend Japan against military attack under treaty and status of forces agreements (Treaty of Mutual Cooperation and Security 1960).

course of action. Instead, the "promise" evolved over the course of several months in the words of many individuals. This chapter explores the genesis of that promise and the interpersonal nature of political promising, as well as ideologies of political promising as an individual speech act. It suggests that, as peace is not merely the absence of war, political accord is not merely the absence of discordant speech.

Political Promising

In "Read My Article," Jane Hill (2001) undertakes an investigation of political promising in the United States by investigating a speech by candidate George H.W. Bush during the 1988 Republican National Convention. In his speech, Bush predicted, "The Congress will push me to raise taxes . . . and I'll say to them, 'Read my lips: No new taxes'" (qtd. in Hill 2001). When President Bush accepted a 1990 budget that included new taxes as well as an increase in rates, newspapers and other commentators accused him of breaking a promise. Members of Bush's White House staff and former campaign staff insisted, on the contrary, that the "Read My Lips" line was not intended as a promise of action but as an expression of leadership style. Bush would go on to lose his 1992 bid for reelection, a loss partially attributed to loss of trust among voters.

Hill (2001) notes that American political speech must fulfill at least two functions, and thus it is judged against two different metrics. First, a politician must give his or her "word," specific information about planned actions and goals. Hill calls this the *discourse of truth* since the speaker is bound by Grice's (1975) maxim of quality to say only what he or she believes to be true and not what he or she believes to be false. If this "word" is seen as false, the politician may be held unworthy of election. At the same time, though, the politician is judged in terms of leadership and thus must speak with an eye toward what Hill calls the *discourse of theater*. In addition to his or her "word," the politician must express a "message," a set of positive emotional themes that draw voters to the candidate or leader. "Message" is expressed through theatrical cues, such as images of the politician and music or colors associated with a campaign, and must also be reflected in the candidate's way of speaking.

In the case of George H.W. Bush, the line "Read my lips: No new taxes" was intended, according to Bush's aides, as an expression of message. In poetic terms, it has two spondee triplets, sets of three stressed syllables, making it highly rhythmic. Its use of reported speech—the candidate's own speech in an imagined future—makes it highly personal. And the words "read my lips" were variously attributed to actor Clint Eastwood (Hill 2001) or various rock and roll musicians (Safire 1988), making it highly masculine.

At the same time, however, the line can be understood not simply as an abstract expression of "message" but also as a specific instance of "word." Since it purports to quote a future utterance by Mr. Bush, it commits him to utter these words or at least to hold to the notion they seem to express. It can be heard as a commissive speech act (Searle 1975, 1980), a promise of future action, and indeed was widely interpreted as such.

Although John Searle (1980) suggests that commissives—promises of future action—are a central speech act in human interaction, research in various settings, especially Michelle Rosaldo's (1982) study of Ilongot speech in the Philippines and Alessandro Duranti's (1988) work on Samoan political oratory, shows that the particular speech acts that are held to be central vary from one setting to the next. Hill (2001) recognizes that judgment in terms of truth and theater are aspects of American political speech and that local linguistic ideologies determine how acts of speech are evaluated. It is within a "regime of personalism" in the United States that the utterances of a politician can be taken as both expressions of personal leadership ability and commitments to future action.

The study that forms the data for this chapter initially set out to investigate certain promises attributed to Japanese Prime Minister Yukio Hatoyama in order to see whether the discourse of truth and the discourse of theater that Hill identifies in US political rhetoric are equally at play in Japan.

In August 2009 Hatoyama became prime minister when his Democratic Party of Japan (DPJ) took control of the Diet, the Japanese parliament, by winning a landslide election victory over the long-time ruling party, the Liberal Democratic Party (LDP). Shortly after the Hatoyama government was formed in September 2009, a public opinion survey found a 72 percent approval rate among respondents. By the spring of 2010, however, that approval rating had fallen to around 20 percent and newspaper editorials, opposition politicians, and even some former coalition partners were calling for Hatoyama's resignation (Japan Times 2010, May 5).

Press coverage cited two causes for the sudden fall in the government's popularity: a financial scandal and a broken promise. The financial scandal involved allegedly improper contributions to Hatoyama's campaign and to that of former DPJ president Ichiro Ozawa. Ozawa would eventually be indicted over his alleged improprieties. More curious, though, is the charge of false promises.

According to news coverage as well as newspaper editorials, Hatoyama had failed to deliver on his campaign promise to remove US Marine Corps Air Station Futenma from Okinawa. What makes this charge curious is not Hatoyama's failure to remove the base—he handled the issue clumsily, and the base is still where it was before his election. Rather, the curiosity comes from the fact that Hatoyama did not mention the base during his campaign. Indeed, an editorial in the *International Herald Tribune Asahi* newspaper before the election lamented the fact that the DPJ made no promises about the base (*IHT/Asahi* 2009, July 27). Yet by the following spring the same newspaper was among those charging that Hatoyama "failed . . . on his promise to move the facility 'at least' out of the prefecture" (*IHT/Asahi* 2010, May 15).

During the 2009 campaign, the Democratic Party of Japan's election platform made only vague allusions to a possible reexamination of US forces in Japan and did not mention the Futenma station by name. Instead, an expectation that arose both during the campaign and after the election was cast in retrospect as a campaign promise, despite a general lack of clear statements on the issue during the campaign. With this in mind, I analyzed a corpus of newspaper articles and editorials to trace how this "promise" came to be jointly constructed by the news media, Hatoyama, members of his cabinet, and partners in the coalition government.

The discourses analyzed here reveal ideologies within contemporary Japanese politics that locate responsibility for truth and leadership in particular individuals. This cluster of ideologies is similar to that described by Hill (2001) among Americans, and it makes political speech similarly "dangerous" in Japan and the United States. In addition, the analysis illustrates how discourses of promising and leading do not issue solely from the individuals held responsible for them. Interlocutors and interpreters contribute to the discourses they then attribute to political leaders.

Metaphorical Promising

In everyday language, the noun *promise* is used in multiple senses, at least two of which are relevant to the discussion here. In one sense, a promise is a linguistic act in which one person expresses a commitment to undertake some activity in the future. In a prototypical promise of this sense a speaker may say, for example, "I promise to pay you twenty dollars tomorrow." By saying these words the speaker commits to pay twenty dollars to the listener the following day. In the philosophy of language this type of speech, along with its required preconditions and its ensuing commitment, is known as a commissive speech act. Searle defines commissive speech acts as "those illocutionary acts whose point is to commit the speaker . . . to some future course of action" (1975: 356).

A second sense of the noun *promise* in everyday language relates not to an act of speaking but to an expectation of future performance. For example, an athlete, a new employee, or a young scholar may be said to "show great promise." A promising scholar does not actually commit herself to particular actions in the future through acts of speaking. Instead, aspects of the scholar's behavior—such as asking insightful questions or writing well, as well as aspects of the scholar's social positioning, such as relationships with prominent teachers or acceptance at prestigious institutions—cause observers to expect future academic or professional success. Unlike a commissive speech act, "showing promise" in this sense does not require sincerity or commitment on the part of the promiser. Still, if the expectations of future success are not met—if, for example, the young scholar does not go on to produce interesting work in her field of study—one may speak of unfulfilled promise.

What both of these ideas have in common is an orientation toward future actions or states. As the speaker who makes a promise commits to some future action, the hearers expect this action to be fulfilled at the appropriate time. When observers label an athlete, scholar, or the like as "showing promise" they expect some positive performance in the future (though neither the nature nor the time of the performance need be precisely specified). Talk of promise in both senses therefore relates to expectations about the future.

In the following case, expectations about the future are built from a combination of discourse and social positioning. Between 1998 and 2009 the Democratic Party of Japan was a major opposition party in Japan's parliament, while the Liberal Democratic Party held parliamentary majority and the position of prime minister. With the election of a DPJ majority in 2009, then, came an expectation that certain government policies would change. These expectations included both specific programs that the party outlined in its election manifesto and general ideas about change and reform that grew simply from the fact that a new party had come to power. As president of the Democratic Party of Japan, Yukio Hatoyama both made promises—he uttered certain locutions that committed him to specific actions—and showed promise; he raised expectations simply by virtue of being the leader of the former opposition party.

Hill (2001) notes that locating responsibility for a promise in a single speaker is part of an American linguistic ideology that she labels the regime of personalism, building on observations by Alessandro Duranti (1993). The truth and meaning of a discourse may be distributed across the range of individuals involved in the discourse's production and uptake, yet traditionally we hold a single individual responsible for the discourse. In the case of a promise, we identify a single promiser and hold this individual responsible if expectations, which are jointly constructed and held, are not met.

In the case that follows, there is no single locutionary act, no utterance in which Hatoyama commits himself to remove the US Marines from Okinawa. Expectations for action, and the ability to act, are widely distributed among participants. Furthermore, these expectations develop not only from linguistic action but also from social positioning. The promise at the center of the events, then, resembles a commissive speech act in some respects and is held to have the effect of such an illocution, even though it has neither the linguistic form nor the distribution of speaker/listener roles of a typical promise. It is instead a metaphorical promise, in the sense that it is regarded as a promise despite the crucial absence of an act of speaking.

The Data

Data for this study come primarily from four English-medium news sources published in Japan. Kyodo News is a cooperative news agency that distributes stories from its own reporters and from member newspapers and broadcasters in Japanese, English, and Chinese throughout Japan and overseas. *Daily Yomiuri* is the English-language publication of *Yomiuri Shimbun*, a center-right broadsheet that is the largest daily newspaper in Japan. *International Herald Tribune Asahi* (hereafter *IHT/Asahi*) is published by *Asahi Shimbun*, Japan's second-largest newspaper, in collaboration with the *International Herald Tribune*, an affiliate of the *New York Times*. The *Japan Times*, a centrist broadsheet published exclusively in English, has a smaller circulation than the other sources.

The newspaper articles and editorials analyzed in this chapter were gathered using both the Factiva and Proquest newspaper archives. Stories published between June 2009 and June 2010 mentioning the Democratic Party of Japan, Yukio Hatoyama, or the US Marine Corps Air Station Futenma were collected. Removing duplicates and minor updates yielded a corpus of approximately 450 pieces, each of which was read and analyzed using qualitative methods of discourse analysis. This corpus of Japanese news stories was supplemented with documents referenced or alluded to in editorials or reportage in the corpus. Two manifestos, published by the Democratic Party of Japan and the Liberal Democratic Party prior to the August 2009 general election, describe each party's platform for governance (DPJ 2009; LDP 2009). In addition, the "United States-Japan Roadmap for Realignment Implementation," the text of a 2006 agreement between Japan and the United States to remove Marines from Marine Corps Air Station Futenma to Guam and other parts of Okinawa, was published by Japan's Ministry of Foreign Affairs (MOFA) on its public website (MOFA 2006). Finally, a guest editorial by Yukio Hatoyama published in the *New York Times* on August 26, 2009, was also included in the corpus (Hatoyama 2009). In addition to these corpus materials, a third election manifesto, that of the DPJ's coalition partner Social Democratic Party, was subsequently consulted (SDP 2009).

Government in Japan

Japan is a constitutional monarchy. The Emperor of Japan is the nominal head of state, but he holds essentially no executive or legislative power. Government is via a parliamentary system comprising two houses, collectively known as the 国会 *kokkai* or Diet. The members of each house are elected by Japan's citizens through a combination of direct election of individual members and proportional election via political parties. Legislation is introduced and voted in the lower House of Representatives. If a bill passes the lower house, it moves on to the upper House of Councilors. If the upper house rejects a bill, it may still become law if it receives support from a two-thirds super-majority in a second vote in the lower house.

The prime minister, elected from the lower House of Representatives by a vote of both houses, serves as the executive head of government. The prime minister in turn selects a cabinet, whose members may come from either the lower or the upper house. Elections for the lower house are held every four years, or following a vote of no-confidence by its members. Members of the upper house serve six-year terms, with elections for approximately half of the members every three years.

Parallel to the cabinet is a strong bureaucratic system. The prime minister appoints ministers of state responsible for foreign affairs, justice, defense, education, and ten other specific functions. Each ministry also features a senior vice minister, the highest-ranking civil servant in the ministry's bureaucracy. Given the short terms in office of most cabinet ministers (often one to two years), these senior bureaucrats traditionally have both managed the ministries' professional civil servants and also led policy direction, with political cabinet ministers simply accepting or rejecting decisions of the senior vice minister (Neary 2004). This arrangement began to change under the government of Prime Minister Junichiro Koizumi from 2001 to 2006 (Estévez-Abe 2006; Neary 2004), a shift that continued under Prime Minister Hatoyama.

Compared to Great Britain or other Westminster-style parliaments, the Japanese Diet features a relatively weak party system. Individual members of parliament tend to owe loyalty not to the party itself but to other individual politicians. Parties tend to be divided into *habatsu* or factions, each loyal to one powerful leader (Estevez-Abe 2006). Prior to the government of Prime Minister Koizumi, cabinet members were often chosen in a manner to maximize the number of factions represented in the cabinet (Neary 2004).

Before becoming party leader Yukio Hatoyama was associated with a faction in the DPJ loyal to Ichiro Ozawa, who led the party immediately prior to Hatoyama. This association would seem to have an important effect on Hatoyama's own government for two reasons. First, Ozawa's alleged fund-raising improprieties, which led to his resignation as party leader, were cited as one reason for Hatoyama's falling poll numbers in early 2010 (Kin 2009). Moreover, unlike Hatoyama, Ozawa actually had expressed a desire to reduce the presence of US forces in Japan early in 2009, several months before Hatoyama became party leader (Furukawa, Murao, and Kuromi 2009). Although one might expect that this fact influenced expectations for Hatoyama's own position on base realignment, news sources in the corpus do not mention Ozawa in regard to the Futenma controversy after August 2009. For that reason, fuller exploration of Ozawa's role in the issue is beyond the scope of this analysis.

Japan's lower house of parliament as well as the cabinet was controlled by the Liberal Democratic Party (LDP) or by coalitions including the LDP almost continuously from 1955 until 2009, with the exception of a coalition government of smaller parties that ruled for eleven months during 1993–94. Since 2006, though, popular discontent with the long-time ruling party had been growing in Japan, and three governments in a row had lasted no more than one year each (see table 7.1). The DPJ swept to power promising to end corruption in the national government, increase direct benefits to individuals, and devolve more power to local governments (DPJ 2009).

The government of LDP Prime Minister Junichiro Koizumi from 2001 to 2006 was generally regarded as successful, and Koizumi himself was quite popular. Koizumi was one of the first leaders to take advantage of changes in Japanese election laws and party rules that allowed for greater concentration of power in the office of prime minister (Estévez-Abe 2006). He was a highly visible party leader who led his party to a substantial electoral victory in 2005 and used his strong majority to push through fiscally conservative policies, including privatization of the postal service. Following Koizumi's retirement as prime minister and party leader, however, the next three LDP prime ministers held the office for only one year each. Shinzō Abe resigned in 2007 amid opposition criticism involving funding scandals; Yasuo Fukuda was censured by the opposition-controlled upper house in 2008 and resigned thereafter; and Taro Aso left the party's leadership in 2009 when the DPJ soundly defeated the LDP in the general election.

In the Democratic Party of Japan's manifesto, its platform for the 2009 elections, party president Yukio Hatoyama promised that if elected his government would rule by five principles. The first three principles—politician-led government, cabinet-centered policy making, and leadership from the prime minister's office—were reminiscent of Koizumi's ruling style. Principle 4, "From a vertically organized society of vested interests to a horizontal society bound by human ties," appeared to be an expression of greater social progressivism, and the details of the manifesto called for increased social spending on

TABLE 7.1

Japan's Recent Prime Ministers

Prime Minister	Political Party	Dates in Office
Junichiro Koizumi	Liberal Democratic Party (LDP)	April 2001–September 2006
Shinzō Abe	LDP	September 2006–September 2007
Yasuo Fukuda	LDP	September 2007–September 2008
Taro Aso	LDP	September 2008–September 2009
Yukio Hatoyama	Democratic Party of Japan (DPJ)	September 2009–June 2010
Naoto Kan	DPJ	June 2010–September 2011
Yoshihiko Noda	DPJ	September 2011–December 2012

child care allowances, free public high schools, and reform of the pension and medical care systems. Under the heading of Principle 5, "From centralized government to regional sovereignty," the manifesto promised to give greater decision-making authority to local governments.

Emergence of the Promise

In 2005 and 2006, negotiators from the United States and Japan developed a plan to "realign" US military installations in Okinawa Prefecture in order to remove US Marine Corps Air Station Futenma while reconstituting many of the base's functions elsewhere in Okinawa and in Guam. On May 1, 2006, US Secretary of State Condoleezza Rice, Secretary of Defense Donald Rumsfeld, Japanese Minister of Foreign Affairs Taro Aso, and Minister of State for Defense Fukushiro Nukaga signed the "United States-Japan Roadmap for Realignment Implementation" (MOFA 2006). The Aso-Rice agreement called for the two countries to build a new air station off the coast of Henoko, Okinawa, near the existing US Camp Schwab base by 2014. Approximately 8,000 US Marines and 9,000 dependents would then be removed from Japan to Guam, other Marines moved to the new air station, and Futenma and other facilities returned to Japanese control.

The Aso-Rice agreement was controversial within Okinawa. Although it would remove the Futenma base from the city of Ginowan, the off-shore replacement facility would still be within Okinawa Prefecture, and its construction would destroy a coral reef and threaten the habitat of a protected marine mammal (*Economist* 2010). The plan was nonetheless acceptable in Tokyo and in Washington, and subsequent governments—including three short-lived LDP governments in Japan—made no moves to change it.

The Democratic Party of Japan made little mention of the controversial Aso-Rice agreement during the summer of 2009, amid preparations for an expected general election. One of the few mentions of US forces in Okinawa in the Diet that summer was a statement by Taro Aso. The former minister of foreign affairs was by this time serving as prime minister. During a debate in June with DPJ president Hatoyama, Aso criticized a past suggestion from the former DPJ president, Ichiro Ozawa, that most US forces should be removed from Japan. Coverage of the debate in *Daily Yomiuri* suggested that Aso "dredged up a past remark" by Hatoyama's predecessor because he was losing the debate (Furukawa, Murao, and Kuromi 2009). For the press and much of the public, the status of US forces was not a central concern that summer.

Okinawa and the status of US military forces was not a major issue for the DPJ, either. It became an issue only when the DPJ began discussion with another opposition party, the Social Democratic Party, about the possibility of forming a coalition government if elected. The SDP is to the political left of the

DPJ and is avowedly pacifist. Under the heading "Peace and human rights" the SDP election manifesto made the following commitment.

米国に在日米軍再編についての再協議を求め、沖縄などの米軍基地の縮小・撤去をすすめます。普天間基地の閉鎖・返還を求め、辺野古への新基地建設など、基地機能の強化に反対します。「グアム移転協定」の廃棄を要求します。

Request new consultations with the United States on the realignment of US forces in Japan, and hasten the reduction/removal of US bases from Okinawa and elsewhere. Seek to hasten the closure/return [to Japan] of the Futenma base, and oppose the construction of a new base at Henoko or the expansion of [existing] bases. Demand repeal of the "Guam transfer agreement." (SDP 2009, my translation)

Unlike the DPJ, which avoided strong statements on the issue, the SDP committed itself not only to support the removal of Air Station Futenma but also to oppose its replacement with the new facilities called for in what it labels the "Guam transfer agreement," the 2006 Aso-Rice agreement.

SDP leader Mizuho Fukushima initially resisted working with the DPJ since it refused to take positions on the US military in Japan or Japan's support of US and British naval operations in the Indian Ocean. Eventually, however, SDP joined DPJ and a third minor party, the centrist People's New Party, in embracing five pledges to be made in each party's manifesto in anticipation of forming a coalition government (*Daily Yomiuri* 2009, June 13). The five pledges related to domestic economic issues and not to military or foreign affairs.

Throughout July of 2009 Hatoyama spoke out on domestic issues. His major goal if elected would be to reform the relationship between the cabinet and government bureaucracies. Under the Koizumi administration, the office of prime minister had begun to take the lead in setting government policy, minimizing the role of civil service senior vice ministers (Estévez-Abe 2006). Hatoyama vowed to take power away from the bureaucracies and to give it not solely to the prime minister but to each of the cabinet's ministers of state (Harris and Murphy 2009).

In addition to restructuring the relationship between the cabinet and the bureaucracy, Hatoyama and the DPJ campaigned on economic issues. At a "next cabinet" meeting in July, they pledged to make high schools tuition free, establish a child care allowance, establish supports for agriculture, and cut several provisional taxes (*Daily Yomiuri* 2009, July 17). Hatoyama avoided making any promises to change Japan's diplomatic or military positions. In response to a formal request from the SDP to help craft legislation banning nuclear weapons, he expressed concern over possible threats from North Korea and said that he would need to consult with the United States before taking any action (Kyodo 2009, July 24).

The Democratic Party of Japan officially released its manifesto for the upcoming election on July 18, 2009, though versions had been leaked to the press some weeks earlier. The manifesto made no explicit mention of Marine Corps

Air Station Futenma. Near the end of the document, however, was a brief mention of the realignment agreement. Point 51 of the manifesto's fifty-five pledges is headed "Build a close and equal Japan-US relationship." As with the rest of the document, this pledge is largely economic, suggesting that the two countries should conclude a free trade agreement while being careful not to harm Japan's agricultural industry. The section's last paragraph discusses US forces and base realignment.

> 日米地位協定の改定を提起し、米軍再編や在日米軍基地のあり方につ
> いても見直しの方向で臨む。

> Propose the revision of the Japan-U.S. Status of Forces Agreement; move in the direction of re-examining the realignment of the U.S. military forces in Japan and the role of U.S. military bases in Japan. (DPJ 2009, official DPJ translation)

This is hardly a clear commitment. It suggests only the possibility of revisiting the Status of Forces Agreement, not a commitment to change that agreement or the Aso-Rice plan in specific ways. In what appears to be a criticism of the DPJ's lack of clarity on this issue, the Liberal Democratic Party's manifesto suggested, "We cannot entrust the safety of Japan to a political party . . . that cannot even reach agreement among its members about their stance on these [military and diplomatic] issues" (LDP 2009).[2]

On August 26, 2009, a guest editorial by Yukio Hatoyama was published in the *New York Times*. In it, he criticized globalization as a form of neo-liberal capitalism centered on US interests and called for "fraternity—as in the French slogan 'liberté, égalité, fraternité'—as a force for moderating the danger" (Hatoyama 2009). An editorial in the *Japan Times* read Hatoyama's criticism of the United States as a signal that he would try to move the Futenma replacement site outside of Japan (*Japan Times* 2009, September 6). But Hatoyama's editorial contained no mention of the realignment plan. His comments on military issues were limited to an offhand criticism of the war in Iraq and an allowance that the United States "will remain the world's leading military and economic power for the next two to three decades" (Hatoyama 2009). The bulk of his criticism related to economic and political philosophy.

The Democratic Party of Japan won the election on August 30 and took enough seats to form a government. The DPJ introduced a coalition government on September 9 with leaders of the People's New Party and the Social Democratic Party in minor cabinet positions. A September 11 report in the

---

[2] The LDP manifesto was released on August 12, 2009, six days before the DPJ manifesto. It therefore cannot be reacting specifically to language in the final document. Nonetheless, the criticism clearly appears to be directed at the DPJ position. The LDP manifesto does not mention US forces or base realignment.

Japan Times suggested that the Futenma realignment had been a sticking point in negotiating the coalition. The SDP reportedly demanded that the new government renegotiate the agreement with the United States, while the DPJ resisted, not wanting to show any disagreement with the United States ahead of a scheduled visit to Japan from President Barack Obama. In the end the parties agreed to "propose revising the SOFA and take a stance toward reviewing the realignment plans" (*Japan Times* 2009, September 11).

Prime Minister Hatoyama and US President Obama met for the first time on September 23. They agreed to work together to face North Korea and to combat global warming but did not discuss any contentious issues (*Japan Times* 2009, September 25). An editorial in the conservative *Daily Yomiuri* urged the DPJ to stick to the 2006 Aso-Rice agreement, saying that this would be the fastest route to removing US Marines from Ginowan (*Daily Yomiuri* 2009, September 24).

Over the next two weeks, conflicting ideas about how to deal with Air Station Futenma were announced from various cabinet offices. State Minister for Okinawa Seiji Maehara suggested that the government might revisit the Aso-Rice agreement (Kyodo 2009, October 3a), but Defense Minister Toshimi Kitazawa said that it would be difficult to find any other solution (Kyodo 2009, October 2). At a press conference in Cambodia, Foreign Minister Katsuya Okada said that he planned to renegotiate the base realignment deal with the United States in exchange for a promise that Japan would continue refueling ships in support of the war in Afghanistan (Kyodo 2009, October 3b).

On October 7, Prime Minister Hatoyama held a press conference to address the conflicting statements from cabinet ministers. He reportedly met with the mayor of Ginowan and the governor of Okinawa, each of whom seemed prepared to accept realignment as described in the Aso-Rice agreement. At his press conference Hatoyama referred to the manifesto's pledge to "move in the direction of re-examining realignment." He suggested that the manifesto might be regarded as a promise, but at the same time intimated that the reexamination process might not be a timely one.

> 国民との約束事だから基本的にそれを守ることが大事だ。簡単に変えるべきではない。[しかし]時間という要素によって変化する可能性は否定しない。(qtd. in *Okinawa Times* 2009)

> What we stated in our manifesto is certainly one promise we have made, and I still don't think we should change that so easily. [But] I would not deny the possibility that it could change in terms of time. (qtd. in Kyodo 2009, October 7)

In framing the manifesto's decidedly weak language as 約束事 *yakusokugoto*—a promise or arrangement—Hatoyama appears to strengthen the illocutionary force of the manifesto somewhat. At the same time, however, he weakens the suggestion that change will happen in the near future. Furthermore, there is no clarification of what that change might be or when it may arrive. Hatoyama offers no clear vision for government action at any definite time in the future.

The following day *Daily Yomiuri* published an editorial by Riichiro Maeki, deputy political news editor of *Yomiuri Shimbun*.[3] Maeki called on the DPJ "to review their electoral promises" (Maeki 2009). After criticizing the government's handling of a separate health care system for the elderly and its abandoning of LDP plans to build a dam, he writes, "In its general election manifesto, the DPJ stated that the realignment plans of U.S. forces in Japan 'must be reviewed,'" a review that Maeki suggests would be a mistake (Maeki 2009). Despite the quotation marks in Maeki's prose, however, the words "must be reviewed" do not appear in the DPJ manifesto. The party's own official English translation only called for a "move in the direction of re-examining." Likewise the original Japanese text contained nothing suggesting strong obligation.

米軍再編や在日米軍基地のあり方についても見直しの方向で臨む。

Concerning the realignment of US military forces or how US military bases in Japan ought to be, look toward reviewing the course of action. (DPJ 2009, my translation)

Maeki calls on the DPJ to be flexible in dealing with these issues. Given the diversity of suggestions emanating from the cabinet, however, obstinacy on the issue of base realignment does not seem to be the problem.

From October 26 to November 30, the parliament convened in extraordinary session. In light of the US Congress's recent vote to accept the 2006 Aso-Rice agreement on Futenma relocation and President Obama's planned visit to Japan in November, editorials in all three newspapers in the corpus called for the government to conclude its review of the relocation plan quickly (*Daily Yomiuri* 2009, October 14; *Japan Times* 2009, October 23; *IHT/Asahi* 2009, October 27). The conservative *Daily Yomiuri* was especially insistent on this point, publishing editorials on November 3, 7, 14, and 18 calling on Hatoyama to accept the 2006 agreement. When the parliamentary session ended with no conclusion on the issue, the paper accused Hatoyama of sacrificing Japan's relationship with the United States in order to keep the Social Democrats in the government (*Daily Yomiuri* 2009, December 4). An editorial in *IHT/Asahi* was less alarmist, suggesting that the US-Japan relationship could weather disagreement on this issue, but warning that if Hatoyama could not make a decision in spite of his coalition partners' intransigence, there would be no political progress before the next general election (*IHT/Asahi* 2009, December 5).

In December, Hatoyama announced that he would not make any decision on the Futenma relocation issue before the end of the year. US Secretary of

---

[3] Maeki's editorial, written in Japanese and translated into English, was undoubtedly prepared before Hatoyama delivered his remarks in Okinawa.

State Hillary Clinton visited Japan's ambassador in Washington to urge implementation of the Aso-Rice agreement (*Japan Times* 2009, December 24). Public approval for the Hatoyama government fell from around 70 percent after the election to less than 50 percent in December, with many respondents expressing displeasure with the prime minister's lack of leadership (*IHT/Asahi* 2009, December 23).

In January, Foreign Minister Katsuya Okada attended a summit meeting in Hawaii with Secretary Clinton in an attempt to shore up relations between the two nations (*IHT/Asahi* 2010, January 11; *Daily Yomiuri* 2010, January 14). In a speech before parliament Prime Minister Hatoyama announced, "The government shall decide on a specific [Futenma] replacement site by the end of May" (Kyodo 2010, January 30). Local elections in Okinawa by that time had made acceptance of the Aso-Rice agreement more difficult, however. In Nago, the city near the proposed replacement site, for the first time a mayor had been elected who opposed building the new facility. A resolution had also passed in the Okinawa assembly opposing the 2006 agreement. With growing opposition to the current plan and no specific alternative on the table, editorials in each of the newspapers in the corpus criticized Hatoyama's lack of leadership (*IHT/Asahi* 2010, January 26; *Japan Times* 2010, January 27; *Daily Yomiuri* 2010, January 30).

Unlike earlier statements in the party manifesto and Hatoyama's addresses to parliament during the extraordinary session, his declaration that "the government shall decide on a specific replacement site by the end of May" was a clear and specific commitment to a future course of action. By April, newspaper editorials were referring to Hatoyama's "promises" (*IHT/Asahi* 2010, March 6; *Daily Yomiuri* 2010, April 15; *Japan Times* 2010, April 24).

Public opinion surveys in May found that approval for the DPJ-led government had fallen to around 20 percent. Of those dissatisfied, 40 percent cited a lack of leadership and 19 percent a lack of trust (*Japan Times* 2010, May 5). In newspaper editorials the lack of trust came in for particular criticism. On May 6, Hatoyama insisted to reporters that his party's manifesto never promised to remove the Futenma replacement facility outside of Okinawa. In making this argument he explained, "Moving it at the very least outside the prefecture merely represented my own thinking" (Asahi.com 2010). Editorials, however, seized upon the words "at least outside the prefecture" and cast this not as an excuse offered in May but as a promise made the previous August. *IHT/Asahi* wrote, "Prime Minister Yukio Hatoyama pledged during an election campaign to relocate the U.S. Marine Corps Air Station Futenma outside Okinawa Prefecture" (May 7, 2010). The *Japan Times* wrote, "Before the August 30 Lower House election last year, Mr. Yukio Hatoyama . . . made a campaign pledge to move U.S. Marine Corps Air Station Futenma, Okinawa, outside Okinawa or even abroad" (May 7, 2010). While he had made vague allusions to the base realignment plan during the campaign, however, Hatoyama had refrained from explicitly making any such promise.

On May 13, the DPJ released its revised base realignment plan. Contrary to expectations, it was substantially similar to the 2006 Aso-Rice plan, with several minor modifications. The replacement facility would still be built at Henoko in Okinawa, but instead of a V-shaped pair of runways on reclaimed land, it would feature a single runway on pilings. Hatoyama seemed to feel that he had delivered on his promise to announce a new plan by the end of May. The *Daily Yomiuri*, though, called the new plan a "hopeless hodge-podge" (May 14, 2010), while *IHT/Asahi* declared Hatoyama "has effectively reneged on his promise" (May 15, 2010).

Most unhappy about the government's lightly revised plan was the Social Democratic Party, which actually had campaigned on a promise to oppose relocation within Okinawa. Mizuho Fukushima, who was SDP president and the cabinet's consumer affairs minister, threatened to resign from the cabinet over the issue. In order to prevent dissension and possible calls to dissolve the government, Chief Cabinet Secretary Hirofumi Hirano suggested that the cabinet could approve a plan with no specifics, and the prime minister would officially announce the details in a speech to the public, not to parliament (JIJI 2010, May 28a). Such legal maneuvering did not satisfy Fukushima, however, and when she refused to sign cabinet approval for the agreement, Hatoyama dismissed her from the cabinet (JIJI 2010, May 28b). On June 2, with the SDP joining the Liberal Democratic Party and minor opposition parties in calling for a new government, Hatoyama suddenly and somewhat unexpectedly announced his intention to resign (JIJI 2010, June 2). DPJ Minister of Finance Naoto Kan was elected new prime minister on 4 June (Kyodo 2010, June 9) (see timeline in table 7.2).

Discussion

The Democratic Party of Japan is, in ideological terms, a broad coalition. The party was formed in 1996 as a centrist party and was soon joined by the Japan Socialist Party, whose members wished to form a stronger rival to the right and center-right Liberal Democratic Party (Christensen 1998). In 1998 the party combined with several smaller centrist or center-left parties, and their own version of history records this as the official beginning of the party (DPJ 2010). Then in 2003 the party was joined by the Liberal Party, a right-leaning party led by former LDP lawmaker Ichiro Ozawa. These parties and factions were united less by political vision or ideology than by a desire to wrest power from the LDP.

Given the broad span of left, right, and center politicians in his party, candidate Hatoyama made few bold and unambiguous promises in this party manifesto or his campaign speeches. After forming a coalition government with the centrist People's New Party and the pacifist left Social Democratic Party, Prime Minister Hatoyama was even more circumspect, often promising to study issues and come to the best possible conclusion, without giving any clear indication of

TABLE 7.2
Timeline of Key Events

Date	Event
1879	Japan annexes Okinawa Prefecture.
April–June 1945	Battle of Okinawa; US military seizes Okinawa.
May 1947	Japan adopts a constitution renouncing the right to wage war.
April 1952	Japan signs the Treaty of Peace officially ending World War II.
1952–1972	US Civil Administration controls Okinawa and the Ryūkyū Islands.
January 1960	US/Japan sign "Treaty of mutual cooperation and security."
May 1972	Okinawa Prefecture returns to Japanese control. US bases remain.
September 1995	Two Marines and a Navy seaman rape a 12-year-old girl in Ginowan.
April 1996	Japanese PM and US Ambassador discuss removal of Futenma.
October 2005	Foreign Minister Aso and Secretary of State Rice agree to move some Marines to Guam and to build a new base in Henoko, Okinawa.
February 2009	DPJ President Ichiro Ozawa suggests a smaller US military presence.
August 2009	SDP manifesto promises to oppose the Henoko replacement base.
August 2009	DPJ suggests "move in the direction of re-examining" base relocation.
December 2009	Hatoyama refuses to decide a base relocation strategy.
January 2010	Hatoyama promises to name a relocation site by May.
May 2010	Hatoyama announces a lightly revised relocation plan.
June 2010	Hatoyama resigns as prime minister.

what he thought those solutions consisted of, and without even framing the problems clearly.

Hatoyama's lack of strong statements or apparent preferences proved problematic in terms of interdiscursive stance-taking. John W. Du Bois defines stance as follows.

> Stance is a public act by a social actor, achieved dialogically through overt communicative means, of simultaneously evaluating objects, positioning subjects (self and others), and aligning with other subjects, with respect to any salient dimension of the sociocultural field. (Du Bois 2007: 163)

Michael Lempert (2009) analyzes American politicians' stance-taking across broad discursive fields, beyond any particular communicative event. Lempert is particularly interested in the notions of "conviction" versus "flip-flopping" in US politics, and how judgments about these attributes relate to stance-taking in multiple speech events over time. A politician who evaluates an object differently in front of different audiences may be charged as an untrustworthy and unreliable flip-flopper.

Hatoyama's personal stance toward military realignment was never clearly or directly stated. His evaluations of various suggestions by members of his coalition and other political actors were not transparently present in Hatoyama's own words but were construed in analysis and interpretation of his words and actions by the news media and the people. This situation parallels what Lempert calls "addressivity by construal" (2009: 228), in which the stance-taker's alignment with particular addressees is achieved through interpretation by others. Observers projected onto Hatoyama's discourses and stances an evaluation of the advisability of various approaches to Futenma's relocation, an evaluation by construal.

While his lack of clear statements may not have opened Hatoyama to charges of flip-flopping (a charge commonly made in the United States) per se, his uncertain stance nonetheless failed to signal conviction (Lempert 2009) or message (Hill 2001). On the issue of the Futenma replacement facility, Hatoyama would later suggest that his personal preference had been to remove the new base to Guam, and that he later concluded that placement in Kagoshima Prefecture, Japan, would be a proper compromise (Kyodo 2009, June 11). While in the prime minister's office, though, he did not clearly state these preferences. In the absence of such statements, the press, the public, and members of his government were free to project their own views on the "revision" and "re-examining" process called for in the party's manifesto.

Prime Minister Hatoyama's principal failure seems to relate to, in Hill's (2001) terms, the discourse of theater. He failed to project a consistent message, an image of the intellectual conviction and emotional appeal understood as leadership ability. Indeed, as his government's approval ratings fell throughout late 2009 and early 2010, respondents to several public opinion surveys cited Hatoyama's lack of leadership as a reason for their disapproval (*Daily Yomiuri* 2009, October 29; *IHT/Asahi* 2009, December 23; *Daily Yomiuri* 2010, April 7; *IHT/Asahi* 2010, April 20). It is curious, then, that so many media analyses of the government's failure blamed Hatoyama for failing to keep a promise (e.g., *Japan Times* 2010, May 7; *IHT/Asahi* 2010, May 7; *Daily Yomiuri* 2010, May 16; *IHT/Asahi* 2010, May 25; *Korea Herald* 2010, May 25; *JIJI* 2010, June 2).

In an editorial published just after he announced his resignation, the *Daily Yomiuri* concluded that Hatoyama had actually delivered on many of his campaign promises. He introduced subsidies for child care and for agriculture and made public high schools tuition-free. He also made progress toward creating a promised East Asia diplomatic community and introduced a law to give the cabinet greater power over the bureaucracies (*Daily Yomiuri* 2010, June 3). The *Japan Times* suggested that despite his successes, two failures came to define Hatoyama: "his failure to keep his promise to relocate the functions of [Futenma] out of Okinawa Prefecture, and a political funds scandal" (June 3, 2010).

Conclusion

The failure of the Hatoyama government illustrates that in Japan, as in the United States, individual leaders are deemed responsible for certain discourses that surround them. Leaders are judged against two yardsticks: their degree of leadership, including conviction and message communicated in a discourse of theater; and their degree of honesty, expressed in the discourse of truth and measured by the degree of fit between words and actions.

What this case further illustrates is that, at least in Japan, the individual leader held responsible for these discourses need not have a central role in their creation. During the general election campaign of 2009, Yukio Hatoyama made no clear statements regarding removal of US forces from Okinawa Prefecture. Yet given his party's pledge to "Move in the direction of re-examining the realignment of the U.S. military forces in Japan" (DPJ 2009), his coalition partners' stated desire to reduce the burden on the people of Okinawa (*Daily Yomiuri* 2009, December 4), and a general expectation that a change of government would result in broad policy shifts (*IHT/Asahi* 2009, October 23; JIJI 2010, June 2), many assumed that he would take action. In the absence of clear statements, Hatoyama, as leader of the government, was held accountable for "promises" that did not come primarily from him.

As regimes of personalism (Duranti 1988, 1993) lead participants to think of discourse as a property that flows from an individual, concomitant ideas lead them to think of leadership and political direction in similarly personalist ways. Yet as this case shows, neither the individual politician nor the state is the sole locus of political discourse. Particularly with democratic systems of governance, but also in other forms of society, political will is emergent from the interaction of multiple, diverse individuals. This includes not only the "speaker" of traditional philosophy of language, but also "hearers" in the broader polity.

The lenses of truth and theater described by Hill (2001) apply not only to uptake of actual statements during a campaign but equally to actions and to the *lack* of clear statements from campaigns and governments. Actions taken while in office that raise expectations of future change may be taken as promises to act. When a metaphorical promise, an expectation of future action that arises among observers but is not related to any particular communicative act, is not met, the individual implicated in the discourse may still be judged as untrustworthy.

The leadership and honesty of a political actor are judged not only against their own locutions but also in light of actions taken or statements made by political allies or opponents. In the case described here, Yukio Hatoyama made few direct statements about the US Marine Corps Air Station Futenma realignment plan. But in an atmosphere of great public interest on the issue, Prime Minister Hatoyama was held accountable for statements made by his foreign minister, defense minister, and chief cabinet secretary, as well as campaign positions by his coalition partner, the Social Democratic Party. Because his party defeated the Liberal Democratic Party in the general election, Hatoyama was also partly defined as "opposite" to LDP campaign positions. Finally, expectations expressed in the press and held among the electorate were recast as promises by the prime minister and his party. In this environment, Hatoyama was held responsible for a metaphorical promise, expectations of future action arising from a broadly co-constructed discourse. Ultimately, Hatoyama was blamed for breaking promises he had only a small role in creating.

As peace is not merely the absence of war, successful political discourse is not merely the absence of divisive or unpopular speech. Political accord arises—or fails to arise—among a broad populace. A would-be political leader needs to find significant accord with the society he or she would lead. As the case of Yukio Hatoyama shows, failure to seek such accord can be a path to loss of position just as surely as failure to deliver one's promises can. Avoiding discord is not a sufficient path to peaceful political engagement. Instead, accord and mutual agreement must be sought through active engagement with individuals and factions throughout society.

References

Asahi.com. 2010, May 7. "Futenma Move 'Not a DPJ' Promise." *Asahi Shimbun*. Retrieved December 4, 2010 from www.asahi.com/english/TKY201005060262.html.

Christensen, Ray. 1998. "The Effects of Electoral Reforms on Campaign Practices in Japan." *Asian Survey* 38(10): 986–1004.

Daily Yomiuri. 2009, June 13. "Can SDP Compromise with DPJ? Security, International Affairs Differences Could Undermine Coalition Talks."

Daily Yomiuri. 2009, July 17. "DPJ Compiles Key Policies."

Daily Yomiuri. 2009, September 24. "Japan, U.S. Must Grasp Nettle of Difficult Issues" (editorial).

Daily Yomiuri. 2009, October 14. "Futenma Move Should Be within Prefecture" (editorial).

Daily Yomiuri. 2009, October 29. "Deepen Talks on Security, Financial Resources" (editorial).

Daily Yomiuri. 2009, November 3. "Hatoyama Should Realize Importance of Base Issue" (editorial).

Daily Yomiuri. 2009, November 7. "Govt Must do More for U.S. Security Alliance" (editorial).

Daily Yomiuri. 2009, November 14. "Settle Futenma Issue to Deepen Alliance" (editorial).

Daily Yomiuri. 2009, November 18. "Restore U.S. Trust by Settling Relocation Issue" (editorial).

Daily Yomiuri. 2009, December 4. "Resolve Futenma Issu [*sic*] by Year-end" (editorial).

Daily Yomiuri. 2010, January 14. "Solve Futenma Issue First to Deepen Japan-U.S. Ties" (editorial).

Daily Yomiuri. 2010, January 30. "Hatoyama Speech Dodged Tough Issues" (editorial).

Daily Yomiuri. 2010, April 7. "Party Politics in Crisis over Rise in Floating Voters" (editorial).

Daily Yomiuri. 2010, April 15. "Deadline Looms for Hatoyama" (editorial).

Daily Yomiuri. 2010, May 14. "Govt's Futenma Plan a Hopeless Hodge-podge" (editorial).

Daily Yomiuri. 2010, May 15. "No One Will Believe Hatoyama's Words" (editorial).

Daily Yomiuri. 2010, June 3. "Hatoyama Out of Power, Out of Time" (editorial).

Democratic Party of Japan [DPJ]. 2009. *2009 Change of Government: The Democratic Party of Japan's Platform for Government.* Retrieved July 6, 2010 from www.dpj. or.jp/english/manifesto/manifesto2009.pdf.

Democratic Party of Japan [DPJ]. 2010. The Democratic Party of Japan (website). Retrieved December 14, 2010 from www.dpj.or.jp/english/about_us/dpj_profile.html.

Du Bois, John W. 2007. "The Stance Triangle." In *Stancetaking in Discourse*, R. Englebretson (ed.), 139–82. Amsterdam: John Benjamins.

Duranti, Alessandro. 1988. "Intentions, Language, and Social Action in a Samoan Context." *Journal of Pragmatics* 12: 13–33.

Duranti, Alessandro. 1993. "Intentions, Self, and Responsibility: An Essay in Samoan Ethnopragmatics." In *Responsibility and Evidence in Oral Discourse*, J. Hill and J. Irvine (eds.), 24–47. Cambridge: Cambridge University Press.

Economist. 2010. "The New Battle of Okinawa." Retrieved December 12, 2010 from www.economist.com/node/15271146.

Estévez-Abe, Margarita. 2006. "Japan's Shift toward a Westminster System." *Asian Survey* 46(4): 632–51.

Fisch, Arnold G. 1987. *Military Government in the Ryūkyū Islands, 1945–1950.* Army Historical Series. Washington: US Government Printing Office.

Furukawa, Hajime, Takashi Murao, and Shuhei Kuromi. 2009, June 19. "Aso Fails to Strike in Debate with DPJ Head." *Daily Yomiuri.*

Grice, H. Paul. 1975. "Logic and Conversation." In *Syntax and Semantics 3: Speech Acts*, Peter Cole and J. L. Morgan (eds.), 41–58. New York: Academic Press.

Harris, Tobias and Colum Murphy. 2009, July 3. "Japan: Can the DPJ Bring Democracy to Japan?" *Far Eastern Economic Review*

Hatoyama, Yukio. 2009. "A New Path for Japan." *New York Times*. Retrieved June 23, 2010 from www.nytimes.com/2009/08/27/opinion/27iht-edhatoyama.html.

Hill, Jane. 2001. "'Read My Article': Ideological Complexity and the Overdetermination of Promising in American Presidential Politics." In *Regimes of Language: Ideologies, Polities, and Identities*, Paul Kroskrity (ed.), 259–92. Santa Fe: SAR Press.

IHT/Asahi (International Herald Tribune Asahi). 2009, July 27. "Minshuto on Policy" (editorial).

IHT/Asahi. 2009, October 23. "Relocating Futenma Base" (editorial).

IHT/Asahi. 2009, October 27. "Hatoyama Policy Speech" (editorial).

IHT/Asahi. 2009, December 5. "Futenma Base Dilemna" (editorial).

IHT/Asahi. 2009, December 23. "Honeymoon is Over" (editorial).

IHT/Asahi. 2010, January 11. "Okada-Clinton Meeting" (editorial).

IHT/Asahi. 2010, January 26. "Nago Mayoral Election" (editorial).

IHT/Asahi. 2010, March 6. "New Futenma Plan" (editorial).

IHT/Asahi. 2010, April 21. "Disenchanted Voters" (editorial).

IHT/Asahi. 2010, May 7. "Weak Leadership" (editorial).

IHT/Asahi. 2010, May 15. "Futenma Impasse" (editorial).

IHT/Asahi. 2010, May 25. "'New' Futenma Plan" (editorial).

Inoue, Masamichi. 2007. *Okinawa and the U.S. Military: Identity Making in the Age of Globalization.* New York: Columbia University Press.

Japan Constitution, Article 9.

Japan Times. 2009, September 6. "DPJ and Japan-U.S. Relations" (editorial).

Japan Times. 2009, September 11. "Coalition on Delicate Foundations" (editorial).

Japan Times. 2009, September 25. "Dancing around Delicate Issues" (editorial).

Japan Times. 2009, October 23. "A Base Okinawans Can Live With" (editorial).

Japan Times. 2010, January 27. "Nago Voters Speak on Futenma" (editorial).

Japan Times. 2010, April 24. "Shift Gears on Base Relocation" (editorial).

Japan Times. 2010, May 5. "Mr. Hatoyama's Rating in a Spin" (editorial).

Japan Times. 2010, May 7. "Mr. Hatoyama at an Impasse" (editorial).

Japan Times. 2010, June 3. "A Disappointing Departure" (editorial).

JIJI Press English News Service. 2010, May 28a. "Hatoyama Keeps Trying to Bridge Gap over Base Issue within Coalition."

JIJI Press English News Service. 2010, May 28b. "Hatoyama Dismisses Fukushima over Futenma Relocation Policy."

JIJI Press English News Service. 2010, June 2. "Update: Japan Prime Minister Hatoyama Announces Resignation."

Kin, Kwan Weng. 2009, July 3. "Opposition Leader Hit by New Scandal." *Straits Times.*

Korea Herald. 2010, May 24. "Hatoyama's Reversal." Seoul.

Kyodo News. 2009, July 24. "SDP Urges DPJ, PNP to Work Together to Legislate Non-nuclear Principles."

Kyodo News. 2009, October 2. "LEAD: Cabinet Members to Continue Talks on Futemma Relocation."

Kyodo News. 2009, October 3a. "LEAD: New Candidate Site Necessary to Move U.S. Base Facility." Maehara.

Kyodo News. 2009, October 3b. "Okada Positive about Reviewing Futemma Relocation Plan." Siem Reap, Cambodia.

Kyodo News. 2009, October 7. "2ND LD: Hatoyama Hints at Possible Change of Stance on Futemma Relocation."

Kyodo News. 2010, January 30. "Full Text of Prime Minister Hatoyama's Policy Speech in Diet. Part 9."

Kyodo News. 2010, June 9. "3RD LD: Cabinet's Support Rate Surges to 62 percent under New PM Kan."

Kyodo News. 2010, June 11. "Hatoyama Regrets Short Deadline to Resolve Futenma Issue."

Lempert, Michael. 2009. "On 'Flip-flopping': Branded Stance Taking in U.S. Electoral Politics." *Journal of Sociolinguistics* 13(2): 223–48.

Liberal Democratic Party [LDP]. 2009. "Liberal Democratic Party: The Ability and Strength to Be Responsible for Protecting Japan." Retrieved July 6, 2010 from www.jimin.jp/jimin/english/pdf/2009_yakusoku_e.pdf.

Maeki, Riichiro. 2009, October 8. "POLITICAL PULSE: DPJ Shouldn't Be so Stubborn: Blind Adherence to Campaign Promises Could Harm Public." *Daily Yomiuri.*

Ministry of Foreign Affairs (MOFA). 2006. "United States-Japan Roadmap for Realignment Implementation." Retrieved June 23, 2010 from www.mofa.go.jp/region/n-america/us/security/scc/doc0605.html.

Ministry of Defense. 2006. 日米安全保障体制の強化 [Strengthening the Japanese-American system to guarantee security]. Retrieved December 12, 2010 from www.clearing.mod.go.jp/hakusho_data/2006/2006/html/i4262000.html.

Nichols, Charles S. and Henry Shaw. 1955. *Okinawa: Victory in the Pacific*. Historical Section, Headquarters U.S. Marine Corps. Retrieved December 20, 2010 from www.ibiblio.org/hyperwar/U.S.MC/U.S.MC-M-Okinawa/index.html.

Okinawa Times. 2009. ［鳩山「普天間」発言］公約実現へ毅然とせよ. [Hatoyama's Futenma speech: Resolve to keep your promise].

Rosaldo, Michelle. 1982. "The Things We Do with Words: Ilongot Speech Acts and Speech Act Theory in Philosophy." *Language in Society* 11(2): 203–37.

Safire, William. 1988, September 4. "On Language: Read My Lips." *New York Times*. Magazine section.

Searle, John. 1975. "A Taxonomy of Illocutionary Acts." In *Language, Mind, and Knowledge*, K. Gunderson (ed.), 344–69. Minneapolis: University of Minnesota Press.

Searle, John. 1980. *Speech Acts: An Essay in the Philosophy of Language*. Cambridge: Cambridge University Press.

Social Democratic Party [SDP]. 2009. 衆議院選挙公約 2009. 概要版. [2009 Lower House election manifesto. Digest edition.] Retrieved January 25, 2011, from www5.sdp.or.jp/policy/policy/election/manifesto02_01.htm.

Treaty of Mutual Cooperation and Security, with Agreed Minute and Exchanges of Notes. 1960. Japan-United States. TIAS 4509.

Treaty of Peace with Japan. 1952. Multilateral. TIAS 2490.

PART THREE

Responding to Armed Conflict

8

"Everyone Has Their Particular Part to Play"

COMMENSURATION IN THE NORTHERN IRISH AND PALESTINIAN
VICTIMS' RIGHTS MOVEMENTS

Candler Hallman

> *Now is the time for you to step into the Bearna Baoil [dangerous gap]*
> *again; not as volunteers risking life and limb but as activists in a national*
> *movement towards independence and unity*
>
> —Gerry Adams, *President of Sinn Fein, asking the Provisional Irish*
> *Republican Army to end the armed conflict, 2005*[1]

Introduction

On June 1, 2010, more than 200 citizens and human rights activists gathered in
front of the Belfast City Hall in Northern Ireland to protest events that had
transpired the previous day off the coast of the Gaza Strip. The events—
colloquially described as the "flotilla raid"—refer to the attack of the *Mavi
Marmara* vessel by Israeli Defence Forces (IDF). The *Mavi Marmara* was one
of six vessels comprising the "Freedom Flotilla" supported by the Free Gaza
Movement. Since 2008, the Free Gaza Movement has endeavored to break the
blockade instituted by the Israelis after Hamas won elections in the Gaza Strip
in 2006 (Free Gaza Movement 2009). In May, the Freedom Flotilla attempted
to run the Israeli blockade. On the morning of May 31, Israeli navy ships surrounded the *Mavi Marmara* and instructed it to surrender. The IDF then
boarded the ship and in the ensuing melee nine activists were killed and scores
were wounded.

The flotilla raid caused particular consternation in Northern Ireland and
sparked a series of public meetings on the subject. Many activists argued that the

---

[1]Quote obtained from http://news.bbc.co.uk/2/hi/uk_news/northern_ireland/4417575.stm. The
translation of "Bearna Baoil" was also obtained from this source.

Israeli government was abandoning efforts to resolve the Palestinian situation peacefully. Indeed, the flotilla raid increased belief, especially among Irish republicans—those who desire a united Ireland—that the Israeli treatment of the Palestinians was analogous to the British treatment of the Irish in the years of the "Troubles."[2] Activists made comparisons between the raid and the killing of fourteen civil rights marchers by the British Army in the Bogside area of Londonderry in 1972; indeed, the flotilla raid was often referred to as a Palestinian "Bloody Sunday."

The circumstances leading to the deaths on board the *Mavi Marmara* are disputed in Northern Ireland, Palestine, and internationally: the IDF claims that the passengers were "terrorists" intent on aiding the militant activities of Hamas, but activists claim that they used "active resistance" and that the Israeli security forces used disproportionate violence in response. Active resistance is a form of "direct action," which is the pursuit of political goals through non-normative means, such as protest, boycotts, and sit-ins. Active resistance describes the use of defensive, non-lethal violence directed at a state's security forces. The purpose of active resistance is to encourage security forces to use disproportionate violence, thus garnering international attention for victims of that violence. This tactic differs from "non-violence" as advocated by Mahatma Ghandi, Martin Luther King Jr., and others, which stipulates that activists should not use violence against antagonists in any way. Instead, non-violent activists engage in protests, boycotts, and more extreme passive methods such as the use of human shields and hunger strikes.[3]

Using active resistance, the *Mavi Marmara* activists achieved much media attention as many outlets criticized the IDF and the blockade. Some of the most scathing rebukes of IDF tactics came from independent and mainstream sources in the United Kingdom, which focused on the rights violations perpetuated by the Israeli government against what they understood as humanitarian workers engaged in legitimate self-defense (McGreal 2010). In the United States, attention focused on the legality of the Israeli actions as well as the intentions of the activists (Kershner and MacFarquahar 2010). These debates were stoked by a United Nations mission that found evidence that passengers were killed at close range (United Nations General Assembly A/HRC/15/1). The self-expressed intentions of the activists to provoke the IDF with active resistance delegitimated their identification as humanitarians

---

[2] The "Troubles" in Northern Ireland began in 1969 and lasted roughly until 1998 when the British and Irish governments, the citizens of Northern Ireland and the Republic of Ireland, and the major political parties in Northern Ireland ratified the Belfast Accord.

[3] Pro-Palestinian groups use non-violent tactics as well. A notable example is Rachel Corrie, who died acting as a human shield for Palestinian homes designated for demolition in the Gaza Strip (see Schulthies, this volume). Both active resistance and non-violent tactics attempt to provoke security forces into violence that will highlight the immorality of their position.

for some commentators, however, including the Israeli ambassador to the United States (Oren 2010). These debates were replicated and intensified in Northern Ireland during the summer of 2010, as they re-awakened fundamental questions about resistance to human rights abuse: What are the morally superior and most effective means for activists to use in responding to human rights abuse perpetrated by a state?

This chapter studies the impact of the flotilla raid and other events during the Gaza blockade on commensuration between Irish and Palestinian victims' rights groups. Commensuration is a common polemic used by advocates to map the abuses in one territory onto another. In order to study this commensuration process, I analyze language use in two public meetings, one from 2008 and another from 2010, in Belfast, Northern Ireland. In the 2008 meeting, a Palestinian advocate casts Irish and Palestinian narratives of rights abuse and resistance as temporally distinct. In the 2010 meeting, an activist portrays the struggle and victimization of the Irish and Palestinians as concurrent. These temporalization effects produce different representations of human rights activists. The representations have different implications for the formation of robust international victims' rights networks as they legitimize certain kinds of activist tactics, which may or may not resonate with the target audience's vision of appropriate and effective methods for ceasing rights abuse. This finding suggests that an anthropological analysis of grammar in human rights debates— focusing on the representations of time that underpin those debates—is a way to study the "microgenesis of political process" in which we may "understand how individual actors collectively and routinely build what we are used to calling the 'political consciousness' or 'worldview' of a given community" (Duranti 1990: 646).

Understanding how transnational advocates align and contest different visions of political action contributes to studies of the process by which human rights theories are translated into local cultural contexts (Merry 2006; Collier 2001; Wilson and Mitchell 2003). Following Merry's (2006) synthesis of the field, anthropologists of human rights focus on the concept of "frame alignment." Frames are ways of organizing an array of "events and experiences together in a meaningful fashion" (Snow and Benford 1992: 138), which prescribe actions and reactions in political and civil society (Merry 2006). Merry uses the concept and asks anthropologists to "map the middle" by following activists as they move between international and transnational institutions and local sites of human rights abuse. These studies share an interest in how local understandings of gendered, economic, social, and political relationships clash and otherwise interface with definitions of cultural and individual human rights suggested in legal forums such as the United Nations and other transnational spaces. This chapter uses linguistic analysis of tense and other markers of temporality to study how transnational activists create commensurability among tales of rights abuse and plans for political action from disparate regions.

The study of frame alignment has some similarities to the analysis of commensuration and incommensurability in cultural, social, and political life. Espeland and Stevens (1998) define commensuration as the comparison of two different entities based upon a common metric. For example, they show how qualitative features of social life are reduced into quantitative measurements, such as the emergence of "quality time" as a metric for evaluating parenting practices (Espeland and Stevens 1998: 314). Anthropologists of commensuration or incommensurability study how actors reconcile seemingly incongruent identities and worldviews (Povinelli 2001), such as how Indonesian Muslims reconcile religion and sexual orientation (Boellstorff 2005). Commensuration is thus a native method for "mapping the middle" or aligning "frames" between different locales with their specific histories, civil, and political conflicts.

I propose an analysis of commensuration that focuses not only on the content of rights debates but also the "chronotopic" underpinnings of those debates. Recent work in linguistic anthropology has used Bakhtin's (1981) theoretical optic, the "chronotope," to understand the interrelatedness of representations of time, space, and person in narratives and talk-in-interaction. Chronotopes focus the analyst on a different order of data from that normally studied by "frame alignment" theorists. In addition to analyzing the semantic content of a narrative, linguistic anthropologists also look at the temporal and spatial underpinnings of the frames of victimization, morality, justice, and citizenship that characterize discussions about human rights abuse.

The concept of the chronotope has been deployed to explain how "referential practice" (Hanks 1990) and Bakhtinian "voicing" are used by interlocutors to align the past and the present, the near and the far, identities, and participation roles in various contexts, such as Western Apache place-naming (Basso 1996), Russian drama (Lemon 2009), Korowai travel literature (Stasch 2011), Tibetan narratives of migration (Lempert 2007), Senegalese story-telling (Perrino 2007), and Lebanese political rhetoric (Riskedahl 2007). These works show that temporal and spatial alignments between here and there, now and then, are often motivated toward the construction of social and political roles in conversation. Theorists focus not only on the lexicon of narratives but also on how speakers deictically mark the "here and now" of interaction and link it to past times and spaces. Perrino (2007) shows how interlocutors transpose characters from their narratives of past events onto participants in the interaction itself. This is transposition from the "denotational text" (the coherent sequence discussed in states of affairs and predications) onto the "interactive text" (the coherence of the interaction itself) (Silverstein 1997).

In a similar fashion this chapter shows how temporalization effects—specifically, the morpho-syntactic and lexical encoding of time in talk—produce certain depictions of human rights advocates and encourage participation in the Palestinian rights movement. Admittedly, the focus in this chapter will be on the temporal alignment of narratives of rights abuse and resistance. In the cases analyzed here, spatial reference is, as compared to temporal and person reference, relatively underused and unelaborated. But the de-emphasis of spatial underpinnings of narratives of violence dovetails with the task of commensuration: the alignment of narratives of rights abuse and resistance is most effective when differences, such as the geographical regions in which abuse occurs, and associated historical and cultural differences are minimized in favor of temporal and thematic similarities.

Analysis

The two Palestinian rights meetings analyzed here were recorded in 2008 and 2010. The first meeting was organized in partnership with Sinn Fein, the leading republican political party in Northern Ireland, for the August West Belfast "Feile an Phobail" (community festival). The Feile is a registered charity that runs events year-round, with a large festival in August. It was started in 1988 to cast the community of West Belfast in a positive light in response to the Troubles in Northern Ireland (Feile Belfast 2010). Many international activists, tourists, and republicans attend the Feile, and it is sponsored by the Belfast City Council, Department of Culture, Arts and Leisure, and the European Union (EU) Programme for Peace and Reconciliation.

During the 2008 festival, organizers held a "Palestinian Day" that included panel meetings, photographic exhibitions, and films on the Israeli/Palestinian conflict. For the most part, speakers focused on the historical circumstances that gave rise to the state of Israel, tracing the roots of Zionism in the nineteenth century to the present day. Many of the speeches focused on the similarities between the Irish and Palestinian conflicts. The public meeting under analysis here consisted of five speakers and a short question and answer period with the audience, which numbered about seventy-five and consisted of Irish republican activists, politicians, and members of the public.[4] The speakers consisted of two Palestinian nationals who write and advocate for Palestinian rights, a Sinn Fein minister of the European Parliament, and a trade union activist. I will focus on "Lina," a naturalized British Palestinian.

In her speech Lina traces out the origins of Zionism, the foundation of the state of Israel, and then cajoles the audience to engage in peaceful efforts at establishing a "one-state" solution to the Israeli/Palestinian conflict.[5] At the beginning of her talk, Lina aligns narratives of victimhood between Ireland and Palestine.

---

[4] Irish republicans are, generally speaking, those who desire a united Ireland. The term also has class connotations as most republicans identify as working class.

[5] The one-state solution entails the establishment of a single democratic state that encompasses Israel and the Palestinian territories with equal rights shared by Jewish and Palestinian peoples.

In the following excerpts I will indicate tense inflections using italics, and underline nouns and modifiers that indicate temporal qualities (please see the transcription key at the end of the chapter).

EXCERPT 1 (LINA)

1. the–the Irish *have* struggl*ed*
2. *have* <u>a history of struggle</u>
3. for rights
4. for their rights
5. a struggle that the Palestinians *are* wag*ing* <u>everyday</u>

At line 1, Lina uses the present perfect to characterize the Irish struggle against rights abuse. In the second line, she references a history of struggle, thus projecting the temporal span of the struggle deep into the past (although not into the present). This is contrasted with the progressive aspect used in line 4 to describe the Palestinian conflict, *are waging*, along with the time expression indicating repetitiveness, *everyday*. The two cases are placed on a linear timeline with the Irish resistance as a past instantiation of the Palestinian struggle. Consider another example in which Lina aligns the Irish and Palestinian narratives of rights abuse:

EXCERPT 2 (LINA)

1. and of course the fact that
2. u—m Britain *has* a very great deal to do
3. with the tragedy that *overtook* your country and mine
4. and u–h of course not least because of a–h the peacemaking efforts *have* really *begun* to bear fruit in Ireland
5. there are lessons I think here for the situation in uh Palestine

Here, she states that Britain had a role in the problems that struck both Palestine and Ireland. The temporal markers, the simple past *overtook* at line 3, situates both of these in the non-specific past. The possessive *your* at line 3 aligns the denotational text with the co-present audience, and thus they become part of the unfolding drama of human rights abuse. At line 4, however, she notes that the *peacemaking efforts have really begun to bear fruit in Ireland*. The verb phrase, *have begun* indicates a present state of *peacemaking* that began in the past. This statement produces a temporal division between the time of conflict and the time of peace in Ireland. Moreover, in line 5 she indicates that the Irish peacemaking process may offer lessons for Palestine. The audience is therefore asked to examine Palestine through the lens of their own past, and perhaps even understand their present as a potential future for Palestine.

By the third excerpt, Lina transitions to an analysis of the Palestinian case with a discussion of how the establishment of Israel has affected the Palestinian people.

EXCERPT 3 (LINA)

1. and i-it *would be* very nice for me to say to you
2. that was something that happen*ed* sixty years ago
3. it *was* terrible but <u>it's in the past</u>
4. and uh <u>we all have to move on</u>
5. of course it isn't like that
6. in the Palestinian case this catastrophe *has been* ongo*ing since that time*
7. <u>there has really not been a let up</u>

Lina begins with the conditional *would be* to describe a hypothetical case in which she could temporalize the Palestinian conflict as a past event. For added effect and to emphasize the expanse of time over which the conflict has occurred, she anchors her hypothetical wish to calendrical time, *sixty years ago*, referencing the establishment of Israel. She voices the hypothetical and states *it was terrible but it's in the past, and uh we all have to move on*. She wishes that, like her description of the Irish case, she could speak in the past tense. At line four, she steps out of this voiced role with the meta-narrative commentary, *of course it isn't like that*.

To summarize, the Irish narrative of past abuse and resistance is characterized as a past instantiation of the Palestinian conflict, and Lina is asking the audience to view the Palestinian case in light of their own history of rights abuse. The two narratives fit onto the same linear timeline and have the same logic of temporal succession. The Palestinian case (potentially) can progress toward peace. In order to facilitate this progression, she implores the audience to agitate for the Palestinian cause using peaceful means:

EXCERPT 4 (LINA)

1. it *can have* a very small action *can have* a very dramatic effect on Israel
2. and *it could be* the *start* of more of these uh groups
3. around the world in terms of ((inaudible))
4. academic wor-cultural work sports work every single work that we *can* think of
5. the more we *do* that
6. the more we *build* an international movement
7. along the lines of the anti-apartheid movement
8. the more I *think* we'*ll have* the sort of success that we *saw* in South Africa

In this excerpt, Lina prescribes certain kinds of action for securing a Palestinian state and ceasing rights abuse perpetuated by Israel. She calls for the establishment of academic, cultural, and sports networks between foreign and Palestinian activists. This kind of transnational advocacy dovetails with the projects promoted at the Feile Palestinian Day, such as a photographic exhibition of Palestinian cultural life, and the "Anti-racism World Cup," which is an international amateur soccer tournament sponsored by Irish republican groups. In concluding her statements, Lina compares this type of activism to the anti-apartheid movement that organized consumer boycotts, economic sanctions, and academic boycotts of apartheid South Africa. Using the simple past, *we saw in South Africa*, she represents the success of transnational activism against the apartheid state as a historical success, much like her portrayal of the Irish case as a relatively successful peace process.

Thus, Lina casts effective advocacy as peaceful efforts aimed at expanding the awareness not only of the Palestinian plight but also of their culture, arts, and sports. Israel should be punished for rights abuse through peaceful activities aimed at damaging their economy and global reputation. At line 8, she has mapped South Africa onto this temporal succession from a state of conflict to a state of peace. This three-way comparison of Northern Ireland, South Africa, and Israel/Palestine is common both as a polemic and an academic comparison in Northern Ireland (Guelke 2008). In all three cases, there is the potential for linear progression from a state of violent conflict to a state of peace. What drives that shift is large-scale transnational activism that uses peaceful methods to promote the oppressed and damage the oppressor's economy and reputation. Her characterization of the Irish as engaged in a relatively successful peace process lends legitimacy to her call for this type of transnational activism.

Two years after the 2008 Palestinian Day meeting, the conflict in Palestine had worsened: in the winter of 2008, the IDF launched an attack on the Hamas-controlled Gaza Strip and further tightened their naval blockade of the region. Pro-Palestinian activists staged a number of rallies in Belfast, including a rally for peace in which a number of activists spoke in the Belfast city center (Strain 2009). In May of 2010, the IDF attacked activists on the Turkish ship, the *Mavi Marmara*, during its attempt to run the blockade and deliver supplies to the Palestinians. One of the activists on board the ship, an American-born Irish national, spoke at a public meeting in Belfast in August 2010. The meeting was sponsored by the Socialist Worker's Party of Ireland[6] and by the Irish Palestinian Solidarity Campaign.[7] The panel was held in a Gaelic Athletic Association club in West Belfast. These clubs support Gaelic athletics, such as Gaelic football, and usually house a pub and meeting hall. The membership of the clubs,

---

[6] The Socialist Worker's Party of Ireland aims to establish a socialist republic in Ireland (Socialist Worker's Party 2011). Although not explicitly republican in perspective, members often express an affinity with the republican cause and suggest that a united socialist republic is the most desired future for the island.

[7] The Irish Palestinian Solidarity Campaign was established in the early 2000s to raise awareness for the plight of Palestinians and advocate for their cause in Ireland. The Campaign claims no political affiliation, but generally speaking, co-hosts many meetings also supported by republican organizations and political parties.

and hence many of those present at the panel, have republican political perspectives.

The keynote speaker, here named "Ben," is an American-born Irish national who has advocated for Palestinian rights over the past decade. Like many of those present, he advocates for direct action against the Israeli government and the IDF in order to attain Palestinian statehood and the protection of Palestinian rights. He also advocates for "active resistance," which is direct action characterized by non-lethal defensive violence. Unlike the non-violent movements of Ghandi or Martin Luther King Jr., these activists attack security forces when they are threatened with arrest. Thus, when the IDF commandos boarded the *Mavi Marmara*, many of the activists responded by attacking the soldiers in an attempt to disarm them. For example, during the raid, Ben asserts that he disarmed a commando and held him prisoner but never threatened the life of the soldier and released him when the attack was concluded.

Transnational activists who condone active resistance see it as a morally superior tactic rather than a "terrorist" tactic or other forms of offensive violence because of its emphasis on defensive and non-lethal force. The emphasis on the non-lethality of the tactic also adds to its moral superiority and potentially highlights the immorality of security forces, as active resistance often tempts security forces to respond with disproportionate force, injuring and killing civilians. In the following passages, Ben contrasts passive and active resistance. Passive resistance is another way of describing non-violent direct action. Activists challenge security and government forces by staging non-violent protests, such as sit-ins or boycotts, but do not in any way violently attack security forces, even if physically harmed themselves. In order to legitimate his support for active resistance, Ben portrays the Irish as conducting present-day resistance against their British oppressors. By emphasizing present-day conflict and de-emphasizing passive resistance, he seeks to compel his mostly Irish audience to join him in active resistance tactics.

During the meeting Ben gave an informal twenty-minute speech about his experiences during the flotilla raid, as well as his general efforts advocating for victims of Israeli violence. In addition, an Irish activist describes his efforts advocating for the Palestinian cause in Ireland. I will focus on Ben's talk because he, unlike the Irish speaker, attempts to link narratives of violence in Ireland and Palestine.[8] After the speeches, a moderator selected audience members to ask the speakers questions about their experiences and political positions. The majority of these responses were directed at Ben. As an American-born Irish

---

[8] This might indicate that commensuration is a common polemic for foreign speakers in Northern Ireland. The absence of commensuration in the Irish activists' speech is an exception to the rule, however. My research, as well as that of Guelke (2008), indicates that commensuration is a common polemic for Irish as well as foreign speakers in Northern Ireland.

national, Ben begins by associating himself with the Palestinians and the Irish in terms of their common struggle against oppression:

EXCERPT 5 (BEN)

1. my wife is Palestinian *born* and rais*ed* in the UK2. these people *are*
3. remarkable
4. absolutely remarkable
5. they'*re* amongst the most generous hospitable patient overwhelmingly non-violent
6. the vast majority of them
7. but of course like the Irish
8. like any people who *are* occupi*ed*
9. when you *reach* <u>a certain point</u>
10. you *fight*
11. a–nd
12. I *relate* to that so much
13. I know that if I *were born* and rais*ed* here in Ireland
14. that I would'*ve been* part of the resistance
15. I *don't have* any doubt of that
16. if I *were* born and rais*ed* in Palestine
17. yeah I *have* no doubt at all
18. that I *would be* involv*ed* in violent resistance
19. I simply *could* not *sit* by and *watch* my family *be* murder*ed* my land *stolen* my rights trampl*ed* on
20. by people who quite frankly *look* at you like you'*re* subhuman

At line 1, the speaker states that his wife is Palestinian. This association—stated at the outset of the speech—lends legitimacy to his advocacy efforts on behalf of Palestinians. He then characterizes the Palestinians as *remarkable* and *hospitable* (lines 3–5), and *overwhelmingly non-violent* (line 5). With this characterization of the Palestinians, Ben deploys a rhetorical device that will be repeated throughout his talk—namely, that a given victimized nationality will only resist violently when given no other choice by oppressive governments. The speaker uses the Irish case to highlight the universal applicability of this maxim, *but of course like the Irish, like any people who are occupied, when you reach a certain point, you fight* (lines 7–10). The Palestinians and Irish are examples of a general evolution of resistance movements, which is indexed by the use of the indefinite *you*, as the process is not only specific to the nationalities involved but cast as a basic causal process (line 9). This discursive move legitimates violence by shifting the responsibility for the instigation of violence to the oppressors. This is common in political talk as actors wish to cast their violent activities as morally superior and portray the other side as being the instigators of violence (Hodges, this volume; Podvornaia, this volume).

The subject then shifts back to the speaker as he states, *I relate to that so much* (line 12). He then aligns the Irish and Palestinian cases saying, *I know that if I were born . . . here in Ireland, that I would have been part of the resistance* (line 13–14); as well as, *that if I were born and raised in Palestine . . . that I would be involved in violent resistance* (lines 16, 18). Ben equates the conflicts in Ireland and Palestine in suggesting that both would qualify as the critical point at which resistance becomes a necessary reaction to oppression. Note also that he uses parallel syntax when describing his hypothetical involvement in violent resistance *if I were born and raised in Ireland, I would have been part of the resistance* (13–14) and, *If I were born and raised in Palestine, I would be involved in violent resistance* (16, 18). The parallel syntax of these two conditional statements and the interchangeability of the two geographical references (Ireland and Palestine) reinforce the similarities between rights abuse and resistance in the two contexts. He continues:

EXCERPT 6 (BEN)

1. but definitely in their treatment of the Palestinians which
2. I think is very similar to the treatment of the Irish
3. under the British
4. as if you *are* dogs
5. even worse than dogs *to be* despis*ed* and beat*en*

The utterances at lines 1, 2, and 3 are temporally unmarked; they could refer to a past or present day situation of ill treatment. The subordinating conjunction *as if* in line 4 offers a comparison between the Irish and dogs. The Irish and Palestinians are both hypothetically, but concurrently, *dogs*. The auxiliary *to be* and the verbs *despised* and *beaten* project the hypothetical future treatment of the Irish and Palestinians based upon this concurrent metaphorical status. Consider another example:

EXCERPT 7 (BEN)

1. and let us recognize the Palestinian people for what they *are*
2. and I think if anyone can *see* them for what they *are*
3. the Irish people surely can *see* them because they *are* you
4. they *are* you
5. and they *are* fighting the same battle that you've *been*
6. fight*ing* for centuries
7. and which continu*es* <u>even</u>

At line 1, Ben cajoles the crowd to *recognize the Palestinian people for what they are*. He then deploys the national category and *you* to refer to the audience, *the Irish people surely can see them because they are you* (line 3). He repeats the transposing clause *they are you* at line 4. The audience is now part of the unfolding drama of rights abuse. The use of the non-past progressive tense and the temporal noun, *centuries* (line 6), characterizes the Irish conflict as having deep historical depth. At line 7, Ben explicitly states that the fight in Ireland *continues even*. This combination of the non-past verb and intensifier *even* extends the historical fighting (*you have been fighting*) from line 5–6 through the present. The Irish and Palestinians are concurrently fighting against oppression.

Ben casts the two narratives of rights abuse and resistance as concurrent in order to portray violent activism (albeit defensive violence) as the *only* effective means for protecting Palestinian rights. By casting the audience as present-day victims and resisters, he seeks to legitimize his claim that active resistance is the most effective way to protect the Palestinian people. In the next excerpt Ben asks the audience to recognize that violent methods are the most effective:

EXCERPT 8 (BEN)

1. listen
2. *keep* lobby*ing* the politicians
3. *keep* writ*ing* letters
4. *keep* go*ing* on the protests
5. keep do*in'* all that but please
6. let us *make* this clear
7. what *will make* the biggest difference
8. which we *can change* things more quickly than anything
9. less than a thousand people on six ships *did* more
10. in an instant
11. than all this work huge amounts of energy and resources *being put* into all sorts of things ((referring to non-violent protest activities))
12. *let* us not *ignore* that

Here, Ben pleads with the audience to recognize the effectiveness of active resistance. The anaphora and parallel syntax, at lines 2 through 5, list the activities undertaken by peaceful activists.[9] The conjunction *but* at line 5 signals his point of contention with peaceful tactics, and how active resistance tactics *can change things more quickly than anything*. Throughout the meeting he has promoted the use of active resistance as a means to force the IDF into confrontations with civilians. Such confrontations, even if they entail loss of civilian life, portray the IDF as morally corrupt. The phrase at line 9 is an indirect reference to this method. Thus, not only is active resistance similar to the resistance of the Irish against the British, but it is also the most effective method for changing world opinion against Israel.[10]

---

[9] The parallel use of syntax adds a qualitative experience of the multitude of tactics used by peaceful activists (cf. Kuipers 1984).

[10] Throughout the Northern Irish conflict, several organizations used only non-violent tactics, the quintessential example being the "Peace People" founded by Mairead Corrigan and Betty Williams. For the most part, however, violent groups received the most attention during the Irish Troubles. These include, on the republican side, the Provisional Irish Republican Army, the Official Irish Republican Army, and the Irish National Liberation Army, among others. By the "resistance of the Irish against the British," it may be inferred that the speaker is alluding to republican paramilitary groups in general.

As we shall see in the question and answer session, this legitimization tactic has limited success. Audience members express concern about Irish combatants engaging in active resistance and suggest that peaceful means are effective as well. When the question and answer session begins, Sean, one of the audience members, responds to a request by Ben that former Irish combatants join the flotilla in 2011 to assist with active resistance efforts.[11]

EXCERPT 9 (SEAN)

1. regard*ing* the u–h
2. combatants from here tak*in'* part in the
3. flotilla
4. do you not *think* that that would make the
5. flotilla more susceptible to attack
6. by the Israelis and do you not *think* the
7. pro-Zionist media *would dance* all over that

Sean worries that combatants' participation will be a public relations problem as they would be labeled "terrorists" and thus play into the Israeli characterization of flotilla participants as militants. In line 2, he uses the membership category of *combatants*. This category is distinctive in that most Northern Irish rights activists refer to themselves or others as "ex-combatants" to signal their past participation in paramilitary activities. In dropping the prefix "ex" he takes up the characterization of the Irish conflict as ongoing. This may signal that Sean has taken up the speaker's "chronotope" of rights abuse and resistance in Palestine and Ireland. This audience member was the only one to explicitly take up the speaker's representations of the two conflicts as concurrent, however.

In the next two examples, audience members express dismay at the speaker's dismissal of peaceful activism and note that many activists will not support direct or violent action against the Palestinians. Consider the following:

EXCERPT 10 (BRENDA)

1. I'm just a wee bit concern*ed* when Ben *was* speak*in'*
2. I just want to put clarity with Ben
3. um because Ben you–you seem*ed* to *be* sort of you know UN EU[12] are all a waste of time
4. um but the example
5. the European Union *has* a statute trade agreement with Israel

---

[11] The phrase *former Irish combatants* likely refers to members of the Provisional Irish Republican Army, which was the primary arbiter of republican violence during the Northern Irish Troubles.

[12] These are references to the United Nations and the European Union. She is alluding to efforts to pursue Palestinian rights and sanction Israel through these mechanisms.

6. and the thing *is* we*'ve been* calling for that to be suspend*ed* after israel breaks international law
7. um but I'm just afraid that people might think that what you were saying *was*
8. that we sh—*should*n't *waste* our time call*ing* for the suspension of that agreement
9. I think it*'s* important for us from an agitational point of view

In this excerpt, Brenda, expresses concern at Ben's dismissal of peaceful activism, such as calling for a trade agreement between Israel and the European Union to be suspended until the blockade is raised. Her concern is evident at lines 3–4 as she notes Ben's comment that pursuing Palestinian rights through international institutions is *all a waste of time*. At line 6 she makes use of the collective *we* to characterize an indeterminate number of activists as engaged in demonstrations against the EU/Israeli trade agreement. Her use of the membership category *people* in line 7 *people might think that what you were saying was*, is a face-saving tactic, which postulates that some people (though not her) might not understand that he is also in favor of peaceful activism. She insists that this kind of activity is important *for us from an agitational point of view*. What is interesting about this example is that she is challenging the speaker's vision of the inefficacy of peaceful tactics, predicated upon the temporal equivalence of the two narratives. The evidence does not suggest that Brenda directly challenges Ben's temporal equation of Irish and Palestinian resistance, but she does challenge the notion that peaceful tactics are inadequate. Her disagreement suggests that the temporal equation—meant to legitimize violent resistance—fails to convince.

As the meeting proceeds, additional audience members express dismay at Ben's dismissal of peaceful activism. At the end of the meeting, one of the meeting organizers, Billy, characterizes both passive and active resistance as advancing the rights of the oppressed in an attempt to create a renewed sense of solidarity between the activists in the room.

EXCERPT 11 (BILLY)

1. I *think* there's an awful lot of
2. people out there
3. who
4. *are* just not in that position
5. where they *would support*
6. for example
7. Palestinian armed resistance
8. or even active resistance on a
9. flotilla
10. but they *would support* the

11. Palestinian case and the
12. Palestinian cause

Similar to the audience member's statement in excerpt 9 that *people might think that what you were saying was that we sh—shouldn't waste our time calling for the suspension of that agreement,* Billy uses the general membership category of *person* to protect the face of individuals in the room who criticize Ben and support peaceful activism. At lines 7–9, he indicates that these hypothetical people would have reservations supporting *armed resistance or even active resistance.* These people would, however, *support the Palestinian case.* He continues:

EXCERPT 12 (BILLY)

1. and I *think* there'*s* an awful
2. lot a people out there who'*d*
3. *be* prepar*ed* to *engage* in people
4. power
5. but we *have* to *remember* where
6. they *are* <u>at this point in time</u>
7. they'*re* not all necessarily where
8. other people *are*
9. and
10. you know there'*s* uh there there
11. there'*s* a guy from this part of
12. the world who once *said*
13. everyone *has* their own particular part to *play*

He again uses the general membership category *people* to indicate that a large number of individuals would engage in *people power,* a common description for direct action. At lines 5–6, he states that *we have to remember where they are at this point in time.* The use of the present tense *are,* the proximal deictic *this,* and the temporal noun *point in time* temporally anchors his characterization of people which follows, *they're not all necessarily where other people are.* The noun *point in time* may also be an indirect reference to the peace process in Northern Ireland.

He concludes by stating, *there's uh there there there's a guy from this part of the world who once said everyone has their own particular part to play.* He is alluding to Bobby Sands who was a Provisional Irish Republican Army (PIRA) volunteer in the 1970s and 1980s, and was convicted in 1977 of firearms possession and sent to prison in Northern Ireland. The paraphrase is borrowed from Sands's prison notebooks: "I have always taken a lesson from something that was told me by a sound man, that is, that everyone, republican or otherwise, has his own particular part to play. No part is too great or too small; no one is too old or too young to do something" (Sands 1989: 169). In 1981, Sands died while on hunger strike aimed at gaining political status in the jails. His death resulted in widespread publicity for the republican cause in Northern Ireland. Riots occurred throughout the province and Europe as well. Sands's death fit into a long tradition of self-sacrifice in Ireland, which values self-destruction as a means to demonstrate the truth and legitimacy of a political perspective (Sullivan 1993: 433). He is a powerful symbol in the current context of debate over human rights in post-conflict Northern Ireland because he took his own life and was not engaged in offensive Provisional Irish Republican military actions at the time of his death. Though opponents to republicanism often brand him a "terrorist," he is associated with popular figures of resistance such as Nelson Mandela, Gandhi, and Martin Luther King Jr.[13] He has become a secular saint for the cause and carries associations of non-violent self-sacrifice for many republicans.[14]

Sands's quote, "everyone has a particular role to play," has become increasingly popular in political discourse in Northern Ireland over the past decade as well. The quote even adorns a mural of Sands on the headquarters of the Sinn Fein office on the Falls Road in Belfast. Danny Devenny—a former combatant and mural artist—describes the meaning that republicans ascribe to the quote in an interview in the late 1990s:

> It's very important what Bobby Sands said, that "everyone has a role to play, no matter how great or how small." We understood that to mean that it didn't have to only be an armed struggle. Bobby's point was correct. If you believed that as an individual you couldn't be involved in that sort of struggle, it didn't mean that you had to walk away or just stay behind your door. There were other avenues, other ways that you could assist the struggle. That was the most important development of the hunger strike. (Conway 2010: 166)

The quote has become particularly important in republican discourse after the signing of the peace accords in Northern Ireland, as it legitimates both violent resistance and non-violent democratic means for protecting minority rights and establishing a united Ireland. Republican politicians use the term to suggest that there was a time when violence was necessary, but that time has passed as democratic avenues have become available to republicans and Catholics in Northern Ireland.

---

[13] See Martin McGuiness's paper on the implementation of the Good Friday Agreement for associations between Sands, other republicans, and these international figures (Arthur and McGuiness 2005).

[14] Like many insurgent movements, Irish republicanism has several ideological divisions. The Provisional IRA split from the Official IRA in 1969 as they determined that armed struggle was an appropriate mechanism for unifying Ireland. The Provisional and Official paramilitaries fought several feuds during the 1970s and thus, Provisional figures such as Bobby Sands are not as revered in some camps of republicanism.

The quote serves a similar purpose in the 2010 Palestinian rights meeting: it legitimates violent and non-violent resistance in both the Irish and Palestinian contexts. As stated in the Palestinian rights meeting, *everyone has their particular part to play*, is cast in the non-past tense. The organizer, Billy, is making no claims about the temporal relationship of the Palestinian and Irish cases. He also avoids spatial reference *and* the national membership categories deployed by Ben and the audience members, such as *Irish* and *Palestinian*. The application of this moral canon—from the prison diaries of the most revered Irish republican—further aligns Palestinian and Irish activism in the pursuit of a common goal. In the words of the main speaker, Ben, alignment of Irish and Palestinian narratives of rights abuse and resistance is motivated toward depicting effective activism and the effective activist, as engaged in active resistance against oppressors. After the meeting finished and in conversation over drinks, I noted that many of the participants repeated the phrase, "everyone has their own particular part to play." Anecdotally, at least, it seems this tactic of commensuration was successful where Ben's temporal alignment was not: it produced a representation of activism (and the activist) based upon common political goals and not on the methods for achieving that goal.

Conclusion

The events on board the *Mavi Marmara* in May 2010 had global effects. One such effect was the revisiting of questions that have long been of political consequence in Northern Ireland: What are the morally superior and most effective means for activists to use in responding to human rights abuse perpetrated by a state? Human rights advocates align Northern Irish and Palestinian narratives of rights abuse and resistance in order to craft and legitimate certain representations of the effective activist and effective activism. In the meetings discussed in this chapter, speakers align the Palestinian and Irish narrative of rights abuse and resistance using different morpho-syntactic and lexical encodings of time, or "chronotopes."

The examples analyzed in this chapter grant a microscopic view of the successes and pitfalls that occur when activists attempt to construct common identities and shared human value across different narratives of rights abuse. The comparison of narratives of resistance in Palestine and Ireland potentially reinforce the legitimacy of both when they are cast as efforts to stop the violation of minority human rights by a more powerful state apparatus. Successful commensuration is vital for human rights advocacy as it reinforces perceptions that events are not just historically specific grievances but also standard forms of rights violation subject to international intervention. In this way, it may foster a sense of shared identity and moral sense of purpose that bridges significant geographical divides.

Despite the discursive differences between the 2008 and 2010 meetings, one should be careful about suggesting a causal relationship between the Gaza blockade, and the shifting temporal markers evident in the practice of commensuration, and different representations of the activist that they produce and legitimate. The world of transnational human rights advocacy is one of circulation as local activists travel to other regions and transnational organizations to distribute their messages. The personnel of local organizations change and individuals who have participated previously in an international exchange may not do so again for some time. This said, the comparison of these two meetings, one occurring at the beginning of the blockade and one in the discursively chaotic aftermath of the flotilla raid, shows interrelationships between the production of spatiotemporal frames, personae, and morality in rights advocacy and the real-time development of conflicts on the ground. The flotilla attacks brought critical attention on Israel, and piggybacking on this, activists may increasingly call for direct action around the world. Moreover, civilian deaths, as occurred during the Gaza War and flotilla attacks, may lend a sense of immediacy to advocacy as well. This changed the nature of international advocacy for some practitioners. It is no longer sufficient to merely educate foreign audiences; one must also compel them to action.

In the case of the pre-blockade meeting, the Irish and Palestinian cases are aligned upon a linear temporal metric; Ireland is a past instantiation of the Israeli/Palestinian conflict. The Irish case, characterized as a peace process, represents a potential future for the Palestinian conflict. The speaker asks her audience to empathize with the Palestinian cause, to gaze through the lens of their history and agree that Israel has wronged the Palestinians in ways similar to past Irish abuse. In the second case, the speaker projects the Irish and Palestinian narratives of rights abuse as concurrent. The Irish *are* victims and they should map the moral outrage born of their experience onto the Israeli government. The use of the un-marked "present" tense for each narrative asks the audience to do something that is perhaps qualitatively different from the pre-blockade temporal alignment. The evidence does not wholly support a conclusion that audience members reject these temporal alignments, but it does show that they challenge the portrayal of activists supported by these alignments as several audience members express ambivalence toward the moral orientation of the speaker.

At the end of the 2010 meeting we see a counterclaim that peaceful activism is effective and that there is a place and a time for legitimate violence. All activist methods are worthy of consideration; for many of the activists, "everyone has a particular role to play." In conclusion, it is important to reflect upon this quote as well as the representation of the Irish conflict as a past instantiation of the Palestinian one. Both seem to achieve a shared activist identity and sense of common political purpose. These narratives are seductive alternatives to the stark moral universe deployed by Ben. It is my impression that this holds for many in the activist audience as well as the foreign researcher in Northern Ireland. "Everyone has a particular role to play" contains an assertion that, to use a biblical allegory, "there is a time for war and a time for peace"; and it has a chronotopic corollary, "there is a person for war and a person for peace." Casting the Northern Irish conflict as a past instantiation of the Israeli/Palestinian conflict engenders a sense of hope not only that the Israeli/Palestinian conflict may arrive at a relative peace, but also that non-violent activism will play a significant role in attaining such a peace.

But the social and political life of the moral maxim, "everyone has a particular role to play" is driven by temporal ambiguity. For Bobby Sands and others after him, both violence and non-violence have their time and space. The idea that past combatants fought when they had to (the time for war) and resorted to democratic means (the time for peace) papers over the historical and moral complexities of the use of non-violent and violent tactics. In the epigraph of this chapter, the former president of Sinn Fein is quoted as asking peaceful republicans to "step into the Bearna Baoil [dangerous gap] again." As activists "step into the gap" or "play their particular role," they may feel at common purpose with the past legitimate arbiters of force. Peaceful activists engage in politics bolstered by semiotic associations with past conflict, yet they do not have to deal with the moral complexities, the loss of life, or wounds that result from political violence. Similarly, the suggestion that Northern Ireland is a past instantiation of the Israeli/Palestinian conflict allows listeners to agree that direct action is required without having to reflect for too long on the moral choice between violence and non-violence.

In Northern Ireland the efficacy of political violence is a common topic of conversation. These conversations are usually confined to the pub or the dinner table, and not public discourse. Northern Irish republicans and otherwise often consider the effect of the nearly forty-year-old campaign against the British state; that is, what did violence achieve politically in 1998 that had not already been achieved by the mid-seventies? There is a sense that the common purpose of attaining civil rights for Catholics—one of the professed aims of the Provisional IRA—was supplanted by a series of ever-escalating revenge killings between republican paramilitaries, loyalist paramilitaries, and the British Army. Violence became the end as well as the means. I have heard many former combatants and victims express a question that must equally apply to those who live and work in other conflict zones; that is, is the human suffering worth potential political gain? Public advocacy for victims' rights in Northern Ireland rarely acknowledges this question. Thus, it is important to note that building solidarity around a common political purpose, particularly between different contexts of conflict, might often require artful evasion, rather than engagement with the question of the morally superior and most effective means for rights abuse prevention and resistance.

Transcription Key

italics	tense inflection
<u>underline</u>	nouns and modifiers that indicate temporal qualities
((comments))	author comments
Capitalization	Used for proper nouns

Acknowledgments

Research for this chapter was funded by a National Science Foundation Dissertation Improvement Grant, the Institute for International and Comparative Area Studies at the University of California, San Diego, and a fellowship from the Human Rights Center, at the University of California, Berkeley. Versions of this chapter have been presented to the 2nd Annual Human Rights Symposium at the University of California, San Diego, the Fellow's Human Rights Conference at the University of California, Berkeley, and the Linguistic Anthropology Workshop at the University of California, San Diego. I thank the audiences for their suggestions. I would also like to thank John Haviland, Kathryn Woolard, Nancy Postero, Rupert Stasch, Joseph Hankins, Gershon Shafir, and Heather Hallman for comments on earlier versions of this chapter.

References

Bakhtin, M. 2008. *The Dialogic Imagination: Four Essays*. Austin: University of Texas Press

Basso, Keith. 2000. *Wisdom Sits in Places: Landscape and Languages among the Western Apache*. Albuquerque: University of New Mexico Press

Boellstorff, Tom. 2005. "Between Religion and Desire: Being Muslim and Gay in Indonesia." *American Anthropologist* 107: 575–85.

Carmack, Robert. 1988. *Harvest of Violence: The Maya Indians and the Guatemalan Crisis*. Norman: University of Oklahoma Press

Conway, Jack. 2010. "Unbowed and Unbroken: A Conversation with Irish Republican Visual Artist Danny Devenny." *Radical History Review* 106: 163.

Davis, Shelton. 1988. *Land Rights and Indigenous Peoples: The Role of the Inter-American Commission on Human Rights*. Cambridge, MA: Cultural Survival

Downing, Theodore E., and Gilbert Kushner. 1988. *Human Rights and Anthropology. Cultural Survival Report, 24*. Cambridge, MA: Cultural Survival

Duranti, Alessandro. 1990. "Politics and Grammar: Agency in Samoan Political Discourse." *American Ethnologist* 17(4): 646–66.

Espeland, Wendy and Mitchell Stevens. 1998. "Commensuration as a Social Process." *Annual Review of Sociology* 24: 313–24.

Feile Belfast. 2010. "About: Feile An Phobail." Retrieved on January 22, 2011 from www.feilebelfast.com/about/.

Free Gaza Movement. 2009. "About: Free Gaza Movement." Retrieved on February 23, 2011 from www.freegaza.org/en/about-us/mission.

Griffiths, Anne. 2001. "Gendering Culture: Towards a Plural Perspective on Kwena Women's Rights." In *Culture and Rights: Anthropological Perspectives*, Jane Cowan, Marie-Bénédicte Dembour, and Richard Wilson (eds.), 102–26. Cambridge: Cambridge University Press

Guelke, Adrian, 2008. "Israeli Flags Flying alongside Belfast's Apartheid Walls: A New Era of Comparisons and Connections." *The Failure of the Middle East Peace Process?*, Guy Ben-Porat (ed.), 30–31. New York: Palgrave Macmillan

Hanks, William. 1990. *Referential Practice: Language and Lived Space among the Maya*. Chicago: University of Chicago Press

Kershner, Isabel and Neil MacFarquhar. 2010. "Pressure Mounts on Israel to Ease Blockade as Activists Vow to Test It Again." *New York Times*, June 2, p. 10.

Kuipers, Joel C. 2008. "Place, Names, and Authority in Weyéwa Ritual Speech." *Language in Society* 13: 455–66.

Lemon, Alaina. 2009. "Sympathy for the Weary State? Cold War Chronotopes and Moscow Others." *Comparative Studies in Society and History* 51: 832–64.

Lempert, Michael. 2007. "Conspicuously Past: Distressed Discourse and Diagrammatic Embedding in a Tibetan Represented Speech Style." *Language & Communication* 27: 258–71.

McGreal, Chris. 2010. "Disproportionate and Brutal: UN Panel Accuses Israel of War Crimes over Aid Ship: Israel Dismisses Report as 'Politicised and Extremist' Rights Body Condemns Blockade of Gaza Strip." *New York Times*, September 23, p. 21.

McGuinness, Martin and Paul Arthur. 2005. "Implementation of the NI Agreement." *Working Papers in British-Irish Studies No. 44*. Institute for British-Irish Studies: University College, Dublin.

Merry, Sally Engle. 2006. "Transnational Human Rights and Local Activism: Mapping the Middle." *American Anthropologist* 108: 38–51.

Oren, Michael. 2010. "An Assault, Cloaked in Peace." *New York Times*, Op-Ed June 3, p. 35.

Perrino, Sabina. 2007. "Cross-chronotope Alignment in Senegalese Oral Narrative." *Language & Communication* 27: 227–44.

Povinelli, Elizabeth A. 2001. "Radical Worlds: The Anthropology of Incommensurability and Inconceivability." *Annual Review of Anthropology* 30: 319–34.

Riskedahl, Diane. 2007. "A Sign of War: The Strategic Use of Violent Imagery in Contemporary Lebanese Political Rhetoric." *Language & Communication* 27: 307–19.

Sands, Bobby. 1982. *Skylark Sing Your Lonely Song: An Anthology of the Writings of Bobby Sands*. Dublin: Mercier Press

Silverstein, Michael. 1997. "The Improvisational Performance of Culture in Realtime Discursive Practice." In *Creativity in Performance*, R.K. Sawyer (ed.), 265–312. Greenwich: Ablex

Snow, David and Robert Benford. 1992. "Master Frames and Cycles of Protest." *Frontiers in Social Movement Theory*, Aldon Morris (ed.), 133–55. New Haven, CT: Yale University Press

Snow, David, E. Burke Rochford Jr., Steven K. Worden, and Robert D. Benford. 1989. "Frame Alignment Processes, Micromobilization, and Movement Participation." *American Sociological Review* 51(4): 464–81.

Socialist Worker's Party. 2011. "What We Stand For: Socialist Worker's Party." Retrieved on February 11, 2011 from www.swp.ie/what-we-stand-for.

Stasch, Rupert. 2011. "Textual Iconicity and the Primitivist Cosmos: Chronotopes of Desire in Travel Writing about Korowai of West Papua." *Linguistic Anthropology* 21(1): 1–21.

Strain, Arthur. 2010. "BBC NEWS | UK | Northern Ireland | Belfast Hears of Gaza Suffering." Accessed December 11, 2010 from http://news.bbc.co.uk/2/hi/uk_news/northern_ireland/7822261.stm.

Sweeney, George. 1993. "Irish Hunger Strikes and the Cult of Self-sacrifice." *Journal of Contemporary History* 28: 421–37.

United Nations General Assembly. 2010. "Report of the International Fact-Finding Mission to Investigate Violations of International Law, including International Humanitarian and Human Rights Law, Resulting from the Israeli Attacks on the Flotilla of Ships Carrying Humanitarian Assistance" (A.HRC.15.21) 15th Session. September 27, 2010.

Wilson, Richard and Jon P. Mitchell. 2003. *Human Rights in Global Perspective: Anthropological Studies of Rights, Claims and Entitlements*. London: Routledge

Wilson, Richard. 2001. *The Politics of Truth and Reconciliation in South Africa*. New York: Cambridge University Press

9

Reasonable Affects

MOROCCAN FAMILY RESPONSES TO MEDIATED VIOLENCE

Becky Schulthies

Introduction

One evening in January 2004, I sat in Fez, Morocco with the extended Bennis family who were engaged in their regular tea visiting routine when the seven forty-five evening news came on the more popular second national television station, 2M. The room was filled with women, including multiple generations of two families and two unmarried and well-educated paternal aunts. They were engaged in their own conversations about familial and community happenings. Several sons were also in and out of the salon, mostly peripheral to the women's discussions until the news broadcast began. Abderazak, a forty-year-old single male cousin, began a comment about the news surrounding the Moroccan king's visit to the famed Egyptian religious school Al-Azhar, followed by a report about another explosion in Iraq that had killed many and wounded many more. No one acknowledged his comments about the king's activities (dubbed "protocol" news by many of the families I visited). However, when he piped up about the Iraqi bombing, the two paternal aunts asked him to change the station from 2M to Rabat (known as *al-ûla*, "the first" Moroccan national television channel) so they could catch the news from the beginning. There was a ten-minute delay between 2M's evening broadcast and the start of Rabat news, so other conversations continued until the second newscast. Abderazak raised the volume as he changed stations and one of his aunts said, *lâ, ghîr lSûra* "No, the image is enough." Despite the overt affirmation of visual primacy, once the news started she actually moved across the room to be closer to the television and the aural broadcast. The aunts responded to the images of carnage left by the bombing with sharp intakes of breath and formulaic religious phrases invoking divine protection on those harmed. Initiated by the aunts, several of the family members present then began to debate causes of the ongoing violence in Iraq, drawing connections between the American occupation, sectarian divisions, and economic distress. This discussion lasted only a few minutes before they moved onto family-related topics.

As illustrated briefly by this vignette, images and stories of human violence and conflict are daily fare on Moroccan television sets. While not a significant portion of all programming (nor of family viewing preferences), news and talk programs provide almost daily accounts of war-related conflict and armed violence within the region with which Moroccan families claim affinity. During my research in urban Fez, Morocco during 2004, these included the Abu Ghraib scandal in Iraq; bombings of Shiite pilgrims in Kerbala, Iraq; Al Qaeda attacks in Saudi Arabia; and Israeli targeted assassinations in Gaza, in addition to reports of clashes between insurgents, soldiers, police, and civilian casualties. News broadcasts corresponded with family gathering times: at lunch and in the evening visiting hours. These representations of violence saturated daily family life. Families collaboratively evaluated these images and accounts, revealing a pattern of dealing with normalized violence. They paired emotional responses with reasoning of who was involved and how it could happen, at times challenging official narratives. The interest in and reactions to regional violence evidenced a strong pan-Arab solidarity, with recognition that conflict involving human harm was morally problematic no matter who was involved.

In this chapter, I examine the ways in which urban Moroccan families co-construct evaluative responses to armed conflict. In doing so, they collaboratively construct affect and jointly analyze mediated violence using the same linguistic resource to express emotion and assess propositions surrounding conflict. For example, an interjection of surprise common in Morocco, such as *wîllî*, may performatively invoke ill consequences toward perpetrators of violence while embedding a critique of actions entailing human casualties. Following Besnier (1990), and Ochs and Schieffelin (1989), I view affect as a socially distributed, multimodal, observable display of emotions, feelings, moods, dispositions, and attitudes toward persons/situations. Studies on language and affect have demonstrated how central assessing the subjective state of another is for responding within ongoing talk (Ochs and Schieffelin 1989). In addition, affect can also be distributed across interlocutors rather than individually located (Besnier 1990), particularly in conversational speech genres. There is also a political ranking of affect by which certain kinds of emotional responses are devalued in interaction and the speakers viewed as irrational (Lutz 1988).

Using transcripts of recorded family television talk (Gillespie 1995), I extend these studies to explore the affective discourse mechanisms utilized by Moroccan family members to collaboratively create stances in relation to images of armed violence in the Arab world. The stances, or positions toward violence they took, involved explicit critiques or reworkings of American and Israeli accounts of armed conflict in the region, signaling their familiarity with international discourses on the Iraq war, the Palestinian-Israeli conflict, and Al Qaeda operations. However, these families also vocally responded in sympathetic ways to representations of violence victims. I argue that affect and evaluations of violence related to war and multiple state projects of control subsumed under the terror rubric are interrelated elements of collective positioning that emerged through family conversations. In Morocco, in particular, familial affective evaluation indexed a counternarrative to the ideology that reasoned discourse entails distancing from emotion. Instead, evaluative emotion emerged as a rational response to the human costs of war, an alternative discourse of affective reason. In this way, these Moroccans implicitly engaged and contested a Western representation of them as irrational because of their passionate responses to violence (Zogby 2010). They challenged international discourses about Arab emotionalism by implying that discourses of peace must include recognition of diverse ways of reasoning in order to reduce structural and armed forms of violence.

Theoretical Context

Conversational interactants convey emotion through many means and employ it to accomplish many tasks. It is not indexed by explicit comments alone but also through grammatical features (such as phonological changes, vowel elongation, syntactic restructuring), voice quality (intonation, speed, pitch), facial expressions, embodied actions, and comportment (Wilce 2009). Despite the long-standing anthropological literature on the socialization of emotion through language and language through emotion (Ochs 1986; Ochs and Schieffelin 1989), and the recognized social construction of emotion and ideologies about emotion (Abu-Lughod 1990; Besnier 1990; Irvine 1982; Lutz 1988; Rosaldo 1984), few analyses emphasize the basic idea that emotion is intersubjective and interactively constructed (Wilce 2009). Emotion continues to be viewed as primarily a subjective state, rather than a particular cultural framing of how affect works. I use discourse analysis of Moroccan family responses to news accounts of violence to illustrate how affect is manifest through a variety of linguistic means (phonological, lexical, voice quality), signals intense involvement in conflict issues, and at the same time indexes analytical reasoning. I explore the collaborative emergence of socially distributed emotion in analyses of two Moroccan domestic viewing events in 2004 involving two different urban families: a lunchtime news report on bombings of Shiite pilgrims in Iraq, and an advertisement for a news magazine program in French about the death of American activist Rachel Corrie in Gaza.

There is a certain danger in analyzing Moroccan emotional discourse of war narratives. As Lutz and others have noted, there exists within academic circles and American society an ideology of emotional talk as irrational, associated with women and colonized "natives," subjective (personal), and a physical rather than intellectual reaction (Lutz 1990; Fanon 1952). Arabs are affiliated with this emotional-talk-as-irrational-character ideology

(Patai 1976; Said 1979). By focusing on affective responses to news narratives, I do not want to reinscribe the "emotionality of Arabs" frame. I do want to foreground how difference in affective ideology can color interactions and their interpretation. Our recognition that particular ways of speaking are associated with certain kinds of speakers or contexts is a widespread social tendency (known as first-order indexicality). We often load these observations with moral, political, and cultural meanings (second-order indexicality or rhematization), such that linguistic features associated with certain groups (social types) are linked to individual intentions and collective natures (Irvine and Gal 2000; Silverstein 2003). This is not simply the ecological fallacy of stereotypes but has a constituting effect on interpretation and interaction, as well as the choices speakers make in reaction to perceived categorizations (Agha 2005). In other words, cultural processes by which communities morally evaluate each other's ways of speaking impact their understandings and responses to events filtered through linguistic representations of those events. At the basic interactional level, assumptions that link emotive behavior with irrationality allow one party to discount the merit of the other's position. At a material level, these language ideologies underlie political alignments and policy development (Irvine 1989; Lynch 2006).

There are many examples illustrating these semiotic processes linking Arabic linguistic practices to logical inadequacies. Historian Michelle Mart used State Department documents and political communiqués of the 1950s to illustrate American political leaders' foreign policy decisions in the Middle East based on their linking Arab emotionalism and perceived irrationality: "A hallmark of fanaticism and irrationality in Arabs, according to some American observers, was their excessive emotion. . . . Not coincidentally, great emotion and irrationality were considered in post-war social understanding to be indications of a lack of masculinity" (Mart 2007: 76–77). Notice how the opposition of gender and reason was nested within the larger linking of irrationality with emotion as part of a "modern" subjectivity (Capps and Ochs 1995; Inoue 2002). Gal and Irvine (1995) called this semiotic process of language ideology "fractal recursivity," where oppositions salient at one relational level become mapped onto another set of oppositions. This is clearly a persistent theme in American political commentary about the failures of Arab political thought and action (Friedman 2006). It emerged in 2008 presidential candidate Mike Huckabee's comments about the cultural conflict in Bagdad at the time: "The problem now is that an Arab culture, much of it pre-modern in its reliance on words, now finds itself cheek to cheek with Americanism, in its technical, unsentimental belief in the bottom line. And so it's yet another battle between ancients and moderns, between poets and scientists, between romantics and rationalizers" (cited in Zogby 2010: 66).

The notion of Arab emotionality is not exclusively the purview of American analysts but also appeared in discussions with some of my American-trained

Moroccan colleagues. In offering the following analysis, this Moroccan colleague cast Arabs as not obtaining the ideal of a reasoning, liberal individual:

> Families usually catch the news before or during lunch, or while gathered together in the evenings. Since Moroccans watch the news with their family, they receive it in a different way than if they were to watch it or read it alone. With the family, there is *awâtif* "emotional" responses to the news, rather than *'aql* "rational" responses, because when you are with the family, one child may be crying, your wife laughing, and the interaction is at the emotional level. When you hear on the news that a Palestinian has been killed, you respond emotionally, rather than by reasoning through the circumstances, or viewing it in light of the factors surrounding the incident.

In this anecdotal account, my colleague foregrounded news viewing as a family affair. While that may not differ from other cultural contexts, he explicitly linked the domestic space to news narratives of Arab violence (Palestine in particular), when any other type of news story would be possible to illustrate the point. Notice, too, how he located affect as a response linked to specific contexts and participants, rather than emotion as reactional norm. When I shared this idea with some of the Moroccan families I worked with, they observed that Arabs self-identify as "hot-blooded" (*dam as-skhûn*), or "excitable" (*Hamâsî*), but only in response to fundamental issues of religion, land, and honor, not as an index of their national character. Instead of pointing to irrationality, affective responses signaled their intense, passionate involvement in the topic, and emerged in interaction (Johnstone 1991; Suchan 2010). Repetition of topic, location, key story points, and evaluative stance are key elements of Arab argument structures (Johnstone 1990). Conversely, the Moroccans viewed the distancing affect of American spokespersons when stating official responses to civilian casualties as unconcern for the people involved: their lack of emotion downplayed the seriousness of the situation as a strategy for minimizing responsibility. Thus, Moroccans employed a different calculus when determining a reasonable response to violence, one that focused on recognizing the human cost and positioning themselves against senseless loss of life. In much the same way, my analysis seeks to disrupt the dichotomy that sets emotion apart from reasoned discourse by providing examples of contexts in which both elements are mapped together to provide an alternative discourse of affective reason.

Research Context

Television viewing in Morocco is largely a family affair. While there were certainly programs, locations (see Graiouid 2007 on cafés), and times of the day when individuals or peers could and did watch together, families formed a key component to collaborative watching, interpreting, and evaluating of television.

I use family as a concept denoting the relational and collaborative contexts in which interpretation occurs. The family here is a unit of cultural production, a fluid term that includes all those participating in domestic television practices, whether blood-related or not. As made clear throughout my research, more than nuclear family members watched television together in the home and participated in television talk. Their presence contributed to the interactional possibilities and interpretive outcomes. Television itself was called a passive member of the family by several Moroccans in my fieldwork, and brought into this relational matrix. It was directly addressed at times, and was the background to everyday relational work.

Moroccans have access, through satellite television, to hundreds of European, Arab, and African stations in many language varieties (standard national languages and social/regional dialects). In terms of languages, Moroccans have greatest exposure to and comprehension of Moroccan Arabic, French, Modern Standard Arabic (MSA), Spanish, Egyptian Arabic, and increasingly, English, given the history of trade, colonialism, migration, education, and regional media flows (Ennaji 2005). Families with variable and alternate educational backgrounds—national public or private schooling, training in Quranic recitation, and "interactional" literacies (spoken French and English fluency and cultural competence through tourism)—made sense together of events encountered via mass media montages: textual, oral, and visual. News programming, the focus in this current analysis, was always in the more formal registers, those taught in schools and associated with literacy: MSA or French. With this range of visual and linguistic resources, the skills and analytical repertoires of all family members were engaged in the interpretive process (Schulthies 2009).

Moroccan Affective Reasoning

Collaborative discourse cues, such as *shûf* (look), *sma'* (listen), and *skût* (quiet) in Moroccan Arabic were everyday phrases pervading family television talk in my research, orienting interaction to what was happening on the television and initiating family commentaries, discussions, and negotiations of television content. These also marked the conversational role, even if passive, of television. Viewers talked to the television while watching, and utilized conversational backchannel cues to encourage discussion, to indicate the truth-value of what they were hearing, or to evidence their emotional response: *îîh* or *wîllî* (interjection of surprise), *ââh* or *eh* (intonation shift, "ok, I get what you are saying"), *îyâh* (can be impatient agreement), *ayawa* (agreement), *mm* (ok), *oaw* (pained), *ûû* (pained), tongue clicks (disapproval). Affective orientation to television content was also signaled through formulaic religious phrases, as well as intense involvement with the event through doubled or tripled replication: *shûf shûf shûf* "look."

In one event I recorded, a Moroccan family responded to a news account of Al Qaeda attacks on expatriate institutions in Saudi Arabia. As they collaboratively responded to images of wounded women and children of Lebanese and German nationalities, they assessed the cause of violence and positioned themselves against the aggressors. They evidenced this through negative interjections damning the Saudi Arab perpetrators (*wîllî*), a verbal exclamation used to enact spitting on the attackers (*tfûh*), religious petitionary phrases asking forgiveness for the evil (*îstaghfir âllah* may God forgive), as well as evoking one of the names of God on behalf of the victims (*yâ laTîf* O Kind One).

Exclamatory interjections and affective prosody fluctuations were sometimes used to initiate a commentary or debate. Attention could be directed by repeating a quote from the television or a simple comment. I also documented pointing and conversational gestures accompanying family dialogues with television as they immediately responded to events unfolding on the screen. These conversational cues fluidly transitioned from interactions with the television to family discussions stemming from viewed content.

Let me provide an illustration from a Moroccan family in this study to demonstrate how affect connected with reasoned argument as they were evaluating a news narrated event. I will provide the context, followed by segments of the transcript interspersed with my analysis. A mother (Zahra) and three of her five children (Toufiq aged twenty-five, Kaltoum aged twenty-four, and Zoubida aged sixteen) were gathered in the smaller, more intimate salon of their home watching television one Friday evening in February 2004. They had just finished watching a state-sponsored television program on Islam. As it ended, the eldest son, Toufiq, initiated a discussion about the meaning of a key MSA term used in the story about Moses they had all just viewed. None of the other family members were interested in a serious religious conversation at that time, and the sister closest in age to him, Kaltoum, playfully tried to derail his attempts. During this discussion, the state television station 2M was cycling advertisements for products and previewing upcoming programs. One announcement was for a Moroccan-produced French language news magazine (*Grand Angle*) episode about American activist Rachel Corrie, killed in Gaza by an Israeli bulldozer driver while protesting Palestinian home demolitions in 2003. As the images of her death rolled across the screen, a disembodied female French-speaking voice invited viewers to tune in for more details the following Monday.

Toufiq 35: سكوت سكوت سكوت[1]

skût skût skût

quiet quiet quiet

(0.02)

---

[1] I choose to iconically reflect Arabic orthography in my transcriptions as a theoretical stance to further represent the voices of the Moroccan families I worked with. It is meant to reconfigure the interpretive flow. Moroccan Arabic, the language variety for most of the interactions transcribed here, often uses a modified MSA, which is written and read from right to left.

سكوت

skût

Quiet

(0.02)

Mon ami le Tip (FR)

my friend "Tip"

(0.04)

هدا غدي يكون مجهد

hadâ ghadî yikûn mjhd

this will be intense

bien sûr (FR)   :Kaltoum 36

of course

(0.02)

شو، شو، شو شو شو]   :Toufiq 37

shu shu shu shu shu[

look look look look look[

كيدربو هادك (.) [المصور]   :Zoubida 38

]*kîdarbû hâdak (.) [lmSawwar]*

]they are beating that (.) [the cameraman]

[شو، شو، شو]   :Toufiq 39

[*shu shu shu*]

[look look look]

قاصو، قاصو (.) إفوو]   :Kaltoum 40

qâSû qâSû (.) ifû[

he smashed (it), he smashed (it), ifuu[

(0.4)

Toufiq directed everyone's attention to the program advertisement with a tripled replication calling for silence, seen in line 35: *skût skût skût* "quiet quiet quiet." As mentioned previously, repetition in Arab argument carries more than straightforward referential meaning; it signals an intense involvement with the issue as well as an imbedded evaluation of its significance (Johnstone 1991). In addition, the level of Toufiq's engagement with the visuals was evidenced in his direct quote of a French documentary title being reviewed on the program *Mon ami le Tip* (FR) "My Friend Tip." Further cementing his affective alignment with Rachel Corrie's sacrifice on behalf of Palestinians, he explicitly stated that the program would be intense: *ʰhadâ ghadî yikûn mjhd* "this will be intense." These consecutive responses (lexical reduplication, repetition of program title, predictive evaluation) verbally evidenced the process by which he was assessing the television transmission's message, both viscerally and logically.

As his sister Kaltoum confirmed her agreement with the aligning French phrase *bien sûr*, the video montage showed an Israeli bulldozer crushing Rachel Corrie in its path, eliciting strong verbal and physical responses, in almost overlapped succession, from all the children present (lines 37–40). Each contribution layered their collective deep emotional response to a human tragedy of the Israeli-Palestinian conflict. Toufiq repeated calls to look *shu shu shu shu shu* "look look look look look" that raised in speed and pitch in correspondence with the unfolding drama. His use of the directive "look" may seem to be a request for family members to attend to the action, but since they were all watching the program at this point, this was more a cry of sentiment: disbelief and distress mapped onto a call for action. Latching onto his directive, his sister Zoubida began to identify the victim, but she was unable to find the right word for cameramen/journalist. She had to use a demonstrative restart *hâdak* "that" before her thoughts caught up with her verbal expression. Her analysis built on Toufiq's multifunctional directive and was followed by the verbal shudder of their sister Kaltoum (*ifû*). Kaltoum's response included a recognition of the single actor (the bulldozer driver) and means of Rachel's hurt prior to, but in seamless conjunction with, her interjection of horror: *qâSû qâSû* (.) *ifû* "he smashed (it), he smashed (it), ifuu." In the midst of Kaltoum's and Zoubida's emotional response, they were identifying the causes and key actors in the unfolding action. This led to collaborative discussion establishing when the program would air, leading into who was ultimately responsible for the ongoing violence in Palestine.

Toufiq 41: هادو مصورين هادو

hâdû mSawarîn hâdû

those are cameramen, those

Zahra 42: مم

mm

hmm

Toufiq 43: فوقاش هدا.. تلاتة وعشرين (FR) fevrier (.) اتناش قل تلوت

fûqâsh hdâ (.) *tlâtah w'ashrîn fevrier (FR)* (.) *itnâsh qal tulût*

when is this? (.) February 23 (.) 11:40

(0.01)

اووه

ûûwh

uwh

(0.03)

هاد النهار ولا البارح   Zahra 44:

had nnhâr wlâ lbâriH

today or yesterday?

اليهود (.) اسرائيل   Toufiq 45:

lyihûd (.) isrâ'îl

Jews (.) Israel

اليوم اه (.)[نهار الإتنين غادي يدوزه؟]   Zoubida 46:

lyom ah (.)[nhâr lîtnayn ghâdî ydûzu]

the day ah (.) [will they air it monday?]

[نهار الإتنين] غيدوزه   Toufiq 47:

[nhâr litnayn] ghaydûzu

[monday] they will air it

(0.02)

Toufiq restated Zoubida's recognition of the participants in the drama as cameramen, a synonym for journalist in Moroccan Arabic, which was subtly confirmed by their mother's *mmm*. Collectively they then began to determine when the program would air in its entirety (lines 43–47). In between the unfolding temporal co-constructions, Toufiq responded affectively to the visual and verbal content of the television, signaling through loaded expressions his displeasure: *ûûwh* "uwh" (midway through 43); *lyihûd isrâ'îl* "Jews, Israel"(line 45). Both evaluations involved voice quality shifts (lowered pitch) and value-laden, declarative intonational contours, and created the context for the following discussion surrounding American support for Israel initiated by his mother. As the commercial programming shifted away from the *Grand Angle* preview, the mother initiated a topic shift, commenting on a recent sale of American war planes to Israel, in which family members layered their further analysis and evaluation of the conflict (lines 48–58)

هد (.) مشفتيش الميريكان [باعت لهوم الطيار] دلحرب لبارح   Zahra 48:

had (.) mashuftîsh lmerîkân bâ't lhûm Ttayâra dalHarb lbariH

this . . . didn't you see America [sold them war] planes yesterday

Zoubida 49: [XXXX]

Toufiq 50: والميريكان هي اللي كدعم تما سميتو

walmerîkân hîya illî kd'am timâ smîtû

and America is the one who supports there, what's it called

Zoubida 51: اه

âh

ah

Kaltoum 52: شكون اللي مزيغ إسرائيل غير [الميريكان]

shkûn illî mazîgh isra'îl ghîr lmerîkân

who encourages Israel except [America]

Toufiq 53: [شكون] شكون اللي مدعمهم بالأسلحة و كيعطيها

shkûn illî md'amhum bil'islaHa wakî'aTîhâ [shkûn]

w[ho] supports them with weapons, and gives it

Zahra 54: مم (0.01) البارح طرأ . . . صيفطت لهم الفوج الاول

mm (0.01) lbariH Tr'. . . SifT lhum frûj l'wâl

mm (0.01) yesterday plan . . . she sent the first group to
them

Toufiq 55: ويلي، [هاد شي معروف]

wîllî, [hâd shî m'arûf]

Whatever (SAR), [this is well-known]

Kaltoum 56: XXX [شي أثما] واعرا مطرطرأ، من الميريكان

XXX [shî 'imâ] wâ'erâ mTarTarâ, mn merîkân

[some list,] wonderful (MOCKING) exploded, from America
(0.01)

من الميريكان

mn merîkân

From America

Toufiq 57: كولها كولها مي عاود لهادي اللي قريا كولها القصة ديال سيدنا موسى

gûlhâ gûlhâ mmî 'âwd lhâdî illî qarîyâ gûlha lqiSa dyâl sîdnâ
musa

Tell her, tell her Mom, narrate to this educated one the story
of our saint Moses

Kaltoum 58: من الميريكان . أآه كي يزيغوا باش يقتلو خوتنا المسلمين (SAR)

mn merîkân. ââh kîzîghû bâsh yiqtlû khûtnâ lmuslimîn

From America, Yeah, they are encouraged so they can kill
our muslim brothers

آههه كي يزيغ باش يقتلو خوتنا المسلمين

ââḥḥh kîzîghû bâsh yiqtlû khûtnâ lmuslimîn

Yah, They are encouraged, in order to kill our Muslim
brothers (SAR)

(POUNDS CHEST, COUGHS, LAUGHS)

مسلمين (INCREASED TEMPO AND PITCH) [كفر بالله]
(RAISED VOICE)

muslimîn (RAISED VOICE) *kufr billah* (INCREASED
TEMPO AND PITCH)

Muslims (RAISED VOICE) unbelievers by God!

Building on his mother's statement about American culpability in the violence, Toufiq referenced her claim and added to the critique: America is well known to provide support as well as weapons (lines 50, 53, 55). Zoubida and Kaltoum collaboratively pile on agreement while furthering the indictment: who else but America supports Israel? (lines 51–52). The family members then collaboratively critique American, Israeli, and Muslim involvement in Palestinian oppression (lines 56–58). In each comment, the bulk of the emotional work was collaborative as family members would finish each other's declarative intonational contours, mirror the pitch and speed values of each other in confirmation of the other's rationale, and overlap lines to signal agreement and add further evidence to this damning evaluation of armed violence and failed diplomacy. Family members co-constructed an affective rationale for ongoing conflict among Palestinians and Israelis.

In the midst of this conversational flow, a phonological slip by one family member became an affective reasoning resource for another. Thus attention to tiny details, at the level of phonological variation, can also contribute to the collaborative construction of a logical argument. In the midst of their discussion about American support for Israeli violence, Kaltoum picked up on her mother's phonological slip in line 54 that sounded like an Old Fassi pronunciation of the word for planes. Old Fassi is a local language variety in Fez that differs from the widespread urban variety that most of the family spoke. It can be aligned with old school elites but has also become associated with the language of old women, since it is a rapidly contracting language style (Hachimi 2005). Though the mother's native variety is from the northern mountains (*jebli*) and her husband and children are consistent speakers of an urban Moroccan koine (new Fassi), she lived for many years in a house filled with Old Fassi–speaking women.

In addition, her neighbor at the time was also an Old Fassi native speaker. She was thus used to accommodating a number of Moroccan Arabic varieties in her conversations.

As Kaltoum parodied her mother's language slip, she drew upon iconic features of the Old Fassi variety: the glottal stop /ʔ/ and alveolar approximate /ɹ/, though the mother had used only the alveolar approximate /ɹ/ variant coupled with vowel changes in her pronunciation of *TTayâra* "planes" (line 48). The more widespread urban variety pronunciation of the word would have included a trilled /r/ instead of the alveolar approximate /ɹ/, the latter indexing old women from Fez. The mother mispronounced the same word later on in the conversation, and it was the second, incomplete form that led to her daughter's parody. She meant to say "planes" again, but restarted mid-word and switched to a different phrasal construction: *lbariH Tr' . . . SifT lhum frûj l'wâl* "yesterday plan . . . she sent the first group to them" (line 54). She said this in reference to American military support for the Israeli occupation. To Kaltoum, it sounded like the Old Fassi pronunciation for *TarTa'* "to explode" (using both Old Fassi glottal stop /ʔ/ and alveolar approximate /ɹ/), so she began an Old Fassi riff on the idea that America provides weapons to Muslims collaborating with Israel (the Palestinian Authority, Egyptian leaders) to explode on their Muslim brothers (lines 56, 58). Kaltoum employed increased tempo and loudness (line 48), as well as a performative religious phrase to constitute Muslims as traitors to their own faith as she pronounced the words *kufr billah* "unbelievers, by God!" In doing this, she playfully, but authoritatively, positioned herself in relation to the complexities of violence in Palestine/Israel. She switched back to new Fassi (the widespread new urban variety) after the first sentence, but the key here was how phonological slips, performative phrases, and voice quality became affective resources for critically evaluating regional political alignments.

These exchanges all took place within a two-minute window of interactional time and demonstrate the wealth of affective layering involved in Moroccan families' collaborative evaluations and analysis of conflict. Bodily gesture (not included in the transcript but present in the interaction) coordinated with voice quality (loudness and speed), evaluatively laden religious phrases, and language variety shifts to recognize the complex structuring of violence and question its moral logic. The family's emotional positioning was not viewed as irrational, but as a natural expression of intense involvement in the death of others, in this case both Palestinians and Corrie as casualties of the violence. It was also the outcome of successive evidence (recounted and understood as common knowledge) supporting their collective critique of those complicit in structuring conflict. The rest of the conversation surrounding the violence in Palestine (which continued for another two minutes) included a co-constructed recounting of Rachel Corrie's story.

Toufiq 59:   لا لا كتشوف هادوك، هاد الصحفيين را فيهوم (0.02)

lâ lâ katshûf hâdûk hâd lSHafîîn râ fîhûm

no, no you see these reporters, they have among them

شتي ديك الصحفية اللي دازو فيها بالطركس؟

shtî dîk lSHafîa illî dâzû fîhâ blTraks

see that reporter who they ran over with the caterpillar?

Kaltoum 60:   هاأأ (0.01)

hââ (0.01)'

No (0.01)

Toufiq 61:   فاش كانت تعرضت ليهم (0.01)

fâsh kânat t'arDat lîhum (0.01)

when she opposed them (0.01)

من داك منضمة حقوق الانسان

mn dâk mnaDma Hqûq lîñsân

from that human rights organization

Toufiq 62:   كانو مشاو [لتمایة] فاش كانو [تیهدمو،] [كيريبو]

kânû mshâw [ltmâya] fâsh kânû [tîhadmû] [kîrîbû]

they went there when they demolished

Aicha 63:   [هآآآ]

[*ââh*]

[oh yeah]

Kaltoum 64:   [سمعتها]

[*sm'athâ*]

[I heard about her]

Zoubida 65:   [آه]

[*âh*]

[yea]

Toufiq 66:   كيريبو المباني، الاسرائيليين

kîrîbû lmbânî lîsra'îlîn

they destroyed the houses, the Israelis

اوو وقفت للجرارات (.) كنو واقفين (.) [آوو]

âww waqft liljârât (.) *knû wâqfîn* (.) [*âww*]

so she stood (.) they stood (.) [oowh[

دَاز [فِيهَا][Zahra 67:

dâz [fîhâ][

he ran [over her][

After the intense riff concerning Muslim on Muslim violence by Kaltoum, Toufiq redirected the family's attention (using distal demonstratives and adverbs such as "those" and "there") to the actors and events involved with Rachel Corrie's death (lines 59, 62). He used the Arabic word for reporters (*lSaHafiîn,* seen as observers and witnesses of civilian casualties in conflict zones) to refer to the human/peace rights organization with whom she was working (line 59). Kaltoum, Zoubida, and another sister (Aicha) who had just entered the room, all briefly signaled their recollection of Corrie's story as the details unfold: "oh yeah," "I heard about her," "yea" (lines 63–65). As Toufiq described the facts building up to the Israeli bulldozer driver's actions, his mother interjected with the climatic detail: *dâz fîhâ* "he ran over her" (line 67). Almost as if carefully orchestrated, at exactly the same time as the mother's statement of the action, Toufiq issued an empathetic exclamation of embodied pain: *âwwh* "oowh" (line 66). Together, mother and son co-articulated event narration with affective response, seamlessly shifting from raconteur to compassionate enactor and back to narrator. They continued this collaborative narration in lines 68–72, while discussing the institutional and individual actors.

]مشي حقوق الانسان، منضمة آآآ   Toufiq 68:

] *mashî Hqûq lînsân mnaDama âââ*

]not from a human rights organization, an organization. . .ahh

اللي كدعي للسلام (0.01) كسميتها؟

îllî kd'aî lilsalâm (0.01) *ksmîthâ*

that one that is calling for peace (0.01) what's its name

(0.02)

يونسكو   Zahra 69:

yûnesko

UNESCO

لا لا لا (0.01) إه.(0.01) شي حاجة بلا حدود   Toufiq 70:

lâ lâ lâ (0.01) âh (0.01) *shî Hâja blâ Hudûd*

No, no, no, no (0.01) Ah (0.01) something "without borders"

(0.02)

Zahra 71:   إوا المهم ماعليناش

îwâ lmuhim mâ'alînâsh

well, no matter, it's not important

Toufiq 72:   ماعليناش كيما گولتي

mâ'alînâsh kîmâ gûltî

it's not important, as you said

مشات وقفت ليهم كتعرض لهم

mshât wqfat lîhum kt'arD lhum

she went, stood in front of them, opposing them

بقاو كيخووهم باش

bqâw kîkhûwhum bâsh

they continued to evacuate in order

يطيحوا الديور

yTîHû ldâr

to collapse the houses

(0.01)

هي مابغاتش (0.01) بغاو

hîya mâbghâtsh (0.01) bghâw

she did not want (this), (0.01) they wanted

لاخر جا بغا يهددها

lâkhr jâ bghâ yihdadhâ

the other (the one driving the caterpillar) came threatening her

ولا مانعرف، كيقيصها بالطراكس

wlâ mân'araf kîqayShâ bilTraks

or I don't know (something like that), he hits her with the catepillar

كيدوز فيها

kaydûz fîhâ

he runs over her

داز فيها بالطراكس

dâz fîhâ bilTraks

(↑RAISED TONE)   he ran over her with the catepillar

(0.02)

Toufiq could not recall the exact name of Corrie's organization, so his
mother proffered a UN agency she knew about from its activities in Morocco,

UNESCO (line 69). She concluded that the name was irrelevant to the story, as the tale was stalling on Toufiq's preoccupation with that detail. He agreed and pressed forward, shifting from a past tense narrative frame into a more vivid present tense account of the greater context for Corrie's activism: foreigners protesting Israeli demolition of Palestinian homes (line 72). They then began discussing how her foreign status would be perceived in relation to the violent act.

Toufiq 73:   مانعرف هي بريطانية ولا ميريكانية

mân'araf hîya brîTânîya wlâ mîrîkânîya

I don't know, (perhaps) she is British or American

Kaltoum 74:   [إي ي]

[ây ây]

ay ay

Zahra 75:   [[ومالهما]] [[شغايديرو لها]]

[[shughâydîrû lhâ]] [wmâlhmâ]

[and who cares] (i.e. Israelis) [[what should they do for her]]

(SAR)

Kaltoum 76:   [[هووووو]]

[[huuuu]]

[[INTAKE OF BREATH]]

Toufiq 77:   وهادو، هاد الصحفيين أغلبيتهم ماشي من لهاه

wahâdû hâd lSHafîîn 'aghlabîythum mâshî min lhayh

and those, those journalists, most of them are not from there

(0.01)

Des Americans (FR) أغلبيتهم (0.01) فرانسيين ولا سبليونيين ولا ↖

↖ *'aghlabîythum (0.01) frânsîîn wlîsbalyûnîîn wlâ (FR) des Americains*

↖ most of them (0.01) are French or Spanish or (FR) Americans

Kaltoum 78:   Des Ètrangers. . . . bien sur Des Ètranger

Foreigners, of course foreigners (FR)

Toufiq ended his account with an observation that Corrie was either American or British. The mother and sister responded to this at the same time, the sister with an emotional intake of breath over Corrie's demise (line 76), and the mother with a sarcastic observation that the Israelis would not care what her nationality was insofar as she was helping Palestinians (line 74). This prompted Toufiq to comment that most of the observers in this story were not Palestinians, restating the idea in both Arabic and French, and raising voice pitch for greater affective emphasis (line 77). While not explicitly stated, this line of reasoning assumed that had Corrie not been a foreigner, her name and death would not have made the news. The eldest sister stumbled over her pronunciation of the French term for foreigners, engaging in an embarrassed self-repair (line 78). This began a collective teasing riff of Kaltoum's poor pronunciation and the conversation returned to the discussion about religion that preceded this interaction.

As demonstrated in this extended analysis, all contributed to the affective response of visual and verbal violence narrations related to the Palestinian-Israeli conflict. The actual logic of violence was collaboratively constructed and shifted as the interactants' inputs altered the telling and evaluated its meaning through emotive and narrative co-articulation. This family interwove affect and analysis, constructing a position against conflict's human toll belied by the professional pace and dispassionate tone of the *Grand Angle* preview.

Gender and Affective Evaluation

As mentioned previously, language ideologies serve to naturalize our linking of speech styles to communal character traits. Ideology does so by evaluating all rationales for ways of speaking in relation to a supposed norm, such as reasoned discourse must be dispassionate in order to serve as a basis for modern society (Briggs and Bauman 2003). This then serves as a basis for hierarchies and disparities on other levels. Gal and Irvine call this *recursivity*, whereby linguistic difference is refracted through multiple levels in society (1995). The "Western" language ideology that links women's emotional expression to irrationality is an example of such recursive nesting of gender and nature (Capps and Ochs 1996; Lutz 1990).

Of course, people refract ideologies in many ways. One example I offered previously: American political leaders viewing Arab leaders' emotive language as emasculating (Mart 2007). In a similar vein, scholarly analyses of Moroccan speech styles register a version of this gendered refraction. They have posited exclamatory interjections, such as *wîllî*, as indexical of women's speech, and linked with illiteracy and emotionalism (Hachimi 2001; Kapchan 1996; Sadiqi 1995, 2003). I found this ideology in everyday Moroccan metalinguistic accounts of gendered language styles. Despite the discourses of gendered forms in Morocco, both men and women used these linguistic features to accomplish a variety of ends in the recordings I analyzed. Sometimes they indexed surprise, but at other times they served other functions, such as teaching morality in relation to television content. Rather than reify notions of gendered speech, I want to further the idea that both men and women used these indexical forms to accomplish many things, including reasoned evaluative positioning based on context and interactants in television talk.

In the following viewing event, a retired father, his two unmarried sons (ages thirty-five and twenty-seven) and I were watching satellite television while waiting for lunch to be served. Lunch arrived while they watched various programs, the eldest son channel surfing to kill time. The twenty-year-old daughter (who prepared the food) stayed in the kitchen while the rest ate, only occasionally coming into the salon. The mother returned home after all had eaten and dessert was being served. The father received national medical training in French and worked as a nurse before he retired. The sons both finished high school and while the younger had gone to Ivory Coast to make his way in the world (returning to Morocco because of civil conflict after seven years), the eldest had earned a university degree in English. All the men were more or less fluent in French and MSA. The eldest son controlled the satellite remote and moved from a Saudi music station to the Arab news channel, *Al Arabiyya,* and finally to English-language *Euronews.* The British broadcaster began with headlines which included a bombing in Iraq while Shi'ites had gathered to celebrate the martyrdom of Husayn (known as *'ashûra*); a separate bombing in Pakistan; a pedophile trial in Belgium; and a recent satellite rocket launch in Europe.

CHANGED TO EURONEWS, MUSIC OF BREAKING HEADLINES (0.09)

:Chafiq 1   نزيد نفهمو شوية الانكليزية (0.01)

nzîd nafhmû shwîyat lînglîzîa

We'll understand a little more English. (0.01)

(LOUDER)

ها بيكي هي اللي غاتفهم وتفسر لي

hâ bîkî hîya îllî ghâtfahm watafsar lî

Now Becky will understand and explain to me

:Father 2   (XXX)

:Chafiq 3   العراق

l'irâq

Iraq

:Becky 4   آ,[

mm[

Oh[

Father 5:   [شوف [شوف شوف]

]shûf [shûf shûf]

]look, [look look]

Younes 6:   [شوف شوف] شوف]

shûf [shûf shûf]

[look, look,] look[

Chafiq 7:   [الشيعة (.) مشكيل هاد صباح

]lshî'a (.) mushkîl hâd SbâH

]The Shia (.) a problem this morning

Father 8:   شكون هاد الشي؟

shkûn hâd shî

Who is this?

Chafiq 9:   الشيعة فإيران، آه (.) فالعراق (0.02)

lshî'a fîrân âh (.) fli'râq (0.02)

The Shia in Iran ah (.) in Iraq (0.02)

اليوم عندهم الديكرة داعشورة (.) ديال الخسين

lyom 'andhum ldîkra da'shûra (.) dyâl lHusayn

Today they have the commemoration of Ashura (.) for Husayn

اليوم عندهم الديكرة (.)

lyom 'andhum ldîkra (.)

today they have the commemoration (.)

(0.03)

Becky 10:   نهار ل . . .

nhâr l . . .

the day of . . .

Chafiq 11:   وقع واحد (FR) لbombardment

waq' wâHd l (FR) bombardment

The (FR) bombing happened

Becky 12:   ام

am

mm

HEADLINES TOPIC CHANGE TO SPACE EXPLORATION
(0.07)

صواريخ   :Younes 13

Swârîkh

rockets

ECHOING THE ENGLISH HEADLINE (0.03)

the mysteries of space (ENG) آ   :Chafiq 14

ah (ENG) the mysteries of space

In this context, the eldest son, Chafiq, positioned himself as a translator, mediating between me as the researcher, the English language news, and his Arabic/French-speaking family. He switched between Arabic, French, and English in his utterances, sometimes to index his skills (lines 5, 14), at other times as part of his regular translator/cultural broker repertoire (line 11). He moved fluidly between affective response and interpretation, both of the unimpassioned English announcers' comments and their significance in terms of Islamic history. His translations encoded evaluations and elaborations he felt necessary to contextualize events for his father and brother (lines 9, 11). The historical account of Husayn's martyrdom and the *'ashûra* mourning ritual are known in Morocco, but not fully understood since the country is almost exclusively Sunni Muslim and the ritual would only ever be observed on television. He used terms indexing specific meanings in Moroccan religious practices (*dîkra*, which in this context means commemoration but in Morocco is associated with mystical religious practice) to convey more than ritual but also an unorthodox connotation (line 9). Throughout this exchange, Chafiq saw his role as cultural broker to include a rationale for and evaluative commentary on events. Similar to the family television viewing event examined earlier, triple repetitions of directives (*shûf shûf shûf* "look look look" in lines 5–6) not only called attention to visual news content but also the intensity of speaker involvement in the topic. During both the headlines and the extended reporting on the bombing in Iraq, these directives were used by the father and his sons to construct collaborative engagement. As the British RP (Received Pronunciation) English-inflected news announced events in Iraq, the visceral bombing sights and sounds elicited the eldest son's automatic recognition of the Shi'ite victims (lines 7 and 9) before his father queried for more details (line 8). Chafiq situated the victims (Shia), the location (Iraq), the context (during *'ashûra*), and the cause (bombing).

The news broadcast moved from headlines to more in-depth coverage of the bombing at the pilgrimage shrine of Hussein in Kerbala, Iraq, during *'ashûra*, the most important religious ritual for Shia Muslims. The video montage included sounds of ambulance sirens, women and men screaming and running frantically from an urban area shrouded in smoke, men carrying the bloodied and maimed bodies of Shia pilgrims in wheelbarrows and carts. As all present watched the violence on screen, emotion and demands for understanding and rationale unfolded in response.

(VISUALS OF DISMEMBERED, WOUNDED AND DEAD)

Younes 15:   شوف شوف كيضربو، شتي كيضربو

shûf shûf kîDarbû, shtî kîDarbû

look, look they struck them, see, they struck them

(0.21)

All 16:   آوو

âww

Oww

(0.3)

Father 17:   آويلي

âwîllî

Oh dear

(0.02)

Younes 18:   ميريكانيين هادوك، منين؟ آدوي

mîrîkânîîn hâdûk, mnîn? âdwî

Are those Americans? Speak!

Chafiq 19:   هادو آبا كان عندهم ديالهم الديكرة ديال الحسين ديال الشيعة

hâdû âbâ kân 'andhum dyâlhum ddîkra dyâl lHsayn dyâl shshî'a

Those, Dad, had their commemoration of Husayn, the Shia

Father 20:   ام

âm

mm

Chafiq 21:   وكيجيو من مختلف [الجمعيات] وتيطلعو بحال يللى كيحجيو تما

wakîjîû mn mkhtalif [lja'mîât] watîTl'aû bHâl îlî kîHajîû tmâ

and they come from different groups and go up like, they pilgrimage there

Father 22:   [إيران]

[îrân]

[Iran]

Younes 23:   إوا

îwâ

and so

Chafiq 24: وقع واحد القانبل واش، شكون اللي دارو؟ مانعرف (.) غيكون دارو غي شي

waq' wâHd lqnâbl wâsh shkûn illî dârû? mân'arf (.) ghîkûn dârû ghî shî

A bombing happened and who did it? I don't know (.) the one who could do it may just. . .

Father 25: آه مايكون غير دوك الباندية

âh mâykûn ghîr dûk lbândîya

ah, certainly just those bandits

(0.02)

Chafiq 26: معرفوش هوما براسهم.

mâ'rfûsh hûmâ brâshum

they don't know themselves

(0.07)

يمكن يكون داك الرجال دصدام حسين

yimkin îkûn dâk rrjâl dSddâm Hsayn

maybe it's Saddam Husayn's men

(0.08)

Father 27: وووووو

ûûûû

ohoooo

(0.06)

Chafiq 28: هادي

hâdî

this. . .

(0.07)

Father 29: وووووو

ûûûû

ohoooo

(0.04)

Younes 30: الجهل الجهل.

ljhil ljhil

ignorance, ignorance

TONGUE CLICK AT IMAGES OF DEAD AND WOUNDED
(HEADLINE MOVES TO BOMBING IN PAKISTAN)

There was a stream of collaborative affective evaluation (including disapproving tongue clicks and embodied pain expressions, *âww, ûûûû*) in response to these television visuals by the men present (lines 16–17, 27–30). This seems a contradiction of the common analytical stereotype that Moroccan women use more emotive interjections than men (Sadiqi 1995:70). The most oft-cited example is *wîllî* (interjection of surprise). The term *wâylûn,* in a decontextualized semantic sense, is a Quranic religious reference to the river in the depths of hell and conveys a bad ending for one's actions. It became *wîllî* in Moroccan Arabic and has a number of functions in everyday discourse. Moroccans use it in a variety of contexts to evoke surprise, to bemoan perceived bad luck, as a moral evaluation of others' choices, to signal disapproval, and to position the speaker as an authority figure. By lengthening and introducing a diphthong to the initial vowel, *wîllî* becomes *wâyllî,* a marker of masculine street toughness and conveys distrust of another speaker's statement. In this interaction, the father used *wîllî,* the "feminine" form, to evince his empathy for the dead and wounded on the screen (line 17).

The collective affective response elicited a demand for responsibility by Younes, the second son. He asked whether Americans were behind this carnage, emphasizing his passionate intent to know with an immediate imperative for someone to respond: *âdwî* "speak!" (line 18). Although Younes requested the answer, Chafiq directed the reply to his father (line 19), who provided recognition with a simple phatic signal *mm* (line 18). As they were eating and only secondarily following the news (notice the pausal lengths between comments), there was quite a bit of topic repetition. Notice too how the eldest son, Chafiq, initiated the extended background comments explaining the Shia commemoration to situate the event (lines 19, 20, 24) and the father and second son, Younes, collaborated in the telling. The father responded to the eldest son's background explanation through a noncommital backchannel cue (line 20), which prompted the eldest son to continue. The father added, in the midst of the extended explanation, that the Shia come from Iran (line 22) and the second son provided the impetus for returning the analysis to assigning responsibility: *îwâ* "and so?" (line 23). Chafiq initially hedged: *waq' wâHd lqnâbl wâsh shkûn illî dârû? mân'arf (.) ghîkûn dârû ghî shî* "a bombing happened and who did it? I don't know the one who could do it may just . . ." (line 24). However, his father blamed those resisting the American occupation (whom he called bandits, line 25) and Chafiq eventually said it may be Saddam loyalists (line 26). Most of Saddam's closest associates were Sunni Muslim, so Chafiq may have been indicating a sectarian shift in the violence.

Much of the interpretation here was framed in evaluative stances taken by the participants present. As images of dismembered and bloodied Shia again dominated the television screen, all the men expressed some level of affective disapproval: verbal utterances of embodied pain (*ûûûû* "ohoooo"), evaluations of the misguided reason for the violence (*ljhil* "ignorance"), or censuring tongue clicks (lines 27–30). In the midst of the extended report on the bombing in Pakistan and the pedophile murder trial in Belgium, the father and Chafiq drew on different assessments of Iraqi history (Iraq as a country of division and hypocrisy, full of difficult people via a famous quote by ninth-century Muslim general al-Hajaj versus Iraq as the cradle of civilization) to construct a reasoned analysis for the area's woes (Schulthies 2009). While there is not space here to examine this interaction, it included emotionally inflected reasoning similar to that in the previous analysis. Making sense of the event was not just explaining the background and parties involved but also entailed a humanizing response to the loss of life and limb. Despite the prevailing stereotype that emotional identification and evaluation are a woman's irrational response, this example included male members of the household situating the news event collaboratively. Their use of affective language features furthered the process of identifying and evaluating rationale for the conflict.

Conclusion

Family evaluations of television news covering war and conflict occurred everyday in relation to the US occupation of Iraq, military actions in Afghanistan, and continued cycles of Israeli/Palestinian violence and reprisals. Morocco may seem far geographically from these conflicts, but in the mediascape of Morocco, they are keenly felt, discussed, debated, and affiliated with in terms of Moroccan identities and meaning-making practices. As one of my Moroccan friends told me, "The Palestinian issue is in our blood. We were born watching it." In other words, Moroccans themselves highlight the way in which news media have contributed to their affiliation with particular sides in regional conflicts. What I analyze in this chapter is their collaborative layering of emotive and reasoned responses while watching montages of visual and verbal violence. Despite assumptions that emotion is an individual expression divorced from reason, I illustrated in this chapter how socially distributed forms of affective reasoning emerged in Moroccan families' television talk surrounding news coverage of regional conflict. The communicative events involved multiple participants' intersubjective cooperation in affective reasoning.

I previously argued that this analysis is not a reinscription of a language ideology mapping emotion to Arab irrationality, but rather a recognition that Moroccan families' take part in alternative language practices in which emotion and reason coexist. They are aware of the "Western" media ideology and practice whereby reason is performed through dispassionate presentation. They challenge this linkage by overlaying emotion, engagement, alignment, and analysis in a reasoning montage. As they do this, they provide a window into Moroccan discourses on violence, which find common cause with victims as they seek reasons for the violence. They don't always agree on the rationale, but they collaboratively build forms of interaction whereby emotion and reason coexist as a signal of cosmopolitan Moroccan sensibilities.

Associations existing at one level of indexical significance, such as emotion and irrationality, become available for mapping onto other oppositions in new contexts. For example, even in Morocco emotional evaluative speech forms are claimed to be indexical of female irrationality. Yet emotional interjection as female indexical is problematic when affect is understood as a collaborative and emergent mechanism signally something other than irrationality. Families watching news reports of violence and conflict engaged in analysis of violence actors, causes, motivations, and outcomes. They simultaneously signaled, through emotive expression, recognition of the human costs and their own connection to violence narratives. In many of the viewing events of war and conflict covered by the news that I observed and recorded, Moroccan families displayed visible and verbal solidarity with Arab and Muslim victims of foreign interventions. Yet they also expressed collectively constructed affective stances toward soldiers, activists, and expatriates as victims of structural power. Responses such as these indicate a broader recognition of conflict victims than might be readily assumed by ethnic or religious affinity. The role of affect here served not only to signal victim solidarity but also a Moroccan means of disrupting dispassionate news presentation styles. As they responded to news representations of violence, they deployed affect (encoded in prosody, phonology, vocables, and phrases) to evaluate and make sense of conflict motivations. Reasoning, for Moroccans, entailed emotion and performed an evaluative stance against distancing ways of discussing violence. In doing so, they implicitly signaled that discourses of peace need to recognize locally salient ways of reasoning if they wish to work toward a reduction in both armed and structural forms of violence.

Transcription Key

ض	ص	ش	س	ز	ر	ذ	د	خ	ح	ج	ث	ت	ب
D	S	sh	s	z	r	dh	d	kh	H	j	th	t	b
ء	ى	و	ه	ن	م	ل	ك	ق	ف	غ	ع	ظ	ط
'	y	w	h	n	m	l	k	q	f	gh	ʿ	Z	T

    ↗   rising intonation or volume

    ↘   falling intonation or volume

    ]   latching

[]	overlap
[[]]	multiple-speaker overlap
(.)	slight pause
(0.02)	pause in seconds
(DIM)	diminutive form
(FR)	French code-switch
(MSA)	Modern Standard Arabic code-switch
(ENG)	English code-switch
HHH	laughter
XXX	incomprehensible talk
(MOC)	mocking
(SAR)	sarcasm
(WH)	whisper
(EMP)	emphasis on word

Long vowels are marked: â, î, û; short vowels as a, i, u. Moroccan Arabic is known for shortening long vowels in MSA to short vowels in the dialect, while short vowels disappear. Sometimes pronunciation will include diphthongs: ay, aw.

References

Abu-Lughod, Lila. 1990. "Shifting Politics in Bedouin Love Poetry." In *Language and the Politics of Emotion*, Catherine Lutz and Lila Abu-Lughod (eds.), 24–45. Cambridge: Cambridge University Press.

Agha, Asif. 2005. "Voice, Footing, Enregisterment." *Journal of Linguistic Anthropology* 15: 38–59.

Briggs, Charles and Richard Bauman. 2003. *Voices of Modernity: Language Ideologies and the Politics of Inequality*. Cambridge: Cambridge University Press.

Besnier, Niko. 1990. "Language and Affect." *Annual Review of Anthropology* 19: 129–51.

Capps, Lisa and Elinor Ochs. 1995. *Constructing Panic: The Discourse of Agoraphobia*. Cambridge, MA: Harvard University Press.

Ennaji, Moha. 2005. *Multilingualism, Cultural Identity and Education in Morocco*. New York: Springer Media.

Fanon, Franz. 2008 [1952]. *Black Skins, White Masks*. New York: Grove Press.

Friedman, Thomas. 2006. "MidEast Rules to Live By." *New York Times*. December 20, sec. A.

Gal, Susan and Judith Irvine. 1995. "The Boundaries of Languages and Disciplines: How Ideologies Construct Difference." *Social Research* 62: 967–1001.

Gillespie, Marie. 1995. *Television, Ethnicity, and Cultural Change*. London: Routledge.

Graiouid, Said. 2007. "A Place on the Terrace: Café Culture and the Public Sphere in Morocco." *Journal of North African Studies* 12: 531–50.

Hachimi, Atiqa. 2005. Dialect Leveling, Maintenance, and Urban Identity in Morocco: Fessi Immigrants in Casablanca. PhD dissertation, Department of Linguistics, University of Hawaii.

Hachimi, Atiqa. 2001. "Arabic. Shifting Sands: Language and Gender in Moroccan Arabic." In *Gender across Languages*, Marlis Hellinger and Hadumod Bußmann (eds.), 27–51. Philadelphia, PA: John Benjamins.

Inoue, Miyako. 2002. "Gender, Language, and Modernity: Toward an Effective History of Japanese Women's Language." *American Ethnologist* 29(2): 392–422.

Irvine, Judith. 1982. "Language and Affect: Some Cross-Cultural Issues." In *Georgetown Roundtable on Language and Linguistics*, Heidi Byrnes (ed.), 31–47. Washington, DC: Georgetown University Press.

Irvine, Judith. 1989. "When Talk Isn't Cheap: Language and Political Economy." *American Ethnologist* 16(2): 248–67.

Irvine, Judith and Susan Gal. 2000. "Language Ideology and Linguistic Differentiation." In *Regimes of Language*, Paul V. Kroskrity (ed.), 35–84. Santa Fe, NM: School of American Research.

Johnstone, Barbara. 1990. "'Orality' and Discourse Structure in Modern Standard Arabic." In *Perspectives on Arabic Linguistics I: Papers from the First Annual Symposium on Arabic Linguistics*, Mushira Eid (ed.), 215–33. Philadelphia: John Benjamins.

Johnstone, Barbara. 1991. *Repetition in Arab Discourse: Paradigms, Syntagms, and the Ecology of Language*. Amsterdam: John Benjamins.

Kaphchan, Deborah. 1996. *Gender on the Market: Moroccan Women and the Revoicing of Tradition*. Philadelphia: University of Pennsylvania Press.

Lutz, Catherine. 1990. "Engendered Emotion: Gender, Power, and the Rhetoric of Emotional Control in American Discourse." In *Language and the Politics of Emotion*, Catherine Lutz and Lila Abu-Lughod (eds.), 69–91. Cambridge: Cambridge University Press.

Lutz, Catherine. 1988. *Unnatural Emotion: Everyday Sentiments on a Micronesian Atoll and Their Challenge to Western Theory*. Chicago, IL: University of Chicago Press.

Lynch, Marc. 2006. *Voices of the New Arab Public: Iraq, Al-Jazeera, and Middle East Politics*. New York: Columbia University Press.

Mart, Michelle. 2007. *Eye on Israel: How America Came to View Israel as an Ally*. Albany: State University of New York Press.

Ochs, Elinor. 1986. "From Feelings to Grammar." In *Language Socialization across Cultures*, Bambi Schieffelin and Elinor Ochs (eds.), 251–72. Cambridge: Cambridge University Press.

Ochs, Elinor and Bambi Schieffelin. 1989. "Language Has a Heart." *Text* 9(1): 7–25.

Patai, Raphael. 1976. *The Arab Mind*. New York: Scribner Press.

Rosaldo, Michelle. 1984. "Toward an Anthropology of Self and Feeling." In *Cultural Theory: Essays on Mind, Self and Emotion*, Richard Shweder and Robert LeVine (eds.), 137–57. Cambridge: Cambridge University Press.

Sadiqi, Fatima. 2003. *Women, Gender and Language in Morocco*. Leiden: Brill.

Sadiqi, Fatima. 1995. "The Language of Women in the City of Fes, Morocco." *International Journal on the Sociology of Language* 112: 63–79.

Said, Edward. 1979. *Orientalism*. New York: Vintage Books.

Schulthies, Becky. 2009. *The Social Circulation of Media Scripts and Collaborative Meaning-Making in Moroccan and Lebanese Family Discourse*. Unpublished dissertation, University of Arizona.

Silverstein, Michael. 2003. "Indexical Order and the Dialectics of Sociolinguistic Life." *Language and Communication* 23: 193–229.

Suchan, Jim. 2010. "Toward an Understanding of Arabic Persuasion." Paper presented at the Annual Convention of the Association for Business Communication, Chicago. Accessed December 5, 2010. www.businesscommunication.org/conventionsNew/.../ABC-2010-22.pdf.

Wilce, James. 2009. *Language and Emotion*. Cambridge: Cambridge University Press.

Zogby, James. 2010. *Arab Voices: What They Are Saying to Us and Why It Matters*. New York: Palgrave Macmillan.

PART FOUR

Promoting Peace

10

Performing Peace

THE FRAMING OF SILENCE IN A QUAKER VIGIL

Anna Marie Trester

Introduction

Every week since October 2002, a group comprised largely of Quakers from the Washington, DC, area has gathered on the lawn of the US Capitol Building to stand together for an hour as part of a silent vigil for peace. As I will explore in this investigation, there are multiple meanings to their silence that may be considered from the perspective of both the sender and the receiver, both literally and metaphorically. Crucially however, gathering together to remain meaningfully silent is understood by participants as a way to bear public witness to peace, resonating with the message on the banner held at the center of the vigil from Psalms 34:14, which reads: "seek peace and pursue it."

As explained to me by one of the original organizers of the event, the most important thing to understand about this group is that they stand for peace; they are not simply opposed to war. This belief manifests in their continuing to hold the event regardless of events occurring on the world stage, and in choosing this Psalm[1] to contextualize their vigil; not because their religious tradition orients to the Bible as its central organizing text, but because this passage is recognizable and communicates in a positive way that peace is an achievement, requiring constant searching and work.

However, given that the majority of passers-by to the vigil are unlikely to be familiar with the Quaker peace testimony (if indeed they even recognize this group to be Quaker), vigilers employ a number of what I will analyze here as *framing devices* (Goffman 1974), or cues to signal "what is going on here?" Specifically, I focus on observed linguistic and visual changes to (1) the banner held at the vigil (as mentioned above), (2) flyers disseminated at the event (which state the goals, purpose, and later history) of the vigil, and (3) *emplacement* or where

---

[1] Currently, a printed version of this Psalm is disseminated at the vigil for those unfamiliar with the passage.

in the physical world this vigil and its surrounding texts and images are located (Scollon and Scollon 2003: 142). Additionally, while many aspects of the vigil changed over the period of ethnographic observation, one passage on the flyer, reading, "we intend our prayerful silence to bring light to our world," has remained consistent, as has the passage printed on the banner and indeed the silence itself. I explore how these texts reflect and produce Quaker beliefs and especially how their use of silence as a text relates to the performance of signs, in this case, drawing on metaphorical meanings of "the light."

STRUCTURE OF THE CHAPTER

I begin by describing my ethnographic engagement with this vigil or "moment of social action" in Scollon and Scollon's (2003, 2004) Nexus Analysis framework. As introduction for the reader, I provide some background about Quakers' beliefs, focusing on their understanding of silence as it relates to their belief in "the light" or "that of God within" each person. To interpret the meanings of silence for this community, I draw from other discourse analytic research that has been done of this aspect of language. In the analysis section of the chapter, I begin by considering shifts in location of the vigil, considering how the meanings of this silent performance are derived by virtue of where it is located in time and space, drawing from Scollon and Scollon's (2003, 2004) concept of emplacement. Then, I use interactional sociolinguistics to explore changes in *framing* (Goffman 1981) devices used to cue interpretation of this silent performance, the banner and the flyer. I consider how visual and semiotic changes in the banner mirror linguistic shifts in the flyer, including use of referring expressions (Schiffrin 2006), and changes in illocutionary force (Searle 1969). Ultimately, I suggest that these devices work to construct shifting relationships with audience(s), which in turn (re)interpret the meaning(s) of silence against an ever-shifting background of US involvement in Iraq from 2003 to the present, performing and reinforcing Quaker beliefs and values of peace and nonviolence.

Background: The Vigil, Quakers, and Silence

DATA AND METHODS: THE VIGIL

Data are drawn from weekly participant observation with this group of vigilers from January through August of 2003. As part of my ethnographic fieldwork, in addition to field notes, I collected materials disseminated at the event and monitored web communication surrounding the vigil (e-mail correspondence and posts to community listservs), noting, as I will describe in greater detail in the analysis section to follow, a number of changes over this span of time including where and when the vigil is held, who participates in and who organizes the vigil, how participation is structured, and how it is described (framed) in the materials that describe and advertise it. Additionally, over the course of participant observation, I came to realize that I could not understand what was happening at the vigil without learning more about Quaker religious practice, thus, my analysis is informed by ongoing involvement in the Quaker community in the DC area including attending meetings for worship at Friends Meeting of Washington (FMW).

My analysis is informed by the approach to the ethnography of communication pioneered by Scollon and Scollon (2004) known as Nexus Analysis. Following this approach, the researcher aims to discover the social actors and actions "crucial in the production of a social issue" in order to bring about social change (153). The research process begins by selecting a *moment of social action*:

> S*ocial action* occurs at the intersection of three factors: historical bodies of the *participants* in that action, the *interaction order* which they mutually produce among themselves and the *discourses in place* which enable that action or are used by the participants as *mediational means* in their action. (153: emphasis mine)

Thus, to understand this particular silent vigil, I needed to understand the participants and their background (as I will describe in the following section), the interaction order of the vigil (which I elaborate on here), and the discourses in place (and how they are used). Among these discourses, I found silence to be of particular importance, and I adopt a functional approach to the analysis of this group's use of silence as part of vigiling. I understand such an approach to mean that "the same interpretive processes apply to someone's remaining meaningfully silent in discourse as to their speaking" (Jaworski 1993: 3). I further understand the silence by exploring it in context with the other discourses in place which surround it such as the banner, the flyer, and metacommentary about the vigil. In so doing, I wish to illuminate how silence both enables the action of the vigil and is used by participants as *mediational means* or a resource brought into use.

In conducting Nexus Analysis, the researcher establishes a "zone of identification" with the actions and participants, such that she comes to be recognized as a fellow participant in the nexus of practice. If here, the moment of social action is that of standing in silence with a banner on the lawn of the US Capitol, I as researcher only came to understand these social actors, their interaction order, the significant cycles of discourse, and indeed how social change is understood and experienced, through regular attendance at and participation in the vigil. I will now illuminate this by recounting a recent moment of engagement, when we were one of four groups gathered on the Capitol lawn that Saturday at noon (the vigil has shifted since the time of observation from being held on Tuesday evenings at 5 pm).

The largest group was gathered that day in support of Planned Parenthood following recent proposed funding cuts in the House of Representatives. While I never actually saw the second group, I was asked twice for directions to their gathering, which was occurring in solidarity with demonstrations happening at the State Capitol in Madison, Wisconsin, because of Democratic legislators who left the state to prevent their Republican colleagues from pushing through a budget control bill directed at collective bargaining organizations (worker's unions). Our closest neighbors shouted angrily into megaphones waving hand-drawn signs and creating new ones even as they stood there being photographed and interacting with passersby. This group was asking for US intervention in Nigeria because of violence there. Hundreds of people walked about, speaking in a multitude of languages, taking in the spectacle, talking to one another and to the protestors, and snapping photographs. A bride with her bridal party posed in their sleeveless dresses and very high-heeled shoes on the Capitol steps amidst the hustle and the bustle. Amid this activity, our group stood in stillness and in silence.

It was a windy day, so we were struggling to hold together our tattered banner, which is beginning to show nearly nine years of weekly use. Gingerly, I handed it to a man from Northern Ireland who asked if he could take over holding the banner for a moment so that his wife could photograph him "standing for peace." Later, as we smoothed it out for a woman from Qatar who wanted a close-up photograph of the word "peace" to have as an image that she could set as the background on her Blackberry, her friend, standing next to me and taking in the spectacle and passersby observed, "Many of them read, but how many of them understand?" My own silent meditation was at times interrupted, as when a man shouted angrily at us that we were naïve to believe in peace when there are situations like the one at that time occurring in Libya where people must engage in violent conflict to secure their own rights. At other times, my prayerful meditation was strengthened, as when a man from Kentucky, overhearing that exchange, shared his own history of violent pro-tests for oppressed workers' rights. "It's complicated" was his assessment, and before leaving, he observed that while all of the protestors on the Capitol that day were expressing opposition to violence and oppression, our group was expressing the message in terms of supporting something positive rather than opposing something negative.

The quality of the vigil itself is always different, owing to the changing social and political context. The biggest vigil I attended was on the evening of the second inauguration of George W. Bush and participation has been consis-tently smaller following the inauguration of Barack Obama. Even for a group who organize themselves around an enduring belief in peace rather than oppo-sition to war, the call to participation seems to ring louder amid crisis and conflict. Indeed, such were the circumstances under which I first encountered the group in the early spring of 2003 leading up to the US invasion of Iraq on

March 20. At that time, having recently moved to Washington, DC, I was looking for a means of adding my own voice to the conversation about my country's actions on the world stage.

I came to understand that some participants had left this particular vigiling group because they felt it did not make enough of an expression of radical and countercultural commitment to peace (indeed even today, as they have been historically, some Quakers feel called to be arrested as a public statement of personal beliefs), but also that those who do feel called to participate in the vigil understand it as *doing* something. Participants sacrifice their time and suffer hardship including standing in the blinding heat of midday in the DC summer and in feet of snow in the winter, enduring at times driving rain, sleet, and even hail because they see participation as doing something active to live their beliefs. For example, the man who is currently clerking (maintaining responsibility for) the vigil is in failing health and his weekly commitment to participate means further sacrificing his health and at times his physical safety to be there (more than once he has gone from vigiling straight to the hospital). To understand the beliefs that guide such practice, I briefly provide some background on Quakerism.

QUAKERISM

Quakers, or the Religious Society of Friends, are a spiritual community whose cultural and religious practices are marked by the core belief in "that of God within" each person, as manifested in practices such as egalitarianism (there is no pastor in Quaker meetings), social activism (pursuit of justice for all people; Quakers were among the first groups to oppose slavery), and historical opposition to war (which as I will show, is perhaps better understood as a belief in peace, not an opposition to war). The Quaker faith emerged in England in the 1600s when George Fox, a soldier, traveled the country (and later parts of Europe and the United States) speaking publicly against military service as well as the pledging of oaths and the practice of tithing. His ministry began in the context of a civil war, providing the context against which the early Quaker relationship to peace should be understood (Orr 1974).

Fox's statement to Charles II in 1660 formed the foundation of the Quaker Peace Testimony (Brock 1990), a statement of belief expressing opposition to war.

> Our Principle is, and our Practices have always been, to seek peace, and ensue it, and to follow after righteousness, and the knowledge of God, seeking the Good and Well-fare, and doing that which tends to the peace of All, Wee know that Warres and Fightings proceed from the Lusts of men, as Jam. 4. 1, 2, 3. out of which Lusts the Lord hath redeemed us; And so out of the Occasion of War; the Occasion of which War, and the War it self (wherein envious men, who are lovers of themselves more than lovers

of God, lust, kil, & desire to have mens lives or estates) ariseth from the lust. (Fox, 1660: 1)

Quaker pacifism has been and continues to be complex, for while Quakers have perhaps been best known in this country for their opposition to wars that were deemed essential, necessary, or just by the larger society (Ryan 2009: 6–7), many early followers of Quakerism were in the army, who in fact provided crucial support for the religious movement in its infancy (Brock 1990). Also, many modern-day Quakers work in or for the military, in the foreign service, and for government. As I will show, the Quaker tradition is one that embraces dualities, and reconciling a standing commitment to peace with participation in military service is but one example of the cultural tolerance for difference of opinion, disagreement, and even dissent, which informs all Quaker practice.

Quakers live a peace testimony that is comprised of concrete actions to work for peace including protesting against wars, refusing to pay taxes unless the money will not be used to fund war, refusing to serve in armed forces if drafted, seeking conscientious objector (CO) status, and working with organizations to support others in those same aims (Meltzer 2002). Importantly, rather than using language to express their belief in peace and their commitment to the peace testimony, actions such as those described earlier are understood as ways of "letting your life speak" which for Quakers are more powerful in that they are less vulnerable to manipulation than is speech. These actions are one way of being *in* the world but not *of* it, as whatever form an individual's living the peace testimony may take, community members share a commitment to living lives that actively pursue social and economic justice rather than being motivated by personal gain, materialism, or indeed results. Thus, the aim of a vigil like this one is not to bring about the end of any particular war but is instead an act of peace, whose effectiveness (if measured at all) would not be measured at the global scale and might indeed be understood at the level of one individual coming to experience peace in one particular moment.

The first Quaker missionaries came to the United States in 1656 to Boston (Dandelion 2007: 250), where they were not welcomed with open arms (Hope Bacon 1999: 1). Early Friends were imprisoned, tortured, deported, even hanged in the Colonies, but by the late 1700s, Quakerism had taken hold, numbering 50,000 of the total population of 1.5 million. Today there are estimated to be approximately 103,000 Quakers in the United States and about 340,000 Quakers worldwide, comprising three principal traditions: Evangelical, Conservative, and Liberal (Dandelion 2008). The largest concentration of Quakers is in Kenya and Burundi, belonging to the Evangelical Tradition. The largest concentration of Quakers in the United States belongs to what is known as the Liberal Quaker tradition. The vigil for peace discussed here is organized and run by or "in the care of" two meetings in the DC area, both of which belong to the Liberal tradition, and more specifically are "unprogrammed Quakers" that, as noted by Ryan (2009), "de-emphasize the Christian legacy of Quaker theology."

QUAKERS AND SILENCE

Unprogrammed weekly hour-long meetings for worship are perhaps most striking for beginning with a period of silence, with a request that any "messages" shared out of the silence by community members be also received with a period of silent reflection. As Saville-Troike (1985) has noted: "Within a single speech community, social values and norms are closely tied to the amount of talk vs. silence that is prescribed to role (sacred or secular), or to age" (4). Within this community, silence is especially valued in sacred contexts and roles, which may be contrasted with religious traditions such as Pentecostals (Maltz 1985), for whom remaining silent as part of worship would be understood as insufficient praise, a failure to adequately observe positive face (both yours and that of God). For Quakers, remaining meaningfully silent accomplishes both observing your own and the negative face wants of your fellow worshippers (allowing them to have the space to listen to God), and allowing space for messages to come through.

As noted by Bauman (1983) in his ethnography of seventeenth-century Quakers, silence in Quaker practice is understood as not merely an end in itself, but a means to the attainment of "the defining spiritual experience" of Quakerism—namely, "the direct personal experience of the spirit of God within oneself" (23). Silence facilitates one's ability to slow down and quiet down enough to be able to achieve openness to and awareness of the spirit of God or "the Light" within (Jaworski 1997b, 1993; Maltz 1985). Quaker ceremonies such as weddings incorporate silence, as do funerals, classes, committee meetings for business, and group discussions. When groups are called to make a decision, the same practice is adopted; thus one evening following an hour of silence as part of the vigil, when members stayed to convene a discussion about the future of the vigil, the convenor asked to begin with "a moment of silence." The meanings and the values attached to silence that exist as part of worship in the sacred context carry over to other contexts and other practices, thus forming not only a central part of Quaker worship practice but also informing Quaker cultural practice more generally.

In their edited volume, Tannen and Saville-Troike (1985) bring together a range of disciplinary approaches to the analysis of silence to explore interpretations, functions, and meanings across disciplines, contexts, and cultures. Saille-Troike advances a broad classification of silences considered at three domains and multiple levels within those: institutionally determined silences, group-determined silence, and individually determined /negotiated silence (16). In considering the silence occurring on the lawn of the US Capitol as part of this vigil, I wish to suggest that it comprises all three. As I have shown, silence is informed by Quaker institutional practices, but the silence has a meaning at the level of the Group, as evidenced in the creation of unifying framing devices such as the banner and the flyer. I will analyze the negotiation of group-level meanings of silence in the analysis section to follow by exploring shifts in their audience-oriented messaging. However, this group is also a collection of individuals, for whom silence is individually practiced, experienced, and understood. In fact, it may even be practiced, experienced, and understood very differently by different participants. Quaker cultural practices, which include tolerance for ambiguity and divergent thinking within the community, allow for considerable internal disagreement about conceptualization of this event as reflected in the diversity of ideas existing at the moment of observation and writing. Revealed in metacommentary about the vigil, another important way such difference expressed itself over the course of observation was through changes to location of the vigil or *emplacement* or where in the physical world this vigil and its surrounding texts and images are located (Scollon and Scollon 2003: 142), as I will now consider.

Analysis

EMPLACEMENT

During the early months of 2003, as tensions escalated on a global scale leading up to the US invasion of Iraq, movement and relocation were very much the norm for this vigil. Changes to location and time were quite frequent and reflective of shifting understandings about the *Key*, *Ends*, and *Genre* (Hymes 1972) of the vigil, responding to growing political pressure. Owing to permit availability for the month of March (large groups holding a banner require police permission to gather in DC), participants made the decision to change the *Setting*, to move the vigil to a location in Upper Senate Park. The US invasion of Iraq took place on March 20. Following this, and through Quaker practices of discernment, when the permit to meet on the West Lawn again become available in April, vigilers decided to hold two vigils simultaneously. One vigil was held at the West Capitol lawn site (the original site) and one in Upper Senate Park, a location farther away from the Capitol and located across the street, but along a major traffic route for commuters to and from Capitol Hill. While both locations are on the Capitol lawn, the latter location is more visible to vehicular traffic and foot traffic. Given that this event takes place at rush hour, the audience (*Participants*) would be largely congressional staffers, while the West Capitol lawn is both closer to the Capitol Building and more visible to tourists (described by one vigiler as a "wider" audience). Example 10.1 features metacommentary about the silent vigil from an e-mail about this decision to hold two separate vigils at these two locations:

Example 10.1: I shall be found on the West Lawn (sent on April 4, 2003)

I read [the choice to have two locations] as recognizing that there are two distinct reasons why people turn up to the vigil.

There are those whose primary purpose is to engage in silent prayer or meditation at the US capitol holding their country and its Administration in the light. There are those who wish to be more observable witnesses for peace carrying their message to a wider audience.

For a while it appeared that both groups could operate at one site. The move from the West Lawn to Upper Senate Park addressed the concerns of the second group.

I shall be found on the West Lawn in future weeks as I feel it is a more suitable place for meditation at this time. I believe that now that it is day-light and the number of tourists has increased, we will experience plenty of 'exposure' at that site. I recognize and support those who wish [to] make a more public statement.

The existence of two *Settings* speaks to divergent perspectives regarding the *Genre* of the event, whether it is internal "silent prayer" and "meditation" or external, something to be witnessed, a "more observable witness for peace." Despite his description of the *Key* of the event as that of solitary prayer and meditation, this participant's simultaneous awareness of and interest in the vis-ibility of the vigil (reflected in his statement "I believe that now that it is day-light and the number of tourists has increased, we will experience plenty of 'exposure' at that site") belies that even for him, this silence is both internal and external (packaged for consumption by an audience). Decisions about which *Participants* are most valued (congressional staffers, tourists), how many are reached, and whether they are audience or object also reflect divergent under-standings of *Genre* and *Ends* of the vigil.

As Saville-Troike (1985) has noted, "silent communicative acts may be an-alyzed as having both illocutionary force and perlocutionary effect" (6), inter-estingly, a primary aspect of the vigil which does not change over time is the *locutionary act* (Searle 1969: 23–24) or the form of the locution, the silence, as I will consider in the following section.

DISCOURSES IN PLACE: SILENCE (PRACTICE AND PERFORMANCE)

While silence inside the walls of the meeting house is framed by context for interpretation as a shared religious practice as allowing access to the voice of God (metaphorically the Light), when silence is decontextualized and collec-tively performed amid the hustle and the bustle surrounding the US Capitol Building, such contextualized meanings are not necessarily available to the var-ious audiences likely to encounter it. As Bauman (1983) explains, "while the ritual frame contextualizes the performance of metaphor and renders it both intelligible and effective" such as might be seen in the context of a religious ceremony, "acting out certain metaphors in other settings may make them more strongly noticeable, but relatively less intelligible as metaphors" (87). Thus, with this silent vigil, I suggest that we are given the opportunity to observe two things: the use of silence, enabling reflection on silence as a meaningful communicative act, but additionally, the performance of silence, which I relate here to Scollon and Scollon's (2004) idea of a discourse in place both enabling that action and serving as a meditational means. Let us explore for a moment how this works.

Example 10.2 is the invitation that appears on the door of the FMW meeting house, which also appears in figure 10.1. While this appears on the door and as such may be understood to be a welcoming into the physical space of the meeting house, what appears instead is in fact an invitation into silence.

Example 10.2: Invitation to Silence (printed on the door of the meeting house)

We gather in silence in the presence of God · In the silence we may worship and listen to the voice of the spirit · Out of the silence His message may also come to us in the spoken word or in prayer · Our meetings for worship are open to all · We invite you to come

—The Religious Society of Friends

As Quakers do not believe in endowing symbolic importance to buildings, nor to language, beliefs manifested in the naming practice of calling this space a

FIGURE 10.1 Invitation to Silence on the door of FMW meeting house

Photo taken by Anna Marie Trester on August 29, 2010

FIGURE 10.2 The Vigil at the Upper Senate Park location, early version of banner
Photo taken by Laura Wright on March 25, 2003

Figure 10.3 shows the new banner and the vigil held in a different *Setting*, namely the West Lawn of the Capitol, as photographed on January 2009 just before the first inauguration of Barack Obama. This original site of the vigil is where it continues to be held at the time of writing, and this image is currently used to publicize the event on the Friends Meeting of Washington[3] listserv.

As mentioned, while the existence of two banners facilitated for a time the ability to hold two vigils simultaneously, at the time of writing, a decision has been made to hold the vigil on the West Lawn site exclusively. The second banner is the only banner used.[4]

Changes to the Banner

The text on the new banner is visually striking for a number of reasons: one is that it is white text on a blue background (instead of blue text on a white background), as may be seen by comparing figures 10.2 and 10.3. The text in the new banner is also bigger, bolder, and in a serif font, features noted as aspects of inscription in Scollon and Scollon's (2003) treatment of place semiotics, which contribute to the interpretation of a more forceful message. This stronger illocutionary force is accompanied also by linguistic changes in the flyer, as I will show in the following section.

Additionally, the new banner is also two-sided, which enables vigilers to perform to at least two audiences at once. Finally, the second banner was accompanied by the decision to move the vigil to the West Lawn, which facilitates the physical orientation of the participants around the banner facing the Capitol (instead of the Mall behind them), indicating that at least symbolically, members of Congress are (for at least some participants) the primary intended audience for this performance, a shift in awareness of audience that is also

---

[3] Friends Meeting of Washington (FMW) currently shares some of the responsibility for the organization of this vigil with the Langley Hill Meeting. The person who currently stores and transports the banner every week is a member at FMW, where the vigil is also often announced as a means for recruiting participants.

[4] In March 2004 a decision was made to move the vigil from Tuesdays at 5 PM to Saturdays from noon to 1 PM, which may be observed to have impacted many aspects of including a reduction in the number of *participants*. Weekly involvement may often be as few as two or three as compared to the previously observed weekly turnout of twenty- or thirty, which can also be understood in terms of the level of urgency that people feel about the situation now that US involvement in Iraq and Afghanistan has been prolonged, and witnessing the change in administration from George W. Bush to Barack Obama.

FIGURE 10.3 The Vigil on the West Capitol Lawn, Banner Version 2

Photo by Jim Kuhn, taken January 2009 (from post to FMW listserv—accessed August 20, 2009)

linguistically constructed, as I will now consider by exploring the shifting construction of relationships to multiple audiences in the flyer.

DISCOURSES IN PLACE: THE FLYER

I focus on three versions of the vigil flyer collected between March and August 2003, which I refer to as versions A through C. A summary of these data is presented in table 10.1, noting aspects relevant to analysis.

In each case, I compare the second paragraph (of three) from the flyer (a sample flyer may be seen in the appendix). On the flyer, this second paragraph

TABLE 10.1

Versions of the Flyer Collected and Analyzed

Version	A	B	C
Date Collected	January 25	March 2	April 11
Summary Characteristics	Speech Act: suggestion agentless passive verbs "to let" "to use"	Speech Act: request "should" "we believe"	Speech Act: request "should" "we believe"
	Addressee: not identified	Addressee: Congress	Addressees: Congress and Nation

speaks to the "meaning" of the vigil, appearing directly after one that describes the location, participants, and history of the vigil, and before a third paragraph detailing any changes of venue, more detailed directions, weather-related clothing suggestions, and other instructions about participation and comportment at the vigil. For ease of analysis and comparison, I have broken this second paragraph into numbered lines, approximating intonation units based on phrase structure.

Speech Acts in the Flyer

In example 10.4, the first version of the flyer I analyze, silence is presented as a suggestion, "we will hold up the option to seek a peaceful path" (line 2). Agentless passive verbs like "to let" and "to use" reinforce the illocutionary force.

Example 10.4: Flyer Version A (Accessed on the web January 25, 20037)

1. Our message is a positive one.
2. Each week of this crisis *we will hold up the option* to seek a peaceful path,
3. *to let* reverence for life guide our actions,
4. and *to use* our country's great strength in the service of the ideal of an international community based on respect and law.
5. No matter what is happening at the time of our vigil,
6. *we intend our prayerful silence to bring light to our world.*
7. Please do not bring additional signs or banners.

A revised version of the flyer was sent out to the mailing list on March 2 by a member of the Langley Hill Friends Meeting (the Quaker group that originally started the vigil in September 2002). In the text of this e-mail, this member explains that he has made "a couple minor edits" from the previous version of the flyer, contextualizing this by providing additional information about other local events and saying that "many of us are intensifying our efforts to avert the potential tragedy in Iraq." In example 10.5, this intensification may be seen as well in the linguistic changes he makes to the text of the flyer—for example, in choosing to use modal verbs like "should" (lines 3 and 4) and the direct articulation of value statements like "we believe" (line 3).

Example 10.5: Flyer Version B (Disseminated via e-mail on March 2, 2003)

1. Our message is a positive one.
2. During the current Iraq crisis, we are *encouraging members of Congress* to seek a peaceful path.
3. *We believe* that a reverence for life *should* guide our nation's actions,
4. and that our country's great strength *should* further the ideal of an international community based on respect and law.
5. We intend our prayerful silence to bring light to the world.

While the *locutionary act* which comprises the vigil "prayerful silence" remains the same, the illocutionary force behind it and perceived perlocutionary effect are quite different in flyer version B, as compared to A. Silence is reframed in version B as a direct suggestion to Congress: "we are *encouraging* members of Congress to seek a peaceful path" (line 2), which may be contrasted with the previous version of the flyer, in which silence was being "held up" as an option. This shift in *illocutionary force* comes into relief when considered along with changes in identified audience, as I will now consider.

Addressee(s) of the Flyer

Arguably the most obvious change in the flyers may be seen in the identification of direct addressees of the silence through use of referring expressions. Whereas in version A, the "prayerful silence" was being "held up," with no use of referring expressions to single out any one particular addressee, version B invokes the referring expression "members of Congress" (line 2) to single out a set of individuals as addressees. It is worth noting here that members of Congress had witnessed and even at times engaged with the vigil and do feature prominently in e-mail discussions about the vigil. For example, appeals to the community for greater vigil participation or decisions to move the vigil via an e-mail post to the listserv will often make reference to congressional activity (i.e., "with several defense spending and international affairs issues before the now busy Congress, it seems a geat [*sic*] time to be continuing our vigil").

The US invasion of Iraq began on March 20, 2003. Following these events, and amid ongoing hostilities, a third version of the flyer was disseminated on April 18, 2003, again via e-mail to the group of vigil participants, but this time with the addition of the referring expression "the Nation," as may be seen in line 2 of example 10.6. The addition of a second addressee here is particularly interesting when you recall that these changes to the flyer occurred at a time when this vigil was being held at two locations simultaneously.

Example 10.6: Flyer Version C (Disseminated via e-mail on April 11, 2003)

1. Our message is a positive one.
2. During the current crisis, we are encouraging the Congress **and the Nation** to seek *and to build* a peaceful path.
3. We believe that a reverence for life should guide our nation's actions,
4. and that our country's great strength should further the ideal of an international community based on respect and law.
5. We intend our prayerful silence to bring light to the world.

Schiffrin (2006) notes that as referring expressions carve up the world to reveal what we know about the world and how we subjectively orient toward it (16), what is *not* said often becomes even more interesting than what is. Similarly, in the address terms used in these flyers, it is worth noting at least two things: first that the president is conspicuously not identified as addressee (as might possibly be expected, given his active and very public role calling for the invasion); also that it is "The Nation" who is being directly addressed despite the fact that a very small percentage of this audience is likely to ever encounter the message. And in fact, the vast majority of those who do view it (at least those who take the step to engage with the vigil) are tourists from other countries.

One final addition of note in version C is the metaphorical extension of the power of silence into that of creation, invoking metaphoric images of construction through use of the text "and to build" in line 2. Thus, while silence may be understood as metaphorically contributing to actions taken to pursue peace, silence in this context may be also understood as reflecting Quaker values including beliefs that "reverence for life should guide action," and in this case *inaction*, a call for the silencing of the activities of war.

Discussion: Performance of Peace and Awareness of Audience

Silence in this context may be understood as an index of literal silence, a literal enactment of prayerful reflection that Quakers prefer to employ in solving problems, and which they seem to desire as the perlocutionary effect on their audience in asking Congress and the Nation to employ silent reflection in decision making. As noted by Bauman (1983), the concepts of speaking and silence were metaphorically extended by early Quakers, speaking coming to be associated with all things human (including violence and corruption), and silence with that of God. Thus, to be silent was to withdraw from the activities of the human world, and in this case to withdraw from war, a metaphorical extension that seems to be palpably present.

Further metaphorical meanings are being accessed as well: recall the aspect of the flyer that was shown not to change: "we intend our prayerful silence to bring light to our world." However, while this light metaphor draws from biblical light imagery and "conveys a sense of God's luster and brilliance and of his spirit as a beacon," it crucially "says little of the substance of his message to man or how it is *communicated*" (Bauman 1983: 24; emphasis in original). And in fact, participants' and recipients' understandings of what is communicated by silence are likely to be widely divergent. For example, while participants in this vigil for peace may understand their silence symbolically as "breaking the silence surrounding the war with a more meaningful silence," as explained to me by one group member, such metaphorical and symbolic meanings and cultural associations of silence are not necessarily available to the various audiences encountering it on the Capitol Lawn, particularly those unfamiliar with Quakers, much less their religious beliefs or cultural practices. Additionally, a perceived incongruity between this textual message and the silent performance at times becomes highlighted. For example, one day I noted in my field notes that a passerby shouted at the group, "seems like your sign should read 'seek peace and then sit back and do nothing!'" Although these vigilers understand their public performance as an embodiment of their intended message of peace, as with the sign performances of the seventeenth-century Quakers described by Bauman, the fuller complexities and layers of metaphorical meaning are, as we have discussed, somewhat less accessible to audiences, of which vigilers are no doubt aware.

However, as this analysis has shown, linguistic changes to the flyer and the banner do reflect a heightened awareness of multiple audiences, both symbolically and visually, along with an attention to context. And while we may observe that the silence of these vigilers is employed verbally and kinesthetically, we may also observe that this event does not employ visual or textual silence. There is a large banner at the center of the event after all, and the vigilers make a deliberate choice to physically interrupt a panoramic tourist vista in a popular tourist destination at a heavily trafficked time. Such choices represent a very powerful way that they chose to *break* visual silence. Further, in strategically choosing to talk about peace (not war), and express their message positively (pro-peace, not anti-war), there are ways in which the vigil is silent about war, while at the same time implicating it by their very act of gathering together in this place at this time (especially when it is observed that there are always bigger groups of people when events of war are taking place).

Recall that when I first began participating with the vigil in January 2003, a single-minded orientation to an audience of Capitol Hill staffers was reflected in the one-sidedness of the banner and location of the vigil, reinforced in version B of the flyer on March 2 by use of the referring expression "Members of Congress." In Goffman's (1981) terminology, Congress was at that time the *addressee*, known, ratified, and addressed. Then, after vigiling at Upper Senate Park, when participants started becoming aware of the potential for being "more observable witnesses for peace carrying their message to a wider audience," passersby who might previously have been viewed as *overhearers*—that is "third parties whom the speaker knows to be there, but who are not ratified participants" (Bell 1984: 159)—became *auditors* both known and ratified. This shift in awareness was mirrored in the addition of the referring expression "the Nation" in version C of the flyer, as well as semiotically in the decision to make the banner two-sided and with a bolder and larger font, and thus visible by even more *overhearers* and *eavesdroppers* from larger distances.

Thus, while the banner may be viewed as setting up a symbolic conversation (by the gaze vector of participants) with the Capitol, given a new banner that renders the vigil more visible by a wider audience, this conversation also becomes an observable performance, triggering new possibilities for metaphorical meanings attributed to the silence on the part of audiences as we have considered. Crucially, some of these meanings are staged for consumption by an audience because such associations are not shared by vigil participants themselves. Recalling that Quaker practice does not endow symbolic importance to buildings, for

Quakers, the Capitol Building is just another building. While they may appear to be engaged in a symbolic conversation with an institution of power, these metaphorical associations may exist entirely in the eyes of their beholders. But if this is the case, such meanings do not arrive there accidentally.

Participants' awareness of both their performance and their audience is reflected in frequent speculation about the trajectories of photographs taken by tourists at the event, including how far their silence may be disseminated for consumption by wider and increasingly more disparate audiences. In discussions about location of the vigil, the West Lawn site was mentioned as desirable because it interrupts the scenic view down the mall all the way to the Washington Memorial, which most tourists would be interested in photographing. Comments recur along the lines of "who knows where a photo of us might end up!" or "through the power of photography, we also have a much greater reach than just an hour at the Capitol." Such comments reference the idea of inserting their image of peace into the cameras of travelers who would take them around the world, thus placing their performance before myriad, unanticipated audiences.

In fact, on one day during the summer of 2008, the vigil was filmed by an artist's collective, which has since been used to create a silent filmic performance art piece based on this vigil. For this performance, the screening of the silent film was accompanied by a group of participants having a conversation about silence at a museum in DC, which was itself filmed.

As may be seen in figure 10.4, the artists' collective created tables and chairs for the conversation out of chalkboard; participants were instructed to visually represent

FIGURE 10.4 A conversation about silence

Photo courtesy of The Floating Lab Collective, taken on October 4, 2008, at Katzen Art Center

their conversation about silence visually and through text, and the artifacts of the conversation were then deconstructed and hung on the walls of the museum for display, as may be seen in figure 10.5. These two films have been shown in a traveling exhibit in Virginia and were recently accepted for a festival in Germany.

Thus, as a performance, silence takes up complex footings to audience (Goffman 1981). As described earlier in this chapter with the example of the gentleman from Northern Ireland, passersby do jump into the vigil to pose (often with fingers in a peace sign) as if they were part of the group, and indeed for those few seconds of silence, they are. Among the texts used by participants, silence is appropriated as a meditational means as easily as grabbing and holding the banner. Thus, perhaps, like the early Quakers, participants do not worry about whether or which of the symbolic aspects of their silent message get communicated. If silence is internal and external, both the process and the product, the message(s) (not to mention the metamessage(s)) cannot be entirely within the control of the sender. The audience is implicated in the contextualized meaning of the performance, and if some deeper meanings get across, it may be "that of God" in the speakers communicating with "that of God" in their hearers.

Conclusion

Heeding Coupland's (2007) call for linguistic studies of performance, the current investigation explores one Quaker group's use of silence both as practice and performance, considered both literally and metaphorically and from the

FIGURE 10.5 **Silence as art**

Photo courtesy of The Floating Lab Collective, taken on October 4, 2008, at Katzen Art Center

point of view of both performer and audience. In so doing, it adds to our understanding of the contemporary language practices of the Quaker community, specifically to their use of silence as a meaningfully communicative practice. I have considered silence as among the texts that enable the action of vigiling and are also used by the participants as *mediational means* in this action. Additionally, I have explored how these texts reflect and produce Quaker beliefs and especially how their use of silence as a text relates to the performance of signs, in this case, drawing on metaphorical meanings of "the light," regardless of how such meanings are received.

Thus, while silent and symbolic engagement with institutions of power may have varying levels of success in generating public discourse, ultimately, regardless of speaker or setting, this silent performance is staged for consumption by multiple audiences, which shapes and generates contextualized meanings. Being both literally and metaphorically silent has been shown to be a way for these participants to both search (internally) for peace and perform it (externally).

Finally, as an ethnographic, contextualized study of silence, this work investigates the religious and political meanings of silence by examining how performances borrow and extend the meanings of silence as a form of religious expression to embody shifting responses to, the experiencing of alienation from, and disagreement with the institutions and structures of power.

Acknowledgments

My gratitude to my colleague Laura Wright who first referred me to this *ongoing silent vigil for Peace* and to George Laufenberg, the third member of our group project for the Ethnography of Communication course taught by Ron Scollon at Georgetown University in the spring semester of 2003. My gratitude goes out to Ron for structuring a collaborative and supportive learning environment in which we all pushed ourselves beyond what we thought was our capacity, and to my classmates for their encouragement and ideas in the very early stages and throughout my work on this project. Earlier versions of this paper were presented at American Anthropological Association meetings in Chicago in November 2003, in Philadelphia in December of 2009, and at Sociolinguistic Symposium 18 in 2010. My thanks for the feedback given to me by my colleagues at these meetings, especially Sonya Fix, Adam Jaworski, Veronika Koller, Barbara Johnstone, and Crispin Thurlow. Special thanks to Deborah Schiffrin who provided critical feedback and very helpful suggestions on multiple versions of this manuscript. My deepest gratitude goes to Friends Meeting of Washington and the Quaker community more broadly for their time and for allowing me to experience their wisdom, patience, and peace. All errors of fact and interpretation are mine alone.

Appendix—Flyer Version B

ONGOING SILENT VIGIL FOR PEACE

Tuesdays, 5:30–6.30 p.m. U.S. Capitol, at Upper Senate Park on Constitution Avenue

Each Tuesday since October 15th, we have held a silent vigil at the U.S. Capitol under the banner "**Seek peace, and pursue it (Psalms 34:14)**". We meet for one hour from 5.30 to 6.30 p.m. Our *NEW LOCATION* is in Upper Senate Park, which is on Constitution Avenue directly across from the north end of the Capitol. All are invited to join us in silent prayer and worship. Battery-operated candles are optional; no open flames are permitted. We meet whenever the weather, so please dress appropriately for the conditions. Please do not bring additional signs or banners.

Our message is a positive one. During the current Iraq crisis, we are encouraging members of Congress to seek a peaceful path. We believe that a reverence for life guide should guide our nation's actions, and that our country's great strength should further the ideal of an international community based on respect and law. We intend our prayerful silence to bring light to the world.

From Union Station: Walk halfway around the circle to Delaware Avenue. Turn right and walk two blocks. Turn right onto Constitution Avenue. Upper Senate Park is between the Russell Senate Office Building (Delaware Avenue) and the Taft Memorial (New Jersey Avenue). From Capitol South Metro: Walk four blocks north along 1st St. SE. and then left onto Constitution.

Please join us.

Peace Committee, Langley Hill Friends Meeting

Contact: Catherine Farrel–703-787-7595 or catherine.farrel—.net

References

Barrett, Rusty. 1999. "Indexing Polyphonous Identity in the Speech of African American Drag Queens." In *Reinventing Identities: The Gendered Self in Discourse*, Mary Bucholtz, A. C. Liang, and Laurel A. Sutton (eds.), 313–31. Oxford: Oxford University Press.

Bauman, Richard. 1983. *Let Your Words Be Few: Symbolism of Speaking and Silence among Seventeenth Century Quakers*. Cambridge: Cambridge University Press.

Bauman, Richard and Charles L. Briggs. 1990. "Poetics and Performance as Critical Perspectives on Language and Social Life." *Annual Review of Anthropology* 19: 59–88.

Bell, Allan. 1984. "Language Style as Audience Design." *Language in Society* 13: 145–204.

Blommaert, Jan. 2009. "Ethnography and Democracy: Hymes' Political Theory of Language." *Text and Talk* 29: 257–76.

Brock, Peter. 1990. *The Quaker Peace Testimony 1660 to 1914*. York, England: Sessions Book Trust.

Bucholtz, Mary. 2001. "Play, Identity, and Linguistic Representation in the Performance of Accent." *Proceedings from the Ninth Annual Symposium about Language and Society (SALSA), April 20–22, 2001*. Texas Linguistic Forum 44(2): 227–51.

Coupland, Nikolas. 2007. *Style: Language Variation, Identity and Social Meaning*. Cambridge: Cambridge: University Press.

Coupland, Nikolas and Adam Jaworski. 2004. "Sociolinguistic Perspectives on Metalanguage: Reflexivity, Evaluation and Ideology." In *Metalanguage: Social and Ideological Perspectives*, Adam Jaworski, Nikolas Coupland, and Dariusz Galasinski (eds.), 15–52. New York: Mouton De Gruyter.

Dandelion, Pink. 2007. *An Introduction to Quakerism*. Cambridge: Cambridge University Press.

Dandelion, Pink. 2008. *The Quakers: A Very Short Introduction*. Oxford: Oxford University Press.

Fox, George. 1660. "A Declaration from the Harmless and Innocent People of God, Called Quakers, Against all Plotters and Fighters in the World, for the Removing the Ground of Jealousy and Suspicion from Both Magistrates and People in the Kingdom, Concerning Wars and Fightings. Given Unto the King, Upon the 21 Day of the 11th Month, 1660." *Earlham School of Religion Digital Quaker Collection*: http://dqc.esr.earlham.edu:8080/xmlmm/docButton?XMLMMWhat=builtPage&XMLMMWhere=E11229469.P00000002-1&XMLMMBeanName=toc1&XMLMMNextPage=/builtPageFromBrowse.jsp.

Goffman, Erving. 1981. *Forms of Talk*. Philadelphia: University of Pennsylvania Press.

Goffman, Erving. 1974. *Frame Analysis*. Cambridge, MA: Harvard University Press.

Hymes, Dell. 1972. "Models of the Interaction of Language and Social Life." *Directions in Sociolinguistics: The Ethnography of Communication*, John Gumperz and Dell Hymes (eds.), 35–71. New York: Holt, Rinehart and Winston.

Jaworski, Adam. 1993. *The Power of Silence: Social and Pragmatic Perspectives*. Newbury Park: Sage.

Jaworski, Adam. 1997a. "Aesthetic, Communicative and Political Silences in Laurie Anderson's Performance Art." In *Silence: Interdisciplinary Perspectives*, Adam Jaworski (ed.), 15–36. Berlin; New York: Mouton de Gruyter.

Jaworski, Adam, ed. 1997b. *Silence: Interdisciplinary Perspectives*. Berlin: Mouton de Gruyter.

Maltz, Daniel. 1985. "Joyful Noise and Reverent Silence: The Significance of Noise in Pentecostal Worship." In *Perspectives on Silence*, Deborah Tannen and Muriel Saville-Troike (eds.), 113–37. Norwood, NJ: Ablex.

Meltzer, Milton. 2002. *Ain't Gonna Study War No More: The Story of America's Peace Seekers*. New York: Random House.

Orr, E. W. 1974. *The Quakers in Peace and War: 1920 to 1967*. Eastbourne: W. J. Oxford and Sons.

Ryan, James Emmett. 2009. *Imaginary Friends: Representing Quakers in American Culture*. Madison: University of Wisconsin Press.

Saville-Troike, Muriel. 1985. "The Place of Silence in an Integrated Theory of Communication." In *Perspectives on Silence*, Deborah Tannen and Muriel Saville-Troike (eds.), 3–20. Norwood, NJ: Ablex.

Schiffrin, Deborah. 2006. *In Other Words: Variation in Reference and Narrative*. Cambridge: Cambridge University Press.

Scollon, Ron and Suzanne Wong Scollon. 2003. *Discourses in Place: Language in the Material World*. London: Routledge.

Scollon, Ron and Suzanne Wong Scollon. 2004. *Nexus Analysis: Discourse and the Emerging Internet*. New York: Routledge.

Searle, John. 1969. *Speech Acts: An Essay in the Philosophy of Language*. London: Cambridge University Press.

Tannen, Deborah and Muriel Saville-Troike, eds. 1985. *Perspectives on Silence*. Norwood, NJ: Ablex.

11

Narrating War and Peace at the Battle Ruins

OKINAWAN TOURISM-ACTIVISM DISCOURSES

Taku Suzuki

Introduction

In the summers of 2008, 2009, and 2010, I joined sightseeing bus tours in southern Okinawa Hontō, the largest and most populated among the Ryūkyū Islands, which featured stops at the sites and memorials that are related to the Battle of Okinawa, the fierce ground battle that killed more than 240,000 American, Japanese, Okinawan, British, Korean, and Taiwanese combatants and noncombatants in the spring of 1945. The sightseeing tour, named "Southern Hontō Battle Ruins Course," daily departs Naha, Okinawa's prefectural capital, to visit several battle-related sites scattered across southern Hontō, led by bus guides ("sightseeing guides" hereafter). I also tagged along with numerous groups of middle and high school students on an educational trip, or *shūgaku ryokō*, from Japanese main islands, or Naichi, touring around the southern Hontō battle ruins and memorials, led by local peace activist guides, or "peace guides" (*heiwa gaido*), on what is usually referred to as a "peace study" (*heiwa gakushū*) program within the *shūgaku ryokō* itinerary.

Despite the similarities between the two group tours' itineraries, I was struck by the differences I felt while being part of these tours. The sightseeing tour was emotionally stirring yet ultimately leisurely, while the peace study was subdued yet thought-provoking. After these tours, I compared travelogues and weblog entries written by those tourists who visited the battle ruins on sightseeing tours with the response letters to the peace guides sent by the *shūgaku ryokō* students. Diverse responses to the tours within each group notwithstanding, their responses largely mirrored my own. The former highlighted how "moving" their experiences were, and the latter were more introspective.

The battle ruins in southern Hontō of Okinawa are among numerous sites of past atrocities and mass violence around the world, such as former battlefields, slave forts, and concentration camps, which are also tourist attractions. These sites are often referred to as touristic "black spots" (Rojek 1997: 62). Many of the institutions that manage these "black spots," such as the Auschwitz-Birkenau

Memorial and State Museum, the Hiroshima Peace Memorial Museum, and the Tuol Sleng Genocide Museum in Phnom Penh, as well as the tour operators at these sites, envision what they do as a form of public education and peace activism. They believe that tourists who visit these sites learn from the horrific past and go home with renewed determination to build peace. While few would question these goals, it is unclear exactly how these institutions and tour operators conceptualize and present peace. How is peace narrated in these tours of war and peace memorials and museums, and how exactly do these tours try to help tourists become peace builders? Do different forms of tourism envision peace and peace building differently through their narratives?

To answer these questions, I draw from my ethnographic research in Okinawa to comparatively analyze the sightseeing bus tours and *shūgaku ryokō* in the southern Hontō battle ruins. The differences in the two travel experiences undoubtedly derive from a number of factors, such as tourists' motivations, preparation before the departure to Okinawa, tourists' age and socioeconomic background, size of touring groups, and travel itinerary. In this essay, I zero in on one key component in tourism: guides' narrations of the Battle of Okinawa and today's Okinawan society. As many sociologists of tourism have noted (Cohen 1985; Holloway 1981; Schmidt 1979), tour guides "play perhaps the most important determining role" (Schmidt 1979: 454) in shaping tourists' experiences. By comparing how sightseeing guides and peace guides represent the past to today's tourists, this chapter seeks to illuminate the potential and limitation of touristic discourses for peace building. More specifically, I argue that sightseeing guides take what Lauren Berlant (2000: 45, 59) calls a "sentimentalist" approach to peace building, which is predicated on the belief that "identification with pain, a universal true feeling, would . . . lead to structural social change" and create a peaceful world where "there is no more [personal] pain." In contrast, peace guides for *shūgaku ryokō* do not romanticize peace as a utopian state in which everyone can find personal comfort. Instead, they encourage the student-tourists to find value in the *act* of learning and thinking about war and peace in itself, and to take action based upon these contemplations.

The two different guiding narrations of war and peace, furthermore, represent two distinct approaches to history. Sightseeing guides narrate the war's details by drawing on the objectivist belief that "history is a simple accounting of 'just the facts'" (Handler and Gable 1997: 78). Referring to Walter Benjamin, Lisa Yoneyama calls this approach to the past "universal history," which aims to create "an inventory of happenings," and, in effect, "endorses the status quo of present knowledge" about the past (Yoneyama 1999: 28). In contrast, peace guides encourage the student tourists to develop what Yoneyama calls a "historical materialist" approach to the past, in which a past tragedy, like the Battle of Okinawa, is "remembered with at once an acute sense of irreversibility and an immense regret that compels us to imagine possible alternative courses of history and to suspect that opportunities to prevent the moment of destruction might have been seized, but were not." The past narrated as such, Yonayama argues, would "remain critically germane to present struggles for social change" (30).

Along with some other chapters in this volume (Dunmire; Hodges), this chapter seeks to demonstrate that narrative performances can play a critical role in shaping and provoking social action. Through the narration of the past war in *shūgaku ryokō*, peace guides attempt to instill in the student-tourists the idea of peace "not as a static concept nor is it something given by somebody," but as part of their "identity . . . generated through reflections and practices" in their everyday lives (Ogawa 2011: 391). This vision of peace that resides within one's sense of self, generated by persistent learning and actions, not only endorses the classic concept of "positive" peace, or an active promotion of a just world, in contrast with "negative" peace, defined by an absence of armed conflict, in peace education scholarship (Galtung 1964: 1971), but also addresses the necessarily political nature of the peace concept, which peace educators often downplay in their theorizations and practices (Ben Porath 2003). Additionally, this chapter's case studies offer unique examples of bodily performed narrations of war and peace. In the *shūgaku ryokō* peace study program, the student-tourists have a polysensual—physical, visual, and audio—encounter with the past war at the former battle ruins, to which peace guides' narrative performance contributes. The *shūgaku ryokō* group's "environmental bubble," formed by the peace guides and student-tourists (Edensor 2000; Suzuki 2012), offers a more coherent and intensive communicative environment in which the participants are compelled to engage the concepts of war and peace more deeply than in commercial sightseeing tours.

I participated in two bus tours to the southern Hontō battle ruins in 2009 and ten *shūgaku ryokō* peace study programs led by peace guides who belong to the Okinawa Peace Network (*Okinawa Heiwa Nettowāku*), or OPN, in 2008, 2009, and 2010. While my analysis of the guiding narrations primarily draws on my participant observation of these tours, I compensate for the small number of samples by drawing on interviews with OPN peace guides, sightseeing guides, and Okinawa prefectural government officials in charge of tourism promotion, as well as on various primary and secondary sources. I will first outline the history of postwar tourism in Okinawa, highlighting the significance of the battle ruins and memorials in the industry. I will then juxtapose the guiding narrations by sightseeing guides and peace guides in two settings. The first setting is the Himeyuri Cenotaph (*Himeyuri-no-tō*), which, along with the Himeyuri Peace Museum (*Himeyuri Heiwa Kinen Shiryōkan*), memorializes the fallen members of the Himeyuri Student Nurse Corps, or *Himeyuri Gakuto-tai* (Himeyuri Corps hereafter), Okinawa's female high school students who cared for Japanese soldiers during the Battle of Okinawa. The second setting is a memorial structure called the Cornerstone of Peace (*Heiwa-no-ishiji*) in the Okinawa Prefectural Peace Memorial Park (*Okinawa Heiwa Kinen Kōen*, Peace

Memorial Park hereafter). Both sites are located in Itoman City, the location of the final battles between the Japanese and the Allied Forces in June 1945, during which most of the Okinawan noncombatant deaths took place. I will conclude by reiterating that touristic discourses of war and peace can take multiple forms, which might or might not encourage the visitors to the sites of past atrocities to take political action to build a more peaceful world after participating in the tours. Throughout this chapter, quotes from the sightseeing guides and peace guides are all spoken in "standard" Japanese, unless otherwise noted, and the English translation of these quotes is my own. For Japanese names, except for those of the scholars whom I cite, I maintain the typical order of family name first, given name second (e.g., "Suzuki Taku" instead of "Taku Suzuki").

History of Postwar Okinawan Tourism

Less than a decade after the devastating Battle of Okinawa in 1945, Okinawa regained its status as a travel destination for Naichi Japanese.[1] The battle ruins and memorials in southern Hontō were the most popular destination from the 1950s to the mid-1970s, which developed a particular style of tour-guiding narrations tailored for the Naichi visitors to the US military-occupied Okinawa. In the 1970s, tour/peace guiding as a form of political activism emerged in part as a response to these tour-guiding narrations at the battle ruins during the US occupation era.

1950S–1970S: BATTLE RUINS PILGRIMAGE

Under the rule of the United States Civil Administration of the Ryūkyū Islands (USCAR) from 1945 to Okinawa's reversion to Japan in 1972, Okinawa was fast transformed into a military stronghold against the perceived threat of Soviet and Chinese aggression. Meanwhile, from 1945 to 1950, despite USCAR's disapproval, municipal leaders in southern Hontō led an effort by local residents to dig and clean the hundreds of abandoned corpses left in the areas surrounding

---

[1] Although there is no scholarly record of the beginning of tourism in Okinawa, it is believed that the first group of Japanese visitors came to Okinawa in 1894, only fifteen years after the Ryūkyū Kingdom was annexed to Japan as Okinawa Prefecture in 1879. During the 1920s and 1930s, fleet service between Kobe and Naha enabled Naichi tourists to visit Okinawa for "sightseeing, tasting of Okinawan cuisine, enjoying famous Okinawan karate, classic theater" (Yamashiro 1964: 1–2). Many of these visitors were intellectuals and artists intrigued by the local sceneries, language, music and visual arts, and customs; even if their curiosity manifested a form of modern Japanese Orientalism toward Okinawa and other Asian neighbors (Tada 2008; Tomiyama 1997), some of them became vocal advocates of Okinawan culture and language against the Japanese government's assimilation efforts to make the Okinawans into Japanese imperial subjects (Ishikawa 1984: 7–10; Tomiyama 2002a). Okinawa tourism went into hiatus in the late 1930s as the war intensified.

the Mabuni Hill in Itoman and Shuri area in Naha, and built several ossuaries and memorials, which were typically simple stone markers.[2] In the 1940s, USCAR enforced strict regulation of travel in and out of Okinawa as it was concerned about infiltration of political activists from Naichi. Pressured by bereaved family member associations and the Japanese government (Awazu 2006; Figal 2007; Hamai 2005), however, USCAR began to make exemptions for those Naichi Japanese whose relatives were among some 66,000 Japanese soldiers killed in the Battle of Okinawa, allowing them to travel to Okinawa to mourn the war dead.[3] USCAR also reluctantly allowed the Japanese government and bereaved family associations to collect bones and build ossuaries and memorials in Okinawa (Figal 2007: 84, 92). Since 1954, hundreds of Naichi Japanese, many of whom were members of prefectural bereaved family associations (Hamai 2006; Kitamura 2005), have traveled to Okinawa for what was called the "battle ruins pilgrimage" (*senseki sanpai*).[4]

In response to the increased interest among Naichi Japanese in visiting Okinawa, the Okinawa Tourism Association (*Okinawa Kankō Kyōkai*, OTA hereafter) was established in 1954. In addition to petitioning USCAR to ease the travel restrictions,[5] the OTA began training bus guides to cater to the increasing visitors by organizing a "sightseeing bus girl training session" (*kankō basu-gāru kōshūkai*) to teach tour-guiding techniques (Yamashiro 1964: 30). In addition to these bus guides trained by the OTA, travel guidebooks written and published by the OTA played a pivotal role in shaping the Naichi visitors' tours to the battle ruins and US bases. A guidebook published by the OTA in 1957 included photographs of the memorials, along with melodramatic descriptions of the deaths of Japanese and Okinawan combatants and noncombatants who were memorialized by them. For instance, for the Himeyuri Cenotaph, the last days of the Himeyuri Corps were described in the guidebook as follows: "Seventeen

---

[2] The most famous cases of corpse collection, burial, and memorial-building efforts were led by Kinjō Washin, mayor of Mawashi Village, who, along with 4,300 villagers, was ordered to move to Miwa Village of the Komesu area near Mabuni Hill. Led by Kinjō, the villagers gathered the remains, some still with flesh and hair, of the Okinawan, American, and other casualties. With cement and coral rocks, they built the first memorial, *Konpaku-no-tō*, or the Tomb of the Unknown, in 1946 (Figal 2007: 89; Ōta 2006: 152–60; see also Kitamura 2006).

[3] In fact, the families and relatives of the war dead were among the first groups of Japanese to travel overseas (i.e., outside Naichi) in the postwar era; they traveled to grieve their losses throughout the South Pacific, including New Caledonia, Papua New Guinea, Saipan, and Guam; Southeast Asia, including Singapore, Burma, Cambodia, and the Philippines; and Northeast Asia, including the Russian Far East (Cooper 2006; see also Yamashita 2000).

[4] The visit to the former battlefields is referred to in many different terms: *sanpai, junpai, junrei, irei,* and *bosan.* While each term has unique connotations, which might not be best translated into the English term "pilgrimage," I stick with the term to avoid confusion.

[5] In the OTA's letter to the prefectural bereaved family associations, and National Bereaved Family Association (*Nippon Izokukai*), the OTA president asked these groups to petition the Japanese government and political parties to grant Naichi Japanese travelers to Okinawa special permission to carry more foreign currency than the Japanese government officially permitted (Yamashiro 1964: 30).

or eighteen year-old pure-hearted maidens tragically ended their lives in this cave, while they cared for, consoled, and encouraged the injured soldiers, being convinced of the Emperor's nation's victory (*kōkoku no shōri*)" (Okinawa Kankō Kyōkai 1957: 54).

Drawing on these storylines established by the OTA, the commercial bus guides assumed the role of "a theatrical director of the tragedy of the Battle of Okinawa and a performer to represent the tragedy" for the Naichi Japanese tourists (Kitamura 2007a: 280). Tsuyoshi Kitamura, in his analysis of bus guides in battle ruins pilgrimages during the 1960s, found that the bus guides narrated two distinct story lines for the Japanese visitors from Naichi: (1) a moving story of Okinawans' sacrifice for the nation (*junkoku bidan*); and (2) Okinawans' desire for reversion to Japan (*fukki ganbō*) (281). Kitamura cites a newspaper reporter who accompanied the Okinawa pilgrimage tour group in 1964; this reporter stated that the Okinawan bus guides were very "nationalistic" (*kokusui-teki*) and that the guides used criticism of the US military rule of Okinawa to express their "earnest wish to revert to the home nation of Japan" (*sokoku Nippon ni fukki shitai to iu higan*) (281–82). Kitamura also quotes a tour-guiding script, circa 1971, for the bus ride heading to the Himeyuri Cenotaph:

> The [Himeyuri] maidens, who absolutely believed in their nation's victory, propelled their bodies, which were about to perish under fatigue and hunger, to care for the wounded soldiers at a makeshift hospital inside a cave, while consoling and encouraging each other. . . . They took a pulse of the dying soldiers, listened to their last words on behalf of their mothers and daughters, wrote down the soldiers' wills and kept their mementos to deliver to their mothers back home. . . . Their precious and unadulterated love for their country, however, was not rewarded, and their side's losing battles forced the maidens into a horrendous state in the end. (Kitamura,2007a: 283; my translation)

For many Naichi Japanese pilgrims, Kitamura argues, the pilgrimage to Okinawa provided an opportunity to consume the Okinawans' "moving stories" of self-sacrifice for the Japanese nation and their "desire" for reversion to Japan, as well as to satisfy their "paternalistic emotion" and wish to rescue and "heal" Okinawa, which, in effect, confirmed their superiority as a rescuer of the Okinawans, who were suffering under US military rule (293).

FROM THE MID-1970S: PEACE STUDIES FOR NAICHI SCHOOLS

After Okinawa's reversion to Japan in 1972, which also allowed the continuing presence of US military bases in Okinawa, the touristic image of Okinawa transformed from the site of brutal deaths and foreign military occupation into a subtropical paradise. Following a dip in tourism after the festivities of the Okinawa

International Ocean Expo ended in 1975, the Okinawa prefectural government, Okinawan tourism businesses, Japanese airlines, and advertisement agencies worked together to promote the image of Okinawa as a tourists' utopia symbolized by its blue ocean and white-sand beaches filled with bikini-clad young women, in addition to the islands' distinct culture and history (Tada 2004: 150–59).[6]

Within this dramatic shift in Okinawa tourism, the legacy of the Battle of Okinawa became a smaller, if still significant, segment of the industry.[7] The southern Hontō battle ruins and memorials changed from sites for the elderly and middle-aged Naichi Japanese visitors to remember and grieve the war dead to sites for young Naichi students to learn about the horror of war and envision the world without it.[8] In pre–World War II Japan, *shūgaku ryokō* developed as a means to bolster youths' patriotism, physical and mental strength, and cultural knowledge about their nation. After a hiatus from 1943 to 1946 due to the war and its aftermath, *shūgaku ryokō* once again became an integral part of Japanese schooling. In the 1950s, when the Japanese economy was firmly on the path to recovery, *shūgaku ryokō* resumed countrywide. The Ministry of Education officially designated it the educational curriculum in the "Guidelines for the Course of Study" (*Gakushū Shidō Yōryō*) and began to provide financial assistance for schools to teach it.

Shūgaku ryokō to Okinawa in the postwar era began as soon as Okinawa reverted to Japan in 1972. The prefectural government intensified its *shūgaku ryokō* recruitment effort in the late 1970s, which resulted in the fast increase of Okinawa *shūgaku ryokō* among Naichi schools in the 1980s, helped by the Naichi school boards' decision to permit school air travels and the increase in the national government's financial aid (Okinawa-ken Kankō Konbenshon Byūrō 2009: 2). In 1980, only 19,988 students from 127 schools visited Okinawa

---

[6] The Okinawan "history" referred to by those engaged in tourism promotion typically does not mean the modern Okinawan experiences of colonization by Imperial Japan and the Battle of Okinawa, but instead the pre-modern history of Ryūkyū Kingdom. See Figal (2008) for the notion of "heritage" expressed in the Okinawa tourism industry.

[7] A 1973 survey revealed that while more than two-thirds of Naichi Japanese visitors considered the ocean and beach to be Okinawa's most attractive features, only 10 percent found the war ruins attractive. The result prompted an Okinawan tourism analyst to conclude that "although traditional war ruins tours may still be significant for their appeal to the tourists' desire for peace, today's [young tourists in their] twenties and thirties would find marine leisure activities more enjoyable" (Ishikawa 1984: 15). In a 2008 survey conducted by the Okinawa prefectural government, 12.7 percent of the visitors to Okinawa listed visiting the battle-related sites as part of their travel plans (Okinawa-ken 2009: 44).

[8] *Shūgaku ryokō* in modern Japan began in 1886 when an elite Tokyo high school organized an *ensoku*, or long walk, to neighboring Chiba Prefecture to enhance students' physical and mental discipline, give them military training, and help them to learn about the cultural heritage and historical ruins of the area. While many other middle and high schools modeled their educational field trips after military camps, others organized their trips focusing on sightseeing and scholarly field research. As Imperial Japan rapidly militarized itself and strengthened its national identity as a unified nation under the Emperor, who was to be revered by his subjects as the living god, shintō shrines in Ise and Kyoto, as well as to the Korean peninsula and Manchuria, became common *shūgaku ryokō* destinations (Zenkoku Shūgaku Ryokō Kenkyū Kyōkai N.d.). Although *shūgaku ryokō* ended in 1943, as World War II intensified, it took only a year to revive the tradition after the war ended in 1945.

for *shūgaku ryokō*; in 2008, 430,878 students from 2,603 schools came to Okinawa, accounting for approximately 7.3 percent of all the tourists visiting the prefecture (Okinawa-ken 2009: 4, 57). In 2008, the vast majority of the Naichi school students who visited Okinawa were from high schools and middle schools; they typically spent three or four days in Okinawa, at least one of which was set aside for learning about the Battle of Okinawa in the southern Hontō battle ruins and memorials (56, 62).[9]

Peace guiding for *shūgaku ryokō* emerged in the 1970s as a critical response to tour-guiding practice in the battle ruins pilgrimages in the previous era (Aniya 1974; Aniya et al. 1974; Ōshiro 2004). Many Okinawan schoolteachers, as well as several commercial bus tour guides, were disturbed by the overdramatic and celebratory descriptions of the battle and its casualties in the battle ruins pilgrimage tour guides' scripts, their exclusive focus on the experience of military personnel at the expense of Okinawan noncombatants, and the numerous factual inaccuracies they contained (Ōshiro 2004: 4; Kitamura 2004: 65–66). They organized study sessions, public forums, and field research trips to the battle-related sites to create alternative guiding scripts and tour itineraries, and began guiding Naichi visitors to the battle ruins and memorials themselves, marking the unofficial beginning of peace guiding as the "antithesis of sightseeing tour guiding" (Asahi Shinbun Seibu Honsha Shakai-bu 1982: 2; Kitamura 2004: 65; Shiroma 2004).[10] In 1974, they formed an organization called the Group to Think about the Battle of Okinawa (*Okinawa-sen wo Kangaeru Kai*), which later became the Okinawa Peace Guide Association (*Okinawa Heiwa Gaido no Kai*) in 1987, and the OPN in 1994 (Ōshiro 2005: 188).[11] As the number of *shūgaku ryokō* groups from Naichi increased in the 1990s, more schools requested peace guiding by the members of the OPN and other groups. The OPN peace guides are Okinawa- and Naichi-born residents of Okinawa of

---

[9] Most high school *shūgaku ryokō* groups are sophomores (i.e., second year of three school years). Typically during the students' freshman year, the teachers in charge choose the travel destination, pick a travel agency to manage logistics, organize teachers' study sessions to learn about the place they will visit, and plan the itinerary, accommodation, and transportation. During the sophomore year before the trip, the teachers prepare the students for *shūgaku ryokō* by teaching them the topics related to the travel destination in various subjects, such as language, art, geography, and history, and by inviting a guest lecturer from the destination (Iijima 2003).

[10] In July 1972, only a few months after the reversion, a national convention of *Nihon Rekishi Kyōikusha Hyōgikai* (Commission of History Educators in Japan) was held in Naha. In preparing to host the convention and guide the Naichi teachers around Okinawa during the convention, local Okinawan teachers chartered a sightseeing bus to tour the former battlefields and US military bases, guided by sightseeing guides. The group was stunned by the guides' jingoistic and often inaccurate narrations of the battle (Kitamura 2004: 65–66; Ōshiro 2004: 4). The local educators, therefore, decided to guide the visitors to the battle ruins and memorials themselves (Kitamura 2004; see also Umeda 2008: 315).

[11] This renewed scrutiny of sightseeing routes and tour-guiding narratives in the battle ruins emerged within a larger movement in the 1970s to reexamine the history of the Battle of Okinawa from the viewpoint of Okinawan noncombatants, not military commanders and government officials (Aniya et al. 1974; Kitamura 2004; Ōshiro 2004).

both genders and various age groups.[12] By 1998, it is reported that more than 60 percent of all *shūgaku ryokō* groups participated in some sort of peace study program, assisted by peace guides (Murakami 1999: 30).

Sightseeing Tours and Peace Studies in the Southern Hontō Battle Ruins

Despite the declines in battle ruins pilgrimages since the 1970s, well-known battle-related sites in southern Hontō, such as the Himeyuri Cenotaph and Peace Memorial Park, continue to attract many tourists.[13] Major tour agencies continue to include these sites in the itinerary for leisure-oriented package tours,[14] but if you are not with a packaged tour or a *shūgaku ryokō* group, a logical option is to join a half-day-long sightseeing tour to southern Hontō, offered by two major bus operators, A Bus and B Bus, in Naha. The itineraries of A Bus and B Bus tours are virtually identical; they stop at three battle-related sites: the Former Navy Underground Headquarters, the Himeyuri Cenotaph and the adjacent Himeyuri Peace Museum, and Peace Memorial Park where the Okinawa Peace Memorial Atrium, the Cornerstone of Peace, the Okinawa Prefectural Peace Memorial Museum, the National Cemetery for the Battle of Okinawa Victims, and dozens of memorial markers for the war dead are located (figure 11.1).

A sightseeing guide gives a description of the Himeyuri Corps in front of the Himeyuri Cenotaph before leading the group to a nearby restaurant/souvenir shop for lunch. Thereafter, tourists have thirty minutes or so to explore the Himeyuri Peace Museum, to which individual tourists must pay admission, or to purchase souvenirs at one of the half dozen shops nearby. At Peace Memorial Park, B Bus's sightseeing guide takes the group inside the Peace Memorial Atrium, where a large sitting Buddha statue is located, while the A Bus guide

---

[12] In addition to tour guiding, Okinawan academics and activists wrote numerous guidebooks specifically for peace study and *shūgaku ryokō* student-tourists, to encourage them to learn not only about Okinawa's pre-modern history and culture, but also Japanese colonization, mass casualties of Okinawans during the battle, and continuing oppression of Okinawans under the US occupation and the US military presence after the 1972 reversion to Japan (Aniya et al. 1985; Arasaki et al. 1983; Okinawa-ken Kōkyōso Nanbu Shibu and Heiwa Kyōiku Kenkyū Iinkai 1986; Okinawa-ken Kōkyōso Kyōiku Shiryō Sentā "Gama" Henshū Iinkai 2009; Ōshiro and Mezaki 2006).

[13] In the surveys conducted by Okinawa Prefecture in 2000, 2003, and 2006, 19.8, 16.3, and 12.4 percent of tourists, respectively, claimed that the main purpose of their visit to Okinawa was a pilgrimage to the battle ruins (Okinawa-ken 2008: 10). In another survey by the prefecture in 2004, the Himeyuri Cenotaph and Peace Memorial Park ranked the seventh and ninth most popular tourist destinations, respectively (Okinawa-ken 2004: 34).

[14] Kinki Nippon Tsūrisuto, one of the largest Japanese travel agencies, for instance, featured the Himeyuri Cenotaph in eighteen Okinawa tour packages from the Tokyo metropolitan area in the autumn of 2010. None of the tours included "war," "battle," or "battle ruins" in the package's title; instead, they highlighted an aquarium in northern Hontō, theme parks, and resort villas as their featured destinations (Kinki Nippon Tsūrisuto 2010).

FIGURE 11.1 Himeyuri Cenotaph

simply describes it outside. A guide then walks the group through the Cornerstone of Peace and gives descriptions of the Cornerstone in front of the Flame
of Peace (*Heiwa-no-hi*), before giving the group a short break. It is long enough
for tourists to walk around the Cornerstone and Peace Memorial Museum's
admission-free area, including its panoramic vista point, but not long enough
to explore the full museum exhibit or the entire park. The park is the last
battle-related stop for the tours; then the bus leaves for a cultural theme park
built around the Gyokusendō natural cave in Nanjō City before heading back
to Naha.

In addition to the sites that sightseeing tours visit, peace study itineraries
typically include those sites that are not included in sightseeing tours, such as
natural caves, or *gama* in Okinawan vernacular. The peace guides are generally critical of the war memorials in Peace Memorial Park, many of which
glorify the deaths of Japanese soldiers (Yasukuni Jinja Kokuei-ka Hantai
Okinawa Kirisuto-sha Renrakukai 1983; Aniya et al. 1985: 40). Therefore,
they take the visitors to what are known as the "backstreet" (*urakaidō*) of the
battle ruins (Asahi Shinbun Seibu Honsha Shakai-bu 1982: 2; Figal 2003;
Kitamura 2004; Tanji 2006: ch.4), such as *gama*. For the sake of comparative
analysis of the guiding narrations, however, I will ethnographically portray
sightseeing guides and peace guides in the same two settings, the Himeyuri
Cenotaph/Himeyuri Peace Museum and the Cornerstone of Peace, in the
remainder of this chapter.

SIGHTSEEING GUIDES AT THE HIMEYURI CENOTAPH

Shortly after departing from the Naha headquarters, the sightseeing guide for A Bus, Ms. Togashi,[15] a woman in her early twenties, finished providing a historical summary of the Battle of Okinawa. While heading to the Himeyuri Cenotaph, Ms. Togashi switched from a textbook-like description of the history of the battle during the previous leg of the bus ride to a more personal tone. Ms. Togashi said that she had been among "the generation of people who do not know, and do not want to know, the war." What had changed her was the video about the Battle of Okinawa, which she watched as part of the peace study program at her school before the June 23 Day to Mourn the Dead (*Irei-no-hi*).[16] She continued: "My image of war before watching the video was one in which soldiers fight with each other with machine guns. But in the video, the major victims were babies, children, and elders. I learned that a war victimizes the weak. . . . As someone who was born and raised in Okinawa, I want to carry on the stories of war."

The personal yet apolitical tone of the narration of the battle continued after we arrived at the Himeyuri Cenotaph. Following the typical guiding scenario, Ms. Togashi meticulously detailed the struggle of the Himeyuri Corps, and suddenly shifted to a dramatic description of the Corps' demise, a reminiscence of the guiding narrations during the battle ruins pilgrimage in the 1950s and 1960s. She referred to the teenage Himeyuri Corps members as "maidens" (*otome-tachi*) and "kids" (*kodomo-tachi*), who were "determined to battle with American soldiers with bamboo spears," but eventually died in the cave, "screaming, 'Mom, Dad!'" Then, Ms. Togashi asked the group to join hands in front of the cenotaph and pray for the victims.

Another sightseeing guide, Ms. Kawashima of B Bus, who is in her late forties, did not insert herself into her narration of the battle.[17] At the Himeyuri Cenotaph, however, Ms. Kawashima graphically described the last days of the Himeyuri Corps in a natural cave, which was used as a field hospital during the battle:

---

[15] The names of sightseeing guides and peace guides in the essay are pseudonyms to protect their confidentiality.

[16] June 23, 1945, is the most popularly recognized date for the end of organized combat between the Japanese and the Allied Forces, and has been the prefectural holiday since 1961. The Day to Mourn the Dead was one of several local holidays designated by *Ryūkyū Seifu*, or the Government of Ryūkyū Islands (GRI), the local administrative, legislative, and judicial authority of Okinawans under USCAR. When Okinawa reverted to Japan in 1972, the prefectural government adopted national holidays and abolished the local ones. The Day to Mourn the Dead remained a holiday for prefectural and municipal workers even after the reversion, but the Local Autonomy Law (*Chihō Jichi-hō*) of 1988 eliminated all prefectural and municipal holidays. In 1991, in response to the strong opposition from the Okinawan public, the national government revised the Local Autonomy Law, and the Day to Mourn the Dead once again became a prefectural holiday (Nakachi 2005: 195–96).

[17] Ms. Kawashima of B Bus added a few anecdotes of the Himeyuri Corps survivors in the postwar era, "who are all eighty years old or older, whose testimonies often appear in the newspapers, especially around the Day to Mourn the Dead." She told the tourists that most Himeyuri survivors became elementary schoolteachers after the war and wrote books about their experiences, upon which, she told the tourists, her guiding narrations were based.

June 19th, when the dissolution order [from the Japanese commanders] was delivered, it was too late to escape. Inside the cave, they held a meeting, or what you may call a farewell party (*Owakarekai*). Each of them sang her favorite song. Then, all sang *Umi Yukaba* (Going Out to Sea, the anthem of the Japanese Imperial Navy) and *Furusato* (Hometown or Home Village, a children's folksong) in a tearful voice. The next morning, the morning of the 20th, a gas bomb was thrown into the cave by the American soldiers who had found them hiding there. . . . When the American soldiers found the local residents and students hiding near the entrance of the cave, they told them to surrender in Japanese, saying, "Come out" (*Dete koi*). There were three calls for surrender, but the [Imperial Japan's anti-American] education at the time was such that they didn't believe them. They didn't come out. After the three calls, the gas bomb attack happened. They were in a panic. They screamed: "I'm in pain! Help!"

In both situations, the sightseeing guides succeeded in keeping the tourists' attention, as they stood quietly during their long—about ten minutes long—narrations. According to the standard scenario used by sightseeing bus guides, the two guides' detailed retelling of the Himeyuri Corps' footsteps from Naha to the southern Hontō battlefield during the Battle of Okinawa and the graphic and melodramatic depiction of their tragic end at the cave, where the cenotaph stands today, were typical (Okinawa Heiwa Nettowāku 2004: 14).

The sightseeing guides' narrations of the battle, unlike those in the battle ruins pilgrimages of the past, included a few critical, if vague, remarks about the Imperial Army. Ms. Togashi, for instance, pointed out the questionable order to the Okinawan civilians made by the Japanese military commanders when they were about to commit suicide: "Japanese military headquarters' order was, 'Fight until the last one dies.' Normally, the war ends when the highest commander of the troops dies or kills himself, doesn't it? But the battle continued after the [Japanese military's] surrender in June, and even after August 15th [when the Japanese government surrendered to the Allies]." Similarly, in her guiding narrations, Ms. Kawashima included a few anecdotes that portrayed Japanese commanders in an unflattering light. She described how the field hospital commanders left the severely wounded soldiers in the cave/field hospital when they decided to further retreat to southern Hontō:

When their field hospital was in danger, the military command ordered it to retreat to the south. . . . They could not transport severely injured patients with them. They sent off those patients who could still walk to the south. What happened to the severely injured patients? They were left alone, abandoned. The military then handed out potassium cyanide to them. After seeing off those patients who could still walk without saying a word, they killed themselves [by drinking the potassium cyanide].

Even in these narrations, the sightseeing guides did not elaborate on the systematic violence within the military, or mention the Japanese soldiers' violence against local Okinawan residents. The discrimination against Okinawans by Imperial Japanese bureaucrats before the war, and by Naichi Japanese soldiers during the battle, were never explicitly raised either, despite the fact that the guides were describing the caves from which some Okinawan noncombatants were forced out into the combat zone, wrested of their food and water, and even killed by the soldiers. Ms. Togashi did touch upon the Japanese military's executions of local Okinawans and Koreans for espionage charges, and the so-called collective suicide (*shūdan jiketsu*) among the residents of Zamami Island, northwest offshore of Hontō, in the wake of the US Force's landing on March 26, 1945 (Jahana 2008; Ōe 1970; Yonetani 2002).[18] Despite raising two of the most revealing incidents of Imperial Japan's structural violence against Okinawans and Koreans, colonized subjects whom Imperial Japan "made" Emperor's subjects (Tomiyama 2006), yet who were regarded "almost but not quite" (Bhabha 1994) the same as Naichi Japanese, Ms. Togashi merely stated: "It is said that killings of local residents for espionage and the currently controversial (*ima mondai ni natteiru*) collective suicide are the epitomes of war's cruelty." She did not address what exactly these incidents were, what was controversial about them, and, most crucially, what these incidents meant for the political-historical relationships between Naichi and Okinawa in the past and present.

SIGHTSEEING GUIDES AT THE CORNERSTONE OF PEACE

At Peace Memorial Park, both Ms. Togashi and Ms. Kawashima guided the group to the Flame of Peace at the center of the Cornerstone of Peace, a massive memorial built to commemorate the fiftieth anniversary of the end of the Pacific War and the Battle of Okinawa. Modeled after the Vietnam Veterans Memorial in Washington, DC, the names of over 240,000 war dead are engraved on marble walls. Both guides highlighted the Cornerstone's unique feature. Ms. Togashi twice stated, "It is said that this is the only place in the world that memorializes the war victims, regardless of their nationalities and the sides they belonged to during the conflict," a fact that is also advertised by the prefectural

---

[18] As soon as the landing took place, some 700 islanders, including elders and children, who had been made to believe that once captured by the US military they would be raped, tortured, mutilated, and eventually killed, killed each other with grenades, guns, and knives. It is widely believed among historians in Okinawa and Naichi alike that the Zamami Islanders' "collective suicide" was triggered by the Japanese military command; the army commander, Lieutenant Akamatsu Yoshitsugu, instilled the noncombatant islanders with the fear of being captured by the enemy and tacitly forced the residents to choose suicide over surrender by distributing grenades among them upon the US landing. Several attempts to discredit the Islanders' claim that they were compelled by the Akamatsu Squadron to kill themselves, most recently in the defamation suit against the Nobel Laureate author Ōe Kenzaburō, who interviewed the survivors in Zamami Island and wrote that Lietenant Akamatsu caused the tragedy, have been made by groups backed by right-wing intellectuals (Ōe 1970; Okinawa Heiwa Nettowāku 2008).

government (Okinawa-ken Bunka Kankyō-bu Heiwa/Danjo Kyōdō Sankaku-ka 2012). In contrast with her detailed and sometimes theatrical descriptions of the last days of the Himeyuri Corps, Ms. Togashi did not mention the mass casualties at the site, including those Okinawan noncombatants and Japanese soldiers who were about to surrender to the Allied Forces and were shot by their fellow Japanese soldiers because they were deemed to be betrayers of the Imperial Army during the last days of the battle near Mabuni Hill. For example, she did not describe *Gēzabanda* in Okinawan vernacular, or "Suicide Cliff" in English, next to Mabuni Hill, where a number of Okinawan noncombatants, escaping from the advancing US troops and facing the US fleets off the coast, jumped off the cliff to kill themselves; she simply pointed to the cliff from a distance and told the group that the cliff is called "sūsaido kurifu," without telling the tourists the reason for its name.

During their narrations at the park, Ms. Togashi and Ms. Kawashima both emphasized the connections between the past war and the current visitors to the memorial. Ms. Togashi reminded the tourists that many uncollected bones of the war dead remained in Okinawa, and that these bones "still lie underneath [where the tourists] were standing." She also noted that there were many blank spaces left on the Cornerstone in order for the names of newly discovered victims to be added: "Even now, when the new bones are found, and their identities are miraculously determined, their names are added to the Cornerstone every June 23rd." She also mentioned the existence of numerous unexploded bombs in Okinawa, citing a recent case where one was found in Naha's bustling Kokusai Dōri, prompting nearby residents to evacuate. She concluded her narration at the Peace Memorial Park by stating, "I hope you understand, and will remember, that the war is not over yet, and it is not just an event in the past." Ms. Kawashima of B Bus also mentioned the unexploded bombs and uncollected bones as the symbolic "scars of war" (*sensō no kizuato*) that continue to haunt the Okinawans' lives today. As the bus approached Peace Memorial Park's parking lot, she described how Okinawans are still profoundly affected by the remnants of the war: "You see it frequently in the newspaper: the problem of unexploded bombs (*fuhatsudan mondai*). On January 14th, a dud exploded, right around here, at a construction site. . . . Around here, it looks like just another farming village, doesn't it? But [the bomb explosion] turned it back to the village [during the war]. . . . It is said that it would take thirty or forty more years to remove all the unexploded bombs [from the Okinawan soil]." She continued: "Like the unexploded bombs, there are bones [of the war dead] that have been sleeping [in the ground] for thirty-seven years. . . . The southern end [of Hontō] is the place many residents threw their bodies off [the cliffs] to die." Before giving the tourists a break, Ms. Kawashima led them to the entrance lobby of the Peace Memorial Museum to show them a deactivated bomb displayed there.

The unexploded bombs and bones of the war dead that remain underground have been powerful symbols of the postwar Okinawan imagery that connect the past war and the present (Kitamura 2010).[19] Medoruma Shun, an Okinawan novelist born in 1960, states, "When I was a child, the bones existed right next to our everyday lives. . . . There were numerous scars of the war around us. . . . Now that bone collection and removal of unexploded bombs have been conducted, the scars of the Battle of Okinawa have disappeared. . . . Because the bones existed, however, the villagers never forgot the war" (Medoruma 2004: 56). The Cornerstone of Peace was, in fact, built to represent the corpses and bones that had lain across Mabuni Hill and surrounding areas in the wake of the Battle of Okinawa. In envisioning the Cornerstone, planners intended the engraved names of more than 200,000 war dead to act as "the substitutes for thousands of corpses that would still have lain in the battlefield," and the engraved names would make "the abstract number of the war victims materially visible" (Ishihara 2002: 320). It is no coincidence, therefore, that the sightseeing guides' narrations at the Cornerstone centered on the bones of the war dead to evoke the connections between the past and present, and to remind the tourists that the war is still present among Okinawans today.

As the bus left Peace Memorial Park, Ms. Togashi concluded her guiding of the battle-related sites in southern Hontō with a quote from Fukuzawa Yukichi, a leading Japanese intellectual in the late nineteenth and early twentieth centuries: "Fukuzawa stated, 'We must follow the example of Ryūkyū.' I was moved. . . . As a peace-loving Okinawan (*heiwa wo aisuru Okinawa-ken-jin to shite*), I believe that I have to continue to tell others how precious peace is (*heiwa no taisetsusa wo tsutaete ikanakareba naranai to omoimasu*)." This self-portrait of Okinawans as bearers of the pacifist tradition is popular (Arashiro 2005; Ōta 2007: 200–212) not only among intellectuals but also within the tourism industry in Okinawa, since the image promotes Okinawa as an attractive vacation destination where the visitors' bodies and minds are "healed" (*iyasareru*).[20] It is not surprising, then, that Ms. Togashi's vision and narration of peace drew on the popularized image of Okinawa in touristic discourse as a perpetually peaceful paradise, which had only momentarily been interrupted by the past war.

At the Cornerstone, the sightseeing guides' narrations of Okinawa's past lacked any critical interrogation of the decisions made by the Japanese government, such as the forced linguistic and cultural assimilation policies under the

---

[19] Figal (2007), Hamai (2005), and Kitamura (2010: ch.1) chronicle a series of negotiations among the Japanese Tokyo government, USCAR, GRI, bereaved families associations, and the US government, over Naichi Japanese travel to Okinawa for collecting bones and mementos of the war dead and constructing memorials for them. Figal argues that the demand for bone collection and burial and the erection of war dead memorials in Okinawa established "beachheads on Okinawa that served as an important presence for reclaiming the prefecture" into Japanese national polity (Figal 2007: 86).

[20] Some Okinawan scholars are critical of this idealized image (Yakabi 2009: 139), pointing out not only the lack of credible evidence to back the claim but also their concerns that the self-image of Okinawans as a peaceful and welcoming people prevent them from aggressively fighting the injustice committed by the Japanese government and US military (Ishihara 2002: 322–23).

Japanese Imperial regime after Okinawa's annexation to Japan in 1879 (Christy 1997; Oguma 1998; Tomiyama 2002a), the transformation of Okinawa into a volatile monoculture economy of sugar cultivation, which resulted in the mass exodus of Okinawans to Naichi (Rabson 2003; Tomiyama 1990) and overseas (Kaneshiro 2002; Sakihara 1981; Suzuki 2010; Tomiyama 2002b), and its abysmal job of collecting corpses and bones left on the ground in Okinawa and determining their identities, especially in the early postwar years (Kitamura 2010: ch.1).[21] They did not bring up the postwar Japanese government's decision to sacrifice Okinawa in exchange for gaining Japan's political independence from the Allied Occupation Forces in the San Francisco Peace Treaty in 1951 and the US-Japan Security Treaty in 1952 by allowing the US government to continue occupying Okinawa and maintaining its military bases there (Yoshimi 2003), nor did they discuss the economic inequality between Okinawa and Naichi prefectures that have existed since the 1972 reversion (Okinawa has long remained the poorest among all forty-seven prefectures in Japan).

Other than indirect reference to Imperial Japan's educational doctrine of "making Emperor's subjects" (*kōminka*) and the Imperial Army's fanatical "shattering of the jewel" (*gyokusai*) strategy that prohibited all Japanese combatants and noncombatants from surrendering and forced them to fight to the death, the sightseeing guides refrained from making any statement that might be construed as criticism of a particular individual or group. In fact, as Ms. Togashi began describing the battle, she asked the tourists to "understand [her] talk from the perspectives of the US Forces, Japanese Forces, and [Okinawan] residents." When I interviewed Ms. Togashi, she told me that she would never create a situation in which "an Okinawan, a person from Okinawa Prefecture, is speaking to [people from] Japan or [Naichi], because [she] would imagine the Japanese military had good reasons to do what it did, and had [she] been in their position, [she] might as well have done the same thing" during the battle.

Instead of encouraging the tourists to critically examine Okinawa-Japan relationships in the past and present, sightseeing guides highlighted the contrast between the horrors of the past war and peaceful Japan today. Ms. Togashi told me that when a tourist asked her what peace is, she told him: "The fact that you can walk outside during the daytime means peace. Had someone been outside

---

[21] Kitamura points out that even though the Japanese government claims that there were approximately 186,500 Japanese war dead in Okinawa and it has collected 186,142 corpses/bones in Okinawa by March 2008, these numbers are likely inaccurate. First, the total number of Japanese war dead in Okinawa does not include a large number of Okinawan noncombatants who died during the Battle of Okinawa. Second, those corpses/bones that had been collected by local Okinawans and returned to the bereaved families in the early postwar years were not counted by the Japanese government. Finally, it is very likely that the numerous excavations that the Japanese government's bone-collecting teams have conducted double- or triple-counted the same war dead because of the deterioration and scattering of the bones (Kitamura 2010: 56–57).

[like we are now] sixty-five years ago, the person would have been killed." Her narration of the connection between the past misery and present pleasure exemplifies a hegemonic pattern of narrating World War II in postwar Japan: it is the people's suffering during the war that somehow made postwar Japan's "peace and prosperity" possible (Field 1997). The contrast between the past and present in her narrative is, then, not only due to her intention to remind the tourists of the pleasure of life that they enjoy today and to imagine the war and its horror in the past, but also responds to the Naichi Japanese tourists' "desire to give meanings to the deaths of the war victims" from their present viewpoints (Kitamura 2007: 55).

What was also missing in both Ms. Togashi's and Ms. Kawashima's efforts to narrate the connection between the Battle of Okinawa and today's Okinawa is an obvious remnant of the war, and arguably more significant than unexploded bombs and uncollected bones—the massive presence of the US military bases. Currently, approximately 75 percent of the total land area exclusively used by US Forces in Japan is located in Okinawa Prefecture, although the prefecture comprises only 0.6 percent of Japan's total land area (Okinawa-ken Chiji Kōshitsu Kichi-Taisaku-ka 2012; see also Nilep in this volume for the political debates surrounding the potential relocation of the US base). The enormous impact of the US bases on Okinawan people's lives during the occupation and after the reversion to Japan have been well documented (Hein and Selden 2003; Inoue 2007; Johnson 1999; Molasky 1999; Tanji 2006). As the United States expanded its Okinawan bases in the wake of the Korean War, it converted nearly 14 percent of Hontō land into military property through expropriation (Ōshiro 1992: 99). Okinawans took on much of the ill effects of militarization, while the Naichi Japanese enjoyed economic development from the 1950s to 1980s without this burden (Yoshimi 2003). There have been many accidents caused by the US military, such as aircraft and vehicle clashes outside the bases, the explosion of stray missiles outside the training areas, and noise problems created by the Kadena Air Base and Futenma Air Station, which are surrounded by civilian residential and commercial areas. The US military servicemen have committed numerous crimes, including (reported and unreported) hit-and-runs, physical assaults and murders, and sexual assaults that victimized local Okinawans throughout the postwar years (Angst 2003; Aniya et al. 2007: 97–101; Francis 1999; Inoue 2007: ch.2; Kichi Guntai wo Yurusanai Kōdō suru Onnatachi no Kai 2004). In addition, the US troops stationed in Okinawa have been dispatched to numerous battlefields in the post–World War II era—the Korean Peninsula, Vietnam, Kuwait, and, more recently, Iraq and Afghanistan. The US military bases' continuing impact on people's lives in Okinawa, and the US military's direct engagement in armed conflicts around the world today are, however, not narrated by the sightseeing guides as a legacy of the Battle of Okinawa. Even when the continuity between the two is brought up, it is presented as a *residue* of the past military violence, rather than the ongoing military violence in and outside Okinawa.

Sightseeing guides' narration of the Battle of Okinawa and its aftermath was an awkward combination of what Richard Handler and Eric Gable call "mimetic realism" (Handler and Gable 1997: 70, 78) and what Berlant calls "sentimentalism," which attempts to bridge the differences, in this case, between the past and present, "through channels of affective identification and empathy" (Berlant 2000: 44). A discursive implication of this "just the facts" (Handler and Gable 1997: 84) and sentimentalist approach to history is uncritical acceptance of the past—that is, the historical narrative from which "the teeth of critical history are pulled" (84). This form of narration of war and peace at the Himeyuri Cenotaph and Cornerstone of Peace reaffirms the "narrative of progress" (84) from the past war to the present peace, and depoliticizes peace building by equating "the eradication of pain" that has survived from the past, such as unexploded bombs and uncollected bones, with "the achievement of justice" (Berlant 2000: 45).

PEACE GUIDE AT THE HIMEYURI CENOTAPH

Unlike sightseeing guides, peace guides can use narrations that take advantage of the sequential processes within *shūgaku ryokō* by building their guiding upon previous learning experiences of the student-tourists. Constructing their guiding within a "peace study" bubble (Suzuki 2012), peace guides can resort to a more explicitly educational tone of narration than sightseeing guides within their commercial tourism context. In their narrations of the past war and present peace, peace guides illuminate the similarities between the Japanese and Okinawan political conditions in the prewar period and today. While peace guides encouraged *shūgaku ryokō* students to identify with the battle victims, they also asked them to confront the present political conditions in which they live. In other words, the past war was narrated by peace guides as a potential future that they could face, providing the audience with a sense of urgency that sightseeing guides' narrations typically lacked.

Ms. Nakasone, an OPN peace guide and a graduate student at the University of the Ryukyus, stood next to the driver's seat of a coach bus filled with high school students from Naichi on *shūgaku ryokō*. As the bus approached the Himeyuri Cenotaph, she briefly described the experiences of the Himeyuri Corps, but did not dwell on their details. Instead, she built her guiding narratives on the student-tourists' visit to *gama*, a natural cave, prior to the ride to the cenotaph, and their struggles with the slippery surface and damp air in a dark cave, to discuss her own engagement with peace activism. She said:

When you entered the *gama*, perhaps you all thought, "Are we really going inside?" When you saw such a steep incline and slippery ground [leading up to the *gama*], you must have said to yourself, "Why do I have to go in there?" . . . I thought so, too. "Oh, I hate this. It is so slippery, dark, and dangerous—why do I need to go into this horrible place?" . . . I entered a cave for the first time when I was a high school student.[22] I felt exactly the same way as you did today. . . . Even though I was born in Okinawa, I, too, thought, "Why do I have to simulate the war experience? We live in peace now. Why do I have to learn about war in this peaceful time? It has nothing to do with me."

By starting the guiding narration this way, Ms. Nakasone, like the sightseeing guides, attempted to make the past atrocity during the Battle of Okinawa relevant in the eyes of the present visitors. What differentiated her approach from the sightseeing guides' is that she did not try to bridge the gap between the past and present by providing the abundant details of the Corps' last days in southern Hontō or (over)dramatically describe the scenes of the deaths of the Himeyuri Corps. She instead told the students how present-day Japan and Okinawa actually resemble the pre–Battle of Okinawa era in which the Himeyuri survivors had lived. Ms. Nakasone continued:

The people who dramatically changed my view were elderly women (*obāchan*) at Himeyuri Peace Museum [i.e., the former Corps who had survived the war, and served as storytellers and guides at the museum] we are heading to now. . . . They often say when we are watching TV and drinking tea together: "Ms. Nakasone, the society today looks more and more like the one we had lived in before we went to war. . . . It is scary." They say things like that in a mundane conversation while watching TV news about . . . the current political trends. . . . Then, they tell us, "Before we went to war, we had no idea. . . . We thought we would care for the soldiers on the battlefields, and return to school and study again after the war ended." The battlefield, in reality, . . . was the place where your friend, who was standing right next to you, got killed; your friend's guts spilled out when she was hit by a bombshell; your friend lost an entire arm; and you could be the next one [to die]. . . . Those who survived these situations tell us, "Please learn what war is. Learning is the first step." When I heard that, a light bulb went on in my head. "I see, we might be living in peace now, but we, who seemingly have no connection to war, still have to learn about war, so that we won't have to go to war again."

---

[22] Most, but not all, Okinawan primary and secondary schools include peace studies in their curriculum, and many peace study programs, like Naichi schools' *shūgaku ryokō*, include visits to a *gama*, war memorials, and museums, as well as battle survivors' storytelling, typically during the month of June, which is designated "Peace Month" (*Heiwa Gekkan*) by the prefectural government.

After getting out of the bus, Ms. Nakasone spent little time in front of the Himeyuri Cenotaph; she simply pointed out the *gama* where the Corps spent the last days before its demise. Unlike most sightseeing guides I have observed, including Ms. Togashi, she did not ask the students to join hands in prayer. Instead, she encouraged them to meet with the Himeyuri survivors who might be inside the museum and to look at the portraits of the Corps who died in the battle: "The museum . . . displays many portraits of the dead [Corps]. I don't think they ever thought they would die before going to war. Looking at these photos, I want you to think to yourself, 'I don't want to be displayed like this,' 'I don't want to go to a war,' and 'What can I do to prevent a war from happening?'"

Like storytelling by an atomic bombing survivor in Hiroshima who has spoken to schoolchildren and the general public about his experiences (Yoneyama 1999), the peace guide deliberately tried to blur the boundary between the past war and the world in which we live today. According to Yoneyama, the Hiroshima survivors narrate the past "to induce young audiences to begin to think critically about their knowledge of the nation's past and its supposedly 'peaceful' present, as well as about the general questions of war, life, and death" (134). The Okinawa peace guide's narration at the Himeyuri Cenotaph was also intended to make the past war resonate across time, not by melodramatically portraying the young women's deaths during the war, like the sightseeing guides did, but by quoting the former Corps in order to help the young students to "imagine the story about the past as a possible future event" (134). Moreover, helping the students to learn about the Battle of Okinawa in the past was not about cultivating their sympathies and helping them to grieve for the victims. Instead of asking the students to pray for the peaceful afterlives of the fallen Corps, the peace guide asked them to face the portraits of the dead, who "never thought they would die" in the war, just like the *shūgaku ryokō* students today who could not imagine their brutal deaths on the battlefield. What was narrated by the peace guide was, then, a call for radical questioning of their supposedly "peaceful" life-world, from which they were innocently "gazing" upon the past atrocities through a touristic lens (Urry 1990).

PEACE GUIDE AT THE CORNERSTONE OF PEACE

A group of high school students from Tokyo were standing in front of the Cornerstone of Peace, accompanied by Mr. Minami, an OPN peace guide and a graduate student at the University of Ryukyus. This was the group's second day of *shūgaku ryokō*. The previous evening, Mr. Minami held a workshop at the hotel where the group was staying. He lectured on a variety of topics that he hoped the group would explore during the trip: Okinawan language, music, vegetation, and geology, as well as the potential future relocation of the Futenma

FIGURE 11.2 Peace guide at the Cornerstone of Peace

Air Station in Ginowan City, a hotly debated subject in Okinawa and Naichi.[23] In so doing, like Ms. Nakasone on her way to the Himeyuri Cenotaph, his guiding narration at the Cornerstone explicitly builds on the knowledge and learning experience that the student-tourists had just acquired through the peace study programming within the *shūgaku ryokō* itinerary. Like Ms. Nakasone, in his narrative, Mr. Minami also explicitly encouraged the tour participants to make a connection between the past war and their lives today, not through feeling sympathetic toward the war dead, but through sharpening their critical understanding of the current politics in Japan and the world (figure 11.2).

Mr. Minami briefly explained the Cornerstone's design, including its unique feature that lists the names of "all those who lost their lives in the Battle of Okinawa, regardless of their nationality or military or civilian status." Unlike the sightseeing guides, he quickly moved on and led the group to a wall that lists the war dead who were originally from Kagoshima

---

[23] In addition to peace guiding, the OPN is also actively involved in the military base removal effort. There are many scholarly publications on the Okinawan "base problem" and Okinawan antimilitary activism available in English. See Inoue (2007) and Tanji (2006) for comprehensive studies of Okinawan anti-military movements. To contextualize the Okinawan bases and resistance against them within the US global military strategy, see Cooley (2008, especially ch.5) and Lutz (2009, especially ch.8). Several websites offer up-to-date information on the issues surrounding the US military bases in Okinawa, including the potential relocation of the Futenma Air Station: Asia-Pacific Journal: Japan Focus (http://japanfocus.org); Peace Philosophy Centre (http://peacephilosophy.blogspot.com); and Close the Base (http://closethebase.org).

Prefecture. He asked the students to find the name of Ushijima Mitsuru, the Japanese Army commander during the Battle of Okinawa. After a student found his name, he outlined the decision-making process of the Japanese Army's retreat to southern Hontō after losing the crucial battle with the US Force in central Hontō:

> By late May, it is reported that the Japanese Forces had lost about 70 percent of their soldiers. At that point, on May 22, the Japanese Army commanders held a meeting at its headquarters [in the Shuri area of Naha]. During that meeting, they discussed three options. . . . First option: to remain in Shuri and battle it out. Second option: . . . to move to Chinen Peninsula [in southeastern Hontō]. Third option: . . . to move to Kyan Peninsula near Itoman. Among these three options, the Commander [Ushijima] chose . . . the third option. . . . The Commander moved here, so, of course, the entire Army moved south, and the battle victimized many local residents in the process.

He continued:

> Why did the Japanese Army move from Shuri to this place? . . . The reason was very simple; although other places had their own merits, the reason Kyan Peninsula was chosen was that this peninsula has numerous natural caves. If [the Japanese Army] took advantage of them during combat, it could buy time even with the small number of remaining soldiers. . . . If Okinawa fell into American hands, the [Japanese] main islands certainly would be the next offensive target. The main islands were not ready [to defend themselves] yet, so they needed to buy time. . . . This makes it sound like [the Army commanders] were well-intentioned, but the point is that many people were victimized by this decision. Had someone in the [May 22] meeting brought up, 'A lot of local [Okinawan] residents had already evacuated to [southern Hontō],' things might have been different. . . . I want you all to know that is why so many people became the victims of the battle around here.

He then concluded the narration by referring to the previous evening's workshop for the students:

> What we can get out of this question relates to today's problem. Okinawans, although there are many different opinions among them, many of them, in contrast with those in the main islands, doubt that the military presence provides them with peace. They doubt that the US military's presence actually protects their safety. . . . Why do they have this doubt? The answer is simple: because of this history [we just discussed]. As I said, Okinawans tried really hard to help the Japanese Army because they believed they had come to protect Okinawa. But what did the Japanese military value most? It was

not Okinawan people's lives. . . . Because of this experience, we, including myself, ask, "Does an armed force really exist to protect people/citizens (*kokumin*)?" One might say that it protects country/state (*kuni*), but . . . what about *kokumin*? These are the questions we must continue to ask today. . . . You all must think for yourselves by seeing with your own eyes and forming your own perspective.

Unlike sightseeing guides and the prefecture's promotional materials, the peace guide was not interested in celebrating the universal pacifism embodied by the Cornerstone, nor did he try to build the bridge between the past and present by bringing up the uncollected bones and unexploded bombs buried in the ground. The guide calmly described Commander Ushijima's decision to retreat to southern Hontō, and his last order to the remaining Japanese soldiers to fight until the end. Like Yoneyama (1999: 29), who calls for a "historical materialist" approach to the past, which "brings to light the numerous counterpoints—the revolutionary 'now-time' (*Jetztzeit*)— to the known course of the past and questions history's inevitability," Mr. Minami refused to depict the mass noncombatant casualties in southern Hontō during the waning days of the Battle of Okinawa as a tragic but unavoidable outcome. He urged the students to think what the outcome could have been had Ushijima and other Army leaders made a decision with more serious consideration for the lives of local Okinawan residents. Instead of gawking at the enormous number of names of the war dead engraved on the Cornerstone and grieving for their deaths, he encouraged the students to question why so many noncombatant Okinawans' names had to be among them, and to "envision the possibility that the suffering and agony of an enormous number of war victims . . . might have been averted, that they were never inevitable" (135).

Furthermore, Mr. Minami attempted to link the Commander's decisions during the Battle of Okinawa, which slighted the safety of civilians for the sake of "national defense," with the heated debate regarding the presence of military bases in Okinawa today. He exemplified how peace guides challenge the visitors not to uncritically accept "just the facts" from the past, but to actively politicize the historical knowledge, so that they could understand and engage the urgent contemporary issues. He acted as a thought provocateur, urging the students to question the conventional wisdom they likely held: the presence of robust armed forces is indispensable for a state to protect its citizens' safety. In front of the Cornerstone of Peace, the peace guide narrated the historical events to impel the student-tourists to imagine what the past could have been had people opted for pursuing peace instead of continuing war, and what the future could become, if people, including those students, accompanying teachers, and the peace guide himself, decide to act upon the militarized world in which they live today.

Conclusion

By contrasting sightseeing guides' and peace guides' narrations at the Battle of Okinawa-related sites, I did not aim to merely criticize the sightseeing guides who encourage tourists to identify with the suffering of the battle victims in the past and appreciate their purportedly peaceful lives today, nor did I suggest that their efforts to provoke the tourists' compassion for Okinawans by bringing up the uncollected bones and unexploded bombs buried in Okinawan soil that continue to haunt the Okinawans today are an ineffective means of fostering the tourists' desire to build a peaceful world. What I wanted to point out is the vulnerability inherent in the peace-building effort that is predicated upon the cultivation of compassion. Berlant argues that "compassion is a term denoting privilege: the sufferer is *over there*," and that such an endeavor has to be "more than a demand on consciousness—more than a demand to *feel right*" to effectively create political and social changes (Berlant 2004: 4; emphasis original). The sightseeing guides' narrations remain a form of "sentimental politics"; its power "asserts the priority of interpersonal identification and empathy for the vitality and viability of collective life," supposedly shared among Naichi Japanese guests and Okinawan hosts (Berlant 2000: 45). Even though today's sightseeing guides' narrations may not be as sensationalistic or jingoistic as those offered by Okinawan bus guides during the battle ruins pilgrimages of the 1950s to 1970s, their narrations of war and peace retain the same key features: incitement of compassion and enactment of sentimental politics, both of which effectively widen, rather than narrow, the distance between the past war and presumably peaceful present. The narration's outcome is a static and passive conception of "negative" peace, which tends to lead to the "foreclosure on political engagement" with the militarized world in which the tourists live (Sturken 2007: 26).

Peace guides at the battle-related sites resist the sentimentalization, and, in effect, the depoliticization of the deaths in the past during their narrations, and attempt to fill the spatiotemporal distance between the battle in the past and the student-tourists' lives today through intellectual and political provocation. In their guiding narratives, the past war does not continue to exist in today's Okinawa merely as a residue, but as a political struggle by Okinawans against the islands' highly militarized state, created and sustained under the US-Japan military regime in the postwar years. The past events narrated by the peace guides to the student visitors, in short, are "made urgently relevant to the present" in their effort to interrupt "the evolutionary continuity between past [war] and present [peace]" (Yoneyama 1999: 30). In so doing, peace guides' narrative performances encourage the student-tourists to cultivate peace as part of their individual selves through tireless introspection, learning, and political engagement.

The two forms of guiding narrations of the past war during the sightseeing tours and peace study programs illuminate the possibility and limitation of tourism in the sites of past atrocities as a means of peace activism. While these sites undoubtedly evoke strong emotion among the visitors, of which deep compassion for the victims is common (Hughes 2008; Thurnell-Read 2009), the "universal" and "sentimentalist" narrations of history are unlikely to succeed in mobilizing the visitors to take action to build peace today. The peace guides' narrative approaches to the past and present that aim to help the student-tourists question the linear evolution of history and reject sentimentalism also suggest that there are ways to make touring and discursive practices at the sites of mass violence in the past a potent tool for mobilizing people to build peace in the future. For scholars who seek to understand popular discourses, including tourism narratives, on war and peace, my case studies suggest that it is imperative to examine the narrators' approaches to history, emotionality, and politics that often implicitly yet crucially contextualize the meanings and effects of these discourses.

References

Angst, Linda I. 2003. "The Rape of a School Girl: Discourses of Power and Women's Lives in Okinawa." In *Islands of Discontent: Okinawan Responses to Japanese and American Power*, Laura Hein and Mark Selden (eds.), 135–57. Lanham, MD: Rowman and Littlefield.

Aniya, Masaaki. 1974. "Kankō basu ni notta!" *Okinawa Shichō* 3: 32–34.

Aniya, Masaaki, Yoshihiro Ōta, Ryōshin Nakayoshi, and Keiji Shinzato. 1974. "Zadankai: Sengoshi to Okinawasen taiken: Okinawa no sensō taiken wo dō ikasu ka." *Okinawa Shichō* 4: 4–18.

Aniya, Masaaki, Yoshikatsu Maeda, Masaru Ōnishi, and Hiroshi Kawabata. 1985. *Okinawa No Senseki To Gunji Kichi: Heiwa No Tame No Gaidobukku*. Naha: Akebono Shuppan.

Aniya, Masaaki, Yasuhide Ōshiro, Yasuhiro Ōkubo, and Takeo Matsumoto. 2007. *Okinawa No Senseki To Gunji Kichi: Heiwa No Tame No Gaidobukku*. Osaka: Kariyushi Shuppan Kikaku.

Arasaki, Moriteru, Masaji Nakasone, Taizan Maezato, Kiyohiko Nakaoji, Masayasu Ōshiro, Kenichi Yamakado, Asao Kinjō, and Tomokazu Takamine. 1983. *Kankō kōsu de nai Okinawa*. Tokyo: Kōbunken.

Arashiro, Yoneko. 2005. "Ryūkyū/Okinawa no heiwa shisō: 'Hibōryoku' no shiten kara." In *Okinawa wo heiwa-gaku suru!*, Masaie Ishihara, Hiroshi Nakachi, and C. Douglas Lummis (eds.), 33–43. Kyoto: Hōritsu Bunkasha.

Asahi Shinbun Seibu Honsha Shakai-bu (ed.). 1982. *Shin Okinawa hōkoku: Fukki kara 10 nen*. Kitakyūshū: Asahi Shinbun Seibu Honsha.

Awazu, Kenta. 2006. "Shūgōteki kioku no porityikusu: Okinawa ni okeru Ajia-Taiheiyō sensō-go no senbotsusha kinen shisetsu wo chūshin ni." *Kokuritsu Rekishi Minzoku Hakubutsukan Kenkyū Hōkoku* 126: 87–117.

Ben Porath, Sigal R. 2003. "War and Peace Education." *Journal of Philosophy of Education* 37(3): 525–33.

Berlant, Lauren. 2000. "The Subject of True Feeling: Pain, Privacy, and Politics." In *Cultural Studies and Political Theory*, Jodi Dean (ed.), 42–62. Ithaca: Cornell University Press.

Berlant, Lauren. 2004. "Introduction: Compassion (and Withholding)." In *Compassion: The Culture and Politics of an Emotion*, Lauren Berlant (ed.), 1–14. London: Routledge.

Bhabha, Homi. 1994. *The Location of Culture*. London: Routledge.

Christy, Alan S. 1997. The Making of Imperial Subjects in Okinawa. In *Formations of Colonial Modernity in East Asia*, Tani E. Barlow (ed.), 141–69. Durham, NC: Duke University Press.

Cohen, Erik. 1985. "The Tourist Guide: The Origins, Structure and Dynamics of a Role." *Annals of Tourism Research* 12(1): 5–29.

Cooley, Alexander. 2008. *Base Politics: Democratic Change and the U.S. Military Overseas*. Ithaca, NY: Cornell University Press.

Cooper, Malcolm. 2006. "The Pacific War Battlefields: Tourist Attractions or War Memorials?" *International Journal of Tourism Research* 8: 213–22.

Edensor, Tim. 2000. "Staging Tourism: Tourists as Performers." *Annals of Tourism Research* 27(2): 322–44.

Field, Norma. 1997. "War and Apology: Japan, Asia, the Fiftieth, and After." *Positions* 5(1): 1–49.

Figal, Gerald. 2003. "Waging Peace in Okinawa. In *Islands of Discontent: Okinawan Responses to Japanese and American Power*, Laura Hein and Mark Selden (eds.), 65–98. Lanham, MD: Rowman and Littlefield.

Figal, Gerald. 2007. "Bones of Contention: The Geopolitics of 'Sacred Ground' in Postwar Okinawa." *Diplomatic History* 31(1): 81–109.

Figal, Gerald. 2008. "Between War and Tropics: Heritage Tourism in Postwar Okinawa." *Public Historian* 30(2): 83–107.

Francis, Carolyn Bowen. 1999. "Women and Military Violence." In *Okinawa: Cold War Island*, Chalmers Johnson (ed.), 189–204. Cardiff, UK: Japan Policy Research Institute.

Galtung, Johan. 1964. "A Structural Theory of Aggression." *Journal of Peace Research* 1: 95–119.

Galtung, Johan. 1971. "A Structural Theory of Imperialism." *Journal of Peace Research* 8: 81–117.

Hamai, Kazufumi. 2005. "Okinawasen senbotsusha wo meguru nichibei kankei to Okinawa." *Gaikōshiryōkanpō* 19: 89–115.

Hamai, Kazufumi. 2006. "Kita no hate kara minami no shima e: Hokureihi junpaidan no Okinawa tokō to sono inpakuto." *Nijusseiki Kenkyū* 7: 53–77.

Handler, Richard and Eric Gable. 1997. *The New History in an Old Museum: Creating the Past at Colonial Williamsburg*. Durham, NC: Duke University Press.

Hein, Laura and Mark Selden. 2003. "Culture, Power, and Identity in Contemporary Okinawa." In *Islands of Discontent: Okinawan Responses to Japanese and American Power*, Laura Hein and Mark Selden (eds.), 1–35. Lanham, MD: Rowman and Littlefield.

Holloway, J. Christopher. 1981. "The Guided Tour: A Sociological Approach." *Annals of Tourism Research* 8(3): 377–402.

Hughes, Rachel. 2008. "Dutiful Tourism: Encountering the Cambodian Genocide." *Asia Pacific Viewpoint* 49(3): 318–30.

Iijima, Yoshinobu. 2003. "Okinawa ni kakeru hashi: Heiwa gakushū no kyōiku-teki kōka ni." *Kikan Okinawa* 25: 34–39.

Inoue, Masamichi S. 2007. *Okinawa and the U.S. Military: Identity Making in the Age of Globalization*. New York: Columbia University Press.

Ishihara, Masaie. 2002. "Okinawa-ken heiwa kinen shiryōkan to 'Heiwa-no-ishiji' no imisuru mono." In *Sōten: Okinawasen no kioku*, Masaie Ishihara, Masayasu Ōshiro, Hiroshi Hosaka, and Katsutoshi Matsunaga (eds.), 308–23. Tokyo: Shakai Hyōronsha.

Ishikawa, Masahide. 1984. *Okinawa no kankō sangyō*. Naha: Okinawa Kankō Sokuhōsha.

Jahana, Naomi. 2008. *Shōgen Okinawa "shūdan jiketsu": Kerama shotō de naniga okitaka*. Tokyo: Iwanami Shoten.

Johnson, Chalmers (ed.). 1999. *Okinawa: Cold War Island*. Cardiff, UK: Japan Policy Research Institute.

Kaneshiro, Edith M. 2002. "'The Other Japanese': Okinawan Immigrants to the Philippines, 1903–1941." In *Okinawan Diaspora*, Ronald Y. Nakasone (ed.), 71–89. Honolulu: University of Hawai'i Press.

Kichi Guntai wo Yurusanai Kōdō suru Onnatachi no Kai (ed.). 2004. Okinawa beihei ni yoru josei e no seihanzai: 1945 nen 4 gatsu–2004 nen 8 gatsu. *Naha: Kichi Guntai wo Yurusanai Kōdō suru Onnatachi no Kai*.

Kinki Nippon Tsūrisuto. 2010. Himeyuri-no-tō tsuā (Ryokō: Shutoken hatsu). www://meito.knt.co.jp/1/cb/20901011.

Kitamura, Tsuyoshi. 2004. "Okinawa senseki no 'omotedōri' to 'uradōri': 'Okinawasen kiroku/keishō undō' no genryū." *Hyūman Saiensu Risāchi* 13: 51–72.

Kitamura, Tsuyoshi. 2005. "Senshisha e/tono tabi: Okinawa senseki junrei ni okeru 'izoku no komyunitasu.'" *Ningen Kagaku Kenkyū* 18(2): 137–52.

Kitamura, Tsuyoshi. 2006. "'Konpaku-no-tō' saikō: Sono ōkikute, fukai, chinmoku no ana." *Okinawagaku* 9: 121–33.

Kitamura, Tsuyoshi. 2007a. "'Okinawabyō' kanja no minzokushi: Himeyuri-no-tō to 'fukki' ni itaru yamai." In *Eko-imaginēru: Bunka no seitaigaku to jinruigakuteki chōbō*, Hiroe Shimauchi, Masamichi Deguchi, and Atsurō Murata (eds.), 273–96. Tokyo: Gensōsha.

Kitamura, Tsuyoshi. 2007b. "Okinawa no 'Mabuni-no-oka' ni miru senshisha hyōshō no porityikusu: Kokumei-hi 'Heiwa-no-ishiji' wo meguru gensetsu to jissen no bunseki." *Chiiki Kenkyū* 3: 49–66.

Kitamura, Tsuyoshi. 2010. *Shisha-tachi no sengo-shi: Okinawa senseki wo meguru hitobito no kioku*. Tokyo: Ochanomizu Shobō.

Lutz, Catherine (ed.). 2009. *The Bases of Empire: The Global Struggle against U.S. Military Posts*. New York: New York University Press.

Medoruma, Shun. 2004. "Intabyū." *Wander* 36: 46–59.

Molasky, Michael S. 1999. *The American Occupation of Japan and Okinawa: Literature and Memory*. London: Routledge.

Murakami, Akiyoshi. 1999. "Okinawa no sensō iseki to heiwa gakushū." *Kēshikaji* 22: 30–33.

Nakachi, Hiroshi. 2005. "Jichitai no heiwa shisaku." In *Okinawa wo heiwagaku suru!*, Masaie Ishihara, Hiroshi Nakachi, and C. Douglas Lummis (eds.), 195–206. Tokyo: Hōritsu-Bunkasha.

Ōe, Kenzaburō. 1970. *Okinawa nōto*. Tokyo: Iwanami Shoten.

Ogawa, Akihiro. 2011. "Peace, a Contested Identity: Japan's Constitutional Revision and Grassroots Peace Movements." *Peace and Change* 36(3): 373–99.

Oguma, Eiji. 1998. *"Nihonjin" no kyōkai: Okinawa, Ainu, Taiwan, Chōsen shokuminchi shihai kara dokuritsu undō made*. Tokyo: Shinyōsha.

Okinawa Heiwa Nettowāku. 2004. "Gaido shinario." *Ne to Waku* 44: 14.

Okinawa Heiwa Nettowāku. 2008. "Ōe/Iwanami Okinawasen saiban tokushū." *Ne to Waku* 67: 1–12.

Okinawa Kankō Kyōkai. 1957. *Okinawa kankō no shiori: Shin Okinawa an'nai*. Naha: Okinawa Kankō Kyōkai.

Okinawa-ken. 2004. *Kankōkyaku idō riben-sei kōjō taisaku chōsa hōkokusho*. Naha: Okinawa-ken.

Okinawa-ken. 2008. *Kankō Yōran: Heisei 19 nendo-ban*. Naha: Okinawa-ken.

Okinawa-ken. 2009. *Kankō yōran: Heisei 20 nendo-ban*. Naha: Okinawa-ken.

Okinawa-ken Chiji Kōshitsu Kichi-Taisaku-ka. 2012 "U.S. Military Bases in Okinawa." www.pref.okinawa.jp/site/chijiko/kichitai/25185.html.

Okinawa-ken Bunka Kankō-bu Heiwa/Dan-jo Kyōdō Sanka-ka. 2012. "Statement of Purpose and Concept: The Cornerstone of Peace." www.pref.okinawa.jp/site/kankyo/heiwadanjo/heiwa/7792.html.

Okinawa-ken Kankō Konbenshon Byūrō. 2008. *Shūgaku ryokō no shiori: Miru, manabu, taiken-suru Okinawa*. Naha: Okinawa-ken Kankō Konbenshon Byūrō.

Okinawa-ken Kankō Konbenshon Byūrō. 2009. *Okinawa shūgaku ryokō setsumei-kai*. Naha: Okinawa-ken Kankō Konbenshon Byūrō.

Okinawa-ken Kōkyōso Kyōiku Shiryō Sentā "Gama" Henshū Iinkai. 2009. *Okinawa no senseki bukku: Gama*. Naha: Okinawa Jiji Shuppan.

Okinawa-ken Kōkyōso Nanbu Shibu and Heiwa Kyōiku Kenkyū Iinkai. 1986. *Aruku, miru, kangaeru Okinawa*. Naha: Okinawa Jiji Shuppan.

Ōshiro, Kōshin. 1986. "Hajimete no kankō basu." *Kankō to keizai* 265: 25.

Ōshiro, Masayasu. 1992. *Ryūkyū Seifu*. Naha: Hirugisha.

Ōshiro, Masayasu. 2004. "Kōshite 'heiwa gaido' ga tanjō shita." *Ne to Waku* 43: 2–4.

Ōshiro, Masayasu. 2005. "Heiwa no bunka no sōzō to hasshin." In *Okinawa wo heiwagaku suru!*, Masaie Ishihara, Hiroshi Nakachi, and C. Douglas Lummis (eds.), 178–91. Kyoto: Hōritsu Bunkasha.

Ōshiro, Masayasu, and Shigekazu Mezaki. 2006. *Shūgaku ryokō no tame no Okinawa an'nai*. Tokyo: Kōbunken.

Ōta, Masahide. 2006. *Shishatachi wa imada nemurezu: "Irei" no imi wo tou*. Tokyo: Shinsensha.

Ōta, Masahide. 2007. *Okinawa no irei no tō: Okinawasen no kyōkun to irei*. Naha: Naha Shuppansha.

Rabson, Steve. 2003. "Memories of Okinawa: Life and Times in the Greater Osaka Diaspora." In *Islands of Discontent: Okinawan Responses to Japanese and American Power*, Laura Hein and Mark Selden (eds.), 99–134. Lanham, MD: Rowman and Littlefield.

Rojek, Chris. 1997. "Indexing, Dragging and the Social Construction of Tourist Sights." In *Touring Cultures: Transformations of Travel and Theory*, Chris Rojek and John Urry (eds.), 52–74. London: Routledge.

Sakihara, Mitsugu. 1981. "History of Okinawa." In *Uchinanchu: A History of Okinawans in Hawai'i*, Ethnic Studies Oral History Project and the United Okinawan Association of Hawai'i (eds.), 3–22. Honolulu: Ethnic Studies Program, University of Hawai'i.

Schmidt, Catherine J. 1979. "The Guided Tour: Insulated Adventure." *Urban Life* 7(4): 441–67.

Shiroma Sachiko. 2004. "Kankō basugaido to Okinawa heiwa gakushū." *Ne to Waku* 43: 7–9.

Sturken, Marita. 2007. *Tourists of History: Memory, Kitsch, and Consumerism from Oklahoma City to Ground Zero*. Durham, NC: Duke University Press.

Suzuki, Taku. 2010. *Embodying Belonging: Racializing Okinawan Diaspora in Bolivia and Japan*. Honolulu: University of Hawai'i Press.

Suzuki, Taku. 2012. "Forming an 'Activism Bubble' in Tourism: Peace Guiding at Okinawa Battle Ruins." *Tourist Studies* 12(1): 3–27.

Tada, Osamu. 2004. *Okinawa imēji no tanjō: Aoi umi no karuchararu sutadīzu*. Tokyo: Tōyō Keizai Shinpōsha.

Tada, Osamu. 2008. *Okinawa imēji wo tabi suru: Yanagita Kunio kara ijū būmu made*. Tokyo: Chūōkōron Shinsha.

Tanji, Miyume. 2006. *Myth, Protest and Struggle in Okinawa*. London: Routledge.

Thurnell-Read, Thomas P. 2009. "Engaging Auschwitz: An Analysis of Young Travelers' Experiences of Holocaust Tourism." *Journal of Tourism Consumption and Practice* 1(1): 26–52.

Tomiyama, Ichirō. 1990. *Kindai Nihon shakai to "Okinawa-jin": "Nihonjin" ni naru to iukoto*. Tokyo: Nihon Keizai Hyōronsha.

Tomiyama, Ichirō. 1997. "Colonialism and the Sciences of the Tropical Zone: The Academic Analysis of Difference in 'The Island Peoples.'" In *Formations of Colonial Modernity in East Asia*, Tani E. Barlow (ed.), 199–221. Durham, NC: Duke University Press.

Tomiyama, Ichirō. 2000. "'Spy': Mobilization and Identity in Wartime Okinawa." In *Japanese Civilization in the Modern World XVI: Nation State and Empire*, National Museum of Ethnology (ed.), 121–32. Senri: Japan National Museum of Ethnology.

Tomiyama, Ichirō. 2002a. *Bōryoku no yokan: Ifa Fuyū ni okeru kiki no mondai*. Tokyo: Iwanami Shoten.

Tomiyama, Ichirō. 2002b. "The 'Japanese' of Micronesia: Okinawans in the Nan'yo Islands." In *Okinawan diaspora*, Ronald Y. Nakasone (ed.), 57–70. Honolulu: University of Hawai'i Press.

Tomiyama, Ichirō. 2006. *Zōho: Senjō no kioku*. Tokyo: Nihon Keizai Hyōronsha.

Umeda, Masaki. 2008. "Honsho 'Kankō kōsu de nai Okinawa' no 'rireki' ni tsuite." In *Kankō kōsu de nai Okinawa*, 4th ed., Moriteru Arasaki, Naomi Jahana, Tsuyoshi Matsumoto, Hiromori Maedomari, Norikazu Kameyama, Masaji Nakasone, and Shizuo Ōta (eds.), 312–18. Tokyo: Kōbunken.

Urry, John. 1990. *The Tourist Gaze: Leisure and Travel in Contemporary Societies*. London: Sage.

Yakabi, Osamu. 2009. *Okinawa-sen, Beigun senryōshi wo manabinaosu: Kioku wo ikani keishō suruka*. Yokohama: Yo'ori Shobō.

Yamashiro, Zenzō. 1964. *Okinawa kankō kyōkai-shi*. Naha: Okinawa Kankō Kyōkai.

Yamashita, Shinji. 2000. "The Japanese Encounter with the South: Japanese Tourists in Palau." *Contemporary Pacific* 12(2): 437–63.

Yasukuni Jinja Kokueika Hantai Okinawa Kirisutosha Renrakukai (ed.). 1983. *Sensō sanbi ni igi ari!: Okinawa ni okeru ireitō hibun chōsa hōkoku*. Sajiki: Yasukuni Jinja Kokueika Hantai Okinawa Kirisutosha Renrakukai.

Yonetani, Julia. 2002. "Contested Memories: Struggles over War and Peace in Contemporary Okinawa." In *Japan and Okinawa: Structure and Subjectivity*, Glen D. Hook and Richard Siddle (eds.), 188–207. London: Routledge.

Yoneyama, Lisa. 1999. *Hiroshima Traces: Time, Space, and the Dialectics of Memory.* Berkeley: University of California Press.

Yoshimi, Shun'ya. 2003. "'America' as Desire and Violence: Americanization in Postwar Japan and Asia during the Cold War." *Inter-Asia Cultural Studies* 4(3): 433–50.

Zenkoku Shūgaku Ryokō Kenkyū Kyōkai. N.d. Shūgaku ryokō no rekishi. http://shugakuryoko.com/museum/rekishi/index.html.

CONTRIBUTORS

Aditi Bhatia, Assistant Professor, Department of English, City University of Hong Kong, Hong Kong

Patricia L. Dunmire, Associate Professor, Department of English, Kent State University, Kent, Ohio, USA

Janis L. Goldie, Assistant Professor, Communication Studies, Huntington/Laurentian University, Sudbury, Ontario, Canada

Candler Hallman, Doctoral Candidate, Department of Anthropology, University of California San Diego, La Jolla, California, USA

Adam Hodges, A.W. Mellon Postdoctoral Humanities Fellow, Department of English, Carnegie Mellon University, Pittsburgh, Pennsylvania, USA

Chad Nilep, Lecturer, Institute of Liberal Arts and Sciences, Nagoya University, Nagoya, Japan

Anna Podvornaia, Graduate, The Norman Paterson School of International Affairs, Carleton University, Ottawa, Ontario, Canada

Becky Schulthies, Assistant Professor, Department of Anthropology, Rutgers University, New Brunswick, New Jersey, USA

Taku Suzuki, Associate Professor, International Studies, Denison University, Granville, Ohio, USA

Anna Marie Trester, Lecturer and MLC Program Director, Department of Linguistics, Georgetown University, Washington, DC, USA

INDEX